INTENSIVE BULGARIAN

Monastery and Rila mountains

INTENSIVE BULGARIAN

A TEXTBOOK AND REFERENCE GRAMMAR

VOLUME 2

BY

RONELLE ALEXANDER

WITH THE ASSISTANCE OF OLGA M. MLADENOVA

THE UNIVERSITY OF WISCONSIN PRESS

The University of Wisconsin Press
2537 Daniels Street
Madison, WI 53718-6722

3 Henrietta Street
London WC2E 8LU, England

Copyright © 2000
The Board of Regents of the University of Wisconsin System
All rights reserved

5 4 3 2 1

Library of Congress Cataloging-in-Publication Data

Alexander, Ronelle, with the assistance of Olga M. Mladenova
Intensive Bulgarian: A Textbook and Reference Grammar, Volumes 1 & 2
Volume 1 = 414 pp.   cm.; Volume 2 = 413 pp.   cm.
ISBN 0-299-16744-5 (Volume 1) (alk. paper)
ISBN 0-299-16754-2 (Volume 2) (alk. paper)
Bulgarian language Textbooks for foreign speakers–English.
I. Title.
PG839.5.E5A44 2000

491.8'082421–dc21 98-17528

Publication of this book has been made possible in part by
a grant from the Peter N. Kujachich Endowment in Balkan Studies
at the University of California-Berkeley.

DEDICATION

To the memory of two friends and colleagues who left us far too soon

> Maksim Slavchev MLADENOV (1930-1992)

> Mihaila Petkova STAINOVA (1940-1987)

Intensive Bulgarian audio tapes and CDs

Audio tapes and CDs that complement this textbook are available from the University of California-Berkeley Language Center. These tapes and CDs---one per volume---contain recordings of all the dialogues (both volumes), most of the sample sentences (volume 1 only), and certain readings (both volumes), as well as brief excerpts of Bulgarian folk music (both volumes).

To order, contact:

> The University of California
> Berkeley Language Center
> Media Duplication Services
> B-40 Dwinelle Hall #2640
> Berkeley, CA 94720-2640
>
> email: LL-dup@socrates.berkeley.edu
> phone: (510) 642-0767, ext. 29
> http://www.ITP.berkeley.edu/blc/mediaduplication.htm

CONTENTS

INTRODUCTION	xv
ACKNOWLEDGEMENTS	xvii

LESSON 16

Dialogue: Куче ли си ни купил, татко?	3
Basic Grammar	
16.1. The past indefinite tense: formation of the L-participle	5
16.2. Agreement in the past indefinite	6
16.3. Word order in the past indefinite	7
16.4. Usage of the past indefinite tense	7
16.5. Imperfective imperatives	9
16.6. Additional imperative forms	10
Exercises	11
Additional grammar notes	
16.3a. Word order rules for the past indefinite tense	12
16.6a. Недей and стига with the truncated infinitive	14
16.7. Motion verbs: the past tense of the verb идвам	14
16.8. Impersonal verbs, continued	15
16.9. Alternating consonant/vowel sequences	16
Sample Sentences	18
Sentences for Translation	19
Reading selection: Кореспонденция - (12)	20
Glossary	22
Cultural Commentary	
City life: street names	24
Folklore: music, dance, costumes; Koprivshtitsa festival	24
Geography: place names	24

LESSON 17

Dialogue: Тежко е човек да е сам	25
Basic grammar	
17.1. Passive participles: formation	27
17.2. Passive participles: usage	28
17.3. Relative pronouns: който	29
17.4. Other relative conjunctions	31
чий "whose?" / чийто "whose"	31
какъв "what [kind of]?" / какъвто "[such] as", колко "how much? how many?" / колкото "as many as, as much as"	32
това, което	33
кога "when?" / когато "when", къде "where?" / където "where" and others	33
17.5. Compound conjunctions	34
17.6. Aspect differentiation in subordinate clauses	34
17.7. Imperfect tense and perfective aspect	36
Exercises	38
Additional grammar notes	
17.3a. The possessive relative pronoun	39
17.3b. Relative pronouns in indefinite expressions	39
17.4a. Indefinite usage of other relative conjunctions	40
17.4b. The conjunction дето	41
17.5a. The conjunction като	41
17.8. Derivation: verbs in -в-, nouns in -ение and -ост	42
The suffix -в-	42
The suffix -ени-	43
The suffix -ост	43

Sample sentences	44
Sentences for translation	45
Reading selections: Кореспонденция - (13)	46
Автобиография	47
Glossary	48
Cultural commentary	
Families: in-laws	51
City life: telephone numbers	51
Literature: Hristo Botev, Tărnovo school	52
Schooling and education: university and academic degrees	52
Academic life: the Bulgarian Academy of Sciences; ethnography as a discipline	52
Work requirements	52

LESSON 18

Dialogue: Ангеле, ти баща, ти майка	53
Basic grammar	
18.1. Verbal aspect: review	55
18.2. Formation of aspect pairs: basic vs. derived	55
Basic pairs: possible correlations between imperfective and perfective forms	56
Simplex imperfectives, and derived pairs	57
18.3. Meaning of derived imperfective	59
18.4. Indirect object pronouns: review	61
18.5. Indirect object of "affect"	61
Exercises	63
Additional grammar notes	
18.2a. Derivation in aspect pairs: derived perfectives	64
18.2b. Verbal derivation: the prefixes по- and за-	65
18.3a. Meaning of derived imperfectives: "holes in the system"?	65
18.4a. Indirect object pronouns and word order	66
18.5a. Idiomatic uses of the indirect object pronoun	69
18.6. Derivation of diminutives, continued	69
Sample sentences	72
Sentences for translation	73
Reading selections: Елисавета Багряна, поетеса	74
Стихии (poem)	75
Glossary	76
Cultural commentary	
City life: landmarks, room rental, public transportation	79
Food and drink: mekhana; grills, salads, sandwiches, wine	79
Home life: repairs	79
Families: children	80
History: Tsar Samuil	80
Literature: Elisaveta Bagryana	80

LESSON 19

Dialogue: Разходка из София	81
Basic grammar	
19.1. The past anterior tense	83
19.2. Word order in the past anterior	85
19.3. Passive participles, continued	85
19.4. Passive constructions with passive participles	88
Exercises	91
Additional grammar notes	
19.2a. Word order in the past anterior	92
19.3a. Complex constructions with passive participles	93
19.4a. Passive agentive constructions	93
19.5. Derivation of agentive nouns and family group names	94
Agentive nouns in -ач	94
Agentive nouns in -тел	94

Agentive nouns in **-ар**	94
Borrowed agentive nouns	95
Family-group possessives	95
Sample sentences	96
Sentences for translation	97
Reading selections: **Кореспонденция - (14)**	98
Молба	99
Glossary	100
Cultural commentary	
Sofia: major streets, yellow tiles; NDK; dogs	102
Official and semi-official life: connections, official requests	103
Forms of address: surnames	103
Academic life: publications by BAN	103

LESSON 20

Dialogue: **Ти знаеш ли как се дресират кучета?**	104
Basic grammar	
20.1. Verbal nouns	106
20.2. Review of се-constructions	108
Reflexivity	108
Reciprocity	108
Intransitivity	108
Idiomatic	109
20.3. Passive constructions with **се**	109
20.4. Impersonal constructions with **се**	112
Exercises	115
Additional grammar notes	
20.5. Derivation: the suffixes **-ство, -ина**, etc.	
The suffix **-ство**	116
The suffix **-ина**	116
Non-productive suffixes	117
Sample sentences	118
Sentences for translation	119
Reading selection: **Кореспонденция - (15)**	120
Glossary	122
Cultural commentary	
Food and drink: soft drinks, kachamak, the making of rakia	125
Geography: the Black Sea	125
Geography: the Balkans	126
City life: books	126
History: general	126
Literature: Zahari Stoyanov	126
Folk customs: săbor	126

LESSON 21

Dialogue: **Не ме ли помните?**	127
Basic grammar	
21.1. The past indefinite tense, continued	129
21.2. The past indefinite as expression of focus on present result	129
21.3. The past indefinite as expression of point of view	130
21.4. The past indefinite as expression of inference or assumption	132
21.5. The past indefinite as expression of indirect discourse	132
21.6. Summary: contrast between aorist/imperfect and past indefinite	133
21.7. Conditional usage of the particle **ли**; use of the perfective aspect with habitual meaning	134
Exercises	135

Additional grammar notes
    21.8. Derivation: causative and stative verbs
        Causative verbs   136
        Stative verbs   136
    21.9. Derivation: substance adjectives   137
Sample sentences   139
Sentences for translation   140
Reading selection: Старобългарските азбуки   141
Glossary
    143
Cultural commentary
    City life: beards, professional unions   145
    Language: Bulgarian tense system; history of Slavic writing systems   146
    Literature: medieval period   146
    Philanthropy   146

LESSON 22

Dialogue: Нали щяхте да дойдете заедно?   147
Basic grammar
    22.1. The future anterior tense   149
    22.2. The future in the past tense: introduction and formation   150
    22.3. The future in the past tense: basic usage   151
    22.4. The future in the past as an expression of surprise or disappointment   153
    22.5. The future in the past in conditional constructions   154
Exercises   156
Additional grammar notes
    22.6. Kinship terminology, continued   157
Sample sentences   158
Sentences for translation   159
Reading selection: Алеко Константинов, "Братя славяни в далечна Америка"   160
Glossary   162
Cultural commentary
    City life: outdoor cafes   165
    Food and drink: wine   165
    Literature: Aleko Konstantinov   165
    Geography: Banat   165
    History   165

LESSON 23

Dialogue: Под сияещото слънце на летния следобед   166
Basic grammar
    23.1. Review of participles   168
        Past passive participle   168
        Past active participle   168
    23.2. The present active participle: formation and usage   169
    23.3. The verbal adverb   171
    23.4. The future anterior in the past tense   172
    23.5. Conditional constructions, continued   173
    23.6. Review of the Bulgarian tense system   176
        BULGARIAN VERBAL TENSES (INDICATIVE MOOD)   176
Exercises   178
Additional grammar notes
    23.7. Derivation of nationality names   179
Sample sentences   181
Sentences for translation   182
Reading selection: Тракийското съкровище от Рогозен   183
Glossary   185
Cultural commentary
    History: Patriarch Euthymius   189

Archaeology: Thracian civilizations	189
Customs: sunburns	189
Geography: Balchik	189
Bureaucracy	189

LESSON 24

Dialogue: Там имало интересен обект	190
Grammar	
24.1. The renarrated mood: introduction	192
24.2. Formation of the renarrated mood: general principles	192
24.3. Renarrated mood: present and imperfect tenses	194
24.4. Renarrated mood: future and future in the past tenses	195
24.5. Renarrated mood: aorist tense	196
24.6. Use of the renarrated mood in narrative context	197
24.7. Summary: use of the renarrated mood	201
Exercises	202
Sample sentences	203
Sentences for translation	204
Reading selection: За вампирите	205
Glossary	207
Cultural commentary	
Religion: mosques and churches	209
History: Georgi Dimitrov	209
Archaeology: recent excavations	209
Geography: citation of place names; local food and drink	209
Folk belief	210

LESSON 25

Dialogue: Ти си бил голям кавалер!	211
Grammar	
25.1. The renarrated mood, continued	213
25.2. Renarrated mood in 1st and 2nd person	213
25.3. Renarrated mood of the past indefinite and past anterior tense	214
25.4. Renarrated mood of the future anterior and future anterior in the past tenses	215
25.5. The "admirative" and "dubitative" moods	218
25.6. Forms expressing "stronger renarration"	219
25.7. Review of the renarrated mood: the general concept of "distancing"	221
TENSE VS. MOOD IN BULGARIAN: TEMPORAL DISTANCE	
VS. "INVOLVEMENT DISTANCE"	222
Exercises	223
Sample sentences	223
Sentences for translation	224
Reading selection: Хитър Петър и ламята	225
Glossary	227
Cultural commentary	
Geography: Vitosha	229
Names	229
Political history: socialist government (and jokes)	229
Folklore	229

LESSON 26

Dialogue: Чудя се аз какъв подарък да му направя	230
Grammar	
26.1. Verbal prefixation, review	232
26.2. *Aktionsarten* and the Bulgarian verb: general principles	232
The prefix в-	232
Aktionsart derivation: в-	233
The prefix из-	234

Aktionsart derivation: из- *(meaning 1)*	234
Aktionsart derivation: из- *(meaning 2)*	235
26.3. The system of *Aktionsarten* in Bulgarian	236
AKTIONSARTEN (Prefixal and prepositional meanings in Bulgarian)	237
26.4. The usefulness of a classification phrased in terms of *Aktionsarten*	238
The prefix по-	238
Aktionsart derivation: по- *(meaning 1)*	238
The prefixes от- and раз-	238
Aktionsart derivation: от- *(meaning 1)*	239
Aktionsart derivation: раз- *(meaning 1)*	239
26.5. Degrees of predictability within the system of *Aktionsarten*	240
The prefix над-	240
The prefix до-	240
The prefixes по- and на-	241
26.6. Word order in certain fixed phrases	241
Exercises	242
Sample sentences	243
Sentences for translation	244
Reading selection: Анна Каменова, "Разказвай, Брезице!"	245
Glossary	247
Cultural commentary	
History: Graf Ignatiev and the treaties of 1878	249
City life: on the streets	249
Geography: the Danube	250
Folklore: the walled-in wife	250
Customs: "topping off"	250
Literature: Anna Kamenova	250

LESSON 27

Dialogue: Без мене не би знаел как да се оправиш	251
Grammar	
27.1. The conditional mood: introduction and formation	253
27.2. Word order in the conditional mood	253
27.3. The conditional mood used to describe hypothetical states	254
27.4. The conditional mood used in attenuated commands and statements	255
27.5. The conditional of impersonal and modal constructions	256
27.6. "Non-conditional" би	257
27.7. The conditional mood in conditional constructions	258
27.8. Archaic case forms	260
Exercises	261
Sample sentences	261
Sentences for translation	262
Reading selection: Йордан Йовков, "Сали Яшар, прочутият майстор на каруци"	263
Glossary	265
Cultural commentary	
Forms of address: "Welcome"	267
Folklore: proverbs; folk medicine	267
Literature: Iordan Iovkov	267

LESSON 28

Dialogue: Кога друг път бихме могли да им го покажем?	268
Grammar	
28.1. Tense, aspect, and mood in the Bulgarian verb	270
28.2. Review of conditional constructions	270
28.3. Tense vs. mood in conditional constructions: general observations	272
28.4. Factive vs. hypothetical conditional constructions	273
28.5. Concrete vs. theoretical conditional constructions	276
28.6. Specific vs. broad interpretation of conditional constructions	277
28.7. Conditional constructions: summary	278

28.8. Modal usage of the future anterior	278
28.9. Factive vs. hypothetical, and the usage of да	279
Exercises	282
Sample sentences	283
Sentences for translation	284
Reading selections: Кореспонденция - (16)	285
Да се завърнеш в бащината къща... (poem)	286
Glossary	287
Cultural commentary	
Geography: Vitosha	289
Literature: Dimcho Debelyanov	289
Guests	290
Food and drink: foreign borrowings	290
History: April uprising	290

LESSON 29

Dialogue: Увлекли са се в спомени за доброто старо време	291
Grammar	
29.1. Tense, mood, and aspect in Bulgarian: general review	293
29.2. Past narration and the renarrated mood	294
29.3. Renarrated forms of the aorist revisited	295
29.4. Renarrated forms of the imperfect revisited	297
29.5. Towards a solution: transcending tense, aspect, and mood	299
29.6. Usage of the generalized past	300
Exercises	302
Sample sentences	302
Sentences for translation	303
Reading selection: Захари Стоянов, "Христо Ботев в село Задунайка"	304
Glossary	306
Cultural Commentary	
Literature: Hristo Botev	308
Literature: Zahari Stoyanov	308
Geography: Bessarabia	309
Village life	309

LESSON 30

Dialogue: Ще се видим ли догодина?	310
Postscript	
30.1. Standard and literary languages: the Bulgarian literary standard	312
30.2. Variation within standard languages, and the concept of "norm"	314
30.3. Dialectology and linguistic geography: the study of rural dialects	316
30.4. Dialectology and sociolinguistics: the study of urban dialects	317
30.5. The Bulgarian language: conclusion	318
Reading selections: Стойко Стойков, "Българският книжовен език и българските диалекти"	319
Glossary	321

CUMULATIVE GLOSSARY: Lessons 1-30	325
INDEX	383

INTRODUCTION

Intensive Bulgarian is designed to introduce the English-speaking student to the essentials of Bulgarian grammar. Volume 2 of this book continues the pattern of Volume 1: each lesson begins with a dialogue, which presents a segment of a continuing story told in contemporary colloquial spoken Bulgarian. These dialogues, which continue a story begun in Volume 1, focus on the interactions between two visiting American students and several small groups of Bulgarians. Each lesson concludes with a reading selection; certain of the reading selections also continue the narrative begun in Volume 1, which is presented as a series of letters between a Bulgarian family and an American family. Other reading selections are intended to expose the student to different styles of contemporary written Bulgarian. All but the final lesson include drill and translation exercises, sample sentences (examples which illustrate usage to a greater extent possible than in the dialogue story script), and "Cultural commentary", containing brief explanatory notes about Bulgarian culture and society. Bulgarian-English glossaries are given at the end of each lesson, and are repeated in a cumulative glossary at the end of each volume. The Bulgarian-English glossary list in this volume contains all the words which occur in both volumes. Although volume 1 contained a brief English-Bulgarian glossary, it is considered that at this point the student should be using a standard English-Bulgarian dictionary; therefore, no English-Bulgarian glossary is included here.

As in Volume 1, the central focus is on the grammar explanations. The subtitle of *Intensive Bulgarian* indicates the book's dual intent. On the one hand, it is a textbook which gives a graded presentation of Bulgarian grammar that can be used either in the classroom or for self-study. Reflecting the fact that second-Slavic language classes are often a combination of undergraduates with no other exposure to foreign languages and graduates specializing either in Slavic languages or linguistics, the first 23 lessons have been split into "Basic grammar" (designed for the first group) and "Additional grammar notes" (designed for the second group). Readings, sample sentences, substitution drills, and translation exercises complete the pedagogical side of *Intensive Bulgarian*. Audio tapes (also available in CD format), as a supplementary aid in the acquisition of pronunciation, may be purchased separately (see p. vi). The assumption throughout, exemplified in the primary focus on grammar, is that speaking will come on its own with practice (especially in a Bulgarian-speaking environment) once students have acquired a solid knowledge of grammatical structure.

The other intent of *Intensive Bulgarian* is to serve as a reference grammar. To this end, the grammar explanations in Volume 1 were made as thorough as possible while still remaining consistent with the textbook format; additionally, the final lesson in Volume 1 presented a concise synopsis of Bulgarian grammar, a full listing of all verbal paradigms (including those to be explicated in the present volume), a full presentation of all word order rules, and a comprehensive index. The current volume, while still maintaining the textbook format, goes into much further detail on analytic issues of Bulgarian grammar, and concludes with a new interpretation both of the Bulgarian conditional and of the entire Bulgarian tense-mood-aspect system.

Both volumes have been written in layman's language, on the assumption that complex grammatical issues can be made accessible to the intelligent layman if specialized jargon (or recourse to theories requiring special formalism) is avoided. During most of the writing of this book, the only other reference grammar available in English required knowledge of a specialized theory. As this book goes to press, however, other accessibly-written reference grammars have begun to appear. The contribution of *Intensive Bulgarian* to a suddenly enriched field lies in its unique dual focus: it is thorough enough to give the student and scholar not only linguistically sophisticated analyses accompanied by extensive examples and furnished with a full index, but it also offers the clarity and fullness of the pedagogical approach which includes lively speech, cultural notes, extensive glossaries and concise, accessible explanations, many of which make explicit reference to structural similarities and differences between Bulgarian and English.

Intensive Bulgarian, therefore, provides a self-contained description of the Bulgarian language, written in textbook format but with a thoroughness approaching that of a reference grammar.

As a textbook, *Intensive Bulgarian* is intended to aid students in acquiring communicative skills (via practice of the conversational phrases embedded in the dialogues, the letters, and included in certain of the sample sentences), structural comprehension (via study of the grammar explanations and the sample sentences), and ability in reading and writing. Language teachers and learners will find all the fundamental points of Bulgarian grammar in the "Basic" section of each lesson. Individual teachers (or self-study students) may choose to include some, all, or none of the more detailed information in the "Additional" notes which follow each "Basic" section. Most students, even those who know Russian and/or who are highly motivated and able to work intensively, will probably need three semesters to finish the book; others may require four semesters. Self-study is possible but (as in all language learning) success is more assured when the text is used in the classroom by an experienced teacher. The extent to which one (or more) of the several language skills are to be emphasized is at the discretion of the instructor. Students and instructors should both note that the glossary lists for each lesson are quite long, since they include all words encountered in all sections of each lesson, and that it is not expected that students attain active mastery of each lesson's vocabulary list before going on to the next lesson. It is suggested that each instructor select from the lists the words that are to be actively memorized for each lesson.

As a reference grammar, *Intensive Bulgarian* offers a thorough account of Bulgarian morphology and syntax according to traditional models, while also introducing several innovations to descriptive Bulgarian grammar. These include:
-- a new analysis of clitic ordering rules together with a new descriptive notation
(this presentation began in Lesson 5, and continued throughout Volume 1 to Lesson 13. It was summarized in schematic form in Lesson 15, and is repeated in abbreviated form in Lesson 16 of the present volume);
-- a newly clarified schematic overview of the verbal system highlighting both the relationship between present and aorist forms (Lesson 12, volume 1) and that between simplex and compound verb forms (Lesson 23 in this volume) and between tense and mood (Lesson 25 in this volume);
-- new contributions to ongoing discussions of tense, mood and aspect (Lessons 28 and 29 in this volume); and, most notably,
-- the addition of the "generalized past" to the roster of Bulgarian verbal paradigms (Lesson 29 in this volume). Indeed, the major contribution of the present volume as a reference grammar is to demonstrate how a conventional description of the Bulgarian system of tense, aspect and mood leads naturally and inexorably to this innovative re-interpretation.

* * * * * * * *

In writing this textbook, I have taken as authoritative sources the following standard dictionaries and grammars:

Т. Атанасова и др., Българо-английски речник
П. Пашов и Хр. Първев, Правоговорен речник на българския език
Л. Андрейчин, Граматика на българския език
Ю. Маслов, Грамматика болгарского языка

Additionally, in an attempt to describe more accurately the language spoken by educated Bulgarians, I have introduced certain interpretations of my own. The data underlying all such interpretations have been checked extensively with university-educated native speakers of Bulgarian.

ACKNOWLEDGMENTS

The division of labor in the writing of this textbook has been as follows. The conception and organization of the book, and the grammatical interpretations, are my own. I have also written all the grammar sections, all the "Cultural Commentary" sections, dialogues 1-14, and dialogues 15-18 in collaboration with Olga Mladenova. The remaining dialogues (19-30), all the reading selections not otherwise identified, all the exercises, and all the sample sentences were composed by Olga Mladenova, who has also checked the earlier dialogues and all the example sentences in the text for accuracy, and has rendered me invaluable service as an informant, both in linguistic and cultural terms. Vladimir Zhobov has also contributed many hours as an informant, and has written the reading selections in Lessons 4, 8, 12 and 14. William S. Nickell gave invaluable help and moral support throughout earlier stages of work on this textbook, and especially in first-round compilations of the glossary lists. Milena Savova (together with Eve Sweetser) and Jonathan Barnes were also of great help in the earlier and later stages, respectively, of this project.

Several classes of students have given helpful feedback on the earlier versions of this textbook. I am grateful to them, and especially to their teachers, who include (in addition to myself) Jonathan Barnes, Grace Fielder, Robert Greenberg, Christina Kramer, John Leafgren, William Nickell, and Catherine Rudin. Others who have rendered aid of various sorts are Lauren Brody, Donald Dyer, Michael Holman, Katia McClain, Yves Moreau, Valentin Paunov, Maksim Stamenov, Andrei Stoevsky, and Maria Todorova. Photos which illustrate the text either were taken by me or were donated by Robin Brooks, Robert Greenberg, Michael Kuharski, Alex Madonick, Olga Mladenova, Dirk Morr, Milena Savova, Eve Sweetser, and Orna Weinroth, to whom I extend my gratitude collectively. Their photos appear on the following pages of this second volume:

Robin Brooks: pp. 80, 97, 250
Robert Greenberg/Orna Weinroth: p. ii
Michael Kuharski: pp. 21, 288
Alex Madonick: p. 45
Olga Mladenova: pp. 90, 117, 138, 146, 290, 305
Dirk Morr: pp. 177, 210, 395
Milena Savova: p. 182
Eve Sweetser: p. 260

The University of Wisconsin Press has produced a beautiful volume, and Steve Salemson has been an ideal editor, without whose efforts the book would not have come to light in its present elegant manner (and with whom it has been a great pleasure to work). Cynthia Ramsey was of great assistance in the final stages of text output.

For having been allowed entry into the world of Koprivshtitsa, the inspiration of which is seen throughout both volumes of the book, I am indebted to Petăr and Vasil Petrov (and most of all to the late Mihaila Stainova); I likewise extend my gratitude to the many Bulgarian friends through whom I came to love this beautiful country and its language, especially my linguist colleagues and friends among whom stand out Tanja Behar, Todor Boyadzhiev, Georgi Kolev, Darina Mladenova, Olga Mladenova, Sabina Pavlova, Vasil Vasilev, Boryana Velcheva, Vladimir Zhobov, and most of all the late Maksim Mladenov. Finally, I am grateful to family members and friends in California for their patience and unflagging support through the years it took for this work to come to fruition.

INTENSIVE BULGARIAN

LESSON 16

DIALOGUE

<u>Кýче ли си ни кýпил, тáтко?</u>

// Пéтър, Тáня и децáта пристѝгат вкъ̀щи. Пéтър отклю̀чва вратáта. Ня̀къде лáе кýче. //

Петър: Добрé дошлѝ, éто ни нáй-накрáя вкъ̀щи.

Надка: А къдé е изненáдата?

Петър: Не я̀ ли чýваш?

Таня: Амá товá кýче у домá ли лáе?

Камен: Кýче ли си ни кýпил, тáтко?

Надка: Къдé е?

Петър: Затвóрил съм го в бáнята, тó е óще мнóго мáлко.

// Децáта изтѝчват до бáнята и намѝрат еднó мáлко пýхкаво чéрно кýченце. //

Надка: Тáтко, кáк се кáзва?

Петър: Не съм му измѝслил ѝме. Измислéте вѝе!

Таня: Тѝ акъ̀л ѝмаш ли? В тáя къ̀ща за нáс ня̀ма мя̀сто, а тѝ кýче си донéсъл!

Камен: Мáмо, амá вѝж кóлко е слáдко! Ѝмето му е Бóби. Бóби, Бóби, елá! Вѝж, мáмо, знáе, че ѝмето му е Бóби.

Таня: Какъ̀в Бóби! Детѝнски рáботи!

Петър: Кýпил съм един учéбник. Ще го десѝраме всѝчки заéдно.

Надка: Вѝж го, кóлко ýмно глéда! Всѝчко разбѝра.

Таня: Пéтре, избѝрай! Или Бóби или áз!

Петър: Бóби тéбе нáй-мнóго те харéсва. Сѝгурно ще те слýша мнóго.

Шестнайсети урок / Lesson 16

Таня: Хем жи́вотно, пък и то́ зна́е кого́ да слу́ша. Не́ като ня́кои...

Камен: Не́ка да изведе́м ку́чето на разхо́дка.

Петър: Добре́, вре́ме му е. Не съм го изве́ждал от сутринта́.

Таня: Ха́йде, изли́зайте вси́чки, а́з ще приго́твя не́що за вече́ря.

Камен: Ни́е с Бо́би и́скаме пържо́ла, нали́ Бо́би?

Таня: Ти́ нали́ до сутринта́ ня́маше ни́що да яде́ш?

Камен: Па́к огладня́х.

Надка: И а́з.

Таня: Не зна́м дали́ и́ма пържо́ли в хлади́лника...

Петър: Ня́ма. И́ма са́мо хля́б, яйца́, дома́ти и ки́село мля́ко. А́з ня́мах вре́ме да и́да на паза́р.

Таня: Но и́маше вре́ме за Бо́би, нали́?

Камен: Ма́мо, ни́е с Бо́би и пъ́ржени яйца́ яде́м.

Таня: Ви́ж ти́, каква́ новина́. И откога́ яде́те пъ́ржени яйца́? До вчера не мо́жех да ви нака́рам да ги опи́тате.

Надка: От дне́с.

Таня: То ма́й не е́ мно́го я́сно ко́й кого́ дреси́ра: ви́е ку́чето или то́ ва́с. Ха́йде, тръ́гвайте. Не го́ ли ви́ждате, че ня́ма търпе́ние да изле́зе навъ́н.

Петър: Неде́й да бъ́рзаш с вече́рята. Ни́е си́гурно ця́л ча́с ще се разхо́ждаме.

Шестнайсети урок / Lesson 16

BASIC GRAMMAR

16.1. The past indefinite tense: formation of the L-participle

The past indefinite tense (**мѝнало неопределе́но вре́ме**) designates a past action within some broader context, usually with reference to the present state of the speaker. It is formed by combining the copula with the past active participle, also called the "L-participle". These participles were presented in Lesson 9 as adjectives made from verbs like **оста́на** (оста́нал), **мѝна** (мѝнал), or **свъ́рша** (свъ́ршил).

The L-participle endings, composed of **-л** plus adjective endings, are added to the aorist stem. This stem is found by dropping the **-х** from the 1sg. aorist form. When the final vowel of the stem is an alternating vowel, the **-е-** form of the alternant appears in the plural L-participle (and the **-а-/-я-** form in all others).

L-PARTICIPLE

1sg.aor	stem	masculine	feminine	neuter	plural
сре́щна-х	сре́щна-	сре́щна-л	сре́щна-ла	сре́щна-ло	сре́щна-ли
гле́да-х	гле́да-	гле́да-л	гле́да-ла	гле́да-ло	гле́да-ли
хо́ди-х	хо́ди-	хо́ди-л	хо́ди-ла	хо́ди-ло	хо́ди-ли
пи́-х	пи-	пи́-л	пи́-ла	пи́-ло	пи́-ли
пи́са-х	пи́са-	пи́са-л	пи́са-ла	пи́са-ло	пи́са-ли
бра́-х	бра-	бра́-л	бра́-ла	бра́-ло	бра́-ли
взе́-х	взе-	взе́-л	взе́-ла	взе́-ло	взе́-ли
живя́-х	живя-	живя́-л	живя́-ла	живя́-ло	живе́-ли
видя́-х	видя-	видя́-л	видя́-ла	видя́-ло	виде́-ли
вървя́-х	вървя-	вървя́-л	вървя́-ла	вървя́-ло	върве́-ли

Note: Refer to the present-aorist chart of verb types in Lesson 12.

For verbs of type 5, however, special rules must be learned. To find the stem, drop both the 1sg. aorist ending **-х** *and* the preceding theme vowel. Then add the L-participle endings directly to the stem (except for the masculine form, where it is necessary to insert the "fleeting" vowel **-ъ-**).

If the stem vowel is an alternating one (as in **обл-е-ка́** vs. **обл-я́-кох**), the **-е-** alternant appears in the plural L-participle. Remember that the stem vowel **-е-** does not necessarily alternate (as in **пека́**).

If the final consonant of a type 5 verb stem is **-т** or **-д**, drop this consonant before adding the L-participle ending. In this case, there is no fleeting vowel in the masculine form.

Шестнайсети урок / Lesson 16

L-PARTICIPLE

1sg.aor	stem	masculine	feminine	neuter	plural
обля́к-ох	обля́к-	обля́к-ъ-л	обля́к-ла	обля́к-ло	обле́к-ли
вля́з-ох	вляз-	вля́з-ъ-л	вля́з-ла	вля́з-ло	вле́з-ли
пе́к-ох	пек-	пе́к-ъ-л	пе́к-ла	пе́к-ло	пе́к-ли
че́т-ох	че-	че́-л	че́-ла	че́-ло	че́-ли
да́д-ох	да-	да́-л	да́-ла	да́-ло	да́-ли

The verb мо́га can form the L-participle from the aorist stem. Usually, however, it forms it from the present stem. Both variants are possible.

The verbs оти́да and до́йда form the L-participle with a stem ending in -ш, and the verb съм forms the L-participle from the stem би-.

L-PARTICIPLE

1sg.aor	stem	masculine	feminine	neuter	plural
мож-а́х	мож-	можа́-л	можа́-ла	можа́-ло	може́-ли
[мо́га]	мог-	* мог-ъ́-л	мог-ла́	мог-ло́	мог-ли́
[оти́дох]	оти́ш-	* оти́ш-ъ-л	оти́ш-ла	оти́ш-ло	оти́ш-ли
[дойдо́х]	дош-	* дош-ъ́-л	дош-ла́	дош-ло́	дош-ли́
[съм]	би-	* би́-л	би-ла́	би-ло́	би-ли́

* The L-participles of съм, до́йда and the less preferred variant of мо́га (могъ́л) are accented on the final syllable; оти́да also has optional final stress (отишъ́л and оти́шъл). All others have the accent of the aorist.

Optional stress shifts in the aorist (for instance, хо́дих or ходи́х) are equally possible in the L-participle (for instance, хо́дил or ходи́л).

16.2. Agreement in the past indefinite

The past indefinite tense consists of the L-participle plus the appropriate present tense form of съм, acting as verbal auxiliary. Both must agree with the subject of the verb. The auxiliary съм agrees in person and number (а́з съм, ти́ си, etc.), and the L-participle agrees in number and (in the singular only) gender.

If the subject is plural, therefore, one need only make sure that the L-participle is plural as well. But if the subject is singular, the L-participle must indicate the gender of the subject. In other words, even though it is part of a verbal tense, it follows the agreement rules of an adjective. Thus:

spoken to or by a woman

| Ку́пила ли си но́ва ро́кля? | Have you bought a new dress? |
| Вче́ра съм била́ с не́го. | I was with him yesterday. |

spoken by or to a man

Ти́ би́л ли си у тя́х?	Have you been at their house?
Дошъ́л съм навре́ме, ама ви ня́ма.	I came on time, but you're not here.

16.3. Word order in the past indefinite

When a verb in the past indefinite has one or more short form pronoun objects, these objects must occur adjacent to the verbal auxiliary. Pronoun objects precede the 3rd singular auxiliary, but follow all other auxiliary forms. The L-participle must stand immediately before (or immediately after) the chain of clitics.

Ку́пил съм им го.	I bought it for them.
А́з съм им го ку́пил.	*(same)*
Ку́пил си им го.	You *(sg.)* bought it for them.
Ку́пили сме им го.	We bought it for them.
Ку́пили сте им го.	You *(pl.)* bought it for them.
Ку́пили са им го.	They bought it for them.
Ку́пил им го е.	He bought it for them.
Та́тко им го е ку́пил.	Dad bought it for them.

In an affirmative question, the interrogative particle follows the L-participle directly. In a negative question it follows the first clitic in the string. For example:

Ку́пил ли си им го?	Did you buy it for them?
Не си ли им го ку́пил?	Didn't you buy it for them?

16.4. Usage of the past indefinite tense

The past indefinite tense makes reference, within the scope of the present, to an action which occurred at some point in the past. It has a number of different meanings. The most simple is that defined by its form: an adjective derived from a verb. In this meaning, the past indefinite describes the state which results from a particular verbal action. For example:

Па́к си закъсня́л.	You're late again.
Тя́ е ве́че зами́нала за Ва́рна.	She's already left for Varna.
Те́ са се́днали на пе́йката.	They're sitting on the bench.

The past indefinite refers not only to a present state, however, but to the result of any verbal action. Like the aorist and imperfect, it is a past tense, recounting an action which happened in the past. Unlike the aorist and imperfect, each of which focuses exclusively on the past (either on the fact of the action itself or on the period of time the action lasted), the past indefinite brings the scope of the action into the moment of speaking. Thus, it refers not only to the action itself but to some aspect of it which is relevant to the present. Consider the following examples:

Та́тко ни е ку́пил ку́че.	Daddy [has] bought us a dog.
Ку́че ли си ни ку́пил, та́тко?	Daddy, have you bought us a *dog*?
	Daddy, did you buy us a *dog*?
Ку́пил съм еди́н уче́бник. Ще го дреси́раме за́едно.	I['ve] bought a manual. We'll train him together.

All the above examples refer to the past action of a purchase, but were spoken in a context which directs attention more to the result of the purchase than to the act itself. The English present perfect ("have bought") is similar in its focus on the present result of past action, and renders the sense of these Bulgarian sentences well. But the scope of the Bulgarian past indefinite is broader, and can often be rendered by the English simple past as well, as seen in the translations given above.

In general, the English speaker learning Bulgarian has a certain advantage, since the verbal systems of the two languages are roughly parallel in a number of ways. When it concerns narration of past action, for instance, speakers of both languages have a choice whether to focus more on the fact of past action or on its result in the present. Thus:

	Fact of past action		*Scope of action extended to present moment*	
English	*past*	I did	*present perfect*	I have done
Bulgarian	*aorist*	(на)пра́вих	*past indefinite*	(на)пра́вил съм

This parallel must *not* be taken as a given, however, because the choices made by a Bulgarian speaker will often not be those made by an English speaker. The concept "scope of action extended to present moment" is quite broad and flexible, and choice of tense in both languages is determined simply by the speaker's focus.

Generalizations and examples given in this lesson and subsequent ones are intended to help the student gain a feel for Bulgarian past tense usage, but (as in all language learning) such generalizations can only lay the groundwork for practice and experience. Sometimes the English present perfect is the best translation for the Bulgarian past indefinite. At other times, the English present perfect will be the best translation for the Bulgarian aorist, and the English simple past will be used to translate the Bulgarian past indefinite.

One context in which the past indefinite occurs particularly frequently (and which does parallel English usage fairly consistently) is that of negation, especially when the speaker wishes to indicate that an action has not been performed yet.

Шестнайсети урок / Lesson 16

Не съм му измислил име.	I haven't thought up a name for him [yet].
Не съм го извеждал от сутринта.	I haven't taken him out since this morning.
В живота си не съм виждала такива планини.	In my whole life I haven't seen mountains like these.
От четирийсет години не е ходил в Париж.	He hasn't been to Paris in 40 years.

16.5. Imperfective imperatives

In general, affirmative commands are given in the perfective aspect and negative commands in the imperfective aspect. The imperfective aspect can also be used when the desired action is a habitual or repeated one. For example:

affirmative single action: perfective

Когато излезеш, затвори вратата!	Close the door when you go out!

affirmative repeated action: imperfective

Когато излизаш, затваряй вратата!	Close the door when[ever] you go out!

negative: imperfective

Не затваряй вратата!	Don't close the door!

Bulgarians may also use the imperfective imperative for a single affirmative action. This choice of aspect exppresses a certain amount of insistence or impatience.

Петре, избирай! Или Боби, или аз!	OK, Peter, choose! Either Bobby or me!
Хайде, излизайте всички.	All right -- out, all of you!

The neutral command is centered on the desire that an action be carried out: the action is perceived in its bounded terms and the perfective aspect is therefore chosen. In a more insistent or impatient command, however, the focus is more on the fact of the action itself, and the speaker's desire that it be initiated. This absence of boundedness prompts the choice of the imperfective aspect.

The sense of impatience need not be as strong as in the above examples. Depending on the context, the imperfective imperative can convey different degrees of focus on the immediacy of the action. For example:

affirmative single action: perfective

Избери едно от тях!	Choose one of these!

Шестнайсети урок / Lesson 16

affirmative single action: imperfective
-- Всé ми е еднó.   "It doesn't make any difference."
-- Ня́ма значéние, избирай!   "Never mind, choose anyway."

16.6. Additional imperative forms

Negative commands can be formed either with **не** and the imperative form of an imperfective verb, as in the example above, or with the aid of various particles.

The particle **недéй(те)**, which is followed by a **да**-phrase, conveys a slightly lesser sense of urgency than "**не** + imperative". The phrase "**стига** + past indefinite" is used when the speaker wishes an action to stop. Both **стига** and **недéй** can be used alone if the action is understood from the context.

Недéй да бъ́рзаш!	Don't hurry!
Недéйте да се притесня́вате!	Don't worry!
Недéй!	Don't!
Стига си я глéдал!	Stop looking at her!
Стига си повта́рял еднó и съ́що!	Stop repeating the same thing!
Стига!	Stop! Enough!

A command can be issued to a third person by means of the particle **нéка**, sometimes followed directly by a perfective verb and sometimes by a **да**-phrase, with no difference in meaning. **Да**-phrases are also sometimes used alone in this meaning.

Да влéзе ли?	Should he come in?
Нéка влéзе.	Have him come in.
Нéка да влéзе.	*(same)*
Да влéзе.	*(same)*
Да ви́дим дали́ ще ста́не.	Let's see if it happens or not.

When used in the 1pl. present, **нéка** is similar to **ха́йде**, but not identical. **Нéка** conveys more of a request or a desire on the part of the speaker, and **ха́йде** conveys a somewhat stronger sense of command. In both cases, the sense of command can be attenuated by adding the interrogative particle **а** at the end.

Нéка да изведéм ку́чето на разхо́дка!	Let's take the dog out for a walk.
Ха́йде да изведéм ку́чето на разхо́дка!	Come on, let's take the dog out for a walk!
Нéка / Ха́йде да изведéм ку́чето на разхо́дка, а?	What about we take the dog out for a walk?

Шестнайсети урок / Lesson 16

EXERCISES

I. Rewrite these sentences in the past indefinite:

1. То́й ще прочете́ кни́гата та́зи се́дмица.
2. Ще ви́диш ли ня́кого на у́лицата?
3. Деца́та ще са мно́го уморе́ни от то́лкова игра́.
4. Та́ня ще оти́де на ки́но, а не́ на ра́бота.
5. Тя́ ня́ма да мо́же да наме́ри беле́жката.
6. Ле́ля Ва́ня живе́е в та́зи къ́ща.
7. Ви́е ще даде́те по една́ би́ра на вси́чки го́сти.

II. Rewrite in the past indefinite:

1. Бра́т ти вче́ра и́маше и́зпит, взе́ ли го?
2. Вре́мето е то́пло, а ти́ си с палто́! Защо́ си го обле́че?
3. Не ви́ждам ключа от по́щенската кути́я. Ко́й ли го изгу́би?
4. Дне́с не я́ видя́х в библиоте́ката.
5. Не ги́ ли но́си ве́че на попра́вка?
6. То́зи фи́лм го гле́дах два́ пъ́ти.
7. За рожде́ния де́н му ку́пиха вратовръ́зка.

III. Transform these sentences to the negative form, using either неде́й *or* сти́га.
Extra credit: give two possible forms for each.

1. Отвори́ си очи́те, а́з запа́лих свещта́!
2. Огле́дай се в огледа́лото!
3. Разкажи́ ми то́зи фи́лм!
4. Помогни́ ми с та́зи кръстосло́вица!
5. Разходе́те се из па́рка!
6. Прибере́те пране́то на су́хо!
7. Стани́ пра́ва!

Шестнайсети урок / Lesson 16

ADDITIONAL GRAMMAR NOTES

16.3a. Word order rules for the past indefinite

When the past indefinite takes pronoun objects, a number of clitic forms occur together. Since the ordering of clitic forms both with respect to each other and to other words in the sentence is very rigid, it is important to review the rules which govern this ordering. The basic components of these rules were studied in detail in Volume 1, and are summarized here briefly:

(1) If two object pronouns are present, the indirect object must precede the direct object.
(2) The verbal copula (съм), which in the past indefinite functions as verbal auxiliary, precedes any object pronoun(s), unless it is the 3rd singular, in which case it follows any object pronoun(s).

Definition of clitic string: "the entire complex of pronoun(s) and copula"

(3) The clitic string must occur immediately after the negative particle, the L-participle, or another stressed word.
(4) If some other word than the L-participle precedes the clitic string, then the L-participle must occur immediately after the clitic string.
(5) The interrogative particle follows the verb directly and precedes any object pronoun(s).
(6) The negative and interrogative particles surround the first clitic in the string.

Examples will be given below, with segments in each case identified according to a notation developed for this purpose. Within this notation, all clitics are identified in upper-case letters, all fully stressed words in lower case letters, and words which belong to neither category, such as the negative particle, are identified by a capitalized abbreviation. Abbreviations relevant to the past indefinite are:

DIR	direct object pronouns, including the reflexive ce
IND	indirect object pronouns, including the reflexive си
COP	plural verbal auxiliaries (сме, сте, са) and 1-2sg. (съм, си)
3rdCOP	3sg. verbal auxiliary (е)
INT	the interrogative particle (ли)
Neg.	the negative particle (не)
part	the L-participle

Шестнайсети урок / Lesson 16

Examples (1) - (4) illustrate basic ordering within the clitic string, and with respect to the L-participle. The sentences are kept simple in order to focus on the elements of word order. Other words may be added, of course, but they may not break up the sequences of elements noted above.

(1) Ку́пил си им го.
     part *COP* *IND* *DIR*

(2) Ти́ си им го ку́пил.
     subject *COP* *IND* *DIR* *part*

You bought it for them.

(3) Ку́пил им го е.
     part *IND* *DIR* *3rdCOP*

(4) То́й им го е ку́пил.
     subject *IND* *DIR* *3rdCOP* *part*

He bought it for them.

Examples (5) through (10) repeat the above sentences, transformed first into interrogative, then negative, then negative-interrogative. Note that while the ordering of the L-participle is flexible in affirmative sentences (it may either stand either before or after the clitic string), it is fixed in non-affirmative sentences.

(5) Ку́пил ли си им го?
     part *INT* *COP* *IND* *DIR*

Did you buy it for them?

(6) Ку́пил ли им го е?
     part *INT* *IND* *DIR* *3rdCOP*

Did he buy it for them?

(7) Не си́ им го ку́пил.
     Neg. *COP* *IND* *DIR* *part*

You didn't buy it for them.

(8) Не и́м го е ку́пил.
     Neg. *IND* *DIR* *3rdCOP* *part*

He didn't buy it for them.

(9) Не си́ ли им го ку́пил?
     Neg. *COP* *INT* *IND* *DIR* *part*

Didn't you buy it for them?

(10) Не и́м ли го е ку́пил?
     Neg. *IND* *INT* *DIR* *3rdCOP* *part*

Didn't he buy it for them?

16.6a. Недей and стига with the truncated infinitive

Недей is usually followed by a да-phrase, and **стига** is usually followed by the past indefinite. Both, however, can also be followed by the so-called "truncated infinitive", which is identical with the 3sg. aorist of an imperfective verb. This usage is common with some speakers and rare with others. For example:

Недей писа! Стига писа!	Don't write! Stop writing!
Недей чете! Стига чете!	Don't read! Stop reading!

16.7. Motion verbs: the past tense of the verb идвам

The verb **идвам** is an imperfective verb meaning "come" (and sometimes "go"). Although it is listed in dictionaries as a simple imperfective, most Bulgarians feel that the perfective verb **дойда** is its de facto partner. In the present and imperfect tenses, **идвам** has the meaning of a regular imperfective verb. For example:

present

Той идва редовно у нас.	He comes to see us regularly.
Към нея идва един висок човек.	A tall man is coming towards her.

imperfect

Той идваше редовно у нас.	He used to come to see us regularly.
Към нея идваше един висок човек.	A tall man was coming towards her.

In the past indefinite, **идвам** can also be used in the meaning "go" with the unbounded meaning of the imperfective aspect. For example:

Той идвал ли е в България?	Has he [ever] been to Bulgaria?
Тя е идвала в Англия.	She has been to England.

In the aorist, however, and in most instances of the past indefinite, **идвам** has a different meaning. Namely, it refers to a single, completed trip: someone came and then went away again. This meaning is perfective in its boundedness; nevertheless it is still broader than the perfective meaning of **дойда** (which refers to a bounded trip in one direction only). Here are examples of **идвам** in this meaning:

-- Идва ли пощаджията?	"Has the postman come?"
-- Не е идвал, още е рано.	"He hasn't come yet, it's early."
Не разбрах защо той идва в канцеларията ми.	I didn't understand why he came to my office.

Помниш ли братовчедка ми? Тя ти идва на гости.	Do you remember my cousin? She came to visit you.
Тя идва ли да ви се обади? Веднага щом се върна в България, първата ѝ работа беше да дойде на гости.	Has she been to see you? The first thing she did when she returned to Bulgaria was to come over [to your house].
Аз съм идвал у вас на гости, но не помня кога беше.	I came to your house [once], but I don't remember when it was.

As is the case with all **a**-conjugation verbs, the 3sg. aorist and 3sg. present are identical. Without context, then, the form идва can mean either "is coming" (present) or "came and went" (aorist). All the instances of идва above have been interpreted as aorist; in the appropriate context, however, they could also have present tense meaning.

Speakers also have the option to shift the accent to the theme vowel of the aorist (see vol. 1, p. 180) to emphasize the distinction. In fact, however, for most speakers context is sufficient to indicate which of the two meanings is intended.

16.8. Impersonal verbs, continued

Each of the four major impersonal verbs, **има, няма, трябва,** and **може,** conveys a particular condition or situation:

verb	present condition	verb	present condition
има	there is	трябва	it's necessary
няма	there isn't	може	it's possible

When impersonal verbs are followed by **да**-phrases, each of these situations becomes relevant to a particular verbal action or state, as follows:

verb	action	state
има да ...	one will...	...will happen
няма да ...	one will not...	...will not happen
трябва да ...	one must...	...is supposed to happen
може да ...	one may...	...might happen

The past tense of each of these impersonal verbs is equivalent to the 3sg. imperfect of the relevant conjugated verb. In the simple form, the past tense meaning of each of these verbs refers to a situational condition, as follows:

verb	past condition	verb	past condition
и́маше	there was	тря́бваше	it was necessary
ня́маше	there wasn't	мо́жеше	it was possible

When followed by a да-phrase, however, the past tense of these verbs is more difficult to translate. This is because each projects a certain potential situation (either an action or a state of affairs) into the past. Depending on the context, therefore, several different meanings are possible. Here is a schematic presentation of the meanings, followed by examples.

verb	projected action	projected state
и́маше да ...	one would have...	...would have happened
ня́маше да ...	one would not have...	...would not have happened
тря́бваше да ...	one ought to have...	...was supposed to have happened
мо́жеше да ...	one could have...	...might have happened

Тя́ и́маше да измѝе съ́довете и да измете́ по́да.	She [still] had to wash the dishes and sweep the floor.
Ти налѝ ня́маше нѝщо да яде́ш?	Weren't you going to not eat anything?
Вла́кът тря́бваше да присти́гне досега́.	The train ought to have been here by now.
Ти мо́жеше поне́ да пи́таш.	You could at least have asked.

The English translation of such constructions, particularly those with ня́маше да..., is at times awkward. The main thing to remember is that a particular situation is being projected into the past. In the case of ня́маше да constructions, the situation is that of not intending ("not going") to do something. This particular construction will be studied in more detail in Lesson 22. The point here is to realize that the idea is a straightforward one; it is the expression of it in English which is difficult.

16.9. Alternating consonant / vowel sequences

Sometimes the sequence -ър- (or -ъл-) within a word can alternate with the sequence -ръ- (or -лъ-) in other forms of the same word. This alternation has been seen already in the first syllable of each of the verbs in the aspect pair връ́щам / въ́рна.

This alternation occurs more frequently in monosyllabic nouns or in derivation. Among the words where this alternation occurs are:

Шестнайсети урок / Lesson 16

ръ alternates with ър			
singular indefinite	*singular definite*	*plural*	*(meaning)*
връх	върх-ъ́т	върх-ове́	summit
гръб	гърб-ъ́т	гърб-ове́	back
гръ́к	гърк-ъ́т	гъ́рц-и	Greek
гръ́м	гърм-ъ́т	гръ́м-ове*	thunder
пръ́в	пъ́рв-ият		first
		*[and гъ́рм-ове]	

ъл, ър alternates with лъ, ръ			
adjective	*(meaning)*	*derived form*	*(meaning)*
пъ́лен	full	плъ́н-ка	filling
дъ́лг	debt	длъ́ж-ен	obliged
зъ́рн-о́	grain	зръ́н-це́	granule

It is important to note that this alternation does not occur in all possible instances where it might. The word пръст, for example, might be expected to participate in this alternation, but it does not. For example:

ръ retained in all forms			
singular indefinite	*singular definite*	*plural*	*(meaning)*
пръ́ст	пръ́ст-ът	пръ́ст-и	finger

Шестнайсети урок / Lesson 16

SAMPLE SENTENCES

1. Тóй никóга не é прáл, кáк можá да го накáраш да перé на ръкá?
2. Такá кáкто хубавичко сме сéднали, сегá да и́ма и по еднó ви́но.
3. Вéче са построи́ли къ́щата, остáва да се обзаведé.
4. Тря́бва да провери́ш óще веднъ́ж адрéса, да не сá смени́ли и́мето на у́лицата.
5. Не съм лежáл в бóлница, откáкто ме опера́ха.
6. Тя́ е завъ́ршила срéдно образовáние, но нé и ви́сше.
7. Недéй плáка, ня́ма ни́що стрáшно.
8. Недéй да прáвиш грéшки и ни́кой ня́ма да ти се кáра.
9. Сти́га сте се смéли, ни́що смéшно не съм кáзала.
10. Сти́га сте хóдили по чужби́на, постóйте мáлко тýка за разнообрáзие.
11. Сти́га са ни у́чили с кóй крáк да стъ́пим.
12. Сти́га вéче, че не мóга да издъ́ржам пóвече.
13. Нéка веднъ́ж и твóят мъ́ж да постои́ с децáта вкъ́щи. Ня́ма сáмо ти́ да ги глéдаш.
14. А́з да и́мам такáва къ́ща, пъ́к нéка ми е злé.
15. Нéка да му кáжем какъ́в подáрък ни е донéсъл Дя́до Мрáз.
16. -- А ако те пи́тат, каквó ще отговóриш?
    -- Нéка сáмо посмéят да пи́тат.
17. Нéка се разби́рате, пъ́к дрýгото ще е нарéд.
18. Ля́гай си вéче, коé врéме стáна.
19. Тръ́гвай, че ще закъснéеш, ще затвóрят магази́ните.
20. Тръгни́ веднáга, мóже и да успéеш.
21. Чу́вай каквó ще ти кáжа.
22. Чу́й кáк пéят пти́ците.

Шестнайсети урок / Lesson 16

SENTENCES FOR TRANSLATION

1. "Won't you try the chops?"
   "Thank you, I've already tried them."
   "You have not tried them! Try some..."

2. I must admit I have never been to Bulgaria, so I can't tell you much about their folk costumes. Have you ever seen them?

3. I don't have the patience to wait until they pass out the awards. Can't we make them do it now? I can't endure it anymore.

4. We have a lot of work to do. We really should have finished it all yesterday, but we were training the dog all day.

5. Is there really nothing to eat in the refrigerator? You might at least have left me some meat or cheese! I have eaten only fried eggs every day since you arrived!

6. "I haven't taken the dog out, because I am afraid of animals."
   "Doesn't he know where the door is? Let him go out by himself!"

7. "Has Angel come by this morning?"
   "Yes, he came to ask you some questions about folk dances, because he knows you have been present at many such festivals. He wants to know how to dance a horo."

Шестнайсети урок / Lesson 16

READING SELECTION

Кореспонденция - (12)

14 април, София

Драга ми Патриша,

 Върнах се вчера от Пловдив и намерих на масата писмото ти. Пристигнало е още преди три дни и ме чака. Бързам да ти отговоря, преди да ми запълнят времето други задачи.

 Даже ми е неудобно да си призная, че ние от народна музика много не се интересуваме. Вие на запад май повече знаете за нашата народна музика и за народните ни танци, отколкото младите хора у нас. Докато учат в прогимназията, децата научават някои основни неща за нашата музика и дори учат стъпките и тактовете на различни хора и ръченици, но после в живота имат малко поводи да покажат умението си. Хоро играят днес обикновено само на сватба. На нашата сватба с Бойко танцьорите от класа бяха все от старото поколение. Бащата на Бойко беше неуморим хороводец. Аз обаче знам само дайчовото хоро -- него много го играят по нашия, по Видинския край.

 Ти ме питаш за фестивала в Копривщица. Аз случайно знам повече за него, защото една година съм присъствувала на него. Ние бяхме там точно по това време, без да подозираме, че ще има такъв фестивал. Даже ходихме да слушаме как пеят бабите. Казвам бабите, тъй като повечето изпълнители бяха възрастни жени, дошли в Копривщица специално за целта. Изпълнителите пееха на дървен подиум на една поляна край града. Слушателите седяха на тревата наоколо. След като изслушахме всички певци, на най-добрите раздадоха награди. На твоята плоча сигурно има запис на такива наградени песни. За разлика от повечето народна музика по радиото и телевизията, тази беше истинска. Пееха като моята баба, когато бях малка, и много ме трогнаха. Една от песните даже съм чувала от нея, --

  Дето беше булката,
  черна асма израсла
  бяло грозде пуснала.
  Дето беше младоженика,
  бяла е асма израсла,
  черно грозде пуснала
  и си върхове заплели.

Шестнайсети урок / Lesson 16

Тази песен има много варианти. Пеят я из цяла България. Ти разбираш, нали, че става дума за двама разделени влюбени. Те умират от мъка. Погребват ги. А на гробовете им израстват две лози. Тия две лози се прегръщат и влюбените, разделени приживе, остават завинаги заедно след смъртта си. Много печална история! Моята баба, Бог да я прости, беше от Старозагорско. Колко приказки ми е разказвала, колко песни съм запомнила от нея.

На фестивала слушахме и свирнята на гайда на един, както по-късно разбрах, страшно знаменит дядо от Добруджа. После го гледах по телевизията като свири. Всички певци бяха в различни народни носии. Нашите носии са много разнообразни: всеки край си има своя носия. Сега вече у нас на село рядко ще видиш селяни в народна носия, но повечето си имат по една, скътана в сандъка. Затова певците в Копривщица и намирисваха на нафталин.

И аз имам народна носия от моето родно село във Видинско. Една моя стринка ми я подари. Изтъка специално за мене фуста и престилка. Ризата ми (също от тъкано на ръка платно и дантели) е стара, от прабаба ми. Само забрадка си нямам. Част от женската носия в планинските райони пък е сукманът -- на моята свекърва ѝ е останал един прекрасен вълнен сукман от майка ѝ. А сребърните ѝ пафти са просто мечта... Но по какъв ли повод човек може да се облече в народна носия в наше време?!

Пиши ми пак. Винаги чета твоите писма с радост. Твоя

Калина

Musicians in folk costume, Koprivshtitsa Festival

Шестнайсети урок / Lesson 16

GLOSSARY

акъ́л	mind, brain, sense	измѝтам / измета́	sweep, sweep off
асма́	trellis vine	изпълнѝтел (ка)	performer; executor
		изра́ствам / изра́сна or израста́	grow, shoot up
Бо́г да я про́сти	may she rest in peace		
булева́рд	boulevard	изслу́швам / изслу́шам	listen to the end, hear out
в живо́та	in the course of life, in daily life	изтѝчвам / изтѝчам	run [out, over, around]
вариа́нт	variant	изтъка́вам / изтъка́ (-че́ш)	weave to completion
вѝсш	high, supreme		
вѝсше образова́ние	higher education		
влю́бени	lovers	кава́л	wooden flute
вре́ме му е	it's time for him [to go/do it, etc.]	канцела́рия	office
		кла́са	social class
все́ ми е едно́	it doesn't make any difference	кое́ вре́ме ста́на	[look] what time it's gotten to be
		ку́ченце	puppy
га́йда	bagpipe		
гро́б	grave	лежа́ в бо́лница	be in the hospital
гръ́м, гърмъ́т (pls. гръ́мове or гъ́рмове)	thunder(bolt)		
		мечта́	dream, fantasy
гъду́лка	rebec, folk violin	мѝнало неопределе́но (вре́ме)	past indefinite (tense)
да вле́зе ли?	should he come in?	мъ́ка	pain, suffering, difficulty
да́йчово хоро́	[name of folk dance]		
данте́ла	lace	на ръка́	by hand, handmade
де́то	where, who, which	на су́хо	in/to a dry place
длъ́жен	indebted, obliged	награжда́вам / наградя́	award (a prize)
дресѝрам	train, break in		
дру́го	other, rest	на́й-накра́я	finally
дру́гото ще е наре́д	the rest will be O.K.	нака́рвам / нака́рам	make [someone] do, induce
дълг, -ъ́т	debt		
		намирѝсвам	smell (slightly) of
же́нски	women's, female, feminine	наро́дна носѝя	folk costume
		нафталѝн	mothballs
		неде́й	don't...
за ра́злика от	as opposed to	не́ка	let, let's
за разнообра́зие	for a change	неопределе́н	indefinite, unspecified
забра́дка	headscarf	неуморѝм	tireless
завѝнаги	forever	носѝя	folk costume
зада́ча	task, assignment	но́ся на попра́вка	take in for repairs
за́пад	west	ня́мам търпе́ние	not be able to wait
запа́лвам / запа́ля	light, turn on	ня́маше да	wasn't/weren't going to
заплѝтам / заплета́	braid, intertwine		
запъ́лвам / запъ́лня	fill, fill up	обзаве́ждам / обзаведа́	equip, furnish
зрънце́	grain, granule		
зърно́	grain, cereals		

Шестнайсети урок / Lesson 16

обзавѐждам се / обзаведа́ се	settle in, get installed
опери́рам	operate
опи́твам / опи́там	try, taste
освободи́тел	liberator
осно́вен	basic, fundamental
оста́ва да	it remains to
от кла́са	"classy", high-grade
отклю́чвам / отклю́ча (-иш)	unlock
откога́	since when
о́ще веднъ̀ж	again, once more
паза́р	market
па́рк	park
па́фта	buckle
пера́ на ръка́	wash out by hand
печа́лен	sad
плани́нски	mountain (adj.)
платно́	cloth, fabric
пла́ча (-еш)	weep, cry
плъ̀нка	filling
погрѐбвам / погреба́	bury
по́диум	platform, dais
поколѐние	generation
поля́на	meadow, clearing
попра́вка	correction, repair
посмя́вам / посмѐя	dare
постоя́вам / постоя́	stay for a bit
построя́вам / построя́	construct, build
праба́ба	great-grandmother
пранѐ	wash, laundry
прегръ̀щам / прегъ̀рна	embrace
прекра́сен	magnificent, splendid
прести́лка	apron
прѝживе	during [one's] lifetime
призна́вам / призна́я	acknowledge, confess
присъ̀ствувам (or присъ̀ствам)	be present, attend
прогимна́зия	junior high
про́ст	simple
про́сто	simply, just
проща́вам / простя́	forgive
пръ̀в, пъ̀рви	first
пу́хкав	fluffy
пъ̀к нѐка ми е злѐ	I should have it so bad!
разде́лям / разделя́	divide, split
ра́злика	difference
разнообра́зен	varied
разнообра́зие	variety, diversity
райо́н	district, region
ру́ски	Russian
ръчени́ца	folk couple dance
сандъ̀к	box, chest
свѐщ, -та́	candle
свѝря	play [musical instrument]
свирня́	playing, tune
сѐлянин	villager, peasant (male)
сѐлянка	villager, peasant (female)
скъ̀твам / скъ̀там	put by, store away
смъ̀рт, -та́	death
специа́лно	especially
специа́лно за целта́	just for that reason
срѐбърен	silver (adj.)
срѐдно образова́ние	secondary education
ста́ва ду́ма за	it's about
сти́га вѐче	[that's] enough already!
сти́га си я глѐдал!	stop looking at her!
стра́шно	awfully, terrifically
стри́на, стри́нка	aunt (father's brother's wife)
стъ̀пвам / стъ̀пя	step, set foot
стъ̀пка	step
сукма́н	(folk) tunic
су́х	dry
съ̀д	vessel, container
съ̀дове	(the) dishes
та́кт	beat, rhythm
тамбура́	folk mandolin or lute
та́нц	dance
танцьо́р	dancer
трева́	grass
тро́гвам / тро́гна	move, touch, affect
тъка́ (тъчѐш)	weave
тъ̀пан	drum
търпѐние	patience
умѐние	ability, skill
фу́ста	(folk) skirt
хоро́	folk line dance
хорово́дец	leader of line dances
цѐл, -та́	purpose
ча́ст, -та́	part, portion

Шестнайсети урок / Lesson 16

CULTURAL COMMENTARY

City life: street names

Since 1989, the names of many streets in Sofia have been changed. For instance, the main boulevard used to be called Ruski (булевард Руски); now it bears once again its prewar name: Tsar Osvoboditel (Цар Освободител), after Tsar Alexander II.

Folklore: music, dance, costumes; Koprivshtitsa festival

Bulgarian folk music is well known in the West, both by folk dance enthusiasts and by fans of "le mystère des voix bulgares". Most urban Bulgarians, however, know this music only through the orchestral arrangements and choreographed performances broadcast on radio and television. With some justification, they regard this predigested version of "folklore" as unworthy of their attention. Practically all Bulgarians will sing together on impromptu occasions, however; and on the occasion of a wedding they will get up and dance either the traditional "horo" (хоро), which is a round dance; or the traditional "răchenitsa" (ръченица), a couple dance (which can also be done as a solo or in line forms with set patterns).

Many different regions have dances particular to that region but it is often the case that only the older people know them. The names of folk dances sometimes reflect the geographical area where they are most often found, such as Yambolsko horo (the round dance from Yambol). Other names have no obvious source: the very common Daichovo horo was probably named after a particular Daicho who either danced it well or first played the music for it.

Along with folk wisdom and folk music and dances, each region also has its characteristic folk costume. In earlier times, everyone wore this costume, and most old people still have their finest costumes packed away. Some keep them in order to be buried in them, but others keep them to give to a favorite younger relative. Each part of the costume has its traditional name, and practically all pieces were made by hand.

The national folk festival of Koprivshtitsa is held every five years. For one long weekend in August, folk musicians, singers and lovers of folk music gather in this picturesque mountain town. Singers, musicians and dancers are from the villages and present the actual music of their own areas. Nevertheless, since the performers are conscious of being on stage and competing for prizes, there is a certain artificiality to these performances. The real pleasure of these festivals is in the music that is performed impromptu once the performers are finished with the "staged" version.

The traditional Bulgarian folk instruments are the gaida (гайда) or bagpipe, the gădulka (гъдулка), or double-stringed folk violin, the kaval (кавал), or wooden flute, the tăpan (тъпан) or large drum, and the tambura (тамбура), or mandolin-lute. More modern folk ensembles also add an accordion (акордеон). The most recent innovation in folk music is the genre called "wedding music", a modern, amplified form of music borrowing from various outside genres and styles including Turkish, Serbian, Greek and western jazz. The instruments include accordion, clarinet, saxophone, electric bass and synthesizer; many of the musicians in these ensembles are Rom (Gypsy).

Geography: place names

Bulgaria is divided into a number of smaller administrative regions. These are identified by the name of the largest town. "Vidinsko" (Видинско) is thus the region around Vidin (Видин), and "Starozagorsko" (Старозагорско) is the region around Stara Zagora (Стара Загора). The names of certain regions (e.g. the disputed region of Dobrudzha (Добруджа) in the northeast) have different origins.

LESSON 17

DIALOGUE

<u>Те́жко е чове́к да е са́м</u>

// Поръ́чаното такси́ ча́ка пред га́рата. Дими́тър, Миле́на и Павли́на се ка́чват в не́го. //

Павлина: Мо́ят адре́с е Патриа́рх Евти́мий № 32. Зна́ете ли къде́ се намира?

Шофьорът: Разби́ра се, госпо́жо.

Павлина: Ще ми́нете по на́й-пре́кия пъ́т, нали́?

Димитър: Зна́е чове́кът откъде́ да ми́не, не се́ вълну́вай.

Милена: Какво́ ка́зват ле́карите? Ка́к ми́на опера́цията?

Павлина: Все́ки си е роде́н с късме́та. А пъ́к а́з съм си късметли́я. Попа́днах на еди́н мно́го талантли́в хиру́рг. Виртуо́з. Ръце́те му като на цигула́р. Дру́ги бо́лни по це́ли се́дмици ча́кат да ги опери́ра, а а́з от къ́щи -- пра́во в операцио́нната.

Димитър: Зна́чи, сега́ си добре́?

Павлина: По́-добре́ съм, но не съ́м добре́.

Милена: Сега́ тря́бва мно́го да се па́зите. Да не вди́гате те́жко, да не се́ преуморя́вате. Добре́ е, че ни́е сме с ва́с. Ще ви пома́гаме.

Павлина: Ама, Миле́нче, ни́е нали́ сме на ти́?

Милена: Да́, ма́йко, на ти́ сме.

Павлина: Бра́во, така́ те и́скам!

// Весели́н, Джу́ли, Де́йвид и А́нгел сти́гат до бло́ка на Джу́ли, бе́з да наме́рят подходя́щ рестора́нт. Бло́кът е построе́н наско́ро и нао́коло и́ма разхвъ́рляни строи́телни отпа́дъци. //

Джули: Ви́е поча́кайте до́лу, дока́то се кача́ да поиска́м от хазя́йката телефо́нния но́мер.

Веселин: Аз ще ви помогна да занесете чантата горе. На кой етаж живеете?

Джули: На четвъртия.

// Джули и Веселин се качват до четвъртия етаж. Стълбището е прясно боядисано и още мирише на боя. //

Джули: Пристигнахме. Много съжалявам, чантата ми е препълнена. Уморихте ли се?

Веселин: А-ми! Нали видяхте аз колко багаж имам! Вашата чанта не е и наполовина толкова тежка, колкото обикновено тежи моята. С моята работа аз ходя натоварен като магаре. По-рано работехме двамата с един приятел, който ми помагаше да нося апаратурата. Петър се казваше. Той беше човек, с когото много се разбирахме. Можеше по цели седмици да пътуваме заедно из България, но никога не се карахме. Сега съм сам.

Джули: Какво стана с него?

Веселин: Нищо. Ожени се, намери си по-добре платена работа в друг вестник. Женен човек други отговорности има. Но от друга страна и семейният живот си има своите радости. Тежко е човек да е сам.

// Те звънят. Хазайката отваря вратата. //

Джули: Здравей, лельо Ваня!

Иванка: О, добре дошла, Джули! Как изкара на морето? А кой е този господин?

Веселин: Аз съм познат на госпожица Джули. Качих се само да попитам за телефонния ви номер. Госпожица Джули го няма записан.

Иванка: Запиши. Номерът е четирийсет и четири, дванайсет, петдесет и девет.

Веселин: Благодаря, аз тогава ще тръгвам. Довиждане. Джули, до утре.

Джули: Лельо Ваня, ако някой ме потърси по телефона тази вечер, кажи, че ме няма. Много съм уморена, искам рано да си легна.

Седемнайсети урок / Lesson 17

BASIC GRAMMAR

17.1. Passive participles: formation

Passive participles are adjectives describing the result of an action. They are formed from all transitive verbs, but most commonly from perfective verbs. They can also be formed from certain intransitive verbs. Passive participle endings are added to the aorist stem of the verb.

There are three sets of endings, **-ан**, **-ен**, **-т**. The ending **-т** is used with verbs of types 4 and 6 (refer to the present-aorist chart of verb types in Lesson 12). The other endings are distributed according to the aorist theme vowel. If it is **-а-**, the ending **-ан** is used; otherwise the ending **-ен** is used. By knowing the verb type, one can predict the type of participle ending.

The examples below illustrate the formation of passive participles. The ending **-т** is added directly to the aorist form, after the theme vowel if there is one. Before the endings **-ен** and **-ан**, the aorist theme vowel is dropped. The ending **-ен** looks like the adjective suffix **-ен**, but the vowel is *not* fleeting. The accent in all cases is that of the aorist. Masculine singular and plural forms are given; neuter and feminine forms are made by adding **-а** or **-о**, respectively, to the masculine form.

PASSIVE PARTICIPLE

Verb	*3sg. aorist*	*Type*	*passive participle (masculine, plural)*
participles in -т-			
позная	позна́	4	позна́т, -и
взе́ма	взе́	4	взе́т, -и
пу́сна	пу́сна	6	пу́снат, -и
participles in -ан-			
напи́ша	напи́са	8	напи́сан, -и
прегле́дам	прегле́да	1	прегле́дан, -и
разбера́	разбра́	9	разбра́н, -и
participles in -ен-			
же́ня	же́ни	2	же́нен, -и
затво́ря	затво́ри	2	затво́рен, -и
уморя́	умори́	2	уморе́н, -и
облека́	обле́че	5	обле́чен, -и

Exceptions to these rules concern primarily verbs of classes 3 and 7. Some verbs of class 7 use the ending **-т** and some use the ending **-ен**. The **-е-** in this ending is not a fleeting vowel. If the ending -ен- is accented and the following syllable does not contain -и-, this ending appears as -ян-. In these verbs, therefore, the -е- is an alternating vowel.

Verbs of type 3 are almost all intransitive and therefore do not form passive participles. The only exception is the verb ви́дя. Its participle is formed like the class 7 verbs which take -ен/-ян.

PASSIVE PARTICIPLE

Verb	*3sg. aorist*	*Type*	*passive participle*
			(masculine, plural)
participles in -ен-/-ан-			
живе́я	живя́	7	живя́н, живе́ни
ви́дя	видя́	3	видя́н, виде́ни
participles in -т-			
изпе́я	изпя́	7	изпя́т, изпе́ти

17.2. Passive participles: usage

Many adjectives which have already been learned are in fact passive participles. They refer to the result of the completed verbal action. The relationship in usage between the Bulgarian aorist tense and passive participle is similar to that between the English past tense and past participle. Here are examples of participles used as adjectives. (For their use in passive verbal constructions, see Lesson 19.)

(о)же́ня
 aorist tense | Оже́них сина́ си. | I married off my son.
 passive participle | Сега́ то́й е же́нен. | He's a married man now.

облека́
 aorist tense | Бъ́рзо се обле́че. | She got dressed quickly.
 passive participle | Мно́го еле́гантно е обле́чена. | She's dressed very elegantly.

затво́ря
 aorist tense | Затво́ри ли врата́та? | Did you close the door?
 passive participle | Врата́та е затво́рена. | The door is closed.

уморя́
 aorist tense | Умори́х ли те? | Did I tire you out?
 passive participle | Мно́го съм уморе́на. | I'm very tired.

пу́сна
 aorist tense | Пу́сна ли писмо́то? | Did you mail the letter?
 passive participle | Пу́снато е. | It's mailed.

Седемнайсети урок / Lesson 17

напи́ша
- *aorist tense* — Написа́ ли писмо́то? — Did you write the letter?
- *passive participle* — Писмо́то е добре́ напи́сано. — The letter is well written.

позна́я
- *aorist tense* — Позна́ ли му и́мето? — Did you guess his name?
- *passive participle* — И́мето (му) е позна́то. — It's a [well-]known name.

взе́ма
- *aorist tense* — Откъде́ взе́ приме́ра? — Where did you get the example?
- *passive participle* — Приме́рът е взе́т от ре́чника. — The example is taken from the dictionary.

прегле́дам
- *aorist tense* — Прегле́да ли те ле́карят? — Did the doctor examine you?
- *passive participle* — Пацие́нтът е ве́че прегле́дан. — The patient has already been examined.

17.3. Relative pronouns: който

A relative pronoun relates one clause to another. Consider the following English examples, in which each set of two simple sentences is made into a single complex sentence by means of the English relative pronouns "who" or "which". When two identical nouns are related in this way in a complex sentence, one of them is replaced by the relative pronoun.

simplex sentences -- Do you know this woman? -- This woman works with us.	*complex sentence* Do you know the woman *who* works with us?
simplex sentences -- This man used to live with us. -- This man moved to Germany.	*complex sentence* The man *who* used to live with us moved to Germany.
simplex sentences -- Where is the child? -- The child was here five minutes ago.	*complex sentence* Where is the child *who* was here five minutes ago?
simplex sentences -- The students are studying. -- She helped the students.	*complex sentence* She helped the students *who* are studying.
simplex sentences -- You brought me flowers yesterday. -- The flowers are beautiful.	*complex sentence* The flowers *which* you brought me yesterday are beautiful.

Седемнайсети урок / Lesson 17

In form, English relative pronouns are exactly like interrogative pronouns; in function, of course, they are different. The Bulgarian system is similar, but far from identical. First, Bulgarian relative pronouns are formally distinguished from interrogative pronouns by the addition of the particle -то. Second, while the particle -то does not change, the pronoun itself must agree with the noun to which it refers.

The most common relative pronoun in Bulgarian is ко́йто, which corresponds to both "which" and "what" in English. As in the interrogative pronoun ко́й, care must be taken to distinguish the masculine singular (which ends in the consonant -й) from the plural (which ends in the stressed vowel -и́).

masculine	feminine	neuter	plural
ко́йто	коя́то	кое́то	кои́то

According to the rules of Bulgarian grammar, the phrase in which ко́йто occurs must always be set off by commas, regardless of the rhythm of the spoken sentence. Here are the Bulgarian translations of the above English complex sentences. The relative pronouns are underlined: note that in each case the relative pronoun agrees with the noun to which it refers.

Позна́ваш ли жена́та, коя́то рабо́ти с на́с?
Чове́кът, ко́йто по́-ра́но живе́еше у на́с, се преме́сти в Герма́ния.
Къде́ е дете́то, кое́то бе́ше ту́ка преди́ пе́т мину́ти?
Тя́ пома́гаше на студе́нтите, кои́то се подго́твяха за и́зпита.
Цветя́та, кои́то ми донесе́, са мно́го ху́бави.

When the relative pronoun joins two simple sentences, it replaces one of the two instances of the noun it refers to. If that noun occurred in an object position, the relative pronoun replacing it must be in the object form. This rule is relevant in Bulgarian only when the noun in question refers to a person who is either male or of unspecified gender, in which case the object form кого́то must be used.

subject
    Позна́вам добре́ чове́ка,   I know the man who lives with you well.
        ко́йто живе́е у ва́с.

direct object
    Чове́кът, кого́то позна́вам добре́,   The man I know well lives with you.
        живе́е у ва́с.

indirect object
    Чове́кът, на кого́то пома́гах,   The man I was helping lives with you.
        живе́е у ва́с.

If the noun object refers to a female person (or to a group or a masculine inanimate object), no distinction need be made. The same pronoun is used in both subject and object meaning.

When two simple Bulgarian sentences are joined in this way (by **който**, etc.), the relative pronoun must *always* be present. This is in contrast to English, where the corresponding pronoun can often be omitted. Consider the following examples. In each case, an English speaker can say both (a) and (b), and would probably be more likely to say the shorter version, (b). The correct Bulgarian translation, however, must have the relative pronoun -- that is, it must correspond literally to (a), the longer of the two possible English sentences. For example:

Цветята, които носиш на работа, са много хубави.	(a) The flowers which you bring to the office are lovely. (b) The flowers you bring to the office are lovely.
Познаваш ли човека, с когото тя говори?	(a) Do you know the man to whom she is talking? (b) Do you know the man she's talking to?
Идеята, за която ми разказваш, е много интересна.	(a) The idea about which you're telling me is a very interesting one. (b) The idea you're telling me about is a very interesting one.

17.4. Other relative conjunctions

Other interrogative pronouns can also be made into relative conjunctions by the addition of the particle -**то**. The relative clauses in which they appear are similar to those with **който** in that the element they refer to must be present. The following compares both form and usage of these interrogative pronouns and the relative conjunctions formed from them.

чий "whose?" / чийто "whose"

Both **чий** in a question, and **чийто** in a relative clause, must agree with the noun modified. The word to which **чийто** relates precedes it directly.

interrogative

Лиляна, знаеш ли чий са тези стихове?	Liljana, do you know whose these verses are [= who is the author of these verses]?

relative

Уважаеми слушатели, да ви представя поета, от чийто стихове вие отдавна се възхищавате.	Allow me to present to the radio audience the poet whose verses it has admired for a long time.

Седемнайсети урок / Lesson 17

interrogative
    Чий са тези деца?   Whose children are these?

relative
    Горко на оная жена, чийто деца умират млади!   Woe to the woman whose children die young!

interrogative
    Чий е този портрет?   Whose portrait is this?

relative
    Какъв ти се пада човекът, чийто портрет виждам на стената?   What relation to you is the man whose portrait I see on the wall?

какъв "what [kind of]?" / **какъвто** "[such] as"
колко "how much? how many?" / **колкото** "as many as, as much as"

The structure of relative clauses with **какъвто** and **колкото** is somewhat different. Sentences in which they appear must be organized around the relationship between two words of parallel shape, as in the following schema:

такъв ...	какъвто
толкова ...	колкото

Because the corresponding English sentence lacks this structure altogether, sentences with **какъвто** and **колкото** are more difficult to translate. Here are examples:

interrogative
    Какви са тези хора?   What are these people like?

relative
    И досега ги помня такива, каквито ги видях за първи път.   Even now I remember them just as I saw them for the first time. [= just the way they were when...]

interrogative
    Какво е това ядене?   What is this dish?

relative
    Сервирам яденето такова, каквото е.   I'm serving you this dish as is. [= just the way it is]

interrogative
    Колко пари имаш със себе си?   How much money do you have with you?

relative
    Харчи толкова пари, колкото имаш.   Spend the money you've got. [= as much money as you have]

Sentences of the above sort can also occur in a "shortened" version, although this is less common. For example:

Харчи́, ко́лкото и́маш.	Spend what [= as much as] you have.

това, което

When a question framed with какво́ refers to something very general, the answer often contains the relative phrase това́, кое́то. Here is an example:

interrogative
Какво́ те трево́жи?	What's bothering you?

relative
Това́, кое́то ме трево́жи, е, че напосле́дък мно́го го мързи́.	What worries me is that lately he's been very lazy.
	It worries me that he's been very lazy of late.
	The fact that he's been lazy lately worries me.

кога "when?" / когато "when"
къде "where?" / където "where"   and others

The student has already encountered the relative conjunctions кога́то "when", къде́то "where" and защо́то "because". Their relationship to the corresponding interrogative forms is parallel to that between ко́й and ко́йто. Students must continue to remember that the two different *meanings* of the English words "when", "where" and the like, correspond to two different (though related) *words* in Bulgarian.

interrogative form		corresponds to	relative conjunction	
	meaning			*meaning*
кога́?	When?		кога́то	when...
къде́?	Where?		къде́то	where...
защо́?	Why?		защо́то	because...
ко́й?	Who?		ко́йто	who... which...
ка́к?	How?		ка́кто	as...

17.5. Compound conjunctions

The most common compound conjunctions, преди́ да "before", след като "after" and без да "without", were discussed in Lesson 14. Here are others, with examples of usage.

тъй като   *inasmuch as*
    Тъй като си бо́лен, тря́бва да   Inasmuch as you are ill, you need to
    взе́меш аспири́н.   take some aspirin.

щом като   *as soon as, since*
    Щом като се въ́рнеш, обади́ ми   Call me as soon as you get back.
    се.

    Щом като сега́ и́маш пари́,   Since you've got some money now,
    почерпи́ ме с едно́ кафе́!   treat me to a cup of coffee!

мака́р (и) да   *although, even though*
    Мака́р и да ми е братовче́д, а́з   Even though he is my cousin, I don't
    не го́ позна́вам.   know him.

мака́р че   *although*
    Ще ти обясня́, мака́р че   I'll explain, although I usually don't
    обикнове́но не обясня́вам.   do so.

са́мо че   *except*
    Ще до́йдем непреме́нно, са́мо че   We'll come without fail, except we'll
    вероя́тно ще закъсне́ем.   probably be late.

освен че   *not only*
    Освен че е ху́бава, тя́ е и бога́та. She's not only beautiful -- she's rich.

17.6. Aspect differentiation in subordinate clauses

Some conjunctions can be followed by verbs of either aspect, depending on the meaning of the sentence. Certain conjunctions, however, contain within themselves the meaning of "boundedness". After these conjunctions, only perfective verbs may be used.

The most frequent type of boundedness is that which relates to time. The tense of the verb in the subordinate clause depends on the meaning of the sentence. In the following examples all the verbs following the conjunctions are of the perfective aspect.

преди́ да
> Ти́ замина́ваш ско́ро, нали́? — You're leaving soon, aren't you?
> Обади́ ми се, преди́ да
> зами́неш. — Call me before you leave.

> Тря́бваше да му се оба́дя,
> преди́ да тръ́гна. — I ought to have called him before I left.

след като
> След като свъ́ршиш с дома́шните
> си, ха́йде на разхо́дка. — After you finish your homework, let's go out.

> След като свъ́ршиха с дома́шните
> си, изля́зоха на разхо́дка. — After they finished their homework, they went out.

кога́то
> Кога́то го ви́диш, поздрави́ го. — When you see him, say hello for me.

> Кога́то го видя́х, не можа́х да
> повя́рвам ко́лко е голя́м. — When I saw him, I couldn't believe how big he was.

Certain conjunctions have two meanings, one unbounded and the other bounded. In the unbounded meaning, they usually occur followed by imperfective verbs. In the bounded meaning, however, they must be followed by perfective verbs. Although most of these conjunctions are by now familiar, they are given below with both bounded and unbounded meanings for the sake of comparison.

unbounded дока́то *while*
> Дока́то прика́зваш по телефо́на,
> вода́та ври́. — While you've been talking on the phone, the water's been boiling.

bounded дока́то *until, by the time*
> Тря́бва да свъ́ршиш вси́чко,
> дока́то се облека́. — You have to finish everything by the time I get dressed.

unbounded като *as, when/if*
> Като у́чехме за́едно в
> университе́та, все́ки де́н се
> сре́щахме. — When we were students together, we used to meet each day.

> Ста́ята изсти́ва, като посто́янно
> вли́заш и изли́заш. — The room gets cold if you keep going in and out.

bounded като *when*
    Ще ти ка́жа, като те ви́дя   I'll tell you next time I see you. [I'll
    дру́гия пъ̀т.   tell you the next time when...]

unbounded щом *since, if*
    Щом те боли́ гъ̀рлото, облечи́   If your throat hurts, put something
    се!   on.

bounded щом *as soon as, when*
    Щом свъ̀рша, ще ти се оба́дя.   I'll call you as soon as I finish.

When conjunctions with bounded meaning are used in the narration of habitual, repeated action, the boundedness of the conjunction outweighs, as it were, the unboundedness of the general time frame. Thus, one must use perfective verbs after these conjunctions *even though* the basic narrative context is one which requires imperfective verbs. Examples will be given on the following page.

17.7. Imperfect tense and perfective aspect

In the narration of a habitual, repeated action, the tense depends on the time frame. If the habitual actions are continuing to occur at the general moment of speaking, all verbs are in the present tense. If they used to occur during some time frame in the past but now no longer do, all verbs are in the imperfect tense. What is important is that in each case, the *aspect* of the verb is determined by the frame *within the sentence*: main verbs are imperfective aspect, but those which occur after bounded conjunctions are perfective aspect.

It is in contexts such as these that the complexity of the concept "aspect" in Bulgarian begins to be seen. Unboundedness of past time is conveyed by the imperfect tense, and unboundedness of action is conveyed by the imperfective aspect. It is possible, however, for there to be a subsidiary boundedness embedded within this "doubly unbounded" context, which is marked by the use of perfective verbs after bounded conjunctions.

To see this, consider the following narrative, which relates a series of habitually performed actions. The narrative is given first in the present tense (where the tense conveys the meaning that the speaker still performs this series of actions whenever the conditions are appropriate). It is then repeated in the imperfect tense (where the tense conveys the meaning that the speaker used to perform this set of actions regularly but now no longer does).

The fact of repeated action is conveyed by the main verbs, which are in the imperfective aspect. After the bounded conjunctions within this narrative, however, perfective verbs are used. The *overall* meaning is still of repeated, habitual action, but the specific meaning within each subordinate clause is the boundedness which is here shared by the conjunction and the verb which depends on it.

Седемнайсети урок / Lesson 17

PRESENT tense

subordininate clause: Perfective	*main clause:* Imperfective
Като <u>се уморя́</u> да чета́,	<u>оти́вам</u> на планина́.

When I get tired of reading, I [get out and] go to the mountains.

| Щом <u>до́йда</u> до ли́фта, | <u>купу́вам</u> си биле́т. |

As soon as I arrive at the ski-lift, I buy a [lift] ticket.

| След като ми <u>до́йде</u> редъ́т, | <u>се ка́чвам</u> в каби́нката. |

When it gets to be my turn, I get into the gondola.

|Ведна́га щом <u>сти́гна</u> върха́, | <u>сла́гам</u> тъ́мните очила́ и <u>ся́дам</u> да чета́. |

The minute I get to the top, I put on my dark glasses and sit down to read.

PAST tense

subordininate clause: Perfective	*main clause:* Imperfective
Като <u>се уморя́х</u> да чета́,	<u>оти́вах</u> на планина́.

Whenever I would get tired of reading, I would [get out and] go to the mountains.

| Щом <u>до́йдех</u> до ли́фта, | <u>купу́вах</u> си биле́т. |

As soon as I would arrive/arrived at the ski-lift, I would buy a [lift] ticket.

| След като ми <u>до́йдеше</u> редъ́т, | <u>се ка́чвах</u> в каби́нката. |

When it got to be my turn, I would get into the gondola.

| Веднага щом <u>сти́гнех</u> върха́, | <u>сла́гах</u> тъ́мните очила́ и <u>ся́дах</u> да чета́. |

The minute I got to the top, I would put on my dark glasses and sit down to read.

Note that the English translation is sometimes able to convey this boundedness. The verbs in the main clauses convey the idea of past habitual action by the addition of "would". Certain verbs in subordinate clauses, however, can be rendered either with or without this particular habitual marker.

Седемнайсети урок / Lesson 17

EXERCISES

I. Fill in the blanks with the correct passive participle of one of the following verbs:
сло́жа, очаро́вам, разби́я, разваля́, сма́чкам, сме́ля, лъ́сна, изпера́, нави́я.

1. Те́ бя́ха _____ от но́вата си кола́.
2. На ма́сата са _____ две́ ва́зи с цветя́ и ку́па с плодове́.
3. Това́ яйце́ е _____ и мири́ше ло́шо.
4. Тарато́р пра́вят от _____ ки́село мля́ко.
5. Карто́фите мо́жеш да поръ́сиш със _____ че́рен пипе́р.
6. Сложи́ та́зи _____ харти́я в ко́шчето за боклу́к.
7. Обу́вките му са _____, чора́пите _____ и часо́вникът _____. То́й ня́ма да закъсне́е у́тре за учи́лище.

II. Fill in the blanks with the correct form of кой́то.

1. Ни́кога не гле́дам фи́лм, _____ ве́че съм гле́дал.
2. Запо́мни ли младе́жа, _____ ни помо́гна с бага́жа?
3. Не се́ доверя́вай на чове́к, _____ не позна́ваш добре́.
4. Потъ́рси ли кни́гата, _____ ти препоръ́чах?
5. Оба́ди ли ти се жена́та, на _____ да́дох телефо́на ти?
6. И́ма о́ще ма́лко от зе́лето, _____ сго́твих вче́ра.
7. Потъ́рсих ду́мата във вси́чки ре́чници, _____ успя́х да наме́ря.

III. Rewrite the passage in the past tense.

Момче́то, с кое́то пъту́ваме в едно́ купе́, изгле́жда е ма́лко не́рвно. Непрекъ́снато зада́ва въпро́си. Щом не му́ отгово́рят внеда́га, се разсъ́рдва -- ту́ тро́пне с кра́к, ту́ се объ́рне с гръ́б. Щом наближи́м ня́коя га́ра, пи́та дали́ е после́дна. Ако вла́кът спре́, не се́ успокоя́ва. Щом тръ́гнем отно́во, и́ска ни биле́тите за прове́рка. Не взи́ма голе́ми гло́би - са́мо по еди́н бонбо́н. Като изле́зем от туне́л, па́к и́ска биле́тите. Ако му ста́не ску́чно, па́к проверя́ва. Не зна́м за не́го, но за ме́не това́ пъту́ване не е́ ску́чно.

Седемнайсети урок / Lesson 17

ADDITIONAL GRAMMAR NOTES

17.3a. The possessive relative pronoun

The idea "whose" can be expressed not only by the relative pronoun чийто, but also by the phrase на кого́ (-то). This phrase is used somewhat more frequently in conversational style than is чий (то). Here are examples.
(For the "indefinite" use of ко́йто, etc., see the following section.)

Виж какво́ наме́рих в ра́ницата. На кого́ са те́зи са́ндвичи?	Look what I found in this backpack! Whose sandwiches are these?
Не пи́тай, а яж. Са́ндвичите са на ко́йто ги наме́ри.	Don't ask, just eat. The sandwiches belong to whoever finds them.

17.3b. Relative pronouns in indefinite expressions

Most relative pronouns can also occur without specific mention of a word they relate to, a usage which is called "indefinite". It is usually translated "whoever", "whichever", etc., and appears frequently in answers to questions containing the corresponding interrogative pronoun.

interrogative
-- На кого́ да ка́жа?   "Who(m) should I tell it to?"
indefinite relative
-- На кого́то и́скаш.   "Whomever you want."

interrogative
-- Кой да уча́ствува?   "Who should take part?"
indefinite relative
-- Ко́йто и́ска.   "Whoever wants to."

Related to this is the use of the relative pronoun ко́йто in proverbial expressions. Sometimes the relative pronoun stands alone as subject of both clauses, and sometimes the masculine pronoun той, то́зи (or тоз, a shortened form of то́зи) is there for it to relate to. In the examples below, the relative pronoun ко́йто is translated "he who" in order to maintain the proverbial tone of the Bulgarian. The translation "whoever" is equally possible.

Ко́йто не рабо́ти, ня́ма да яде́.	He who doesn't work won't eat.
Ко́йто мно́го зна́е, бъ́рзо остаря́ва.	He who knows a lot grows old quickly.

Ко́йто се у́чи, то́й ще сполу́чи.	He who studies will succeed.
То́з ко́йто па́дне в бо́й за свобо́да, то́й не уми́ра.	He who perishes fighting for freedom does not die.

(Verse from a poem by Hristo Botev; accentuation according to verse structure.)

The phrase това́, кое́то can also occur simply as кое́то. This meaning is *not* indefinite. Rather, it is simply a shortened version of това́, кое́то. For example:

Напосле́дък то́й е мно́го мързели́в, кое́то ме трево́жи.	Lately he's been very lazy, [a fact] which worries me.

Similarly, the phrases то́лкова ... ко́лкото and какъ́в ... какъ́вто can also occur in shortened variants without taking on the meaning "indefinite".

И досега́ ги по́мня, какви́то ги видя́х за пъ́рви пъ́т.	Even now I remember them just as I saw them for the first time.
Серви́рам я́денето, какво́то е.	I'm serving you this dish just as it is.
Харчи́, ко́лкото и́маш.	Spend what [as much as] you have.

17.4a. Indefinite usage of other relative conjunctions

A similar "indefinite" meaning is present when relative conjunctions occur in a phrase together with ...и да. In this case the meaning is intensified, as demonstrated by the different possible English translations.

Ка́кто и да го мо́лих, не пожела́ да до́йде.	No matter how [much] I pleaded, he didn't want to come. [= Nothing I said could make him want to come.]
Какво́то и да му ка́жеш, оби́жда се.	He gets offended no matter what you say to him. [= Whatever you say to him, he will take offense.]
Ко́йто и да ме тъ́рси по телефо́на, кажи́, че ме ня́ма.	No matter who calls, tell them I'm not here. [= Tell anyone who calls that I'm not here.]

Another sort of indefinite meaning is obtained when the "inquisitive" doubling of the interrogative pronoun is combined with the negative marker. Recall that the combination of an interrogative pronoun and the interrogative marker ли adds a sense of inquisitiveness, roughly translated by the English "I wonder".

Какъ́в ли е то́зи чове́к?	What sort of a man is he, I wonder?

When the accented negative marker is added to such a phrase, the meaning is roughly equivalent to the English phrase "all sorts of".

Какви́ ли не́ пе́сни пе́ят хо́рата.	People sing all sorts of [strange] songs.
За не́го гово́рят какво́ ли не́.	People say all manner of things about him.
У тя́х мо́жеш да сре́щнеш кого́ ли не́.	You meet all kinds of people at their house.

Finally, interrogative pronouns can convey the indefinite meaning usually translated by English "so-and-so" or "such-and-such". In this meaning, the interrogative occurs in a phrase composed of the particles еди́ and си with an interrogative form intervening. A hyphen always joins еди́ and the question word. Here are examples:

Павли́на твърди́, че пра́ви ба́ница са́мо с еди́-какво́ си си́рене.	Pavlina claims that she makes banitsa only from such-and-such kind of cheese.
Тя́ си игра́е с едно́ момче́ на и́ме Пе́тър еди́-ко́й си.	She's playing with a boy called Peter something-or-other.
Ха́йде, да рече́м, ще присти́гнеш еди́-кога́ си, ще му ка́жеш еди́-какво́ си...	Well, let's see. You'll get there at such-and-such a time, you'll tell him such-and-such...

17.4b. The conjunction дето

The informal conjunction де́то does not change form. In colloquial language, it can be substituted for къде́то or ко́йто, in either referential or indefinite meanings.

| Иди́, де́то и́скаш. | Go wherever you want. |
| Е́то го чове́ка, де́то те тъ́рсеше. | There's the man who was looking for you. |

17.5a. The conjunction като

The conjunction като deserves mention for two reasons. One is that it cannot always be translated simply by the corresponding conjunction in English. Sometimes its meaning of "concurrent activity" can only be translated by an English gerund.

| Децата тичаха бързо, като размахваха ръце да се стоплят. | The children ran quickly, waving their hands about to get warm. |

The other is that it can be combined with the conjunction **че** and the interrogative particle **ли**. This compound conjunction has two meanings. One corresponds to English "as if", and the other to English "apparently, it seems". Note that in both cases this compound conjunction carries the accent on the interrogative particle **ли**.

| Той затваря очи, като че ли спи. | He closes his eyes as if in sleep. |
| Вие на запад като че ли повече знаете за това, отколкото младите хора у нас. | It appears that you in the West know more about that than the youth do here. |

17.8. Derivation: verbs in -в-, nouns in -ение and -ост

The suffix -в-

Many verbs are formed with the suffix **-в-**, to which are added endings of the a-conjugation. Verbs can be derived in this way either from nouns, or from perfective verbs. In the latter case, an aspect pair is created.

noun	stem	+ в ›	derived verb	(meaning)
обяд	обяд-	+ в ›	обядв-ам	eat lunch
съвет	съвет-	+ в ›	съветв-ам	advise
рад-ост	рад-	+ в ›	радв-ам	make happy

verb	stem	+ в ›	derived verb	(meaning)
по-чак-ам	почак-	+ в ›	почакв-ам	wait
по-зна-я	позна-	+ в ›	познав-ам	know, guess
по-бърз-ам	побърз-	+ в ›	побързв-ам	hurry up
пре-кар-ам	прекар-	+ в ›	прекарв-ам	spend
кач-а	кач-	+ в ›	качв-ам	carry up
за-кус-я	закус-	+ в ›	закусв-ам	eat breakfast

Седемнайсети урок / Lesson 17

The suffix -ени-

The suffix **-ени-** (with predictable stress), plus the neuter ending **-е**, is added to a verbal stem to form a noun denoting an abstract concept. Since most nouns of this sort have been borrowed from Russian, the derivation process cannot be said to be a productive one in Bulgarian today.

Because Bulgarian does have many verbs corresponding to the Russian verbs that these nouns were derived from, it is useful to be aware of this derivational relationship.

Bulgarian verb	*(meaning)*	*derived noun* *	*(meaning)*
съжал-я́	regret	съжале́ние	pity
предло́ж-а	propose	предложе́ние	proposition
съобщ-я́	announce	съобще́ние	announcement
допълн-я	supplement	допълне́ние	supplement
тек-а́, теч-е́ш	flow	тече́ние	current
зна́ч-а	mean	значе́ние	meaning
не + търп-я́	not + endure	нетърпе́ние	impatience
сти́х + твор-я́	verse + create	стихотворе́ние	poem

* *(Russian borrowing)*

The suffix -ост

Many abstract nouns are formed from adjectives by adding the suffix **-ост** to the adjective stem, which is found by dropping the vocalic ending of a non-masculine form. Nouns with this suffix are always feminine.

adjective	*(meaning)*	*derived noun*	*(meaning)*
благода́рн-а	grateful	благода́рност	gratitude
ва́жн-а	important	ва́жност	importance
си́гурн-а	sure	си́гурност	certainty
опа́сн-а	dangerous	опа́сност	danger
тру́дн-а	difficult	тру́дност	difficulty
мла́д-а	young	мла́дост	youth
ста́р-а	old	ста́рост	old age
ми́л-а	dear	ми́лост	compassion

Седемнайсети урок / Lesson 17

SAMPLE SENTENCES

1. Той не е който и да е. Трябва да го посрещнеш, както подобава.
2. Виж тия чиновници как не си стоят на мястото. Когото и да потърсиш, не можеш да го намериш.

3. Каквото и да стане, не се бой. Нали съм с тебе.
4. Животните са такива, каквито ги създаде природата.

5. Той може да си го позволи. Има толкова пари, колкото звезди има на небето.

6. Върви гордо изправен, като че ли наоколо не стрелят.
7. Ти като че ли от небето падаш!

8. -- Прощавайте, май ви настъпих.
   -- Няма нищо.

9. Щом като е в чужбина, няма да плаща данък.
10. Не ми е удобно да му поискам такава услуга, макар че го познавам добре.

11. Макар и да е син на богати родители, той е много работлив.
12. Той не си отваря устата, макар и да знае всички отговори.

13. Много го ценят, макар че е още млад.
14. Само партия, чиито членове са готови на всякаква саможертва, може да разчита на успех.

15. Какви ли не нови машини измислят да облекчат живота на хората.
16. У нас можеш да чуеш какво ли не за живота в Америка.

17. Ти казваш "Гледай хората какво правят и прави като тях." Защо? Ако еди-кой си тръгне гол по улицата, и аз ли да направя като него?

18. Всеки път, когато тя обличеше нова рокля, той разливаше чашата си върху нея. Никой не знаеше нарочно ли го прави, или без да иска.

19. Лиляна беше приятелка на Мария, докато Мария не ѝ отне мъжа. Сега не си говорят, макар че мъжът ѝ отдавна починa.

Седемнайсети урок / Lesson 17

SENTENCES FOR TRANSLATION

1. The dinner I promised you is all prepared. You can serve it as it is. Only I need to go to the store to buy some appropriate wine. If we want to eat this dish as is fitting, we need some red wine. If you can wait until I return, we can eat as soon as I get back.

2. They hold all manner of folk festivals here. But I have never been to one. Every time as soon as I would arrive, I would learn that all the tickets were already sold.

3. Don't worry! The house is built, the walls are painted, and the staircase is repaired. We don't have half as much work to do tomorrow as we had today. The man we bought it from will be very surprised.

4. Whoever comes looking for me, tell them I went out to buy cigarettes.

5. What worries me is that I've seen the man standing on that corner several times today. He seems to be everywhere where I am.

6. So it's decided then. We will speak to each other as "ti" even though you are the teacher and I am the student.

7. What a lucky fellow I am! Although I have lots of responsibilities, nonetheless while everyone else is working I will watch television. All last year I would work right up until I went to sleep. But now no matter how much TV I watch it's not enough for me.

Tsarevets Hill, Veliko Tărnovo

Седемнайсети урок / Lesson 17

READING SELECTION

Кореспонде́нция - (13)

20 апри́л, Со́фия

Дра́ги Бо́б,

И́мам една голя́ма молба́ към те́бе. Нали́ не си забра́вил мо́ята братовче́дка Кръсти́на, коя́то ти идва́ на го́сти в Сан Франци́ско? Ка́кто зна́еш, тя́ се занима́ва със славя́нски фолкло́р. Напи́сала е мно́го неща́, кои́то специали́стите ценя́т. А́з ни́що не разби́рам от те́зи ра́боти, зна́м са́мо, че тя́ е све́стен чове́к. Тя́ и́ма в моме́нта голе́ми тру́дности. Разве́доха се с мъжа́ ѝ и тя́ оста́на сама́ с две́ деца́ на глава́та. И́ма слухове́, че ще съкраща́ват те́хния институ́т. Тя́ си е науми́ла да си тъ́рси ра́бота в чужби́на, но за вси́чки конку́рси е ну́жно да предста́виш не са́мо нотариа́лно заве́рени пре́води на вси́чки докуме́нти, но и автобиогра́фия. Ни́е ту́ка не зна́ем ка́к пи́шат на за́пад автобиогра́фии. Вероя́тно в разли́чните за́падноевропе́йски страни́ и́ма разли́чни станда́рти. Тъ́й като си́гурно от на́чина, по ко́йто е напи́сана автобиогра́фията, зави́сят до голя́ма сте́пен ша́нсовете на чове́ка да си наме́ри ра́бота, а́з и́скам да те помо́ля да соста́виш на англи́йски една́ автобиогра́фия на Кръсти́на, като изпо́лзуваш да́нните от не́йната автобиогра́фия, коя́то ти пра́щам.
    Ако́ и́маш о́ще ня́какви въпро́си по пъту́ването до Бълга́рия, неде́й да се колеба́еш, непреме́нно пиши́. Сти́га да мо́га, ще ти отгово́ря с пъ́лни подро́бности. Мно́го ни е прия́тно, че то́лкова ско́ро ще мо́жем да ви ви́дим.
    Накра́я не́ка пожела́я на те́бе и ця́лото семе́йство здра́ве и бо́дрост.

Тво́й

Бо́йко

АВТОБИОГРА́ФИЯ

на Кръсти́на Петро́ва Йорда́нова
живу́ща в Со́фия, ЖК "Дианаба́д", бл. 28, вх. Б, ап. 107, тел. 52-20-18

    Роде́на съм на 21.XI.1954 г. в г. Со́фия в семе́йство на слу́жещи. Баща́ ми, Пе́тър Димитро́в Петро́в, е роде́н в Пе́рник на 2.II.1926 г. То́й бе́ше счетоводи́тел в Металурги́чния комбина́т "Креми́ковци", понастоя́щем е пенсионе́р. Ма́йка ми, Грозда́нка Или́ева Петро́ва, е роде́на в Смо́лян на 30.VII.1930 г. и сега́ е пенсионе́рка. Тя́ рабо́теше като медици́нска сестра́ в XXII поликли́ника в Со́фия. И два́мата са безпарти́йни. Бра́т ми, Ива́йло Петро́в Петро́в, роде́н на 3.XII.1955 г. заги́на при автомоби́лна катастро́фа през 1970 г.
    Завъ́ршила съм сре́дното си образова́ние с пъ́лно отли́чие през 1972 г. Постъ́пих съ́щата годи́на в Софи́йския университе́т "Кли́мент Охри́дски" в специа́лност Не́мска филоло́гия. През сле́дващата годи́на се прехвъ́рлих във Факулте́та по славя́нска филоло́гия, специа́лност Славя́нска филоло́гия, и през 1977 г. успе́шно завъ́рших ви́сшето си образова́ние. О́ще през студе́нтските си годи́ни проявя́вах интере́с към фолкло́ра и старобъ́лгарската литерату́ра. Уча́ствувала съм във фолкло́рни експеди́ции из страна́та, организи́рани от Кате́драта по бъ́лгарска литерату́ра. През 1977-79 г. бях аспира́нтка на проф. П. Ди́неков в Институ́та по фолкло́р към БАН. През 1980 г. успе́шно защити́х дисерта́цията си на те́ма "Фолкло́рни моти́ви в оригина́лните среднобългарски па́метници от Тъ́рновската шко́ла" и полу́чих сте́пен кандида́т на филологи́ческите нау́ки. От 1980 г. и понастоя́щем рабо́тя в Институ́та по фолкло́р. През 1989 г. се хабилити́рах ("Сва́тбените пе́сни на бъ́лгарите в съпоста́вка със сва́тбените пе́сни на дру́гите южнославя́нските наро́ди") и бя́х избра́на за ста́рши нау́чен сътру́дник II сте́пен. Во́дила съм упражне́ния по фолкло́р за студе́нтите от Бъ́лгарска филоло́гия в Великотъ́рновския университе́т. През перио́да 1983-1986 г. уча́ствувах с ле́кции по фолкло́р и старобъ́лгарска литерату́ра в Ле́тния семина́р по бъ́лгарски ези́к и култу́ра за чуждестра́нни бълга́ристи и слави́сти.
    Разве́дена съм и и́мам две́ деца́. Би́вшият ми съпру́г, Па́вел Димитро́в Йорда́нов, е инжене́р в Кре́миковци. От 1990 г. е член на БЗНС "Нико́ла Петко́в". Си́нът ми Дими́тър (роде́н на 1.II.1981 г.) и дъщеря́ ми Грозда́на (роде́на на 25.VII.1985 г.) са учени́ци.
    От 1968 до 1982 г. членува́х в ДКМС.

    В увере́ние на вернотта́ на гореизло́женото се подпи́свам.

20.IV.19--   [по́дпис]
Со́фия

Седемнайсети урок / Lesson 17

GLOSSARY

автобиогра́фия	autobiography, CV	да́нни	data
автомоби́лен	automobile *(adj.)*	да́нък	tax
автомоби́лна катастро́фа	auto accident	дисерта́ция	dissertation
акаде́мия	academy	до голя́ма сте́пен	to a great extent
апарату́ра	apparatus, equipment	доверя́вам / доверя́	confide, entrust
аспира́нт (ка)	graduate student	доверя́вам се на	confide in
аспиранту́ра	graduate studies	до́ктор	doctor
		докуме́нт	document
БАН = Бъ́лгарска акаде́мия на нау́ките		допъ́лвам / допъ́лня	supplement, expand
безпарти́ен (-и́йна)	[someone who is] not a party member	е́ди-ка́к си	in such-and-such way
би́вш	ex, former	е́ди-какво́ си	such and such [a thing]
благода́рен	grateful	е́ди-какъ́в си	such-and-such sort of
бо́дрост	liveliness, cheer	е́ди-кога́ си	at such-and-such a time
бо́й	battle, beating	е́ди-ко́й си	so-and-so
бо́лни	sick people, patients	експеди́ция	expedition, field trip
бълга́рист (ка)	specialist in Bulgarian studies	живу́щ	resident, residing
Бъ́лгарската акаде́мия на нау́ките	Bulgarian Academy of Sciences	ЖК = жи́лищен кварта́л	
		заверя́вам / заверя́	notarize, endorse
в съпоста́вка с	compared with	завъ́ршвам / завъ́рша (-иш)	finish, wind up
в увере́ние на верността́ на	in certification of	заги́вам / заги́на	perish, die
ва́жност	importance	зада́вам / зада́м (-даде́ш)	give, assign
ва́за	vase		
ве́рност	truthfulness, veracity	зада́вам въпро́с	ask a question
вероя́тен	probable	за́падноевропе́йски	West European
вероя́тно	probably	запи́свам / запи́ша (-еш)	write down, record
виртуо́з	virtuoso		
вся́какъв	all sorts of	защища́вам / защитя́	defend
възхища́вам / възхитя́	enrapture, fill with admiration	звезда́	star
вълну́вам	excite, agitate	земеде́лски	agricultural
вълну́вам се	be agitated, excited	зна́ча (-иш)	mean
върху́	on, over		
		изка́рвам / изка́рам	take out, finish
г. = град		изпо́лзувам *(or* изпо́лзвам)	use
г. Со́фия	the city of Sofia	изпра́вен	erect
гло́ба	fine, penalty	изпра́вям / изпра́вя	set upright, correct
го́л	naked		
голе́ми тру́дности	big problems	институ́т	institution, institute
го́рд	proud		
гореизло́жен	aforementioned	к.м.н.	M.D. equivalent
горко́	woe	к.ф.н.	Ph.D. equivalent
го́рък	bitter	каби́нка	[ski-lift] gondola

Седемнайсети урок / Lesson 17

ка́кто подоба́ва	in a fitting manner
какъ́в ти се па́да?	what [relation] is he to you?
какво́то и да	no matter what
ка́кто и да е	no matter how; never mind
какъ́вто	such [...as]
какъ́вто и да е	whatever / however [he is]
кандида́т	candidate
карто́ф	potato
катастро́фа	accident, disaster
кате́дра	department
кого́то	whom (conjunction)
ко́йто, коя́то, кое́то, кои́то	who, which - (conjunction); whoever/whichever
ко́йто и да	no matter who
колеба́я се	hesitate, vacillate
ко́лкото	as much as
комбина́т	works (factory)
комунисти́чески	communist (adj.)
конку́рс	competition
ко́шче	basket
ко́шче за боклу́к	wastebasket
ку́па	bowl
къде́то	where (conjunction)
късметли́я	fortunate [person]
ле́тен, ля́тна	summer (adj.)
литерату́ра	literature
лифт	ski-lift
лъ́скам / лъ́сна	polish, shine
мага́ре	donkey
мака́р (и) да	even though
маши́на	machine, engine
медици́нска сестра́	nurse
медици́нски	medical, health (adj.)
металурги́чен	metallurgical
ми́лост	mercy, compassion
мири́ше (3d person only)	smell of
младе́ж	youth, young man
младе́жки	youth (adj.)
мла́дост	youth
молба́	request
моти́в	motive, motif
мързели́в	lazy
мързи́ (3d person only)	be lazy
мързи́ го	he's lazy
на глава́та	in need of support
наближа́вам / наближа́ (-и́ш)	approach, draw near
нави́вам / нави́я	wind up, roll up
накра́я	finally
нами́рам се	be, be located
наполови́на	in half, by half
наро́чно	
наско́ро	recently
натова́рвам / натова́ря	burden, load down
нау́ка	science
нау́мявам си / нау́мя си	take it into one's head
нау́чен	scientific
не ми́ е удо́бно	I feel awkward
не се́ вълну́вай(те)	take it easy
небе́ (poetic pl. небеса́)	sky
не́мски	German
непрекъ́снат	continuous, unbroken
непрекъ́снато	constantly, always
не́рвен	nervous
нотариа́лен	notarized
ну́жен	necessary
ну́жно е (да)	you have (to)
ну́ла	zero
ня́ма ни́що	no problem
оби́ждам / оби́дя	offend, insult
оби́ждам се / оби́дя се	take offense
облекча́вам / облекча́ (-и́ш)	lighten, facilitate
обръ́щам се с гръб	turn one's back
обя́двам	have lunch
обясня́вам / обясня́	explain
опа́сност	danger
опера́ция	operation
операцио́нен	operating (adj.)
операцио́нна (за́ла)	operating room
оригина́лен	original
осве́н че	not only
остаря́вам / остаре́я	grow old
отгово́рност	responsibility
от дру́га страна́	on the other hand
откъде́ да ми́на	which way to go
отли́чие	distinction
отне́мам / отне́ма	take away, deprive
отпа́дъци	refuse, waste
очаро́вам	charm, fascinate
па́дам се / па́дна се	fall to, go to
па́метник	monument, manuscript

49

Седемнайсети урок / Lesson 17

патриа́рх	patriarch
пенсионе́р (ка)	retired
перио́д	period (of time)
пипе́р	pepper (spice)
подоба́вам	befit
по́дпис	signature
подпи́свам се / подпи́ша се (-еш)	affix one's signature
подро́бност	detail
подходя́щ	suitable, appropriate
поликли́ника	clinic, polyclinic
понастоя́щем	at present
попа́дам / попа́дна	fall, land, happen on
портре́т	portrait
поръ́свам / поръ́ся	sprinkle
постъ́пвам / постъ́пя	proceed, act, enter
постъ́пвам в университе́т	enter university
пра́во	straight, directly
пре́ки see пряк	
преме́свам / преме́стя	move
препоръ́чвам / препоръ́чам	recommend
препъ́лнен	overfilled
преумори́вам се / преумори́ се	be overworked, get overtired
прия́тно ни е	we're [very] pleased
прове́рка	control, verification
проща́вайте	excuse me
пряк, пре́ки	direct
пъ́лни подро́бности	complete details
пъ́лно отли́чие	high honors
ра́бота	thing, matter
работли́в	hard-working
рабо́тник	worker
ра́двам	make happy
разби́вам / разби́я	break, beat
развали́м / развали́	spoil, destroy
разве́ден	divorced
разве́ждам / разведа́	take about; divorce
разве́ждам се с	get divorced from
разма́хвам / разма́хам	swing, brandish
разма́хвам ръце́	wave [one's] hands
разхвъ́рлям / разхвъ́рля	throw about, scatter
ра́ница	backpack, knapsack
ре́д, -ъ́т (pl. редове́)	row, range, line
редъ́т ми и́два	my turn is coming
роде́н	born
роде́н(а) съм	I was born
са́мо че	except (conjunction)
саможе́ртва	self-sacrifice
све́стен	decent
семина́р	seminar
си́гурност	certainty, security
слави́ст (ка)	specialist in Slavic studies
славя́нски	Slavic
служе́щ	(state) employee
слу́х, -ъ́т (pl. слухове́)	hearing, ear; rumor
слухове́	gossip
слуша́тел	listener
слуша́тели	audience
сма́чквам / сма́чкам	crush, crease
сми́лам / сме́ля	grind, mill
специали́ст (ка)	specialist
специа́лност	specialty; univ. major
сполу́чвам / сполу́ча (-иш)	succeed
среднобъ́лгарски	medieval Bulgarian
станда́рт	standard
старобъ́лгарски	Old Bulgarian, Old Church Slavic
ста́рост	old age
ста́рши	senior
ста́рши нау́чен сътру́дник	senior research associate
стена́	wall
сте́пен, -та́	degree
сте́пен к.ф.н.	Ph.D. degree
сти́га да мо́га	as/if I can
стих, -ъ́т	verse
сто́плям се / сто́пля се	get warm
стоя́ на мя́сто	stay in one place
стре́лям	shoot
студе́нтски	student (adj.)
стъ́лбище	staircase
счетоводи́тел	bookkeeper
създа́вам / създа́м (-даде́ш)	create, establish
съкраща́вам / съкратя́	curtail, lay off
съпоста́вка	comparison
съста́вям / съста́вя	compose, make up
сътру́дник	collaborator, associate
талантли́в	talented
творя́	create
твърдя́	assert, claim
тежа́ (-и́ш)	weigh, be heavy
те́жко	heavy (things)

Седемнайсети урок / Lesson 17

те́жко е	it's hard	филоло́гия	philology
те́жък	heavy; difficult, serious	филологи́чески	philological
		фолкло́р	folklore
те́ма	subject, theme	фолкло́рен	folklore (adj.)
това́, кое́то	what [that which]		
трево́жа (-иш)	bother, worry	хабилити́рам се	attain academic rank beyond Ph.D.
тро́пвам / тро́пна	rap, knock		
тро́пвам с кра́к	stamp one's foot	ха́рча (-иш)	spend
тру́дност	difficulty	хиру́рг	surgeon
туне́л	tunnel		
тъ́й като	inasmuch as	ценя́	esteem, value
тъ́мен	dark	цигула́р	violinist
тъ́рновски	of Tărnovo		
търпя́	endure	чи́йто, чия́то, чие́то, чии́то	whose (conjunction)
уважа́ем	honored, esteemed	чино́вник	official, functionary
увере́ние	assurance	член	member
упражне́ние	exercise, drill	члену́вам	be a member
услу́га	favor	чора́п	sock
успе́шно	successfully	чуждестра́нен	from foreign countries
успокоя́вам / успокоя́	soothe		
		шанс	chance
успокоя́вам се / успокоя́ се	calm down	шко́ла	school
у́ча се (-иш)	study, learn	щом като	as soon as, since
уча́ствувам	participate		
		южнославя́нски	South Slavic
факулте́т	faculty, university division		

CULTURAL COMMENTARY

Families: in-laws

The relationship between mother-in-law and daughter-in-law is a traditional one in that the son's new wife becomes as a daughter to her husband's mother. She must obey her wishes and defer to her in all matters.

City life: telephone numbers

Practically all phone numbers in Sofia are six digits long, and are thought of as a series of three two-digit numbers. The zero is called "nula" (ну́ла).

Седемнайсети урок / Lesson 17

Literature: Hristo Botev, Tărnovo school

Hristo Botev (Христо Ботев, 1848-1876) is perhaps Bulgaria's most famous poet. The volume of his verse is small, but all his poems are considered masterpieces. His work inspired the revolutionary movements which led to Bulgaria's liberation from the Turks in 1878.

One of the most famous periods of medieval Bulgarian literature is connected with the capital city of Tărnovo (Търново), now the modern city of Veliko Tărnovo (Велико Търново). Literature and culture flowered there especially during the latter part of the 14th century, under the leadership of Patriarch Euthymius (ca.1317 - ca.1402), the last head of the independent Bulgarian church before the fall to the Ottoman Turks. Among other things, Euthymius reclarified the writing system and promoted new literary forms. After the Ottoman occupation, the fame of the Tărnovo school (and of Bulgarian medieval literature) was spread to Romania, Serbia and especially Russia, by Euthymius's many talented pupils who sought refuge in these countries and who introduced elements of the Tărnovo school into local literary practice.

Schooling and education: university and academic degrees

The university at Veliko Tărnovo is the second best known in the country. The first-place university, of course, is Sofia University.

To complete secondary education (средно образование) in Bulgaria means to finish the course at a gymnasium or a technical school. To complete higher education (висше образование) means to complete the undergraduate university course, or a course at a higher technical college. Graduate studies (аспирантура) lead to the academic degree of "kandidat", equivalent to a Ph.D. in the West, which can be obtained in any of a number of areas. True academic status and rank is only attained with the second degree, however. This carries the same name as, and is parallel to, the German degree of "Habilitation"; it is roughly equivalent to the attainment of tenure in U.S. universities.

The highest academic degree (equivalent to the rank of full professor in universities in the West) is the doctorate, for which one must undergo a formal public defense of his published research. A "kandidat" may place the title к.ф.н. (кандидат на филологическите науки) or к.м.н. (кандидат на медицинските науки) or the like after his name, and a "doktor" the title of д.ф.н. As Bulgaria's ties with the West increase, the title кандидат is tending to be replaced by that of доктор. To differentiate this rank from that which is officially termed доктор, the latter rank is now informally (and unofficially) referred to as "голям доктор".

Academic life: the Bulgarian Academy of Sciences; ethnography as a discipline

The Bulgarian Academy of Sciences (Българската академия на науките) sponsors a large number of research institutes in various academic fields. Research positions in these institutes carry the titles "scientific associate" (научен сътрудник) and "senior scientific associate" (старши научен сътрудник), with several degrees of seniority within each rank.

Bulgarian ethnography is a well-developed science. Researchers are highly conscious of the ethnographic riches in Bulgarian village culture (ranging from folk beliefs to farm implements, weaving patterns, planting customs, and the like). Folklorists are equally conscious of the variety of verbal art in this same village culture. Although the two academic fields belong to separate disciplines in Bulgaria, both are busily at work recording and documenting. Many small groups, both of folklorists and ethnographers, travel into the "field" to record this information from villagers.

Work requirements

During the socialist period, all Bulgarians were required to keep up-to-date copies of their autobiographies on file at their workplace. These documents summarized not only one's own academic and work career, but were also required to specify the relevant statistics for all members of one's immediate family. Such statistics included the social status of one's parents. Within the socialist schema there were only three possible classes: villager/peasant (селянин), worker (работник) or official serving the state (служещ). These statistics also included party memberships. All children, for instance, once belonged to the ДКМС (Димитровски комунистически младежки съюз), and it was necessary to include this information in the biography. A party which is very popular at present is the БЗНС (Български земеделски народен съюз), especially those branches which were outlawed during the socialist period.

LESSON 18

DIALOGUE

Áнгеле, ти́ бащá, ти́ мáйка

// Весели́н изли́за от вхóда и ви́жда, че Áнгел и Дéйвид са сéднали на еднá пéйка в гради́нката от дрýгата странá на ýлицата. //

Ангел: Áз тъ́кмо разпи́твах Дéйвид къдé е отсéднал, та да потъ́рсим кръ́чма ня́къде в тáя посóка.

Дейвид: Мóята квартѝра е в цéнтъра, на еднá от ýличките зад пáметника на Цáр Освободи́тел.

Веселин: А-а, на опáшката на кóня. Тáм набли́зо мóжете да оти́дете в Рýския клýб.

Дейвид: Амá вѝе ня́ма ли да дóйдете с нáс?

Ангел: Елá с нáс, бé. Без тéбе ня́ма да е такá вéсело. Джýли се измъ́кна, а сегá и ти́... Пъ́к и не гó знáм тóя клýб къдé е.

Веселин: За съжалéние, áз си спóмних тóку-щó, че един прия́тел обещá да намѝне тáя вéчер към нáс.

Ангел: Откъдé го извáди сегá тóя прия́тел? Ако не мé лъ́же памeттá, ти́ днéс тря́бваше по плáн да си в Гáброво. Налѝ такá? Амá кáкто и да é.

// Áнгел и Дéйвид се сбогýват с Весели́н на трамвáйната спи́рка. Весели́н се упъ́тва към къ́щи, а двáмата нóви познáйници реши́ват всé пáк да вечéрят зáедно. //

Ангел: Добрé че не си́ и ти́ вегетериáнец като Джýли, че къдé ще ти тъ́рсим пóстни мáнджи по товá врéме.

Дейвид: Амá не серви́рат ли вегетериáнски я́стия в ресторáнтите?

Ангел: Откъдé да знáм?! Не съ́м ги пи́тал. Ти́ ми кажи́ на мéне кой мъ́ж мóже да се наядé с тревá?

Дейвид: Зеленчýците са мнóго полéзни за здрáвето.

Ангел: По тáя рáбота спóр ня́ма. Амá знáеш áз как оби́чам да си пи́йна раки́йката с мéшана салáтка. Или с кьóпоолу... Пръ́стите да си обли́жеш. Амá налѝ знáм, че след товá ще и́ма и скáричка.

53

Осемнайсети урок / Lesson 18

Дейвид: Ти сам ли живееш?

Ангел: Къде ти! Аз живея с нашите. Майка и татко са вече пенсионери. Вечер, като се върна от работа, им помагам из градината. Ако не са ме поканили някъде на гости, де. Аз имам много приятели в Балчик.

Дейвид: Аз разбирам, че Балчик е много хубав град. Жалко, че ние с Джули не знаехме нищо за него и затова не отидохме да го видим.

Ангел: Човек не може да види всичко на един път. Остави си нещо и за догодина. Ти нали ще дойдеш пак в България?

Дейвид: Може и да дойда.

Ангел: Ела непременно. И се отбий и при мене в Балчик. Майка ми има да се радва.

Дейвид: Аз не съм решил още какво ще работя другото лято. Рано ми е да правя планове.

Ангел: Какво толкова ще му мислиш?! Аз, без много да му мисля, станах плочкаджия и хич не съжалявам. Иде ми отръки. Клиентите много ме търсят. Ето и оня ден една ми се обади по телефона и направо плаче. "Ангеле, ти баща, ти майка, какво ли не опитвах, падат пустите му плочки и това е. Ела веднага." Ясно ти е каква е работата. Те строиха къща по-миналата година. Аз им сложих плочките в банята и стана като картинка. За кухнята обаче хубави плочки не можа да намери. То, да ти кажа, не че няма плочки, но нали ги знаеш жените какви са -- искат нито една съседка да няма като техните плочки. Да са уникални. Та, докато тя избере плочките, аз минах на друг обект. Като ме потърси, аз ѝ отказах -- нямам свободно време. Хората чакат по цели месеци. Наложи се тя да извика друг майстор и на. Ама съжалих я, де. Отидох един неделен следобед и на бърза ръка ѝ оправих кухничката.

Дейвид: Ангеле, виж тая механа отсреща. Да влезем там, а?

Ангел: Дали ще има свободни места?

Осемнайсети урок / Lesson 18

BASIC GRAMMAR

18.1. Verbal aspect: review

For practically every verbal meaning in Bulgarian, there exist two different verbs: one perfective and one imperfective. The difference in meaning between them corresponds to the speaker's point of view as to whether there exists, for the specific verbal action in question, some sort of boundedness. Every time a Bulgarian uses a verb, s/he is obliged to choose which of these two aspects, or points of view, s/he wishes to emphasize.

The rules governing these choices are difficult to formulate because there are different sorts of "boundedness" depending on the meaning of the particular verb. The best (and almost only) way is simply to get a feel for it through practice and exposure. By now the student has been exposed to this distinction long enough for such a process to have begun. The examples of usage given in later portions of this lesson are intended simply to bring this process onto a more conscious level.

Once having made the conceptual choice of which aspect to use, students must then produce the proper form, perfective or imperfective. Predicting the imperfective form from the perfective (or vice versa) takes some practice, but fortunately there is a system of sorts. In the discussion below, aspect pairs will be given in the standard format, in which the imperfective is listed first.

18.2. Formation of aspect pairs: basic vs. derived

The essence of the aspect system is that verbs come in pairs. There are two sorts of pairs, basic and derived. To the "basic" type belong many very common verbs. The ones listed below, for instance, happen to occur in the dialogue for this lesson, and should be very familiar to the student by now.

imperfective	*perfective*	*(meaning)*
виждам	видя	see
връщам	върна	return
казвам	кажа	say
намирам	намеря	find
отивам	отида	go
падам	падна	fall
слагам	сложа	put
ставам	стана	stand up, become
сядам	седна	sit down

55

Осемнайсети урок / Lesson 18

Because for basic verbs it is impossible to say which is the more fundamental of the two forms, there is no sure way to predict the imperfective form from the perfective, or vice versa. Certain correlations can be noted, however. In each case, the verbs from the above list will be repeated, followed by additional examples.

Basic pairs: possible correlations between imperfective and perfective forms

(1)   If a verb ends in -вам, it is likely to be imperfective; it is also possible for its perfective partner to have a different form of the stem final consonant. Sometimes the imperfective form will end in -áвам.

imperfective	*perfective*	*(meaning)*
кáз-вам	кáж-а	say
отѝ-вам	отѝд-а	go
дá-вам	дáм (дад-éш)	give
закýс-вам	закýс-я	eat breakfast
кáч-вам се	кач-á се	mount, go up
полýч-áвам	полýч-а	receive
реш-áвам	реш-á	decide
свъ́рш-вам	свъ́рш-а	finish

(2)   If a verb ends in -на, it is likely to be perfective. The imperfective partner will usually end in -ам; sometimes there is a shift in the shape of the stem as well.

imperfective	*perfective*	*(meaning)*
връ́щ-ам	въ́р-на	return
пáд-ам	пáд-на	fall
стáв-ам	стá-на	stand up, become
ся́д-ам	сéд-на	sit down
помáг-ам	помóг-на	help
пýск-ам	пýс-на	drop, mail
срéщ-ам	срéщ-на	meet
стѝг-ам	стѝг-на	arrive

(3)   Stem-final -д or -т in the perfective often corresponds to stem-final -жд or -щ, respectively, in the imperfective.

imperfective	*perfective*	*(meaning)*
вѝжд-ам	вѝд-я	see
обáжд-ам се	обáд-я се	call, contact
плáщ-ам	плáт-я	pay
сéщ-ам се	сéт-я се	think of, recall

(4) There can be a variation in root vowels, according to which the imperfective partner will have **-a-** or **-и-** in the root, and the perfective partner will have **-e-** or **-o-** (and in one exceptional case, **-я-**).

imperfective	perfective	(meaning)
нам-и́-рам	нам-е́-ря	find
сл-а́-гам	сл-о́-жа	put
вл-и́-зам	вл-я́-за	enter
дон-а́-сям	дон-е-са́	bring
обл-и́-чам	обл-е-ка́	put on, clothe
отв-а́-рям	отв-о́-ря	open
отгов-а́-рям	отгов-о́-ря	answer

Simplex imperfectives, and derived pairs

A large number of Bulgarian verbs exist only in the imperfective. These are called "simplex imperfectives", and they all denote basic, general activities. Examples (again, from the dialogue) are

пи́там	ask
пи́я	drink
пра́вя	do, make
тъ́рся	look for
я́м, яде́ш	eat

To make these verbs perfective, one adds a prefix. It is at this point that such verbs become part of the Bulgarian aspect system, in which (as on Noah's ark) all verbs come in pairs. That is, every perfective verb derived in this way from a simplex imperfective, must then give rise, via derivation, to a corresponding imperfective verb.

The formal relationships between verbs in derived pairs are partly predictable. When one adds a prefix, the meaning and aspect of the verb change, but its conjugation pattern is unaltered.

imperfective	+ prefix ›	perfective	(meaning shift)
бера́	+ раз- ›	раз-бера́	gather › understand
Conjugation		Conjugation	
1sg. бера́		1sg. разбера́	
2sg. бере́ш		2sg. разбере́ш	
3sg. бере́		3sg. разбере́	
etc.		etc.	

Осемнайсети урок / Lesson 18

Other examples which occur in this lesson's dialogue are:

imperfective	+ prefix ›	perfective	(meaning shift)
бия	+ от- ›	от-бия се	beat › drop in
вадя	+ из- ›	из-вадя	take out › take out
лижа	+ об- ›	об-лижа	lick › lick off
питам	+ о- ›	о-питам	ask › attempt

For each of these new perfectives -- a new verb with a new meaning -- it is then necessary to derive an imperfective partner. This process of derivation is accomplished by suffixation. The meaning of the verb does not change (except for the removal of the sense of "boundedness"), but the form changes considerably. Furthermore, one must know which of the several possible suffixes is the appropriate one for the verb in question. One element is common, however: all derived imperfectives end in -ам, and all belong to the **a**-conjugation.

The majority of imperfectivizing suffixes contain -в-; indeed, the most frequently occurring one consists solely of -в-. In these instances, one forms the imperfective simply by adding -вам directly to the stem. The accent is always on the syllable immediately preceding the -в-.

Sometimes there is a shift in the stem-final consonant or in the root vowel before the suffix -в-. These shifts usually follow the general patterns seen in the "basic" types above. Other verbs expand the suffix to -ава-/-ява- or (more rarely) -ува; this suffix is always accented. Finally, the verb can simply shift to the **a**-conjugation, often with a change in the stem-final consonant as well.

Here are examples of all these patterns.

perfective	derived imperfective	formal marker	(meaning)
запозна́-я	запозна́-вам	-в-	acquaint
опи́т-ам	опи́т-вам	-в-	attempt
отби́-я	отби́-вам	-в-	drop in
пока́н-я	пока́н-вам		invite
наре́ж-а	наря́з-вам	-в-, cons. shift	cut into pieces
обли́ж-а	обли́з-вам	-в-, cons. shift	lick off
препи́ш-а	препи́с-вам	-в-, cons. shift	rewrite
забра́н-я	забра́н-явам	-ава-	forbid
зами́н-а	замин-а́вам	-ава-	depart
ку́п-я	куп-у́вам	-ува-	buy
нау́ч-а	науч-а́вам	-ава-	learn
извá́д-я	извá́жд-ам	cons. shift	take out
изпра́т-я	изпра́щ-ам	cons. shift	send off
разгле́д-ам	разгле́жд-ам	cons. shift	examine
събу́д-я	събу́жд-ам	cons. shift	wake

18.3. Meaning of derived imperfectives

In its general outlines, the Bulgarian aspect system is straightforward. Certain imperfective verbs denote an action which is so general and basic that it is by nature perceived as unbounded: for this reason, these "simplex imperfectives" have no perfective partners. One adds the idea of boundedness to such verbs by placing a prefix on them: in this way a perfective verb is created.

The essence of verbal aspect, however, is that the idea of "boundedness" can only exist in opposition. According to the Bulgarian system, a perfective verb requires an imperfective partner to complete its semantic range. That is, it cannot exist unless it is paired with a corresponding imperfective verb, a verb which itself exists only to express the unbounded point of view of the very same action. Thus, for every perfective verb derived from a simplex imperfective by prefixation, there must be an imperfective verb derived by suffixation. Here is a schematic depiction of this process:

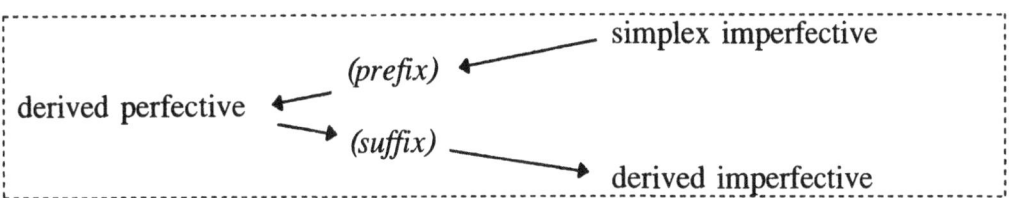

Most simplex imperfectives give rise to at least several perfectives, each of which has a different meaning. The meaning which a particular prefix will impart can only sometimes be predicted (for more on this topic, see Lesson 26). For example:

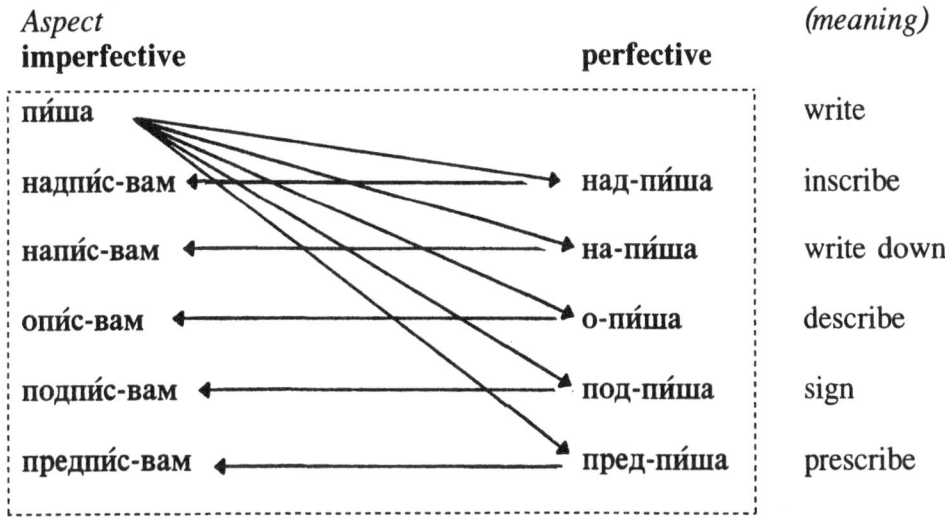

Thus, even though the aspect system is basically a binary one (imperfective - perfective), in many instances there is in practice a three-fold distinction. Consider the following example, where the derivational process moves from one verb through a second to create a third.

Осемнайсети урок / Lesson 18

1. *simplex imperfective: basic action*
   Тя пи́ше пое́зия.   She writes poetry.

2. *derived perfective: newly limited meaning, bounded version*
   Ми́налата годи́на тя напи́са пе́т   Last year she wrote [= finished]
   стихотворе́ния.   five poems.

3. *derived imperfective: newly limited meaning, unbounded version*
   Тя напи́сва по едно́ стихотворе́ние   Every day she writes [and finishes]
   преди́ заку́ска все́ки де́н.   a poem before breakfast.

The base activity, expressed by the simplex imperfective **пи́ша**, is writing. The newly limited meaning created by adding the prefix **на-** (**напи́ша**) is that of a single completed instance of writing a particular text (such as a letter or a poem). The derived meaning created by adding the imperfectivizing suffix **-вам** (**напи́свам**) retains the idea of writing a text to completion but removes the idea of boundedness.

Unboundedness can take several forms, of course. The correct meaning of aspectual marking usually can be determined only in context. In the above instance, the idea of unboundedness is conveyed in the repeated nature of the action: numerous poems are written (but each one written to completion). The following examples presents another sort of unboundedness, with the meaning of duration.

1. *simplex imperfective: basic action*
   То́я бло́к отсре́ща го строя́т   They've been building the apartment
   поне́ от пе́т годи́ни.   house across the way for at least
                                              five years.

2. *derived perfective: newly limited meaning, bounded version*
   Ни́кога ня́ма да го построя́т --   They're never going to finish it --

3. *derived imperfective: newly limited meaning, unbounded version*
   -- построя́ват еди́н ета́ж за два́   -- they take two months to put together
   ме́сеца и изче́зват.   a single floor and [then] they
                                              disappear.

The base activity, expressed by the simplex imperfective **строя́**, is that of construction. The newly limited meaning created by adding the prefix **по-** (**построя́**) is that of completion of a particular sort of construction activity. The derived meaning added by the imperfectivizing suffix **-авам** (**построя́вам**) retains the idea of completing this type of construction activity but removes the idea of boundedness. Here the idea of unboundedness is conveyed as one of duration: the speaker focuses upon the fact that it takes the builders two entire months to finish a single floor.

18.4. Indirect object pronouns: review

Constructions with the indirect object are very widespread in Bulgarian, and cover a broad range of meanings. The neutral expression of the indirect object is with the short form pronouns (**ми, ти, й, му**, etc.). The long form pronouns (**ме́не, те́бе, не́я, не́го**, etc.) can be used instead for contrastive or emphatic meaning.

The "doubled" form of pronoun objects (**на ме́не ми, на те́бе ти, на не́я й, на не́го му**, etc.) is very common. Most indirect object constructions can utilize either the short form or the doubled form of the pronoun, with relatively little difference in meaning. Examples of such constructions are indirect object of the verb, experiencer constructions, and relational expressions such as **Гео́рги ти е брат (на те́бе)**. Pronoun objects in all of these obey the basic word order rules for clitics.

Short form indirect object pronouns can also be used to indicate general possession. Here two points are to be noted. First, pronoun objects used in this meaning cannot appear in the doubled form. Second, they are placed not next to the verb but to the definite article (or, in the case of kinship terms, to the noun). Thus, when the verb of the sentence has a "true" indirect object, there can be a sequence of what looks like two instances of indirect object pronouns. For example:

Но́вата ми кни́га е на ма́сата.	My new book is on the table.
Ма́йка ми им да́де сладоле́д на деца́та.	My mother gave ice cream to the children.

18.5. Indirect object of "affect"

The similarity among all indirect object constructions is that the person denoted by that object pronoun is affected somehow by an action, a state or a relationship. Often this state of "affectedness" is such that it is difficult to find an appropriate English translation for the pronoun. Consider the following examples, in which only the broader context can convey the full meaning.

bare example
    Ще ми ми́не.

    It'll go away.
        [*literally:* it will pass to me]

context of example
    Изведна́ж си́лно ме заболя́ коре́мът. Ми́слех отнача́ло, че ще ми ми́не, и продължи́х да го́твя. Но не отми́на и тря́бваше да изви́кам бъ́рза по́мощ.

    All of a sudden I got a sharp pain in my abdomen. I thought at first it would go away, and resumed cooking. But it didn't go away, and I had to call an ambulance.

Осемнайсети урок / Lesson 18

bare example
    Врéме ѝ е.

It's high time.
    [*literally:* it's time to her]

context of example
    Тя́ е на двáйсет и пéт годи́ни! Врéме ѝ е вéче да се ожéни.

She's 25 years old [already]! It's high time she got married.

bare example
    Рáно ми е.

It's still early.
    [*literally:* it's early to me]

context of example
    Áз не съм реши́л óще каквó ще рабóтя. Рáно ми е да прáвя плáнове.

I haven't yet decided what I'm going to do. It's still early to be making plans.

bare example
    Нéщо ми и́ма.

Something's wrong.
    [*literally:* something is to me]

context of example
    Знáех, че нéщо ми и́ма, но не можáх ни́що да напрáвя досегá.

I knew something was wrong [with me], but I couldn't do anything about it till now.

bare example
    Тя́ ми глéдаше на кáрти.

She read my fortune. [*literally:* she looked at the cards to me]

context of example:
    (Fortune-telling: the fortune-teller looks at the cards with attention focused on a particular person, who can be said to be "affected" by this action.)

This construction, called here the "indirect object of affect", is similar in both form and meaning to "experiencer" constructions: pronouns can be single or doubled, and the person experiencing or affected by a particular situation is the one denoted by the pronoun object.

Grammatically, however, the two sentence types are often different. In an experiencer construction, there is no grammatical subject (although the person experiencing the state is the logical subject of the sentence, and is expressed as such in the English translation). In an "affect" construction, however, the subject - verb relationship is usually as in other Bulgarian sentences. The English translation of "affect" sentences, though, usually has no subject other than the "dummy *it*".

Experiencer:	Бéше ми мнóго студéно.	I was very cold.
Affect:	Ще ми ми́не.	It'll pass.

Осемнайсети урок / Lesson 18

EXERCISES

I. Rewrite the following in the present tense, imperfective aspect.

В събота ще отидем на планина. Ще поканим и колегите от службата. Отначало ще тръгнем с коли. Ще преценим колко човека ще бъдем и ще решим колко коли ни трябват. От паркинга ще продължим пеша. Пътят няма да е лек и ще спрем няколко пъти за почивка. Предварително ще си приготвим закуска и ще вземем освежителни напитки. Всеки ще избере най-подходящи дрехи и още по-важно -- обувки. Аз ще обуя специални маратонки. Иначе ще хвана мазоли. Разходката трябва да е удоволствие, а не мъчение.

II. Fill in the blanks with the appropriate form of one of the following verbs:
опиша, препиша, напиша, надпиша, подпиша, разпитам, опитам, попитам.

1. Нямам търпение да _____ тортата.
2. Не зная пътя до театъра и трябва да _____ хората по пътя.
3. Баща му е известен в селото, можеш да _____ всеки за него.
4. Трудно е да ти _____ красотата на този курорт.
5. Момчето не си _____ домашното вкъщи и трябваше да го _____ на училище.
6. Господине, трябва да се _____ под молбата.

III. Rewrite the sentences using short form indirect object pronouns when possible.

1. На тях помогнахте, а на мене ще помогнете ли?
2. На тебе казвам, не на шапката си.
3. На нея дадох книгата, а тя не я върна.
4. На него не обяснявай, той знае пътя добре.
5. Занесохте ли на него подаръци?
6. Голямата чест се падна на нас.
7. Твоят часовник ме буди всяка сутрин в 6 ч.

Осемнайсети урок / Lesson 18

ADDITIONAL GRAMMAR NOTES

18.2a. Derivation in aspect pairs: derived perfectives

Whenever a prefix is added to a simplex imperfective, a new perfective verb is created. Each individual concatenation of "prefix + stem" has a unique lexical meaning which can only be partially predicted (see Lesson 26 for more on this topic). For every new prefixed perfective verb, an imperfective verb is derived via suffixation. Each of these new verbs keeps the unique individual lexical meaning of its prefixed partner. The meaning added by imperfectivization, however, is general to all derived imperfectives: it is the "absence of boundedness".

It is also possible to derive perfective verbs from simplex imperfectives with the suffix -н-, which adds the meaning of one-time instantaneous action. This suffix can also add attenuative meaning (to do something "a little bit"). Only certain simplex verbs can undergo this derivational process, but for those which do, the meaning of the derived form is clear. As do all derived perfectives, these also give rise to a secondarily derived imperfective. Here is the model of derivation, followed by examples both of derivational patterns and of usage.

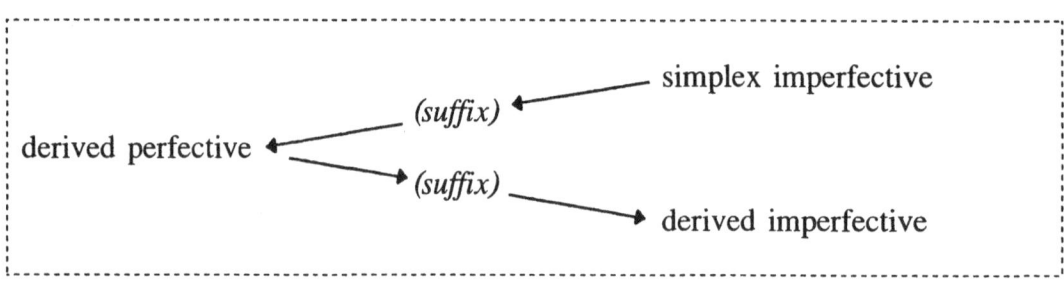

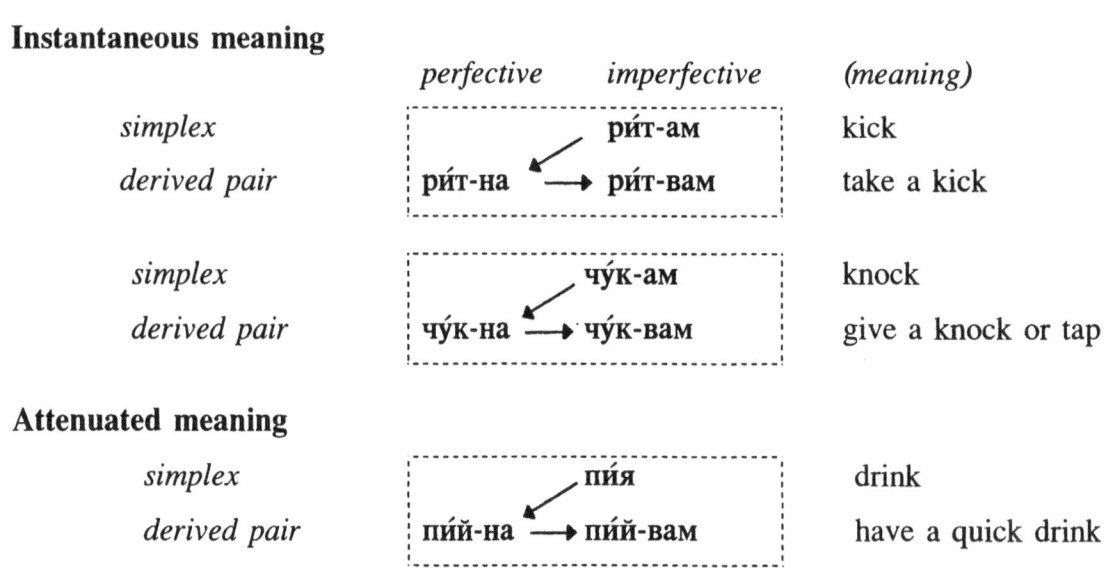

simplex	хáп-я	bite
derived pair	хáп-на ⟶ хáп-вам	have a bite

(хáп-на derives from хáп-я)

Áх, кáк обѝчам да си пѝйна ракѝйката с мéшана салáтка!	Oh, how I love to have a shot of rakia with a bit of mixed salad!
Тáя вéчер трябва да вечéряме рáно, на óбед сáмо хáпнахме мáлко.	We should have dinner early tonight, we only had a small bit at lunch.
-- Тѝ разбрá ли, че Пéтър е удáрил колáта? -- Áу! -- Не сé притеснявай дé, тóй сáмо я е чýкнал мáлко.	"Did you hear that Peter smashed up his car?" "Oh no!" "Don't worry, he just bumped it a bit."

18.2b. Verbal derivation: the prefixes по- and за-

Certain prefixes impart a particular meaning to a verb. Among these are по-, which adds the meaning "for a little while", and за-, which normally adds the meaning of the beginning of an action. This type of perfectivization will be studied in more detail in Lesson 26.

Седнéте до мéне, ще ви почетá и от двéте кнѝги.	Come sit by me, and I'll read you a bit of both books.
Трябва да мѝна някой пъ̀т да си поприкáзваме.	I should come by sometime so we can chat for a bit.
Хáйде да се поразхóдим.	Let's go for a little walk.
Пáк завалях, а áз не сѝ нóся чадъ̀р.	It's begun to rain again, and I don't have an umbrella.
На стáри годѝни всяка женá заприлѝчва на мáйка си.	As she gets on in years, every woman starts to resemble her mother.

18.3a. Meaning of derived imperfectives: "holes in the system"?

It is a cardinal rule of the Bulgarian aspect system that the addition of a prefix to a simplex (unpaired) imperfective always creates a new verb pair with a new meaning, and such pairs are always listed separately in the dictionary from the original simplex verb. In most instances, this reflects the actual state of the language:

the new, derived meaning is palpably and clearly distinguished from that of the basic simplex verb. For instance, the pairs **разпи́твам / разпи́там** "interrogate" and **опи́твам / опи́там** "attempt" are both clearly distinct in meaning from **пи́там** "ask".

In the case of some verbs, however, this structural model seems somewhat forced. Certain imperfective verbs have clearly been formed by derivation from a perfective which itself has been derived from a simplex imperfective. The perfective verb which represents the necessary intermediate stage, however, has fallen out of existence. One is left with two imperfective verbs which function essentially as synonyms. Examples of pairs which are completely synonymous are **ча́кам -- оча́квам** "wait", **зна́я -- позна́вам** "know". Another pair which is almost complete synonymous is **гово́ря -- разгова́рям** "talk". In each case, the presumed intermediate verb (**оча́кам / позна́я, разгово́ря**) is not in existence or is only used very rarely in that meaning.

18.4a. Indirect object pronouns and word order

A number of different constructions utilize short form indirect object pronouns. In most of these, the indirect object pronouns follow the rules learned earlier: they occur adjacent to the verb, immediately before the direct object pronoun, and after all copula forms except 3rd singular. In possessive constructions, however, they must occur immediately after the definite marker of the possessed noun (or in the case of kinship terms, immediately after the noun itself).

Examples are given below of both types of word order patterns. Indirect object pronouns are labeled *IND* wherever they are attached to the verb -- in indirect object constructions, experiencer expressions, relational-possessive expressions, and when used as the indirect object of affect. When used to express possession of a noun, however, they are labeled *POS*. When the verb of such a sentence takes an actual indirect object, there can be a sequence of what looks like two instances of *IND*, but which in fact is a sequence of *POS - IND*.

Indirect object of the verb

Да́дох	им	сладоле́д.
verb	*IND*	

I gave them ice cream.

Experiencer expressions

Хареса́	ми	фи́лмът.
verb	*IND*	

I liked the film.

Студе́но	ми	е.
	IND	*3^{d}COP*

I'm cold.

Осемнайсети урок / Lesson 18

Relational possessive expressions

Георги	ти	е	брат.
	IND	*3ʳᵈCOP*	*predicate*

Georgi is your brother.

Ти	си	ми	приятел.
	COP	*IND*	*predicate*

You are my friend.

Indirect object of affect

Ще	ми	мине.
Fut.	*IND*	*verb*

It'll pass.

Possessive constructions

Новата	ми	книга	е	на масата.
adj. def.	*POS*	*noun*	*verb*	

My new book is on the table.

Майка	ми	им	даде	сладолед	на децата.
subj	*POS*	*IND*	*verb*	*dir. obj.*	*ind. obj.*

My mother gave the children ice cream.

Despite the difference in word order patterns, these short form possessive pronouns share the overall category of "affectedness". In terms of meaning, they express an idea very similar to that of relational possessives. What is interesting, however, is that in certain instances a possessive pronoun object may appear to move away from its position adjacent to the definite article and take up position next to the verb. In other words, in certain instances it sheds the identity of *POS* and takes on that of *IND*.

In the examples below, *poss. noun* identifies the noun to which the possessive short form pronoun is normally attached. In the first sentence of each pair, the possessive pronoun occurs next to its noun, according to the rules for a short form pronoun in the *POS* function. In the second sentence(s), this same pronoun occurs in the *IND* position, which is next to the verb. The English translation, given between the different versions, cannot usually convey the difference in meaning between them.

possessive rules

Значи,	виртуозът	отряза	апандисита	ти.
	subj.	*verb*	*poss. noun*	*POS*

So this virtuoso took out your appendix.

indirect object rules

Значи,	виртуозът	ти	отряза	апандисита.
	subj.	*IND*	*verb*	*poss. noun*

possessive rules

Смени́ха	имена́та	им.
verb	*poss. noun*	*POS*

They changed their names.

indirect object rules

Смени́ха	им	имена́та.
verb	*IND*	*poss. noun*

На тя́х	им	смени́ха	имена́та.
ind. obj.	*IND*	*verb*	*poss. noun*

A similar relationship is seen in the following pairs of sentences, in each of which the indirect object pronoun replaces a prepositional phrase in **на**, once with the meaning of possession and once with the meaning of indirect object of affect.

possessive rules

Ръце́те	на На́дка	са	мръ́сни.
poss. noun		*verb*	

Nadka's hands are dirty.

Ръце́те	й	са	мръ́сни.
poss. noun	*POS*	*verb*	

Her hands are dirty.

indirect object rules

Та́ня	й	ми́е	ръце́те.
subj.	*IND*	*verb*	*poss. noun*

Та́ня	й	ми́е	ръце́те	на не́я.
subj.	*IND*	*verb*	*poss. noun*	*ind. obj.*

Tanya washes her [Nadka's] hands.

In all of the above examples, the meaning of "possessiveness" is still present: the appendix belongs to the speaker, the names belong(ed) to the streets, and the hands belong to Nadka. Yet sometimes this possessive appears to be absorbed into the broader meaning of "affectedness". That is, the attention of the speaker shifts from the more concrete idea of possession to the more subtle idea of affect, and this shift of focus is conveyed by a shift in word order. The fact that the two different meanings -- that of possession and that of indirect object -- can be expressed with the preposition **на** is certainly relevant here.

Two points are significant here: 1) not every instance of a possessive construction can make this shift; and 2) the presence of the shifted word order indicates not so much a change in meaning as a shift in the speaker's range of perception.

18.5a. Idiomatic uses of the indirect object pronoun

All the uses of indirect object pronouns studied in this lesson refer to a person. That person is either the possessor, the experiencer, the recipient, the relative, or is in some way affected by the action. Certain idioms, however, include indirect object pronouns which have no real-world referent (but which still obey the appropriate word order rules).

An example is the use of the 3rd singular masculine indirect object form **му** used with the verb **мисля** (or alone). The meaning added by **му** is simply a highly emotional one (there is no reference to any person or thing of masculine gender).

Какво́ то́лкова ще му ми́слиш!	Why so much thinking?!
А́з, без да му ми́сля, ста́нах пло́чкаджия.	I became a tile-layer without a second thought.
Па́дат пу́стите му пло́чки и това́ е.	Those stupid tiles fall off and there's nothing I can do about it.

18.6. Derivation of diminutives, continued

As seen in Lesson 13, the suffix **-ч-** is used to form nouns that designate smaller versions of the base noun -- hence the name "diminutive". Numerous other suffixes also are used to form diminutives. The characteristic mark of all of them is the presence of one or more of the following consonants or consonant groups: **-ч-, -ц-, -чк-, -нц-**. Depending on the degree of diminution speakers wish to convey, they can add more than one of these suffixes to a word.

All of these suffixes can also be used to convey the sense of endearment and affection. This usage of words meaning "little" is not unknown in English. For instance, a speaker of English might refer to a shop she is fond of, regardless of its size, in the following manner:

"There's this little shop down the street where they have...."

In Bulgarian, such usage is much more widespread than in English. Diminutive suffixes can be added to nouns, adjectives, and even verbs. Depending on the context (and on the noun itself), the same suffixes can signify either smallness or affection (and, of course, sometimes both). Personal names are also often modified by means of these suffixes.

The suffix **-к-** is freely added to many words. In the following instances, where it refers to items of food and drink, it clearly does not indicate smallness of portions. Rather, it expresses the speaker's fondness for the experience of eating and drinking.

Осемнайсети урок / Lesson 18

neutral word	root	+ -к- ›	derived diminutive	(meaning)
ракия	ракий-	-к- ›	ракий-ка	rakia
салата	салат-	-к- ›	салат-ка	salad
скара	скар-	-ич-к- ›	скарич-ка	grilled meat

The sequence -чк- in скаричка in fact is a double occurrence of the suffix -к-; the first -к- shifts to -ч- before the second one.

Another diminutive suffix is -ен-ц- (always followed by the neuter ending -е). It forms nouns signifying both the young of certain animals, and endearing forms of personal names. For example:

base	stem	+ ен-ц-	derived diminutive	(meaning)
кот-ка	кот-	-ен-ц-	кот-енце	kitten
куч-е	куч-	-ен-ц-	куч-енце	puppy
прас-е	прас-	-ен-ц-	прас-енце	piglet
пил-е	пил-	-ен-ц-	пил-енце	
Над-ка	Над-	-ен-ц-	Над-енце	
Мит-ко	Мит-	-ен-ц-	Мит-енце	

Words in the first half of the above chart illustrate the "true" diminutive use of this suffix: these are the neutral forms used to refer to small (that is, the young of) animals. Words in the second half of the chart illustrate the "endearing" use of this suffix: all these words refer to humans. In turn, most are derived from a word which already has a diminutive meaning.

The word пиленце, for instance, which is used in the sense of "sweetheart", is derived from пиле. Пиле, in turn, is the neutral diminutive referring to the young of a chicken. The other two diminutives are nicknames derived from names which themselves are already diminutive forms of the given names Надежда and Димитър. This second degree of diminution (with -енце) would be used only to a child, or to someone to whom one felt extremely close.

The following examples illustrate the usage of these derived forms. In each case the speaker is a child or is speaking to a child. Translations are of necessity approximate, as much depends on the context.

NOTE: diminutive formations of this sort are not included in glossary lists.

Осемнайсети урок / Lesson 18

Мáмо, вѝж товá кóтенце кóлко е хýбавичко!	Mommy, look at the kitten, how little and cute it is!
Ѝскаш ли чáйче, пѝленцето ми?	Do you want a bit of tea, my little sweetheart?
Óх, на мáма злáтното момѝченце!	Oh, [see] Mommy's little golden girl!

Diminutives of proper names end in either **-о** or **-е**. If the diminutive form of the personal name ends in **-е**, it takes the definite article when used in any form other than the vocative.

Вéско, каквó прáвиш?	Vesko, what are you doing?
Нѝе с Вéско ще хóдим тáм.	I'm going there with Vesko.
Милéнче, каквó прáвиш?	Milenche, what are you doing?
Нѝе с Милéнчето ще хóдим тáм.	I'm going there with Milenche.

Another commonly heard example of a diminutive suffix used endearingly is the series of words formed from the rarely used indefinite adjective **гóрък** "bitter, wretched". In the definite form, this adjective is used to convey sympathy. More frequently, the series of diminutive suffixes **-ич-к-** is added in order to achieve a heightened sense of sympathy. For example:

Мнóго му бéше трýдно, горкѝят.	It was hard for him, poor fellow.
Горкѝчкият -- прóсто не можá.	The poor thing -- he just couldn't [manage].

Осемнайсети урок / Lesson 18

SAMPLE SENTENCES

1. Който търси, намира.
2. Много почнах да забравям. Не помня кое къде слагам. Каквото и да потърся, не мога да го намеря.

3. Не можеш да очакваш от него да ти намери книга за превод. Него ще го домързи да търси. Той за себе си не потърсва, ама превежда каквото му попадне.

4. -- Твоите деца френски ли учат в училище, или английски?
   -- Моите деца учиха немски шест години, но нищо не научиха.
   -- Така не можеш да научиш чужд език. Трябва поне по два часа на ден да учиш, за да има някакъв резултат.

5. Нека да вземем някакво решение най-после. Размишляваме от една седмица и още нищо не сме измислили. Ти идваш всяка сутрин с нови идеи, а вечерта казваш: "Аз размислих, тази идея за нищо не става, трябва да измислим нещо ново."

6. Те и двете плетат много хубаво. Майката обаче е по-бърза и изплита по един чорап на ден. А дъщерята е по-бавна -- на нея ѝ трябват два дена да изплете един чорап.

7. Някой чука на вратата. А аз си седя тихичко в стаята и не отварям. Чуден човек. Чуква веднъж, после -- след дълга пауза -- още веднъж. Точно когато реша, че си е тръгнал, той чуква пак. Питам се кой ли е? Дали да не отида да отворя?! Ето, пак чукна.

8. След дългата студена зима слънцето грейна и гората изведнъж се разлисти. Слънцето грее сега.
9. Много е странно времето това лято: сутрин слънцето грейва за малко, но след обед винаги завалява дъжд.

10. Чудни хора. Те в тяхното семейство гълтат маслините с костилките. Пръв започна да ги гълта бащата. Глътна две. Хареса му. После и другите последваха неговия пример. На децата обаче не разрешават да гълтат по много. Те глътват само по три преди закуска. Не повече.

11. Често минавах покрай тази къща. Лампата пред нея винаги светеше. Оня ден обаче пред къщата беше тъмно. После изведнъж лампата светна. Посвети малко и угасна. Оттогава винаги, когато минавам покрай лампата, тя светва. Сигурно ме поздравява.

12. Катеричките са големи къщовници. Каквото намерят, занасят го в хралупата си. Ето, и тази сега носи един орех. Да видим дали пак ще си го занесе в хралупата.

Осемнайсети урок / Lesson 18

13. Очи́те му са отво́рени.
14. Отво́рени са му очи́те.

15. Гранича́рят ѝ взе́ паспо́рта и сле́зе от вла́ка. Като тръ́гна вла́кът, не́го о́ще го ня́маше с паспо́рта. Тя́ ужасе́но се притесни́.

16. Дека́нът връ́чи дипло́мата на студе́нта и му сти́сна ръка́та.

17. Бо́же, какво́ ху́баво бе́бе си ми ти́! Какви́ са ти́я си́ни очи́чки! Ами́, ти́я ма́лки ръчи́чки!
18. Ка́мене, що́м те боли́ глави́чката, тря́бва да пи́йнеш то́пло млечице́.

19. -- Ма́мо, да́й ми пари́чки за бонбо́ни.
    -- На́ ти пари́!

SENTENCES FOR TRANSLATION

1. This rakia is no good at all. I don't like it. I usually have a little bit of rakia with my salad. I wanted to have a little now, but I have changed my mind.

2. The dentist wants to extract another of my teeth. He always sings as he is pulling them out. I think I'll find myself a new dentist.

3. A month ago it would start raining every day in the afternoon. But it hasn't rained in a long time. Maybe it will start raining now!

4. I used to read the newspaper every morning when I got up. It was always too early for me to do any work, and so every morning I would read at least two newspapers. But then I decided I had to renounce this habit.

5. When people say goodbye to each other, they often shake hands.

6. "What's wrong with you?"
   "I don't know. I don't feel well. My stomach just suddenly started hurting."
   "Your stomach always starts hurting when you have to sit down and do a bit of work. There's nothing wrong with you!"

7. Let's try to sneak out of here. It's time for me to go to bed.

READING SELECTION

Елисаве́та Багря́на, поете́са

Елисаве́та Багря́на е псевдони́мът, с ко́йто поете́сата Елисаве́та Бе́лчева подпи́сва о́ще пъ́рвата си кни́га със сти́хове "Ве́чната и свя́тата", изля́зла през 1927 г. Под това́ и́ме тя́ зае́ма бля́скаво мя́сто в бъ́лгарската литерату́ра. Ни́кога преди́ Багря́на на бъ́лгарски ези́к не е́ прозвуча́вала пое́зия с такава́ въ́трешна свобода́ на и́зраза и на духа́! При вси́чки бъ́лгарски пое́ти преди́ не́я стихъ́т -- дали́ тро́мав, или виртуо́зен -- но́си следи́те на тво́рческата мъ́ка. Кога́то оба́че се вслу́шваме в не́йната пое́зия, ни́е ся́каш забра́ваме, че това́ е пое́зия, то́лкова прили́ча тя́ на есте́ствената чове́шка ре́ч. Това́ не е про́сто индивидуа́лно откри́тие на Багря́на, то́ е и резулта́т от обекти́вния разво́й на бъ́лгарското поети́чно сло́во; отнача́ло отделе́но от обикнове́ния го́вор и превъ́рнато в "сти́х", то́ след това́ дости́га поети́чно съвърше́нство и се завръ́ща -- на дру́го ниво́ -- та́м, откъде́то е тръ́гнало -- при чове́шкия гла́с.

Характе́рното за Багря́на ця́лостно хармони́чно съзна́ние я отлича́ва от мнози́нството съвре́менни бъ́лгарски творци́. Тя́ твори́ в хармо́ния със се́бе си и със света́ и възпри́ема живо́та пълноце́нно. Така́ тя́ примиря́ва мечта́та и спо́мена, у́трото и ноща́, тя́лото и духа́, греха́ и светостта́. Не́йната пое́зия не са́мо изразя́ва най-широ́ката емоциона́лна га́ма -- от радостта́ до скръбта́ -- но и най-пъ́лния биологи́чен ци́къл на чове́ка. В пое́зията на Багря́на ня́ма по́зи и метафизи́чески бе́здни, тя́ ня́ма дори́ ня́каква осо́бена своя́ те́ма, в коя́то да изче́рпва се́бе си. Тво́рчеството на Багря́на е в съ́щото вре́ме една́ от пъ́рвите изя́ви на на́шето национа́лно и балка́нско самосъзна́ние. И не́йната чове́шка фигу́ра дори́, не по́-ма́лко от не́йната пое́зия, излъ́чва красота́ и благоро́дство, ня́какво го́рдо досто́йнство. И́ма удиви́телна мя́ра и сдъ́ржаност в поведе́нието ѝ. И не е́ чу́дно, че те́зи, кои́то я позна́ваха, па́зят в паметта́ си све́тлия ѝ о́браз.

Адапти́рано от Светозар Игов, <u>История на българската литература, 1878-1944</u>.

Осемнайсети урок / Lesson 18

Стихи́и

Мо́жеш ли да спре́ш ти́ вя́търа, де́то и́два от моги́лите,
префуча́ва през боа́зите, вди́га о́блак над дика́ните,
гра́бва стре́хите на къ́щите, на кару́ците черги́лата,
сва́ля по́ртите, огра́дите и деца́та по мегда́ните --
в ро́дния ми гра́д?

Мо́жеш ли да спре́ш ти́ Би́стрица, де́то и́де про́лет я́ростна,
разтроша́ва ледове́те си, на мосто́вете подпо́рите
и изли́за от кори́тото, и завли́ча, мъ́тна, па́костна --
къ́щиците и гради́нките, и доби́тъка на хо́рата --
в ро́дния ми гра́д?

Мо́жеш ли да спре́ш ти́ ви́ното, щом веднъ́ж е закипя́ло то́
в бъ́чвите огро́мни, взи́дани, с вла́га лъ́хаща наси́тени,
на кои́то с бу́кви ки́рилски пи́ше "че́рното" и "бя́лото" --
в ро́дния ми гра́д?

Ка́к ще спре́ш ти́ ме́не -- во́лната, ски́тницата, непоко́рната --
ро́дната сестра́ на вя́търа, на вода́та и на ви́ното,
за коя́то е прима́мица непости́жното, просто́рното,
де́то все́ съну́ва пъ́тища -- недости́гнати, неми́нати --
ме́не ка́к ще спре́ш?

-- Елисаве́та Багря́на

Осемнайсети урок / Lesson 18

GLOSSARY

ако не ме́ лъ́же паметта́	if memory serves me correctly	домързя́ва ме / домързи́ ме (3rd ps.)	not feel like, be too lazy
апандиси́т	appendix, appendicitis	дости́гам / дости́гна	reach, achieve
балка́нски	Balkan (adj.)	досто́йнство	worth, dignity
бе́бе	baby	ду́х, -ът (pl. ду́хове or духове́)	spirit
бе́з да му ми́сля	not a second thought		
бе́здна	abyss		
биологи́чен	biological	емоциона́лен	emotional
би́я	beat	есте́ствен	natural
благоро́дство	nobility		
бля́скав	brilliant, sparkling	за ни́що не ста́ва	isn't worth anything
боа́з	defile, gorge	забраня́вам / забраня́	forbid
бу́дя	awaken, arouse		
бъ́рза по́мощ	first aid, ambulance	завли́чам / завлека́ (-че́ш)	drag off, wash away
бъ́чва	barrel, cask		
ва́дя	take out, get issued	завръ́щам се / завъ́рна се	turn, return
ве́чен	eternal		
взе́мам реше́ние	arrive at a decision	закипя́вам / закипя́	begin to boil; be in full swing
взи́дан	"walled-in"		
виртуо́зен	masterly	заприли́чвам / заприли́чам	begin to resemble
вла́га	dampness, moisture		
во́ин	warrior		
во́лен	free, independent	и́де ми о́тръки	be good at, handy at
връ́чвам / връ́ча (-иш)	hand, deliver, present	изве́стен	well known, familiar
все́ па́к	nevertheless	излъ́чвам / излъ́ча (-иш)	radiate, emanate
вслу́швам се / вслу́шам се	listen closely	измъ́квам се / измъ́кна се	make off, slip away
възприе́мам / възприе́ма	perceive, apprehend	и́зраз	expression
въ́трешен	internal	изразя́вам / изразя́	express, manifest
		изче́рпвам / изче́рпя	exhaust, wear out
га́ма	scale, gamut		
гле́дам на ка́рти	read [some]one's fortune by cards	изя́ва	manifestation
		импера́тор	emperor
го́вор	speech, dialect	индивидуа́лен	individual, personal
горки́ят, горка́та	wretched one, poor thing	кару́ца	cart, carriage
гра́бвам / гра́бна	snatch up, carry off	кате́ричка	squirrel
гради́нка	small garden	ки́рилски	Cyrillic (adj.)
грани́ча́р	border guard	ки́рилски бу́кви	Cyrillic letters
гре́йвам / гре́йна	start to shine (of sun)	клие́нт	client, customer
гря́х, грехъ́т (pl. грехове́)	sin	клу́б	club, clubhouse
		кори́то	trough; river bed
		кости́лка	pit, stone
дека́н	dean	ко́тенце	kitten
дика́ня	threshing board	красота́	beauty
ди́плома	diploma	кръ́чма	pub, tavern
доби́тък	cattle, livestock	къде́	far, infinitely

Осемнайсети урок / Lesson 18

къде́ ти	how could that be?
къщо́вница	sterling housewife
кьо́поолу	eggplant caviar
ла́мпа	lamp, light
лед, -ъ́т (*pl.* ледове́)	ice
ли́жа (-еш)	lick
лъ́жа (-еш)	tell a lie, deceive
лъ́хащ	smelling of, giving off
мазо́л	corn, callous, blister
ма́йстор	master [worker], craftsman
ма́нджа	dish, food
марато́нка	training shoe
масли́на	olive
мегда́н	[public] square
ме́ри *see* мя́ра	
механа́	tavern
ме́шана сала́та	garden salad
мнозинство́	majority
моги́ла	hill, mound
му	(*conversational particle; see p. 69*)
мъ́тен	muddy, dull
мъче́ние	torment, torture
мя́ра (*pl.* ме́ри)	measure, fit
на́ (*emphatic particle*)	here, there
на бъ́рза ръка́	hastily
на́ ти пари́	here's [your] money
надпи́свам, надпи́ша (-еш)	inscribe
нала́гам / нало́жа (-иш)	put, impose, force
нала́гам се / нало́жа се (-иш)	impose, necessitate
нала́га се / нало́жи се (*3rd ps.*)	be necessary
намина́вам / намина́	drop in
напра́во	directly, openly
Наро́дното събра́ние	Parliament
наря́звам / наре́жа (-еш)	cut into pieces
наси́щам / наси́тя	saturate
национа́лен	national
неде́лен	Sunday (*adj.*)
недости́гнат	unattained
неми́нат	"untrodden"
непоко́рен	disobedient, rebellious
непости́жен	unattainable
ниво́	level
обе́кт	object, project, site
обекти́вен	objective
о́блак	cloud
обли́звам / обли́жа (-еш)	lick
о́браз	image, form
огра́да	fence
огро́мен	huge, enormous
опра́вям / опра́вя	settle, put in order
освежи́телен	refreshing
отби́вам се / отби́я се	drop in
отде́лям / отделя́	separate, detach
откри́тие	discovery
отку́де да зна́м	how should I know
отку́дето	whence, from where (*relative conjunction*)
отлича́вам / отлича́ (-и́ш)	distinguish
отря́звам / отре́жа (-еш)	cut off, cut out
отсре́ща	across the way
отся́дам / отсе́дна	put up, stay at
оттога́ва	from that time
па́костен	harmful, pernicious
па́мет, -та́	memory
па́ркинг	parking lot, carpark
паспо́рт	passport
па́уза	pause, break
пи́йвам / пи́йна	have a drink/shot
пи́ле	chick, chicken; sweetheart
пи́там се	wonder
пленя́вам / пленя́	take captive, captivate
плета́	knit, braid, plait
пло́чкаджия	tile-layer
площа́д	[city] square
по та́я ра́бота	on that score
по́-ми́налата годи́на	the year before last
поведе́ние	behavior, conduct
подпи́свам / подпи́ша (-еш)	sign one's name
подпо́ра	support, pillar
пое́зия	poetry
пое́т	poet
поете́са	poetess
поети́чен	poetic
по́за	posture, attitude
поздравя́вам / поздравя́	greet
по́рта	gateway

Осемнайсети урок / Lesson 18

посве́твам / посве́тна / посветя́	shine for a while
после́двам	follow
прасе́	pig
прасе́нце	piglet
преве́ждам / преведа́	translate
превръ́щам / превъ́рна	transform
предвари́телен	preliminary
предвари́телно	in advance
предпи́свам / предпи́ша (-еш)	prescribe
префуча́вам / префуча́ (-и́ш)	rush past
преценя́вам / преценя́	estimate, assess
прима́мвам / прима́мя	entice, allure
приме́р	example
примиря́вам / примиря́	reconcile
прозвуча́вам / прозвуча́ (-и́ш)	sound, ring out
просто́рен	spacious, roomy
псевдони́м	pseudonym
пълноце́нен	complete, full value
развой́	development
разли́ствам се / разли́стя се	burst into leaf
разми́слям / разми́сля	ponder; change one's mind
размишля́вам	speculate
разпи́твам / разпи́там	inquire, interrogate
разреша́вам / разреша́ (-и́ш)	allow, permit
разтроша́вам / разтроша́ (-и́ш)	break up, crumble
резулта́т	result
реч, -та́	speech
реше́ние	decision, solution
ри́там	kick
ри́твам / ри́тна	take a kick
ро́ден град	hometown
ро́дна сестра́	birth sister (same parents)
самосъзна́ние	self-awareness
сбогу́вам се	say goodbye, take leave of
сва́лям / сваля́	remove, throw down
све́твам / све́тна	flash, go on (of a light)
све́ти see свят	
све́тост	sanctity
све́тъл о́браз	a noble figure
све́тя	shine
свят, све́ти	holy, sacred
сдъ́ржаност	reserve, restraint
ска́ра	grill
ски́тница	wanderer
скръб, -та́	grief, sorrow
следа́	trace, track
сло́во	word, speech
спо́мен	memory, recollection
спор	argument
спор ня́ма	it goes without saying
сти́скам / сти́сна	squeeze, press
сти́скаме си ръце́те	shake hands
сти́скам ръка́та	shake another's hand
стра́нен	strange, unusual
строя́	build
стря́ха (pl. стре́хи)	eaves
събра́ние	meeting, gathering
съвре́мен	contemporary
съвършéнство	perfection
съзна́ние	consciousness
ся́каш	as if
та	and, even; so that
творе́ц	creator; artist
тво́рчески	creative
тво́рчество	creative work
ти баща́, ти ма́йка	you're my only hope
тих	quiet
ти́хо	quietly; quiet!
то́рта	cake
тро́мав	clumsy, ungainly
тя́ло (pl. тела́)	body
уга́свам / уга́сна	go out
удиви́телен	amazing
удово́лствие	pleasure
у́дрям / уда́ря	hit, strike
ужася́вам / ужася́	horrify, appall
у́личка	small street
уника́лен	unique
упъ́твам се / упъ́тя се	make one's way to
фигу́ра	figure
формули́рам	formulate, phrase
фре́нски	French

Осемнайсети урок / Lesson 18

ха́пя	bite	черги́ло	awning
характе́рен	characteristic	чест, -та́	honor
хармони́чен	harmonious	чове́шки	human; decent
хармо́ния	harmony	чу́ден	wonderful; strange
хва́щам мазо́ли	get blisters	чу́кам	knock
хич	nothing, not at all		
хралу́па	cavity in a tree	я́ростен	furious, fierce
		я́стие	dish
ци́къл	cycle, series		
ця́лостен	entire, total		

CULTURAL COMMENTARY

City life: landmarks; room rental; public transportation
    The square in front of the Parliament building in Sofia (площа́д Наро́дно събра́ние) is often identified by the statue at its center. The statue is of the Russian Tsar Alexander II, known in Bulgaria as Tsar Osvoboditel (the emperor who liberated the serfs). With respect to Bulgaria, he led the armies victorious over the Turks in the Russo-Turkish war of 1877-78 which won Bulgaria her independence from the Ottoman Empire. He is highly revered for this feat; the great cathedral named after Alexander Nevsky (his own patron saint) was built to honor him. Since the statue is of a mounted solider facing towards the parliament building, the portion of Sofia located behind the statue is often referred to as "behind the tail of the horse".
    One of the best restaurants in Sofia is called Кри́м ("Crimea"). It is colloquially referred to as Ру́ски клу́б ("The Russian Club").
    It is common for foreign visitors to rent rooms within Bulgarian households. Use of the bathroom and telephone is assured; use of the kitchen is less usual and must be negotiated. Heating water for tea or coffee in one's room, and eating take-out food there, is usually the norm. Landladies are friendly and helpful (and often naturally curious about foreign ways).
    Public transportation in Sofia is quite good: a combination of trams, trolleys and buses covers the city well. The same tickets work for all public transport. One can buy individual tickets, but most Sofia residents buy long-term tickets at a reduced rate. Tickets are shown only when asked for (but a heavy fine is assessed if one is caught traveling without a ticket).

Food and drink: mekhana; grills, salads, sandwiches, wine
    The salad called кьопоолу is made of eggplant, peppers and garlic. It is known in Yugoslavia as "ajvar" and in some parts of the West as "eggplant caviar". It is a very popular accompaniment to rakia.
    Those smaller restaurants serving grilled meats often advertise themselves as "skara" (ска́ра), after the name of the outdoor grill itself. Another popular type of restaurant is that called "mekhana" (механа́). Such restaurants usually have traditional decor (colorful folk tablecloths and earthenware cups and dishes), and the servers usually wear folk costume. The food is also simple and traditional.
    "Sandwiches" in Bulgaria used to be open-faced -- a slice of bread with cheese or salami on it; now Western-style sandwiches are just as common. Yogurt is purchased in standard sized containers. It is either eaten with a spoon, or the container is shaken and the yogurt then drunk. Traditionally the main meal is still taken at midday; yogurt and bread is a very common supper.
    Red wine in Bulgaria is sometimes colloquially referred to as "black" wine, especially in certain western villages. Certain types of very dark grapes are regularly called "black grapes".

Home life: repairs
    Most Bulgarians do as many home repairs (or home improvements) as they can by themselves, since workmen who specialize in these jobs are expensive and in constant demand. A workman who is reliable and good at one of these jobs, such as the laying of tiles in kitchens and bathrooms, is highly sought after.

Осемнайсети урок / Lesson 18

Families: children

Children are doted upon, and the language reflects this through the extremely expressive means by which one talks to or about children. Children are often not addressed by name at all, but by various terms which translate roughly as "Mommy's [Daddy's] dear one".

History: Tsar Samuil

One of the most famous medieval Bulgarian rulers was Emperor Samuil (**Цáр Самуи́л**), who ruled from 980-1014. His capital was in Ohrid (**О́хрид**, now part of modern Macedonia). He successfully expanded the Empire through a series of conquests, but then lost a significant battle to forces under the Byzantine emperor Basil in 996. However, it was his final defeat by Basil (in 1014) which gave the latter the nickname of "the Bulgar-slayer": after taking 14,000 Bulgarian soldiers captive, Basil ordered all of them to be blinded and sent back to Ohrid, sparing only one man in 100 so as to lead them home. When Samuil saw the fate of his army, he died from the shock.

Literature: Elisaveta Bagryana

Elisaveta Bagryana (1893-1990) is Bulgaria's first great woman poet, and one of its most famous and beloved of all poets. She was the first emancipated woman artist in a very patriarchal society, and was admired both for her literary achievements and her personal courage. Her biographer and critic, the poet Blaga Dimitrova (**Бла́га Димитро́ва**, 1922-), is seen by many as the successor of her feminist artist mantle.

Statue of Tsar Alexander the Liberator, Parliament Square, Sofia

LESSON 19

DIALOGUE

Разхо́дка из Со́фия

// Ра́но сутринта́ на дру́гия де́н заку́ската е изя́дена, кафе́то изпи́то и чини́ите изми́ти от трима́та с о́бщи уси́лия. Дне́с Павли́на и Дими́тър и́скат да разхо́дят Миле́на из Со́фия. Павли́на взе́ма и голя́мото си ку́че. //

Павлина: Миле́нче, ти́ откога́ не си́ и́двала в Со́фия?

Милена: О-о, отда́вна. Си́гурно и́ма ше́ст-се́дем годи́ни.

Димитър: Оттога́ва Со́фия мно́го се е промени́ла... Ня́ма да я позна́еш.

Павлина: Да́. Що́м то́лкова отда́вна не си́ и́двала в Со́фия, си́гурно ще я наме́риш мно́го промене́на.

Милена: Къде́ оти́ваме?

Димитър: А́з предла́гам да ми́нем по Рако́вски до булева́рд Ру́ски.

Павлина: Не́ булева́рд Ру́ски, а Ца́р Освободи́тел. Нали́ му смени́ха и́мето.

Димитър: Ня́ма значе́ние. На то́лкова у́лици имена́та са им смене́ни. Не мо́га да им свикна на те́зи но́ви имена́. Та, отта́м по жъ́лтите паве́та покрай Вое́нния клу́б до Наро́дното събра́ние и Алекса́ндър Не́вски.

Павлина: Ма́лко жъ́лти паве́та оста́наха... Ми́не не ми́не ня́коя годи́на и току́ ви́диш о́ще ня́коя ча́ст замене́на с асфа́лт.

Димитър: Мно́го пра́вилно. Ще си изпочу́пят хо́рата крака́та по ти́я хлъ́згави паве́та през зи́мата.

Павлина: Ама́ пъ́к асфа́лтът не е́ то́лкова ху́бав. Нали́ зна́еш, Миле́нче, че ни́къде друга́де в Бълга́рия ня́ма таки́ва паве́та. Ма́йка, бо́г да я прости́, ми бе́ше разка́звала, че са били́ внесе́ни от Че́хия в нача́лото на века́. В тога́вашните ве́стници и́ма карикату́ри на натъже́ни софи́йски коке́тки с вди́гнати до гле́зена поли́. Ня́мат, горки́те, ве́че по́вод да си пока́зват крака́та. Нали́ ня́ма ве́че ка́л...

Димитър: От Университе́та мо́жем да взе́мем троле́я до Двореца́ на култу́рата. Ти́ вли́зала ли си́ в не́го?

Милена: Не́ съм, мака́р че то́й ве́че бе́ше постро́ен тога́ва. И́маше веднъ́ж една́ учи́телска конфере́нция та́м, но а́з не можа́х да вля́за.

Деветнайсети урок / Lesson 19

Димитър: Не беше ли поканена?

Милена: Разбира се, че ме бяха поканили, но áз си бях забравила поканата в хотела.

Павлина: Аз съм ходила там много пъти, но всé с връзки. Бях веднъж на откриването на една изложба, организирана от един мой приятел. И аз бях пропуснала да си взема поканата, но моят приятел познаваше всички на пропуска...

Милена: А Митко, виж! Онези хора на другия тротоар не са ли нашите вчерашни спътници?

Димитър: Ами да, те са. И те имат куче. Я да пресечем улицата и да им се обадим. Те май не са ни забелязали още. Виж как са унесени в разговор.

Павлина: Чакай да светне зелено!

// След като изчакват светофарът да смени светлините, те пресичат улицата. //

Милена: Камене, Надке, здравейте!

Димитър: Здравейте, Таня!

Таня: А, каква изненада. Здравейте, здравейте.

Милена: Таня, запознайте се. Това е майка.

Таня: Много ми е приятно.

Камен: Мамо, виж какво куче има тази леля.

Надка: Как се казва?

Павлина: Барт. Съкратено от Бартоломей. То е расова порода.

Надка: Лельо, хапе ли породата?

Павлина: Не хапе, миличко. Барт много обича малки деца.

Димитър: И вие сте излезли да се поразходите, нали? Да вървим тогава заедно. Ние сме към Народното събрание.

Таня: Да вървим.

Деветнайсети урок / Lesson 19

BASIC GRAMMAR

19.1. The past anterior tense

The Bulgarian past anterior tense (мина́ло предвари́телно вре́ме) designates an action which had been completed prior to another specific action in the past. It is a compound tense, formed by combining the past tense of съм with the L-participle. In all three persons of the singular, the form of the L-participle agrees in gender with the subject: the masculine form оти́шъл is given below, but оти́шла or оти́шло (variant forms отишъ́л, отишла́, отишло́, отишли́) would be used with feminine or neuter subjects.

In the third person singular, the auxiliary бе́ is also frequently encountered; there is no difference in meaning.

	singular	plural
1st	бях оти́шъл	бя́хме оти́шли
2nd	бе́ше оти́шъл	бя́хте оти́шли
3rd	бе́ше оти́шъл бе́ оти́шъл	бя́ха оти́шли

The student should exploit the similarites between the Bulgarian and English past tense systems (at least at this point). Both languages have a simple past tense (which refers to completed past actions), a resultative past tense (which considers the relevance of past action in the present moment) and a doubly marked past tense (which indicates a time frame specifically located in a more distant past). Thus:

Bulgarian   English

aorist	а́з оти́дох	simple past	I went
past indefinite	а́з съм оти́шъл	present perfect	I have gone
past anterior	а́з бях оти́шъл	pluperfect	I had gone

The simple past tense is always a single word, while the other two tenses are composed of an auxiliary and a participle. The two compound tenses utilize the same auxiliary; the only difference is in the tense of the auxiliary. When the meaning is "relevance to the present moment", the auxiliary is in the present tense (Bulgarian съм / English "have"), but when the meaning is "time frame removed in the past", the auxiliary is in the past tense (Bulgarian бях / English "had").

The usage of the Bulgarian past anterior is almost exactly parallel to that of the English pluperfect: each indicates that one of two completed past actions occurred before the other one. In each of the examples below, for instance, two past events are identified. The earlier one is described with the past anterior, and the later one is either described with the aorist or is assumed from the context.

Деветнайсети урок / Lesson 19

А́з го бя́х да́л ве́че, кога́то ти́ ми пи́са, че не мо́жеш да до́йдеш.	I had already submitted it when you wrote me that you wouldn't be able to come.
Ва́шият младе́ж бе́ше дошъ́л да го ча́ка о́ще преди́ 8.00 и те́ изля́зоха за́едно.	Your young man had come before 8:00 to meet him, and [then] they left together.

For the past anterior to be used, it is always necessary that there be two sequential events in the mind of the speaker, whether or not both are explicitly described. If the later event is not mentioned, it can always be assumed from the context. The verb in the past anterior can be of either aspect, although the perfective is usually used unless the speaker wishes especially to emphasize the durative or repeated nature of the earlier action. For example:

Ни́е наро́чно бя́хме отпеча́тали по́вече екземпля́ри, за да ги разпространя́ваме сред коле́ги, кои́то не са́ могли́ да присъ́ствуват.	We had purposefully printed a surplus of copies in order to send them to colleagues who weren't able to come.

(It is clear from the context that at the moment of speaking the conference has concluded; the use of the past anterior specifies that the printing of the copies had been completed before the conference had taken place.)

Ма́йка, Бо́г да я прости́, ми бе́ше разка́звала, че са били́ вне́сени от Че́хия в нача́лото на века́.	My mother, God rest her soul, had told me [repeatedly] that they had been imported from the Czech lands at the turn of the century.

(The speaker is of course aware of the fact that her mother is no longer alive. Even though there is no real necessity to mark the sequence of the events -- since it is obvious that the mother must have told the tale about the tiles prior to the event of her death -- the speaker chooses to focus on that sequence by using the past anterior. She uses the participle of the imperfective verb (разка́звала) to emphasize the repeated nature of the action.)

Не ги́ бя́х ви́ждала ни́кога за́едно и ми́слех, че не се́ позна́ват.	I had never seen them together before, and [therefore] thought that they didn't know each other.

(This speaker mentions two past actions, both of which occurred prior to another past action which is not mentioned. It must be assumed from the context that the speaker has just seen the pair in question and has realized that they are acquainted. The present moment from which she is speaking encompasses both this more recent event and the longer period prior to that event. The durative nature of that long period is communicated both by the imperfective aspect of the past anterior [бях виждала] and the imperfect verb describing a state concurrent with that period [мислех]).

19.2. Word order in the past anterior

The past anterior is similar to the past indefinite in that it is composed of an auxiliary and an L-participle. Word order rules are also similar: the auxiliary precedes the object pronouns, the negative particle must precede the auxiliary, the interrogative particle comes after the first element in the string, and the entire string of clitics must be adjacent to the L-participle. For instance:

past indefinite
    Не сме́ му го да́ли.   We haven't given it to him.
    Не сте́ ли му го пока́зали?   Haven't you shown it to him?

past anterior
    Не бя́хме му го да́ли.   We hadn't given it to him.
    Не бя́хте ли му го пока́зали?   Hadn't you shown it to him?

There is one major difference between the past indefinite and the past anterior, however. The auxiliary in the past indefinite, съм, is a clitic and must obey all the rules for clitics. The auxiliary in the past interior, бя́х, is not a clitic however. Thus it may stand at the beginning of a sentence; indeed, it often occupies this position.

Бя́хме ти пра́тили по́-ра́но програ́мата, сега́ ти пра́щам за информа́ция материа́лите от конфере́нцията.	We'd sent you the program [some time] earlier, now I'm sending for your information materials from the conference.
Бя́ха им ка́зали това́, но те́ го забра́виха.	They'd been told about it, but they forgot.
Бя́х напра́вила ня́кои гре́шки, а то́й ги попра́ви.	I'd made several errors, and he corrected them.
Бе́ше ли научи́ла уро́ка навре́ме?	Had you [indeed] learned the lesson on time?

19.3. Passive participles, continued

Passive participles are adjectives which express a completed action, and which consequently retain a great deal of their original verbal meaning. Like all adjectives, they can be used either attributively (to modify nouns) or predicatively (after the verb съм). Both these usages are similar to English.

Деветнайсети урок / Lesson 19

attributive

Оттáм ни мáха еднá мнóго добрé облéчена дáма.	A very well-dressed woman is waving to us from over there.
Нúе ще ядéм пъ́ржени яйцá.	We'll have fried eggs.

predicative

Материáлите ще бъ́дат публикýвани в окончáтелен вариáнт след двá мéсеца.	The papers will be published in their final version in two months.
Вúе сúгурно сте уморéни от пъ́тя.	You're no doubt tired out from the trip.

Attributive passive participles are used much more frequently in Bulgarian than in English, and most such usages cannot be translated by English passive participles. Instead, English must usually resort to verbal phrases. The closest literal translation, using a related adjective which has no verbal meaning in it, often completely fails to render the sense of Bulgarian. For example:

Сúгурно ще я намéриш мнóго променéна.	You'll certainly find that it has changed a lot. [*literally:* You'll certainly find it very changed.]
Мúне не мúне нáкоя годúна и токý вúдиш óще нáкоя чáст заменéна с асфáлт.	A year or so passes, and all of a sudden you see that they've replaced yet another part with asphalt. [*literally:* ...you see yet another part replaced with asphalt.]
На твóята плóча сúгурно úма зáпис на такúва награденú певцú.	On your disk is certainly a recording of singers who were awarded such a prize. [*literally:* ...of such awarded singers.]
Рúзата ми (сúщо от тъкáно на ръкá платнó и дантéли)...	My folk costume shift (also made from fabric and lace which was woven by hand)... [*literally:* from woven by hand fabric and lace...]

Predicative passive participles are also used quite frequently. They indicate that a particular action has taken place or will take place. As in English, they can appear after any tense form of the copula. Thus:

present	Хлябът е наряан.	The bread is/has been sliced.
past	Хлябът бéше нарязан.	The bread was sliced.
future	Хлябът ще бъ́де нарязан.	The bread will be sliced.

Деветнайсети урок / Lesson 19

The system seems straightforward, but it can cause problems for the speaker of English. This is because only in the future tense is the English translation relatively exact. In these (and certain other) constructions, the Bulgarian present tense covers a much wider range of meaning than the English present tense. For Bulgarians, the fact that an action may already have been accomplished in the past is seen as less important than the fact that its results are still very present. The following sentence, although it does not contain a passive participle, illustrates this:

От снощи не се чувствувам добре.   I've been feeling bad since last night.

An English speaker must use the present perfect here and in other instances where s/he needs to specify the point in the past at which the state began. For the English speaker, the use of the present perfect (a past tense whose scope extends into the present) is sufficient to indicate that the state is still in effect. A Bulgarian speaker, however, must use the present tense: the fact that the state is still in effect outweighs any other consideration.

Constructions with passive participles are especially tricky in this regard. All of the following examples, for instance, are considered "present tense" in Bulgarian, despite the fact that all the predicative participles refer to events which were completed long before the moment of speech. The reference to the present results of the events allows (and requires) the use of the present tense in Bulgarian. By contrast, only the first example is considered "present tense" in English. In turn, present tense in English is possible in this first sentence only because no time period is specified; compare the second example, which must use the present perfect tense in English:

Разведена съм.	I am divorced.
Разведена съм вече от три години.	I've been divorced for three years.
Родена съм на трети април.	I was born on April 3.
Рилският манастир е създаден през X век.	Rila monastery was founded in the 10th century.
Днес той е превърнат в национален музей.	Now it has been transformed into a national museum.

The English speaker learning Bulgarian must pay attention to the broader scope of "present" tense in Bulgarian. One consequence of this broader scope is that the use of past tense in Bulgarian predicative constructions has a pluperfect meaning: it indicates that the action denoted by the participle was completed prior to some other past action. For example:

Не съм влизала в Двореца, макар че той вече беше построен тогава.	I didn't go into the Palace [when I was here before], although the construction had been completed at that point.

| Кога́то си дойдо́х, вси́чко бе́ше напра́вено. | When I got home, everything had [already] been done. |

Considerable context is often necessary to interpret the tense choice in such sentences. For instance, each of the following two passive sentences could be said about one and the same event, and both have the same English translation:

| Ни́е сме тро́гнати от ва́шето внима́ние. | We were touched by your consideration. |
| Ни́е бя́хме тро́гнати от ва́шето внима́ние. | *(same)* |

In both cases the speaker refers to an instance in the past when s/he was shown a certain consideration for which s/he now expresses gratitude. The difference between the two sentences concerns not time but rather the speaker's point of view. The first speaker focuses on the emotional state in general (indeed, it is almost as if she is reliving that state in the present). By contrast, the second speaker focuses more upon that state at a particular past moment and the fact that other events have intervened between that moment and the moment of speech -- despite the fact that he still feels the gratitude.

19.4. Passive constructions with passive participles

Many of the above sentences are examples of "passive constructions". Such sentences presume an underlying active one. The relationship between the two in Bulgarian is parallel to that in English: the direct object of the transitive verb in the active sentence becomes the subject of the passive sentence, and the transitive verb of the active sentence is expressed as a passive participle in the passive sentence.

active sentence

Someone	will send	the letter	on time.
Ня́кой	ще изпра́ти	писмо́то	навре́ме.
subject	*transitive verb*	*direct object*	

passive transformation of above sentence

The letter	will be	sent	on time.
Писмо́то	ще бъ́де	изпра́тено	навре́ме.
subject	*auxiliary*	*passive participle*	

In the above example, the subject of the active sentence (the "agent" of the action) goes unmentioned in the passive sentence. If the speaker wishes to name the agent in the passive sentence, this is done by a prepositional phrase. Again, the structure is like English; the student need only remember that Bulgarian uses от where English uses "by". For example:

active sentence

I	wrote	the letter
Áз	напи́сах	писмо́то.
subject	*transitive verb*	*direct object*

passive transformation of above sentence

The letter	was	written	by me.
Писмо́то	е	напи́сано	от ме́не.
subject	*auxiliary*	*passive participle*	*agent*

In fact, passive constructions are used frequently when it is not necessary (or desirable) to specify the actor (or agent of the action). In the first "active" variant given above, the indefinite form **ня́кой** appears as the subject, but this is simply because an active sentence requires an explicitly identified subject. If the speaker cannot (or does not wish to) specify the agent of the action, s/he will usually choose to express the idea in the passive. Passive constructions are also used when the speaker wishes to focus more on the result of the action than on its actors. For example:

Ра́но сутринта́ на дру́гия де́н заку́ската е изя́дена, кафе́то изпи́то и чини́ите изми́ти.	It's early morning on the next day -- breakfast is done [eaten], the coffee is all gone [drunk up], and the dishes all washed.
Сле́д като вси́чкото ви́но бе́ше изпи́то и вси́чките пе́сни изпе́ти, ста́на вре́ме за съ́н.	When all the wine had been drunk and all the songs sung, it was time to sleep.

If the speaker had wished to specify the subject of the actions in the second sentence, s/he would probably have used an active construction such as

Сле́д като бя́ха изпи́ли ви́ното и изпе́ли пе́сните, го́стите се разоти́доха.	After they had drunk [all] the wine and sung [all] the songs, the guests went their separate ways.

Similarly, while some sentences are perfectly natural in the passive form, the same sentences sound awkward with an agentive phrase. In principle they can be said, but speakers would normally not say them. Here, too, English usage is parallel:

Ма́сата е сло́жена. Ко́й я е сло́жил?   The table is set. Who set it?

and not   *and not*
От кого́ е сло́жена?   By whom was it set?

The same idea (of passivity without specific expression of the subject) is often expressed by a verb in the 3rd plural; this usage is also parallel to the English. In this type of construction it is not possible to specify the agent grammatically by a prepositional phrase. If such a phrase occurs, a third-person subject is understood.

-- Добре́ ли пра́вят омле́та?	"Do they make a good omelet?"
-- Ту́к вси́чко го́твят добре́.	"They do [cook] everything here well."
Та́м го пра́тиха [ня́кои] от реда́кцията.	He was sent there by [some people from] the editorial office.

Although the two types of passives are not interchangeable, their meaning is very similar. This is seen in the frequent substitution of one type for the other in English translations of Bulgarian passive constructions. For instance:

На то́лкова у́лици имена́та са им смене́ни.	They've changed the names of so many streets. [*literally:* The names of so many streets have been changed.]

The idea of "passive" in English can be rendered by one of these two constructions, both of which find nearly exact parallels in Bulgarian. There is also a third way to render passives in Bulgarian, one which has no parallel in English. These constructions, with **се**, are the subject of the next lesson.

Eagle's Bridge, Sofia

EXERCISES

I. Rewrite in the past.

1. Сърдя се, защото ме излъга.
2. Очаква се сняг, въпреки че зимата почти отмина.
3. Плащат му, защото е свършил работа.
4. Всички, които са дошли, слушат внимателно.
5. Сигурен съм, че никой не те е търсил.
6. Търсят кандидати, които са работили повече от две години.
7. Мисля, че всички вече са се събрали.

II. Rewrite as passive.

1. Разделиха тортата на равни парчета.
2. В края на годината ще наградят най-добрите ученици.
3. Вече продават билети за концерта.
4. Изпуснаха и последния срок да подадат молба.
5. Оставиха колата на най-близкия паркинг.
6. В центъра на града ще строят нова театрална сграда.
7. Глобиха шофьора на автобуса за превишена скорост.

III. Rewrite, replacing past tense verbs by passive participles.

1. Прогнозата за времето ги уплаши и те останаха вкъщи.
2. Любимият му отбор го разочарова и той вече не ходи на стадиона.
3. Дъждът го измокри и той трепереше от студ.
4. Упорството му ме учуди и аз не искам да го виждам.
5. Слънцето го заслепи и той не вижда пътя добре.
6. Предупредиха го за последствията и той стана много внимателен.
7. Новината я зарадва и тя я съобщи на всичките си приятели.

Деветнайсети урок / Lesson 19

ADDITIONAL GRAMMAR NOTES

19.2a. Word order in the past anterior

Word order rules in the past anterior are less strict than in the past indefinite. This is partly because the auxiliary бях is not a clitic and therefore is not bound to obey the rules applying to clitics. Among other things, it can (and often does) begin a sentence.

Short form pronoun objects, which are always clitics, continue to obey the relevant rules: they cannot stand in initial position and they must occur adjacent to the verb. In the past indefinite, the verb form they depend on is the L-participle; and they must therefore always be adjacent to it. In the past anterior, however, they can depend on one of two forms: either the auxiliary бях, or the L-participle. For many sentences, therefore, two different basic word orders are possible. In the notation below, the auxiliary бях will be designated *Aux*: the capitalization indicates that it is neither a clitic nor a fully independent stressed word.

In a neutral interrogative sentence, however, only one word order is possible. That is, when the particle ли must be fitted into the verb phrase, it must follow the auxiliary directly. In this case, the pronoun objects are required to depend upon the L-participle. (When the particle ли occurs elsewhere, as an emphatic, it does not affect the word order within the verb phrase.)

Following are examples of word order in the past anterior:

| Беше | ми | го | казала | по-рано. |
| *Aux.* | *IND* | *DIR* | *participle* | |

You had told me that earlier.

| Не | бях | му | се | обадила. |
| *Neg.* | *Aux.* | *IND* | *DIR* | *participle* |

| Не | мý | се | бях | обадила. |
| *Neg.* | *IND* | *DIR* | *Aux.* | *participle* |

I hadn't called him.

Още ли | не | беше | му | се | обадила?
| | *Neg.* | *Aux.* | *IND* | *DIR* | *participle* |

Още ли | не | мý | се | беше | обадила?
| | *Neg.* | *IND* | *DIR* | *Aux.* | *participle* |

Hadn't you called him *yet*?

| Беше | ли | му | се | обадила? |
| *Aux.* | *INT* | *IND* | *DIR* | *participle* |

Had you called him?

Не	бе́ше	ли	му	се	оба́дила?
Neg.	Aux.	INT	IND	DIR	participle

Hadn't you called him yet?

19.3a. Complex constructions with passive participles

When passive constructions are embedded within longer sentences, especially within да-phrases, the structure of these sentences sometimes seems very opaque to the English speaker. This is largely because of the very common word order rules connected with да: the verb of the да-phrase must follow immediately after the да.

In passive constructions, the unit of "copula + passive participle" is considered the "verb", and must follow да immediately. Due to the structure of such sentences, however, the subject of this да-phrase is sometimes separated from the да-phrase by one or more intervening clauses. Such constructions are common in the written language (and extremely so in certain official styles). In the following example, the да-phrase and its subject are underlined.

| .... предложе́нието <u>материа́лите</u> от Осмата междунаро́дна конфере́нция по но́ви ме́тоди за лече́ние на онкологи́чните заболя́вания, състоя́ла се в Со́фия от 4 до 7 апри́л та́зи годи́на, <u>да бъ́дат публику́вани</u> от изда́телството като отде́лно изда́ние. | ...the proposal that the papers of the Eighth international congress on new methods of cancer research, held in Sofia on April 4-7, be issued by the publishers in book form. |

19.4a. Passive agentive constructions

Students of Russian will note that certain Bulgarian prepositional phrases using от correspond to the instrumental case in Russian. One example is the use in passive agentive constructions. Another instance of this correspondence is after the verb **интересу́вам се**. For example:

| Бях веднъ́ж на откри́ването на една изло́жба, организи́рана от еди́н мой прия́тел. | Once I was at the opening of an exhibition organized by a friend of mine. |
| Тя́ се интересу́ва от Средновеко́вието. | She's interested in the Middle Ages. |

19.5. Derivation of agentive nouns and family group nouns

There are several suffixes which are used to form "agentive nouns": nouns indicating the performer of an action (or more rarely, the instrument). The noun formed refers to males, to mixed company, or to the general category. The suffix **-ка** can be added to form a noun designating a female member of this category. Some verbal roots, however, give rise only to masculine agentive nouns.

Agentive nouns in -ач

The most common agentive suffix is **-ач**. It is always accented, is added to the present stem of the verb, and is usually limited to imperfective verbs.

verb (pres.)	stem	+ ач (ка) ›	agentive noun	meaning shift
изпра́щам	изпращ-	+ ач (ка) ›	изпращ-а́ч (ка)	send › shipper
прода́вам	продав-	+ ач (ка) ›	продав-а́ч (ка)	sell › salesperson
чи́стя	чист-	+ ач (ка) ›	чист-а́ч (ка)	clean › cleaning person
мета́	мет-	+ ач (ка) ›	мет-а́ч (ка)	sweep › sweeper, scavenger
разда́вам	раздав-	+ ач (ка) ›	раздав-а́ч (ка)	distribute › postman
копа́я	коп-	+ ач ›	коп-а́ч	dig › digger, hoe
ора́	ор-	+ ач ›	ор-а́ч	plough › ploughman

Agentive nouns in -тел

Another common agentive suffix is **-тел**. It is also added to verbal roots, although usually to the aorist stem. The accent is always on the syllable immediately preceding -тел.

verb (aor.)	stem	+ тел (ка) ›	agentive noun	meaning shift
у́чих	учи-	+ тел (ка) ›	учи́-тел (ка)	teach › teacher
пи́сах	писа-	+ тел (ка) ›	писа́-тел (ка)	write › writer
създа́дох	създа-	+ тел (ка) ›	създа́-тел (ка)	establish › creator, founder
победи́х	победи-	+ тел (ка) ›	победи́-тел (ка)	win › victor

Agentive nouns in -ар

A third suffix is **-ар**. This is added to noun roots. Most nouns in **-ар** do not form the female counterpart in **-арка**, although a few do. This may be partly because most of these words designate occupations or actions normally performed only by men. This suffix is almost always accented.

noun	stem	+ ар (ка) ›	agentive noun	meaning shift
ри́ба	риб-	+ ар ›	риб-а́р	fish › fisherman
млека́ (pl.)	млек-	+ ар ›	млек-а́р	milk › milkman
гъ́ба	гъб-	+ ар ›	гъб-а́р	mushroom › mushroom gatherer
обу́ща	обущ-	+ ар ›	обущ-а́р	shoe › shoemaker
овца́	ов-ч-	+ ар ›	овч-а́р (ка)	sheep › shepherd(ess)
ле́к	лек-	+ ар ›	ле́к-ар (ка)	remedy › physician

Borrowed agentive nouns

Certain names for professions are borrowed into Bulgarian from Western languages. One can sometimes predict the suffix from the English, but not always.

специал-и́ст (ка)	special-ist		
журнал-и́ст (ка)	journal-ist		
би-оло́г	bi-ologist		
архе-оло́г	archae-ologist	*but:*	
теоре́т-ик	theoret-ician	физ-и́к	physi-cist
матема́т-ик	mathemat-ician	хим-и́к	chem-ist
техн-и́к	techn-ician	гимнаст-и́к (-и́чка)	gymnast

Family-group possessives

Nouns indicating a family group are formed with the possessive suffixes -ин- and -ов-. The suffix -ин- is added to a female personal name, and the suffix -ов- to a male personal name. The resulting plural form refers to the family group associated with that person. For example:

name	stem	+ -ин-	/ -ов-	plural form
Миле́на	Милен-	+ -ин-		Миле́нини
Сто́йко	Сто́йк-		+-ов-	Сто́йкови

The particular size and composition of the family group is known from the context. Translations out of context are somewhat awkward, as the following example shows:

Преди́ сре́щата у Миле́нини те́ се бя́ха ви́ждали ня́колко пъ́ти.

Before they met at Milena's family's place, they had seen each other several times.

Деветнайсети урок / Lesson 19

SAMPLE SENTENCES

1. Вие с него май не се познавате. Когато вие пристигнахте в София, той си беше заминал.
2. Таня вече беше купила ягодите, когато се сети, че вкъщи няма захар.
3. Вече бяха затворили магазините, когато ти се обади. Какво можех да направя?
4. Преди срещата у Миленини те се бяха виждали няколко пъти, но никога не бяха разговаряли. Веднъж даже бяха пътували няколко часа в едно купе, без да се поздравят.
5. Тя беше чувала за тази библиотека, но никога не беше ходила там.
6. Иван я беше поканил, но тя не можа да дойде.
7. Иван беше я поканил, но тя не можа да дойде.
8. Беше я поканил, но тя не можа да дойде.
9. Не ти ли бяха останали малко от онези пари? Не бяха ли ти останали малко от онези пари?
10. Бяха им казали за това, но те го бяха забравили.
11. Което е преживяно, няма да бъде забравено.
12. Решението беше взето от всички нас. Не можем току-така да го променяме.
13. Предложението беше направено от Съюза на писателите.

14. -- Масата е сложена. Заповядайте да вечеряме!
    -- Ама кой я е сложил? Ти беше през цялото време с нас.

15. Всичко, което виждате наоколо, е създадено от трудолюбивите ръце на нашите ученици.

16. Аз бях измила прозореца и до преди малко той блестеше измит на слънцето. Сега обаче по него има много следи от малки ръчички. Изглежда, малкият ми приятел пак е идвал на гости, докато ме е нямало.

17. -- Ти това копче ли ши вчера?
    -- Едва ли. Това липсва. Аз когато правя нещо, правя го. Щом съм зашил копче, то стои зашито и след като ризата се скъса.

18. Непрекъснато го канят на международни симпозиуми и конференции. Поканен е и на конгреса в Амстердам. Видях името му в списъка на почетните гости.

19. Надка е вече сресана и измита. Облечена е в новата си рокля. Връзките на обувките ѝ са завързани. Тя стои пред вратата и чака с нетърпение да я заведат в зоологическата градина.

Деветнайсети урок / Lesson 19

SENTENCES FOR TRANSLATION

1. I had been to Bulgaria several times already, but when I arrived there this time, so many things had changed that I couldn't even get my bearings in Sofia, a city I knew well.

2. The meeting organized by our society was very successful. I am sorry you couldn't come.

3. I was quite surprised to hear that you had already left by the time I arrived. I quickly figured out, however, why you had to leave.

4. I had a look around for yesterday's newspaper, but it had already been thrown out.

5. Look what has happened! The beautiful young maiden has been turned into a frog by the evil magician. By the time I learned about it, she had already been sold to the zoo.

6. That dog doesn't bite. It was trained by some very nice people.

7. I found him on Patriarch Evtimij completely lost. He still hasn't got used to walking around Sofia by himself.

People's Palace of Culture (NDK), Sofia

READING SELECTION

<u>Кореспонде́нция - (14)</u>

12 апри́л, Со́фия

Дра́ги Бо́б,

    Пи́ша ти по по́вод на конфере́нцията по но́ви ме́тоди за лече́ние на онкологи́чните заболя́вания. Ка́кто зна́еш, на́шият институ́т съби́ра през две́ годи́ни най-до́брите специали́сти в та́я о́бласт за обмя́на на о́пит. Жа́л ми е, че ти́ не можа́ да прису́ствуваш. Бя́хме ти пра́тили по-ра́но програ́мата, сега́ пра́щам за тво́я информа́ция материа́лите от конфере́нцията. Ни́е наро́чно бя́хме отпеча́тали по́вече екземпля́ри, за да ги разпространя́ваме сред коле́ги, кои́то не са́ могли́ да прису́ствуват. Ви́ждаш, че резюме́то на тво́я докла́д е вклю́чено на съотве́тното мя́сто. А́з го бях да́л ве́че, кога́то ти́ ми пи́са, че не мо́жеш да до́йдеш. Ми́сля, че ста́на добре́. Сега́ ще мо́жем да вклю́чим и пъ́лния те́кст на докла́да ти в сбо́рника (ни́що, че не си́ го изне́съл), ако ни го изпра́тиш навре́ме. Кра́йният сро́к е 15 септе́мври.
    На конфере́нцията и́маше, ка́кто обикнове́но се слу́чва, мно́го и най-разли́чни га́фове. А́з като организа́тор се стара́ех да бъ́да едновре́менно на три́ места́, но нали́ не съм слъ́нце да огре́я нався́къде... За пъ́рви път успя́хме да убеди́м профе́сор Бе́нсен от Хола́ндия да прису́ствува. Бя́хме прикрепи́ли към не́го еди́н аспира́нт да му пома́га да се ориенти́ра нао́коло. Пъ́рвия де́н ча́кахме Бе́нсен да се появи́, ча́кахме и накра́я по́чнахме без не́го. Притесни́х се, нали́ той тря́бваше да чете́ плена́рен докла́д, пък не е́ ве́че то́лкова мла́д чове́кът... Ка́кто и да е́. Загря́х телефо́на да въртя́ да го търся́. От хоте́ла ми ка́заха, че профе́сорът е изля́зъл. Ва́шият, ка́зват, младе́ж бе́ше дошъ́л да го ча́ка във фоайе́то о́ще преди́ о́сем часа́ и те́ изля́зоха за́едно. Къде́ са тога́ва? Пъ́тят е са́мо де́сет мину́ти. Най-се́тне, в де́сет без де́сет двама́та присти́гат по́тни. На́шият хубо́стник да взе́ме да се загу́би, мо́ля ти се. Профе́сор Бе́нсен по́сле се сме́еше: "Добре́, че мо́га да се ориенти́рам по слъ́нцето, та наме́рихме пъ́тя с Мари́н!" Сра́м и позо́р!
    А́з мно́го се вълну́вах от реа́кцията на профе́сор Дюпо́н от Бе́лгия по по́вод на мо́я докла́д. А́з та́м оспо́рвам едно́ не́гово положе́ние. Дока́то изна́сях докла́да, все́ погле́ждах към не́го. Глава́та му през ця́лото вре́ме бе́ше наве́дена и той не се́ помръ́дваше. Ре́кох си, то́я ще ме напра́ви на бъ́зе и копри́ва, като свъ́рша. И изведнъ́ж разби́рам, че той спи́! В па́узата дъ́лго ми сти́ска ръка́та и хва́ли докла́да ми. И досега́ не ми́ е я́сно дали́ зна́е за крити́чните ми беле́жки по не́говия ме́тод, или не зна́е.
    И́мам ну́жда от тво́я съве́т по по́вод предложе́нието на Изда́телството на БА́Н да публику́ва докла́дите като отде́лно изда́ние. Разби́ра се, мно́го по-ху́баво ще е докла́дите да бъ́дат изда́дени така́, а не́, ка́кто бя́хме реши́ли първонача́лно, поотде́лно в на́шето списа́ние. И изда́нието ще е по́-ху́баво, и по́вече чита́тели ще наме́ри. Те́ оба́че ни да́ват мно́го кра́тки сро́кове.

Пращам ти копие от писмото си до тях. Как мислиш, добре ли е формулирана молбата ми за повече време?

Поздрави вкъщи от всички ни
Твой

Бойко

До г-н Директора на
Издателството на БАН
София

М О Л Б А

от Бойко Атанасов, к. м. н.,
научен секретар на
Института по онкология

Уважаеми г-н Директор,

Нашият институт е много признателен на Издателството на БАН за предложението материалите от Осмата международна конференция по нови методи за лечение на онкологичните заболявания, състояла се в София от 4 до 7 април тази година, да бъдат публикувани от издателството като отделно издание. Аз като научен редактор на изданието имам обаче една забележка относно предполаганите срокове на изданието.
Изискването на издателството материалите да бъдат представени в окончателен вариант в течение на два месеца не е реално изпълнимо. Вашето предложение беше направено след края на конференцията. Повечето участници от чужбина няма да бъдат в състояние да спазят този срок, още повече, че на самата конференция беше обявен 15 септември като краен срок.
Моля, като се имат пред вид изложените по-горе обстоятелства, срокът на издателството да бъде удължен до средата на септември. Надявам се, че това закъснение няма да повлияе на решението Ви да издадете материалите от конференцията.
С дълбоко уважение

[подпис]
(Бойко Атанасов, к.м.н.)

10. IV. 19--
София

Деветнайсети урок / Lesson 19

GLOSSARY

асфа́лт	paving, asphalt	изда́вам / изда́м	give out, reveal; betray; publish
био́лог	biologist	изда́ние	edition, publication
блестя́	shine, sparkle	изда́телство	publishing house
бъ́зе	danewort (*Sambucus ebulus*)	изи́скване	requirement
		изла́гам / изло́жа (-иш)	exhibit; set forth
в тече́ние на 2 ме́сеца	within 2 months	изло́жба	exhibition
		излъ́гвам / излъ́жа (-еш)	lie, deceive
вна́сям / внеса́	import, bring in		
вое́нен	military	изна́сям / изнеса́	take out, export; make public
връ́зки	connections		
въ́преки	despite	изна́сям докла́д	read/deliver a paper
въ́преки че	despite the fact that	изпочу́пвам / изпочу́пя	break [all up]
гаф	gaffe, blunder	изпраща́ч (ка)	sender, shipper
гимнасти́к, -и́чка	gymnast	изпълни́м	feasible
глобя́вам / глобя́	fine, impose penalty	изча́квам / изча́кам	await, wait for
гъба́р	gatherer, grower or seller of mushrooms	и́мам пред ви́д	bear in mind
		информа́ция	information
дворе́ц	palace		
дру́гаде	elsewhere	кал, -та́	mud
дълбо́к	deep	карикату́ра	cartoon, caricature
		коке́тка	flirt, coquette
едва́	with difficulty, hardly, just	конгре́с	congress
		конце́рт	concert
едва́ ли	hardly, not likely	копа́ч	digger; hoe
екземпля́р	copy	копри́ва	nettle
		ко́пче	button, knob
жал	pity, sorrow	кра́ен, кра́йна	endmost, final, extreme
жал ми е	be sorry, be grieved	кра́ен срок	deadline
жълт	yellow	крити́чен	critical
		крити́чни бележки	criticisms
забеле́жка	note, observation		
заболя́вания	[cases of] illness	лек, -ъ́т (*pl.* ле́кове *and* леково́)	remedy, cure
загря́вам / загре́я	heat up; catch on		
загу́бвам / загу́бя	lose	лече́ние	treatment, cure
загу́бвам се / загу́бя се	get lost	ли́псвам / ли́псам	be missing, lack
заме́ням / заменя́	substitute, replace	математи́к, -и́чка	mathematician
зара́двам	please, delight	материа́л	material
заслепя́вам / заслепя́	blind, dazzle	междунаро́ден	international
заши́вам / заши́я	sew up, sew in	мета́	sweep
заши́вам ко́пче	sew on a button	мета́ч (ка)	sweeper; scavenger
зоологи́ческа гради́на	zoo	ме́тод	method
зоологи́чески	zoological	ми́нало предвари́телно вре́ме	past anterior tense

Деветнайсети урок / Lesson 19

ми́не не ми́не годи́на	every year or so	побежда́вам / победя́	conquer, defeat, win
млека́р	milkman	повлия́вам, повлия́я	influence, affect
музе́й	museum		
НДК = Наро́ден дворе́ц на култу́рата		пода́вам молба́	submit a request
на про́пуска	at the clearance point	позо́р	disgrace
наве́ждам / наведа́	bend down; suggest	пока́на	invitation
нався́къде	everywhere	пола́	skirt
надя́вам се	hope	положе́ние	position
най-се́тне	finally	помръ́двам се / помръ́дна се	budge
Наро́ден дворе́ц на култу́рата	People's Palace of Culture	поотде́лно	separately
натъжа́вам / натъжа́ (-и́ш)	sadden	попра́вям / попра́вя	fix, correct, mend
нача́ло	beginning	поро́да	breed, race
ни́къде дру́гаде	nowhere else	после́дствие	consequence
		по́тен	sweaty, perspiring
о́бласт, -та́	region, sphere	по́четен	honored; honorary
обмя́на	exchange	пра́вилен	right, straight, true
обмя́на на о́пит	pooling experience	пра́вилно	correctly, rightly so
обстоя́телство	circumstance	пра́вя на бъ́зе и копри́ва	make mincemeat of
обуща́р	shoemaker		
обявя́вам / обявя́	announce, proclaim	преви́шавам / превиша́ (-и́ш)	exceed, surpass
овца́	sheep		
овча́р (ка)	shepherd(ess)	предпола́гам / предполо́жа (-иш)	suppose, presume
огря́вам / огре́я	illuminate, light up		
оконча́телен	final, definitive	предупрежда́вам / предупредя́	warn, caution; advise
онкологи́чен	oncological, cancer-related		
онкологи́чни заболя́вания	[cases of] cancer	преживя́вам / преживе́я	experience, survive
онколо́гия	oncology	преси́чам / пресека́ (-че́ш)	intercept, interrupt; cross (the street)
о́пит	attempt, try		
ора́	plough, till	призна́телен	grateful
ора́ч	ploughman	прикре́пвам / прикрепя́	attach, join; support
организа́тор	organizer, sponsor		
ориенти́рам	orient, put on the right track	прогно́за	prognosis
		прогно́за за вре́мето	weather forecast
ориенти́рам се	get one's bearings	про́пуск	pass; omission
оспо́рвам / оспо́ря	contest, dispute	публику́вам	publish
отде́лно изда́ние	separate book/edition	първонача́лен	original, initial
откри́ване	opening (ceremony)		
относ́но	concerning	ра́зговор	conversation
отпеча́твам / отпеча́там	print up	раздава́ч (ка)	postman, letter-carrier
		разоти́вам се / разоти́да се	disperse, go separate ways
оча́квам се	be liable to occur, be expected	разочаро́вам	disappoint
о́ще по́вече	all the more	разпространя́вам / разпространя́	distribute
паве́	paving-stone, cobble	ра́сов	racial
парче́	piece, portion	ра́сова поро́да	pedigreed
плена́рен	plenary	реа́кция	reaction
плена́рен докла́д	keynote paper	реа́лен	real, practicable
победи́тел (ка)	victor, winner	реда́ктор (ка)	editor

Деветнайсети урок / Lesson 19

реда́кция	editor's office	тога́вашен	of that time
резюме́	summary, résumé	току́	just, suddenly
риба́р	fisherman, fishmonger	трепе́ря	tremble
		трудолюби́в	industrious
с о́бщи уси́лия	working all together		
светлина́	light	удължа́вам /	prolong, lengthen
светофа́р	traffic light	удължа́ (-и́ш)	
сгра́да	building	уна́сям / унеса́	carry away, transport
се́тне	afterwards	упла́швам /	frighten
симпо́зиум	symposium	упла́ша (-иш)	
ско́рост	speed	упо́рство	tenacity
скъ́свам / скъ́сам	tear, break; break off	уси́лие	effort
спа́звам / спа́зя	observe, adhere to	уча́стник	participant
спи́сък (*pl.* спи́съци)	list, roll	учи́телски	teacher's
спъ́тник	fellow traveler	учу́двам / учу́дя	surprise, astonish
срам и позо́р!	for shame!		
сред	among, amidst	физи́к, -и́чка	physicist
сре́свам /	comb	фоайе́	foyer, lobby
сре́ша (-еш)			
срок	term, time limit	хва́ля	praise
стара́я се	try, take pains	хими́к, -и́чка	chemist
създа́тел (ка)	creator, founder	хлъ́згав	slippery
съотве́тен	corresponding; appropriate	хубостни́к	good-for-nothing
съ́рдя се	be/get angry	чини́я	plate, dish
състоя́ние	state, condition	чиста́ч (ка)	cleaner, cleaning person
		чи́стя	clean
театра́лен	theater *(adj.)*	чита́тел (ка)	reader
те́кст	text		
теорети́к, -и́чка	theoretician	ши́я	sew
те́хник	technician	шофьо́р	driver

CULTURAL COMMENTARY

Sofia: major streets, yellow tiles; NDK; dogs

One of the most fashionable streets in Sofia, Rakovska (у́лица Рако́вска), is named after an early Bulgarian revolutionary, Georgi Rakovksi (Гео́рги Рако́вски, 1821-1867). Rakovski was a key figure in the movement for Bulgarian independence, as well as a journalist and scholar. In an attempt to raise Bulgarian national self-consciousness, he researched and published a great deal of early and folk Bulgarian literature.

The main street of Sofia, Tsar Osvoboditel (Bulevard Ruski during the socialist period), enters the city proper at Eagle's bridge (О́рлов мо́ст), runs through Parliament square and ends in front of the large building which was the royal palace until 1944. It is said that sooner or later one meets all one's acquaintances strolling along this street (whether one wants to or not).

Деветнайсети урок / Lesson 19

To mark both the prestige of this main street in the capital city and the entry of independent Bulgaria into the new century, the government paved this street in 1907 entirely with yellow bricks imported from Prague. Newspaper cartoons at the time poked fun at the consequent unhappiness of flirtatious upper-class women: now that the street was paved, they had no more excuse to flash a well-turned ankle by lifting their skirts above the mud in inclement weather. In postwar years the bricks have been gradually replaced by asphalt pavement, to the chagrin of many to whom these yellow bricks carry special nostalgic meaning.

The People's Palace of Culture (Народен дворец на културата) is often referred to by its initials, NDK (НДК, pronounced ендека). It was built at great expense in the early 1980s, causing both a massive rearrangement of the city center, and considerable anguish to those who considered (correctly) that Bulgaria could ill afford such extravagance. Until 1989 it bore the name of its instigator, socialist Bulgaria's Minister of Culture, Lyudmila Zhivkova (Людмила Живкова, 1942-1981), who was also the daughter of socialist Bulgaria's leader, Todor Zhivkov (Тодор Живков, 1911-1998).

NDK consists of numerous meeting, concert and exhibition halls and is fronted by a large landscaped promenade. Trams and buses run underneath this area and there are many shops in the underground passageway. During the socialist period, conventional wisdom claimed that this complex was also connected by underground tunnels to important Party headquarters; otherwise, went the logic, why was security so tight simply for a cultural meeting house? The complex was usually heavily guarded, and one could gain admittance to scholarly and cultural events there only by showing an approved pass.

As in many large Western cities, it has become a symbol of social status to own a dog. The larger the dog and the more obviously purebred it is, the higher the status.

Official and semi-official life: connections, official requests

"Connections" (връзки) are essential in Bulgaria as elsewhere. If one has the right connections, one can bypass many a bureaucratic requirement or obstacle. It is a mark of pride to obtain something (either for oneself or for a friend) through "connections". Bribes are considerably less common than in other Eastern countries, however; often the person to whom the bribe is offered may take offense and the reverse effect will obtain. It is almost as if the attempt to bribe is an indication that the person lacks "connections".

Whenever an individual wishes (or needs) to interact with some bureaucratic agency, s/he must produce a written request in the form of a "molba" (молба). The format is similar to that of a business letter except for the particular heading.

Forms of address: surnames

Family names in Bulgaria frequently consist of a personal name followed by the suffix -ов or -ев (feminine -ова, -ева), athough they also may end in -ски/ска or -ин/ина; for instance Rakovski (Раковски), Andreichin (Андрейчин). The surnames in -ов(а) or -ев(а) in fact are simple patronymics: possessive forms indicating the father-child relationship. Thus, Димитър Стойков literally means "Dimitar son of Stoyko", and Кръстина Колева literally means "Krystina daughter of Kolyo". The parallel to English Anderson and Wilson is obvious. The name preceding the possessive suffix need not be a proper name; it can also be the name of a profession such as бояджия (painter) or поп (priest) -- hence the surnames Бояджиев and Попов.

Many Bulgarians even today have a choice of surname. For instance, Ivan son of Andrei Rakovski (and grandson of Naiden) may take either the surname Andreev, the surname Naidenov or the surname Rakovski. The fact that his brother or sister may not make the same choice can mean that children of the same parents will have different surnames. The custom which dictates that all children and grandchildren of the same man should bear the same surname is an import from the West which is only now gradually taking hold (see also the cultural notes to Lesson 25).

Academic life: publications by BAN

The Bulgarian Academy of Sciences runs an extensive publishing house, producing all manner of scholarly volumes. Some of these are part of established series themselves associated with individual institutes of the Academy, and some are separate editions.

LESSON 20

DIALOGUE

Ти́ зна́еш ли ка́к се треси́рат ку́чета?

// Миле́на и Дими́тър вървя́т по Патриа́рх Евти́мий, хва́нати за ръка́. На ня́колко ме́тра след тя́х се дви́жат Павли́на и Та́ня с две́те деца́. Ку́четата ска́чат нао́коло. //

Надка: Ле́льо, нали́ и на́шият Бо́би, като пора́сне, ще заприли́ча на Ба́рт?

Павлина: Ка́к мо́же Бо́би да ста́не като Ба́рт?! Те́ са разли́чна поро́да.

Надка: Ами ще се нау́чи. И́маме вкъ́щи уче́бник по дреси́ране на ку́чета.

Павлина: А ти́ зна́еш ли ка́к се дреси́рат ку́чета?

Надка: Ка́к?

Камен: Взи́ма се една́ пръ́чка и се хвъ́рля надале́че. По́сле ка́рат ку́чето да я донесе́.

Надка: Ами ако не ще́? Би́ят ли го? А́з не да́вам да би́еш на́шия Бо́би.

Павлина: Не се́ пра́ви така́. Ку́чето мно́го оби́ча господа́ря си и и́ска да му угоди́. Са́мо тря́бва да му се обясни́ какво́ се разреша́ва и какво́ -- не́.

Надка: Ма́мо, нали́ Бо́би е мо́е ку́че?

Камен: Не е́ тво́е, а е мо́е. А́з съм по́-голя́м.

Таня: Ма́й па́к ще тря́бва да се взе́мат ме́рки. Ко́лко пъ́ти съм ви ка́звала, че не би́ва да се ка́рате. Бо́би е ку́чето на та́тко ви. Нали́ то́й го ку́пи.

Камен: То́й го е ку́пил, но ни́е ще го дреси́раме. Та́тко и без това́ ни́кога не си́ е вкъ́щи.

Таня: Та́тко ви ня́ма вре́ме за гу́бене. То́й тря́бва да пече́ли пари́чки за вси́чки на́с.

Павлина: Ва́шият мъ́ж какво́ рабо́ти?

Таня: То́й е спо́ртен журнали́ст и мно́го пъту́ва. Хо́ди из ця́ла Бълга́рия да пра́ви репорта́жи. Ми́налата годи́на да́же го пра́тиха от реда́кцията в чужби́на за олимпиа́дата.

Павлина: Така́ ли? Те́ мо́же би са се позна́вали с поко́йния ми съпру́г. То́й и́маше мно́го прия́тели в спо́ртната реда́кция на телеви́зията. Велими́р Карастоя́нов, си́гурно сте чу́вали за не́го?

Надка: Ма́мо, ма́! Ако а́з ка́жа: "Та́я вода́ не е́ за пи́ене, не я́ пи́й, Бо́би!", то́й ня́ма ли да ме послу́ша?

Камен: Ви́жда се, че ни́що не разби́раш от ку́чета.

Надка: А ако му ви́кна?

Камен: Ви́кането не пома́га. Защо́ ще те слу́ша, ако е жа́ден? И а́з ако съм, и а́з ня́ма да слу́шам.

Павлина: И ще сбъ́ркаш. Добре́ възпи́таните ку́чета ни́що не пи́пат, ако не и́м се позволи́. Ти́ да не си́ по́-глу́пав от ку́чето?

Димитър: Я́ ви́жте! Ба́рт и Бо́би ма́й се сприятели́ха.

Милена: Току́-що се запозна́ха и ве́че си игра́ят, а ви́е се ка́рате.

Таня: Ка́мене! На́дке! От ва́с не мо́жем да си чу́ем прика́зката. Върве́те напре́д и кроту́вайте. Ако слу́шате, на връ́щане ще ви ку́пя сладоле́д.

Надка: Не и́скам сладоле́д. Яда́т ми се пу́канки.

Камен: А́з пъ́к и́скам и пу́канки, и сладоле́д. А на Бо́би си́гурно му се пи́е шве́пс.

Павлина: За ку́четата е вре́дно да пи́ят гази́рани напи́тки.

Камен: Тога́ва а́з ще изпи́я шве́пса на Бо́би.

Надка: И на ме́не ми се пи́е шве́пс.

Таня: Ти́хо! Не се́ зна́е дали́ въобще́ ще и́ма шве́пс, ако продължа́вате да се надви́квате. Ня́ма са́мо ва́с да слу́шаме.

Двайсети урок / Lesson 20

BASIC GRAMMAR

20.1. Verbal nouns

Nouns referring to the fact of verbal activity are called verbal nouns. Such nouns are formed only from imperfective verbs. One of two suffixes (either **-ен-** or **-ан-**) is added, followed by the neuter ending **-е**.

Like passive participles, verbal nouns are formed from the *aorist* stem of the verb. The final vowel of the 3rd singular aorist is dropped and the verbal noun suffix is added. If the aorist theme vowel is **-а-/-я-**, the suffix is **-ан-/-ян-**; otherwise it is **-ен-**. The only exceptions are verbs like **пе́я** and **живе́я**, which form the verbal noun not from the aorist stem (**пя́-, живя́-**) but from the present stem (**пе́-, живе́-**).

The accent is normally as in the aorist. A very few verbal nouns carry accent on the final syllable.

3sg. aorist	*stem*	+ -ан/-ен ›	*verbal noun*	*(meaning)*
тръ́гва	тръгв-	+ -ан ›	тръ́гв-ане	leaving
връ́ща	връщ-	+ -ан ›	връ́щ-ане	returning
представя	представ-	+ -ян ›	предста́в-яне	presenting
пу́ши	пуш-	+ -ен ›	пу́ш-ене	smoking
че́те	чет-	+ -ен ›	че́т-ене	reading
брои́	бро-	+ -ен ›	бро-е́не	counting
бра́	бр-	+ -ан ›	бран-е́	picking
пра́	пр-	+ -ан ›	пран-е́	washing
спа́	сп-	+ -ан ›	спан-е́	sleeping

3sg. present	*stem*	+ -ан/-ен ›	*verbal noun*	*(meaning)*
пе́е	пе-	+ -ен ›	пе́-ене	singing
живе́е	живе-	+ -ен ›	живе́-ене	living

In general, verbal nouns carry the meaning of durational activity. A few have lost this sense and have taken on the meaning of true nouns (sometimes in idiomatic expressions). The stem for such nouns is often composed of a phrase. For instance:

verb or phrase	*verbal noun*	*(meaning)*
пъту́вам	пъту́ване	trip
ям	я́дене	food, dish
пребива́вам	пребива́ване	stay, sojourn
до + ви́ждам	дови́ждане	farewell
са́м + обслу́жвам	самообслу́жване	self-service [establishment]

Most verbal nouns, however, denote the actual process of the action. On occasion these nouns can be translated by the corresponding verbal noun in English (ending in "-ing"). Sometimes they can be translated by an infinitive form, and sometimes by an actual verbal phrase. The most usual translation is simply with another noun.

The proper translation depends both on the noun itself and on the context. Verbal nouns are particularly common in the so-called "historical present", in which past historical events are narrated in the present tense. For example:

Вто́рото бъ́лгарско ца́рство приклю́чва с па́данетo на Бълга́рия под ту́рско ро́бство.	The second Bulgarian empire ended with the fall of Bulgaria to the Turks. [= when Bulgaria came under the Turkish yoke.]
Ва́жен моме́нт в проце́са на наро́дностното ни само-утвържда́ване е прие́манетo на христия́нството.	The acceptance of Christianity was an important factor in the process of our national self-determination.
С покръ́стването на Бълга́рия е свъ́рзано създа́ванетo на славя́нската пи́сменост.	The founding/origin of Slavic literacy was connected with Bulgaria's conversion to Christianity.

Verbal nouns can appear either with or without the definite article, according to the rules for definiteness which apply to all nouns.

indefinite
    Ще и́ма тържéствено откри́ване.   There will be a formal opening ceremony.

definite
    Пъту́ването не бе́ше удо́бно.   The trip was not a comfortable one.

"generic" definite
    Пу́шенето е мно́го опа́сно за здра́вето.   Smoking is very bad for one's health.

    Ту́ка преси́чането е забране́но.   Crossing is not allowed here.
    Ви́канетo не пома́га.   Shouting won't help.

A prepositional phrase composed of "на + verbal noun" refers to the time of a specific action. In such phrases, verbal nouns always occur in the indefinite form.

На тръ́гване затвори́ прозо́реца, мо́ля.	Please close the window on leaving/ when you leave.
На връ́щане ще ти ку́пя сладоле́д.	On the way back I'll buy you an ice cream.

20.2. Review of се-constructions

The particle **се** is used with verbs in a number of different meanings. In certain of these meanings, **си** can also be used. Four meanings have already been learned. These can be summarized as follows:

Reflexivity

Reflexive verbs are those in which the action is performed on ("reflected back on") the subject. The particle **се** is used as a direct object, indicating that the subject is the direct recipient of the action; the particle **си** is used as an indirect object, indicating that the subject performs the transitive action for his or her own benefit. For example:

На́дка се ми́е, докато́ Ка́мен се обли́ча.	Nadka washes while Kamen dresses.
На́дка си ми́е лице́то, а Ка́мен си обли́ча пуло́вера.	Nadka is washing her face and Kamen is putting his sweater on.
Тя́ се черви́ дъ́лго пред огледа́лото.	She spends a long time in front of the mirror putting on her lipstick.
Ще си ку́пя но́в ре́чник.	I'm going to buy myself a new dictionary.

Reciprocity

Reciprocal verbs occur only in the plural, with multiple subjects. In reciprocals, like reflexives, the action is reflected back on the subjects. The added meaning is that each of the subjects performs the action on or for the benefit of the other (this is often denoted in English translation by the phrase "each other"). Reciprocals may occur with either **се** or **си** according to whether the verb in question normally takes a direct or an indirect object. For example:

Ба́рт и Бо́би ма́й се сприятели́ха.	It looks like Bart and Bobby have made friends [with each other].
Ко́лко пъ́ти съм ви ка́звала, че не би́ва да се ка́рате?	How many times have I told you that you mustn't argue [with each other]?
От ва́с не мо́жем да си чу́ем при́казката.	Because of you we can't talk. [*literally:* hear each other's speech]
Те́ не си́ гово́рят.	They're not on speaking terms.

Intransitivity

The intransitive use of **се** is extremely frequent. Most transitive verbs (those which take a direct object) can be used with **се**. When **се** is added to these verbs, the meaning becomes one of simple verbal activity, specifically lacking an object. For example:

По тази линия трамваите се движат често.	Trams run frequently on this line.
Ами ще се научи!	So he'll learn!
Той ще се мести да живее в друг град.	He's moving to (live in) another town.
Децата се скриха от погледа ни.	The children are hiding from us. [*literally:* from our gaze]

Idiomatic

This usage is very verb-specific. Certain verbs do not exist without **се**; it is a part of their identity. For others, adding **се** changes their meaning sufficiently that one cannot simply call them "intransitive". For example:

Казвам се Милена.	My name is Milena.
Магазинът, който търсиш, се намира отсреща.	The store you're looking for is across the street.
Той се черви, когато ти му говориш така.	He blushes when you talk to him like that.

There are two more **се**-constructions in Bulgarian: which will be presented below. These are the **Passive** and the **Impersonal**.

20.3. Passive constructions with се

The preceding lesson presented Bulgarian passive constructions which can be translated directly by passive constructions in English. The most common means of expressing the idea "passive", however, is with **се**. Compare the following examples:

active

| Взимам една пръчка и я хвърлям. | I take a stick and throw it. |
| Взимат една пръчка и я хвърлят. | They take a stick and throw it. |

passive

| Взима се една пръчка и се хвърля. | (a) You take a stick and throw it. (b) A stick is taken and thrown. |

It is impossible to give a literal English translation of this Bulgarian passive sentence. Translation (a), using the English impersonal "you", is more correct in that it is closest to the meaning of the Bulgarian **се**-passive. In grammatical terms, however, translation (b) is more correct, since it renders the subject of the Bulgarian sentence (**пръ́чка** "stick") with a similar subject in the English sentence.

Ce-passives are thus active and passive at the same time. They are passive in meaning: the grammatical subject of the sentence is that which undergoes the action. But the verbs in them are grammatically active in that the main verbal meaning is expressed by a conjugated verb (and not a passive participle). Compare first the "active/passive" pair presented in the previous lesson, in which the structure of Bulgarian passives matches that of English passives; following that compare the same idea expressed as a **ce**-passive:

active sentence

Someone	will send	the letter	on time.
Ня́кой	**ще изпра́ти**	**писмо́то**	**навре́ме.**
subject	*transitive verb*	*direct object*	

passive transformation of above sentence

The letter	will be	sent	on time.
Писмо́то	**ще бъ́де**	**изпра́тено**	**навре́ме.**
subject	*auxiliary*	*passive participle*	

above sentence expressed as **ce**-*passive*

The letter	will be sent	on time.
Писмо́то	**ще се изпра́ти**	**навре́ме.**
subject	*active [intransitive] verb*	

Strictly speaking, **ce**-passives are a special sub-type of the intransitive category. What makes them a unique construction is the fact that the grammatical *subject* of an active verb is at the same time its logical *object*.

Here are some additional examples of **ce**-passives. Since there is no direct equivalent in English, translations will vary. Note that a good English translation must often be fairly loose, and that a more literal passive one (given after each "good" translation, in italics) is usually rather awkward.

А ти́ зна́еш ли ка́к се дреси́рат куче́та?	Do you know how to train dogs? *Do you know how dogs are trained?*
Кажи́ му какво́ се разреша́ва и какво́ -- не́.	Tell him what he can do and what he can't. *Tell him what is allowed and what isn't.*
Па́к ще тря́бва да се взе́мат ме́рки.	I'm going to have to put my foot down again. *Measures will have to be taken again.*

Двайсети урок / Lesson 20

Откакто той замина, нищо не се чува за новата му книга.	Since he left, no one's heard anything about his new book. *Since he left, nothing has been heard about his new book.*

There are thus three different ways to express the meaning "passive" in Bulgarian: with a passive participle, with a 3rd plural form of the verb, and with a 3rd singular or plural verb form plus **ce**. Here are examples of the same general idea expressed in each of these three formats:

passive participle

Тази баница е направена както трябва.	This banitsa was made the way it should be.
Откриването на изложбата ще бъде показано от културната редакция на телевизията.	The opening of the exhibition will be shown on TV [by those responsible for cultural programming].

3rd plural subjectless

Тука правят хубава баница.	They make good banitsa here.
Ще покажат откриването на изложбата по телевизията.	The opening of the exhibition will be shown on TV.

ce-passive

Баница се прави от сирене и яйца.	Banitsa is made from white cheese and eggs.
Откриването на изложбата ще се покаже от културната редакция на телевизията.	The opening of the exhibition will be shown on TV [by those responsible for cultural programming].

There is a certain amount of overlap in the usage of these three passive constructions. All place more focus on the activity itself than on the actor, and all refer to the eventual accomplishment of the activity (either explicitly or implicitly). The three types are not interchangeable, however. Not all can be used in all possible instances of "passive" meaning.

The order in which the three types are listed above corresponds roughly to the frequency of usage in modern Bulgarian: constructions with the passive participle are the most limited and **ce**-passives are the most widespread. Participial constructions tend to occur more in formal speech; in such constructions the emphasis is on the specificity of the action (and for such reasons, perfective verbs are more frequent). **Ce**-constructions are widely used in all styles of speech; they tend to focus more on the general nature of an activity, either in bounded or unbounded form (verbs of both aspects are frequent). Third-plural subjectless sentences convey roughly the same "general" meaning as **се**-passives and can usually be substituted for a **се**-passive. The most "Bulgarian-sounding" of the three, however, is undoubtedly the **се**-passive.

20.4. Impersonal constructions with се

Impersonal sentences are similar to passive constructions with **се** in that both express the logical object of the verb as its grammatical subject. They differ in the matter of the logical "actor". In a passive sentence, the speaker always has such a potential actor in mind, whether or not s/he expresses it.

Impersonal sentences, however, derive their meaning precisely from the absence of such an actor. The focus is purely on the action itself. English translations therefore vary: if the verb is reproduced at all it can have the impersonal "you" or "one" as its subject, or it can be in the passive; sometimes a nominal construction is best. For example:

Не сé прáви такá.	Don't do that! You can't act like that.
Тáзи водá не сé пи́е.	This isn't drinking water. You can't drink this water.
Оттýк не сé минáва.	There's no way through here. You can't get through this way.
Тáзи врáта не сé отвáря. Вли́за се сáмо през антрéто.	That door doesn't open. You can only get in through the entryway.
От тóзи прозóрец се ви́жда трамвáйната спи́рка.	The tram stop is visible from this window. You can see the tram stop from this window.
До Óрлов мóст се сти́га за 10 минýти.	It takes 10 minutes to get [from here] to "Eagle's bridge".
Сáмо трябва да му се обясни́ каквó се разрешáва и каквó -- нé.	You simply have to explain to him what's allowed and what isn't.
Добрé възпи́таните кýчета ни́що не пи́пат, ако не и́м се позволи́.	Well-trained dogs don't touch anything they're not permitted to [touch].

Не сé знáе далѝ тáм въобщé ще ѝма сѝрене.	There's no way to know if there will be any cheese there at all.
Тýк не сé пýши.	There's no smoking here.
Налáга се да рабóтя по двá чáса извънрéдно.	I will have to work two hours overtime.

All the above verbs are active. None of the activities referred to above can be performed in a vacuum; rather, each must be done by someone. The point here is that the speaker of these sentences has no actor in mind. His focus is purely on the action itself, and on how or whether it can be accomplished.

Indeed, the speaker often uses an impersonal sentence to place emphasis on this very absence of an actor. In the following, for instance, what is important to the speaker is that the action be accomplished. A central part of the sentence's meaning is that she does not care who does it. She only cares that it get done.

Мóля телегрáмата да се изпрáти веднáга.	Please see that this telegram is sent immediately.

Another type of impersonal sentence with **се** (and verbs of the imperfective aspect) expresses the speaker's inclination towards a particular action. This meaning is hard to translate directly into English. The speaker wants to do something, but in a somewhat more indirect manner. Part of this meaning is captured by the English phrase "feel like...". For instance:

Не мѝ се пѝе.	I'm not in the mood for drinking.
Пѝе ми се водá.	I'm thirsty. [I want some water]
Ядя́т ли ти се черéши?	Do you feel like [eating] some cherries?
Óх, че е хýбаво! Не мѝ се тръ́гва оттýк!	It's so beautiful here! The last thing I want to do is leave!
Ѝмето ми е хýбаво. Не мѝ се щé да го смéням.	My name is a good one. I don't really want to change it. This is a good name. I don't really feel I can change it.
Ядáт ми се пýканки; на Бóби сѝгурно му се пѝе швéпс!	I'm in the mood for some popcorn, and Bobby surely would like a soft drink!

Двайсети урок / Lesson 20

In structure, such sentences are a mixture of the impersonal sentences seen above and the "experiencer" constructions studied earlier. Their similarity to impersonal sentences is in the appearance of the logical object as grammatical subject. The logical object is not always stated, but if it is (such as the cherries which one feels like eating), it will be the subject of the sentence, and therefore the verb must agree with it in number. Compare "body-ache" constructions such as **Болят ме зъбите**.

Their similarity to "experiencer" constructions, of course, is that the person who feels the inclination towards the action is expressed as an indirect object. This shift (from logical subject to grammatical indirect object) attenuates the expression of desire somewhat. The use of imperfective verbs in such expressions also shifts the focus from the external fact of the action to the speaker's attitude towards it. For instance:

Не и́скам да тръ́гна отту́к.	I don't want to leave [this place].
Не ми́ се тръ́гва отту́к.	I really don't feel like leaving [this place].

Certain other impersonal constructions also share these two characteristics -- an indirect-object experiencer, and the main verb expressed with **се**. Some of these are straightforward in their structure and some are quite idiomatic. In certain instances (exemplified by the last two examples below) the main verb can be conjugated.

Стру́ва ми се, че ня́ма да сти́гнем навре́ме.	It seems to me that we're not going to make it on time.
Ще́ ми се да му ка́жа и́стината в очи́те.	I'd just love to tell him the truth to his face.
Слу́чва ми се поня́кога да мина́вам по та́зи у́лица.	It happens on occasion that I go down that street.
Счу́ва ми се, че ня́кой се кри́е в хра́ста.	I think I hear someone [hiding] in that bush.
Ви́ждаш ми се мно́го уморе́н.	You look really tired [to me].
Те́зи обу́вки не ми́ се стру́ват мно́го здра́ви.	These shoes don't seem very sturdy [to me].

Двайсети урок / Lesson 20

EXERCISES

I. Fill in the blanks with a verbal noun made from one of the following verbs:
плу́вам, чета́, изда́вам, пи́ша, сека́, владе́я, въве́ждам.

1. Интересу́ва ме вси́чко, свъ́рзано със _____ на моне́ти.
2. Не́гово голя́мо преди́мство е _____ на ня́колкоези́ка.
3. _____ е еди́н от люби́мите ми спо́ртове.
4. _____ на уче́бник мо́же да ти взе́ме здра́вето.
5. _____ на сла́ба светлина́ вреди́ на очи́те.
6. Гла́вна причи́на за подобря́ването на ра́ботата е _____ на компю́три.
7. Изми́наха два́ ме́сеца от _____ на кни́гата.

II. Rewrite as passive.

1. В то́я рестора́нт предла́гат италиа́нска ку́хня.
2. Не прода́ваме цига́ри на малоле́тни.
3. Получа́ваме по́щата о́ще преди́ де́вет часа́ сутринта́.
4. На ю́жното Черномо́рие откри́ват сезо́на по́-ра́но, отко́лкото на се́верното.
5. В това́ ма́лко село́ прожекти́рат са́мо по два́ фи́лма се́дмично.
6. Ни́е пра́вим качама́ка от царе́вично брашно́.
7. На село́ пера́т че́ргите на река́та.

III. Rewrite the sentences to have the same meaning without the particle се.

1. На тече́ние не се́ стои́.
2. Прозо́рците не се́ отва́рят.
3. На дома́тена сала́та оце́т не се́ сла́га.
4. На то́зи де́н го́сти не се́ връ́щат от пра́га.
5. Не се́ разреша́ва вно́сът на алкохо́лни напи́тки в страна́та.
6. Възра́стните тря́бва да се уважа́ват.
7. Те́зи гъ́би са отро́вни. Те́ не се́ яда́т.

Двайсети урок / Lesson 20

ADDITIONAL GRAMMAR NOTES

20.5. Derivation: the suffixes -ство, -ина, etc.

The suffix -ство

The suffix -ств-, always followed by the neuter ending -о, forms nouns of abstract quality. The stem to which it is added can be either from a noun or an adjective. For example:

base noun	derived noun	(meaning shift)
лékар	лекáр-ство	physician › medicine
рóб	рóб-ство	slave › slavery
цáр	цáр-ство	emperor › empire
християн-ин	християн-ство	Christian › Christianity
издáтел	издáтел-ство	publisher › publishing house
минúст-ър	министéр-ство	minister › ministry

base adjective	derived noun	(meaning shift)
дежýр-ен	дежýр-ство	on duty › duty
семé-ен	семéй-ство	family (adj.) › family (noun)
óбщ	обще-ствó	common › society
електрúч-ески	електрúче-ство	electrical › electricity

The suffix -ина

The suffix -ин-, always followed by the accented feminine ending -а, also forms nouns. Sometimes the meaning is abstract, and sometimes it is more concrete. The stem is usually based on the plural form of the adjective; if the final consonant is к- or г-, it shifts to ч- or ж- before this suffix. For example:

base adjective	derived noun	(meaning shift)
рáвн-и	равн-инá	flat › level plain
нóв-и	нов-инá	new › [piece of] news
свéтл-и	светл-инá	light (adj.) › light (noun)
горéщ-и	горещ-инá	hot › heat
голéм-и	голем-инá	big › size
дъ́лг-и	дълж-инá	long › length
висóк-и	височ-инá	tall › height
дълбóк-и	дълбоч-инá	deep › depth
шир-óк-и	широч-инá	wide › width

Двайсети урок / Lesson 20

Non-productive suffixes

Verbs designate activity, and nouns designate objects or concepts. It is often the case that the same root forms both a verb and a noun in such a way that the relationship of meaning is clear. The formal relationship is less clear, however.

This is partly because the suffixes (and in certain cases, prefixes) in question are not productive (are not readily used in the language to form nouns) and partly because one cannot say with certainty whether it is the noun or the verb that is primary. The best one can do is be aware of the relationships. Here are some examples:

verb	noun	(meaning relationship)
вя́р-вам	вя́р-а	believe / faith, belief
мо́л-я	мол-ба́	beseech / petition, request
надя́вам се	наде́жда	hope (verb) / hope (noun)
стро-я́	стро-е́ж	build / structure, construction
у́ч-а	уч-и́лище	learn / school
хо́д-я	хо́д	go / walk, gait
	в-хо́д	go / entrance
	и́з-ход	go / exit

National Assembly (Parliament) Building, Sofia

Двайсети урок / Lesson 20

SAMPLE SENTENCES

1. Тéзи гъ́би са отрóвни. Не стáват за я́дене.
2. -- Кáк си?
   -- А бé, не é за прикáзване.

3. Водáта не é за пи́ене.
4. Ня́мам изли́шни пари́ за хáрчене.

5. Гóтвенето отнéма мнóго врéме. Токý-що си сгóтвил и вси́чко вéче е изя́дено.
6. Ми́енето на чини́и бéше мóе задължéние като детé.
7. Раки́я се вари́ от сли́ви, грóзде и -- пó-ря́дко -- от дрýги плодовé. Из плани́нските крáища, къдéто лозáта не вирéе, варя́т раки́ята от сли́ви.

8. Равнини́те на Бъ́лгария са мнóго плодорóдни. Тáм се отглéждат вся́какви плодовé и зеленчýци.
9. Мнéнието, че да се летýва на морé е пó-хýбаво, откóлкото на планинá, нé от вси́чки се споделя́.
10. Мóрските ни курóрти се посещáват от гóсти от разли́чни страни́.

11. -- Бáбо Пéно, прáви ли се във вáшето сéло качамáк?
    -- Кáк да не сé прáви! Прáвят го и с пръ́жки, и със си́рене, и кáк ли нé.

12. Ни́е не смé задължéни да нóсим вратовръ́зки на рáбота. Задължáват ни обáче да хóдим на рáбота всéки дéн.
13. Слъ́нцето залéзе и вéче не сé ви́жда зад хоризóнта.

14. -- Извиня́вайте, че закъсня́х. Áз се загýбих.
    -- Не ти́ ли обясни́ха къдé се нами́ра Университéтът?

15. -- Ви́ждаш ми се мáлко омърлýшен. Да не си́ бóлен?
    -- Нéщо съм насти́нал. Гърбъ́т ми е схвáнат и главáта ме понаболя́ва.

16. Тóзи писáтел бéше мнóго висóко оценéн от култýрната обществéност. Кни́гите му се разкупýват светкáвично. Удостоéн е с мнóго нáши и чýжди нагрáди.

17. Тъ́й като не бя́х известéн наврéме за резултáтите от и́зпитите, áз пропýснах срóка за подáване на докумéнти.
18. Сли́сани бя́ха да ви́дят нóвите си тéниски след пъ́рвото пранé. Тé се бя́ха смали́ли с двá нóмера, а нáдписът бéше почти́ напъ́лно изтри́т.

19. Обстоя́телствата не налáгат бъ́рза реáкция.
20. Поради ремóнта се налáга да се спрé движéнието по тáзи ýлица.

Двайсети урок / Lesson 20

SENTENCES FOR TRANSLATION

1. Smoking is forbidden in the university buildings. Here one does not smoke. Except for him over there. He smokes wherever he feels like it.

2. I feel like drinking a little champagne. Champagne is usually drunk only in Russia and France. But no matter. Will this bottle here do for drinking?

3. Quick! Buy two round-trip tickets. We'll just have to hurry up a bit. We have no time to waste.

4. That's not how you make a "shopska salata"! Look, you'll mess up the whole thing. Give it to me! I pride myself on my salads, and making a proper "shopska salata" is no easy matter.

5. I don't feel like sleeping, but it really won't do for us to go to bed late tonight.

6. It seems to me that translating these sentences is going more slowly than usual. I have no desire to finish them. Unfortunately, one is not allowed to miss classes here.

7. The dog-walking is all my responsibility. For a while my brother walked him, but it became evident that only I know how it is properly done.

Detail of church, Nesebăr

Двайсети урок / Lesson 20

READING SELECTION

<u>Кореспонде́нция - (15)</u>

30 апри́л, Со́фия

Дра́ги Патри́ша и Бо́б,

    Зна́м, че мно́го се интересу́вате от исто́рията на Бълга́рия. А́з и́скам да ви разка́жа подро́бно за това́. Я́сно е оба́че, че обзо́рът на та́зи огро́мна те́ма тря́бва да бъ́де по необходи́мост кра́тък.
    На́шите земи́ и́мат бога́та исто́рия о́ще преди́ бъ́лгарите да се появя́т на истори́ческата сце́на. С те́зи земи́ са свъ́рзани имена́та на тра́ките и ста́рите македо́нци, се́верните съсе́ди на дре́вните гъ́рци. Орфе́й е тъ́рсил своя́та Евриди́ка и́менно из люби́мите на Бо́йко Родо́пи. От на́й-ста́ри времена́ се зна́ят таки́ва гръ́цки коло́нии по на́шето Черномо́рие като Месе́мврия, дне́шният Несе́бър, или Одесо́с, дне́шната Ва́рна.
    През 1981 годи́на в Бълга́рия тържествено се отпразну́ваха 1300 годи́ни от основа́ването на бъ́лгарската държа́ва. Все́ки бъ́лгарин се горде́е със съби́тията от 681 годи́на. Тога́ва са се обедини́ли в държа́вен съю́з две́ наро́дности с разли́чен етни́чески произхо́д: пра́българите, дошли́ от равнини́те край Во́лга под предводи́телството на своя́ ха́н Аспару́х, и славя́нските племена́, чи́ето прису́ствие на Балка́ните е засвиде́телствувано в истори́ческите па́метници два́-три́ ве́ка по́-ра́но. От пра́българите, немногобро́йно нома́дско пле́ме, дне́с се па́зи са́мо и́мето и ня́колко десе́тки ду́ми. Ни́е, мака́р и славя́ни, нари́чаме се́бе си с и́мето на еди́н отда́вна изче́знал тю́ркски наро́д.
    Ва́жен моме́нт в проце́са на наро́дностното ни самоутвържда́ване е приема́нето през 865 г. на християнството в не́говата и́зточна фо́рма от Цариград. Това́ е де́ло на ца́р Бори́с I, еди́н от на́шите на́й-знамени́ти владе́тели. Християнството е игра́ло през ця́лата ни исто́рия положи́телна ро́ля за консолиди́рането на на́шия наро́д. С покръ́стването на Бълга́рия се свъ́рзва създа́ването на славя́нската пи́сменост от солу́нските бра́тя Св.Св. Кири́л и Мето́дий. От Бълга́рия славя́нската пи́сменост се разпространя́ва в Съ́рбия, Румъ́ния (къде́то се изпо́лзува до нача́лото на XIX в.) и Руси́я.
    Исто́рията на Бълга́рия се дели́ на́й-о́бщо на три́ пери́ода, който се нари́чат ца́рства. Пъ́рвото бъ́лгарско ца́рство завъ́ршва през 1018 г. с попа́данетo на Бълга́рия за почти́ два́ ве́ка под византи́йска вла́ст. Второ́то бъ́лгарско ца́рство (1185 - 1396 г.) пък приклю́чва с па́данетo на Бълга́рия под петвеко́вно ту́рско ро́бство, завъ́ршило ча́к в резулта́т на Ру́ско-ту́рската война́ от 1877-1878 г. Са́мо за ня́колко годи́ни мла́дата бъ́лгарска държа́ва се изпра́вя на крака́. През 1879 г. се прие́ма Тъ́рновската конститу́ция. Това́ уско́рено разви́тие мо́же да се ви́ди и в живо́та на отде́лни ли́чности. Заха́ри

Двайсети урок / Lesson 20

Стоя́нов, наприме́р, се у́чи да чете́ на два́йсет годи́ни, а на три́йсет и пе́т е призна́т писа́тел и полити́к. Съби́тията през после́дния ве́к и не́що бъ́лгарска исто́рия са мно́го бу́рни: те́ включват уча́стие в ня́колко войни́ и почти́ полови́н ве́к тоталитари́зъм.

Ни́е с Бо́йко зна́ем за интере́са на Бо́б към на́й-но́вата исто́рия и предви́ждаме безкра́йно би́стрене на поли́тиката през ве́черите край о́гъня на Ри́ла или в Родо́пите.

Бъ́лгарската наро́дна култу́ра и ези́кът ни са резулта́т от взаимоде́йствието на еле́менти изко́нни, доне́сени от славя́нската прароди́на, и еле́менти от култу́рата и ези́ка на съсе́дните балка́нски наро́ди, с кои́то от векове́ живе́ем в симбио́за. Вси́чко така́ се е препле́ло, че в по́вечето слу́чаи не мо́же да се устано́ви ни́то първои́зточникът на да́дено явле́ние, ни́то пъ́тят на прони́кването му в култу́рата на отде́лните балка́нски наро́ди. Еди́н приме́р. Ви́е ве́че зна́ете ко́лко прили́ча на́шата ку́хня на ту́рската и гръ́цката. В Съ́рбия и Румъ́ния съ́що се го́твят мно́го от на́шите го́зби. И имена́та им поня́кога си прили́чат: гюве́ч, мусака́, сарми́, чорба́. Съ́щото се отна́ся и за мно́го обича́и. Ма́ртеници наприме́р се но́сят и в Румъ́ния, и в Алба́ния, и в Се́верна Гъ́рция. О́бща е и тради́цията на събо́рите. Във вся́ко се́ло се пра́ви събо́р в деня́ на ме́стния свете́ц покрови́тел. Ця́л де́н на площа́да се чу́ват зву́ците на га́йди и кава́ли, ви́ят се хора́. На паза́ра в то́я де́н се прода́ва какво́ ли не́. Сти́чат се го́сти от съсе́дните села́, а -- спо́ред тради́цията -- го́сти на то́я де́н не се́ връ́щат от пра́га.

Тру́дно е вси́чко да се ка́же в едно́ писмо́. На мя́сто неща́та се науча́ват по́-добре́. Ако и́мате о́ще въпро́си, пи́тайте. Ще се постара́я да отгово́ря, доко́лкото мо́га.

Пожела́вам ви вси́чко ху́баво. По́здрави от Бо́йко, И́во, Я́на

Кали́на

Двайсети урок / Lesson 20

GLOSSARY

алкохо́лен	alcoholic	гюве́ч	clay pot; Balkan one-pot stew
антре́	entryway		
безкра́ен	endless	XIX в.	the 19th century
би́вам	occur, be	де́ло	deed; case
би́стря	clarify	деля́	divide, split up
би́стря поли́тиката	discuss politics	десе́тка	ten
брашно́	flour	доко́лкото	as far as
бря́г, брегъ́т (pl. брегове́)	coast, bank	до́лен	lower
		долина́	valley
бу́рен	stormy, tempestuous	дома́тен	tomato (adj.)
		дре́вен	ancient
в резулта́т на	as a result of	дру́жба	friendship; society
в. = ве́к		дълбочина́	depth
ва́жен моме́нт	an important point	дължина́	length
ве́че не се́ ви́жда	one can no longer see	држа́ва	state
взаимоде́йствие	interaction	държа́вен	state (adj.), public
взе́мам здра́вето на	be the death of		
ви́квам / ви́кна	call to, yell at	електри́чески	electrical
виря́	thrive, flourish	електри́чество	electricity
височина́	height, elevation	елеме́нт	element
ви́я	curve, wind	етни́чески	ethnic
владе́тел	ruler, owner		
владе́я	rule, control	за ня́колко годи́ни са́мо	in the space of just a few years
владе́я ези́к	have command of a language	задължа́вам / задължа́ (-и́ш)	oblige, bind
вла́ст	power, authority		
внос	import	задълже́ние	duty, obligation
вре́ден	harmful, injurious	за́писка	note, recording
вредя́	harm	засвиде́телствувам	bear witness, certify
вредя́ на здра́вето	be bad for the health	звук	sound
вредя́ на очи́те	be hard on the eyes	здра́ви обу́вки	sturdy shoes
връ́щам / въ́рна	turn away	земя́	earth, land
въве́ждам / въведа́	bring in, introduce		
възпи́тавам / възпи́там	bring up, educate	известя́вам / известя́	notify, inform
въста́ние	uprising, rebellion	извънре́ден	extraordinary, special
вя́ра	faith, belief	изда́тел	publisher
		и́зконен	ancient, original
гази́ран	fizzy, carbonated	изли́шен	superfluous; surplus
глу́пав	stupid, foolish	измина́вам / изми́на	cover; elapse
големина́	size, magnitude		
горде́я се	take pride in	и́зточен	eastern
горде́я се с	be proud of	изтри́вам / изтри́я	erase, rub [out]
горещина́	heat	и́зход	exit
господа́р	master	и́менно	namely, exactly
гръ́цки	Greek (adj.)	истори́чески	historical
гърбъ́т ми е схва́нат	my back is stiff	италиа́нски	Italian

122

Двайсети урок / Lesson 20

ка́звам на ня́кого в очи́те	say to someone's face	не ми́ се ще́	I don't feel like
ка́рам да донесе́	get [someone] to bring [something]	не ста́ва за я́дене	isn't for eating
		немногобро́ен	not numerous
качама́к	hominy, polenta	необходи́мост	necessity
коло́ния	colony	не́що съм насти́нал	have a bit of a cold
компю́тър (*pl.* компю́три)	computer	нома́дски	nomadic
консолиди́рам	consolidate	ня́колко десе́тки ду́ми	a few score words
конститу́ция	constitution		
край	along, by	обединя́вам / обединя́	unify
кри́я	hide	обзо́р	survey
кроту́вам	keep quiet	обслу́жвам / обслу́жа (-иш)	serve, cater for
културна обще́ственост	cultural circles	обще́ственост	public
лету́вам	spend the summer	олимпиа́да	Olympic games
ли́ния	line, course	омърлу́шен	down in the mouth, low-spirited
ли́чност	personality, character	оре́л (*pl.* орли́)	eagle
ма́!	(*appellative particle, to a woman*)	о́рлов	eagle's
		основа́вам / основа́	found, establish
Ма́мо, ма́!	hey, Mom!	отгле́ждам / отгле́дам	grow, cultivate
македо́нец	Macedonian (male)		
малоле́тен	minor, underage	откри́вам / откри́я	open
мерки, see мярка		отна́сям / отнеса́	take away
ме́стен	local, native	отна́сям се / отнеса́ се	apply to
ме́стя	move		
ме́стя се	move, change residence	отпразну́вам	celebrate
		отро́вен	poisonous
мини́стър	minister	оценя́вам / оценя́	value, estimate
мне́ние	opinion	оце́т	vinegar
мо́ля	ask, beseech		
моме́нт	point, feature	петвеко́вен	five centuries' (*adj.*)
мусака́	moussaka (Balkan dish)	пече́ля	earn, gain
		пи́сменост	writing, literacy
мя́рка (*pl.* ме́рки)	measure; step	пле́ме (*pl.* племена́)	tribe, clan
на море́	at the seaside	плодоро́ден	fertile
на мя́сто	on the spot	по два́ се́дмично	two a week
надале́че	far	по́глед	look, glance; view
надви́квам / надви́кам	outshout, outcry	подобря́вам / подобря́	improve, ameliorate
напъ́лно	completely	поко́ен, -о́йна	late, deceased
наро́дност	nationality	покрови́тел (ка)	patron
наро́дностен	national, concerning nationality matters	покръ́ствам / покръ́стя	convert to Christianity
наро́дностно самоутвържда́ване	national self-determination	полити́к	politician
		поли́тика	politics
насти́вам / насти́на	catch cold	положи́телен	positive
насти́нал съм	have a cold	понаболя́ва (3rd ps.)	hurt a little; ache from time to time
науча́вам се / науча́ се (-иш)	learn to; get used to		
		поради́	because of
не е́ за пи́ене	not fit to drink		

Двайсети урок / Lesson 20

послу́швам / послу́шам	take advice, obey
постара́вам се / постара́я се	try, do one's best
пра́българи	proto-Bulgarians
пра́г	threshold
прароди́на	land of origin
пребива́вам	stay, sojourn
предви́ждам / предви́дя	foresee; provide for
предводи́телство	leadership
преди́мство	priority, advantage
препли́там / преплета́	interweave
приклю́чвам / приклю́ча (-иш)	end, conclude
прису́ствие	presence
причи́на	reason, cause
прожекти́рам	show, project
произхо́д	origin, descent
прони́квам / прони́кна	penetrate, infiltrate
проце́с	process
пръ́жки	cracklings, suet
пръ́чка	stick, switch
първоизто́чник	prime source, origin
пя́сък	sand
равнина́	level plain
разви́тие	development, progress
разкупу́вам / разку́пя	buy up
ремо́нт	repairs
репорта́ж	descriptive report
ро́б	slave
ро́бство	slavery, bondage
ро́ля	role
самообслу́жване	self-service
самоутвържда́ване	self-affirmation
сбъ́рквам / сбъ́ркам	err, get confused
Св. = Свети́, Света́	
Св.Св. Ки́рил и Мето́дий	Sts. Cyril and Methodius
свете́ц	saint
светка́вичен	like lightning
светка́вично	with lightning speed
свъ́рзвам / свъ́ржа (-еш)	tie, bind; connect
се́верен	northern
се́дмично	weekly
сезо́н	season
сека́ моне́ти	mint coins
симбио́за	symbiosis
скри́вам се от по́гледа	drop out of sight; hide from view
сла́ба светлина́	poor light
славя́нин	Slav (male)
сли́ва	plum
сли́свам / сли́сам	amaze, astound
слу́чвам / слу́ча (-иш)	run across, happen on
слу́чвам се / слу́ча се (-иш)	happen
смаля́вам / смаля́	reduce in size, shrink
смале́н с два́ но́мера	shrunk two sizes
солу́нски	from/of Solun (modern Thessalonike)
споде́лям / споделя́	share
според	according to
спо́рт	sport
сприятеля́вам се / сприятеля́ се	make friends
сро́к за пода́ване на докуме́нти	application deadline
сти́чам се / стека́ се (-че́ш)	flow down; flock together
строе́ж	structure, construction
стру́вам се	seem
стру́ва ми се	it seems to me
схва́щам / схва́на	grasp, comprehend
схва́щам се / схва́на се	get stiff, cramped
сце́на	scene
счу́ва се / счу́е се	seem to hear
счу́ва ми се	I think I hear
събитие	event
събо́р	fair; convention, council
съсе́ден	neighboring, adjacent
съ́щото се отна́ся до/за	the same applies to
така́ не би́ва	it won't do, it can't be
те́ниска	T-shirt
тоталитари́зъм	totalitarian rule
тради́ция	tradition
тра́ки	Thracians
ту́рски	Turkish
ту́рско ро́бство	the Ottoman yoke
тържествен	solemn, official, ceremonial
тю́ркски	Turkic
уважа́вам	respect, honor
уга́ждам / угодя́	indulge, please

Двайсети урок / Lesson 20

удостоя́вам / удостоя́	honor, vouchsafe	християни́н	Christian
удостоя́вам с награ́да	confer a prize	христия́нство	Christianity
ускоря́вам / ускоря́	hasten, accelerate	ца́ревичен	corn *(adj.)*
установя́вам / установя́	determine, establish	ца́ревично брашно́	cornmeal
		ца́рство	kingdom, realm
утвържда́вам / утвърдя́	confirm, endorse		
уча́стие	participation	червя́ се	blush; apply lipstick
		черга́	rug
фо́рма	form	чорба́	soup
		шве́пс	soft drink
ха́н	khan		
хва́нати за ръка́	hand in hand	широчина́	width
хвъ́рлям / хвъ́рля	throw, toss	ю́жен	southern
хо́д	walk, gait		
хоризо́нт	horizon	явле́ние	phenomenon
хра́ст	bush, shrub		

CULTURAL COMMENTARY

Food and drink: soft drinks; kachamak; the making of rakia

For many years the most popular soft drink in Bulgaria was Schweppes, licensed to be produced in Bulgaria under the same name (**шве́пс**). Gradually the Bulgarian versions came to be so different from the original that the license was revoked; by then, however, Bulgaria was producing its own soft drinks under different names. However, the general name "shveps" is still often used colloquially for soft drinks which have some sort of fruit flavor (such as orange, lemon-lime or the like). Cola, however, has always been called "kola" (and has never been referred to as "shveps").

Kachamak (**качама́к**), or fried cornmeal, is a dish known throughout the Balkans; it is similar to polenta. The Bulgarian version is much thicker than its Romanian counterpart (mamaliga). Whereas mamaliga is more like a mush, kachamak is often baked in the oven like a pie or cake. Often white cheese or **пръ́жки** (small bits of fried lard or meat) are added to it.

The production of rakia is a state-owned monopoly. Private individuals may make rakia only from the fruit of their own trees or vines (thus only in small quantities). Each village or town has its own large home-made still, for the use of which individuals pay a small fee. To make the rakia one boils the fruit mash (usually plums, or the leftover grape mash from wine production) in the still. It is necessary to feed the wood fire constantly and watch the boiling process carefully over a long period of time. Since the making of rakia is normally done outdoors in the colder months, this takes dedication. It is a special treat to be present at the first "pressings". Empty bottles are gathered all year long in order to be filled with homemade rakia. A filled bottle is one of the most valued gifts.

Geography: the Black Sea

The entire Black Sea resort area is often referred to by the general term "Chernomorie" (**Черномо́рие**). The adminstrative center of the northern half is Varna, and the major resorts are Zlatni pjasătsi (**Зла́тни пя́съци**), Druzhba (**Дру́жба**), Albena (**Албе́на**) and Rusalka (**Руса́лка**). The administrative center of the southern half is Burgas (**Бурга́с**), and the major resorts are Slănchev bryag (**Слъ́нчев бря́г**) and the International Youth Center (**Междунаро́ден младе́жки це́нтър**). All these resorts are large hotels with self-contained tourist services; most are quite luxurious. Many vacationers prefer to stay instead in small towns or villages along the seashore, camping or else renting bungalows or rooms in private homes.

Двайсети урок / Lesson 20

Geography: the Balkans

The concept "Balkan" is a complex one, signifying much more than just geographical position. The peoples of the Balkans (Bulgarians [and their closely related neighbors, Macedonians], Romanians, Albanians and Greeks) have lived together for many centuries in the land which was first Byzantium and then Ottoman Turkey in Europe. As a result, all these peoples share many cultural elements on a very deep level. Their languages are structurally very similar, they have many folk customs in common, their cuisine is practically identical; even their jokes are shared. It is useless to try to find the original source of any one of these shared elements, although scholars of each of the different peoples have made intense efforts to do so.

City life: books

Like most other Slavs, Bulgarians are voracious readers and follow the current press hungrily. A new printing of a book, especially by a well-known author (or one whom conventional wisdom says is "up and coming"), can sell out within hours.

History: general

Bulgarians are proud of their long and rich history. They know that their lands were settled by ancient folk such as the Thracians and Dacians, and are enamored of the legend that Orpheus and Eurydice lived in their own Rhodope mountains. Byzantine culture flourished on their soil (especially on the Black Sea coast) even before the coming of the Slavs. The founding of Bulgaria as such is dated to 681, when the leader or khan (хан) of the Bulgars, Asparukh (Аспарух), crossed the Danube and founded a state. Slavic tribes, who had settled in the Balkans not long before, intermarried with the Bulgars, who were ethnically Turkic. Within a few centuries, the resulting mixed population had taken nearly completely Slavic form, and from that time is called "Bulgarian". Only a few words (primarily proper names) are left of the original Turkic language.

The Bulgarians were converted to Christianity during the rule of Boris I. A major element of the conversion was the introduction of a newly formed Slavic literary language, which had been developed by the missionaries Constantine-Cyril and Methodius, who were natives of Solun, which is the Bulgarian name corresponding to the Greek name Thessalonike (for more on Cyril and Methodius, see the cultural notes to Lesson 21). Both the Christian religion and the language associated with it were important factors in Bulgarian cultural history, keeping the idea of Bulgarian nationhood alive during both the conflicts with Byzantine rule and the long period of Ottoman rule. Modern Bulgaria was freed from Ottoman rule only after the Russo-Turkish war of 1877-78. In the 20th century, Bulgaria took part in four wars (the first and second Balkan Wars, and the two World Wars) and endured nearly a half century of totalitarian rule.

Literature: Zahari Stoyanov

Zahari Stoyanov (Захари Стоянов, 1850-1889) is an extremely popular Bulgarian author. Born into a peasant family, he was completely self-taught. His voluminous eye-witness account of the events leading to the liberation of Bulgaria, *Notes on the Bulgarian uprisings of 1870-1876* (Записки по българските въстания 1870-1876), has been one of the most widely read books of the last hundred years.

Folk customs: săbor

A "săbor" (събор) is a rural gathering of the folk, usually on the occasion of a saint's day. Each village is considered to be under the protection of a particular saint, and celebrates its communality and well-being on that saint's day. Events include the holy liturgy, a communal meal in the churchyard, singing, dancing and competitive sport events. It is traditional that the communal meal include a large meat stew, cooked in an enormous kettle in the churchyard itself. Churchladies work from early dawn preparing this meal, and each villager must take a small portion from this communal pot to ensure the health and well-being of his family during the coming year.

LESSON 21

DIALOGUE

<u>Не мé ли пóмните?</u>

// Телефóнът у г-жа Петрóва звъни́. //

Иванка: А́ло!

Веселин: Добрó у́тро! А́з съм Весели́н Хри́стов. Удóбно ли е да говóря с Джу́ли? Тя́ нали́ óще не é изля́зла?

Иванка: Здравéйте. Весели́н ли? Кóй Весели́н? Не знáех, че Джу́ли познáва ня́какъв Весели́н.

Веселин: Ви́е вчéра ме видя́хте. А́з нóсех чáнтата на Джу́ли.

Иванка: Че тъ́й кажи́! Ти́ си знáчи óня брадáтият... Ти́ ми кажи́ на мéне какви́ са ти́я пу́сти мóди? Като че ли́ в горáта са ви глéдали.

Веселин: С брадá е пó-лéсно. Стáнеш су́трин, пли́снеш си двé шéпи водá на лицéто и си готóв. И хéм ня́ма кáк да се порéжеш. Но за товá мóже ня́кой дру́г пъ́т да си поговóрим, а сегá мнóго бъ́рзам. Ще мóжете ли да изви́кате Джу́ли?

Иванка: Сегá ще проверя́ да не é изля́зла. Не съм я чу́ла да изли́за, дé. Ама áз съм мнóго оглушáла напослéдък. Си́гурно си е в стáята. Почáкай мáлко.

Джули: А́ло!

Веселин: Здравéйте, Джу́ли! На телефóна е Весели́н. Нали́ ме пóмните от пъту́ването вчéра.

Джули: Дá, дá, пóмня, разби́ра се. Кáк сте?

Веселин: Добрé съм, благодаря́. Обáждам се да изпъ́лня обещáнието си.

Джули: Каквó обещáние?

Веселин: Кáк каквó! Обещáл съм да ви свъ́ржа с профéсор Попóв и да ви уредя́ срéща с нéго. А́з съм сериóзен човéк. Кáжа ли нéщо, прáвя го. Дéто и́ма една при́казка: кáзана ду́ма, хвъ́рлен кáмък.

Джули: Дá, дá. И каквó стáна?

Двайсет и първи урок / Lesson 21

Веселин: Амѝ, а́з о́ще сно́щи се оба́дих у тя́х, но отнача́ло ни́кой не вди́гаше слуша́лката.

Джули: Си́гурно не са́ били́ вкъ̀щи.

Веселин: Ве́че и́сках да се отка́жа, кога́то се оба́ди жена́ му. Ка́за, че Са́шо си е ле́гнал и тя́ не и́ска да го бу́ди. Ця́л де́н е изпи́твал студе́нти и е ка́пнал от умо́ра. Разбра́хме се да се оба́дя па́к дне́с ра́но сутринта́, преди́ да е оти́шъл на ра́бота.

Джули: Неудо́бно ми е, че сте загу́били то́лкова мно́го вре́ме с уре́ждането на та́зи сре́ща. Тя́ наи́стина е мно́го ва́жна за на́с с Де́йвид...

Веселин: Не се́ притесня́вайте! За какво́ гу́бене на вре́ме мо́же да ста́ва ду́ма? Дра́го ми е, че мо́га да напра́вя не́що за ва́с. Та, сутринта́ ра́но-ра́но вди́гнах телефо́на и хва́нах Са́шо на врата́та. Тъ̀кмо изли́заше. Ка́за, че дне́с ще рабо́ти в кабине́та си в Университе́та. Ка́за да ви заведа́ напра́во при не́го. По́-удо́бно е да оти́дем след обя́д. Към три́ часа́ добре́ ли е?

Джули: Да́, мно́го добре́.

Веселин: Тога́ва в три́ без петна́йсет на Ректора́та?

Джули: Къде́ по́-то́чно?

Веселин: На стъ̀лбите пред гла́вния вхо́д. Между ста́туите на бра́тята Евло́ги и Хри́сто Георги́еви.

Двайсет и първи урок / Lesson 21

BASIC GRAMMAR

21.1. The past indefinite tense, continued

There are three major past tenses in Bulgarian: the aorist, the imperfect, and the past indefinite. All refer to past action, but in different ways. The aorist relates the simple fact of past action, and the imperfect is opposed to the aorist by the fact of its concentration on the duration of that past action. Both these tenses convey a sense of vividness, as if one were present in that past time. By contrast to both, the past indefinite extends the scope of the past action into the present moment of speaking, and conveys a certain distancing from the past action to which it makes reference.

This element of "distancing", which can take several different forms, is the essence of the past indefinite. As the student moves further into the complexities of the Bulgarian past tense system, this concept will take on more and more importance. For the purpose of the present lesson, which is a detailed discussion of the meanings and usage of the past indefinite, it provides a useful yardstick. Ultimately it will be seen as one of the central organizing principles of the entire Bulgarian tense-mood system.

The meanings of the past indefinite, to be discussed below, are

Focus on present result, including state of non-achievement;
Focus on non-specific, generalized view of an action;
Focus on inference or assumption;
Expression of indirect discourse or reported speech.

21.2. The past indefinite as expression of focus on present result

The most basic meaning of the past indefinite is the extension of the scope of past action into the present moment of speaking. The speaker refers both to the past action and to the effect of that past action on his or her present state. For example:

Неудо́бно ми е, че сте загу́били то́лкова мно́го вре́ме.	I feel bad that you've lost so much time.
Ка́кто са нацъфте́ли те́зи ро́зи, са́мо са за сни́мка.	These roses have burst into bloom such that you can't not photograph them.
Така́ ка́кто хуба́вичко сме се́днали, сега́ да и́ма и по едно́ ви́но.	Now that we're sitting in such a nice spot, all we need is glass of wine apiece.
Тя́ си е ле́гнала.	She's lying down.

In each of the above examples the speaker relates a past action, but it is clear that her focus is more on her own present state and its relationship to that past action. For this reason she uses the past indefinite and not the aorist. The English translation as present perfect usually reproduces this meaning well.

The idea of "present result" is also central in many negated sentences. Here speakers often choose the past indefinite to indicate their focus on the result of the non-occurrence of the action in question.

Тя нали още не е излязла?	She hasn't left yet, has she?
Откакто замина, не ни е написал нито ред.	He hasn't written us a single word since his departure.
-- Аз мислех, че тя учи в университета преди няколко години.	"I thought she was a student several years ago."
-- Учи, но не завърши и не е получила диплома.	"She was, but she didn't finish and never got a diploma."

The final example illustrates the contrast between all three past tenses. The first speaker describes a durative event in the past using the imperfect -- she thought (for a long period which lasted until just before the moment of speech) that a particular fact had been the case, that someone had been enrolled at a university. The second speaker restates this fact (by way of affirmation) and adds another fact: the person had been enrolled, but had failed to graduate. All these three are viewed as facts of past action, and are communicated in the aorist.

To state the final fact, however, the speaker shifts to the past indefinite, indicating thereby that her point of view has shifted: she apparently considers that the non-receipt of the diploma is more relevant to the present state than the other actions related.

21.3. The past indefinite as expression of point of view

In relating past events, Bulgarian speakers can choose to view certain actions as more vivid, concrete, specific points in the past, and others as more generalized and non-specific. They will choose the aorist (or imperfect) to speak of the former, and the past indefinite for the latter. As an example, consider the following narration, drawn from the reading selection in Lesson 17:

past indefinite
Завършила съм средното си образование с пълно отличие през 1972 г.	I completed my secondary education with straight A's in 1972.

Двайсет и първи урок / Lesson 21

aorist
 Постъ́пих съ́щата годи́на в Софи́йския университе́т и през 1977 г. успе́шно завъ́рших ви́сшето си образова́ние.

 The same year I enrolled in Sofia University, and in 1977 successfully completed my higher education.

imperfect
 О́ще през студе́нтските си годи́ни проявя́вах интере́с към фолкло́ра.

 Already during my student years I was interested in folklore.

past indefinite
 Уча́ствувала съм във фолкло́рни експеди́ции из страна́та.

 I participated in several field trips throughout the country.

aorist
 През 1980 г. успе́шно защити́х дисерта́цията си и полу́чих сте́пен к.ф.н.

 In 1980 I successfully defended my dissertation and received the degree of Ph.D.

past indefinite
 Во́дила съм упражне́ния по фолкло́р за университе́тските студе́нти.

 I led tutorials on folklore for university students.

aorist
 През перио́да 1983-1986 г. уча́ствувах в Ле́тния семина́р.

 Between 1983 and 1986 I participated in the Summer seminar.

 The author of this text gives a summary description of her academic life. In the excerpt above, which includes seven sentences, there are four verbs in the aorist, three in the past indefinite and one in the imperfect. The English translation, by contrast, renders all the verbs with the simple past. The English present perfect (the "literal" translation of the Bulgarian past indefinite) would sound very wrong to an English ear in the first sentence, although it might be a possible variant in the other two Bulgarian usages of the past indefinite. To a Bulgarian, however, the contrast between the tenses is necessary to express the several shifts in point of view.

 The essential difference in focus is one of specific vs. general. When the writer of the above text concentrates on the several different specific facts of what she *did* in her academic life, she relates these facts in the aorist. In each case, she pins the action to a specific point in the past. But there are three instances where her focus is more general.

One is at the beginning of the passage, in (1). Although this event is also located at a specific point in the past, the telling of it is important for the general frame of the narrative in that it sets the scene for the events which follow. The other two instances of past indefinite, (4) and (6), concern events which the author has chosen not to specify with time reference. Had she connected these events with a specific point in time she might well have used the aorist for them too. Since she used the past indefinite, one concludes that her view of these events (at least at the moment of this narration) is a more generalized and less concrete one.

21.4. The past indefinite as expression of inference or assumption

Another expression of the "distancing" effect of the past indefinite is the idea of inference or assumption. If a Bulgarian relates a past event in the past indefinite (and not the aorist), s/he often does this to indicate that s/he is inferring the fact of past action from a present result. The results are evident, and therefore the action can be inferred with certainty. For example:

Сигурно не са́ си били́ вкъ́щи.	Most likely they were not home.
Не съм я чу́ла да и́злезе.	I didn't hear [= don't think I heard] her go out.
На́шите съсе́ди па́к са си пи́йнали и вди́гат шу́м.	Our neighbors have had a bit to drink again and are making noise.
Ви́ждам, че си напра́вила то́рта.	I see you've made a cake.
Къде́ е? Навя́рно е оти́шъл в ку́хнята да опи́тва то́ртата.	Where is he? Probably he went to the kitchen to taste the cake.
Какви́ са ти́я пу́сти мо́ди? Като че в гора́та са ви гле́дали.	What kind of crazy fashions are these? It's as if you were brought up in the wild.
А́з съм мно́го оглуша́ла напосле́дък.	I've gotten [= seem to have gotten] a lot deafer lately.

21.5. The past indefinite as expression of indirect discourse

The past indefinite is also used to relate reported speech. The original speaker may have used either the aorist or the past indefinite, but the speaker who conveys the news always uses the past indefinite. S/he fully believes the news s/he is reporting; nevertheless the distancing from the actual event requires the use of the past indefinite. For example:

Съсе́дката ка́за, че ги е видя́ла вче́ра да се целу́ват.	The neighbor woman said she saw them kissing yesterday.
Ка́заха ни, че си дошъ́л ма́лко преди́ на́с.	They told us you had arrived a little before we did.
Ка́за, че Са́шо си е ле́гнал и тя́ не и́ска да го бу́ди. Цял ден е изпи́твал студе́нти и е ка́пнал от умо́ра.	She said that Sasho had gone to bed and she didn't want to wake him. He'd been examining students all day and was exhausted.

The English pluperfect in most of the above examples is due to the English rule requiring indirect discourse to be related in a tense which is one degree removed from that of the original statement.

21.6. Summary: contrast between aorist/imperfect and past indefinite

In each of the above instances the speaker is distanced in one way or another from the events s/he is relating. This generalized distancing may carry one or more of the above shades of meaning; if one in particular is meant, it is usually clear from the context. By contrast, the aorist and imperfect convey a greater vividness, specificity and concreteness. Often a speaker will shift from the generalized past indefinite to the more concrete and vivid aorist to express the idea of direct verification. In these instances, the corresponding English distinction (between present perfect and simple past) is often the most correct translation. For example:

Не зна́я дали́ е изля́зла. Ча́кай да ви́дя. Сега́ изле́зе.	I don't know if she's gone out. Let me see. [Yes,] she left.
Ми́сля, че е заку́сила ве́че. Лиля́на, заку́си ли?	I think she's already had breakfast. Lilyana, did you eat breakfast?
Не съм я чу́ла о́ще. Еди́н моме́нт, чух, че врата́та ѝ се отво́ри.	I haven't heard [anything from] her yet. Just a minute, I heard her door open.

The concept of "vivid" vs. "distanced" narration is an important element in the verbal system of Bulgarian, and will be treated in more detail in subsequent lessons.

Двайсет и първи урок / Lesson 21

21.7. Conditional usage of the particle ли; use of the perfective aspect with habitual meaning

When used with a perfective verb, the interrogative particle ли expresses conditional meaning. That is, if a certain action occurs, the speaker considers it the case that another will follow on its heels.

In such sentences, the "trigger" action, that followed by the particle ли, is expressed with a perfective verb. The action which is predicted as a result is expressed with an imperfective verb. The overall context is one of predictable, repeated, habitual action. In this sense, ли acts as a "bounded" conjunction of the sort seen in Lesson 17. For example:

Ка́жа ли не́що, пра́вя го.	If I say something, I do it.
То́й не забеля́зва деца́та. Забеле́жи ли ги, го́ни ги.	He takes no notice of children. If he sees them [at all], he chases them away.

The same construction can refer to action which was predictable in the past but is no longer. In this case, the verbs are in the imperfect tense, and the same aspectual relationship is maintained. For example:

Ка́жех ли не́що, пра́вех го.	If I said/were to say it, then I would do it.
Забеле́жеше ли ги, го́неше ги.	If he noticed/were to notice them, he would chase them away.

Perfective verbs can be used to refer to this sort of habitual action even without the presence of the particle ли. The meaning is one of a repeated action that is visualized in sharp and concrete fashion. For example:

С брада́ е по́-ле́сно. Ста́неш су́трин, пли́снеш си две́ ше́пи вода́ на лице́то и си гото́в.	It's easier with a beard. You get up in the morning, splash a bit of water on your face, and you're ready.

Двайсет и първи урок / Lesson 21

EXERCISES

I. Rewrite the following sentences, replacing ли *with either* ако *or* дали, *according to the meaning.*

1. Питах я иска ли да дойде с нас.
2. Отвори ли се някъде врата, тя трепва.
3. Не знаеш той сърди ли се, или не.
4. Разбери подал ли е молба да го приемат в Съюза на преводачите.
5. Отвориш ли сутрин очи, виждаш голямото кафяво мече да се смее.
6. Те не пишат в писмото добре ли се развива лозата на двора.
7. Наведа ли се, прерязва ме силна болка в кръста.

II. Rewrite the following sentences, replacing each instance of ставам + *adjective (or adverb) with a verb form.*

1. Когато го заболи стомахът, той става бял като платно.
2. Ако напрежението стане силно, ще разкажеш някой виц.
3. Ако гледаме живота през черни очила, всичко става черно.
4. Аз не държа килима на слънце, да не станат бледи цветовете му.
5. Виждам, че ви става спокойно като слушате всичко това.
6. На нея ѝ става весело, когато слуша песни от трийсетте години.
7. Време е да се прибираме. Виж, небето стана тъмно.

III. Fill in the blanks with aorist or past indefinite forms of one of the following verbs, as appropriate: надмина, направя, позная, обадя се, боядисам, откажа се, идвам, вляза, казвам.

1. Ти знаеше, че той _____ вече сутринта, нали? Защо тогава не ми каза?
2. Няма да повярваш, но вчера той _____ пицата за петнайсет минути. Ако не бях свидетел и аз нямаше да повярвам. Той много пъти ми _____, че я прави бързо, но това, което видях, _____ очакванията ми.
3. Много ще ми е мъчно, ако той _____ по телефона, докато ни нямаше.
4. Веднага след като гостите _____, те им казаха голямата новина.
5. Тя _____ старата приятелка на майка си, още преди да е чула името ѝ.
6. Вече не го виждам в Университета. Сигурно вече _____ от следването.
7. Ние _____ яйцата за Великден, както пожелахме.

Двайсет и първи урок / Lesson 21

ADDITIONAL GRAMMAR NOTES

21.8. Derivation: causative and stative verbs

Causative verbs

Many adjectives which describe a state can give rise to a perfective causative verb (a verb signifying the action necessary to bring that state into being).

The stem is taken from a non-masculine form of the adjective (which may be slightly altered). A perfective verb is created by adding a prefix and the endings of the и-conjugation (which are usually accented but not always). The corresponding imperfective is derived by one of the means learned in Lesson 18.

adjective	prefix	causative verb		(meaning shift)
		perfective	*imperfective*	
велик-и	у-	увелич-а́	увелич-а́вам	great › increase
готов-и	при-	пригот́в-я	пригот́в-ям	ready › prepare
прав-и	из-	изпра́в-я	изпра́в-ям	straight › straighten
	по-	попра́в-я	попра́в-ям	straight › fix
добр-и	по-	подобр-я́	подобр-я́вам	good › improve
дълг-и	про-	продълж-а́	продълж-а́вам	long › continue
	у-	удълж-а́	удълж-а́вам	long › lengthen
лесн-и	у-	улесн-я́	улесн-я́вам	easy › facilitate
ма́л-ки	на-	намал-я́	намал-я́вам	small › decrease
споко́й-ни	у-	успоко-я́	успоко-я́вам	calm › soothe
шир-о́к-и	раз-	разшир-я́	разшир-я́вам	wide › broaden

Adding **се** to the verbs given above makes them intransitive.

Stative verbs

Explicitly intransitive verbs (sometimes called stative verbs) can also be formed from an adjective by means of the suffix **-ей**, to which are added endings of the е-conjugation.

These verbs take their meaning from the adjective identifying a state, and denote the process of becoming, or coming into, that state. The derivation process sometimes produces a simplex imperfective and sometimes a perfective from which the imperfective must be derived.

Двайсет и първи урок / Lesson 21

adjective	prefix	stative verb		(meaning shift)
		perfective	imperfective	
къ́сн-и	за-	закъсн-е́я	закъсн-я́вам	late › be late
ма́л-к-и	на-	намал-е́я	намал-я́вам	small › decrease

adjective			stative verb		(meaning shift)
	simplex imperfective	prefix	perfective	imperfective	
зеле́н-и	зелен-е́я	по-	позелен-е́я	позелен-я́вам	[be/get] green
ста́р-и	стар-е́я	о-	остар-е́я	остаря́-вам	[be/grow] old
червѐн-и	червен-е́я	по-	почервен-е́я	почервен-я́вам	[be/get] red

21.9. Derivation: substance adjectives

Adjectives indicating the substance of which something is made are formed with various suffixes, all of which are added to a noun root.

The most frequent of these suffixes is **-ен**, before which stem-final **к-** or **г-** shift to **ч-** or **ж-**. The vowel in this suffix is never a fleeting vowel.

noun	+ -ен ›	adjective	(meaning shift)
карто́ф	+ -ен ›	карто́фен, -ена	potato (noun) › potato (adj.)
дома́т	+ -ен ›	дома́тен, -ена	tomato (noun) › tomato (adj.)
ри́б-а	+ -ен ›	ри́бен, -ена	fish (noun) › fish (adj.)
въ́лн-а	+ -ен ›	въ́лнен, -ена	wool › woolen
дърв-о́	+ -ен ›	дъ́рвен, -ена	wood › wooden
ко́ж-а	+ -ен ›	ко́жен, -ена	skin, leather › leather (adj.)
копри́н-а	+ -ен ›	копри́нен, -ена	silk › silken
ле́н	+ -ен ›	ле́нен, -ена	linen, flax › linen (adj.), flaxen

Adjectives derived from the names of animals usually take either the suffix **-шки,** or a zero suffix. The latter suffix does not contain any segments, but it does cause softening of a preceding consonant (in which **-ц** is replaced by **-ч**), and causes the neuter form to end in **-е** rather than **-о**. Masculine forms of all these adjectives must have the ending **-и**.

Двайсет и първи урок / Lesson 21

noun	adjective		meaning shift
	masculine	neuter	
áгне	áгнешки	áгнешко	lamb *(noun)* › lamb *(adj.)*
тéле	тéлешки	тéлешко	calf *(noun)* › calf *(adj.)*
крáва	крáви	крáве	cow *(noun)* › cow *(adj.)*
овцá	óвчи	óвче	sheep *(noun)* › sheep *(adj.)*

These adjectives are often used without a corresponding noun when they refer to food, and when the unit of food is thought to be self-evident. For instance, **тéлешко** means "veal" (in which case, the neuter noun **месó** "meat" is understood). The adjective **óвче** "sheep's" refers either to soft cheese, yogurt or milk made from sheep's milk (in which case one of the neuter nouns **сúрене** "white cheese", **млякó** "milk" or **кúсело млякó** "yogurt" is either understood or specified).

National Library "Cyril and Methodius", Sofia

Двайсет и първи урок / Lesson 21

SAMPLE SENTENCES

1. Кракъ́т им не е́ стъ́пвал на събра́нията ни.

2. Сърце́ не ми́ да́ва да му ка́жа, че съм се отка́зала от пъту́ването.

3. Не ни́ се е слу́чвало да чу́ем та́зи глаго́лна фо́рма.

4. И по́-ло́шо му се е слу́чвало.

5. Ще ви́диш ли дали́ са си оти́шли ве́че?

6. Ако чу́еш, че па́к са се разпе́ли, обади́ се на поли́цията.

7. -- Ни́кога не сме́ я́ли кита́йско я́дене.
   -- А ни́е веднъ́ж сме про́бвали, но не ни́ харе́са.

8. А́з съм у́чил ру́ски, но вси́чко съм забра́вил.

9. -- Сви́рите ли на пиа́но?
   -- Не. У́чил съм 10 годи́ни, но по́лза ни́каква.

10. По́-ра́но и́дваше че́сто, но от пе́т годи́ни не се́ е мя́ркал.

11. Те́ не са́ и́двали в на́шия кра́й след смъртта́ на ма́йка си.

12. И́ма едно́ тако́ва пра́вило: изми́я ли прозо́рците, заваля́ва дъ́жд.

13. Чу́ех ли шумоле́не в ку́хнята, сърце́то ми тре́пваше.

14. Сре́щнем ли я, любе́зно я поздравя́ваме.

15. Сре́щнеха ли се, оти́ваха да пи́йнат по една́ раки́я.

16. Внима́вай какво́ прика́зваш пред не́я: чу́е ли не́що, ведна́га му го ка́зва.

17. Хи́ч не ми́ върви́: реша́ ли да се изкъ́пя, то́плата вода́ спи́ра.

Двайсет и първи урок / Lesson 21

SENTENCES FOR TRANSLATION

1. She says he didn't come to class today. As far as I know, he hasn't come for weeks. And whatever cafe I go to these days, I see him there.

2. How can it be that you can't arrange the meeting?! You just pick up the phone, call the person, and that's that. If he refuses to come, I will happily help you convince him. Hasn't he promised many times to meet with us?

3. "Excuse me, could you lean over and pick up my book? It seems to have fallen."
   "Sorry, I can't. The bus is too crowded. Every time I try to take a step, someone pushes me."

4. "Don't get angry, but the neighbor seems to have taken your car again."
   "What a terrible neighbor! It's as if he thinks it's his own car. Why did I give him the keys?"

5. "Have you seen Boryana today?"
   "No, she's not here now. Let me go see if she's come in at all today. Hm, I see that her dog is in her office, so she must have arrived."

6. I worked in many restaurants when I was in school. I worked in one for three years, then I started working in another, then in another, and finally they drove me out of that one too. Every time I cook something, someone suddenly falls ill!

7. I notice you haven't got much sleep recently. Would it be more comfortable if we tried to get in touch again another time?

READING SELECTION

Старобъ́лгарските а́збуки

Ако запи́таш гръ́цките книжо́вници, като рече́ш: "Ко́й ви е създа́л бу́квите или преве́л кни́гите, или в кое́ вре́ме?", то ря́дко измежду тя́х зна́ят. Оба́че ако запи́таш славя́нските азбука́рчета, като рече́ш: "Ко́й ви е създа́л а́збуката или преве́л кни́гите?", вси́чки зна́ят и в о́тговор ще река́т: "Свети́ Константи́н Филосо́ф, наре́чен Ки́рил: то́й ни създа́де а́збуката и преве́де кни́гите и бра́т му Мето́дий." И ако попи́таш в кое́ вре́ме, то зна́ят и ще река́т, че през вре́мето на гръ́цкия ца́р Михаи́л и на Бори́с, бъ́лгарския кня́з, и на Расти́ца, мора́вския кня́з, и на Ко́цел, бла́тенския кня́з в годи́ната 6363 (855) от създа́ването на света́.

Чернори́зец Хра́бър, За бу́квите (IX в.)

През IX в. сред славя́ните назря́ва необходимостта́ да се приобщя́т към достиже́нията на цивилиза́цията и сами́ да създада́т своя́ со́бствена култу́ра. А в осно́вата на вся́ка култу́ра лежи́ писмеността́. Чернори́зец Хра́бър е засвиде́телствувал о́питите да се пи́ше на славя́нски, като се изпо́лзват гръ́цки и лати́нски бу́кви. Но те́зи отде́лни проя́ви о́ще не са́ писмо́. Ну́жно е да се създа́де еди́нна пи́смена систе́ма, коя́то да отразя́ва ця́лостния зву́ков съста́в на ези́ка. Необходи́мо е та́зи графи́чна систе́ма да полу́чи официа́лно призна́ние и подкре́па. През IX в. на две́ места́ възни́кват благоприя́тни усло́вия за създа́ване на официа́лна славя́нска пи́сменост -- във Виза́нтия, в среда́та на бъ́лгарските славя́ни около Со́лун, и в Бълга́рия.

През 862 г. в о́тговор на молба́та на мора́вския кня́з Ростисла́в да бъ́дат изпра́тени в Мора́вия славя́нски учи́тели и пропове́дници, византи́йският импера́тор Михаи́л III възла́га на бра́тята Ки́рил и Мето́дий да създада́т славя́нска пи́сменост. Мотиви́ровката на и́збора е: "Ви́е двама́та сте солунча́ни, а вси́чки солунча́ни гово́рят чи́сто славя́нски" (Простра́нното житие́ на Мето́дий). Напъ́лно есте́ствено славя́нските първоучи́тели изгра́ждат своя́та книжо́вна де́йност върху осно́вата на своя́ славя́нски диале́кт. Ка́кто посо́чват истори́ческите свиде́телства, създа́ването на пъ́рвата старобъ́лгарска и славя́нска а́збука -- глаго́лицата, е ли́чно де́ло на Ки́рил. То́й създа́ва съвърше́на а́збука, а в проце́са на пъ́рвите прево́ди форми́ра книжо́вен старобъ́лгарски ези́к с висо́ка сто́йност и пола́га соли́дни осно́ви за изгра́ждане на старобъ́лгарската и славя́нската култу́ра. Пи́смената систе́ма, коя́то създа́ва славя́нският първоучи́тел, то́чно отразя́ва зву́ковия съста́в на бъ́лгарските гово́ри в Со́лунско през IX в. Тя́ е напъ́лно своеобра́зна и не повта́ря начерта́нията на ни́то една́ от изве́стните тога́ва а́збуки. Пъ́рвата старобъ́лгарска а́збука е полу́чила и́мето глаго́лица от старобъ́лгарския глаго́л глаголати, който означáва "говóря". Глагóлицата, създáдена във Византия, е въвéдена от сóлунските брáтя в Морáвия и Панóния по врéме на тя́хната културна дéйност сред зáпадните славя́ни. От Панóния тáзи áзбука е прониќнала в Хървáтско и там здрáво се е задържáла в богослужéбните тéкстове чак до XVIII в. От Морáвия глагóлицата се е разпространила в чéшката държáва и се е употребя́вала там докъм крáя на XI в. Учениците на Кирил и Метóдий въвéждат глагóлицата в Бългáрия.

В българските земи, най-вероя́тно в Преслáв, под въздéйствие на глагóлицата се е доразвила прáктиката да се изпóлзва гръ́цкото писмó за записване на старобългáрската реч. Според Кириловата áзбука тó се допъ́лва с бу́кви за специфичните бъ́лгарски зву́кове, приéма последователността́ на нéйните бу́квени знáци и се офóрмя във втóра старобългáрска áзбука -- кирилица. Името си нóвата áзбука е получила пó-къ́сно, в чест на създáтеля на славя́нската писменост -- Кирил. От Бългáрия кирилицата е била́ пренéсена в Руси́я, Сърбия и Влáхо-Молдáвските княжества.

През цéлия старобългáрски периóд (IX - XI в.) в двáта културни цéнтъра на държáвата -- Преслáв и Óхрид -- едновремéнно се употребя́ват и двéте áзбуки. Но постепéнно, óще към крáя на старобългáрския периóд, кирилицата започва да се изпóлзва пó-чéсто поради практическото удóбство на опростéните си бу́квени очертáния. През слéдващите векóве тя окончáтелно измéства глагóлицата. Тóзи прéходен периóд е намéрил отражéние в редица кирилски ръкóписи, в който са вмъ́кнати отдéлни бу́кви, ду́ми, израз́и, пасáжи, писани на глагóлица. През XII - XIV в. всé óще са знáели áзбуката на Константин-Кирил Филосóф и са чéли глаголически тéкстове. Но нóви прéписи на глагóлица са престáнали да се прáвят. Такá постепéнно е изчéзнало от Бългáрия глаголическото писмó и е остáнала сáмо кирилицата.

Адаптирано от "Старобългарските азбуки" (Екатерина Дограмаджиева, Кирило-Методиевски страници).

Двайсет и първи урок / Lesson 21

GLOSSARY

а́гне	lamb	зву́ков	sound *(adj.)*
а́гнешки	lamb *(adj.)*	здра́во	well, soundly
а́збука	alphabet	зелене́я	appear green
благоприя́тен	favorable, auspicious	изгра́ждам / изградя́	build, construct
бла́тенски	of the Blaten area	изме́жду	among
богослуже́бен	liturgical	изме́ствам / изме́стя	move away, displace
брада́т	bearded		
бу́квен	letter *(adj.)*	изпи́твам / изпи́там	test; experience
бу́квени зна́ци	alphabet characters		
бя́л като платно́	white as a sheet	изпълня́вам / изпъ́лня	carry out, fulfill
вели́к	great		
Вели́кден	Easter		
вла́хо-молда́вски	Wallacho-Moldavian	ка́мък (*pl.* ка́мъни)	stone
вмъ́квам / вмъ́кна	insert		
въздей́ствие	influence, impact	ка́пвам / ка́пна	drop
възла́гам / възло́жа (-иш)	assign, delegate	ка́пнал от умо́ра	exhausted
		карто́фен, -ена	potato *(adj.)*
възни́квам / възни́кна	arise, originate	кафя́в	brown
		кили́м	carpet, rug
въ́лна	wool	кири́лица	Cyrillic [alphabet]
		кита́йски	Chinese
г-жа = госпожа́		княже́ство	kingdom
глаго́л	verb	книжо́вен	literary, learned
глаго́лен	verbal	книжо́вник	man of letters
глаго́лица	Glagolitic [alphabet]	ко́жен, -ена	leather
го́ня	chase	копри́на	silk
градя́ върху осно́вата на	build on the foundations of	копри́нен, -ена	silken
		кра́ва	cow
графи́чен	graphic	кра́ви	cow *(adj.)*
		кръст	cross; small of back
де́йност	activity		
диале́кт	dialect	лати́нски	Latin
до́към	until approximately	лежа́ в осно́вата на	underlie
доразви́вам / доразви́я	develop fully		
		лен	linen, flax
достиже́ние	achievement	ле́нен, -ена	linen *(adj.)*, flaxen
дра́го ми е	I'm pleased	ли́чен	prominent; personal
държа́ се здра́во	hold tight, hold fast		
		мо́да	fashion
еди́нен	uniform, united	молда́вски	Moldavian
есте́ствено	naturally	мотивиро́вка	motivation
		мя́ркам се / мя́рна се	show, put in an appearance
житие́	saint's life		
задъ́ржам / задържа́ (-и́ш)	keep, hold back	наве́ждам се / наведа́ се	lean over, bend down
за́паден	western	надмина́вам / надмина́	outdistance, surpass
запи́твам / запи́там	inquire [of]		

Двайсет и първи урок / Lesson 21

назря́вам / назре́я	ripen, mature; come to a head
намаля́вам / намале́я	decrease, dwindle
намаля́вам / намаля́	decrease, reduce
нацъфтя́вам / нацъфтя́	burst into bloom
начерта́вам / начерта́я	draw, sketch, outline
необходи́м	necessary
обеща́ние	promise
о́вчи	sheep (adj.)
оглуша́вам / оглуше́я	go deaf
означа́вам / означа́ (-и́ш)	mark, mean, signify
о́коло	around, in vicinity of
опростя́вам / опростя́	simplify
осно́ва	base, grounding
отка́звам се / отка́жа се (-еш)	give up, cancel
отраже́ние	reflection; repercussion
отразя́вам / отразя́	reflect
официа́лен	official, formal
офо́рмям / офо́рмя	shape, fashion
оча́кване (pl. -ния)	expectation
очерта́ние	outline, delineation
паму́к	cotton
паму́чен	cotton (adj.)
паса́ж	passage
пиа́но	piano
пи́смен	written; for writing
писмо́	[system of] writing
пи́ца	pizza
пли́свам / пли́сна	pour; fling
подкре́па	support
позеленя́вам / позелене́я	turn green
пола́гам / поло́жа (-иш)	lay, put
поли́ция	police
поря́звам / поре́жа (-еш)	cut
последова́телност	sequence, order; consistency
посо́чвам / посо́ча (-иш)	indicate, point out
постепе́нен	gradual
почервеня́вам / почервене́я	turn red
пра́ктика	practice
практи́чески	practical
прево́дач (ка)	translator
прена́сям / пренеса́	transfer; transport
пре́пис	copy, transcript
преря́зва ме	I feel a sharp pain
преря́звам / преря́жа (-еш)	cut through
преста́вам / преста́на	cease, stop
пре́ходен	transitional
призна́ние	acknowledgment
приобща́вам / приобщя́	incorporate
приобща́вам се / приобщя́ с	affiliate with
приобща́вам се към тях	join them
про́бвам	try
проло́жен	[part of] a prologue
про́повед	sermon
простра́нен	spacious, extensive
проя́ва	manifestation, act
първоучи́тел	founder of a doctrine
разви́ва се лоза́	the vine is putting out leaves
разви́вам, разви́я	develop, cultivate
разпя́вам се / разпе́я се	burst into song
разширя́вам / разширя́	extend, broaden
реди́ца	row, series
ректора́т	university president's office
ри́бен, -ена (or ри́бна)	fish (adj.)
ръ́копис	manuscript
Свети́ Константи́н	St. Constantine
свиде́тел	witness
свиде́телство	certificate; evidence
своеобра́зен	original; odd
свъ́рзвам / свъ́ржа (-еш)	connect, put [someone] in touch
серио́зен	serious
систе́ма	system
сле́двам	follow, pursue; study
сле́дване	college studies
слуша́лка	telephone receiver, headphone
соли́ден	solid, firm
солунча́нин	native of Solun
специфи́чен	specific

Двайсет и първи урок / Lesson 21

споко́ен	calm, peaceful	усло́вие	condition
ста́туя	statue	фило́со́ф	philosopher
сто́йност	value, worth	форми́рам	form, shape, set up
съвърше́н	perfect, consummate		
съста́в	composition	цвят, цветъ́т (*pl.* цветове́)	color
те́ле	calf	цивилиза́ция	civilization
те́лешки	calf *(adj.)*, veal	червене́я	redden, grow red
тре́пвам / тре́пна	wince, flinch	чернори́зец	monk
тъ́жен	sad	че́ли са	they read *(generalized past, see L. 29)*
увелича́вам / увелича́ (-и́ш)	increase	че́шки	Czech
удо́бство	convenience	ше́па	hollow of hand; handful
улесня́вам / улесня́	facilitate	шумоле́не	rustling
умо́ра	fatigue		
употребя́вам / употребя́	use; use up		

CULTURAL COMMENTARY

City life: beards; professional unions

Traditionally, a well brought up Bulgarian male shaves regularly (unless he is an Orthodox priest, for whom beards are the rule). Beards are considered by many of the older generation to be a sign of bohemianism and loose living. During the post-socialist elections, beards were associated with the political opposition, UDF (United Democratic Front -- СДС, Съю́з на демократи́ческите си́ли). In the present generation, however, beards are more and more frequent among young males.

Journalists, translators, and authors each have their separate unions in Bulgaria. Only the more distinguished members of these professions are admitted into the respective unions. To become a member of the Union of Translators, for instance, one must have published several thousand pages of translations (as well as meet various criteria of excellence). There are complex procedures to follow to join each of these unions, one of which is certainly the submission of the appropriate "molba". During the socialist period, there was essentially only one union for each profession. Since then many more unions have been created, differing among themselves primarily as to political orientation.

Language: Bulgarian tense system; history of Slavic writing systems

Bulgarians are both proud of, and rueful about, their very complex verbal system. They even make jokes about it, introducing new verbal "tenses" to describe common human failings. One joke, for instance, characterized "work" (in the sense of the time spent at one's job) during the socialist regime as "wasted time" (ми́нало загу́бено вре́ме). The joke is a play on the double meaning of вре́ме (which means both "time" and "verbal tense"). Since many jobs seemed superfluous, the activity of going to work seemed for many to be "lost" time.

The invention of the Slavic alphabet, and the introduction of literacy to the Slavs, are events to which Bulgarians feel very close. The creators of Slavic literacy, Constantine and Methodius, were brothers living in Solun (Greek Thessalonike). When the Moravian prince Rastislav requested missionaries so that his people might "learn the whole truth about" Christianity not in Latin but in their native Slavic, the Byzantine emperor Michael chose these two brothers from Solun to create the Slavic alphabet because, as he is claimed to have said, "everyone from Solun knows Slavic"; additionally, the two brothers had already served on a missionary journey to the Crimean Khazars in 860.

In 862-863, the brothers were sent to Moravia (modern Czech Republic) to carry out their literary and missionary work. The Slavic alphabet created by Constantine (often called "the Philosopher") for their translation work was called Glagolitic. After a somewhat difficult time at Rastislav's court, they were invited to the court of Prince Kotsel on Lake Balaton (in modern

Hungary), where their work was more successful. From the outset, however, their mission was politically complex, and they eventually went to Rome to defend the rights of Slavs to have the liturgy in their language. Constantine died in Rome in 869 having taken the name Cyril (and holy orders); on his deathbed he urged Methodius to continue the mission. Methodius and their disciples returned to Pannonia where they worked assiduously, despite numerous difficulties, until Methodius' death in 885. The disciples were then persecuted and imprisoned; three of them managed to build a raft and travel down the Danube back to the Balkans. Along the way, they taught Slavs the Glagolitic alphabet, which continued to be used in the Slavic liturgy on the northern Croatian coast until the early 20th century.

The disciples who returned to Bulgaria introduced literacy (in Slavic) to Boris's Bulgarian court. Since most scribes at this court already knew Greek, the returning disciples derived a writing system for Slavic based on the Greek alphabet and named it after its founder, St. Cyril: this is the modern Cyrillic alphabet. During the pre-Ottoman times, there were two main centers of medieval South Slavic (Bulgarian/Macedonian) culture. One was in Preslav (near modern Shumen), associated with the reign of Emperor Boris and his son Simeon, and the other was in Ohrid (in modern southwestern Macedonia), associated with the reign of Emperor Samuil.

Literature: medieval period

Much of the preceding information is known to us from writings of contemporaries. Important sources are the Lives of the Saints Cyril and Methodius, and the treatise written by a monk named Khrabar who lived during the time of the alphabet's creation. The literary genre of a "saint's life" ocupies a special place in the medieval literary canon. There are two kinds, the full, or extensive (**простра́нен**) life, and the abbreviated (**проло́жен**) life, which serves as a prologue in church services.

The dates in medieval religious texts are usually reckoned not from the birth of Christ but from the traditionally transmitted date of creation. The most current belief is that the world was thought to have been created 5508 years before the birth of Christ.

Philanthropy

The brothers Evlogi and Hristo Georgiev (**Евло́ги и Хри́сто Георги́еви**), merchants from Karlovo, founded a philanthropic organization which both laid the groundwork for the Bulgarian Academy of Sciences and furnished the funds for the construction of Sofia University. The statues of the philanthropist-merchant brothers are found at the main entrance to the University.

Sofia University

LESSON 22

DIALOGUE

Нали́ щя́хте да до́йдете за́едно?

// Весели́н ча́ка пред Университе́та. Джу́ли и́два запъхтя́на. //

Весели́н: Здраве́йте, Джу́ли! А къде́ е Де́йвид? Нали́ щя́хте да до́йдете за́едно?

Джу́ли: Здраве́йте! Мо́ля да ме извини́те. А́з ма́лко закъсня́х. Не ми́ се и́скаше да тръ́гна от къ́щи, преди́ Де́йвид да е дошъ́л. Но то́й така́ и не дойде́.

Весели́н: Надя́вам се, че ни́що ло́шо не му́ се е случи́ло?

Джу́ли: Зави́си от гле́дната то́чка. Тря́бваше да се сре́щнем с не́го о́ще сутринта́. Щя́хме да хо́дим в библиоте́ката. Ча́ках, ча́ках, а не́го го ня́ма ни́какъв. Оба́дих му се по телефо́на към двана́йсет и го събу́дих. Си́гурно ще́ше да спи́ до дове́чера, ако не бя́х се оба́дила.

Весели́н: Да не е́ бо́лен?

Джу́ли: Ще́ше да е по́-добре́, ако бе́ше бо́лен. Вче́ра с А́нгел са реши́ли, че вся́ко кюфте́ тря́бва да се поле́е с бути́лка сухиндо́лска гъ́мза. Така́ че дне́с си почи́ва.

Весели́н: Вси́чки зна́ят, че черве́но ви́но на гла́дно сърце́ не се́ пи́е.

Джу́ли: Е́х, и Де́йвид сега́ ве́че зна́е.

Весели́н: Тря́бва ли тога́ва сре́щата с профе́сора да се отмени́?

Джу́ли: Не зна́м. Де́йвид ще́ше да го пи́та за то́лкова мно́го неща́. Но от дру́га страна́, сре́щата е угово́рена, чове́кът ни ча́ка. Не ми́ се ще́ да я отме́няме.

Весели́н: Наи́стина. Ха́йде да върви́м наго́ре.

// Джу́ли се подхлъ́зва на стъ́лбите. Весели́н я хва́ща под ръка́. //

Джу́ли: За ма́лко щя́х да па́дна.

Двайсет и втори урок / Lesson 22

Веселин: Джу́ли, защо́ не се́ отби́ете след ра́зговора с профе́сора в Криста́л. А́з тъ́кмо ще съм свъ́ршил ра́ботата си в реда́кцията. Ще пи́ем по едно́ кафе́ на споко́йствие. Нали́ зна́ете къде́ е кафе́-сладка́рница Криста́л?

Джули: Да́, зна́м я къде́ е. В гра́дската гради́на на Рако́вска. Ще до́йда с удово́лствие.

// Джу́ли и Весели́н сти́гат до кабине́та на профе́сор Попо́в. Весели́н чу́ка, но о́тговор ня́ма. //

Веселин: Къде́ ли е оти́шъл? Нали́ ще́ше да ни ча́ка? А врата́та е отво́рена. То́й не ни́ е чу́л. Са́шо, здраве́й. Ви́ж кого́ ти во́дя.

Александър: Здраве́йте. Заповя́дайте, вле́зте.

Веселин: Да ти предста́вя госпо́жица Джу́ли Бе́йкър. Тя́ е студе́нтка. От Аме́рика.

Александър: Дра́го ми е. Попо́в. Алекса́ндър Попо́в.

Джули: А́з съм Джу́ли Бе́йкър.

// Ръку́ват се. //

Веселин: Джу́ли ще ти разка́же от какво́ се интересу́ва, а а́з да вървя́. Да ви оста́вя да си поприка́звате.

Александър: Седни́, де. А́з бя́х с впечатле́ние, че щя́ха да до́йдат два́ма америка́нски студе́нти.

Джули: Мо́ят коле́га Де́йвид Бо́йд ще́ше наи́стина да прису́ства на сре́щата, но в после́дния моме́нт бе́ше възпрепя́тстван.

Веселин: Не мо́га да оста́на. Тръ́гвам. Притесня́вам се, че ме ча́кат в реда́кцията.

Александър: За къде́ бъ́рзаш? Седни́. Ра́ботата не е́ за́ек да избя́га.

Веселин: Не́, не́. Ще вървя́. Са́шо, благодаря́ ти. Ще ти се оба́дя тези дни́. Джу́ли, ще ви ча́кам в пе́т в Криста́л.

Двайсет и втори урок / Lesson 22

BASIC GRAMMAR

22.1. The future anterior tense

The future anterior tense in Bulgarian (бъдеще предварително време) is similar in meaning to the future perfect in English. In both cases, speakers use it to envisage a completed result in the future. The two tenses are also similar in form: in both cases, there is a sequence of "future auxiliary + present perfect auxiliary + resultative participle". Namely:

Ще	съм	дошла́	до 5 ч.
I	will	have arrived	by 5 o'clock.

The future anterior tense is thus a combination of the future (а́з ще до́йда) and the past indefinite (а́з съм дошла́). Since the form and the meaning of both these tenses are by now well known to the student, the future anterior tense should pose no problem. The full conjugation (given with a perfective form of the verb чета́) is as follows:

FUTURE ANTERIOR

	affirmative	*negative*
1ˢᵗ singular	ще съм проче́л	ня́ма да съм проче́л
2ⁿᵈ singular	ще си проче́л	ня́ма да си проче́л
3ʳᵈ singular	ще е проче́л	ня́ма да е проче́л
1ˢᵗ plural	ще сме проче́ли	ня́ма да сме проче́ли
2ⁿᵈ plural	ще сте проче́ли	ня́ма да сте проче́ли
3ʳᵈ plural	ще са проче́ли	ня́ма да са проче́ли

In meaning, the future anterior tense projects a completed state into the future: the speaker envisages as complete an action which has not yet taken place. The future anterior is most frequently encountered with perfective verbs, although imperfective ones may occur in the case of repeated completed actions.

Like the past anterior, this tense makes reference to two different points in time: the completion of the action itself and the point of future time by which this action will be completed. The essential meaning of the past anterior (то́й бе́ше дошъ́л) is to describe an action which occurred prior to some other past action. In similar fashion, the future anterior describes an action which is expected to take place prior to some other action (or time point) envisioned in the future. The second action is not always specifically mentioned, but it is necessarily clear from the context. Indeed, were it not clearly present in the speaker's mind, s/he would have no reason to use the future anterior. For example:

Защо́ не се́ отби́ете след ра́зговора с профе́сора в Криста́л? А́з тъ́кмо ще съм свъ́ршил ра́ботата си в реда́кцията.	Why don't you drop by the cafe 'Kristal' after your meeting with with the professor? [By then] I will just have finished my business at the office.
Ня́ма ну́жда да яде́м по пъ́тя. Докато сти́гнем та́м, ба́ба ве́че ще е опе́кла а́гнето а дя́до ве́че ще е наля́л ви́но.	There's no need to eat along the way -- by the time we get there, Grandma will already have roasted the lamb and Grandpa will have poured out some wine.

22.2. The future in the past tense: introduction and formation

Just as Bulgarian can project an envisioned action into the future (by means of the future anterior tense), it can also project the envisioning of this action into the past. The tense with the somewhat unwieldy name, "future in the past" (бъдеще в ми́налото) means exactly what it says. A statement of future action which is made in the present moment is then shifted into a past tense time frame.

At first, this definition may seem strange to one whose language does not have such a formalized tense. In practice, however, it is straightforward. In English, one says in the present

"I will do that in an hour's time."

Once one is removed from this present moment, one often has occasion to look back on it and recall one's thinking at that moment. To do so in English, one says one of a number of things:

"I was about to do that after an hour."
"I was to do that in an hour's time."
"I intended to do that in an hour's time."
"I would have done that in an hour's time."

The exact meaning depends, of course, both on the actual outcome of events and on the extent to which the speaker is aware of and makes reference to this outcome. Examples of usage, and of the ways in which these several meanings are communicated, will be given below.

The shape of this tense is in many ways parallel to that of the simple future -- a form of the auxiliary ще plus a conjugated present tense form of the verb. In the simple future the auxiliary ще is an unaccented, unchanging particle which is identical with the 3rd singular of the verb ща́. In the future in the past, however, this auxiliary is the fully conjugated imperfect tense form of the verb ща́, which is accented like any other word. Additionally, whereas the simple future auxiliary ще is followed directly by the present tense form of the verb, in the future in the past the two forms are joined by the conjunction да.

Similarly, the negative forms of the future in the past resemble the negative forms of the simple future. Both are composed of "auxiliary + present tense"; in both cases the auxiliary is unchanging for person or number. Only the tense of the auxiliary is different: present tense (**няма**) in the simple future and past tense (**нямаше**) in the future in the past.

Here are the forms of the future in the past, both affirmative and negative. They are given alongside the simple future for comparison:

FUTURE IN THE PAST (contrasted with simple future)

	AFFIRMATIVE		*NEGATIVE*	
	Future in the past	*(future)*	*Future in the past*	*(future)*
1ˢᵗ sg	щях да чета́	ще чета́	нямаше да чета́	няма да чета́
2ⁿᵈ sg.	ще́ше да чете́ш	ще чете́ш	нямаше да чете́ш	няма да чете́ш
3ʳᵈ sg.	ще́ше да чете́	ще чете́	нямаше да чете́	няма да чете́
1ˢᵗ pl.	щя́хме да чете́м	ще чете́м	нямаше да четем	няма да четем
2ⁿᵈ pl.	щя́хте да чете́те	ще чете́те	нямаше да чете́те	няма да чете́те
3ʳᵈ pl.	щя́ха да чета́т	ще чета́т	нямаше да чета́т	няма да чета́т

22.3. The future in the past tense: basic usage

The simple future tense describes an event the speaker thinks will (or will not) happen. Sometimes a statement made in the future tense implies intention on the part of the speaker (that the event happen or not happen), and sometimes it simply expresses a belief, guess or projection. Whatever that statement meant when it was made is what the future in the past reports. The various possible meanings are thus quite different, and so are the various English translations.

What is common to all meanings is the projection into the past of a non-past state. The relationship between future and future in the past is thus exactly parallel to that between present and imperfect.

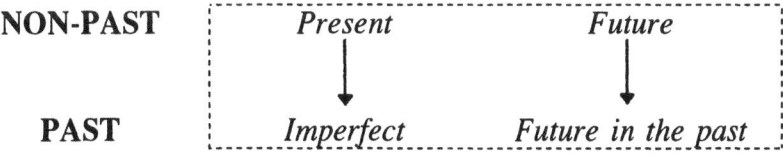

NON-PAST *Present* *Future*

PAST *Imperfect* *Future in the past*

Consider the following two narratives. In the first, a speaker describes to a friend his current state, including his thoughts, intentions and projections in the future. A certain period of time passes, after which the speaker wants to recapture for someone else, as exactly as possible, the state of his thinking at that moment. The only changes in the text, therefore, are of verbal tense: present is transformed into

Двайсет и втори урок / Lesson 22

imperfect, and future is transformed into future in the past. To make these correspondences clearer, the relevant verb forms are underlined and the sentences numbered.

NON-PAST time frame

1. <u>Чу́дя се</u> какво́ да пра́вя.
   I wonder what I should do.
2. То́лкова неща́ <u>и́мам</u> да довъ́рша, преди́ да зами́на!
   I have so many things to get done before my departure!
3. <u>Тря́бва</u> про́сто да запо́чна с не́що.
   I simply have to start somewhere.
4. <u>Ще оти́да</u> пъ́рво до ба́нката,
   First I'll go to the bank
5. къде́то <u>ще си обменя́</u> пари́те,
   where I'll change some money,
6. и <u>ще ку́пя</u> пода́ръци.
   and [then] I'll buy some presents.
7. <u>Ня́ма да мо́га</u> да се оба́дя на Мари́на,
   I won't have time to phone Marina,
8. напра́во <u>ще се отби́я</u> при не́я.
   so I'll just drop in on her.
9. <u>Ще си поговори́м</u> ма́лко,
   We'll talk for a bit
10. а по́сле <u>ще си тръ́гна.</u>
    and then I'll leave.
11. Мно́го ми <u>се хо́ди</u> с не́я на конце́рт та́зи ве́чер,
    I really want to go to the concert with her this evening,
12. но <u>ня́ма да и́мам</u> вре́ме.
    but I'm not going to have the time.

PAST time frame

1. <u>Чу́дех се</u> какво́ да пра́вя.
   I was wondering what to do.
2. То́лкова неща́ <u>и́мах</u> да довъ́рша, преди́ да зами́на!
   I had so many things to get done before my departure!
3. <u>Тря́бваше</u> про́сто да запо́чна с не́що.
   I simply had to start somewhere.
4. <u>Щях да оти́да</u> пъ́рво до ба́нката,
   First I was going to go to the bank
5. къде́то <u>щях да си обменя́</u> пари́те,
   where I was going to change some money,
6. и <u>щях да ку́пя</u> пода́ръци.
   and [then] I was going to buy some presents.
7. <u>Ня́маше да мо́га</u> да се оба́дя на Мари́на,
   I wouldn't have had the time to phone Marina,
8. напра́во <u>щях да се отби́я</u> при не́я.
   so I was just going to drop in on her.
9. <u>Щя́хме да си поговори́м</u> ма́лко,
   We would have talked for a bit,
10. а по́сле <u>щях да си тръ́гна.</u>
    and then I would have left.
11. Мно́го ми <u>се хо́деше</u> с не́я на конце́рт та́зи ве́чер,
    I really wanted to go to the concert with her that evening,
12. но <u>ня́маше да и́мам</u> вре́ме.
    but I wouldn't have had the time.

In the "real time" of the moment of speech, the speaker usually knows whether or not these events have occurred as predicted. This is irrelevant to a narration of the above sort, however, whose only purpose is to recapture the moment exactly as it was. Nevertheless, as the English translation suggests, it is hard for a speaker to completely ignore his or her present knowledge (of whether or not the event happened as intended or predicted).

Thus, there are often several additional elements of meaning present in any instance of the future in the past tense. One or more of the following may contribute to the "meaning" of this tense:

-- whether or not the event actually happened as predicted;
-- if it did not happen (which is usually the case), how close it came to happening;
-- the degree of the speaker's expectation that it would happen (and consequently, of his surprise or disappointment);
-- the degree of his intention to make the event happen after all;
-- the nature of his speculation about why the event failed to happen.

22.4. The future in the past as an expression of surprise or disappointment

Sometimes an unexpected event almost happens, and the future in the past is used to express the speaker's surprise and (sometimes) relief at the "near miss".

Щях да забравя! Добре, че ми каза навреме.	I almost forgot! It's good you told me in time.
За малко щях да падна.	I nearly fell.

The first speaker above was reminded in time of something important he nearly forgot, and the second speaker managed to regain her balance (and not fall). The future in the past here gives a very vivid picture of the moment immediately prior to an action that almost happened but did not.

This tense can also convey this same vividness even if the event did happen. In the following, for instance, a speaker locates the time of a past event with reference to his own imminent action:

Когато той дойде, тъкмо щях да излизам.	I was just on the verge of leaving when he arrived.

The implication again is of a "near miss". Whether or not the speaker then continued with his intentions to go out is not relevant; what is important is that he had not done so yet. (In the larger context of speech, of course, the result would be clear.)

Sometimes a speaker uses the future in the past to express his or her disappointment upon realizing that an expected event has not taken place. In such cases, the future in the past can even carry a tinge of accusation. For instance:

Нали щеше да ни чака?	I thought he was going to wait for us! [= Wasn't he going to wait for us?]

| Áз бях с впечатле́ние, че щя́ха да до́йдат два́ма америка́нски студе́нти. | I was under the impression that two American students were coming to see me. |
| Ти́ нали́ до сутринта́ ня́маше ни́що да яде́ш? | I thought you weren't going to eat another thing till morning! [= Wasn't it the case that you weren't going to eat till morning?] |

The meaning of such a sentence can also include the speaker's underlying intention to make the event happen after all. For instance, if someone has not returned a book as promised, the following can serve not only as a statement of surprise but also as a "gentle reminder":

| Нали́ ще́ше дне́с да ми въ́рнеш та́зи кни́га? | Weren't you going to get that book back to me today? |

22.5. The future in the past in conditional constructions

Probably the most common usage of the future in the past is in a conditional sentence, in which the speaker offers his interpretation of a sequence of causation.

| Ще́ше да е по́-добре́, ако бе́ше бо́лен. | It would be better if he had been sick. |

A conditional sentence consists of a prediction of the nature "if A then B". If a speaker believes there to be a causal relationship between A and B, and sees that A is the case, then he will predict that B will follow. Note that the prediction "B will follow", is phrased in the future tense. Thus:

present	*future*
ако ста́ва А	ще ста́не Б
If A happens,	then B will happen.

If one shifts this entire construction from the non-past into the past, according to the schema given earlier, one has

imperfect	*future in the past*
ако ста́ваше А	ще́ше да ста́не Б
If A were to happen,	then B would happen.

Двайсет и втори урок / Lesson 22

Many conditional sentences in Bulgarian follow the pattern

IF *[imperfect]*, THEN *[future in the past]*.

This pattern is most frequently found in sentences where the prior condition described constitutes a state. For instance:

Ако знаех, че ми има нещо, щях да взема мерки предварително.	If I had known there was something wrong with me, I would have done something about it earlier.
Ако бях още болен, щях ли да се разхождам така?	If I were still ill, would I be out walking around like this?
Ако можехме, щяхме да отидем.	If we could have, we would have gone.
Ако не беше студено, цветята нямаше да измръзнат.	If it hadn't been [so] cold, the flowers wouldn't have frozen.
Ако не искахме, нямаше да излезем.	If we hadn't wanted to, we wouldn't have gone out.

If the prior condition is a completed action, however, it is usually expressed in the past anterior. The following pattern then obtains:

past anterior	*future in the past*
ако беше се случило А	щеше да стане Б
If A had happened,	then B would have happened.

The prediction continues to be expressed by the future in the past. For instance:

Сигурно щеше да спи до довечера, ако не бях се обадила.	If I had not called, he would certainly have slept through till this evening.
Той щеше да умре, ако не бях се върнала бързо.	He would have died if I hadn't come back right away.

Двайсет и втори урок / Lesson 22

EXERCISES

I. Rewrite the following passage to express a point of reference further in the future. Begin with: Ще се стара́ем да сме стана́ли ...

      Стара́ем се сутринта́ да ста́нем ра́но, но от о́пит зна́ем, че ко́лкото и да е ра́но, Ми́рко е ста́нал ве́че. Нали́ слъ́нцето ве́че е изгря́ло?! Събра́л е дърва́, накла́л е о́гъня и е сва́рил вода́ за кафе́то. Ку́чето съ́що се е събу́дило. Гле́да го пре́дано в очи́те и върти́ опа́шка. То е, защо́то то́й му е да́л вку́сен ко́кал -- или мо́же би́ про́сто от о́бич? Простре́ните на въже́то дре́хи са изсъ́хнали. То́й е почи́стил ка́лните обу́вки. Оста́ва са́мо да изпи́ем кафе́то, да се качи́м в ло́дката и да поте́глим.

II. Rewrite the following passage to express a point of reference further in the past. Begin with: Зна́ех ...

      Зна́м, че и то́зи де́н ще бъ́де като дру́гите. Ще ста́нем ра́но, ще заку́сим и ще провери́м и́ма ли писма́ за на́с. По́сле деца́та ще оти́дат на учи́лище, а възра́стните -- на ра́бота. Са́мо а́з (ко́тката) ще оста́на да скуча́я сами́чка. Ми́шки ве́че ня́колко ме́сеца ня́ма, а врабче́тата са дале́че. Ня́ма и да се опи́твам да хва́на ня́кое. Пъ́рво, те́ са мно́го дале́че. И второ́ -- не са́ вку́сни, ако ги яде́ш с пера́та. Ще лежа́ на кили́ма и ще ча́кам ня́кой да се прибере́ вкъ́щи.

III. Complete the sentences, using one of the following verbs: пи́там, проверя́, помо́гна, измръ́зна, ча́кам, оба́дя се, до́йда.

1. Ако не бя́ха то́лкова си́гурни в успе́ха си, те́ ...
2. Ако не зна́еш пъ́тя, ...
3. Ако ги бя́хме пока́нили, те́ ...
4. Ако оти́дат ня́кой пъ́т отно́во та́м, те́ ...
5. Мно́го е студе́но. Ако бя́хме ку́пили цветя́, те́ ...
6. Ако се бе́ше объ́рнал към те́бе за по́мощ, ти́ ...
7. Ако зна́я, че ще до́йдеш, а́з ....

Двайсет и втори урок / Lesson 22

ADDITIONAL GRAMMAR NOTES

22.6. Kinship terminology, continued

Basic kinship terminology, learned in Lesson 10, is for the most part parallel to that of English. There is greater complexity in the system of aunts, uncles and in-laws, however. This is because Bulgarian specifies not only the type of relationship but also the blood-line. For aunts and uncles it is necessary to specify *whose* sister (or brother), and for in-laws it is necessary to specify *whose* parents (or siblings).

Many Bulgarians now use a simplified version of the system given below. If the relatives in question are considered part of a Bulgarian's immediate family, however, s/he will probably know and use the more precise form. The separate forms for parents-in-law are distinguished by everyone.

relationship	*Bulgarian term*	*English term*
father's sister; mother's sister	ле́ля	aunt
father's brother's wife	стри́нка	aunt
mother's brother's wife	ву́йна	aunt
father's brother	чи́чо	uncle
mother's brother	ву́йчо	uncle
mother's (or father's) sister's husband	сва́ко	uncle
husband's father	све́към	father-in-law
wife's father	тъст	father-in-law
husband's mother	свекъ́рва	mother-in-law
wife's mother	тъ́ща	mother-in-law
daughter's husband	зет	son-in-law
son's wife	снаха́	daughter-in-law
sister's husband	зет	brother-in-law
wife's sister's husband	баджана́к	brother-in-law
wife's brother	шу́рей	brother-in-law
husband's brother	де́вер	brother-in-law
brother's wife	снаха́	sister-in-law
husband's sister	зъ́лва	sister-in-law
wife's sister	балдъ́за	sister-in-law
wife's brother's wife	шурена́йка	sister-in-law
husband's brother's wife	етъ́рва	sister-in-law

Note that there is an interesting overlap in the terms **снаха́** and **зет**, which cross generations. **Снаха́** refers to the wife of either one's son or brother, and **зет** refers to the husband of either one's daughter or sister.

Двайсет и втори урок / Lesson 22

SAMPLE SENTENCES

1. Когáто се върнем вкъщи, тóй ще е пригóтвил вечéрята.
2. Тръгнéте рáно. Когáто слънцето изгрéе, вие ще сте стигнали върхá на планинáта.

3. Мнóго сте далéче. Децáта ще са порáснали, преди да се накáним да дóйдем пáк при вáс.
4. Рáно е. НЯма да са заспáли, когáто се обáдим.

5. Мóжем да се обáдим и пó-късно. Тé нЯма да са заспáли.
6. Гóстите се бáвят, ще сме изпили винóто и изЯли слáдките, когáто дóйдат.

7. Нали ти щéше да хóдиш в Бългáрия?
8. Сиренето щéше отдáвна да се свърши, ако всички го ядЯха.

9. Детéто дръпна покривката и вáзата за мáлко щéше да пáдне.
10. Всичко щéше да е Ясно, ако го бéше обяснил като хóрата.

11. НЯмаше ли да ти е мъчно, ако не бéше дошъл с нáс на концéрта?
12. Ако цветЯта не бЯха увéхнали, нЯмаше да ги изхвърлят.

13. Ако се бéше подгóтвила, щéше да се предстáви пó-добрé на изпита.
14. Тáзи срéща щéше да се състои утре, нали?

15. В тéхния клáс ти щéше да си нáй-висóката. Другите момичета в тóзи клáс са пó-ниски.

16. Ако не бéше избухнала войнáта, всичко щéше да бъде съвсéм различно.
17. Елá в пéт часá. Áз тъкмо ще съм свършил рáбота.

Двайсет и втори урок / Lesson 22

SENTENCES FOR TRANSLATION

1. Come at five if you want. Only I won't have finished the job yet. I was going to start it earlier, but Ivancho called and we chatted a while. We will have to change the deadline.

2. Had I known he was going to slip, I would have grabbed him. He might at least have informed me of his intentions. Then I wouldn't have stepped on him, and he wouldn't have fallen.

3. There are so many words for different relatives in Bulgarian. I wouldn't even have known he was my "badzhanak" if he hadn't told me.

4. I was going to set up a meeting with her for tomorrow, but everything depends on when she will get back from Varna. She wasn't going to come back until Friday, but I hear it's been raining a lot there so perhaps she will arrive sooner.

5. I have the deepest respect for our teacher. He has made a great impression on me.

6. I was going to sit here and prepare for the test. But if that bothers you, I can leave.

7. I'm afraid the meeting will not be long enough. We won't even have shaken hands yet and it will be time for us to leave.

Melnik, in the Pirin Mountains

READING SELECTION

Алеко Константинов, "Бра́тя славя́ни в дале́чна Аме́рика"

Бя́хме се запъ́тили да пи́ем по една́ би́ра. Заведе́ ни на́шият чичеро́не в едно́ до́ста обши́рно и чи́стичко помеще́ние. Вси́чките ма́си бя́ха пра́зни, ако и да ня́маше 9 часа́ вечерта́. Около бюфе́та и́маше постоя́нно движе́ние; посети́тели дохо́ждат, поръ́чат си би́ра или уи́ски, изпи́ят, запла́тят и се оттегля́т мълчали́во. Сла́ва бо́гу, че та́зи пи́вница не бе́ше чи́сто америка́нска, а то и ни́е ня́маше да и́маме удово́лствието да се разполо́жим около ма́сата и със сла́дка при́казка да си изпи́ем по ня́коя ча́ша би́ра, а тря́бваше, като оне́зи не́ми хла́дни посети́тели, като че изку́ствени, човекоподо́бни маши́ни, да се изпра́вим при бюфе́та, ка́кто у нас пра́вят пияни́ците, и мълчали́во да си изпра́зним ча́шите. В пи́вниците, съдъ́ржани от америка́нци, ня́ма места́ за ся́дане; вся́ка консума́ция ста́ва пред бюфе́та; та́м са насла́гани всевъзмо́жни заку́ски на разположе́нието на посети́телите безпла́тно. Ако си с дебели́чки очи́, мо́жеш да изпи́еш са́мо една́ би́ра, а да се нахра́ниш хубави́чко със заку́ски и ще пра́виш та́зи "иконо́мия" дотога́ва, дока́то еди́н де́н стопа́нинът не те́ улови́ за яка́та и ти помо́гне да изхвъ́рнеш из врата́та.

За на́ше ща́стие стопа́нинът на та́зи пи́вница бе́ше не́мец, не успя́л още да се американизи́ра. Ни́е забеля́захме, че ра́зни хо́ра дохо́ждат, пи́ят и си оти́ват, но еди́н от тя́х постоя́нно стърче́ше при бюфе́та и все́ си сръ́бва по ча́ша и се вслу́шва в на́шия ра́зговор. По едно́ вре́ме дойде́ да го пови́ка едно́ моми́че. То́й ѝ ка́за не́що по англи́йски, па приба́ви "Иди́ си, бо́га ти!" То́й наро́чно пу́сна ти́я ду́ми като въ́дица, за коя́то ни́е ту́такси се закачи́хме.

-- Ви́е сте съ́рбин? -- попи́та го до́кторът.
-- Ест, србин, и ви сте срби? * -- полюбопи́тсвува то́й кра́йно зара́дван.
-- Бъ́лгари сме.
-- Све едно́, ща су срби, ща су бугари -- брача словени! **

-- и бе́з да ча́ка покана́, то́й се́дна при на́с, като пода́де ка́ртичката си.

Ока́за се, че е бана́тски съ́рбин, Неде́лкович; след дъ́лги скита́ния по Евро́па дошъ́л в Ню Йо́рк преди́ четирина́йсет годи́ни, кожуха́рин, же́нен за немки́ня. Засмя́н до уши́ от ра́дост, че се сре́щнал с "бра́ча", то́й не зна́еше ка́к да изка́же удово́лствието си. Преди́ вси́чко залови́ се да че́рпи. Разка́за си на́две-на́три биогра́фията: спо́мняше си епизо́ди от живо́та, осо́бено от дети́нството. Четирина́йсет годи́ни, уверя́ваше ни то́й, не би́л проду́мал по сръ́бски, та сега́ като че и́скаше да се наприка́зва за це́ли 14 годи́ни. Не му́ млъ́кнаха уста́та. И на вся́ка фра́за пи́таше дали́ вя́рно се изразя́ва, проверя́ваше дали́ не е́ забра́вил ро́дния си ези́к. Ця́л ро́й впечатле́ния, кои́то са спа́ли то́лкова годи́ни покри́ти с но́ви впечатле́ния, сега́ се пробу́диха и забръмча́ха през уста́та му. Спо́мни си то́й за ра́зни обича́и, о́бреди, сва́тби,

---

* Да, съ́рбин, и ви́е ли сте съ́рби?
** Все́ едно́ -- съ́рби ли са́, бъ́лгари ли са́. Бра́тя славя́ни!

почна да проверява дали не е забравил молитвите по славянски, запя най-сетне "Христос воскресе" за крайно удивление на американците в пивницата.

Стопанинът, едър, красив, във висша степен добродушен и вечно засмян баварец, и жена му, една пълна, бяла саксонка -- преситени от желязната студенина на американците, възхитиха се от сантименталностите на доволния до блаженство бай Неделкович и с позволение се присъединиха към нашата маса, която любезната госпожа затрупа с всевъзможни закуски. България, Сърбия, Бавария и Саксония си подадоха ръце, за да отразят с общи сили американски егоизъм и студенина. И победиха....

Както Неделкович, тъй и баварецът са вече американски граждани. Те са откъснати от отечествената си почва и виждаш, че искрено, с гордост се наричат американци. На бившето си отечество гледат като на нещо останало някъде там далече, в мъглата. Интересите на щата и на града Ню Йорк са и техни интереси. Те винаги четат вестници и са постоянно в течение на американските работи, като не забравят и Европа.

Адаптирано от Алеко Константинов, До Чикаго и назад.

Sofia City Baths

Двайсет и втори урок / Lesson 22

GLOSSARY

ако и да	even though
американизи́рам	Americanize
бава́рец	Bavarian
баджана́к	brother-in-law (wife's sister's husband)
балдъ́за	sister-in-law (wife's sister)
бана́тски	of the Banat region
ба́нка	bank
безпла́тен	free of charge, gratis
биогра́фия	biography
блаженство́	bliss, beatitude
бути́лка	bottle
бъ́деще в ми́налото (вре́ме)	future in the past (tense)
бъ́деще предвари́телно (вре́ме)	future anterior (tense)
бюфе́т	sideboard, buffet, refreshment bar
в после́дния моме́нт	at the last minute
в тече́ние на	informed about
вои́стина	in truth *(archaic Slavonic)*
вои́стина воскре́се	in truth Christ has risen (ritual Easter formula)
воскре́се	arose *(3sg. aorist, archaic Slavonic)*
впечатле́ние	impression
врабче́	sparrow
всевъзмо́жен	all sorts of, every possible
ву́йна	aunt (mother's brother's wife)
във ви́сша сте́пен	eminently, in the highest degree
въ́дица	fish-hook; fishing rod
въже́	rope, line
възпрепя́тствувам	prevent, hinder
възхища́вам се / възхитя́ се	admire, be enraptured by
въртя́	turn, spin
въртя́ опа́шка	wag tail
гле́дна то́чка	point of view
го́рдост	pride
градска́ гради́на	town garden; central park
гра́дски	town, municipal; urban
гра́жданин	citizen
гъ́мза	particular sort of dark red wine
дебе́л	thick, fat
де́вер	brother-in-law (husband's brother)
дети́нство	childhood
добродушен	good-natured, kind-hearted
дово́лен до блаженство́	blissfully content
довъ́ршвам / довъ́рша (-иш)	finish off, bring to a close
до́ста	fairly
дотога́ва	until then, by that time
дотога́ва, дока́то	until
дръ́пвам / дръ́пна	pull, tug
егои́зъм	egotism
епизо́д	episode
етъ́рва	sister-in-law (husband's brother's wife)
желе́зен, желя́зна	iron, steel-like
забръмча́вам / забръмча́ (-и́ш)	begin to buzz
за́ек	rabbit
зака́чвам се / закача́ се (-и́ш)	get caught on
заку́ска	hors d'oeuvre
зала́вям се / заловя́ се	catch hold of; set about
запла́щам / заплатя́	pay, pay up
запъ́твам се / запъ́тя се	set out, be off
запъхтя́н	out of breath
запя́вам / запе́я	begin to sing, break into song
засмя́н	smiling
засмя́н до уши́	grinning from ear to ear
зет, -ят *(pl. зе́тьове)*	son-in-law; brother-in-law (sister's husband)
зъ́лва	sister-in-law (husband's sister)

Двайсет и втори урок / Lesson 22

из	out of	наприка́звам се	talk one's fill, talk to one's heart's content
избу́хвам / избу́хна	burst, explode	насла́гам / насло́жа (-иш)	put out, lay
избу́хна война́	war broke out		
избя́гвам / избя́гам	run away, get loose	насла́гам всевъзмо́жни заку́ски	serve all sorts of snacks
изгря́вам / изгре́я	rise, come up (of the sun)	нахра́нвам се / нахра́ня се	eat one's fill
изка́звам / изка́жа (-еш)	express; reveal	не́мец	German (male)
изку́ствен	artificial, unnatural	немки́ня	German (female)
измръ́звам / измръ́зна	freeze, die from cold	ни́сък	low, short, of small stature
изпра́звам / изпра́зня	empty, drain	ням (pl. не́ми)	mute, silent, dumb
изразя́вам се вя́рно	say [it] right	о́бич, -та́	love
изсъ́хвам / изсъ́хна	dry out, become dry	обме́ням / обменя́	exchange
изхвъ́рквам / изхвъ́ркна	fly out	о́бред	ritual, ceremony
изхвъ́рквам из врата́та	fly out the door	обши́рен	wide, extensive, spacious
изхвъ́рлям / изхвъ́рля	throw out, eject	ока́звам се / ока́жа се (-еш)	turn out, prove to be
иконо́мия	economy, saving	опи́чам / опека́ (-че́ш)	roast, bake
и́скрен	sincere, genuine	оте́чествен	of one's native land; patriotic
ка́лен	muddy	оте́чество	native land
ка́ртичка	business card, visiting card	откъ́свам / откъ́сна	tear, break off, uproot
като́ хо́рата	properly	отме́ням / отменя́	abolish, cancel
кожуха́р (archaic form кожуха́рин)	furrier	отразя́вам / отразя́	refute
		оттегля́м се / оттегля́ се	withdraw, retire
консума́ция	consumption, use		
кра́йно удивле́ние	utter amazement	па	and, but
краси́в	beautiful, handsome; noble	перо́	feather
		пи́вница	pub, saloon
кюфте́	meatball	пода́ваме си ръце́	[we] join hands
		подхлъ́звам се / подхлъ́зна се	slip, trip
ло́дка	boat, dinghy	позволе́ние	permission
млъ́квам / млъ́кна	fall silent, hush up	покри́вам / покри́я	cover, overlay
моли́тва	prayer	покри́вка	cover (tablecloth, bedspread)
мъгла́	mist, fog		
мълчали́в	silent, tacit	полюбопи́тствувам	inquire, show curiosity
		помеще́ние	room; premises
на гла́дно сърце́	on an empty stomach	посети́тел	visitor; patron, customer
на споко́йствие	at leisure	поте́глям / поте́гля	set out, set off
на тя́хно разположе́ние	at their disposal, available to them	по́чва	soil, ground
		почи́ствам / почи́стя	clean, clean up
на́две-на́три	helter-skelter, in a disorganized manner	пре́дан	devoted, faithful
нака́нвам се / нака́ня се	get round to, find time to	представя́м се / предста́вя се	arise; introduce oneself
накла́ждам / наклада́	make, light	преси́тен	satiated; fed up
		приба́вям / приба́вя	add, supplement
накла́ждам о́гън	light a fire	присъединя́вам се / присъединя́ се	join, associate with
нали́вам / нале́я	pour out, fill [a glass]		

Двайсет и втори урок / Lesson 22

пробу́ждам се / пробу́дя се	awaken, be aroused	студенина́	cold, frigidity
проду́мвам / проду́мам	utter, say a word	стърча́ (-и́ш)	stand out; hang about
		съдържа́м	contain, hold
(не би́л проду́мал)	had not uttered *(renarrated mood, see L. 24-25)*	сърби́н	Serb (male)
		те́зи дни́	one of these days
		това́ тря́бва да се поле́е	this calls for a drink
пъ́лен	plump	то́чка	point, dot
ра́зни	various, diverse	ту́такси	immediately, right off
ра́зни хо́ра	all sorts of people	уверя́вам / уверя́	assure
разпола́гам се / разполо́жа се (-иш)	settle down	увя́хвам / увя́хна	wither, fade
		угово́рен	stipulated, agreed-upon
разположе́ние	situation, disposition	удивле́ние	amazement
ро́ден ези́к	native language	уи́ски	whiskey
ро́й, ро́ят (*pl.* ро́еве)	swarm, host	ула́вям / уловя́	catch, seize
ръку́вам се	shake hands	фра́за	phrase
с впечатле́ние съм	be left with the impression	хва́щам под ръка́	take [someone's] arm
		хла́ден	cool; wintry
с дебе́ли очи́	shameless	Христо́с	Christ
саксо́нка	Saxon (female)	Христо́с воскре́се	Christ has risen (Easter formula)
сантимента́лност	sentimentality		
сва́ко	uncle (aunt's husband)		
свъ́ршвам се / свъ́рша се (-иш)	end, run out, sell out	чи́стичък	neat
		чичеро́не	cicerone, guide
ски́тане (*pl.* -ния)	wandering	човекоподо́бен	anthropoid
скуча́я	be bored		
сла́дка при́казка	pleasant chat	шуре́й	brother-in-law (wife's brother)
сла́дки	pastries, sweetmeats		
снаха́	daughter-in-law; sister-in-law (brother's wife)	шурена́йка	sister-in-law (wife's brother's wife)
споко́йствие	calm, quiet	ща́стие	happiness, good fortune
сръ́бвам / сръ́бна	take a nip, sip		
сръ́бски	Serbian *(adj.)*	яка́	collar
стопа́нин	owner, proprietor		

Двайсет и втори урок / Lesson 22

CULTURAL COMMENTARY

City life: outdoor cafes

The Crystal cafe (кафе́ Криста́л) is situated in the center of town at the corner of Rakovska street and Tsar Osvoboditel boulevard. It is both an indoor and outdoor restaurant which borders on the main city park. The outdoor garden cafe is an extremely pleasant place to take afternoon coffee and sweets, particularly in the summer months.

Food and drink: wine

Several regions in Bulgaria are known for their excellent red wines. One of these is the area near the southwestern Bulgarian town of Melnik (Ме́лник); the best wines from here are from the Merlot and Cabernet Sauvignon grape varietals. The area around Haskovo (Ха́сково) in southeastern Bulgaria also produces very fine wines. There is also a dark, rich red wine grape which is apparently unique to Bulgaria, called gămza (гъмза), grown in northern Bulgaria. Two areas which produce this wine are Novo Selo (Но́во село́) in northwestern Bulgaria, and Suhindol (Су́хиндол) in northeastern Bulgaria. The high quality of Bulgarian wines has yet to be discovered by importers in most western countries.

Literature: Aleko Konstantinov

The name of Aleko Konstantinov (1863-1897), despite his relatively brief life, is known to nearly all Bulgarians through his lively and irreverent writings. An inveterate traveler, Konstantinov published spirited and engaging descriptions of his travels throughout Bulgaria, Europe and across the Atlantic. The best-known of these is До Чикаго и назад ("To Chicago and Back" [1894]), in which he describes his adventures on the way to the 1893 Chicago exposition via Paris, New York and Niagara Falls. While in the U.S., Konstantinov was simultaneously entranced by the technological advances and repelled by what he perceived as the lack of Balkan, personal warmth. His most famous literary creation, however, is the parvenu Bay Ganyo, the corrupted nouveau city dweller who has lost his traditional roots but has not (and most likely never will) become "civilized". Through the adventures of this character, hypocrisy of all sorts is unmasked. Konstantinov, who had worked within the legal system and refused to take part in widespread bribing and corruption, was such a sharp critic of governmental failings that when he was assassinated "by accident" (the bullet, from the gun of a paid killer, had been intended for his traveling companion), many who had suffered his critiques said that the bullet had in fact been well placed.

Geography: Banat

The Banat is a region encompassing westernmost Romania, northeastern Serbia (covering part of the former autonomous province of Vojvodina), and a small part of Hungary. The large number of Bulgarians living north of the Danube in Romanian Banat (who moved there in the 17th and 18th centuries and have retained their language and customs to this day) are called the Banat Bulgarians; Serbs living in the Banat (on both sides of the political border) are called the Banat Serbs. Although many different languages are spoken in the Banat, the customs, music and other characteristics of folk life are very similar throughout the region.

History

Serbs and Bulgarians share a common history on many points, and although the two languages are clearly distinct from one another, there are sufficient similarities that with good will Serbs and Bulgarians can usually understand one another's speech. Both peoples spent many centuries under the so-called "Ottoman yoke", both are of the Orthodox Christian religion, and both owe much of their sense of identity during the Ottoman occupation to their religion and its practices. Church rituals, and the archaic Slavic language (called simply "Slavonic" [славянски]) in which these rituals were carried out, were especially important in this maintenance of identity. Prayers, and especially formulas like Христо́с воскре́се ("Christ has risen") and the ritual answer Вои́стина воскре́се ("Indeed he has risen") play a major role, especially as Easter is the central festival of the year for Orthodox Christians (as opposed to Catholics and Protestants, for whom Christmas is the central festival).

LESSON 23

DIALOGUE

Под сия́ещото слъ́нце на ле́тния следо́бед

// На ъ́гъла на Патриа́рх Евти́мий и Рако́вска Та́ня и Павли́на насти́гат Дими́тър и Миле́на. Под сия́ещото слъ́нце на ле́тния следо́бед младоже́нците изгле́ждат осо́бено щастли́ви. Ку́четата ве́село джа́фкат, преска́чайки се. Деца́та се зали́ват от смя́х. //

Таня: Чу́вам, че не сте́ могли́ да прису́ствувате на сва́тбата на сина́ си?

Павлина: Уви́, разболя́х се. Това́ ще́ше да бъ́де най-ва́жният де́н в мо́я живо́т, а а́з го прека́рах в бо́лницата. Бя́х си уши́ла специа́лно за целта́ бя́л ле́нен костю́м. Щя́ха да ме зака́рат до Ва́рна едни́ прия́тели с ме́рцедеса.

Димитър: Те́зи дни́ ще ста́нат сни́мките от сва́тбата и ще ти ги пока́жа. С те́бе ще́ше да е по́-ве́село, но какво́ да се пра́ви. Съдба́...

Павлина: А́з съм то́лкова фотогени́чна. Щя́х да бъ́да мно́го ху́бава на сни́мките, ако бя́х сти́гнала до Ва́рна.

Милена: Помисли́ си, ма́йко, ко́лко по́-стра́шно ще́ше да бъ́де, ако кри́зата се бе́ше случи́ла по пъ́тя.

Таня: Каква́ кри́за?

Павлина: Апандиси́т. Присви́ ме в деня́ преди́ сва́тбата. Взе́ха ме в бо́лницата по спе́шност и ме опери́раха о́ще съ́щия де́н. Ако зна́ех, че ми и́ма не́що, щя́х да взе́ма ме́рки предвари́телно.

Таня: Възпале́нието на апандиси́та мо́же да доведе́ до мно́го неприя́тни после́дици. Ра́двайте се, че сте се отърва́ли е́втино.

Павлина: Дока́то бя́х в бо́лницата, съсе́дката се гри́жеше за Ба́рт. То́й то́лкова се бе́ше изму́чил без ме́не, че ще́ше да умре́, ако не бя́х се въ́рнала бъ́рзо. Мно́го стра́да, кога́то ме ня́ма. Пъ́к и съсе́дката не зна́е с какво́ да го хра́ни. Да му да́ва пи́лешки дро́бчета, мо́ля ви се. Ако бя́х прека́рала о́ще ня́колко дни́ в бо́лницата, щя́х да го загу́бя.

Таня: Сега́ по́-добре́ ли се чу́вствувате?

Двайсет и трети урок / Lesson 23

Павлина: Добре́ съм, благодаря́. Ако не бя́х добре́, щя́х ли да се разхо́ждам по Рако́вска? А́з си гле́дам здра́вето. Здра́вето е най-голя́мото съкро́вище на чове́ка.

Милена: Докато го и́маш, не му́ обръ́щаш внима́ние, но горко́ ти, ако го изгу́биш.

Димитър: А бе́, то, го́лото здра́ве си е жи́ва бо́лест. Без пари́ живо́тът не му́ се усла́жда на чове́к, ко́лкото и да е здра́в.

Таня: Ако си здра́в да рабо́тиш, и пари́ ще има́ш.

Милена: Така́ си е ...

Таня: А сва́тбеното ви пътеше́ствие къде́ бе́ше?

Милена: На́шите ку́мове и́мат ви́ла в Балчи́к, на брега́ на море́то. Вера́ндата е построе́на така́, че по вся́ко вре́ме на деня́ и́ма ся́нка. Мо́же да се хо́ди по ба́нски до пла́жа - то́й е под сами́те прозо́рци. Прека́рахме та́м де́сет дни́.

Димитър: Миле́на така́ се ра́дваше на слъ́нцето, че ако не бя́х я прибра́л наси́ла на ся́нка, ще́ше да е изгоря́ла до вечерта́. И така́ на дру́гия де́н бе́ше черве́на като ра́к и се наложи́ да я ма́жа с ки́село мля́ко.

Таня: За пъ́рви пъ́т ли бя́хте в Балчи́к?

Димитър: Преди годи́ни щя́х да лету́вам та́м с едни́ прия́тели, но не́що ста́на и пла́новете ни не се́ осъществи́ха.

Милена: А́з съм хо́дила ня́колко пъ́ти и зна́ех, че на Ми́тко ще му харе́са.

Димитър: А́з то́лкова мно́го ка́ктуси, ко́лкото в Ботани́ческата гради́на та́м, не бя́х ви́ждал събра́ни на едно́ мя́сто.

Павлина: Ви́жте деца́та и ку́четата ко́лко дале́че отидо́ха. Докато сти́гнем до гради́нката при Криста́л, те́ ще са пи́ли вода́ от чешма́та. А Ба́рт не би́ва да пи́е студе́на вода́.

Димитър: Не́ка да побъ́рзаме тога́ва. Да ги насти́гнем.

Двайсет и трети урок / Lesson 23

BASIC GRAMMAR

23.1. Review of participles

Participles are adjectives which are formed from verbs. They function as adjectives but retain verbal meaning. There are three participles in Bulgarian, the past passive, the past active and the present active.

The past participles, learned in previous lessons, both refer to actions which have been completed. The usage of these two participles is summarized briefly below. The present active participle, which refers to actions that are in progress, will be learned in this lesson.

Past passive participle
The past passive participle is formed from the aorist stem of the verb. It can be formed from verbs of both aspects. It is used as an adjective, both attributively and predicatively. For example:

attributive
    Една добре облечена дама ни маха.   A well-dressed woman is waving to us.
predicative
    Тя е много добре облечена.   She is very well dressed.

It is also used in forming passive constructions. For example:

    Филмът ще бъде показан утре.   The film will be shown tomorrow.
    Това писмо е написано от самия директор.   This letter was written by the director himself.

Past active participle
The past active participle, otherwise known as the L-participle, is also formed from the aorist stem of the verb. Practically every verb stem can form the L-participle. Although this participle can be used as an attributive adjective, it is much more commonly used predicatively. For example:

attributive
    Зрелите плодове са винаги предпочитани.   Ripe fruits are always [to be] preferred.
predicative
    Тези плодове са много зрели.   These fruits are very ripe.

The primary use of the L-participle is in the various compound verbal tenses. For review, these are:

past indefinite
    Той го е свършил.   He's finished it.

past anterior
    Той вече го беше свършил,   He had already finished it when
        когато дойдохме.   we arrived.

future anterior
    Той ще го е свършил преди 5 ч.   He'll have finished it by 5 PM.

future anterior in the past (see below)
    Той щеше да го е свършил   He would have finished it by 5 PM.
        преди 5 ч.

23.2. The present active participle: formation and usage

The present active participle is used only adjectivally. It is formed from the present tense stem, of imperfective verbs only. To make the present active participle, add the suffix -щ- to the 3rd singular present of **a**-conjugation verbs and stem-stressed **e**-conjugation verbs.

For **и**-conjugation verbs, replace the theme vowel by -е-, and for all end-stressed verbs, replace the theme vowel by -я-. This vowel, spelled -а- after ч, ш or ж, does *not* alternate with -е- before the plural ending. Adjectival endings are then added.

3sg. present	**PRESENT ACTIVE PARTICIPLE**			
	masculine	*feminine*	*neuter*	*plural*
a-*conjugation*				
чак-а	чакащ	чакаща	чакащо	чакащи
вечер-я	вечерящ	вечеряща	вечерящо	вечерящи
e-*conjugation*				
зна-е	знаещ	знаеща	знаещо	знаещи
бъд-е	бъдещ	бъдеща	бъдещо	бъдещи
чет-е́	четящ	четяща	четящо	четящи
и-*conjugation*				
търс-и	търсещ	търсеща	търсещо	търсещи
нос-и	носещ	носеща	носещо	носещи
сед-и́	седящ	седяща	седящо	седящи
сп-и́	спящ	спяща	спящо	спящи

If the meaning of the verb includes the particle **се**, then this particle must always accompany the participle, following it directly.

Двайсет и трети урок / Lesson 23

The present participle describes an action in progress: the noun it modifies denotes the person who is performing the action. Sometimes it can be translated by an English adjectival form in "-ing"; more frequently, one must use either a verbal phrase or a noun which subsumes the verbal idea. Only in the case of the adjective бъдещ "future" does a participle correspond directly to an English adjective.

1. Той е бъдещ студент.	He's a future student.
2. Следващият месец е април.	The coming [= following] month is April.
3. Въртящата се врата беше постоянно в движение.	The revolving door was in constant motion.
4. Под сияещото слънце на летния следобед младоженците изглеждат особено щастливи.	In the bright sunlight [= shining sun] of a summer's afternoon, the newlyweds look particularly happy.
5. Движещите се отдясно коли имат предимство.	Cars [moving] on the right have the right of way.
6. Пишещият тези редове не знае по-нататъшната съдба на своите герои.	The writer of these lines [= the one writing these lines] knows nothing of the subsequent fate of his characters.
7. Познаваш ли седящия в ъгъла студент?	Do you know the student sitting in the corner?

In each case, the participle is grammatically equivalent to a relative clause. The list below gives the relative clauses which correspond to the participles used in the example sentences above. The difference between participles and relative clauses is not so much in meaning as in usage. Participles are used frequently in written and formal language, while in the spoken language the same meaning is expressed almost exclusively with relative clauses.

1. бъдещ студент.	[този,] който ще бъде студент
2. следващият месец	месецът, който следва
3. въртящата се врата	вратата, която се върти
4. сияещото слънце	слънцето, което сияе
5. движещите се отдясно коли	колите, които се движат отдясно
6. пишещият тези редове	[този,] който пише тези редове
7. седящия в ъгъла студент	студента*, който седи в ъгъла.

* [object form]

23.3. The verbal adverb

English has two different verb forms in "-ing": an adjective which modifies a noun (and corresponds to the Bulgarian present participle), and an adverb which modifies the main verbal phrase and expresses simultaneity of action with it. This, the English gerund, corresponds to the Bulgarian verbal adverb. For example:

English and Bulgarian present participle

| Прелистващият книгата случайно се натъкна на името си. | The person leafing through the book happened upon his own name. |

English gerund, Bulgarian verbal adverb

| Прелиствайки книгата, Иван случайно се натъкна на името си. | Leafing through the book, Ivan happened upon his own name. |

Like present participles, verbal adverbs are formed from the 3rd singular present tense form. The ending, -йки, is added directly to the 3sg form, with the important provision that и-verbs replace the theme vowel by -е. The verbal adverb is unchanging in form (as opposed to present participles, which add adjectival endings).

	3sg. present	**VERBAL ADVERB**
а-conjugation	чак-а	чакайки
	вечер-я	вечеряйки
е-conjugation	пиш-е	пишейки
	зна-е	знаейки
	чет-е́	четейки
и-conjugation	уч-и	учейки
	сед-и́	седейки

A verbal adverb expresses a time relation: the action it refers to is simultaneous with the one in the main clause. The same person must be performing both actions -- that of the verbal adverb and that of the main clause. In addition, the verbal adverb can only be used with reference to the subject of the sentence.

subject reference: verbal adverb possible

| Връщайки се обратно, ще отидем и там. | On our way back we'll go there too. |
| Обръщайки се назад, аз не мога да намеря грешка в неговото поведение. | Looking back [= as I look back on it], I can't find anything wrong in his behavior. |

| Те́ се опи́таха да напра́вят това́, пренебре́гвайки съве́та ни. | They tried to do it despite [ignoring] our advice. |
| Оти́вайки на поку́пки, сре́щнах Боря́на. | I met Boryana [as I was] on my way to the store. |

object reference: verbal adverb not possible

| Сре́щнахме ги като оти́ваха на поку́пки. | We met them as they were on their way to the store. |

23.4. The future anterior in the past tense

The future anterior describes an event in the future which the speaker predicts will be completed prior to another future event. For example:

| Кога́то се въ́рнем вкъ́щи, то́й ще е приго́твил вече́ря. | By the time we get home, he will have made dinner. |

That is, by the time event B (the return home) takes place, event A (the cooking of dinner) will have been completed.

Because of the complexity involved, it is not frequent that a speaker will cast such a prediction into the past. Nevertheless it can happen, and Bulgarian has a tense for it. The name of this tense, as expected, is the future anterior in the past (**бъ́деще предвари́телно в ми́налото**). In form, it is a mixture of the future anterior and the future in the past. The auxiliary is equivalent to that of the future in the past, and the conjugated verb is equivalent to that of the future anterior.

This tense occurs almost exclusively in conditional constructions, and usually with perfective verbs. Here are the forms, followed by an example of usage:

FUTURE ANTERIOR IN THE PAST

	affirmative	*negative*
1sg.	щя́х да съм проче́л	ня́маше да съм проче́л
2sg.	ще́ше да си проче́л	ня́маше да си проче́л
3sg.	ще́ше да е проче́л	ня́маше да е проче́л
1pl.	щя́хме да сме проче́ли	ня́маше да сме проче́ли
2pl.	щя́хте да сте проче́ли	ня́маше да сте проче́ли
3pl.	щя́ха да са проче́ли	ня́маше да са проче́ли

| Тя́ така́ се ра́дваше на слъ́нцето, че ако не бя́х я прибра́л наси́ла на ся́нка, ще́ше да е изгоря́ла до вечерта́. | She was so happy in the sun that if I had not forced her to come into the shade, she would have gotten completely burned by evening. |

Двајсет и трети урок / Lesson 23

23.5. Conditional constructions, continued

Conditional sentences take the form "if A, then B". The technical terms for these two parts of the sentence are:

```
PROTASIS    APODOSIS
  if A        then B
```

The following examples of conditional sentences will be split into these two halves, each of which will be designated by the corresponding abbreviation *(PRO or APO)*.

Conditional sentences make reference to three factors: time, reality of the condition, and likelihood of its fulfillment. Time can be past or non-past, the condition can be a real or an unreal one, and the hypothetical possibility of its fulfillment can be present or absent.

As an example, consider the following three English sentences (all of which concern the relationship between the presence of money in one's pocket and the ability to buy a ticket for a particular film) and note the choice of verbal tense and mood by which these meanings are expressed in English:

(1) English indicative

section of sentence   PRO   APO
tense   *present*   *future*
                        If I have the money **I'll go.**

Analysis of meaning   *Situational context*

Time: non-past | The time is now -- the film has not yet begun.
Condition: real | The speaker thinks it likely he might have the
Fulfillment: possible | money. Therefore it's possible he will go.

(2) English conditional

section of sentence   PRO   APO
tense   *past*   *conditional*
                        If I had the money **I would go.**

Analysis of meaning   *Situational context*

Time: non-past | The time is now -- the film has not yet begun.
Condition: unreal | The speaker doesn't believe he has the money.
Fulfillment: possible | However, should the money turn up from some-
                          | where, it's still conceivably possible for him to go.

Двайсет и трети урок / Lesson 23

(3) English past conditional

section of sentence	PRO	APO
tense	pluperfect	past conditional
	If I had had the money	**I would have gone.**

Analysis of meaning *Situational context*

Time:	past	The time is later -- the film is over. This fact,
Condition:	unreal	plus the verified fact of there having been no
Fulfilment:	impossible	money, makes it obvious both that the condition
		is unreal and its fulfillment is/was impossible.

Now consider the Bulgarian translation of these three sentences:

(1)

section of sentence	PRO	APO
tense	present	future
	Ако имам пари,	ще отида.

(2)-(3)

section of sentence	PRO	APO
tense	imperfect	future in the past
	Ако имах пари,	щях да отида.

The translations of (1) and (2) into Bulgarian are relatively straightforward: when the time frame of sentence (1) is moved into the past, the result is sentence (2). The parallel is even closer than the English terms suggest, because the English phrase "would go" carries the meaning of *both* conditional (as in "He *would go* if he could") and future in the past (as in "He said he *would go*").

But whereas English moves sentence (3) even further into the past, Bulgarian seems to make no distinction between present and past (and consequently real and unreal conditions). Yet in other instances, Bulgarian can and does make this distinction. Here is a conditional sentence in which the tenses appear to be parallel to English (3), in that they are both shifted further into the past.

section of sentence	APO	PRO
tense	future anterior in the past	past anterior
	Досега щяхме да сме умрели от студ,	ако не се бяхме сетили за старото одеяло.

meaning	We would have died of the cold by now if we hadn't remembered about that old blanket.

Двайсет и трети урок / Lesson 23

The differences between English and Bulgarian usage are not random but are rather a direct consequence of the underlying grammatical organization of each language. English conditionals are concerned more with the concept of past vs. present time, whereas Bulgarian ones are concerned more with particular verbal actions and the degree of boundedness inherent in them.

In other words, English gives precedence to tense but Bulgarian gives precedence to aspect (including the several ways in which boundedness can be included into the meaning of individual verbs). For instance, the general idea of the above sentence could also have been expressed as follows:

section of sentence	APO	PRO
tense	*future in the past*	*imperfect*
	Щя́хме да умре́м от сту́д,	ако ня́махме те́зи одея́ла.

meaning   We would have died of cold if we hadn't had these blankets.

The choice of tense in Bulgarian conditional sentences, therefore, depends upon the degree of specificity and boundedness inherent in the individual verb, and on the limitations of the time frame of the action. If the protasis concerns a general, unbounded idea (such as "having blankets"), the imperfect tense is usually chosen. But if it concerns a specific completed action (such as "having remembered [one had] a certain old blanket"), then the past anterior can be chosen.

Similarly, if the projected result expressed in the apodosis concerns a general idea (such as "dying of cold"), the future in the past is usually chosen. But if the speaker visualizes that scene vividly enough to see it in terms of two sequential actions ("we would have died [first action] by the time we had remembered [second action]"), then s/he can use the future anterior in the past in the apodosis. Indeed, Bulgarian speakers can also combine these possibilities. For instance:

section of sentence	PRO	APO
tense	*imperfect*	*future anterior in the past*
	Ако и́сках,	щя́х да съм дошла́ преди́ то́й да зами́не.

meaning   If I [had] wanted to, I would have come before he left.

section of sentence	PRO	APO
tense	*past anterior*	*future in the past*
	Ако бя́ха ми ка́зали навре́ме,	ня́маше да зами́на.

meaning   If they had told me on time, I wouldn't have left.

Again, the concept of "distancing" comes into play. The further the condition (or its potential fulfillment) is distanced from the speaker, the more complex the tense of its expression. In Bulgarian, however, "distancing" is viewed not so much in terms of time, but rather in terms of the nature and specificity of the verbal action.

23.6. Review of the Bulgarian tense system

The student has now learned the entire system of verbal tenses in Bulgarian. It is good at this point to review this system, particularly as concerns the constructions with some sort of future (or potential) meaning.

The chart below summarizes the nine verbal tenses, and points out formal and functional relationships between them. To keep the chart concise, only 3rd singular forms are given. The verb чета is used throughout, always in its simplex (imperfective) form, despite the fact that certain of these tenses occur almost always with perfective verbs. Some tense names are given in abbreviated form: ANT signifies "anterior", INDEF signifies "indefinite" and /PAST is shorthand for "...in the past".

There are four future-related tenses, each of which is listed together with the non-future tense to which it corresponds. Only the final tense in the chart, the aorist, has no partner with a meaning which can be seen as cast further into the future.

Although there seem to be many tenses, it is important to see that the same forms are repeated in all of them, with minor variations. Furthermore, the variations are of a systematic nature, especially in the six compound tenses.

BULGARIAN VERBAL TENSES (INDICATIVE MOOD)

	AFFIRMATIVE				NEGATIVE			
PRESENT	той			чете	той	не		чете
FUTURE	той	ще		чете	той	няма да		чете
IMPERFECT	той			четеше	той	не		четеше
FUT./PAST	той	щеше да		чете	той	нямаше да		чете
PAST INDEF.	той		е	чел	той	не	е	чел
FUT.ANT.	той	ще	е	чел	той	няма да	е	чел
PAST ANT.	той		беше	чел	той	не	беше	чел
FUT.ANT./PAST	той	щеше да	е	чел	той	нямаше да	е	чел
AORIST	той			чете	той	не		чете

Двайсет и трети урок / Lesson 23

In each of the four future-related tenses, for example, the auxiliary is either a form of **ще** (affirmative) or **няма да** (negative). This auxiliary appears either in its present tense form or in its imperfect tense form. The conjugated form of the verb is either in the present tense or in the past indefinite. Two compound tenses, the past indefinite and the past anterior, are composed of the auxiliary **съм** and the L-participle; again, the auxiliary appears either in its present tense form or in its imperfect tense form.

There are three simplex tenses: present, imperfect and aorist. The forms of two of these, the present and the imperfect, are repeated throughout the system in the auxiliaries. Of the three simplex tenses, therefore, only the aorist tense stands alone. Its form is not repeated anywhere else in the system.

The systematic nature of the Bulgarian tense system will be taken up again in Lesson 29 after the student has learned the parallel system represented by the renarrated mood, the topic of the next two lessons.

Statue of Patriarch Euthymius, Sofia

Двайсет и трети урок / Lesson 23

EXERCISES

I. Rewrite the following passage, shifting the verbs further in the past.

Пе́тър и Па́вел са близна́ци. Дне́с е рожде́ният им де́н. Те́ навъ́ршват 10 годи́ни. Преди́ да се въ́рнат от учи́лище, ма́йка им ще е пригото́вила обе́да. В ця́лата къ́ща ще бъ́де то́пло. Раздава́чът ще е и́двал и ще е доне́съл поздрави́телните телегра́ми от ба́би и дя́довци. Ма́йка им ще е подреди́ла на легла́та им краси́во украсе́ни паке́ти. Какво́ ли ще са сло́жили роди́телите им в паке́тите?

II. Transform the sentences by using a present participle form.

1. Слъ́нцето сия́е и хвъ́рля светлина́ върху поля́ и планини́.
2. Вода́та ка́пе от кра́на на чешма́та и го дра́зни.
3. По́гледът му я тъ́рси и я нами́ра на една́ ма́са в ъ́гъла на рестора́нта.
4. Вси́чки гле́дат как дво́йката танцу́ва.
5. Тя́ с у́жас забеля́зва, че врата́та ти́хо се отва́ря.
6. Самоле́тът кръжи́ над града́ и кла́ти криле́ за по́здрав.
7. Деца́та разгова́рят и не ви́ждат, че учи́телката ги ви́ка.

III. Rewrite each sentence replacing one of the main verbs by the corresponding verbal adverb.

1. Те́ замина́ваха от Со́фия и се оба́диха да се сбогу́ват с вси́чките си прия́тели.
2. Ни́е обсъ́ждахме предложе́нията и взи́махме реше́ния по вся́ко едно́ от тя́х, като съобща́вахме редо́вно на заинтересо́ваните лица́.
3. А́з у́дрях печа́т на писма́та и забеля́зах, че едно́ от тя́х не е подпи́сано.
4. Той откри́ изло́жбата и ка́за, че дебю́тът на мла́дия худо́жник ще предизви́ка одобре́нието на пу́бликата.
5. Тя́ сла́га ча́йника на пе́чката и забеля́зва, че вче́ра е забра́вила да я изклю́чи.
6. То́й отва́ря врата́та и устано́вява, че ня́кой е вли́зал в ста́ята в не́гово отсъ́ствие.
7. Григо́р преми́сля възмо́жните о́тговори и ви́жда, че ни́кой от тя́х не е подходя́щ.

Двайсет и трети урок / Lesson 23

ADDITIONAL GRAMMAR NOTES

23.7. Derivation of nationality names

Names of members of different nationalities or ethnic groups are formed with several different suffixes. One of the most common is **-ец**; the corresponding feminine suffix is usually **-ка,** but can exceptionally be **-киня**. Since the vowel in **-ец** is fleeting, masculine plurals end in **-ци.**

place name	*stem*	*masculine/ generic*	*feminine*	*place name (English)*
А́встрия	австрий-	австри́ец	австри́йка	Austria
Аме́рика	амери́к-	америка́нец	америка́нка	America
Герма́ния	герман-	герма́нец	герма́нка	Germany
	нем-	не́мец	немки́ня	
Евро́па	европей-	европе́ец	европе́йка	Europe
Ирла́ндия	ирланд-	ирла́ндец	ирла́ндка	Ireland
Испа́ния	испан-	испа́нец	испа́нка	Spain
Ита́лия	италиан-	италиа́нец	италиа́нка	Italy
Кита́й	китай-	кита́ец	кита́йка	China
Коре́я	корей-	коре́ец	коре́йка	Korea
Норве́гия	норвеж-	норве́жец	норве́жка	Norway
Румъ́ния	румъ́н-	румъ́нец	румъ́нка	Romania
Си́рия	сирий-	сири́ец	сири́йка	Syria
Со́фия	софиян-	софия́нец	софия́нка	Sofia
Украи́на	украи́н-	украи́нец	украи́нка	Ukraine
У́нгария	унгар-	унга́рец	унга́рка	Hungary
Финла́ндия	финланд-	финла́ндец	финла́ндка	Finland
Швейца́рия	швейцар-	швейца́рец	швейца́рка	Switzerland
Шотла́ндия	шотланд-	шотла́ндец	шотла́ндка	Scotland
Япо́ния	япон-	япо́нец	япо́нка	Japan

Another common suffix is **-ин**. This suffix, cognate to English "one", is dropped in the plural. If the stem ends in **-ан**, the singular form will end in **-анин** and the plural in **-ани**. If the stem ends in **-к**, this consonant will shift in various ways, which must be learned. The stem to which the suffix is added is not always directly predictable from the country name. Sometimes the masculine form takes no suffix at all.

The feminine forms take different shapes; the most common are with the suffixes **-ка** or **-киня**. Note that the masculine form for "Russian" takes an irregular suffix, and that the suffix denoting a "Frenchwoman" is irregular and unpredictable.

Двайсет и трети урок / Lesson 23

place name	stem	masculine/generic	feminine	place name (English)
А́нглия	англичан-	англича́нин	англича́нка	England
Ара́бия	араб-	ара́бин	ара́бка	[Arab country]
Белору́сия	белорус-	белору́син	белору́ска	Belarus
Бълга́рия	българ-	бълга́рин	бълга́рка	Bulgaria
Гъ́рция	гръ́к-/гърк-	гръ́к *	гъркиня	Greece
Да́ния	датчан-	датча́нин	датча́нка	Denmark
По́лша	поляк-	поля́к	поляки́ня	Poland
Руси́я	рус-	русна́к, ру́син	руски́ня	Russia
Слова́кия	словак-	слова́к	слова́чка	Slovakia
Съ́рбия	сърб-	съ́рбин	сръбки́ня	Serbia
Ту́рция	турк-	ту́рчин **	турки́ня	Turkey
Фра́нция	француз-	францу́зин	францу́зойка	France
Хърва́тска	хърват-	хърва́тин	хърва́тка	Croatia
Че́хия	чех-	че́х	чехки́ня	Czech republic
Шве́ция	швед-	шве́д	шве́дка	Sweden

* definite form гъ́ркът, plural гъ́рци
** plural ту́рци

Certain other nouns are formed according to these derivational patterns. Most of them follow the rules as articulated above (although the corresponding feminine form is not always readily predictable). Practically all masculine forms in -ин drop this suffix in the plural; an exception is домаки́н. The most common of these are:

stem	masculine/generic	feminine	(meaning)
господ-	господи́н (*pl.* господа́)	госпожа́ (*pl.* госпо́жи)	sir, Mr./Ma'am, Mrs. gentlemen/ladies
граждан-	гра́жданин	гра́жданка	citizen
домак-	домаки́н (*pl.* домаки́ни)	домаки́ня	host, householder
пев-	певе́ц	певи́ца	singer
плув-	плуве́ц	плувки́ня	swimmer
чужд-	чужден́ец	чужденка́	foreigner, stranger

Двайсет и трети урок / Lesson 23

SAMPLE SENTENCES

1. Прелитайки над вашата прекрасна страна, президентът ви изпраща сърдечните си поздрави и пожеланията си за светли бъднини.

2. Изтъквайки необходимостта от допълнителни капиталовложения, министърът благодари на присъствуващите банкери за участието им в проекта.

3. Изхождайки от тези и други подобни данни, комитетът реши временно да закрие завода.

4. Пренасяйки отрицателното си отношение от бащата на сина, богатият чичо реши да го лиши от наследство.

5. Всички официални писма в България трябва да имат изходящ номер.
6. Не можем да приемем писмото им, защото няма изходящ номер.

7. Четящата публика добре познава този автор.
8. Излизащите от страната трябва да попълват митнически декларации.

9. В съседната къща живеят две постоянно лаещи кучета.
10. Не можейки да понесе нападките на колегите си, той напусна залата.

11. Боледуващите от грип са заплаха за здравето на околните.
12. Влакът пътуващ от Пловдив има 1 час закъснение.

13. -- Как мислиш, той идвал ли е тука, докато не ни е имало?
    -- Едва ли. Ако беше идвал, щеше да е видял обявата. А той нищо не знаеше за нея, когато говорих с него сутринта.

14. Димитър щеше да си е сменил името три пъти досега, ако таксата не беше толкова висока.

15. Преживелите войната още не предполагаха, че пет години по-късно животът в градовете щеше да е замрял и много от тях нямаше да са възстановили изгубените си домове.

Двайсет и трети урок / Lesson 23

SENTENCES FOR TRANSLATION

1. The people who missed the fast train had to take the slow one. The train they missed was very fast indeed. They would have already been in Sofia by now.

2. Smearing the yogurt on my back, I thought that if I had just gone inside an hour earlier, I would not have gotten burned so badly.

3. The plan was to have been implemented by now. We will have to take measures so that no one will notice how lazy we are.

4. The neighbors with their party clearly believe that they are not bothering anyone. Nowadays no one pays any attention to the consequences of their actions.

5. Someone translating these sentences must know a lot of Bulgarian. Had they known in advance how complicated the Bulgarian verbal system is, would they have ever begun to learn it?

6. Overtaking the man, I saw that he was not the person I thought he was.

7. If you don't look after your health, it can lead to unpleasant consequences.

Seaside scene in Balchik, near Varna

Двайсет и трети урок / Lesson 23

READING SELECTION

Тракийското съкровище от Рогозен

През 1986 г. в село Рогозен, Белослатинско, намиращо се в зоната, от която произхожда преобладаващият брой тракийски скъпоценни изделия, бе открито най-голямото засега тракийско съкровище в България. То има общо тегло 20 кг. Копаейки канал в градината си, тракористът Иван Димитров случайно се натъква на част от съкровището. Повиканите срочно от Окръжния исторически музей във Враца археолози бързо разбират, че са изправени пред "находката на века".

Съкровището се състои от 165 сребърни съда с позлата от преди елинистичната епоха -- от V-IV в. преди н. е. На тринайсет от фиалите и две от каните има надписи с гръцки букви. Смята се за най-правдоподобно мнението, че личните тракийски имена сред надписите са имена на притежатели и на майстори, изработили предметите. Разчетени бяха и имена на отдавна изчезнали тракийски селища. Сложните композиции в орнаментиката на съдовете са подчинени на определен ритъм и утвърдени канони, а оригиналните символични мотиви са почерпени от архаичната местна традиция.

Иконографията и епиграфиката на съкровището предоставят богата пряка и косвена информация за идеологията, светоусещането и естетическите критерии на траките. Голяма част от съдовете принадлежат към продукцията на местна работилница. Освен тях обаче има и други, следващи гръцки, малоазийски или персийски образци.

Разумно е да се смята, че богатата колекция е била собственост на тракийски владетелски род от племето трибали. Предметите са събирани в продължение на няколко поколения през периода на най-големия разцвет на тракийската култура и изкуство и отразяват стремежа на тракийската аристокрация да демонстрира могъщество чрез богатство и разкош. Предполага се, че причината съкровището да бъде заровено в две плитки ями съвсем близко една до друга, е обществената несигурност, последвала военните походи на македонските царе Филип II и Александър III Велики.

Оскъдни са сведенията за трибалите у древните автори, но рогозенското съкровище привлече вниманието на специалистите към тях и ще го задържи задълго. Археологическите паметници, открити досега в земите на трибалите, показват високо за времето си развитие на металургията и занаятите.

Особено интересни са каните с образи и сюжети от древната тракийска митология. Сцените, изобразяващи Великата богиня Бендида, хвърлят обилна светлина върху нейния култ като повелителка на природата и ловджийка, за който доскоро почти нищо не беше известно. Едно друго, по-добре известно божество от пантеона на траките -- Тракийският конник, символизиращ избавителя от злото -- е герой на няколко ловни сцени. Изобразената върху друга кана пък фантастична процесия от животни дава ключ за разчитане на редица образи върху предмети, намерени у нас и в Южна Румъния.

Двайсет и трети урок / Lesson 23

През последните десетилетия в централната част на Северна България бяха открити десетина съкровища и още толкова богати погребения, датиращи приблизително от първата половина на IV в. пр. н. е. Те са свидетелство за икономическия подем и политическата мощ на трибалската държава. Естествено е, че това общество има силна и богата аристокрация. Трибалските аристократи са били погребвани в съседство с родовите си домове, в пълни със скъпи дарове гробници, над които има издигнати високи насипи. Така в продължение на десетилетия и векове около родовите имения се натрупвали много надгробни могили. По тях ние днес можем да съдим къде са били тези имения. Съставените карти на тракийските могили позволяват да бъдат локализирани такива имения около съвременните селища Враца, Царевец, Мизия, Галиче, Търнава и Бреница.

Адаптирано от Тракийското съкровище от Рогозен, София, 1988.

Thracian gold and silver pitcher from Rogozen

Двайсет и трети урок / Lesson 23

GLOSSARY

австри́ец	Austrian (male)	дати́рам	date, go back to
австри́йка	Austrian (female)	датча́нин	Dane (male)
а́втор	author	датча́нка	Dane (female)
ара́бин	Arab (male)	дебю́т	artist's debut, opening
ара́бка	Arab (female)	деклара́ция	declaration
аристокра́т	aristocrat, noble	демонстри́рам	demonstrate, display
аристокра́ция	aristocracy, nobility	десетиле́тие	decade
архаи́чен	ancient, archaic	десети́на	ten or so; half a score
археологи́чески	archaeological	джа́фкам / джа́фна	yap
		дове́ждам / доведа́	bring; bring about, lead to
банке́р	banker, money-agent		
белору́син	Belarusian (male)	домаки́н	householder, manager, host
белору́ска	Belarusian (female)		
близна́к	twin	домаки́ня	housewife, hostess
бога́тство	riches, wealth	допълни́телен	supplementary
боги́ня	goddess	доско́ро	until recently
божество́	divinity, deity	дра́зня	irritate
боледу́вам от грип	have the flu	дро́бче	liver [food]
бо́лест	illness, ailment		
бъ́деще предвари́телно в ми́налото	future anterior in the past (tense)	европе́ец	European (male)
		европе́йка	European (female)
бъднина́	days to come	една́ до дру́га	next to each other
бъднини́	the future	елинисти́чен (*also* ели́нски)	Hellenistic
в продълже́ние на	during, throughout	епигра́фика	epigraphy
вера́нда	veranda, porch	епо́ха	epoch
ви́ла	villa	естети́чески	aesthetic
владе́телски	ruling, ruler's		
вре́менен	temporary	заво́д	factory, plant
вре́менно	for the time being	задъ́лго	for a long time
входя́щ	incoming	заинтересо́ван	concerned, partial
възмо́жен	possible	заинтересо́вани лица́	parties concerned
възпале́ние	inflammation		
възстановя́вам / възстановя́	restore, rebuild	зака́рвам / зака́рам	take, drive over
		закри́вам / закри́я	hide; shut down
		зали́вам / зале́я	overflow
герма́нец	German (male)	зали́вам се от смя́х	roar with laughter
герма́нка	German (female)	зами́рам / замра́	die away, decline
геро́й	hero; character (in a literary work)	занаят	craft, trade; vocation
		запла́ха	threat
гра́жданка	citizen (female)	зара́вям / заро́вя	bury
гри́жа се (-иш)	care	зло́	evil
гри́жа се за	look after	зо́на	zone, region
гро́бница	tomb	зря́л (*pl.* зре́ли)	ripe, mature
гърки́ня	Greek (female)		
		идеоло́гия	ideology
да́р, -ъ́т (*pl.* дарове́)	gift, donation; talent	избави́тел	savior, deliverer
		изде́лие	article, product, handicraft

Двайсет и трети урок / Lesson 23

издигам / издигна	raise, build, put up	ловджийка	huntress
изключвам / изключа (-иш)	exclude; turn off	ловен	hunting (adj.)
изкуство	art; skill	локализирам	localize, locate
измъчвам се / измъча се (-иш)	suffer, have a terrible time	мажа (-еш)	spread, smear
		македонски	Macedonian (adj.)
изобразявам / изобразя	portray, depict	малоазийски	Anatolian, of Asia Minor
		металургия	metallurgy
изправен пред	confronted with	митнически	customs (adj.)
изработвам / изработя	produce, work out	митология	mythology
		могъщество	power, might
изтъквам / изтъкна	emphasize	мощ	power, might; vigor
изхождам / изходя	travel all over; originate	на брега на морето	on the seacoast
изходящ	outgoing	навършвам / навърша (-иш)	complete
иконография	iconography		
икономически	economic	навършвам 20 г.	turn 20 years old
имение	estate	надгробен	sepulchral, grave (adj.)
ирландец	Irishman	назад	back, backwards
ирландка	Irishwoman	нападки	attacks, incrimination
испанец	Spaniard (male)	напускам / напусна	leave
испанка	Spaniard (female)		
италианец	Italian (male)	насила	by force
италианка	Italian (female)	насип	mound, embankment
		наследство	inheritance
кактус	cactus	настигам / настигна	overtake, catch up with
кана	pitcher, jug		
канал	canal, drain	нататъшен	far (adj.)
канон	canon, rule	натрупвам / натрупам	heap up, amass
капиталовложение	capital investment		
капя (-еш)	drip, dribble; leak	натъквам се / натъкна се	come across, run into
карта	map, chart		
кг = килограм	kilogram	находка	find
китаец	Chinese (male)	не бива да пие	[one] mustn't drink [it]
китайка	Chinese (female)	неприятен	unpleasant
клатя	shake, roll	несигурност	insecurity, uncertainty
комитет	committee	норвежец	Norwegian (male)
композиция	composition	норвежка	Norwegian (female)
конник	horseman, rider		
кореец	Korean (male)		
корейка	Korean (female)	обилен	abundant
косвен	indirect	образец	model, pattern
кран	faucet	обратно	back, the other direction
криза	crisis	обръщам се назад	turn back, look back
крило (pl. крила or криле)	wing	обръщам внимание на	pay attention to
критерий	criterion	обсъждам / обсъдя	discuss, consider
кръжа (-иш)	circle, go around	обществен	social, public
култ	cult	общество	society, community
		обява	announcement, advertisement
лишавам / лиша (-иш)	deprive of, rob		
		одеяло	blanket
лишавам от наследство	disinherit	одобрение	approval

Двайсет и трети урок / Lesson 23

око́лен	neighboring; roundabout	поче́рпвам / поче́рпя	treat someone to; draw from
окръ́жен	county, regional	правдоподо́бен	likely, probable
определе́н	definite, precise	предме́т	object, article
орнаме́нтика	ornamentation	предоста́вям / предоста́вя	give, concede
оскъ́ден	scarce, meager	президе́нт	president
осъществя́вам / осъществя́	fulfill, carry out	прели́ствам / прели́стя	leaf through
оти́вам на поку́пки	go shopping	прели́там (or прелетя́вам) / прелетя́	fly over
отноше́ние	attitude, relationship		
отрица́телен	negative	преми́слям / преми́сля	think over, ponder
отрица́телно отноше́ние	disapproval	пренебре́гвам / пренебре́гна	neglect, ignore
отсъ́ствие	absence	пренебре́гвам съве́т	disregard [someone's] advice
отърва́вам се / отърва́ се	get rid of, get off	преоблада́вам	predominate, prevail
паке́т	pack, package	преска́чам / преско́ча (-иш)	jump over
пантео́н	pantheon		
певи́ца	female singer	приблизи́телен	approximate
перси́йски	Persian (adj.)	приблизи́телно	roughly
печа́т	stamp, seal; printing press	принадлежа́ (-и́ш)	belong to, pertain to
пе́чка	stove	присви́вам / присви́я	bend
пи́лешки	chicken (adj.)	присви́ва ме ко́рем	feel sharp pains in my abdomen
пи́лешки дро́бчета	chicken livers		
пли́тък	shallow	притежа́тел (ка)	owner, possessor
плуве́ц	swimmer	проду́кция	production, output
плувки́ня	female swimmer	продълже́ние	continuation; sequel
по-ната́тъшна съдба́	subsequent fate	прое́кт	project
по спе́шност	as an emergency case	произхо́ждам	come/descend from
повели́телка	lady sovereign, queen	проце́сия	procession
погребе́ние	funeral, burial	работи́лница	workshop
подем	upsurge, revival	разболя́вам се / разболе́я се	fall ill
подре́ждам / подредя́	arrange, put in order		
подчиня́вам / подчиня́	subordinate, subject	разко́ш	luxury, splendor
пожела́ние	wish	разцве́т	flowering; zenith
поздрави́телен	congratulatory	разчи́там / разчета́	make out, decipher
поздрави́телена телегра́ма	telegram of congratulations	ра́к	crayfish, crab
позла́та	gilt, gold-leaf	ри́тъм	rhythm
поку́пка	purchase	ро́д -ът (pl. родове́)	family, clan; genus, sort; gender
полити́чески	political	ро́дов	family, lineal; generic
поля́ (poetic pl.)	fields	румъ́нец	Romanian (male)
поля́к	Pole (male)	румъ́нка	Romanian (female)
поляки́ня	Pole (female)	ру́син (archaic)	Russian (male)
попъ́лвам / попъ́лня	replenish; fill in	руски́ня	Russian (female)
после́дица	consequence	русна́к	Russian (male)
похо́д	campaign, march		

Двайсет и трети урок / Lesson 23

сведе́ние	some information
сведе́ния	information, knowledge
све́тли бъднини́	a bright future
светоусе́щане	world outlook
се́лище	settlement
символизи́рам	symbolize, stand for
символи́чен	symbolic
сири́ец	Syrian (male)
сири́йка	Syrian (female)
сия́я	shine, be radiant
скъпоце́нен	precious
слова́к	Slovak (male)
слова́чка	Slovak (female)
со́бственост	property
спе́шност	urgency
сро́чен	urgent, pressing
сръбки́ня	Serb (female)
стра́дам	suffer
стреме́ж	striving, aspiration
съдба́	fate, destiny
съ́дя	judge; put on trial
серде́чни пожела́ния	best wishes
съсе́дство	neighborhood
сюже́т	subject[-matter], storyline
ся́нка	shade, shadow
та́кса	charge, fee
танцу́вам	dance
тегло́	weight
телегра́ма	telegram
траки́йски	Thracian (adj.)
тракто́ри́ст	tractor driver
триба́ли	Thracian sub-tribe
турки́ня	Turk (female)
ту́рчин (pl. ту́рци)	Turk (male)
уви́	alas
украи́нец	Ukrainian (male)
украи́нка	Ukrainian (female)
украся́вам / украся́	decorate, adorn, trim
унга́рец	Hungarian (male)
унга́рка	Hungarian (female)
услажда́м се / усладя́ се	give pleasure
услажда́ ми се	enjoy
уши́вам / уши́я	sew, tailor
уши́вам си костю́м	have a suit made; make oneself a suit
фантасти́чен	fantastic, fabulous
фиа́ла	libation bowl
финла́ндец	Finn (male)
финла́ндка	Finn (female)
фотогени́чен	photogenic
францу́зин	Frenchman
французо́йка	Frenchwoman
худо́жник	artist; painter
хърва́тин	Croat (male)
хърва́тка	Croat (female)
черве́н като́ ра́к	red as a lobster
чех	Czech (male)
чехки́ня	Czech (female)
чешма́	fountain; tap
швед	Swede (male)
шве́дка	Swede (female)
швейца́рец	Swiss (male)
швейца́рка	Swiss (female)
шотла́ндец	Scotsman, Scot
шотла́ндка	Scotswoman, Scot
я́ма	pit
япо́нец	Japanese (male)
япо́нка	Japanese (female)

Двайсет и трети урок / Lesson 23

CULTURAL COMMENTARY

History: Patriarch Euthymius
One of the "best" streets in downtown Sofia is that named after Patriarch Euthymius (Патриа́рх Евти́мий, ca. 1317 - ca. 1402), the last head of the autocephalic Bulgarian church before the fall of Bulgaria to the Ottomans. Patriarch Euthymius supervised the defense of the besieged capital of Tărnovo in 1393, and negotiated the surrender to the Turkish sultan with minimal loss of life. He himself was exiled to the Rhodopes, but several of his pupils escaped to Romania and southern Russia, where they were very influential in the course of medieval letters.

In terms of cultural history, Patriarch Euthymius is associated with the Byzantine movement of Hesychasm (quiet contemplative prayer) and with the Tărnovo literary school, noted for restoration of linguistic and liturgical clarity to the original Church Slavic legacy. The influence of both of these movements (and consequently of Patriarch Euthymius) throughout the late medieval Orthodox world was very great.

Archaeology: Thracian civilizations
Bulgarians are proud of their country's rich and old heritage, and especially of the original group of settlers called Thracians. Relatively little is known of the Thracians, and much of what is known has been deduced from the objects which have been excavated on Bulgarian soil. Numerous finds of buried treasure have been discovered at various points throughout Bulgaria, indicating that the Thracians had settled most of the country. These finds include various sculptures, finely worked vessels of silver and gold (some with inscriptions), jewelry and other objects which are indicative of a highly cultured civilization.

The Thracian language largely remains a mystery: all that linguists know about it is based on a few inscriptions found on buried objects. The fact that these inscriptions are written in Greek letters indicates that Thracians knew Greek as well. The identity of their gods and goddesses is also best deduced by objects left behind. One of the most frequently pictured is the horseman, whose carved image appears in numerous areas.

Customs: sunburns
Bulgarians regularly put yogurt on sunburn and claim that it is very efficacious.

Geography: Balchik
There is a large botanical garden in Balchik, with an extensive collection of cactuses. The garden was created for the Romanian Queen Marie in the earlier part of the century during the period (1913-1940) when this northeastern part of Bulgaria belonged to Romania. The garden is on the grounds of what used to be the Romanian royal summer palace, itself an exotic, oriental architectural creation full of towers of different shapes.

Bureaucracy
All official letters must have the appropriate bureaucratic stamp or seal (печа́т) on them. Any official institution also keeps a record book of all its correspondence. All documents are entered into this book and given a formal index number. Incoming documents are given an "incoming number" (входя́щ но́мер) and outgoing documents are given an "outgoing number" (изходя́щ но́мер). These numbers help one to trace such a document to its source should the need arise.

Bulgarian citizens must fill out customs declarations both on entering and on leaving the country. The amount of type of goods that may be exported is limited and strictly regulated.

LESSON 24

DIALOGUE

Та́м и́мало интере́сен обе́кт

// Джу́ли е в гради́ната пред Криста́л и тъ́рси с по́глед Весели́н по ма́сичките на кафе́-сладка́рницата. Весели́н се нади́га от сто́ла, на ко́йто е се́днал, и ѝ ма́ха с ръка́ да привлече́ внима́нието ѝ. //

Веселин: Джу́ли! Наса́м!

Джули: Здраве́йте. Ко́лко е ху́баво ту́к на въ́здух.

Веселин: Ка́к ми́на ра́зговорът с профе́сора?

Джули: А́з стра́шно се притесня́вах, че Де́йвид го ня́ма, но профе́сорът бе́ше мно́го любе́зен. Пока́за ми ня́кои свои́ кни́ги и ми разка́за за на́й-но́вите нахо́дки. Ка́за, че се ка́нел дру́гата се́дмица да зами́не на разко́пки в Топо́лница и мо́жел да взе́ме със се́бе си и на́с с Де́йвид.

Веселин: Къде́ бе́ше това́ Топо́лница? В Пе́тричко ли?

Джули: Да́, на сама́та бъ́лгаро-гръ́цка гра́ница. Та́м и́мало мно́го интере́сен обе́кт.

Веселин: Ма́й съм чу́вал не́що за не́го. Не бя́ха ли наме́рили та́м зла́то?

Джули: Не́. Та́м и́ма предистори́ческо се́лище и некро́пол. По́сле профе́сорът ме поведе́ по ста́ите да ме запозна́е с коле́гите си. Еди́н от тя́х вдру́гиден ще ме разведе́ из Археологи́ческия музе́й.

Веселин: В Че́рната джами́я, нали́? А́з та́м не съм вли́зал от учени́к.

Джули: Де́йвид ще е мно́го дово́лен, като му ка́жа за пока́ната на профе́сора.

Веселин: Ако А́нгел не ви́ е изпрева́рил да го пока́ни ня́къде на гроздобе́р.

Джули: Какъ́в гроздобе́р? Сега́ е о́ще ля́то.

Веселин: И е́сен ще до́йде. По́-добре́ каже́те ка́к си пи́ете кафе́то? Съ́с или бе́з за́хар? И не се́ ли умори́хте да си прика́зваме на вие́?

Джули: С една́ лъжи́чка за́хар, мо́ля. Ви́жте оне́зи деца́ та́м на чешма́та не са́ ли На́дка и Ка́мен?

Двайсет и четвърти урок / Lesson 24

Веселин: Né вижте, а виж. Да́. Те́ са. С ма́йка си. С тя́х е она́зи дво́йка от Ва́рна.

Джули: Да ги пока́ним на на́шата ма́са.

// Весели́н дове́жда Та́ня с деца́та, и дру́гите. Ку́четата се сгу́шват под ма́сата. //

Димитър: Ко́лко е ма́лък светъ́т! Това́ ни е за дне́с вто́рата случа́йна сре́ща. Ма́йко, това́ е Джу́ли, на́шата спъ́тничка. Тя́ е от Аме́рика, но мно́го ху́баво зна́е бъ́лгарски.

Милена: Я́ си призна́йте, ви́е ка́к се наме́рихте? Ма́й не é било́ мно́го случа́йно...

Таня: Не притесня́вайте момче́то, ви́жте го ка́к се изче́рви.

Веселин: Не съ́м се изче́рвил. Ту́к про́сто е мно́го горе́що.

Джули: Весели́н ми уреди́ сре́ща с профе́сор Попо́в.

Веселин: Джу́ли тъ́кмо ми разпра́вяше, че дру́гата се́дмица замина́вала на разко́пки. Сре́щата с профе́сора ми́нала мно́го добре́, мака́р че Де́йвид го ня́мало. То́й да́же ѝ пока́зал свои́ кни́ги и ѝ разка́зал за на́й-но́вите нахо́дки. Еди́н от сътру́дниците на институ́та щя́л вдру́гиден да я разведе́ из музе́я.

Димитър: А Де́йвид защо́ не é дошъ́л?

Джули: Те́ вче́ра до средно́щ се нали́вали с А́нгел с черве́но ви́но и Де́йвид дне́с е махмурли́я.

Таня: Джу́ли, значи в неде́ля ще сте о́ще в Со́фия?

Джули: Така́ изли́за.

Двайсет и четвърти урок / Lesson 24

GRAMMAR

24.1. The renarrated mood: introduction

Verbs express both "tense" and "mood". Tense refers to the time of an action, and mood refers to the speaker's attitude towards the action. The student has now learned all nine of the Bulgarian tenses. Each of these refers to an action that is taking place, or that did or will take place.

The assumption made by speakers of Bulgarian is that the person speaking of these events knows of what s/he speaks, and that unless otherwise indicated the transmission of information is a direct one. This general attitude constitutes one of the four moods; it is termed the "indicative mood" (изявително наклонение).

The other three moods are the imperative mood (повелително наклонение), the conditional mood (условно наклонение) and the renarrated mood (преизказно наклонение). The imperative is known to the student, and the conditional will be learned in Lesson 27.

The fourth mood, the renarrated, is the subject of this and the following lesson. It is one of the most unique and intriguing elements of Bulgarian grammar. With it, a Bulgarian can communicate a certain distance from the information s/he is transmitting. If s/he has heard the information from another source (and therefore cannot vouch directly for its reliability), or if s/he wishes for some other reason to express some distance from that which s/he is saying, s/he will use a form of the "renarrated mood".

This mood takes its name from the fact that it is used most often to restate (renarrate, преизказва) that which one has heard from another. Its several meanings, however, are all best grouped under the more general concept of "distancing". The most basic meaning, that of renarration, will be studied in this lesson and the other meanings will be studied in the following lesson.

24.2. Formation of the renarrated mood: general principles

Since every verbal tense in Bulgarian has parallel indicative and renarrated forms, the student must now learn several new verbal paradigms. Fortunately, while there are nine distinct tenses in the indicative mood, there are only five distinct paradigms in the renarrated mood.

Two things are common to all renarrated paradigms: all are compound forms involving an auxiliary and an L-participle, and all omit the auxiliary in the 3rd person (both singular and plural). Simplex tenses are made into their renarrated counterparts by using the L-participle of the tense form. Compound tenses are made into their renarrated counterparts by using the L-participle of the auxiliary.

Двайсет и четвърти урок / Lesson 24

The L-participle which the student already knows is the past active participle. For the verb чета́, for instance, this participle is чел (feminine че́ла, neuter че́ло, plural че́ли). It is used to form four compound tenses: the past indefinite (чел съм), the past anterior (бях чел), the future anterior (ще съм чел), and the future anterior in the past (щях да съм чел). This participle, which is formed from the aorist stem, is used to form a number of renarrated forms, but not all of them.

The renarrated mood of the present and imperfect tenses, for instance, is based on an L-participle formed from the imperfect stem. The imperfect endings are dropped, and the L-participle endings added. If the imperfect stem vowel is an alternating one, this alternation is maintained in the L-participle form.

Verbs which permit two forms in the imperfect (those with stems ending in -ч, -ж, -ш or -й) permit two L-participles as well.

imperfect	**L-PARTICIPLE**			
	masculine	*feminine*	*neuter*	*plural*
четя́-х, чете́-ше	четя́-л	четя́-ла	четя́-ло	чете́-ли
пи́ше-х	пи́ше-л	пи́ше-ла	пи́ше-ло	пи́ше-ли
държа́-х	държа́-л	държа́-ла	държа́-ло	държа́-ли
/ държе́-х	държе́-л	държе́-ла	държе́-ло	държе́-ли

Of the two variants, most speakers would probably choose държе́л. This is because the aorist participle, държа́л, if used in the renarrated, has a different meaning. Most speakers would choose the form which makes the greater distinction.

Renarrated forms which are built on the L-participle of the auxiliary use one of three auxiliaries: съм, ще, or ня́ма да.

The L-participle of съм is well known to the student, and the L-participle of ня́ма да is the unchanging 3rd singular neuter. The L-participle of ще is formed from the imperfect stem of ще, and has the same -я-/-е- alternation as in the imperfect.

imperfect	**L-PARTICIPLE**			
	masculine	*feminine*	*neuter*	*plural*
бя́х, бе́ше, etc.	бил	била́	било́	били́
ня́маше да			ня́мало да	
щях, ще́ше	щял	щя́ла	щя́ло	ще́ли

Двайсет и четвърти урок / Lesson 24

In the following sections, renarrated paradigms will be given alongside the corresponding indicative ones. The verb **чета́** will be used in all examples. Only the masculine singular form of the participle will be given; if the subject is feminine or neuter, the participle must of course agree with it.

24.3. Renarrated mood: present and imperfect tenses

	Present tense		*Imperfect tense*	
	indicative	**RENARRATED**	indicative	**RENARRATED**
1st singular	чета́	четя́л съм	четя́х	четя́л съм
2nd singular	чете́ш	четя́л си	чете́ше	четя́л си
3rd singular	чете́	четя́л	чете́ше	четя́л
1st plural	чете́м	чете́ли сме	четя́хме	чете́ли сме
2nd plural	чете́те	чете́ли сте	четя́хте	чете́ли сте
3rd plural	четя́т	чете́ли	четя́ха	чете́ли

The renarrated forms of the imperfect are *identical* with those of the present. One must therefore pay attention to the context to know whether present or imperfect meaning is intended. The following examples illustrate this.

Present renarrated

| Ка́за, че се ка́нел дру́гата се́дмица да зами́не на разко́пки и мо́жел да ни взе́ме със се́бе си. | He said that he was intending to go on a dig next week and that he could take us with him. |

Imperfect renarrated

| Ка́за, че по́-ра́но мо́жел да хо́ди по 10 киломе́тра без почи́вка. | He said that he used to be able to walk 10 kilometers without stopping. |

In both examples, the renarrated forms **мо́жел** (as well as **ка́нел** in the first example) indicate to a listener that the speaker knows the information s/he relates only second hand. It is from the context that the listener must (and can) infer that the verb forms used by the original speaker were in the first instance **ка́ня** and **мо́га** (present tense) and in the second instance **мо́жех** (imperfect tense).

Двайсет и четвърти урок / Lesson 24

24.4. Renarrated mood: future and future in the past tenses

Future tense

	indicative	**RENARRATED**
1ˢᵗ singular	ще чета́	щял съм да чета́
2ⁿᵈ singular	ще чете́ш	щял си да чете́ш
3ʳᵈ singular	ще чете́	щял да чете́
1ˢᵗ plural	ще чете́м	щели сме да чете́м
2ⁿᵈ plural	ще чете́те	щели сте да чете́те
3ʳᵈ plural	ще чета́т	щели да чета́т

Future in the past tense

	indicative	**RENARRATED**
1ˢᵗ singular	щях да чета́	щял съм да чета́
2ⁿᵈ singular	ще́ше да чете́ш	щял си да чете́ш
3ʳᵈ singular	ще́ше да чете́	щял да чете́
1ˢᵗ plural	щя́хме да чете́м	щели сме да чете́м
2ⁿᵈ plural	щя́хте да чете́те	щели сте да чете́те
3ʳᵈ plural	щя́ха да чета́т	щели да чета́т

As in the case of the present and the imperfect, so are the renarrated forms of the future *identical* with those of the future in the past. Again, one must deduce from the context which tense was used in the original statement. Here are examples:

Future renarrated
    Пе́тър се ме́сти в дру́г гра́д, щял да полу́чи по́-добра́ ра́бота.
    Peter is moving to another town, [he says] he will get a better job.

Future in the past renarrated
    Ку́пиха му биле́т, но му се оба́диха къ́сно -- ве́че щял да хо́ди на дру́го мя́сто.
    They bought him a ticket but let him know [too] late -- he [said he] was already on the verge of going somewhere else.

In both examples, the renarrated auxiliary щял indicates to the listener that the speaker knows the information only second-hand. From the context, the listener deduces that the verb form used by the original speaker in the first instance was ще полу́ча (future tense) and that used by the original speaker in the second instance was щях да хо́дя (future in the past tense).

24.5. Renarrated mood: aorist tense

	Aorist tense		*Past indefinite tense*
	indicative	**RENARRATED**	
1st singular	че́тох	чел съм	чел съм
2nd singular	че́те	чел си	чел си
3rd singular	че́те	чел	чел е
1st plural	че́тохме	чели сме	чели сме
2nd plural	че́тохте	чели сте	чели сте
3rd plural	че́тоха	чели	чели са

By contrast to the renarrated mood of the first four tenses, in which one renarrated paradigm serves for two tenses, the renarrated mood of the aorist is unique. When the verb forms given above are used in the meaning "renarrated", only the aorist tense is meant. Because the forms of the aorist renarrated are extremely similar to those of the past indefinite indicative, the two have been given together for the sake of comparison.

In the 1st and 2nd persons, in fact, the renarrated aorist is identical to the past indefinite indicative, and only context can distinguish them. This means that the entire formal burden of the distinction between these two paradigms (which cross the boundaries of tense *and* mood) rests on the tiny clitic forms **е** and **са**. The potential confusions to which this gives rise will be discussed in Lesson 29.

Consider the contrast between the following two sentences, which illustrate well the subtlety of the distinction between indicative and renarrated.

Past indefinite indicative
    Ви́ждам, че е свъ́ршил вси́чко,
      преди́ да зами́не.
    I see that he finished everything
      before he left.

Aorist renarrated
    Ка́за, че свъ́ршил вси́чко, преди́
      да зами́не.
    He said that he finished everything
      before he left.

In the first example, the speaker conveys that he has seen sufficient evidence to make an inference, and that he is content with his deduction as a true statement of fact. In the second example, by contrast, the speaker conveys that he is reporting words spoken by another, and emphasizing that in so doing he is simply transmitting a report -- he is noncommittal as to his belief in the actual truth of the report.

Note that neither speaker actually saw the completed action. Neither, therefore, can speak of it using the aorist indicative, but must rather choose between the past indefinite indicative and the aorist renarrated, each of which communicates a different stage of distancing. The first stage of distancing, represented by the past indefinite indicative, is that of inference: the speaker evaluates the evidence and makes a deduction for which he takes responsibility. The second stage, represented by the aorist renarrated, is that of simple transmission: the speaker reports what someone else has said without taking any responsibility for the truth value.

It is important to realize that the use of the renarrated mood is *not* obligatory, and that a speaker can shift "stages" if s/he wishes. For instance, if the speaker of the second sentence quoted above had found the words s/he heard sufficiently convincing (despite the fact that they were the only evidence available) s/he could have used the form **е свършил** with the meaning "He said he finished everything and I fully believe him". The speaker of the first sentence, however, could not have said ****Виждам, че свършил.** (The asterisk means the sentence is impossible.) That is, one cannot use a verbal form that both claims responsibility for an inference (**Виждам**) and then abdicates that responsibility (**свършил**).

In addition to its use in the renarration of events communicated by others in the aorist indicative, the aorist renarrated is the norm in certain types of writing which are by nature distanced. One of these is folktale or fairytale narration, and another is historical prose, especially about events which happened more than one generation prior to the time of writing.

24.6. Usage of the renarrated mood in narrative context

As its name indicates, the renarrated mood is used to retell information one has heard from another source. Its function is to mark the communication as an indirect one. In principle, speakers of Bulgarian are obliged to use these forms to relate every verbal action they have not witnessed directly and have learned through a communication from a third party. In practice, Bulgarian speakers utilize the option of renarrated forms to express their attitude towards what they are saying. Although they usually use renarrated forms to communicate that which they hear from someone else, they may on occasion use indicative forms to emphasize their faith in the truth of what they report. Conversely, they may use a renarrated form to communicate a fact which is not necessarily quoted from another's speech, but from which they wish explicitly to distance themselves in one way or another.

The distinctions involved are multileveled, and speakers will often shift between indicative and renarrated forms as their own attitudes towards what they are saying shift in varying ways. Indeed, most speakers are only partially conscious of these attitudes. Many Bulgarians, although they certainly understand the basic meaning of the renarrated mood, would be at a loss to explain each and every instance of its use (or non-use) in their speech.

Двайсет и четвърти урок / Lesson 24

The entire verbal category is extremely subtle. Those learning Bulgarian should content themselves with learning to understand and appreciate this subtlety before trying to use these forms actively.

To give a concrete example of this, a portion of the current lesson's dialogue will be analyzed below. In order to see the use of the renarrated mood properly, it will be necessary to quote a selection large enough to contain several shifts of stance. Narrative sections are numbered, and the verbs to be discussed in the subsequent analysis are underlined.

1. -- Как мина разговорът с професора?

    --Аз страшно се притеснявах, че Дейвид го няма, но професорът беше много любезен. Показа ми някои свои книги и ми разказа за най-новите находки. Каза, ...

    "How did your talk with with the professor go?"

    "I was terribly nervous because David wasn't there, but the professor was very kind. He showed me some of his books and told me about his newest finds. He said..."

2. ... че се канел другата седмица да замине на разкопки в Тополница и можел да вземе със себе си и нас с Дейвид.

    ...that he intended to go on a dig to Topolnitsa next week, and that he could take David and me with him."

3. -- Къде беше това Тополница? В Петричко ли?

    "Remind me where this Topolnitsa is. In the Petrich area?"

4. -- Да, на самата българо-гръцка граница. Там имало много интересен обект.

    "Yes, right on the border between Bulgaria and Greece. There's supposed to be a very interesting site there."

5. -- Май съм чувал нещо за него. Не бяха ли намерили там злато?

    "I've maybe even heard of it. Didn't they find gold there [or something]?"

6. -- Не. Там има предисторическо селище и некропол.

    "No. There's a prehistoric village and a graveyard there.

7. -- После професорът ме поведе по стаите да ме запознае с колегите си. Един от тях вдругиден ще ме разведе из Археологическия музей.

    Then the professor took me around the department to introduce me to his colleagues. The day after tomorrow one of them is going to take me to the archaeological museum."

The dialogue begins in the indicative mood (1), with a straightforward question in the aorist indicative (**мина**). Веселин, addressing his question to Julie, assumes a neutral stance: he knows she had met with the professor and is simply asking how the meeting went. The first part of Julie's answer is likewise in the

Двайсет и четвърти урок / Lesson 24

indicative. She starts by reporting her own past state in the indicative imperfect (**притеснявах се**), and then continues to report events which she herself witnessed, using the indicative aorist (**беше, показа, разказа, каза**).

She then shifts to the renarrated mood (2) as she reports the professor's words. Since she has clearly identified this statement as one of indirect discourse (by saying **каза, че** ...), she could theoretically have used the past indefinite. Her choice of the renarrated present (**канел, можел**) explicitly communicates a certain distance. She heard the professor say these things but she is not yet certain whether to believe him fully enough to get involved.

Veselin continues in the neutral indicative (3), asking for information about the location of the dig. His use of the past indicative (**беше**) for a present-tense question communicates informality and his desire to recall (or be reminded of) certain information.

Julie's response (4) begins ambiguously: she answers Veselin's question with a prepositional phrase only, thus sidestepping the choice between indicative (**това е**) and renarrated (**това било**). Her underlying stance is apparently still distanced, however, since she continues with a verb in the renarrated present (**имало**). She still explicitly refuses to get directly involved in the circumstances surrounding the information she is reporting.

Veselin then resumes his neutral indicative stance (5) with a statement in the past indefinite indicative (**чувал съм**). His use of the past anterior indicative (**бяха намерили**) for a past indefinite question continues the informal, somewhat impatient stance of his speech in (3).

Julie's answer to his question (6) is stated in the present indicative (**има**). She then resumes her first-hand report (7) of the afternoon's activities using the indicative aorist (**поведе**) and indicative future (**ще разведе**). It is natural for her to return to the indicative mood to report witnessed events. What is interesting, however, is her shift from the renarrated **имало**, in (4) to the indicative **има**, in (6). To a listener this suggests two possibilities.

One is that Julie has now moved onto firmer ground in her attitude towards what she is saying, since it appears from the context that both statements contain information she has learned from her conversation with the professor (and is therefore reporting second-hand). Because the first follows directly upon a statement (2) about which she clearly feels some uncertainty, she retreats into the distance of the renarrated; but since the second follows a question by Veselin (5) which has apparently put her more at ease, she moves back into the indicative. The other possibility is that in (6) Julie could have moved briefly outside the frame of reporting the day's events in order to state something from her own knowledge about the general topic.

Двайсет и четвърти урок / Lesson 24

Later in the same conversation, several new characters enter the scene, and the following dialogue ensues:

8. -- Весели́н ми уреди́ сре́ща с профе́сор Попо́в.	"Veselin arranged a meeting for me with Professor Popov."
9. -- Джу́ли тъкмо ми разпра́вяше, ...	"Julie was just telling me...
10. .. че дру́гата се́дмица замина́вала на разко́пки. Сре́щата с профе́сора ми́нала мно́го добре́, макар че Де́йвид го ня́мало. То́й да́же ѝ пока́зал свои́ кни́ги и ѝ разка́зал за най-но́вите нахо́дки. Еди́н от сътру́дниците на институ́та щя́л вдру́гиден да я разведе́ из музе́я.	...that next week she's going on a dig. Her meeting with the professor went really well, though David never showed up. [The professor] even showed her his books and told her about his newest finds. One of his colleagues is going to take her around the museum the day after tomorrow."
11. -- А Де́йвид защо́ не е́ дошъ́л?	"And why didn't David come?"
12. -- Те́ вче́ра до средно́щ се нали́вали с А́нгел с черве́но ви́но ...	"Apparently he and Angel were drinking red wine well into the night, ...
13. ... и Де́йвид дне́с е махмурли́я.	...and today David has a hangover."

Julie sets the scene by a report (8), of an event of which she has first-hand knowledge, for which she uses the aorist indicative (уреди́). Veselin then takes over (9-10) and retells the story she had told earlier. He begins (9) by reporting an event he has witnessed, using the indicative imperfect (разпра́вяше). He then shifts (10) to the renarrated to tell of events which it is clear he has not witnessed. His narration includes verbs in the renarrated present (замина́вала), renarrated aorist (ми́нала, ня́мало, пока́зал, разка́зал), and renarrated future (щя́л да разведе́).

He has no obvious basis to disbelieve what Julie has told him. Thus he could theoretically have narrated this sequence using indicative verbs. It is true that he could not have used aorist indicative for the past tense forms (since he was not a direct witness), but he could have used the past indefinite. The social situation, however, is such that it would be inappropriate for him not to keep a certain communicative distance. The use of the renarrated is the norm in such a situation. For Veselin to use the indicative here would indicate a markedly strong insistence on his belief in the truth of what Julie has told him.

The next speaker changes the subject and asks a question (11), using the past indefinite indicative (дошъ́л е). It is true that this speaker knows the factual information in question only second-hand. His purpose in mentioning it, however, is not to retell what someone else has told him but rather to ask a question; thus the use of the neutral mode (indicative) is normal and expected.

Julie answers first (12) by transmitting information she learned from someone else, using the renarrated imperfect (**се наливали**). Her use of this mode specifically marks her distance from the event, and emphasizes the fact that she was not present. Her subsequent shift to indicative in the same sentence (13) underscores the difference between her distance from the events of the previous evening, and her certainty of the present result of those events (arrived at via her own powers of deduction). To communicate this certainty, she uses the present-tense indicative (**махмурлия е**).

24.7. Summary: use of the renarrated mood

The above passage, which represents a typical (and quite neutral) use of the renarrated mood, shows some of its subtlety and complexity. It is important to remember that the use of the renarrated mood is never absolutely obligatory. The choice to add the stance of "distancing" to one's speech is always an option. Thus, it is theoretically possible for a Bulgarian to communicate everything in the indicative if s/he chooses not to add this optional element of distancing. The narration of past-tense events poses something of a limitation in that it is impossible for Bulgarians to use the aorist or imperfect indicative for events they are explicitly reporting from another's words. They do, however, always have the option to use the past indefinite indicative.

At the same time, their language gives Bulgarians the option to add the element of distancing at all levels of their speech, and it is an option of which they take frequent advantage. It adds a nuance to the language that is extremely difficult to convey adequately in translation. A possible (but limited) correspondence in English would be the shift to past tense in indirect discourse, which constitutes a "distancing" of sorts in that it adds temporal distancing without a corresponding shift in real time. Otherwise, the only way English can convey the meaning of the Bulgarian renarrated mood is by phrases such as "apparently", "it is said", and through intonation and gestures. Most of the time it must go untranslated (and remain an unmined richness of the Bulgarian linguistic soul).

Двайсет и четвърти урок / Lesson 24

EXERCISES

I. Retell the following sentences to someone else, emphasizing that you are not a direct witness.

1. Той отива за пет месеца в Германия.
2. Те си строят къща на морето.
3. Вие правите най-хубавата пица във вашето заведение.
4. Те настояват за преразглеждане на делото.
5. Тя е изненадана, но не е обидена.
6. Ти отключваш библиотеката сутрин.
7. Тя знае, че той обича да си пийне.

II. Retell the following passage to someone else, emphasizing that you are not a direct witness.

    Малката Мая отиде с майка си в зоологическата градина. Понеже много обичаше животните, тя носеше за тях семки, лешници, бонбони и дори един сандвич със сирене. Първо стигнаха до клетката на маймуните. Клетката беше празна. Пазачът разказа на Мая и майка ѝ за случилото се. Маймуните бяха болни. Децата постоянно им даваха да ядат бонбони и те се разболяха. Мая никога вече не хранеше животните в зоологическата градина.

III. Retell the following passage to someone else, emphasizing that you are not a direct witness.

    Преподавателят закъсняваше. Събралите се студенти отначало седяха по местата си и тихо разговаряха. После някой каза: "Много ми се пуши. Ще се върна след една цигара време." Двама-трима тръгнаха с него. Минаха още няколко минути, а вратата не се отваряше и преподавателят не влизаше. Колко жалко! Лекцията обещаваше да бъде интересна. Най-накрая дойде секретарката и обяви, че преподавателят е болен. Един от студентите се оплака: "Ако знаех, че преподавателят няма да дойде, щях да си остана вкъщи да се наспя." Другите му казаха: "Нищо. Друг път ще спиш. Сега отиваме на кино."

Двайсет и четвърти урок / Lesson 24

SAMPLE SENTENCES

1. Той твърдеше, че щял да чете целия следобед, но когато се обадих, него го нямаше.

2. Те ни убеждаваха, че новината нямало да се разчуе.
3. Те ни убедиха, че новината няма да се разчуе.

4. Тя разказва на всички, че четяла по цял ден, но аз редовно я виждам да пуши с часове на балкона.

5. Той казва, че работел. Ако на това му викат работа, какво ли правят, когато си почиват?

6. Петър смята, че чушките имали нужда от още малко оцет.
7. Тя мисли, че конкурсът бил предрешен.
8. Научи ли, че баба ѝ била много болна?

9. Казаха ми, че най-хубава скара правели в Самоков, а най-хубаво кисело мляко предлагали в Ябланица. Вярно ли е?

10. Той каза, че нямало да излиза преди вечеря.
11. В Русия хората не обичали българско сирене.

12. Цените на самолетните билети щели да се увеличават.
13. Мързеливи сме били, поне така говорят хората зад гърба ни.

14. От подслушания разговор излезе, че никой не искал да поеме ръководството на съюза.

15. Знаеш ли, че на гущерите им израствали нови опашки на мястото на откъснатите?

16. През турско време българите не служели войници.

17. Приятелите на родителите ми водели по това време приятен живот в Марсилия.

18. През 1933 година Георги Димитров прекарал девет месеца в затвора по обвинението, че е подпалил Райхстага.

19. В семейство, където децата умирали малки, по обичай давали на децата "грозни" имена, та смъртта да не ги хареса.

20. Казаха, че щели да дойдат, ако намерили с кого да оставят децата.

Двайсет и четвърти урок / Lesson 24

SENTENCES FOR TRANSLATION

1. Karakonjuls are said to go about in the time between Christmas and Iordanovden. They are big and scary, but not very smart. One can trick them quite easily.

2. As far as I know, he was intending to arrive at six, but I heard that while he was traveling he had some trouble on the border, so he'll be getting to Sofia very late.

3. They were trying to convince us that they had turned into vampires. I'm not sure if I believe them.

4. What could have happened to Pencho? They said he was going to come to the restaurant between 7 and 8, but there's no sign of him.

5. I heard that he didn't come to the exam because he had fallen ill, and I don't doubt it, because he always tells the truth.

6. A long time ago there were no people on the Earth. There were only monkeys and fish.

7. Surely he is exhausted from his travels. Didn't he say he was going to bed early? He is always claiming he is tired, but he never goes to bed on time.

Mosque, Samakov

Двайсет и четвърти урок / Lesson 24

READING SELECTION

За вампирите

Вя́рата във вампи́ри съществу́ва навре́д у бъ́лгарите до към нача́лото на XX в. На́й-че́стото обясне́ние за вампиря́сването на мъртве́ц, умря́л от есте́ствена смъ́рт, е, че то́й, преди́ да бъ́де погре́бан, е би́л преско́чен от ко́тка, от коко́шка или от дру́го ня́кое живо́тно или е па́днала ня́каква ся́нка върху не́го. Твъ́рде че́сто като причи́на се изтъ́ква греховността́ на мъртве́ца. Интере́сно е вя́рването, че хо́рата, кои́то уми́рат мно́го ста́ри, след смъртта́ си вина́ги вампиря́сват. Вампи́ри ста́ват и хо́ра, чия́то смъ́рт е била́ неесте́ствена -- обе́сени, уда́вени, уби́ти.

Ра́зказите и анекдо́тите за вампи́ри из бъ́лгарските села́ са извънре́дно мно́го. Мо́же с пра́во да се ка́же, че ня́ма се́лище, в кое́то да ня́ма по ня́колко таки́ва преда́ния, кои́то че́сто са свъ́рзани и с определе́ни, изве́стни на разказва́чите лица́; те́ че́сто са те́хни родни́ни, бли́зки, позна́ти.

Предста́вите за въ́ншния ви́д на вампи́рите са разнообра́зни. Вампи́рът се явя́ва във ви́д на чове́к или на ра́зни живо́тни. Явя́ва се вина́ги но́щем. То́й оби́ча да произве́жда шу́м по тава́ните. Чу́пи и обръ́ща съди́ни, я́зди и измъ́чва доби́тъка. Запи́сано в Родо́пите свиде́телство гласи́, че вампи́рът вся́ка но́щ изпъ́ждал кра́вите. Фуча́л като чекръ́к. Пра́ните дре́хи, кои́то били́ сла́гани в една́ ка́ца, вся́ка но́щ ста́вали къ́рвави. Вси́чки в село́то се боя́ли да спя́т ве́че по домове́те си. Кога́то отишли́ на гро́ба, наме́рили ѝ то́лкова голя́ма ду́пка. Тога́ва напра́вили пи́тки с ме́д и ги сло́жили на кръстопъ́тя извън село́то. И оттога́ва го ня́мало ве́че.

Сред предста́вите и вя́рванията за вампи́ра е и това́, че вампи́рите са страхли́ви същества́. Те́ се боя́т напри́мер от ши́пка. Затова́ до мъртве́ца сла́гат ши́пкова пръ́чка, та да го убоде́, кога́то запо́чне да вампиря́сва. Вя́рва се, че ку́четата, роде́ни в съ́бота мо́гат да ви́ждат но́щем вампи́рите. На мно́го места́ съ́що така́ вя́рват, че вампи́рите се боя́т от вода́ и о́гън.

Вампи́рите са наи́вни и мо́гат ле́сно да бъ́дат изма́мвани. В Бе́ли Искъ́р, Са́моковско изпра́тили еди́н вампи́р у́ж на сва́тба. Излъ́гали го и го качи́ли на една́ кола́, изпре́гнали воло́вете край село́то и оста́вили та́м кола́та. През нощта́ дошъ́л въ́лк и го изя́л. И в Говеда́рци, Са́моковско вя́рват, че въ́лците оби́чали да да́ват вампи́рите. Бана́тските бъ́лгари пък смя́тат, че вампи́рът оби́чал да яде́ пръ́ст. Затова́ преди́ стоти́на годи́ни, кога́то върлу́вал вампи́рът, ня́кой си Бе́гов, родни́ните му го подма́мили с еди́н чува́л пръ́ст от гро́ба му, като му пу́скали по пъ́тя ма́лко от не́я. Така́ го отве́ли до река́та и хвъ́рлили чува́ла с пръстта́ в не́я. Вампи́рът ско́чил след не́го и се уда́вил във вода́та.

Вампи́рът пра́ви па́кости обикнове́но до четири́десет де́на и ако дотога́ва не се́ унищожи́, то́й се окостеня́ва и ста́ва о́ще по́-стра́шен. Доживе́е ли до ше́ст ме́сеца, вампи́рът получа́ва плъ́т и ста́ва чове́к, какъ́вто е би́л и преди́ смъртта́ си, са́мо че ня́ма но́кти. Такъ́в окостене́н вампи́р оти́вал да живе́е дале́че в дру́го село́, къде́то не го́ позна́ват, и та́м се занима́вал с

Двайсет и четвърти урок / Lesson 24

търговия́ и занаят. Той се же́ни, ка́кто вси́чки хо́ра, и и́ма деца́, кои́то по́сле ста́ват "вампирджи́и", защо́то мо́гат да ви́ждат вампи́рите и да ги уби́ват. Таки́ва вампи́ри ста́вали мно́го пакостли́ви, ако преживе́ели до три́ годи́ни. Широ́ко разпростране́но е вя́рването, че друговерците че́сто ста́ват вампи́ри.

Страхъ́т от вампи́рите е мно́го голя́м у наро́да. Чу́е ли се, че е́ди-ко́й си е ста́нал вампи́р, вси́чки изтръ́пват от стра́х, дори́ из око́лните села́.

В мно́го слу́чаи отстраня́ването на вампи́рите ста́ва чрез пла́шене. По врати́те на къ́щите сла́гат че́репи от живо́тни, от кои́то вампи́рите се пла́шат и не вли́зат. Дру́гаде ока́чват по врати́те слъ́нчогле́д или пра́вят маги́я.

На ня́кои места́ вя́рват, че вампи́рите хо́дят са́мо зи́мно вре́ме. Пъ́рвата гръмоте́вица ги унищожа́вала.

В Бо́тевградско разпъ́ждали вампи́рите, като ока́чвали на врата́та на къ́щата си́то и реше́то и ка́звали: "Кога́то вампи́рът преброи́ вси́чки те́зи ду́пки на си́тото и реше́тото, тога́ва да вле́зе въ́тре." Вампи́рът не мо́жел ни́кога да ги преброи́: той ви́наги се объ́рквал при броене́то, а щом се съ́мнело, той бя́гал от светлина́та. Ако се слу́чело да му се ка́же и́мето тъ́кмо кога́то петли́те пе́ят през нощта́, той ста́вал на пихти́я.

Адаптирано от Христо Вакарелски, Български погребални обичаи, София, 1990.

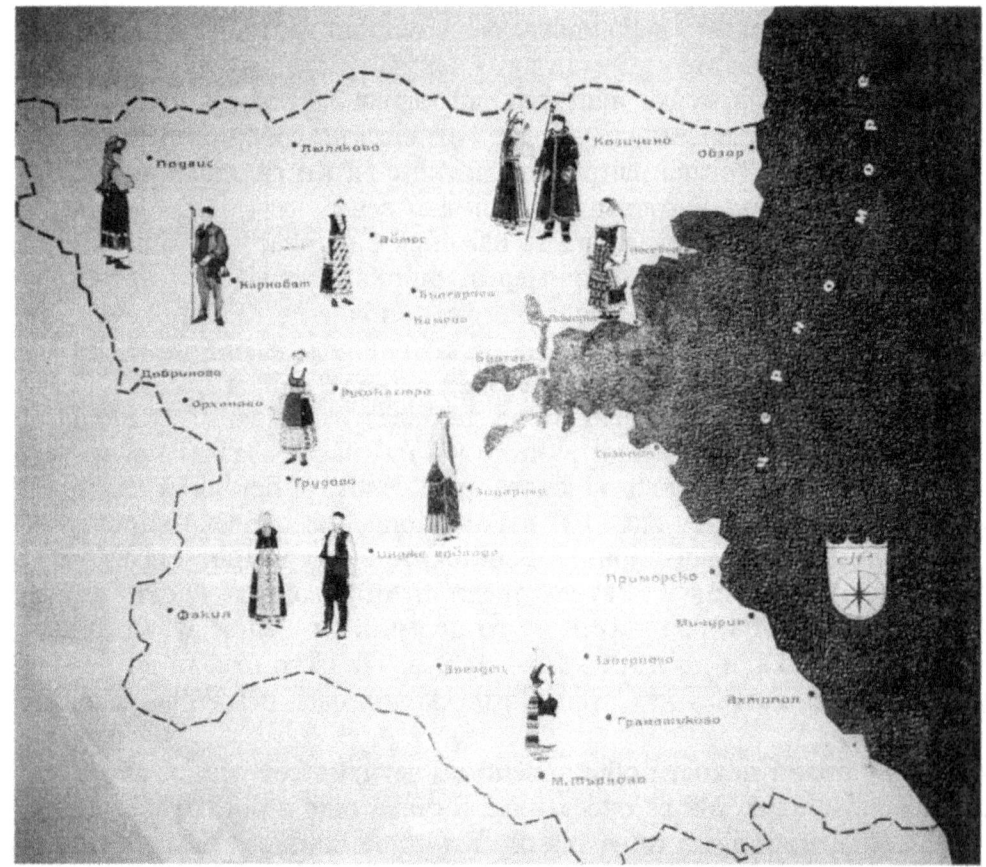

Folk costume map of southeastern Bulgaria, Ethnographic Museum, Nesebăr

Двайсет и четвърти урок / Lesson 24

GLOSSARY

анекдо́т	anecdote	изчервя́вам се / изчервя́ се	blush, turn red
боя́ се от	be afraid of	изяви́телен	declarative
бя́гам	run, run away; avoid	изяви́телно наклоне́ние	indicative mood
вампи́р	vampire		
вампирджи́я	vampire fighter	ка́ца	cask, vat
вампиря́свам	turn into a vampire	киломе́тър	kilometer
вдру́гиден	on the next day	кле́тка	cage
вол	ox	кръстопъ́т, -ят	crossroads
въ́ншен	outside, external	кърва́в	bloody
върлу́вам	rage, run rampant		
вя́рване (*pl.* -ния)	belief	ле́шник	hazelnut
глася́	state, indicate; intend, prepare	маги́я	magic, sorcery
		майму́на	monkey, ape
грани́ца	border; limit	ма́хам с ръка́	wave one's hand
грехо́вност	sinfulness	махмурли́я (съм)	[have] a hangover
гроздобе́р	grape harvest	мед, -ъ́т	honey
гро́зен	ugly, hideous	мъртве́ц	dead person, corpse
гръмоте́вица	peal of thunder		
гу́щер	lizard	на въ́здух	in the open air
		навре́д	everywhere
да́вя	drown; suffocate	нади́гам се / нади́гна се	rise
джами́я	mosque		
доживя́вам / доживе́я	live to see	наи́вен	naive, guileless
		наклоне́ние	(*grammatical*) mood
друговерец	person of another faith	нали́вам се / нале́я се	drink heavily, booze
ду́пка	hole, gap	наса́м	this way, over here
		настоя́вам / настоя́	insist
ей то́лкова	this much (*conversational device*)	неесте́ствен	unnatural
		некро́пол	necropolis
		но́щем	at night
заведе́ние	establishment, public place	обвине́ние	accusation
затво́р	prison; imprisonment	обе́свам / обе́ся	hang (by the neck)
зла́то	gold	обръ́щам / объ́рна	turn, turn over
		обърквам / объ́ркам	confuse, perplex, bewilder, frustrate
изма́мвам / изма́мя	deceive; betray		
измъ́чвам / измъ́ча (-иш)	torment	обясне́ние	explanation
		ока́чвам / окача́ (-иш)	hang, suspend
изнена́двам	take by surprise		
изпре́варвам / изпреваря́	outrun; anticipate	окостеня́вам / окостеня́	take skeletal shape
изпря́гам / изпре́гна	unharness	отве́ждам / отведа́	lead off, take away
изпъ́ждам / изпъ́дя	chase away	отстраня́вам / отстраня́	remove, eliminate
изтръ́пвам от стра́х	get shudders down one's spine		

Двайсет и четвърти урок / Lesson 24

пазáч	guard, keeper	слýжа войнѝк	do military service
пáкост	mischief, harm	слънчоглéд	sunflower
пакостлѝв	mischievous, naughty	спѝтничка	fellow traveler (female)
петéл (*pl.* петлѝ)	cock, rooster	среднóщ	middle of the night
пѝтка	cake, flat loaf	стотѝна	a hundred or so
пихтѝя	jelly; pulp	страхлѝв	cowardly, timid
плът, -тá	flesh, body	съдѝна	vessel, container; pan
повелѝтелен	authoritative	сѝмва се / сѝмне се (*3rd person*)	dawn, day breaks
повелѝтелно наклонéние	imperative mood		
подмáмвам / подмáмя	entice, lure	съществó	being, creature
		съществýвам	exist
подпáлвам / подпáля	set fire to, ignite		
подслýшвам / подслýшам	eavesdrop	тавáн	ceiling; attic
		твърде	rather, very
прáвя пáкост	make mischief, cause damage	търговѝя	trade, commerce
предáние	legend	убѝвам / убѝя	kill, murder
предисторѝчески	prehistoric	убóждам / убодá	prick, stab
предрешáвам / предрешá (-ѝш)	decide in advance, predetermine	удáвям / удáвя	drown
		уж	as if, ostensibly
предстáва	notion, concept	универесáлен	universal
преизкáзвам	renarrate, retell	унищожáвам / унищожá (-ѝш)	destroy, annihilate
преизкáзно наклонéние	renarrated mood		
		услóвен	provisional
преразглéждам / преразглéдам	reconsider, re-examine	услóвно наклонéние	conditional mood
произвéждам / произведá	produce, make; cause	фучá (-ѝш)	whiz; rage
пръст, -тá	earth, soil	халвá	halva, sesame candy
работнѝчески	workers'; labor (*adj.*)	ЦУМ = Централен универсáлен магазѝн	Central universal store (department store)
разказвáч	narrator, storyteller		
разкóпки	excavations		
разпъ̀ждам / разпъ̀дя	drive away, disperse		
разчýвам се / разчýя се	get out, get around	чекръ̀к	spinning wheel
		чéреп	skull
решéто	screen, colander	чувáл	sack
ръковóдство	leadership	чýпя	break
с часовé	for hours		
самолéтен	airplane (*adj.*)	шѝпка	wild rose; rose hip
сгýшвам се / сгýша се (-иш)	huddle together	шѝпков	of wild rose; made of rose hips
сéмка	seed		
сѝто	sieve	явя̀вам се / явя̀ се	appear, show up
слýжа (-иш)	serve, work	я̀здя	ride, straddle

Двайсет и четвърти урок / Lesson 24

CULTURAL COMMENTARY

Religion: mosques and churches
During the Ottoman period, there were many mosques in Sofia. The main one, located near the main department store (Централният универсален магазин, or ЦУМ), still functions as a mosque. Most others now serve other purposes. The mosque referred to colloquially as the "black mosque" (чéрната джамия) has been transformed into the Orthodox church of Свети седмочисленици (The Holy Seven, by whom are meant Cyril, Methodius, and the five of their disciples who worked in Bulgarian lands in the 9th and 10th centuries -- Kliment, Gorazd, Naum, Sava, and Angelarij). Another now houses the archaeological musuem of Sofia (one of whose central exhibits is a large stone-wall carving of the "Thracian horseman"). Many Bulgarians are only dimly aware that some of these buildings once were mosques, and few of them remember which building was which mosque.

History: Georgi Dimitrov
Georgi Dimitrov (Георги Димитров, 1882-1949) is best known to Bulgarians as the central figure of the Communist party, and as the leader of his country after the Communists took power. After his death in 1949, a mausoleum was built in downtown Sofia across from the previous Tsar's palace, where he lay in state under honor guard, embalmed after the manner of Lenin in Moscow. After the fall of the socialist regime, his body was removed and given a normal burial, and the mausoleum was torn down.
Dimitrov had been politically active since 1902, when he joined the Bulgarian Workers' Social-Democratic Party (Българска работническа социал-демократическа партия, БРСДП). This party, which had been formed in 1891 by Dimităr Blagoev (Димитър Благоев, 1856-1924), split in 1903 into two wings. Dimitrov allied himself with the more radical wing, which eventually became the Bulgarian Communist Party. After the government put down the anti-fascist uprising which he helped lead in 1923, Dimitrov went into exile; he lived in Europe between 1923 and 1934, and in the USSR between 1934 and 1945. During 1942 he helped found the Fatherland Front (Отечествен Фронт), which was first a resistance movement to Bulgaria's Axis-sponsored government and later the core of Bulgaria's socialist government.
Dimitrov became world-famous for his role in the Reichstag fire of early 1933. Accused by the Nazis of having conspired with other Communist leaders to burn the Reichstag, Dimitrov conducted his own defense at the trial. By skillful argumentation, he outwitted the Nazi prosecution and won acquittal.

Archaeology: recent excavations
Bulgaria is rich not only in settlements from early historic times (Thracian and Byzantine) but also from prehistoric times. In recent years, archaelogists have been excavating numerous important sites. The largest efforts, by a joint Bulgarian-Austrian team. have been devoted to the Neolithic tell-settlement of Karanovo (Караново), located near Nova Zagora (Нова Загора) in central Bulgaria. Other important excavation efforts have included those at the Bronze Age site of Yunatsite (Юнаците) in southern Thrace (by a joint Russian-Bulgarian team) and the Eneolothic site of Durankulak (Дуранкулак) on the northern Black Sea coast. Excavations in southwestern Bulgaria include a significant Neolithic site at Kovachevo (Ковачево), where a French-Bulgarian team has been working; another smaller site in the same area is in the Struma river valley on the Greek border at Topolnitsa.

Geography: citation of place names; local food and drink
For ease of orientation, village names are cited together with the name of the larger town identifying their location. Thus, Говедарци, Самоковско means the village of Govedartsi in the region of Samokov. It is parallel to the practice of naming a city together with its state in the U.S., e.g. Laramie, Wyoming.
Samokov (Самоков) is a town in southwestern Bulgaria and Yablanitsa (Ябланица) is a town in northwestern Bulgaria, in the Balkan mountains. Bulgarian folk wisdom claims that the best yogurt and halva (халва, or sesame candy) are made in Yablanitsa, that the best outdoor grills are in Samokov, and that the best beer, Zagorka (Загорка), is that made in Stara Zagora.

Двайсет и четвърти урок / Lesson 24

Folk belief

Folk tradition believes that Death will take children whom she finds attractive. For this reason, village children were often given names that were meant to horrify or repel. Examples of such names are Groza or Grozyo (Гро́за or Гро́зьо, related to the word гро́зен "ugly"), Strashimir (Страшими́р, which includes the word стра́х "fear"), and Vulko or Vulkana (Въ́лко or Вълка́на, derived from въ́лк "wolf", an animal who was generally feared).

Folk belief is very alive in Bulgaria. Many in the villages (and not a few in towns as well) will insist that certain legends recount events that "actually happened". Ethnographers have researched and described these beliefs in detail, taking care to identify the geographical sources of the particular variations. One belief common both among the folk and in the Orthodox religion is that the soul of the departed stays close to its mortal remains for forty days, and only then makes the transition to the "other world". Many rituals are necessary during this period to protect both the recently-departed soul and those left behind. It is believed that if these rituals are not properly observed, the soul can be locked forever in the intermediate zone and---willingly or not---cause harm and havoc. Another common folk belief, connected with the widespread conviction that vampires exist, is that certain individuals are born with sufficient knowledge of vampires to be able to fight and outwit them.

Church of the Holy Seven (Sveti Sedmochislenici), Sofia

LESSON 25

DIALOGUE

Ти́ си би́л голя́м кавале́р!

Таня: Хру́мна ми една иде́я. Защо́ да не оти́дем вси́чки за́едно на Ви́тоша? Тъ́кмо и мъжъ́т ми ка́зваше, че в неде́ля щя́л да бъ́де свобо́ден.

Камен: А́з ще пока́жа на Бо́би море́ните. Бо́би, събуди́ се! Не се́ ли наспа́? У́тре оти́ваме на Ви́тоша!

Надка: А а́з ще пока́жа на ле́ля Джу́ли ку́клите си. Ма́мо, нали́ ще ги взе́мем вси́чките с на́с?

Таня: Са́мо те́ ще са ни кусу́рът на Ви́тоша. Ще ги взе́мем, ако обеща́еш ти́ да си ги но́сиш сама́.

Камен: Слу́шай я ти́ не́я какво́ обеща́ва. Ще обеща́е, пъ́к по́сле като ви́ди зо́р, ще ка́же, че не била́ обеща́вала, и ще ти ги даде́ на те́бе да ги но́сиш.

Павлина: А ти́ ня́ма ли да помо́гнеш на сестри́чката си да си но́си ку́клите?

Камен: Те́ са не́йни, тя́ да си ги но́си. А́з ще но́ся Бо́би, ако се е умори́л.

Милена: Ти́ си би́л голя́м кавале́р, бе Ка́мене. Ако еди́н де́н като пора́снеш, то́лкова пома́гаш на жена́ си, горко́ й.

Камен: Ако е ру́са, ще й пома́гам.

Таня: Джу́ли, тря́бва непреме́нно да доведе́те и Де́йвид.

Джули: Не зна́м дали́ ще и́ска да до́йде. То́й разпра́вяше, че наско́ро си би́л чу́пил кра́к. Ле́сно се умори́вал. Не мо́жел дъ́лго да хо́ди пеша́.

Веселин: Си́гурно го е ка́зал като оправда́ние, за да се́днете в ня́кое заведе́ние.

Милена: Е́й, ама́ сте ло́ши. Веднъ́ж му се е слу́чило на момче́то да попрекали́ с черве́ното ви́но и ведна́га му изле́зе сла́ва че би́л голя́м пия́ница.

Димитър: Ти́ си била́ мно́го демократи́чна като ста́ва ду́ма за чу́жди хо́ра. А ако бя́х а́з, ко́й зна́е ка́к ще́ше да ми три́еш со́л на глава́та.

Павлина: Ама Митенце, ти нали не пиеш. В нашето семейство не се е случвало да има мъже пияници.

Димитър: А жени?

Павлина: Какви са тези приказки! Леля Марийка, Бог да я прости, обичаше да си сръбне едно ликьорче, като й дойдат гости... Но не повече.

Димитър: А после по цял ден спеше, уж че я боляла главата.

Павлина: Да, тя страдаше горкичката от страшно главоболие.

Таня: Откога мечтая аз да отидем на Витоша. Ще вземем с нас одеяла. Ще направим шишчета, салатки. Децата ще глътнат чист въздух, а ние ще си поприказваме, ще си починем. А то все работа, работа. Работата край няма.

Джули: Аз мислех, че вие предлагате да се качим на Черни връх с по една раница.

Павлина: Ако ще ходим на Черни връх, аз не мога да дойда. Докторите не ми разрешават да се преуморявам.

Таня: Ако ще е на Черни връх, ще е с лифта. И децата бързо се уморяват.

Димитър: Какво се разбираме тогава?

Таня: Хайде да се срещнем утре в осем часа на последната спирка на петицата в Княжево.

Милена: Добре. Ние ще сме там и тримата, нали майко?

Павлина: Щом настоявате. А сега е време да си вървим.

Таня: И ние тръгваме. До утре.

Двайсет и пети урок / Lesson 25

GRAMMAR

25.1. The renarrated mood, continued

The renarrated mood expresses the speaker's desire to establish a certain distance from the information s/he is transmitting. This distancing can take different forms, and thus impart different meanings to a speaker's choice to use the renarrated mood. The most neutral meaning, which gives rise to the name of the mood itself, is that the content of the speech was heard from a third party and is being transmitted without any committment as to its veracity.

Other meanings convey more emotional involvement on the part of the speaker. Sometimes s/he expresses surprise at a previously unknown fact; if the context permits, this usage can also convey an implied compliment. On other occasions the speaker conveys varying degrees of disbelief, which can imply irony, sarcasm and even bitterness. All of these meanings are, of course, quite dependent on the content of the speech and the context within which it is spoken. The point is that it is through the verbal form itself that the speaker expresses these emotions.

Some grammarians use the special terms "admirative" and "dubitative" for these meanings; the use these terms will be discussed below.

25.2. Renarrated mood in 1st and 2nd person

To a certain degree, elements of this more "emotional" usage are present every time the renarrated mood is used in the 1st or 2nd person. The nature of reported speech is to report what some third party has said; the neutral renarrated usage is thus almost completely restricted to 3rd person forms. It stands to reason that it is somewhat unusual to speak in one's own voice (1st person) or to make a statement directly to someone (2nd person), while at the same time emphasizing one's refusal to take responsibility for the content of one's speech. When such statements are marked by the use of renarrated forms, one or another of the above emotional overtones is usually present.

This is not to say that one cannot "renarrate" 1st or 2nd person speech; the point is simply that it is difficult for such renarration to maintain a completely neutral tone. The following examples, for instance, in which speakers relate what someone else has said either about themselves or the person they are speaking to, also communicate a certain amount of disbelief on the part of the speaker:

Мáмо, глýпав ли съм? Любéн кáзва, че съм бил глýпав.	Mama, am I stupid? Lyuben says that I'm stupid.
Каквó? Щя́ла съм да отúда послéдна? Не é вя́рно!	What? [They say that] I'll be the last one to go? That's not true!
Защó тóй кáзва тогáва, че не си билá готóва?	So then why is he saying that you're not ready?

| Била́ съм заспа́ла по вре́ме на ки́ното. | I fell asleep during the film, is that what you're saying? |

Another common meaning, conveyed by 2nd person renarrated form, is surprise.

| Ти́ си би́л голя́м кавале́р. | Well, you're quite the gentleman! |
| Ко́лко си би́л голя́м! | What a big boy you are! |

Finally, the renarrated mood can convey the expression of irony or sarcasm. Depending on the degree of sarcasm, the appropriate speech intonation usually accompanies such usage. For example:

| Ти́ си била́ мно́го демократи́чна, като ста́ва ду́ма за чу́жди хо́ра. | I must say, you're quite "democratic" when it concerns other people. |

One of the primary formal characteristics of the renarrated mood is that the 3rd person forms lack the auxiliary. Given the plethora of compound tenses in Bulgarian which consist of the L-participle plus an auxiliary, the use of the L-participle standing alone, as the main verb in a sentence, is very marked. This unaccompanied L-participle immediately communicates to a Bulgarian that the speaker intends to send a message which is in some way "distanced".

In the 1st and 2nd person, however, such marking is not possible: all renarrated forms are accompanied by auxiliaries. Formally, therefore, there is potential ambiguity. A student seeing paradigms in a book, or a printed word on a page, probably wonders how s/he is to know whether the words **ти́ си би́л** mean "you were" (past indefinite) or "you are [said to be]" (present renarrated). In practice, though, there is little ambiguity, since the context usually indicates whether the appropriate "distanced" emotional overtones are present or not.

25.3. Renarrated mood of the past indefinite and past anterior tenses

	Past indefinite tense		*Past anterior tense*	
	indicative	**RENARRATED**	*indicative*	**RENARRATED**
1st singular	чел съм	бил съм чел	бях чел	бил съм чел
2nd singular	чел си	бил си чел	беше чел	бил си чел
3rd singular	чел е	бил чел	беше чел	бил чел
1st plural	чели сме	били сме чели	бяхме чели	били сме чели
2nd plural	чели сте	били сте чели	бяхте чели	били сте чели
3rd plural	чели са	били чели	бяха чели	били чели

Двайсет и пети урок / Lesson 25

As in the case of most other renarrated forms, a single paradigm renarrates two different indicative tenses. The renarrated forms of the past anterior are identical with those of the past indefinite. Context gives the information as to tense.

Past indefinite

| Часъ́т би́л запо́чнал навре́ме, зна́чи, часо́вникът ми изоста́ва. | Class started on time [so I hear]; that means my watch is slow. |

Past anterior

| Писмо́то ве́че било́ присти́гнало, кога́то а́з се оба́дих по телефо́на. | [He said] the letter had already arrived when I called. |

The renarrated auxiliaries **би́л** and **било́** indicate to the listener that the speaker knows the information second-hand. From the context, the listener deduces that the verb form used by the quoted speaker in the first sentence was past indefinite indicative (**запо́чнал е**), and that the verb form used by the quoted speaker in the second sentence was the past anterior tense indicative (**бе́ше присти́гнало**).

25.4. Renarrated mood of the future anterior and future anterior in the past tenses

Future anterior tense (affirmative)

	indicative	**RENARRATED**
1ˢᵗ singular	ще съм че́л	щя́л съм да съм че́л
2ⁿᵈ singular	ще си че́л	щя́л си да си че́л
3ᵈ singular	ще е че́л	щя́л да е че́л
1ˢᵗ plural	ще сме че́ли	ще́ли сме да сме че́ли
2ⁿᵈ plural	ще сте че́ли	ще́ли сте да сте че́ли
3ᵈ plural	ще са че́ли	ще́ли да са че́ли

Future anterior tense (negative)

	indicative	**RENARRATED**
1ˢᵗ singular	ня́ма да съм че́л	ня́мало да съм че́л
2ⁿᵈ singular	ня́ма да си че́л	ня́мало да си че́л
3ᵈ singular	ня́ма да е че́л	ня́мало да е че́л
1ˢᵗ plural	ня́ма да сме че́ли	ня́мало да сме че́ли
2ⁿᵈ plural	ня́ма да сте че́ли	ня́мало да сте че́ли
3ᵈ plural	ня́ма да са че́ли	ня́мало да са че́ли

Future anterior in the past tense (affirmative)

	indicative	**RENARRATED**
1st singular	щях да съм чел	щял съм да съм чел
2nd singular	щеше да си чел	щял си да си чел
3rd singular	щеше да е чел	щял да е чел
1st plural	щяхме да сме чели	щели сме да сме чели
2nd plural	щяхте да сте чели	щели сте да сте чели
3rd plural	щяха да са чели	щели да са чели

Future anterior in the past tense (negative)

	indicative	**RENARRATED**
1st singular	нямаше да съм чел	нямало да съм чел
2nd singular	нямаше да си чел	нямало да си чел
3rd singular	нямаше да е чел	нямало да е чел
1st plural	нямаше да сме чели	нямало да сме чели
2nd plural	нямаше да сте чели	нямало да сте чели
3rd plural	нямаше да са чели	нямало да са чели

This final set of renarrated forms also corresponds to a pair of tenses in the indicative. As in the other instances, one must use context to know which tense is meant.

Future anterior

Много са самонадеяни -- щели да са завършили строежа още преди Великден.	They're full of self-confidence -- they say that they will have finished building [it] by Easter.

Future anterior in the past

Няма да повярваш колко е нахален -- нямало да съм взел и половината изпити, ако не бил ми помогнал.	You won't believe how impudent he is -- [he said] I wouldn't have passed even half of my exams if he hadn't helped me.

The renarrated auxiliary phrases headed by щели да and нямало да, as well as the renarrated auxiliary бил, indicate to the listener that the speaker knows the information second-hand. From the context, the listener deduces that the original information of the first sentence was conveyed by a verb in the future anterior indicative tense (ще сме завършили), and that the original information in the second sentence was conveyed by verbs in the future anterior in the past tense indicative (**нямаше да си взе́л** and **ако не бя́х ти помо́гнал**).

Renarrated forms of these two tenses occur less frequently when the verb is affirmative. This is probably because of the degree of distancing necessary. To be able to use the future anterior (and the future anterior in the past), a speaker must envisage two completed actions in the future. The need to express yet further distance from such a sequence seems to create something of an overload. Consider the following example, spoken in the future anterior indicative by a workman:

В сря́да ще съм свъ́ршил по́вече от полови́ната рабо́та.	By Wednesday I'll have finished more than half the job.

His pleased employer, retelling this to another, should theoretically use the renarrated future anterior form **щя́л да е свъ́ршил**. Many Bulgarians, however, would be tempted to use the simple future renarrated instead. That is, they would retain the distancing of the renarrated, but relinquish the complex temporal distancing of the future anterior:

Ви́ж ко́лко добре́ рабо́ти чове́кът -- в сря́да щя́л да свъ́рши по́вече от полови́ната рабо́та.	Look how well this guy is working -- he says by Wednesday he'll finish half the job.

In negative expressions, however, speakers tend to maintain the distinctions. This is probably because the idea of an action's *not* taking place before another one is more consistent with the distancing expressed by the renarrated mood. The same workman, for example, could also have said the following:

Съжаля́вам, ама до сря́да ня́ма да съм свъ́ршил и полови́ната рабо́та.	I'm sorry, but I won't even have finished half the job by Wednesday.

His disgruntled employer, retelling this to another, would almost certainly maintain the sequence of tenses required by the future anterior. That is, instead of collapsing the two into **ня́мало да свъ́рши** (which would be parallel to the example given for the affirmative above), he would be more likely to say:

Чу́ ли то́зи мързели́вец на́шия бояджи́я -- до сря́да ня́мало да е свъ́ршил и полови́ната рабо́та.	Did you hear what that lazy painter of ours said, that by Wednesday he won't even have finished half the job?!

Двайсет и пети урок / Lesson 25

25.5. The "admirative" and "dubitative" moods

The terms "admirative mood" and "dubitative mood" refer to expressions of surprise or doubt, respectively, by means of renarrated forms. The term "dubitative" carries in it directly the idea of doubt, but the term "admirative" must be interpreted broadly: sometimes admiration is indeed meant, but more often the intended emotion is one of sarcasm or irony.

Although renarrated forms in the 1st and 2nd person usually express one of these emotions to some degree or another, 3rd person renarrated forms are more ambiguous. They can indicate simple transmission of information (without emotional overtone), they can indicate such transmission with emotional overtone added, or they can communicate simply "pure" emotional response.

The list below, phrased in the form of two sets of gradations (2-4 and 5-8), gives most of the possible meanings of the renarrated forms. Varying degrees along each of the two scales are also possible. The terms "admirative" and "dubitative" have been applied by grammarians to all but usage (1).

(1) report of someone else's words without emotion but with intent to stay neutral and noncommittal as to the truth value;

(2) report of someone else's words with caution, implying the need to be convinced further before accepting those words as true;

(3) report of someone else's words with considerable doubt, and intent to pass this doubt along to the listener;

(4) report of someone else's words with heavy irony or sarcasm, implying clear disbelief;

(5) pleasant surprise at a previously unknown fact, often intended as an implied compliment;

(6) strong surprise at a previously unknown fact, no other emotion present;

(7) strong surprise at a previously unknown "fact" together with unwillingness to accept this fact at face value; and

(8) highly negative, usually strongly sarcastic or ironic reaction to a supposed "fact" which can be (but is not necessarily) previously known.

Here are examples of various "admirative" and "dubitative" usages. No attempt is made to classify them according to the above scale. In an (admittedly inadequate) attempt to translate these overtones into English, quote marks, or supplemental expressions like "would you believe", "now I ask you", have been inserted into the English translations. Although the translations attempt to convey what the speaker meant in each case, the larger context is obviously crucial for the proper understanding of such sentences.

Веднъ́ж му се е слу́чило на момче́то ... и вднага́ му изле́зе сла́ва че би́л голя́м пия́ница.	Come on! It happens just once to the poor boy and then all of a sudden everybody "knows" he's a souse!
А по́сле по ця́л де́н спе́ше, у́ж че я боля́ла глава́.	And then she'd sleep all day, because she "had a headache"!!
Чу́й какво́ ка́за! Не би́л чу́л. Възмо́жно ли е такова́ не́що?	Listen to him! He says he "didn't hear". Now I ask you, is such a thing possible?
В това́ ма́лко затъ́нтено градче́ серви́рали скари́ди!	Would you believe that in this backwater town they actually serve shrimp?!

The eight numbered meanings given earlier (which roughly cover the numerous possible interpretations of the renarrated mood) can all be subsumed under the general category of "distancing". Speakers may distance themselves from the neutral truth value of a statement in many different ways. It is up to each listener and speaker in any one speech situation to interpret the intended meaning correctly. Because so many different emotions are involved, it is well for the foreigner to listen and observe before trying to use these forms in the many different possible situations.

25.6. Forms expressing "stronger renarration"

The L-participle of съм (би́л, била́, било́, били́) is the auxiliary in the renarrated past indefinite and past anterior. For example:

Past indefinite renarrated
Тя́ била́ прочела́ <u>Война́ и ми́р</u>.   She [said she]'s finished reading *War and Peace*.

Past anterior renarrated
То́й би́л изля́зъл дъ́лго преди́   He [said he] had gone out quite some
дру́гите да напу́снат.   time before the others left.

The self-standing L-participle is also, of course, the renarrated form for both the simple present and past of съм. In 3rd person forms it stands alone, as follows:

Двайсет и пети урок / Lesson 25

	Present tense		*Past tense*	
	indicative	**RENARRATED**	indicative	**RENARRATED**
3rd sing. masc.	той е	той бил	той бе́ше	той бил
3rd sing. fem.	тя е	тя била́	тя бе́ше	тя била́
3rd plural	те́ са	те́ били́	те́ бя́ха	те́ били́

In addition to these several meanings, the form бил has begun to take on something like a life of its own: it can be added to *any* renarrated form to increase the degree of distancing. Although it is clear that this бил conveys various of the stronger degrees of dubitativity and admirativity, Bulgarian grammarians call it simply a "form of stronger renarration" (фо́рма за по́-си́лно преизка́зване).

Here is an example of the gradation from the most direct witnessed through the degrees of distancing to the "strongest" form of renarration:

Imperfect indicative

По́мниш ли Ива́н? Той пи́шеше най-добре́ в класа́.

Do you remember Ivan? He's the one who wrote the best [essays].

Intention of the speaker: to identify Ivan, and to stress the reliability of his information, which he has first-hand.

Generalized past

От вси́чките учени́ци в кла́са Ива́н е пи́шел най-добре́.

Of all the students in the class, Ivan used to write the best [essays].

Intention of the speaker: to make a simple statement without any specification as to its source, other than to imply that the source is reliable. (For the forms of the generalized past, see Lesson 29.)

Neutral renarrated imperfect

По́мниш ли Ива́н? Той пи́шел най-добре́ в класа́.

Remind me who Ivan was -- the one they say was the best writer.

Intention of the speaker: to get identification of Ivan, and to mark lack of involvement on his part by stressing that he is quoting from another source.

Renarrated imperfect marked for "stronger" renarration
    Dubitative/admirative

По́мниш ли Ива́н? Той бил пи́шел най-добре́ в класа́!

You remember Ivan, don't you -- the one who was the "best" writer!?

Intention of the speaker: to stress his opinion, through the means of emotion and sarcasm, that Ivan was in fact one of the least talented in the class.

There is thus a three-way gradation of distancing possible in the narration of events in the present or imperfect, and a four-way gradation possible in the narration of events in the aorist.

Consider the following sets of sentences: in each case the literal translation is the same. The added meanings, conveyed in each case simply by the choice of verbal form, are:

>(1) I see or saw this happen.
>(2) I saw evidence to convince me that this happened.
>(3) I've heard this said.
>(4) I've heard this said -- but I don't believe it.

Present
(1) Тя работи 8 часа без почивка.   She works 8 hours straight.
(3) Тя работела 8 часа без почивка.
(4) Тя била работела 8 часа без почивка.

Imperfect
(1) Тя работеше.   She was working.
(3) Тя работела.
(4) Тя била работела.

Aorist / Past indefinite
(1) Той свърши всичко.   He finished everything.
(2) Той е свършил всичко.
(3) Той свършил всичко.
(4) Той бил свършил всичко

Version (4) within the final example is ambiguous: it can be either the "more strongly renarrated" aorist or the neutral renarrated past indefinite or past anterior. Intonation and context are usually sufficient to distinguish which is meant.

25.7. Review of the renarrated mood: the general concept of "distancing"

The nine different Bulgarian indicative paradigms correspond to five different renarrated paradigms. The following chart summarizes these correspondences. The tenses are given in pairs to emphasize the fact that the renarrated mood collapses each of these pairs into a single form. Only the aorist tense stands outside this grouping.

For brevity's sake, only the 3rd singular (masculine) forms are given. In addition, while some tenses occur almost exclusively with perfective verbs, the same verb, чета, is given throughout for clarity of comparison.

Двайсет и пети урок / Lesson 25

TENSE VS. MOOD IN BULGARIAN:
TEMPORAL DISTANCE VS. "INVOLVEMENT DISTANCE"

		X INDICATIVE	Y RENARRATED
A.	present	чете́	четя́л
B.	imperfect	чете́ше	
A.	future	ще чете́	щя́л да чете́
B.	future in the past	ще́ше да чете́	
A.	future anterior	ще е чел	щя́л да е чел
B.	future anterior in the past	ще́ше да е чел	
A.	past indefinite	чел е	бил чел
B.	past anterior	бе́ше чел	
*	aorist	че́те	чел

    The grouping of pairs is by no means accidental; indeed, it is highly significant. Each of the pairs marked A and B exemplifies an instance of temporal distancing. Moving vertically in the chart (from A to B) means to move into a more "past" time frame. However, when one moves horizontally in the chart (from X to Y, or from tense to mood), this temporal distinction is lost. In other words, a move from the indicative to the renarrated (from X to Y), requires that one relinquish the ability to move between present and past (from A to B).

    Both directional shifts represent types of distancing, therefore. Temporal distancing (from A to B) is inherent in all languages which express verbal tense. All these language express it in grammatical terms; some languages, such as English and Bulgarian, are capable of expressing very fine shades of temporal distancing.

    Involvement distancing (from X to Y) -- whether it concerns doubt, surprise, irony, sarcasm, or simple non-commitment -- is also common in languages, but it is not always expressed in grammatical terms. Languages such as Bulgarian, which express both temporal and involvement distancing grammatically, tend to have very complex verbal systems. It is not surprising that a speaker's choice to express distancing of involvement (i.e. to use the renarrated mood) will require him to override certain of the fine points of temporal distancing. What is intriguing is that the mechanics of "temporary temporal override" are so systematic and elegant.

Двайсет и пети урок / Lesson 25

EXERCISES

I. Someone has said the following to you. Retell it to another person, indicating your surprise or disapproval.

Братовчед ми ще ходи на почивка на море с приятели. Ще живеят в къмпинг на палатка. Ще си готвят сами: ще ловят риба и ще я пържат на скара. От магазина ще купуват само хляб и вино. Ще плуват и ще лежат на плажа по цял ден. Какви безделници! Жените им ще копаят през това време в овощните градини.

II. Retell the following to another, emphasizing that you are not a direct witness.

Нашата страна е вече модерна. Всичко това несъмнено влияе на хората, когато кръщават своите внучета на дядовците и бабите. От една страна, тази традиция трябва неизменно да бъде спазвана, а от друга страна -- тя разумно трябва да бъде модернизирана с оглед на новата обстановка. Ето интересни, оригинални примери:

1. Дядото има званието "Герой на социалистическия труд", а внучката е кръстена Гертруда.
2. Бабата много работи по ОФ линия, внучката ще носи достойно името си Офелия.
3. Дядото е Ламби, а внучката ще кръстят Електра.

(виц от 1987 г.)

Кирил Василев, 45 години вицове, София, 1990.

SAMPLE SENTENCES

1. Ти си бил голям лъжец, бе!
2. Гледаше ме в очите, моля ти се, и ме лъжеше, че винаги ме бил защитавал от нападките на колегите.

3. Щяла била да става киноактриса! Вятър работа!
4. Тя закъсняла, защото си била забравила портмонето вкъщи и се наложило да се връща да го вземе.

5. Когато спектакълът започна, него го нямаше. Той умирал за едно кафе и уж за малко влязъл в кафенето срещу театъра. Там обаче срещнал познати и съвсем забравил, че ние го чакаме тук.

6. Те всички твърдяха, че били "против", но като дойде време да гласуваме, гласуваха "за".

Двайсет и пети урок / Lesson 25

7. Радиацията била предизвиквала рак.
8. Когато го обвиниха в плагиатство, той заяви, че бил написал книгата още преди много години и я бил давал на много колеги да я четат.

9. Твърди се, че това били негови думи, но аз мисля, че ги е казал Марк Твен.
10. Ти чул ли си, че те били направили вече филма, за който ставаше дума?
11. Вярно ли е, че белият хляб вредял на здравето?

12. Не можел да чуе за месо, а ходи тайно да си прави сандвичи с шунка, когато мисли, че никой не го вижда.

13. Цените на самолетните билети щели да се увеличат до следващата седмица.
14. Тя разказва на всички, че била прочела цялата руска класическа литература.

15. Потърсих го в кабинета му и видях само разхвърляни книги. Зарязал е работата и си е тръгнал.
16. Няма да повярваш какъв номер им е направил той вчера! Зарязал работата и си тръгнал.

SENTENCES FOR TRANSLATION

1. Why, you're a real lazy bones! You supposedly work so much (at least you claim to), but I can see from the results of your work that you didn't do a thing this weekend. For shame!

2. He is always telling lies about me. Supposedly I spend every evening in bars and never do my homework.

3. He wasn't going to have eaten all the sandwiches before we got home. He just "suddenly got very hungry" while we were in town and now there are no sandwiches left for us. Like he didn't know the whole time that he would eat them all!

4. She says she won't even have started the lesson by next week.

5. He didn't eat all the snacks! Hah! I suppose that cat ate them all then!

6. The bus was supposed to have arrived an hour ago. What has happened to it?

7. It won't be the slightest problem for him to translate that book, since he -- supposedly -- knows English so well.

READING SELECTION

Хи́тър Пе́тър и ламя́та

Еди́н пъ́т Хи́тър Пе́тър отишъ́л в гора́та да яде́ чере́ши. Тъ́кмо по́чнал да яде́ и се зада́ла една́ ламя́. Хи́тър Пе́тър се упла́шил и приклекнал до дърво́то, да не го́ ви́ди ламя́та. Но тя́ го видя́ла и се прови́кнала:

-- Ей, побра́тиме, ти́ какво́ пра́виш ту́ка?

-- Ами́, чере́ши я́м.

-- Ха́йде за́едно да яде́м, да ви́дим ко́й ще изяде́ по́вече, -- рекла́ ламя́та.

Тя́ хва́нала чере́шата за върха́, наве́ла я и по́чнала да яде́ наре́д: чере́ши, шу́ма, кло́нки. Хи́тър Пе́тър държа́л съ́щия клон и едва́ преглъ́щал. Когато изя́ла вси́чко по върха́, ламя́та пу́снала клона, за да хва́не друг. Клонъ́т се изпра́вил и хвъ́рлил Хи́тър Пе́тър дале́че върху еди́н храст. Изпод храста изско́чил за́ек. Хи́тър Пе́тър ху́кнал презглава́, де́то му очи́ ви́дят, за да избя́га от ламя́та, но тя́ го съгле́дала и тръ́гнала след не́го. Насти́гнала го и рекла́:

-- Ей, побра́тиме, ти́ си би́л голя́м юна́к! Такъ́в скок и а́з не мо́жех да напра́вя.

Хи́тър Пе́тър се поусми́хнал и скрои́л лъжа́та:

-- Ами́, видя́х, сестри́це, о́ня за́ек и ско́чих да го хва́на, но то́й избя́га.

Се́днали и ламя́та го попи́тала откъде́ и́ма та́я си́ла да ска́ча. Хи́тър Пе́тър ре́къл:

-- А́з съм кале́н и съм мно́го си́лен. Ти́ мо́жеш ли да сти́снеш ка́мък така́, че да пу́сне вода́?

Ламя́та сгра́бчила еди́н ка́мък и го сти́снала така́, че то́й ста́нал на пра́х. През това́ вре́ме Хи́тър Пе́тър изва́дил от торби́чката си една́ бу́чка си́рене, сти́снал я и от не́я поте́кла вода́.

-- Е́, кажи́ сега́, ко́й е по́-голя́м юна́к?

Ламя́та се изпла́шила. Преди́ да си тръ́гне, тя́ пока́нила Хи́тър Пе́тър ня́кой де́н да й госту́ва и да й разка́же ка́к е ста́нал то́лкова си́лен, като намислила да го уби́е.

Хи́тър Пе́тър не и́скал ламя́та да си поми́сли, че то́й се страху́ва от не́я и да му напа́кости и отишъ́л на го́сти. Ламя́та свари́ла еди́н во́л, сло́жила го на ма́сата и ре́кла:

-- Ха́ да ви́дим ко́й ще изяде́ по́вече!

Почнала да кърши цели бутове от вола и да яде́. Не след дълго, когато волът се свършвал, пред лама́та се натрупала ка́мара кости, а пред Хитър Петър имало само няколко кокалчета.

Хитър Петър почнал да я лъже:

-- Я виж, се́стро, ей там на оная планина оня черен облак. Това е по-големият ми брат.

Докато лама́та се взирала към облаците, Хитър Петър привлякъл всичките кости пред себе си. Когато омели чиниите, Хитър Петър казал:

-- Я виж сега кой е изял повече!

Лама́та се упла́шила още повече от него, като видяла колко е голяма неговата ка́мара с кости в сравнение с нейната. Упла́шила се и твърдо решила да го убие.

Вечерта́ легнали да спят и лама́та веднага захъркала, а Хитър Петър се повъртял и по едно време станал от леглото, изскочил навън, донесъл камъни и ги завил със завивките си. После излязъл навън и се сгушил до стена́та.

По едно́ време лама́та се събудила и станала. Взела една брадва и започнала със всички сили да удря по камъните. Направила ги на прах. След това си легнала и пак заспала. Хитър Петър тихичко влязъл, разчистил строшените камъни и си легнал. Когато лама́та се събудила сутринта и видяла Хитър Петър да седи на леглото си и да се прозява, тя не могла да повярва на очите си.

-- Добро утро, се́стро, -- рекъл той. -- Ти как спа? Аз цяла нощ не мигнах. Много бълхи имаш, хапаха ме цяла нощ.

Лама́та преглътнала от страх и решила да си признае:

-- Така и така, аз бях решила да те убия. Право да ти кажа, страх ме е от тебе. Как си могъл да станеш толкова силен?

-- Ами, нали ти казах, калил съм се, -- рекъл Хитър Петър.

-- А не може ли и аз да стана силна като тебе?

-- Може, -- рекъл Хитър Петър. -- Трябват само два казана с вода, единият с вряла вода, а другият със студена. Трябва два-три пъти да се топнеш ту в единия, ту в другия казан. Аз така съм се калил.

Когато лама́та приготвила всичко необходимо, Хитър Петър казал:

-- Хайде! Скачай!

Лама́та скочила във вря́лата вода, попарила се и умряла. Оттогава вече няма лами!

(Народна приказка)

Двайсет и пети урок / Lesson 25

GLOSSARY

безде́лник	idler, indolent	кале́н	hardened, seasoned
бра́два	axe	каля́вам / каля́	temper, harden
бут	leg, round; thigh	ка́мара	heap, pile
бу́чка	small lump	като́ ви́ди зо́р	when it gets hard
бълха́	flea	кафене́	cafe, coffeehouse
		киноактри́са	movie actress
взи́рам се / взра́ се	peer	класи́ческа литерату́ра	"the classics"
влия́я	influence		
вя́тър ра́бота!	nonsense, baloney	клон	branch
		кло́нка	twig
главобо́лие	headache	кръща́вам / кръстя́	christen, name
гласу́вам	vote	кусу́р	fault, flaw
гласу́вам за́	vote in favor of	кусу́рът ни е	that's the last straw
голя́м лъже́ц	consummate liar, swindler	къ́мпинг	camping site
		кърша́ (-иш)	break; wring
госту́вам	stay with, visit		
госту́ва ми	s/he's staying with me	лами́я	dragon
		ликьо́р	liqueur
де́то (or къде́то) ми очи́ ви́дят	wherever my feet lead me	лъжа́	lie, falsehood
		лъже́ц	liar
досто́ен	worthy, just		
досто́йно	with dignity	мечта́я	dream, yearn
		ми́гвам / ми́гна	wink
ей та́м	all the way over there	мир, -ът	peace
		модернизи́рам	modernize
зави́вка	blanket, wrap	море́на	moraine
зада́вам се / зада́м се (-даде́ш)	come into view	мързели́вец	lazy person
заря́звам / заре́жа (-еш)	abandon, give up	нами́слям / нами́сля	set one's mind to
затъ́нтен	obscure, desolate	напакостя́вам / напакостя́	harm, injure
затъ́нтено градче́	godforsaken burg		
захъ́рквам / захъ́ркам	start snoring	напра́вя на пра́х	reduce to dust
заявя́вам / заявя́	declare, announce	наре́д	in succession
зва́ние	rank, title	наспи́вам се / наспя́ се	have enough sleep
зор	effort; need		
		наха́лен	insolent, impudent
избя́гвам / избя́гна	escape, avoid	неизме́нно	constantly, always
изоста́вам / изоста́на	lag behind, be slow	несъмне́н	undeniable
изпла́швам се / изпла́ша се (-иш)	be afraid	несъмне́но	without question
изпод	from under	обвиня́вам / обвиня́	accuse, blame
изпра́вям се / изпра́вя се	stand/straighten up	обвиня́вам в	accuse of
изска́чам / изско́ча (-иш)	jump out	обстано́вка	situation, context
		ово́щна гради́на	fruit orchard
		ово́щен	fruit (adj.)
кавале́р	cavalier; gentleman	о́глед	view, inspection
каза́н	cauldron, vat	оми́там / омета́	sweep clean

Двайсет и пети урок / Lesson 25

оправда́ние	justification
Оте́чествен Фро́нт	Fatherland Front
ОФ-ли́ния	party line of the Fatherland Front coalition
пала́тка	tent
пети́ца	№ 5 tram or bus
плагиа́тство	plagiarism
по вре́ме на	during
побра́тим	blood brother
повъртя́вам се / повъртя́ се	rotate, hang around for a while
поми́слям си / поми́сля си	think it over
попа́рвам / попа́ря	steam, scald
попреква́лявам / попрекаля́	overdo
портмоне́	purse, change-purse
поусми́хвам се / поусми́хна се	smile faintly
пра́х, -ъ́т (*pl.* прахове́)	dust
прегла́щам / прегла́тна	swallow down, gulp
предизви́квам / предизви́кам	cause, evoke, induce
пре́зглава	headlong
прикля́квам / прикле́кна	squat
прови́квам се / прови́кна се	exclaim, call out
прозя́вам се / прози́на се	yawn
проти́в	against
ра́ботата край ня́ма	[there's] no end of work
радиа́ция	radiation
разу́мно	judiciously, sensibly
разчи́ствам / разчи́стя	tidy up, clear away
ра́к	cancer
ру́с	blond, fair
с о́глед на	with an eye to
самонаде́ян	self-reliant; presumptuous
сгра́бчвам / сгра́бча (-иш)	clutch, grasp
скари́да	shrimp
ско́к	jump, leap
скроя́вам / скроя́	cut out; concoct
сла́ва	reputation
спекта́къл	performance, show
сравне́ние	comparison
строша́вам / строша́ (-и́ш)	break, smash
съгле́ждам / съгле́дам	notice, catch sight of
та́ен, та́йна	secret, covert
то́пвам / то́пна	immerse, dip
три́я	rub
три́я [на ня́кого] со́л на глава́та	haul [someone] over the coals
тру́д, -ъ́т	labor, work
упла́швам се / упла́ша се (-иш)	take fright, be scared
фро́нт	front; facade
ха́	now, well ; ha
хи́тър	sly, clever
хру́мва / хру́мне (*3rd ps. only*)	occur
хру́мна ми една́ иде́я	I just got an idea
ху́квам / ху́кна	bolt, dart off
ча́с, -ъ́т (*pl.* часове́)	class
чере́ша	cherry tree
ши́шче	skewer; grilled meat on a skewer
шу́ма	foliage, leaves
юна́к	hero, brave fellow

Двайсет и пети урок / Lesson 25

CULTURAL COMMENTARY

Geography: Vitosha

Although Mount Vitosha is not a glacial formation, its flanks contain many piles of rocks which look like glacial moraines; they are thus commonly called морените. These pseudo-moraines are among the various sights and landmarks on this extremely popular site. The chair lifts and gondolas which take skiers up to the summit in winter also operate in summertime. Hardy visitors climb up via one of the many paths; a common outing is to take one of the lifts up and then to walk back down.

Names

It is traditional to name children after grandparents. Names thus have a tendency to alternate through the generations. This is seen graphically in the case of full legal names, which are obliged to repeat the father's name (in the possessive form) as a middle name.

Grandfather:	Ivan Petrov [Rakovski]
Father:	Peter Ivanov [Rakovski]
Son:	Ivan Petrov [Rakovski]

Of course, since there are two sets of grandparents, this pattern can be shifted. Nevertheless, custom heavily favors the paternal line.

The shortened form of the Greek name Haralampios has been taken into Bulgarian as Lambi (Ламби). The loanword for "lamp" has also been borrowed into Bulgarian from Greek. In the dialects nearest to the Bulgarian-Greek border, the [p] sound is pronounced as [b] in both words.

Political history: socialist government (and jokes)

The anti-fascist enemies of Bulgaria's Axis-sponsored government were organized together into the "Fatherland Front" (Отечествен фронт), usually abbreviated "OF" (ОФ). The political stance of this coalition "party" was referred to as the "OF-line" (ОФ-линия).

During the socialist regime, it was a great honor to be named a "Hero of [socialist] labor" (Герой на труда). This title was patterned after its Soviet counterpart, and the comic name Гертруда is a pun on the Soviet tendency to shorten long names of this sort and create new words out of them.

Folklore

Hităr Petăr is a well-known trickster character in folk tales. He is a cast as a simpleton who embodies the highest of folk wisdom. Similar characters are found in other folk traditions of the Balkans and Near East, the best known of which is the Turkish Nasreddin Hodja. There are many stories in which Hităr Petăr and Nasreddin Hodja compete to see who is cleverest. In the Bulgarian versions, Hităr Petăr naturally wins.

A "pobratim" (побратим) is a blood brother. This traditional relationship, known from folk tales, songs and legends, is an extremely strong one.

LESSON 26

DIALOGUE

<u>Чу́дя се а́з какъ́в пода́рък да му напра́вя</u>

Веселин: Джу́ли, ще взе́меш ли един со́к, или мо́же би па́ста? Погледни́, на съсе́дната ма́са подна́сят парфе́.

Джули: Не́, не́, благодаря́. Не и́скам да си разва́лям вече́рята. Тря́бва да позвъня́ на Де́йвид да ви́дя ка́к се чу́вствува, сле́д като се е наспа́л.

Веселин: Телефо́н и́ма на ъ́гъла. И а́з ще до́йда с те́бе.

// Джу́ли набира́ но́мера на Де́йвид. //

Джули: Звъни́, но ня́ма ни́кого. Дали́ не е́ оти́шъл ня́къде?

Веселин: Завърти́ па́к. Мо́же да е гре́шен но́мер.

// Джу́ли се вгле́жда в тефте́рчето си. //

Джули: Не́. Това́ е но́мерът.

Веселин: Да́й а́з да избера́. А, е́то. Ня́кой вди́га слуша́лката. Де́йвид, здраве́й.

Дейвид: Здраве́й.

Веселин: А́з съм Веселин. Вче́ра се запозна́хме във вла́ка. А́з но́сех мно́го бага́ж: ви́деокамера, касетофо́н, фотоапара́т.

Дейвид: А, да́. Спо́мням си. А́нгел ти помо́гна да ги внесе́ш в купе́то.

Веселин: Джу́ли се притесня́ва ка́к си.

Дейвид: Ни́що ми ня́ма. Добре́ съм. Нака́нил съм се да изли́зам.

Веселин: Къде́ ще хо́диш?

Дейвид: И́маме сре́ща с А́нгел в се́дем часа́ в една́ механа́ на Гра́ф Игна́тиев. То́й обеща́ да ми донесе́ подро́бна ка́рта на Бълга́рия. Та́м ще мо́га да намеря всички селища, където има археологически разкопки. Чудя се аз какъв подарък да му направя.

Веселин (към Джули): Дейвид пак отива с Ангел на кръчма.

// Джули го изглежда ужасена. //

Джули: Кажи му, че и аз искам да отида.

Веселин: Дейвид, и ние с Джули ще дойдем в механата.

Дейвид: Елате. Ние ще ви чакаме.

// Веселин и Джули тръгват бавно към "Граф Игнатиев". По улиците има много хора. Млад човек с дълга коса раздава на минувачите листовки. Той се заглежда по Джули. Една стара жена продава лалета. Двама гъдулари се надсвирват. Единият, който е облечен в народна носия, свири много високо. Джули ги разглежда с интерес. Веселин купува едно лале и го подава на Джули. //

Джули: Благодаря. Аз много обичам лалета. Ние имаме в Америка голяма градина. Майка ми сади в нея всяка година различни цветя, но най-често лалета. Насажда луковиците рано през пролетта и после ги разсажда из градината.

Веселин: А пък моята майка сади лук, домати, чушки. И аз ходя през пролетта да й помогна да ги посади.

Джули: Значи ти не си софиянец. Откъде си?

Веселин: От едно село тука близко, в Кюстендилско. В нашия край отглеждат много плодове и зеленчуци.

Джули: Вече е седем и половина. Още много път ли имаме до механата?

Веселин: Не, тя е тука на една крачка. Не бой се, няма да ни избягат Дейвид и Ангел.

Двайсет и шести урок / Lesson 26

GRAMMAR

26.1. Verbal prefixation: review

Adding a prefix to a verb accomplishes two things: it endows it with the quality of boundedness (makes it perfective), and it changes its meaning in a particular way. Creating a new imperfective by suffixation removes the boundedness, but keeps the new meaning. Prefixation is thus a very important part of the Bulgarian verbal system, in that it allows a single basic verbal idea to take on many different incarnations.

The classic example is the simplex verb пиша "write" and the group of its several derivatives, which includes подпиша "sign", надпиша "inscribe", опиша "describe", предпиша "prescribe", препиша "rewrite" and the like. The derivational process creating these verbs was described and schematized in Lesson 18. The similarity between these various meanings is significantly reinforced by the fact that except for the prefix, all conjugational verb forms are exactly the same in each case.

Learning to predict these several meanings, and to see the relationships between the different possible prefixed forms of a verb, is a very important tool in vocabulary building. The fact that prefixes correspond by and large to prepositions, and at times even carry through some of the same meanings as these prepositions, is another potential aid in vocabulary building. Although one must be wary of the temptation to equate prefixes with prepositions, one can to a certain extent assign meaning to some verbal prefixes. Grammarians disagree on the extent to which this can be done successfully, but they all agree that there is a system of sorts.

26.2. *Aktionsarten* and the Bulgarian verb: general principles

When one can predict with sufficient certainty the type of meaning that a particular prefix will add to a verb, this meaning (together with the general cluster of verbs it produces) is designated by the German term *Aktionsart*, which means "type of action". Since it has become standard practice among linguists and grammarians to use this term to describe these kinds of aspectual phenomena, it will be used here as well. The focus is not on terminology, but rather on the regularities which can be described, and on the ways in which these regularities can aid the student in acquiring mastery of the Bulgarian verb.

The prefix в-

A clear example of an *Aktionsart* is the use of the prefix в-. In practically all instances, this prefix adds the same meaning to a verb as the preposition в gives to a prepositional phrase: that of "into". For instance:

Двайсет и шести урок / Lesson 26

Влéзте в стáята!	Come into the room!
Джýли се вглéжда в тефтéрчето си.	Julie looks in [takes a look into] her address book.
Áнгел ти помóгна да ги внесéш в купéто.	Angel helped you bring them into the compartment.
Вдúшвайте, задъ́ржайте въ́здуха, кóлкото мóжете, и издúшвайте.	Inhale, hold your breath as long as you can and then exhale.
Тря́бва да го включим в спúсъка за екскýрзията.	We have to include him in the list of those going on the trip.

The tentative rule to be derived from these examples is that when a simplex imperfective verb (I*) is prefixed with в-, the general verbal action it describes becomes limited in a specific way: the new verb includes the meaning "motion into" in some way or another. The newly prefixed perfective (P) gives rise to its imperfective (I) partner by means of the suffixation processes studied earlier.

Aktionsart derivation: в-

Derivation			Meaning		
simplex	*prefix*	*derived*	*simplex*		*derived*
глéдам	+ в-	вглéдам › вглéждам	look I *	›	look into I / P
дúшам	+ в-	вдúшам › вдúшвам	breathe I *	›	inhale I / P

Aspect pairs of the basic (that is, non-derived) type cannot be listed according to the above schema. This is because there are no separate unprefixed verbs corresponding to pairs such as

perfective	*imperfective*	*(meaning)*
вклю́ча	вклю́чвам	include
вля́за	влúзам	enter
внáсям	внесá	import

Nevertheless, it is clear that these verbal roots also participate in the general schema of *Aktionsarten*, in that the prefix в- adds its generally predictable meaning to them in the same manner as it does to self-standing simplex imperfectives.

Двайсет и шести урок / Lesson 26

One must remember that verbal prefixes and prepositions are never identical in meaning. Even in the above instance, which represents the closest correspondence between the two categories, there is a significant difference between the preposition and the prefix. Namely, whereas **в** as a preposition can mean both "in" and "into", **в-** as a verbal prefix can mean only "into".

The prefix из-

The extent to which caution must be exercised can be illustrated by the prefix/preposition pair **из**. As a preposition, **из** means almost exclusively "move about without direction within an enclosed space". For example:

Ще разведа́ жена́ си из града́.	I'm going to show my wife around town.

But as a prefix, it has two quite different meanings. One is "out of" -- the opposite of "into". Indeed, for verbs prefixed with **из-** in the meaning "out" there is usually a corresponding verb prefixed with **в-** in the meaning "in". Compare the following examples with those given above:

Излезте от ста́ята!	Come out of the room!
Нака́нил съм се да изли́зам.	I was planning on going out.
Той ще ти помо́гне да ги изнесе́ш от купе́то.	He'll help you carry them out of the compartment.
Вди́швайте, задържа́йте въздуха, ко́лкото мо́жете, и изди́швайте.	Inhale, hold your breath as long as you can and then exhale.
Не тря́бва да го изклю́чим от спи́съка за екску́рзията.	We mustn't omit him from the list of people going on the trip.

Aktionsart derivation: из- *(meaning 1)*

Derivation			Meaning	
simplex	*prefix*	*derived*	*simplex*	*derived*
ди́шам	+ из-	изди́шам › изди́швам	breathe I *	exhale I / P

As in the case of в-, aspect pairs of the non-derived type cannot be listed according to the above schema, because there are no separate unprefixed verbs. In terms of their meaning, however, the following verbs are part of this group:

perfective	*imperfective*	*(meaning)*
изклю́ча	изклю́чвам	exclude
изля́за	изли́зам	leave
изна́сям	изнеса́	export

The other meaning of из- is "thorough completion". For example:

Те́ ве́че изгради́ха къ́щата, оста́на да я покри́ят.	They've already built the house, they just have to finish the roof.
Ха́йде да изми́слим не́що.	Let's think of something.
Компю́трите изме́стиха пи́шещите маши́ни.	Computers have completely replaced typewriters.
Ве́че си изпи́х ча́я, мо́га да тръ́гна.	I've finished my tea, I can leave [now].

Aktionsart derivation: из- *(meaning 2)*

Derivation			Meaning	
simplex	*prefix*	*derived*	*simplex*	*derived*
градя́	+ из-	изградя́ › изгра́ждам	build I *	finish building I / P
ми́сля	+ из-	изми́сля › изми́слям	think I *	think up, invent I / P
ме́стя	+ из-	изме́стя › изме́ствам	move I *	move out, replace I / P
пи́я	+ из-	изпи́я › изпи́вам	drink I *	drink up I / P

Note the way in which this second meaning of the prefix из- is harder to pin down concretely. Indeed, the verbs in the above examples seem at first glance to convey nothing other than simple boundedness. The finer line between "thorough" completion and other sorts of completion will be discussed below. The point here is that there is no obvious connection between the prefix из- and the preposition из.

Двайсет и шести урок / Lesson 26

26.3. The system of *Aktionsarten* in Bulgarian

While not all grammarians agree on the exact extent to which generalized meanings can be assigned to verbal prefixes, nor on exactly which meanings to assign, all agree on the possibility (and desirability) of systematizing these meanings, and most conceive of them as an interdependent network.

The chart on the following page gives one conception of that network. Prepositions and prefixes are listed together to aid the student in realizing the extent (and limitations) of overlap. For many prefixes, two different meanings are possible. One of these relates more to the temporal quality of the action, and the other more to its spatial quality. These two meanings are identified below as "T" and "S". The notation *"none"* does not mean that the prefix does not occur; it means simply that one cannot make any generalization about the types of meaning it gives to a verb.

The list is not exhaustive: not all prepositions have been included, nor have all prefixes. Furthermore, it is clear even from this incomplete listing that not every verbal prefix corresponds to a preposition (or vice versa). It is important to note that there is no standardized list of *Aktionsarten*. The outline given below will seem conservative to some grammarians and radical to others. Its intent is to be a guide to students.

It is not possible to give examples of all the usages suggested by the chart. The student is encouraged to review the Bulgarian verbs learned till now with this list in mind. The system of verbal meaning in any language is complex and subtle, and every speaker must construct for himself the categories which correspond best to his understanding of these interlocking meanings. The following (or any) formulation should be utilized only insofar as it is useful in helping one to understand and retain already learned meanings, and to acquire new ones as quickly (and correctly) as possible.

Двайсет и шести урок / Lesson 26

AKTIONSARTEN (Prefixal and prepositional meanings in Bulgarian)

Preposition	meaning	Prefix	meaning
в	in, into	в-	T: *none* S: move into
до	to, up to, until	до-	T: finish to the end S: *none*
за	for, about	за-	T: begin S: move (or be) behind
из	[movement] within	из-	T: complete thoroughly S: move out of
на	on, to, of	на-	T: complete specific instance S: [appropriate to place]
над	on top of	над-	T: surpass S: move on or over
		о-	T: *none* S: from all sides
от	from	от-	T: separation S: move away from
по	along	по-	T: for a short while S: move about a surface
под	under	под-	T: get going S: activity under
		пре-	T: redo S: move through
при	with, by	при-	T: *none* S: move towards
		про-	T: *none* S: move through
		раз	T: get involved in; disperse or scatter S: move in various directions
с	with, from	с-	T: *none* S: *none*
у	with, at	у-	T: *none* S: *none*

26.4. The usefulness of a classification phrased in terms of *Aktionsarten*

The correspondences given on the preceding page are guidelines of possible meanings. The extent to which the meaning of any verbal prefix can be predicted depends largely on the semantics of the verbal stem to which it is added. If the meaning given in the above chart harmonizes sufficiently with the meaning of the verb stem, it is possible (though still not guaranteed) that one can predict the general meaning of the newly prefixed verb, as each of the prefixes listed above can have a number of different meanings.

The prefix по-

Consider the prefix по-, which can add the meaning "to do for a short while." If the meaning of the verb is inherently durative, it is reasonable (though not assured) to predict that the prefixation of по- will add the meaning of "for a short while".

Aktionsart derivation: по- *(meaning 1)*

Derivation			Meaning	
simplex	prefix	derived	simplex	derived
седя́	+ по-	поседя́ › поседя́вам	sit I *	› sit for a bit I / P
прика́звам	+ по-	поприка́звам	chat I	have a short chat I

Often, however, the prefix по- adds a different meaning. When added to the verb садя́ "plant", for instance, its meaning is more of simple completion. For example:

| И а́з хо́дя през пролетта́ да ѝ помо́гна да ги посади́. | I also go there in spring to help her plant them. |

The prefixes от- and раз-

Similarly, the degree to which the meaning of the prefixes от- and раз- can be predicted is at least partially dependent on the semantics of the verb stem. If the meaning of the verb is sufficiently goal-oriented, then it is likely that the prefix от- will add to it the meaning of "separation", or the prefix раз- the meaning of "dispersal". Consider the following examples:

| То́й отско́чи то́чно от кра́я на трампли́на. | He jumped right off the edge of the trampoline. |

Двайсет и шести урок / Lesson 26

Aktionsart derivation: от- *(meaning 1)*

Derivation			Meaning	
simplex	*prefix*	*derived*	*simplex*	*derived*
ско́ча	+ от-	отско́ча › отска́чам	jump I *	jump off of I / P

Мла́д чове́к с дъ́лга коса́ разда́ва на минува́чите листо́вки.	A young man with long hair hands out leaflets to passersby.
Наса́жда лу́ковиците ра́но през пролетта́ и по́сле ги разса́жда из гради́ната.	She sets the bulbs out early in the spring and later she sets them out at various spots in the garden.

Aktionsart derivation: раз- *(meaning 1)*

Derivation			Meaning	
simplex	*prefix*	*derived*	*simplex*	*derived*
садя́	+ раз-	разсадя́ › разса́ждам	plant I *	plant around I / P
да́вам да́м	+ раз-	разда́вам разда́м	give I / P	hand out I / P

Again, one must be wary. With other verbs, the prefixes от- and раз- give a different, more general sort of bounded meaning. For example:

Джу́ли ги разгле́жда с интере́с.	Julie examines them with interest.
В на́шия кра́й отгле́ждат мно́го плодове́ и зеленчу́ци.	In our part of the country they raise lots of fruits and vegetables.
А́з тъ́кмо разпи́твах Де́йвид къде́ е отсе́днал.	I was just asking David where [= at which temporary lodging] he's staying.

26.5. Degrees of predictability within the system of *Aktionsarten*

In general, the degree of predictability of the meaning of a prefix is related to the concreteness of its meaning as a preposition; this meaning is most predictable when it has a spatially-defined element to it. The prepositions with the highest degree of predictability seem to be в-, до- and над-, whose meanings as prepositions are "in/into", "up to/until" and "over/atop", respectively. Verbs with the prefix в- were discussed above; examples are given below for the prefixes над- and до-.

The prefix над-

The prefix над- often corresponds to the English prefix "out-", in the sense of "outdo". For example:

Двама гъдулари се надсвирват.	Two folk fiddle players are trying to outplay each other.
Не се знае дали въобще ще има швепс, ако продължавате да се надвиквате.	It's not clear if there will be any soft drinks at all if you [two] continue trying to outshout each other.

The prefix до-

Verbs prefixed with до- gain the meaning "completion up to an end-point." The idea of the end-point is important to the meaning of such verbs, and often clearly differentiates them from verbs with the more general idea of completion. For example:

Свещта догоря и стана тъмно.	The candle burnt through to the end, and darkness fell.
Долей ми още малко чай, моля ти се.	Top my glass off with a bit more tea, please.

The difference between до- and из-, both of which refer to the completion of an action, can be seen in the following exchange:

-- Метеш ли? Ще ми услужиш ли с метлата, след като изметеш?	"Are you sweeping? Will you lend me the broom when you're done?"
-- Не съм свършила. Като домета, ще ти я дам.	"I haven't finished yet. When I do, I'll give it to you."

Both speakers are referring to a completed instance of sweeping. The first one is concerned with the completed job as a whole, and uses the prefixed form **измета́** to emphasize this focus. The second, however, is more concerned with the amount of work she has yet to do before she reaches the end-point, and uses the prefixed form **домета́** to emphasize this focus on the end-point. Note that the English translation is incapable of rendering this difference. It can only use the perfective form of the auxiliary "do" to emphasize the idea of general completion.

The prefixes по- and на-

The prefixes with the least degree of predictability seem to be **на-** and **по-**, both of which usually give a verb the idea of completion in relatively general terms. Each, however, does have more precise meanings in more limited contexts. The meaning "for a little while" of **по-** was discussed earlier. When the prefix **на-** is combined with the particle **се**, the verb acquires the meaning "do to satiation". For instance:

И́скам да ви́дя Де́йвид ка́к се чу́вствува, сле́д като се е наспа́л.	I want to find out how David feels after he's slept it off.
Мммм! Ще се ная́м!	Yum! I'm going to stuff myself!
Те́ са се напи́ли ве́че.	They're already drunk.

26.6. Word order in certain fixed phrases

According to the rules of word order, clitics must follow the negative particle directly and precede the verb directly. This word order is especially marked for speakers of Bulgarian because it causes the clitic to be accented. For example:

Не го́ позна́вам.	I don't know him.

In certain phrases, another word order has become acceptable. In the most common of these examples (cited below), the majority of Bulgarians can use both word orders (and both are correct).

Не бо́й се!	Don't be afraid!
Не се́ бой!	*(same)*

Двайсет и шести урок / Lesson 26

EXERCISES

I. Fill in the blanks with the proper form of one of the following verbs: наглеждам, раздавам, заглеждам се, придавам, подавам, преглеждам, оглеждам.

1. Сутрин времето за нищо не ми стига: закуся, _____ вестника и то станало обед.
2. Как е по-учтиво: мъжете да _____ първо ръка на жените или обратното?
3. Преди да купиш ризата, трябва да я _____ от всички страни, да няма нещо скъсано по нея.
4. Аз излизам за малко, кой ще _____ кафето ми да не изкипи?
5. Кога пораснаха тези деца?! Нашият Пешо вече е почнал да се _____ по момичетата.
6. Той от малък си е такъв -- _____ всичките си играчки на другарчетата си.
7. Тази шапка много й отива -- _____ й загадъчен и романтичен вид.

II. Fill in the blanks with the proper form of one of the following verbs: влитам, преплувам, политам, заплувам, отлитам, отплувам, долитам.

1. През есента птиците _____ на юг.
2. Той плува много добре. Сигурно ще _____ басейна преди тебе.
3. Орелът разперва криле и _____ над полята.
4. Лодката вече _____ от брега. Виж я там в далечината.
5. Шумът ме стресна. Ято врабчета _____ в пещерата.
6. Информацията няма нужда от криле, за да лети. До нас _____ новини от най-отдалечените кътчета на земята.
7. Детето си пое дълбоко дъх и _____ към острова.

III. Rewrite the following as impersonal expressions.

1. Той искаше да дойде с нас, но никой не се сети да го покани.
2. Тя искаше да си облече нещо ново и хубаво за празника.
3. В наше време публиката иска да слуша само лека музика.
4. Децата не искат сутрин да стават рано и вечер да си лягат рано.
5. Гостите искат да пият още от същото старо вино.
6. Тя не иска да гледа мача по телевизията, но той настоява.
7. Те не искат да признаят правотата й.

Двайсет и шести урок / Lesson 26

SAMPLE SENTENCES

1. Ду́навът се вли́ва в Че́рно море́.

2. Деца́та си бя́ха изми́слили но́ва игра́. Изли́ваха вода́ от шише́тата на балко́на върху глави́те на минува́чите.

3. Еди́н от най-трога́телните сюже́ти на бъ́лгарската наро́дна пое́зия разка́зва за ма́йстор Мано́л, ко́йто вгради́л мла́дата си невя́ста в цъ́рквата, коя́то строя́л, за да придаде́ тра́йност на сгра́дата.

4. Дого́ниха го да му ка́жат, че е изпу́снал шофьо́рската си кни́жка.
5. Ку́чето подго́ни вълка́ и го го́ни, докато́ го изго́ни.

6. Са́мо канди́ло се доли́ва. Ви́но нали́ват в ча́шите, след като наля́тото преди́ е било́ изпи́то.

7. Момче́тата се надбя́гваха по це́ли дни́.

8. Жени́те и́мат по́-голя́ма продължи́телност на живо́та от мъже́те и редо́вно ги надживя́ват.

9. Мо́ят екземпля́р от кни́гата е надпи́сан, не мо́жем да го сбъ́ркаме с твоя́.
10. Препрочето́х о́ще веднъ́ж писмо́то и го подпи́сах.

11. Тя́ ше́та по ця́л де́н, бе́з да подви́е кра́к.
12. Таки́ва при́казки подкопа́ват усто́ите на на́шия обще́ствен стро́й.

13. Подложи́ не́що под покри́вката да не изца́паме ма́сата.
14. Ня́кога отси́чали глави́те на непоко́рните, а сега́ са́мо ги критику́ват.

15. Това́ бе́ше стра́нно сраже́ние, пъ́рво една́та а́рмия настъ́пваше, но по́сле ѝ се наложи́ да отстъ́пи под напо́ра на дру́гата.

16. Ко́пието го пробо́де пра́во в сърце́то.
17. Забо́ждам ви́лицата в масли́ната.

18. Ако не внима́ваш, мо́же да се убоде́ш с игла́та.
19. Ве́че се бя́х унесъ́л в съ́н, кога́то телефо́нът иззвъня́.

20. Ни́е уреди́хме то́зи въпро́с о́ще преди́ да ни ка́жете.
21. Момче́то отску́бнало еди́н ко́съм от гри́вата на ко́ня.

Двайсет и шести урок / Lesson 26

SENTENCES FOR TRANSLATION

1. Every year I plant lots of flowers in our garden. This year I planted them inside early, when it was still cold. Then later I transplanted them into the garden. If you plant them all around the garden in winter, it will be difficult to implant them in the ground. Anyway, they will probably die.

2. "Did you get enough sleep last night?"
"No, Angel and I went out to a pub and the whole evening tried to outdrink each other. I'm afraid we both drank too much, because as we were leaving the pub started to spin before our eyes."

3. "Could you help me make a phone call? Every time I pick up the receiver and dial, I hear a voice speaking Chinese."
"What is it saying?"
"Probably that I have the wrong number, but I'm not sure because the connection is so bad."
"Here, let me dial."

4. Ivancho got involved in his newspaper and forget to get off the tram.

5. When I saw my professor, I tried to look as if I was staring intensely at my book. But alas, I could not avoid the meeting.

6. "Should we include a story about vampires in the textbook?"
"Of course, the vampires will get very angry if we exclude them!" They will come and do lots of mischief if we forget them."
"Don't worry, I'll go lock the doors. They won't get in here!"

READING SELECTION

Анна Каменова, "Разказвай, Брезице!"

-- Разказвай, Брезице.

-- Баща ми беше няколко години горски. Така се случи, че не можеше повече да остане в града. Принуден беше да си търси друго препитание. Обичаше гората. "Между горски и лесничей" - твърдеше той - "няма голяма разлика. Важното е да обичаш и да познаваш едно нещо. Може и да нямам кой знае каква обща култура, обаче гората познавам до дъно." А после, когато отраснах и стигнах до по-горните класове, той реши, че аз трябва да получа по-богата култура, и се преместихме в съседния град.

-- За гората разкажи.

-- Всяка сутрин баща ми взимаше пушката и ме повеждаше през байрчето на училище. Беше много добросъвестен. Трепереше за всяко дърво, за всяка фиданка. За него дърветата бяха живи същества, по-съвършени от нас: хранят се само с вода и светлина. На някои дървета даваше най-невероятни имена. Веднъж в къщи стана недоразумение. Вечеряхме, а той:

-- Днес минах покрай Ружица. Свежа, усмихната.

Майка ми изпусна лъжицата.

-- Ти знаеш ли какво приказваш?

Баща ми най-спокойно сложи залък в устата и продължи:

-- Боях се да не залинее. А тя изправила снага, наперила се. Види се, от дъжда.

Дълго майка ми не можеше да си поеме дъх. А на другия ден ме заразпитва от къде минава баща ми, отбива ли се в селището и има ли там някоя Ружица.

-- Баща ти е бил поет. Виж какво име ти е дал. Няма втора Брезица. А може би и ти пишеш тайно стихове. Признай си.

Какви стихове! Тогава тя четеше само читанката. Вечер баща ѝ взимаше от лавицата някоя от своите книги, предимно за дървета и растения, и четеше на глас. Понякога говореше за гората. Да, наистина говореше като поет: за тишината в гората -- само там се чува тишината; за мъглата -- спуснала призрачни завеси; за песента и благоуханието; всяко дърво има свой глас и свое ухание -- стига да доловиш техния говор.

-- Разказвай!

-- Училището беше доста далеч. За да не газя калта, минавах край самата гора по една пееща пътечка: изсъхналите листа се стелеха под стъпките ми и шумоляха.

Двайсет и шести урок / Lesson 26

-- Затова́ ли зна́еш то́лкова лекови́ти би́лки?

-- Ба́ба ми бе́ше знаха́рка.

Тя́ тръ́гна на учи́лище като вси́чки седемгоди́шни деца́. Ле́ко ѝ бе́ше, кога́то тичешко́м мина́ваше по го́рските пъте́чки и се стъпи́сваше пред огро́мните жи́лищни дворци́ на мра́вките. Закъсня́ваше, за да наблюда́ва ма́йския бръ́мбар: ле́гнал гъ́рбом, то́й разма́хваше два́ чи́фта краче́та и се мъ́чеше да се объ́рне. Тя́ се опи́та с кле́чка да му помо́гне. То́й ня́ма ну́жда от не́йната по́мощ. Упори́т е. Е́то, са́м се объ́рна и бъ́рзо запъ́пла ната́тък. Ма́лко невзра́чно животи́нче, а не се́ отча́йва, не тъ́рси чу́жда по́мощ, бо́ри се и успя́ва.

В гора́та вси́чко ѝ е позна́то. Въпреки́ че ня́ма пъ́тни зна́ци и светофа́ри, тя́ не се́ препъ́ваше о ко́рените или дъ́нерите. Ни́кой не я́ предупрежда́ва да се па́зи от бодли́в хра́ст или да не се́ наве́жда под надве́сен кло́н. Към вси́чко се отна́сяше с дове́рие и о́бич. Защо́то расте́нията и живо́тните не са́ пота́йни.

Зооло́гията изуча́ва вси́чки ви́дове живо́тни: влечу́ги и насеко́ми, хи́щници и кате́рички; вси́чки разнови́дности на мра́вките и терми́тите. Бота́никата ни предпа́зва от по́длите, изма́мни гъ́би. А ка́к да определи́м чове́шките ви́дове и те́хните сво́йства? У хо́рата ня́ма чи́сти ти́пове. Сво́йствата им са сло́жни и препле́тени. Към тя́х се приба́вят чу́вства, ми́сли, преживя́вания, така́ че объ́ркват биоло́зите, антрополо́зите, психоло́зите, че и социоло́зите.

Адапти́рано от "Калейдоско́п" (Анна Каменова, <u>Часовник без стрелки</u>, София, 1980.)

Двайсет и шести урок / Lesson 26

GLOSSARY

антрополо́г	anthropologist	зага́дъчен	enigmatic, mysterious
		загле́ждам / загле́дам	begin to look at; look steadily at
байр	hill, mound		
басе́йн	pool, reservoir	загле́ждам се по	stare at
би́лка	herb	залиня́вам / залине́я	languish, pine
благоуха́ние	fragrance, aroma		
бодли́в	prickly; barbed	за́лък	bite; morsel
бо́ря се	fight, strive	заплу́вам	begin to swim
бота́ника	botany	знаха́р (ка)	folk healer
бреза́	birch	зооло́гия	zoology
бръ́мбар	bug, beetle		
		игла́	needle; thorn, quill
в на́ше вре́ме	nowadays	игра́чка	toy
вгле́ждам се / вгле́дам се	stare, peer closely	избира́м но́мер	dial a phone number
		изгле́ждам / изгле́дам	examine, scrutinize
вгра́ждам / вграда́	build in; immure		
вди́швам / вди́шам	inhale	изго́нвам / изго́ня	chase away; expel
вече́ря	dinner, supper	изди́швам / изди́шам	exhale
влечу́го (pl. влечу́ги)	reptile		
вли́вам / влея́	infuse, pour into	изли́вам / излея́	pour out
вли́вам се / влея́ се	flow into, empty into	изма́мен	deceptive, misleading
вли́там / влетя́	dash, rush	изца́пвам / изца́пам	soil, stain
вре́мето не ми́ сти́га	I'm pressed for time		
га́зя	wade, tread on	канди́ло	icon-lamp
га́зя калта́	flounder in the mud	кле́чка	stick
го́рен	upper, higher, top	коли́ба	cabin, lodge; hut
го́рски	wood, forest (adj.)	ко́пие	spear, javelin
го́рски	forest ranger	ко́рен	root
граф	count, earl	ко́съм	hair, filament
гре́шен	sinful; wrong	краче́	tiny leg
гри́ва	mane	кра́чка	step
гъдула́р	gudulka player	критику́вам	criticize; review
гъ́рбом	with/on one's back	кът (pl. къ́тища)	nook, recess
далечина́	distance	ла́вица	shelf, rack
добросъ́вестен	conscientious	лале́	tulip
дове́рие	confidence, trust	лекови́т	curative, medicinal
дога́рям / догоря́	burn low, burn out	лесниче́й	forester
дого́нвам / дого́ня	run after, overtake	летя́	fly, soar
дола́вям / доловя́	catch, make out	листо́вка	newssheet, flyer
доли́вам / доле́я	top up, pour in more	лу́ковица	bulb, tuber
доми́там / домета́	finish sweeping		
дъ́нер	trunk, stump	ма́йски	May (adj.)
дъ́но	bottom	ма́йски бръ́мбар	May-bug, chafer (Melolontha melolontha)
заве́са	curtain	метла́	broom
зави́вам зад ъ́гъла	turn the corner	минува́ч	passer-by
завъртя́вам / завъртя́	turn, spin	ми́съл, -та́	thought, idea
		мра́вка	ant

Двайсет и шести урок / Lesson 26

мъ́ча се (-иш)	suffer, agonize, have a hard time	отси́чам / отсека́ (-че́ш)	cut off; cut down
		отси́чам глава́	behead
на глас	aloud	отска́чам / отско́ча (-иш)	jump off, rebound
на две́ кра́чки	very close by		
наби́рам / набера́	gather, compose	отску́бвам / отску́бна	pluck out; wrest from
наби́рам но́мер	dial a phone number		
наблюда́вам	observe, examine	отча́йвам се / отча́я се	get discouraged
нагле́ждам / нагле́дам	inspect; look after		
надбя́гвам / надбя́гам	outdistance, outrun	парфе́	parfait, ice-cream dish
		па́ста	cake, pastry; paste
надбя́гвам се / надбя́гам се	race	пещера́	cave, grotto
		пи́шеща маши́на	typewriter
надве́сен	overhanging	пове́ждам / поведа́	lead, conduct
наджи́вявам / наживе́я	outlive, survive	подви́вам / подви́я	bend, tuck under
		подго́нвам / подго́ня	chase, drive away
надсви́рвам / надсви́ря	outplay		
		подкопа́вам / подкопа́я	undermine
надсви́рвам се / надсви́ря се	compete in playing	подла́гам / подло́жа (-иш)	put under, subject to
напе́рвам се / напе́ря се	strut, become perky	по́дъл	base, vile
		покрай	alongside, past
напи́вам се / напи́я се	get drunk	поли́там / полетя́	fly off, soar
		поседя́вам / поседя́	stay/sit for a while
напо́р	pressure	пота́ен	secret, mysterious
наса́ждам / насадя́	plant, set out	правота́	rightness, justice
насеко́мо (pl. насеко́ми)	insect	преди́	previously, before
		предпа́звам / предпа́зя	protect, safeguard
ната́тък	thither, further		
не бо́й се	don't be afraid	преживя́ване	experience
не подви́вам крак	be on the move	преме́ствам се / преме́стя се	move, change residence
невероя́тен	improbable; inconceivable		
невзра́чен	insignificant	препита́ние	subsistence
невя́ста (or неве́ста)	bride, wife	преплу́вам	swim/sail across
недоразуме́ние	misunderstanding	препрочи́там / препрочета́	reread
ня́кога	at one time, formerly		
		препъ́вам се / препъ́на се	stumble, trip; falter
о	against		
определя́м / определя́	define, specify	прида́вам / прида́м (-даде́ш)	add, lend; impart
о́стров	island	при́зрачен	ghostly, shadowy
отдалече́н	remote, distant	принужда́вам / прину́дя	compel, coerce
оти́вам	suit, go with		
отли́там / отлетя́	fly away	пробо́ждам / пробода́	pierce, transfix
отна́сям се / отнеса́ се	treat		
		пробо́ждам в сърце́то	stab in the heart
отна́сям се с дове́рие към	trust in/rely on		
		продължи́телност	duration
отплу́вам	set sail, embark	продължи́телност на живо́та	life expectancy
отра́ствам / отра́сна	grow up		
		психоло́г	psychologist

пу́шка	rifle, gun	трога́телен	touching, moving
пъ́пля (-еш)	creep, crawl	тъ́рся препита́ние	try to make a living
пъ́тни зна́ци	road signs		
		уна́сям се в съ́н	drift off to sleep
разнови́дност	variety	упори́т	tenacious, stubborn
разпе́рвам / разпе́ря	spread, stretch out	услу́жвам /	
разса́ждам / разсадя́	set out [seedlings]	услу́жа (-иш)	do a service, oblige
расте́ние	plant	услу́жвам с	lend
романти́чен	romantic	усми́хвам се /	smile
		усми́хна се	
садя́	plant	усми́хнат	smiling
свеж	fresh	усто́и (pl. only)	buttress; mainstay
сво́йство	characteristic	усто́ите на	the pillars of society
седемгоди́шен	seven-year old (adj.)	обществото	
снага́	body, figure		
социо́лог	sociologist	уха́ние	scent, aroma
спу́скам / спу́сна	let down, drop	учти́в	polite
сраже́ние	battle		
сте́ля се	drift, spread	фида́нка	sapling
строй	system, order		
стъпи́свам се /	be taken aback	хи́щник	beast/bird of prey
стъпи́сам се			
		чита́нка	school reader
		чифт	pair
терми́т	termite	чу́вство	feeling, emotion
тефте́р	register, account book	чужд	someone else's
тефте́рче	notebook		
тичешко́м	at a run	шофьо́рска кни́жка	driver's license
тишина́	silence, quiet	шофьо́рски	driver's
тра́йност	stability, endurance	шумоля́	rustle, murmur
трампли́н	trampoline		
трепе́ря за	be anxious about	я́то	flock

CULTURAL COMMENTARY

History: Graf Ignatiev and the treaties of 1878
  One of the busiest streets in Sofia is Graf Ignatiev, which is named after Count Nikolai Pavlovich Ignatiev (Граф Никола́й Па́влович Игна́тиев, 1832-1908), a Russian diplomat who played a significant role in Bulgaria's liberation. As Russian ambassador in Constantinople from 1864 to 1878, he was sympathetic to the various movements through which the Greek and South Slav subjects of the Porte wished to gain independence from their Ottoman rulers. He is best known (and revered) by Bulgarians as the negotiator of the Treaty of San Stefano (March, 1878) which, as the concluding treaty of the Russo-Turkish war, created the Greater Bulgaria which many Bulgarians still consider to be their rightful state. At the Congress of Berlin in July of that year, the San Stefano treaty was dissolved, and replaced with one whose provisions were distinctly less advantageous to both Russia and Bulgaria.

City life: on the streets
  Street life in Sofia and other large Bulgarian cities is becoming increasingly more lively. There always were old women selling bouquets of flowers, nuts and the like; but now there are tables and stalls selling all manner of things, as well as leafleters, strolling musicians and other colorful characters. Long hair on men, once highly frowned on, is now common. Often folk musicians will dress in national costume, judging (correctly) that this will increase the amount of tips they receive from tourists.

Двайсет и шести урок / Lesson 26

Geography: the Danube

The Danube, which forms the majority of the border between Bulgaria and Romania, turns north when it reaches the area of Dobrudzha and flows into the Black Sea in the large marshy area known as the Danube Delta. The mouth of the Danube itself is Romanian territory; it is the somewhat loosely-defined area of Dobrudzha to the south of it which is disputed between Bulgaria and Romania.

Folklore: the walled-in wife

The ballad of the walled-in wife (вгра́де́на неви́ста) is widespread throughout many countries, but is particularly well-known in the Balkans. The best known Bulgarian version is that of a builder named Manol who was told by spirits that he would not be able to complete the church he was building unless he sacrificed his young bride by entombing her alive in the church structure. In the Greek version, the young woman is built into a bridge and in the Serbian version she is built into the city walls. For many, the cruelty of the sacrifice is balanced by the awareness of the deeper meaning of the ballad -- that individuals must suffer for the advancement of society, that men and women suffer in different ways, and that in many cases the extent of the suffering is extremely great.

Customs: "topping off"

Bulgarian custom decrees that one cannot top off someone's glass; it must be drunk to the bottom before it can be refilled. This is encapsulated in the saying that only icon-lamps can be topped off. The icon lamp in the corner of a religious Eastern Orthodox household must not be allowed to go out; therefore, the oil in it is frequently topped off.

Literature: Anna Kamenova

Anna Kamenova (А́нна Ка́менова, 1894-1982) was a well known author and translator of children's books, a writer of essays, short stories, novellas and novels, and a prominent figure in Bulgarian letters. She was especially active as president of the Bulgarian PEN club, and wrote frequently on the "woman question". Among the books she translated from English were *Uncle Tom's Cabin* (Чи́чо То́мовата коли́ба) and *The Wizard of Oz* (Вълше́бникът от О́з).

"Moraines" on Mount Vitosha, outside Sofia

LESSON 27

DIALOGUE

Без ме́не не би́ зна́ел ка́к да се опра́виш

// Весели́н и Джу́ли ви́ждат о́ще през витри́ната, че Де́йвид и А́нгел са се́днали на една́ ъ́глова ма́са в механа́та. //

Весели́н: Де́йвид ни́как не прили́ча на чужденец́. Не би́х допу́снал, че и́два ча́к от Аме́рика, ако го сре́щна случа́йно на у́лицата.

Джу́ли: А а́з на америка́нка прили́чам ли?

Весели́н: О, да́. Ру́сите жени́ в Бълга́рия са ря́дкост. Би́х се гле́дал по ця́л де́н в огледа́лото, ако и́мах таки́ва ху́бави си́ни очи́.

// А́нгел и Де́йвид на́й-по́сле забеля́зват Весели́н и Джу́ли. Те́ им ма́хат с ръка́. //

А́нгел (към компа́нията младе́жи на съсе́дната ма́са): Проща́вайте, би́хте ли се дръ́пнали ма́лко госпо́жицата да ми́не.

Де́йвид: Добре́ дошли́!

Весели́н: Добре́ сме ви зава́рили. Ви́ждам, че не сте́ си гу́били вре́мето. Преполови́ли сте бути́лката.

А́нгел: От ця́л ча́с сме ту́ка. Ня́ма като коне́ на пра́зни я́сли да стои́м, я.

Весели́н: А́з ако ча́ках да́ма, би́х потърпя́л, докато до́йде.

А́нгел: Я́ си представи́, че въобще́ не до́йде. Какво́ ще пра́виш тога́ва?

Джу́ли: Нали́ дойдо́хме. Де́йвид, и́мам за те́бе две́ нови́ни, една́ ху́бава и една́ ло́ша. С коя́ да започна́?

Де́йвид: Почни́ с ху́бавата, да ви́дим.

Джу́ли: Профе́сор Попо́в ни ка́ни дру́гата се́дмица да оти́дем на разко́пки в Топо́лница. Ка́за, че би́ ни пока́зал и дру́ги обе́кти, но в кра́я на ме́сеца тря́бва да зами́не на конфере́нция в чужби́на.

А́нгел: Е́х, какво́ по́-ху́баво от разко́пки в Топо́лница. Та́м пра́вят едно́ ху́баво ме́лнишко ви́но... Ама ти́, Де́йвид, без ме́не не би́ зна́ел ка́к да се опра́виш... Пък а́з съм зае́т, не мо́га да до́йда с те́бе.

Дейвид: А каква е лошата новина?

Джули: Днес случайно срещнахме вчерашните спътници от влака. Канят ни утре на Витоша. И ти си поканен, но сигурно няма да можеш да дойдеш. Има да скучаеш в тая жега в София.

Дейвид: Защо да не мога да дойда?

Джули: Ами дали ще издържиш? Кракът ти съвсем ли зарасна?

Дейвид: О, аз отдавна съм забравил за него. За нищо на света не бих пропуснал възможността да дойда утре на Витоша.

Ангел: Да знаех, че за утре има такива планове, бих казал на брат си да отложи леенето на плочата за другата неделя.

Джули: За каква плоча става дума?

Ангел: Брат ми строи вила край Курило. За утре е пазарил майстори. Ще изливат бетонната плоча на основата. Та, и аз обещах да помогна. Братя сме, не може... Нали знаеш: брат брата не храни, но горко му, който го няма.

Веселин: Нищо. Витоша, ей я къде е. Друг път ще идеш.

Ангел: Ти май нищо не разбираш. Мене ми е за компанията, бе човек, а не за витошките камънаци. Аз душата си давам за хубави хора.

Дейвид: Веселине, би ли ми казал какво трябва да донеса със себе си утре?

Веселин: Вземи си за всеки случай пуловер, ако захладнее. За другото ще се погрижим ние.

Дейвид: Да бях си взел фотоапарата, щях да направя страхотни снимки на Витоша.

Веселин: Аз бих могъл да донеса моя.

Джули: Значи, срещата ни с Таня, Димитър и Милена е в осем часа на последната спирка на петицата в Княжево. Би трябвало да сме точни.

GRAMMAR

27.1. The conditional mood: introduction and formation

The fourth of the Bulgarian moods is called the conditional mood (усло́вно наклоне́ние). Its meaning and usage are roughly similar to those of the conditional mood in English. The state it describes is usually a hypothetical one -- something which is distanced from reality in one way or another. Speakers make use of this "reality distancing" in several ways. One is to express a general prediction about a more or less hypothetical situation. Another is to add a degree of politeness or modesty to a request or a statement. A third, which falls somewhat between the above two, is to heighten the modality of constructions with "ought" or "might". The final usage is that which gives the mood its name: conditional constructions of the type studied in Lessons 22 and 23. Examples of all these usages are given below.

The Bulgarian conditional mood is parallel in form to most Bulgarian compound tenses: it is composed of an auxiliary plus the L-participle. The conditional mood does not express tense differences. The single conditional paradigm can convey present, future and past.

The forms of the conditional auxiliary are extremely similar to the past tense forms of съм (which itself functions as the auxiliary of the past anterior). For comparison, the past anterior tense is given alongside the conditional mood:

	CONDITIONAL mood	*Past anterior tense*
1ˢᵗ singular	бих чел	бях чел
2ⁿᵈ singular	би чел	бе́ше чел
3ʳᵈ singular	би чел	бе́ше чел, бе́ чел
1ˢᵗ plural	би́хме че́ли	бя́хме че́ли
2ⁿᵈ plural	би́хте че́ли	бя́хте че́ли
3ʳᵈ plural	би́ха че́ли	бя́ха че́ли

27.2. Word order in the conditional mood

Word order rules are also similar to those of the past anterior. The conditional auxiliary is a fully accented word, and often stands at the beginning of a sentence. At the same time, the relevant clitics and particles must take their appropriate positions next to it. Namely, the negative particle precedes it directly, the interrogative particle follows it directly, and any pronoun objects must intervene between this sequence and the L-participle. The rules are exactly as those for бях in the past anterior except that pronoun objects must precede the L-participle. There is no variation permitted in word order.

Here are examples of word order in the conditional:

Бихме	ли	отказали?	
Aux.	INT	participle	

Would we refuse?
Would we have refused?

Не	бихте	ли	казали	това?
Neg.	Aux.	INT	participle	

Wouldn't you say that?
Wouldn't you have said that?

Бих	ти	го	дал.	
Aux.	IND	DIR	participle	

I'd [be able to] give it to you.
I'd [have been able to] have given it to you.

Бихте	ли	ми	го	показали?
Aux.	INT	IND	DIR	participle

Would you show it to me?
Would you have showed it to me?

Не	бихте	ли	му	го	дали?
Neg.	Aux.	INT	IND	DIR	participle

Wouldn't you give it to him?
Wouldn't you have given it to him?

27.3. The conditional mood used to describe hypothetical states

To make a prediction about a hypothetical state, a Bulgarian uses the conditional mood. Whether or not the state is real is not at issue; the speaker's intent is simply to state a hypothesis. The tense of the statement must be inferred from the context. Taken out of context, therefore, the following could refer to several different points in time.

Тя би стояла там часове.
She could (might) stand there for hours.
She would/used to stand there for hours.
She would have stood there for hours.

Ти без мене не би знаел как да се оправиш.
You wouldn't know how to manage without me.
You wouldn't have known how to manage without me.

The above translations demonstrate the fluidity of the English conditional form "would" as well. That is, the English conditional mood can collapse the distinctions "future/present" and "past/pluperfect". It must, however, distinguish past from non-past. In Bulgarian, the same form has all these possible meanings.

Двайсет и седми урок / Lesson 27

Questions about a hypothetical situation are also expressed in the conditional mood; again, context is necessary to understand which tense is meant.

Ка́к би́хте постъ́пили ви́е в такъ́ва ситуа́ция?	How would you act/have acted in such a situation?
С какво́ ли би́ могъ́л да ги изнена́даш?	What could you surprise/have surprised them with?

Often the speaker envisions a hypothetical state in order to enhance or strengthen the point s/he is making, or to express the strength of emotion.

То́й прекратя́ваше ра́ботата си в еди́н ча́с, кой́то за вси́чки дру́ги би́ би́л твъ́рде ра́нен.	He would stop work at an hour which would be too early for most other people.
...таки́ва фо́рми, какви́то то́й не би́ могъ́л да напра́ви и при на́й-ба́вната и внима́телна ра́бота.	...forms the like of which he wouldn't have been able to make even with the slowest and most careful work.
Това́ то́й чете́ше ба́вно, тържéствено и напе́вно, ка́кто би́ го проче́л в чéрква.	He read this [piece] slowly, in a solemn chanting style, just as he would have read it aloud in church.
Това́ би́ било́ чуде́сно!	That would be fantastic!
За ни́що на света́ не би́х пропу́снал та́зи възмо́жност!	I wouldn't miss that chance for anything in the world!

27.4. The conditional mood used in attenuated commands and statements

The conditional mood is also used when one wishes to tone down the force of an expression. Bulgarians frequently use it in the formation of requests; this usage is similar to English. What is being communicated is in essence a command, but the social situation is such that to use the imperative would be highly impolite and abrupt. The conditional is used, therefore, to soften the force of the command, and turn it into a polite request.

Проща́вайте, би́хте ли се дръ́пнали ма́лко госпо́жицата да ми́не?	Excuse me, could you move aside a bit so the young lady can get through?
Би́ ли ми ка́зал какво́ тря́бва да донеса́ със себе́ си у́тре?	Could you tell me what I should bring along tomorrow?

Бихте ли показали тези картини и на него?	Could you show these pictures to him also [please]?

Speakers also often have occasion, for varying reasons, to tone down questions or statements of intent. As in the case of the commands seen above, the underlying meaning is factual and could be expressed in the indicative mood. If the speaker finds the situation appropriate, however, s/he may attenuate the statement or question by expressing it in the conditional mood. Again, this usage is similar to English.

	Literal translation (conditional)	*Underlying meaning (indicative)*
Би ли знаел къде ...	Would you know where...	Do you know where...
Бих те помолил да ...	May I request...	I am requesting...
Бих казал, че ...	I would say that...	I am saying that...
Би било възможно ...	It might be possible to...	It is possible to...
Аз бих могъл да донеса моя.	I could bring mine.	I can bring mine.
Не би било преувеличено да се каже ...	It would not be an exaggeration to say...	It is not an exaggeration to say...

All the above questions or statements concern present-time events, and the speakers have an underlying present-tense indicative meaning in mind. Their choice to use the conditional instead of the indicative allows them to add the meaning of politeness.

27.5. The conditional of impersonal and modal constructions

The conditional forms of the impersonal verbs може and трябва are:

би могло	it might be possible / one might
би трябвало	one ought / one should

These terms can be used in situations of attenuation, when it is necessary to add a more polite or more softened tone, as in the first example below. The basic meaning of these conditional impersonals, however, is to convey that the speaker is thinking more in hypothetical terms than in real-life terms. The relatively loose translations of the remaining examples attempt to define better the "hypothetical" nature of these conditional forms:

	Literal translation	*Underlying meaning*
Би трябвало да сме точни.	We ought to come on time.	We need to be on time.

Here are more examples of this usage:

Би могло́ да ста́не.	It might [possibly] come about.
Такова нещо би било възмо́жно.	Such a thing might be possible [in theory].
Така́ би тря́бвало да напра́вя.	That's what I ought to do [but I probably won't].
Защо́ се ка́рате? Би тря́бвало да се разби́рате.	Why do you fight? You ought to get along!
На твоя́та въ́зраст би оти́вало по-скро́мно облекло́.	More conservative dress might suit your age group better.

27.6. "Non-conditional" би

The form **би** (functioning as an irregular truncated infinitive form of **съм**) also appears in two set phrases with quasi-conditional meaning. One of these is **мо́же би**, which is exactly equivalent to English "maybe". The negative form is **мо́же би не́**. (Note, in the examples below, the distinctly different, non-conditional, meaning when the bounded form of **съм** is used with **не мо́же**.)

The other is the question marker **да не би́...**, which allows a speaker to express a supposition in the form of a question. More often than not the supposed event is one with potential negative consequences for the speaker. (Note, in the examples below, that the final one contains an embedded question.)

-- Ще до́йдеш ли днес?	"Will you come today?"
-- Мо́же би.	"Maybe."
-- А у́тре?	"And tomorrow?"
-- Мо́же би не́.	"Maybe not."
Не мо́же да бъ́де!	That's not possible! That can't be!
Ня́ма го. Да не би́ да е оти́шъл без нас?	He's not here. Could it be that he left without us?
Да не би́ да си че́л ня́коя от те́зи отврати́телни кни́ги на у́жасите?	Can it be/Don't tell me that you've read one of those disgusting horror stories?
Буди́лникът ми е разва́лен и ця́ла нощ не съм ми́гнал от страх да не би́ да закъсне́я.	My alarm clock is broken, and I didn't sleep all night for fear that I'd be late.

27.7. The conditional mood in conditional constructions

Finally, the conditional mood is used in the apodosis of conditional constructions. The general structure, "if A, then B", was reviewed earlier in Lessons 22 and 23. In most such sentences, Bulgarians can use either the conditional mood or the future in the past tense. For instance, most Bulgarians would say that there is no difference in meaning between the following two statements:

Ако можех, щях да дойда.	If I could (have), I would (have) come.
Ако можех, бих дошъл.	*(same)*

The two constructions *are* different, however. The reason it is difficult for Bulgarians to perceive the difference (and for grammarians and writers of textbooks to define it precisely) is that it depends largely on factors of supposition and interpretation (the degree to which individual speakers perceive things to be hypothetical or real, possible or impossible), factors which are not always accessible to an outside observer.

These questions will be taken up in detail in the next lesson. As an introduction to this issue, however, consider the differences in form between conditional sentences using бих (the conditional mood) and conditional sentences using щях (the future in the past) in the apodosis. The essence of this difference is that conditional sentences using бих do not distinguish tense -- the same form is used to express all degrees of past and non-past -- while conditional sentences with щях must use past tense forms. The protasis *(PRO)* must be either in the imperfect or the past anterior, and the apodosis *(APO)* must be either in the future in the past or the future anterior-in-the-past.

Schematically, this can be seen in a revised and compacted version of the model given in in Lesson 23:

FUTURE IN THE PAST

section of sentence tense	PRO imperfect	APO future in the past
	Ако имах пари,	щях да отида.

                                          If I had the money, I would go.
                                If I had had the money, I would have gone.

section of sentence tense	PRO imperfect	APO future anterior in the past
	Ако исках,	щях да съм дошла преди той да замине.

                    If I had wanted to, I would have come before he left.

Двайсет и седми урок / Lesson 27

CONDITIONAL

section of sentence	PRO	APO
tense	past anterior	future in the past
	Ако бяха ми казали навреме,	нямаше да замина.

If they had told me on time, I wouldn't have left.

section of sentence	PRO	APO
tense	past anterior	future anterior in the past
	Ако бяха му казали навреме,	щеше да е дошъл досега.

If they had told him on time, he would be here by now.

Conditional sentences with **бих** always use the same form in the apodosis. In these sentences, it is the protasis that carries the meaning of "tense". When the protasis contains a past-tense form, the meaning of a conditional with **бих** looks, on the surface, equivalent to that of a conditional with **щях**. Consider again the example given earlier:

Ако можех, щях да дойда.	If I could (have), I would (have) come.
Ако можех, бих дошъл.	(same)

When the protasis contains a present tense form, the difference is more clearly seen. If such a sentence is expressed in the indicative, the apodosis must be in the present tense, and the meaning is clearly "real".

Ако мога, ще дойда.   If I can, I'll come.

In the Bulgarian conditional, however, it is possible to combine the present tense (in the protasis) with a **бих** conditional in the apodosis.

Ако мога, бих дошъл.   If I can, I'll [try to] come.

It is difficult to give an exact translation of this sentence, precisely because the rules for English conditional sentences are closer to those formulated for Bulgarian **щях**-conditionals than for Bulgarian **бих**-conditionals. That is, if a prediction is made in the present tense, the speaker considers the condition to be a real one; it is therefore difficult for him to use a "hypothetical" form.

In Bulgarian, on the other hand, a certain degree of this hypothetical meaning is present in all **бих** conditionals, even in those with present tense meaning. An English speaker can only express such meanings by adding words like "probably" or "might" in the apodosis (as in the above example), or by shifting the protasis to an English conditional (as in the following example):

Не бих допуснал, че идва чак от Америка, ако го срещна случайно на улицата.	If I were to meet him by chance on the street, I wouldn't think he was from faraway America.

Neither method of translation manages to render the Bulgarian meaning fully. The distinction between "real" and "hypothetical" depends so much on each individual speaker, and on each instance of speech context, that one must be content with approximations.

27.8. Archaic case forms

In certain fixed expressions such as proverbs, masculine animate nouns are found with a direct object case ending. This ending happens to look like the definite object case ending: both are spelled **-a**. For example:

Брат брата не храни...	Brother feeds not brother...

Fresco, Church of the Nativity, Arbanasi

Двайсет и седми урок / Lesson 27

EXERCISES

I. Finish the sentences using the conditional mood.

1. Ако не валéше, нúе ...
2. Ако тогáва знáехте за товá, вúе ...
3. Ако мóжех да променя́ програ́мата си, ...
4. Ако не бя́ха тóлкова уморéни, тé ...
5. Ако не бéше гръ́мката ѝ слáва, нúе ...
6. Ако úмаше врéме, тú ...?
7. Ако му бя́ха съобщúли наврéме за товá, тóй ...

II. Transform the following sentences using the conditional mood.

Model: Áз мóжех да дóйда, но úмах мнóго рáбота.
         Áз бúх дошъ́л, ако ня́мах мнóго рáбота.

1. Тóй мóжеше да си пригóтви закýска, но се успá.
2. Кáмен мóжеше да кáже товá на мáйка си, но не остáна врéме.
3. Тя́ мóжеше да глéда фúлма, но я задържáха до къ́сно в слýжбата.
4. Книгата мóжеше да úма голя́м успéх, но не бéше напúсана на ня́кой от международните езúци.
5. Тé мóжеха да напазарýват на връ́щане, но не нóсеха парú.
6. Лозя́та мóжеха да дадáт мнóго плóд, но не гú полúвахме.
7. Новогодúшният прáзник мóжеше да е мнóго пó-вéсел, но покáнените гóсти не сé познáваха.

SAMPLE SENTENCES

1. Бúхте ли ми подáли солтá?
2. Извиня́вай, бú ли затвóрил прозóреца? Дýха ми.

3. Сúгурна съм, че вúе бúхте го харéсали мнóго.
4. Бú билó стрáнно да се предполóжи, че нúкой не гó е усéтил да излúза.

5. Бúхте ли ми кáзали кóлко е часъ́т, мóля?
6. Тóй лéсно бú се спрáвил с едúн хулигáн, но двáма са му мнóго.

7. Тé бúха го приéли пó-бъ́рзо, ако тóй не бéше тóлкова пó-възрастен.
8. Бúхте ли предáли на съпрýга си нáй-сърдéчните ми пóздрави?

9. Те́ би́ха зна́ели какво́ да пра́вят с не́го, ако́ го хва́нат на своя́ терито́рия.
10. Ни́е би́хме се чу́вствали по́-добре́ в самостоя́телно жи́лище.

11. Не би́ ме учу́дило, ако́ то́й се ока́же шпио́нин.
12. Живо́тът ми да зави́си от това́, не би́х могъ́л да го напра́вя.

13. Това́ не би́ и́мало значе́ние, ако́ се бе́ше слу́чило в дру́го вре́ме.
14. Не би́х те помо́лил за та́я услу́га, ако́ мо́жех да се спра́вя са́м със ситуа́цията.

15. Да не би́ да си хо́дил да го ви́диш?
16. Ня́ма ни́кой. Да не би́ да са забра́вили, че ще и́дваме?

17. Не би́хте ли се дръ́пнали да ми́на?
18. Тря́бваше не́я да пока́ниш за гла́вната ро́ля. Тя́ ни́кога не би́ ти създа́вала таки́ва пробле́ми.

SENTENCES FOR TRANSLATION

1. It would be good if you were to manage without help this time.

2. "Mightn't we be able to postpone the meeting for some other time?"
   "You know, I just can't imagine why you couldn't just once do something on time."

3. I wouldn't say he is a very smart fellow, but he has been helping us pour concrete since time immemorial. Once, though, we caught him sleeping on the job. That didn't bother us, but we had to wake him up and make him move over a bit so we wouldn't have to pour the foundation on him.

4. "Excuse me, could you please tell me where I could mail this letter?"
   "Of course. If you mail it at the central post office, in principle it ought to arrive without trouble."

5. "It wouldn't surprise me a bit if he has eaten all the kebabches by now."
   "Can it really be that they are all eaten up already?"

6. I didn't leave the house last night for fear that the karakonjul would see me. That would have been very bad indeed. I don't know if he is still looking for me, but I am always very careful at night just in case.

7. If I had the opportunity to go to Bulgaria, I would certainly not decline.

Двайсет и седми урок / Lesson 27

READING SELECTION

<u>Йорда́н Йо́вков, "Сали́ Яша́р, прочу́тият ма́йстор на кару́ци"</u>

Сла́вата на Сали́ Яша́р, прочу́тия ма́йстор на кару́ци от Али́ Анифе́, сти́гаше ве́че твъ́рде надале́ч. Такъ́в ма́йстор като не́го ни́кога по́-ра́но не бе́ше има́ло в Али́ Анифе́. Ко́й зна́е дали́ ще́ше да и́ма и по́-къ́сно. За око́лните села́ и ду́ма не мо́жеше да ста́ва, там такъ́в ма́йстор ня́маше. Ня́маше дори́ и в града́, и то тъ́кмо в то́я град, ко́йто бе́ше в среда́та на безкра́йна равнина́, от ко́йто изли́заха пъ́тища по вси́чки посо́ки като лъчи́те на звезда́, и къде́то откра́й вре́ме о́ще на́й-пъ́рвите ма́йстори са били́ ма́йсторите на кару́ци. Но това́ поня́кога се слу́чва.

Сали́ Яша́р бе́ше се изди́гнал над вси́чки по божа́ да́рба, появи́л се бе́ше случа́йно, ка́кто случа́йно се появя́ват по села́та они́я прочу́ти знаха́ри, кои́то леку́ват на́й-те́жки бо́лести и че́сто пъ́ти с ня́коя би́лка, с върха́ на нагорещено́ желя́зо или са́мо с ня́колко ду́ми връ́щат живо́та на мно́го уми́ращи.

Сали́ Яша́р наи́стина и́маше не́що, кое́то го оприлича́ваше на ти́я хо́ра. Като все́ки кова́ч, той бе́ше здра́в и си́лен чове́к, но и́нак бе́ше благ, тих, вдълбоче́н в се́бе си. То́й прика́зваше ма́лко, но и ма́лкото, кое́то ка́жеше, бе́ше я́сно, у́мно, отме́рено, а на они́я, кои́то го слу́шаха, ви́наги се стру́ваше, че в очи́те на Сали́ Яша́р и́маше друг кова́ч, ко́йто съ́що рабо́теше, съ́що кове́ше, а не се ви́ждаше, и са́мо искри́те и отбля́съците от това́ вътре́шно огни́ще гре́еха в зами́слените очи́ на Сали́ Яша́р. Така́ Сали́ Яша́р бе́ше прост чове́к, с изца́пани ръце́, кове́ше желя́зото и пра́веше кару́ци, но и́маше вид на мъдре́ц и нево́лно вдъ́хваше уваже́ние дори́ и на они́я, кои́то не го позна́ваха и ни́що не зна́еха за изку́ството на ръка́та му.

То́й и́маше и еди́н друг на́вик, ко́йто съ́що тъ́й бе́ше добре́ позна́т на хо́рата от не́говото се́ло. Вся́ка ве́чер, ма́лко преди́ да зале́зе слъ́нцето, в еди́н час, ко́йто за вси́чки дру́ги би бил твъ́рде ра́нен, Сали́ Яша́р прекратя́ваше отведнъ́ж вся́ка рабо́та и затва́ряше работи́лницата си. Чира́ци и ка́лфи бъ́рзо изми́ваха изца́паните си от въ́глищата лица́ и се разоти́ваха. Ни́какви увеща́ния, ни́какви молби́ не мо́жеха да нака́рат Сали́ Яша́р да оста́не до по́-къ́сно и да довъ́рши ня́коя рабо́та, ко́лкото и бъ́рза да бе́ше тя. "Ще я напра́вим," гово́реше той, "и у́тре е бо́жи ден." И той ка́зваше това́ кро́тко, но твъ́рдо -- и ся́каш бе́ше ве́че дале́ч ня́къде, откъ́снат от вси́чко, забра́вил за вси́чко, потъ́нал в та́я стра́нна зами́сленост, коя́то пъ́лнеше очи́те му, скри́ти под гъ́стите ве́жди. И, наме́тнал ня́коя дре́ха на изпоте́ните си пле́щи, той тръ́гваше за до́ма си, прегъ́рбен ма́лко, споко́ен и загле́дан в земя́та. А хо́рата, кои́то го сре́щаха, след като почти́телно го поздравя́ваха, гле́даха го учу́дено и си ми́слеха, че ня́каква бо́лка тря́бва да гло́жди сърце́то на Сали́ Яша́р и че ако то́й бъ́рза да си оти́де, не е́ за да си почи́не, а за да оста́не сам със се́бе си и ми́слите си.

И пра́ви бя́ха хо́рата от Али́ Анифе́: и́маше не́що, кое́то мъ́чеше Сали́ Яша́р, и вся́ка ве́чер по това́ вре́ме той си ми́слеше за не́го.

Двайсет и седми урок / Lesson 27

Работите му отиваха добре. Беден и прост ковач някога, сега той беше прочут майстор, при когото идеха с поръчки от най-далечни краища. Работа имаше повече, отколкото му трябваше. Сали Яшар не обичаше да връща никого, пък и колкото повече работа имаше, колкото повече трябваше да бърза, толкоз по-добре работеше. Идеха му неподозирани и от него самия сили, разпалваше се, работеше със страст, с увлечение, ръката му ставаше сигурна, погледът точен и желязото под неговия чук добиваше неочаквано такива съвършени форми, каквито той не би могъл да направи и при най-бавната и внимателна работа. А тъкмо такава работа беше по сърце на Сали Яшар и от неговите ръце излизаха каруци, които бяха истинско чудо: леки, като че сами щяха да тръгнат, напети и гиздави като невести, с шарила и бои, които грееха по тях като цъфнали цветя. Но най-чудното в тия каруци бяха звуковете, които те издаваха, когато вървяха. Като че в железните им оси беше скрита някаква музика. Как ги правеше Сали Яшар, един господ знаеше, но неговите каруци не дрънчаха, не хлопаха като другите коли, а пееха по пътищата.

Каруците пееха по пътищата и сякаш разказваха как един човек може да бъде много богат, но и много злочест.

Адаптирано от Йордан Йовков, <u>Песента на колелетата</u>.

Street scene in Koprivshtitsa

Двайсет и седми урок / Lesson 27

GLOSSARY

бе́ден	poor, meager	зава́рвам / заваря́	find
бето́нен	[made] of concrete	зами́слен	thoughtful, preoccupied
би́	would *(2d-3d sg.)*	зами́сленост	pensiveness, reverie
би́х	would *(1sg.)*	зара́ствам / зара́сна	heal, close up
би́ха	would *(3pl.)*		
би́хме	would *(1pl.)*	захладня́вам / захладне́я	turn cool
би́хте	would *(2pl.)*		
бла́г	gentle, kindly	злоче́ст	miserable, unfortunate
бо́жи	God's, divine		
буди́лник	alarm clock	изди́гам се / изди́гна се	rise, advance
бъ́рз	urgent		
		изди́гам се над	tower over
вдълбоча́вам се / вдълбоча́ се (-и́ш)	be absorbed in	изпотя́вам се / изпотя́ се	sweat, perspire
вдъ́хвам / вдъ́хна	breathe in; inspire	и́мам голя́м успе́х	be wildly successful
вито́шки	Vitosha *(adj.)*	ина́че *(archaic* ина́к*)*	otherwise
витри́на	window (shop or public place)	и́скра *(and* искра́*)*	spark
въ́глища	coal	ка́лфа	journeyman
възмо́жност	possibility, chance	камъня́к	stones, stony ground
въ́зраст, -та́	age	карти́на	picture
		кова́	forge, hammer
ги́здав	pretty, comely	кова́ч	smith, blacksmith
гла́вна ро́ля	the lead	компа́ния	company, crowd
гло́ждя	gnaw; rankle		
Го́спод	God, the Lord	леге́нда	legend, myth
гръ́мка сла́ва	resounding fame	леку́вам	cure, treat
гръ́мък	loud, high-sounding	ле́я	pour
гъ́ст	thick, heavy	лъ́ч, -ъ́т *(pl.* лъчи́*)*	ray, glimmer
гъ́сти ве́жди	bushy eyebrows		
		ме́лнишки	Melnik *(adj.)*
да	if	мъдре́ц	wise man, sage
да зна́ех	had I known	мъ́ча (-иш)	torment, bother
да́вам душа́ за	be crazy about		
да́рба	gift, talent		
доби́вам / доби́я	get, acquire	нагореща́вам / нагореща́	heat, heat up
добре́ зава́рили	well-found *(answer to* добре́ дошли́*)*	намя́там / наме́тна	throw on, throw over
допу́скам / допу́сна	allow, admit	напазару́вам	do the shopping
дрънкам / дрънча́ (-и́ш)	rattle, clank	напе́вен	melodious, lilting
дръ́пвам се / дръ́пна се	stand clear	напе́т	sprightly, handsome
душа́	soul, heart	нево́лно	involuntarily
		неоча́кван	unexpected, sudden
еди́н Го́спод зна́е	God only knows	неподози́ран	unsuspected, unexpected
		новогоди́шен пра́зник	New Year's celebration
же́га	sweltering heat		
желя́зо	iron, iron bar		
жи́лище	lodging, residence		

Двайсет и седми урок / Lesson 27

облекло́	clothing, apparel	самостоя́телен	independent
огни́ще	fireplace, hearth; center	самостоя́телно жи́лище	separate living quarters
опра́вям се / опра́вя се	work out, get better; manage	ситуа́ция	situation
оприлича́вам / оприлича́ (-и́ш)	liken, compare [to]	скро́мен	modest; humble
		скро́мно облекло́	low-key/simple dress
ос, -та́	axis; axle	спра́вям се / спра́вя се	cope with, manage
отбля́сък	reflection, gleam		
отведна́ж (or отведнъ́ж)	suddenly, all at once	страст, -та́	passion
		те́жка бо́лест	grave illness
отврати́телен	disgusting	террито́рия	territory, area
откра́й	from the beginning	то́лкоз = то́лкова	
откра́й вре́ме	from time immemorial	уваже́ние	respect, esteem
отла́гам / отло́жа (-иш)	put off, postpone	увеща́ние	admonition; coaxing
		увлече́ние	enthusiasm, animation
отме́рен	measured, deliberate	усе́щам / усе́тя	feel, notice
		успи́вам се / успя́ се	oversleep
пазаря́	hire		
пле́щи	shoulders	хло́пам / хло́пна	knock, clatter
поръ́чка	order, commission	хулига́н	hoodlum, hooligan
потъ́нал	sunk, absorbed		
потърпя́вам / потърпя́	have a little patience	цъ́фвам / цъ́фна	blossom, burst
почти́телен	respectful, reverential	цъ́фнали цветя́	flowers in bloom
прегъ́рбвам се / прегъ́рбя се	stoop	чак	only; that much
преда́вам / преда́м (-даде́ш)	deliver, transmit	чак от Аме́рика	all the way from America
прекратя́вам / прекратя́	cease, suspend	че́рква	church
		че́сто пъ́ти	time and again
преполовя́вам / преполовя́	halve, be halfway through	чира́к	apprentice
		чу́до	miracle, wonder
преувелича́вам / преувелича́ (-и́ш)	exaggerate, overstate	чук, -ъ́т	hammer, mallet
прочу́т	famous, renowned	шари́ло	painted decoration
		шпио́нин	spy
разва́лям / развали́	damage, break		
разпа́лвам се / разпа́ля се	flame up, become intense	ъ́глов	angular; corner (adj.)
ря́дкост	rarity	я́сла	manger; crib

Двайсет и седми урок / Lesson 27

CULTURAL COMMENTARY

Forms of address: "Welcome"

When a new arrival is welcomed with Добре́ дошли́! (literally, "well come"), it is customary for him or her to answer with Добре́ зава́рили! (literally, "well found"). These are literal translations of the Turkish expressions used on identical occasions: *hoş geldiniz* ("well you came") and *hoş bulduk* ("well we found"). Literal translations of Turkish idiomatic phrases into the various Balkan languages abound in the several Balkan countries.

Folklore: proverbs; folk medicine

Slavic languages are very rich in proverbs, phrases which encapsulate folk wisdom in highly concise and poetic form. Often the literal translations leave a great deal to be desired. Literally, for example, the proverb Бра́т бра́та не хра́ни, но горко́ му ко́йто го ня́ма would be rendered "Brother feeds not brother but woe to him who has none." The meaning, however, is universal: one takes family members for granted and pays them no special heed until they are needed; at that time, the absence of family to help is sorely felt.

Folk medicine was widespread until recently (and is still practiced in many villages). The healer was called a "knower" (знаха́р). Healing rituals include passing a burning iron rod over the wound or ailing body part, speaking or chanting of spells, and the preparation of medicinal herbs. Most Bulgarians still believe in the efficacy of the latter. Medicinal herbs are available in most city pharmacies.

Literature: Iordan Iovkov

Nineteenth century life in Bulgaria, particularly in the small towns, had a marked flavor to it, which is best described as "Balkan-Oriental". Life retained its Balkan and Slavic style, but was unavoidably influenced by the many centuries of Ottoman domination. Much of Bulgarian prose writing of the late 19th and early 20th century consists of stories and novels set in such milieus. The highly Turkish sounding names of characters and certain of their occupations help create this atmosphere. Examples are the personal name Сали́ Яша́р (in Turkish, *Salih Yaşar*), the place name Али́ Анифе́, and the terms чира́к (Turkish *çirak* "apprentice" and ка́лфа (Turkish *kalfa*, "assistant master, overseer"). The latter word, of course, derives from the term Caliph, which in the political bureaucracy of Muslim states designated the representative of Muhammad.

One of the best writers in the above genre is Iordan Iovkov (Йорда́н Йо́вков, 1880-1937). He worked most of his life as a small-town teacher in Dobrudzha and as a clerk in the Bulgarian embassy in Bucharest, completing his prose writing on the side. His best known stories are collected in Старопланинските леге́нди (1927) and Ве́чери в Анти́мовския ха́н (1928). He was a man of ideals, and believed in the transforming power of beauty, heroism and love. Many consider him to be Bulgaria's best prose writer of all time.

LESSON 28

DIALOGUE

<u>Когá друг пъ́т би́хме могли́ да им го покáжем?</u>

// Ди́митър, Милéна и Павли́на с кýчето чáкат на трамвáйната спи́рка в Кня́жево. Часъ́т е тóчно óсем. //

Павлина: Ни́е ли сме нáй-ранобýдните? Ня́маше ли да е пó-добрé да бя́хте ме остáвили спокóйно да си допи́я кафéто, вмéсто да виси́м тýка да чáкаме?

Димитър: Си́гурно ще дóйдат всéки момéнт. Вéче ще са се качи́ли в трамвáя.

Павлина: Не щé да са се качи́ли, защóто ги ня́ма.

Милена: Акó слъ́нцето не свéтеше прáво в очи́те ми, щя́х да мóга да ви́дя дали́ в тóя трамвáй дéто и́два, ня́ма ня́кой от нáшите.

Димитър: Ви́ж, ми́ло, óня, висóкият човéк не бéше ли Весели́н?

Павлина: Тóй е. Каквá голя́ма рáница е нарáмил. Като че ли́ ще векýва на Ви́тоша.

Веселин: Добрó ýтро! Буди́лникът ми е развалéн и ця́ла нóщ не съм ми́гнал от стрáх да не би́ да закъснéя за срéщата.

Павлина: Не бóй се. Твóята изгóра óще я ня́ма.

Милена: Ни́е нóсим сáмо рýска салáта, хля́б, салáм и кафé в тéрмоса. Ти́ каквó тóлкова си се натовáрил?

Веселин: Нóся от вси́чко по мáлко. Когá друг пъ́т би́хме могли́ да покáжем на ти́я америкáнци каквó е бъ́лгарско гостоприéмство, акó не сегá?

Павлина: С каквó ли би́ могъ́л да ги изненáдаш? Тé тáм вси́чко си и́мат.

Веселин: Чáк вси́чко не вя́рвам да и́мат. А и да и́мат, еднó е тáм да го и́мат, а съвсéм дрýго -- тýка.

// Дéйвид изни́ква неочáквано иззáд гърбá им. //

Дейвид: Добрó ýтро. Щя́х да се загýбя, акó не бя́х взéл такси́. Слáва бóгу, шофьóрът знáеше къдé е Кня́жево.

Двайсет и осми урок / Lesson 28

// В то́я моме́нт присти́га сле́дващият трамва́й и от пре́дната врата́ сли́зат Пе́тър, Та́ня, деца́та, и Бо́би. От за́дната врата́ после́дна сли́за Джу́ли. //

Джули: Добро́ у́тро. Да бях зна́ела, че сте в съ́щия трамва́й, щях да до́йда да си поприка́зваме по пъ́тя.

Таня: А́з ми́слех, че це́лият трамва́й ни е чу́л. То не бя́ха пи́съци, не бя́ха кря́съци... Ка́мен се опи́тваше да завъ́рже уши́те на Бо́би на фльо́нга, а Бо́би и На́дка се съпротивля́ваха.

Веселин: Кого́ ви́ждат очи́те ми? Това́ про́сто не мо́же да бъ́де!!

Петър: Ве́ско, ама ти́ ли си това́?

Веселин: Пе́шо, пи́пнах те на местопрестъпле́нието! Ко́лкото пъ́ти те сре́щна през после́дните годи́ни, все́ не мо́жем да се наприка́зваме. У́ж все́ си мно́го зае́т, ту́ замина́ваш в командиро́вка, ту́ се връ́щаш от командиро́вка и жена́ ти те ча́ка...

Петър: Ама то не е́ лъжа́.

Веселин: Ама да хо́диш по екску́рзии нами́раш вре́ме, нали́?

Таня: Не по́мня откога́ не ни́ се е случвало да изле́зем ня́къде вси́чки за́едно.

Веселин: О́ня де́н, като се запозна́хме с тво́ята жена́, на ме́не и през у́м не ми́ мина́, че това́ мо́же да е съ́щата Та́ня, за коя́то се оже́ни мо́ят прия́тел. Джу́ли, по́мниш ли, а́з ти разпра́вях за прия́теля си, с кого́то така́ ху́баво се разби́рахме. Да зна́еш, Пе́шо, ако бе́ше оста́нал на ра́бота в реда́кцията, с тво́ята да́рба досега́ така́ва карие́ра ще́ше да си напра́вил...

Таня: То́й и ту́ка си е добре́. Гла́вният реда́ктор мно́го го цени́. Пъ́к и пари́те са по́вече.

Павлина: То́зи предста́вителен мла́д чове́к би тря́бвало да е ва́шият мъ́ж, Та́ня.

Таня: Ах, да́. Запозна́йте се. Пе́тьо, да ти предста́вя Павли́на, ма́йката на Дими́тър.

Петър: Прия́тно ми е. А́з ве́че чу́вах за ва́с от жена́ си. Напра́вили сте ѝ мно́го си́лно впечатле́ние.

Димитър: Ни́е ма́й се събра́хме вси́чките. Ни́кого по́вече не ча́каме, нали́?

Джули: Вси́чки ся́каш са ту́к.

Милена: Тога́ва да потегля́ме.

Двайсет и осми урок / Lesson 28

GRAMMAR

28.1. Tense, aspect, and mood in the Bulgarian verb

The Bulgarian verbal system is quite complex on a number of levels. The idea of aspect (opposing bounded and unbounded views of an action) pervades the verbal system as a whole. The concepts of tense and mood are also central to understanding the meaning of the many different verbal forms. Tense refers not only to the time when a verbal action took place (or will take place), but also to the internal relationships between different points along the time scale which speakers can choose to envision. Mood, by contrast, refers to a speaker's attitude about that which s/he is saying, and how it relates to the overall context within which the speech act is situated.

There are two significant areas within Bulgarian grammar where the concepts of tense and mood overlap, neither of which is sufficiently understood by descriptive grammarians. One will be the subject of this lesson and the other of the following lesson. This lesson is concerned with the question of conditional constructions.

It is a striking feature of Bulgarian grammar that the idea of "conditional" can be expressed both by means of forms marked for tense, and by means of forms marked for mood. The future in the past tense (and other tenses related to it) are ideally suited to express the idea that something "would have happened" (or not); it is thus natural that the idea of "conditional" should be communicated in this form. The conditional mood is also ideally suited to express this idea. Mood, after all, is a means whereby the speaker communicates his attitude about what he is saying -- and the question of one's belief about whether or not something might happen certainly qualifies as an attitude.

Since Bulgarians use both of these means to express the idea "conditional", it makes sense to examine this situation in some detail. Why are both used so commonly? Why does the language seem to need them both? Furthermore, why, when they are formally so very different from each other, do Bulgarians tend to say that these two constructions "mean the same thing" in so many instances?

28.2. Review of conditional constructions

Conditional constructions look straightforward on the surface. What makes analysis of them difficult is that they make reference to a number of very subtle factors.

In order for successful communication to take place, every speaker who produces a sentence with conditional meaning (as well as every one of his listeners) must make the correct decisions about three quite different issues. These are:

Двайсет и осми урок / Lesson 28

(1) Time of the action;
(2) Realness of the condition; and
(3) Likelihood of fulfillment of the condition.

Given that a conditional sentence always takes the form "if A *(protasis)*, then B *(apodosis)*", these factors may be analyzed as follows:

(1) The *time* of the action refers to the entire sequence of "if A, then B". Of the three factors, it is the only one that can be determined objectively. Non-past time is not always expressed with non-past verbs, however. Often the only way the other two factors can be expressed properly is by moving the tense of one of the two verbs (either A or B) into the past.

(2) The *realness* of the condition refers only to A. Does (or did) the condition described in A actually exist, or is it a hypothetical one? If the actual condition described does (or did) not exist, does the speaker have in mind another concrete one that does (or did)?

(3) The *likelihood of fulfillment* refers only to B. If A turns (or had turned) out to be the case, what is the likelihood that B will ensue (or would have ensued)? That is, what is the speaker's assessment of the causal relationship between A and B, given the other relevant circumstances of time and realness of condition?

The correct choice of forms depends on a successful analysis of the above factors. Although there are three possible constructions (identified below as **A, B, C**), the vast majority of conditional statements are made according to the first two models (**A** or **B**).

A. TENSE in the apodosis: either future in the past or future anterior in the past.

This type will henceforth be called the "щях-conditional". If the speaker chooses this form, s/he is limited to past tense forms of the verb in the protasis, but among these, may choose either imperfect or past anterior.

B. MOOD forms in the apodosis: the conditional.

This type will henceforth be called the "бих-conditional". If the speaker chooses this form, s/he may use any tense form in the protasis, although complex forms like future in the past, future anterior, and future anterior in the past are unlikely to occur.

C. MOOD forms (conditional) in *both* the protasis and the apodosis.

When this (much less frequently occurring) option is chosen, the conjunction да is used in place of ако. This construction is for the most part limited to archaic and traditional expressions. For instance:

Да би се я́ло, не би́ вися́ло.	It's not worth it anyway. [*literally:* If it could be eaten it wouldn't be hanging.]

The conjunction да can also be used with indicative forms to express conditionality. These constructions will be discussed at the conclusion of this lesson.

28.3 Tense vs. mood in conditional constructions: general observations

The primary meaning of the future in the past tense is that something "would have happened", while the primary meaning of the conditional mood is that something "could well" happen (or have happened). That is, the future-in-the-past communicates a concrete statement of belief, while the conditional communicates a more general and hypothetical statement of opinion. It would follow, therefore, that when speakers use a щях-conditional, they are stressing their belief in the fulfillability of the condition -- "if A, then *certainly* B"; and that when they use a бих-conditional, the meaning would be closer to "if A, then *possibly* B".

The above yardstick can be applied in certain very clear-cut cases. Consider first two examples in which only the щях-conditional is possible:

Ако́ и́скаше, ще́ше да до́йде.	If she had wanted to, she would have come.
А́з щя́х да се загу́бя, ако́ не бя́х взе́л такси́.	I would have gotten lost if I hadn't taken a taxi.

Both speakers are referring to a real past event, and both are offering an justification for that event. The reason the first speaker chose not to come is that she didn't want to, and the reason the second speaker managed to avoid getting lost was that he took a taxi. Each speaker is certain of his deduction, and each uses the щях-conditional to convey that certainty. Had either speaker used a бих-conditional, this choice would have moved the realm of thought into the hypothetical, thereby contradicting the intended meaning.

Now consider two examples where only the бих-conditional is possible:

Би́х се гле́дал по ця́л де́н в огледа́лото, ако́ и́мах таки́ва ху́бави си́ни очи́.	If I had such beautiful blue eyes, I would spend all day staring at myself in the mirror.
Кога́ дру́г пъ́т би́хме могли́ да пока́жем на ти́я америка́нци какво́ е бъ́лгарско гостоприе́мство, ако́ не се́га?	If we don't do it now, when would we [ever] have another chance to show these Americans what Bulgarian hospitality is?

In each instance, the speaker constructs a hypothetical situation in order to emphasize a particular emotional stance: how beautiful he considers the girl's eyes to be, and how important he considers it to be to seize the chance to demonstrate the Bulgarian conception of hospitality. The use of the щях-conditional would have implied that these conditions were real, which is clearly not the case.

In most instances of conditional sentences, however, the speaker has a choice: s/he may use either a щях-conditional or a бих-conditional. Sometimes the meanings are nearly identical, but in the majority of cases there is at least a slight difference. To think of this difference only in terms of "certainty" vs. "possibility" or "reality" vs. "imagination", however, is misleading. There are several factors involved, each of which must be visualized as a continuum. These are:

	щях-conditionals	бих-conditionals
basis of belief	fact	hypothesis
kind of situation	concrete	theoretical
frame of reference	specific	broad

These three conditions overlap to a considerable extent; very few speech events are such that each can be identified discretely. Furthermore, most speech events must be defined in terms of a gradation (and not in "yes/no" terms). Finally and perhaps most significantly, each speech event is unique, and the point of view taken at any moment ultimately depends upon the speaker himself.

Nevertheless, specifying these three factors does at least allow one to discuss the difference between щях-conditionals and бих-conditionals more objectively. The more explicitly one can define the idea of the sentence in terms of the first of these, "factive" vs. "hypothetical", the greater will be the potential difference in meaning between the two types of possible conditional constructions. If only the latter two shades of meaning can be detected, the more likely it is that Bulgarians will call the two usages synonymous. In addition, it must be noted that the above schema is an idealization. Many Bulgarians will claim that practically all instances of щях- and бих-conditionals mean essentially the same thing.

28.4. Factive vs. hypothetical conditional constructions

Many conditional sentences focus upon the likelihood of fulfillment of the condition. The use of a щях-conditional means that the speaker relies upon factual evidence to make this prediction, while the use of a бих-conditional means that s/he is constructing a hypothetical situation. This was the primary factor at work in the examples given above.

In fact, such an opposition is so clear-cut that it often determines the tense of the sentence as well. Recall that щях-conditionals must use past-tense forms in the apodosis, but that бих-conditionals may use any tense form. The more factive the situation, however, the more impossible it is to use a past tense form in the бих-conditional. That is, if the speaker's intention is to make an explicitly hypothetical statement, then s/he usually chooses the more general non-past tense.

The following examples demonstrate the different ways in which щях-conditionals and бих-conditionals are used to state predictions. If the speaker has in mind a particular factual event and visualizes an alternative phrased in terms of this actual incident, s/he must use the щях-conditional in order to convey the intended meaning. If, however, the speaker presents the same potentially factive event in hypothetical terms, s/he must use the бих-conditional to stress the more general nature of the prediction. Бих-conditionals with past tense forms in the apodosis are less factive than щях-conditionals, but also less hypothetical than бих-conditionals with present tense forms in the apodosis.

Here is a schematic survey of this three-way distinction, followed by examples. The English translations attempt to convey these distinctions, but are only approximate.

> (a) *factive, actual event*
> (b) *hypothetical, potentially factive*
> (c) *purely hypothetical*

(a) Те щя́ха да зна́ят какво́ да пра́вят с не́го, ако́ го хва́неха на своя́ терито́рия.
 If they had caught him on their own territory, they would have known how to deal with him.

(b) Те би́ха зна́ели какво́ да пра́вят с не́го, ако́ го хва́неха на своя́ терито́рия.
 If they caught him on their own territory, they would know how to deal with him.

(c) Те би́ха зна́ели какво́ да пра́вят с не́го, ако́ го хва́нат на своя́ терито́рия.
 If they were to catch him on their own territory, they would know how to deal with him.

(a) Ня́маше да се учу́дя, ако́ то́й се бе́ше оказа́л шпио́нин.
 It wouldn't have surprised me if he actually had turned out to be a spy [after all].

(b) Не би́х се учу́дила, ако́ то́й се бе́ше оказа́л шпио́нин.
 It wouldn't surprise me if he turned out to be a spy.

(c) Не би́х се учу́дила, ако́ то́й се ока́же шпио́нин.
 It wouldn't surprise me if he turns out to be a spy.

Двайсет и осми урок / Lesson 28

(a)	Áз лéсно щях да се спрáвя с едúния хулигáн, но двáма ми бя́ха мнóго.	I could easily have dealt with one thug, but two of them were too much for me.
(b)	Áз лéсно бих се спрáвил с едúния хулигáн, но двáма ми бя́ха мнóго.	I could easily have dealt with one thug, but two would have been too much for me.
(c)	Áз лéсно бих се спрáвил с едúния хулигáн, но двáма са ми мнóго.	I could easily deal with one thug, but two are too much for me.

Some conditional sentences exist in shortened form, i.e. without the protasis. These also require speakers to make the same choice (between щях-conditionals and бих-conditionals) according to the same gradation of factors.

(a)	Нúкой ня́маше да напúше тáзи кнúга пó-добрé от нéго.	No one could have written that book better than he could have.
(b)	Нúкой не би напúсал тáзи кнúга пó-добрé от нéго.	Nobody could write such a book better than he could.

In some cases the English translation admits of both a factive and a hypothetical meaning. In Bulgarian, only the factive meaning is possible for a щях-conditional, while a бих-conditional can, depending on the semantics of the sentence, have either meaning. In the following example, the possible Bulgarian underlying meanings are given in italics.

Conditional sentence:		"We would never go without first being invited."
(a)	Нúе ня́маше да отúдем непокáнени.	*The fact that we went obviously means that we were invited.*
(b)	Нúе не бúхме отúшли непокáнени.	*The fact that we went obviously means that we were invited.* -- OR -- *We wouldn't do such a thing; what kind of people do you think we are?!*

Not all conditional sentences can be described according to the factive/hypothetical continuum. Whether this can be done at all depends to some extent on the verb itself. That is, the meaning of some verbs is markedly more "factive" than that of others: if the verb (and the meaning of the sentence) is sufficiently factive, it is easier to perceive a difference in meaning between a щях-conditional and a бих-conditional.

Двайсет и осми урок / Lesson 28

28.5. Concrete vs. theoretical conditional constructions

Other conditional constructions focus less on the factivity of the condition, and more upon the nature of the condition itself. The event itself is usually hypothetical. But if the speaker visualizes it in concrete terms, usually as a comparison to some other specific event, then s/he is more likely to use a **щях**-conditional. Usage of a **бих**-conditional in such a case would mean that the speaker's focus is more on a general, theoretical level.

Nevertheless, since such events are not necessarily grounded in actual fact, there is considerable overlap between the two usages. Some Bulgarians would say that all of the following examples are interchangeable, while others would accept (at least to a certain degree), the italicized explanations which propose a distinction between them.

Conditional sentence:
  "We wouldn't be able to last so long without electricity in the winter."

(a) През зи́мата ня́маше да мо́жем да прека́раме то́лкова дъ́лго вре́ме без електри́чество.   *We were able to manage without electricity that time only because it wasn't winter.*

(b) През зи́мата не би́хме могли́ да прека́раме то́лкова дъ́лго вре́ме без електри́чество.   *We wouldn't be able to manage in the winter without electricity.*

Conditional sentence:
  "If she lived that close to the park, she'd be out walking every day."

(a) Тя ще́ше да се разхо́жда все́ки ден, ако живе́еше то́лкова бли́зо до па́рка.   *It's amazing that he lives next to a park and never walks there. She, on the other hand...*

(b) Тя би се разхо́ждала все́ки ден, ако живе́еше то́лкова бли́зо до па́рка.   *She loves nature, and living close to a park would be her idea of heaven.*

Conditional sentence:
  "It wouldn't have mattered [so much] if it had happened at a different time."

(a) Това́ ня́маше да и́ма значе́ние, ако се бе́ше слу́чило в дру́го вре́ме.   *Such a situation may not have mattered at some other time, but it certainly does now.*

(b) Това́ не би и́мало значе́ние, ако се бе́ше слу́чило в дру́го вре́ме.   *Times change, and you can never predict what will happen.*

Conditional sentence:
"No fish could live in that water."

(a)	Всяка риба щеше да умре в тая вода.	*I hear they found a dead trout in that pond and I'm not surprised.*
(b)	Всяка риба би умряла в тая вода.	*The current state of water pollution is despicable. Just look at that pond!*

28.6. Specific vs. broad interpretations of conditional constructions

Some conditional sentences describe an event which is clearly hypothetical and which is usually presented as a metaphor. That is, the underlying meaning of the sentence is much broader than the actual event named. In these cases, most Bulgarians would say there is no difference between щях-conditionals and бих-conditionals. Nevertheless, some do admit the possibility of a certain difference in the specificity vs. broadness of the metaphor. For example:

Conditional sentence:
"Someone like Balzac would never have written such nonsense."

(a)	Един Балзак нямаше да напише такава глупост.	*The writer of this piece is most certainly not Balzac -- he wouldn't have written this.*
(b)	Един Балзак не би написал такава глупост.	*Someone with Balzac's talent would never have written such drivel.*

Conditional sentence:
"Gimme five leva!"
"If I had five leva, I'd go off and get married!"

(a)	-- Дай пет лева! -- Ако имах пет лева, щях да се оженя.	*I am totally without money; you know that's an absurd request.*
(b)	-- Дай пет лева! -- Ако имах пет лева, бих се оженил.	*If I had any money to spare, there's all sorts of things I might do!*

Finally, there are a number of instances in which the condition is phrased so generally that practically all Bulgarians would say there is no difference at all between a щях-conditional and a бих-conditional. For instance:

Conditional sentence:
"We would travel constantly if we had the time and the money."

(a) Ни́е щя́хме да пъту́ваме непрекъ́снато, ако и́махме вре́ме и пари́.
(b) Ни́е би́хме пъту́вали непрекъ́снато, ако и́махме вре́ме и пари́.

28.7. Conditional constructions: summary

The *future in the past tense* usually refers to an actual situation. It visualizes the potential outcome that would have resulted if one or more elements of that situation had progressed differently, and conveys the speaker's certainty that this outcome would have ensued in such a situation. Grammatically, the future in the past is part of the indicative mood; as such it narrates events in a neutral tone. The *conditional mood* usually refers to a non-existing, hypothetical situation, almost visualizing (in a sense) a different time line. It conveys the speaker's belief about how things might happen (or have happened) along that imagined time line. Grammatically, the conditional is a mood all of its own; as such it expresses a speaker's attitude.

The above summarizes the definitions usually given in Bulgarian grammars for the two forms, together with the explanation of the difference in meaning between them. However, most of these grammars are attempting to prescribe the way Bulgarians should speak, largely by describing the way they probably used to speak. That is, it is likely that Bulgarians of past generations used to make a sharper distinction between щях-conditionals and бих-conditionals, and that they made this distinction along the lines just stated. The point of the present discussion is that they by and large no longer do so. Despite the significant structural, formal and semantic difference between the "future in the past tense" and the "conditional mood", the two are now synonymous in the meaning "conditional" for most Bulgarians in most instances.

Language changes. The above discussion is an attempt to characterize one of the changes currently in progress.

28.8. Modal usage of the future anterior

Normally, the future anterior describes an action whose future completion is projected to take (or have taken) place before some other future point. Allowing for the fact that all future tenses carry a certain amount of presumptive meaning, the future anterior is as "indicative" as possible, in that it gives a neutral statement of a particular future action.

The future anterior can also be used to make explicit predictions; in this sense it functions more as a mood than as a tense. On the basis of evidence s/he sees, the speaker can presume that a particular event has already taken place. In terms of the moment of speech, the time line is not future but rather past. The actual tense form, then, is the past indefinite. The future marker ще is added to this tense to indicate the speaker's guess that the action or state described must indeed be the case.

The future marker can also be added to the present tense to achieve this same meaning in the present. In addition, some speakers can add the particle да to these constructions to increase the sense of hypotheticalness. Essentially, therefore, the particle ще means that the speaker is presuming something to be so (or to have happened). Without the particle да, this usage is formally identical with the affirmative future or future anterior. In the negative, the particle да is always present, either in the neutral future anterior (няма да) or the variant form не щé да..., which is specifically marked for the meaning of presumptiveness. Examples:

Сигурно ще дойдат всеки момент. Вече ще са се качили в трамвая.	Surely they'll come any minute. [I'm sure that] they've already gotten on the tram.
Не щé да са се качили, защото ги няма.	They [surely] haven't gotten on yet, because they're not here.
Който е отварял хладилника, ще да е бил вегетерианец -- шунката не е пипана.	Whoever opened the refrigerator must have been a vegetarian -- the ham hasn't been touched.
Те ще се познават -- съседи са вече 5 години.	Surely they know each other -- they've been neighbors for 5 years now.

28.9. Factive vs. hypothetical, and the usage of да

The conjunction да is used most frequently with the variety of meanings expressed by the English infinitive. It also is used to introduce a wish, command, or suggestion, and as part of compound conjunctions such as без да..., преди да..., колкото и да..., да не би да..., and the like.

All of these usages express a less than complete degree of factivity. Infinitives by definition lack the specification of tense; wishes and commands by definition imply non-factivity; and all the conjunctions listed above mark the verbal action in question as hypothetical in some way (if only in the sense of not yet having occurred).

In addition, да can be used in place of (or in addition to) more neutral conjunctions when the speaker wishes to add a greater nuance of hypotheticality. When да is used in place of ако in conditional constructions, for instance, it places a slightly greater emphasis on the unrealness of the condition. For example:

Да знаех, че за утре има такива планове, бих казал на брат си да отложи работата.	If I had known such plans were afoot for tomorrow I would have told my brother to postpone the job.
Нямаше ли да е по-добре да бяхте ме оставили спокойно да си допия кафето?	Wouldn't it have been better if you'd left me in peace to finish my coffee?
Да бях знаела, че сте в същия трамвай, щях да дойда да си приказваме по пътя.	If I'd known you were in the same tram, I'd have come to chat along the way.
Животът ми да зависи от това, не бих могъл да го направя.	I wouldn't be able to do that (even) if my life depended on it.

When да is preceded by the conjunction и, the sense of unrealness increases dramatically, as seen by the English translation "even if":

Чак всичко не вярвам да имат. А и да имат, едно е там да го имат, а съвсем друго -- тука.	Well, I don't think they have everything. And even if they did, it's one thing to have it there and quite something else to have it here.
И да ме попитат, няма да кажа нищо.	Even if they (were to) ask me, I wouldn't/won't say a thing.

Да can also occur after relative conjunctions, such as който. Although the added meaning can be roughly captured by the addition of an English conditional term like "might" or "would", many Bulgarian speakers might reject such a translation as too strong, and would say that there is in fact very little difference between който and който да. The translations of the following examples attempt to render these added shades of meaning by the material enclosed in parentheses.

Нужно е да се създаде единна писмена система, която да отразява цялостния звуков състав на езика.	It is necessary to create a unified writing system (such as might serve) to reflect the complete sound system of the language.
Ако има нещо, за което да ни е мъчно, то е, че не успяхме да отидем там.	If there's anything that (might have) made us sad, it's that we didn't manage to get there.

When the main clause contains няма, however, the inherent meaning of hypotheticalness requires който to be accompanied by да. For example:

Ко́лкото и да е изве́стен, ня́ма да е тру́дно да се наме́рят хо́ра, кои́то да не са́ че́ли не́говите кни́ги.	No matter how well known he is, it will/would not be hard to find people who haven't read his books.
Сега́ ня́ма се́лище, кое́то да не е електрифици́рано.	There aren't any villages left which haven't/won't have gotten electricity.
Ня́ма ни́що, за кое́то да ни е мъ́чно.	There's not a single thing that we are/might be unhappy about.

Finally, да can occur in place of че or как after verbs of perception. When such verbs are used in the main clauses of affirmative statements, speakers have a choice of relative conjunction: they can use че to emphasize the fact of the action, как to describe the manner of the action, or да to shift the focus to some other nuance, the exact nature of which is usually evident from the larger context. In the examples below, speakers could have used any of these three conjunctions. The translations attempt to render a possible implicational nuance conveyed by the choice of да (rather than че or как). The actual meaning, of course, would depend upon the real-world situation in which the sentence was spoken.

А́з редо́вно я ви́ждам да пу́ши с часове́ на балко́на.	I regularly see her out on the balcony smoking for hours at a time.

possible implication: It's not true that she has stopped smoking.

Съсе́дката ка́за, че ги е видя́ла да се целу́ват.	The neighbor woman said she saw them kissing.

possible implication: It is indeed likely that they are more than "just friends".

In negative statements or in questions, however, the increased degree of hypotheticalness usually requires the choice of да as a subordinate conjunction introducing the final clause. The substitution of че or ка́к in the sentences below would not be possible.

Спо́мняш ли си, то́й да е но́сел със се́бе си голя́ма че́рна ча́нта?	Do you remember him ever carrying a big black bag?
Не съ́м я чу́ла да изле́зе.	I haven't heard her go out.
Би́ било́ стра́нно да се предполо́жи, че ни́кой не го́ е усе́тил да изли́за.	It would be very strange to suppose that no one would have noticed him go out.

Двайсет и осми урок / Lesson 28

EXERCISES

I. Fill in the blanks with the proper form of the verb given in parentheses.

1. Ние толкова си приличаме, че никой _____, ако аз отидех вместо него на гарата.   (не се усъмня)

2. Ти _____ такъв гаф, ако беше на негово място?   (направя)

3. Можеш да разчиташ на мене. И да ме попитат, аз _____ нищо.   (не кажа)

4. На сватбата ни гощаваха с имам-баялдъ. Ти _____ тази гозба, нали обичаш патладжани.   (харесам)

5. -- Какви са вашите планове за лятото?
   -- Ние _____ да отидем на планина за няколко дни.   (искам)

6. Той добре я познава. Той _____ веднага, че тя не се чувствува добре и я закара в болницата.   (разбера)

II. Explain the context that differentiates each pair of sentences.

1a. Какво би казал, ако те помолех да ми станеш кум?
1b. Какво щеше да кажеш, ако те бях помолил да ми станеш кум?

2a. Бихте ли се зарадвали, ако те се обадят?
2b. Щяхте ли да се зарадвате, ако те се бяха обадили?

3a. Това би било много приятно пътуване.
3b. Това щеше да бъде много приятно пътуване.

4a. Би ли се оправил, ако те пуснат без карта из непознат град?
4b. Ти щеше ли да се оправиш, ако те бяха пуснали така из непознат град?

5a. Какво би станало, ако земята се разтвори и те погълне?
5b. Какво щеше да стане, ако земята се беше разтворила и те беше погълнала?

6a. Да би мирно седяло, не би чудо видяло.
6b. Ако беше седял мирен, нямаше да се намери в чудо.

Двайсет и осми урок / Lesson 28

SAMPLE SENTENCES

1. Катéрехме се към върхá. Валéше. Подхлъ́знах се и за мáлко щях да пáдна.
2. Той е тóлкова óпитен алпинист. Той не би могъл да пáдне такá нелéпо и да загине.

3. Твóята дъщеря за съжалéние не пée в хóра. А тя щéше да изпълнява мнóго по-добрé тáзи пéсен.
4. Купи си пóйна птица. Тя би те рáдвала всяка сýтрин с пéсните си.

5. Добрé, че се върнах пó-рáно от рáбота, инáче кóтката щéше да изядé канáрчето.
6. Тáзи кóтка е тóлкова глéзена. Тя не би помирисала мишка, за ядене да не прикáзваме.

7. Ако бяхме забрáвили да помóлим лéля Вáня да полива цветята, тé щяха да изсъ́хнат.
8. Цветята биха изсъ́хнали, ако не ги поливат.

9. Вие закъсняхте. Чáят щéше да изстине, ако не бях слóжил чáйника на пéчката.
10. Бихме могли да напрáвим такá. Аз ще пригóтвя чáя и ще го държá на тóпло на пéчката. Той не би изстинал до половин -- един час. Вие елáте, когáто мóжете.

11. Щях да дóйда, но в послéдния момéнт ме домързя.
12. Вие бихте ли могли да отговóрите на тóзи въпрóс?

13. Ако знáеше, щéше да дóйде.
    Ако знáеше, би дошъ́л.

14. Нáшите деди биха отговóрили на тóзи въпрóс достóйно.
    Нáшите деди щяха да отговóрят на тóзи въпрóс достóйно.

15. Да го бях родила, нямаше да прилича тóлкова на мéне.
16. Ти каквó би предпочéл: да бъ́деш здрáв и богáт или да бъ́деш бéден и бóлен?

17. Ти би ли се облякла в такáва рóкля?
    Ти щéше ли да се облечéш в такáва рóкля?

18. Óще мáлко и би повярвал на рáзказа му.
    За мáлко щéше да повярва на рáзказа му.

19. Добрé че товá не продължи пóвече. Той би умрял от мъ́ка.
    Добрé че товá не продължи пóвече. Той щéше да умрé от мъ́ка.

Двайсет и осми урок / Lesson 28

20. На нас би ни било интересно да чуем доклада ви.
    На нас щеше да ни е интересно да чуем доклада ви.

21. Той е в Москва пет месеца, руският му ще се е подобрил.
22. Само преди 10 минути бяха тука, не ще да са стигнали до киното.

23. Не знам откога го познавам, но ще е от много време, защото го помня с коса.
24. Той ще да е бързал много сутринта -- дори леглото му не е оправено.

SENTENCES FOR TRANSLATION

1. Would you have shouldered such a heavy backpack if you had known the trip was going to be so long?

2. Would you go to Bulgaria this summer if you get the opportunity?

3. His Bulgarian would improve a lot if he studied more.

4. His Bulgarian would have improved if he had studied more. I know that I, for example, would certainly have studied a lot.

5. His alarm clock is probably broken. He wouldn't have missed class otherwise.

6. We are already home, and they (doubtless) haven't even reached the central station yet. I would have taken a taxi in such a situation.

7. Aha, you must be the repairman I called! Won't you please tell me what is going on with my car?

8. I wouldn't have been so surprised, if you had warned me that the professor always says such strange things. Actually, now he could say anything at all and I wouldn't be the least bit surprised.

Двайсет и осми урок / Lesson 28

READING SELECTION

<u>Кореспонде́нция - (16)</u>

10 септе́мври, Со́фия

Дра́ги Патри́ша и Бо́б,

    Не би́ било́ преувеличено́ да се ка́же, че ва́шето госту́ване в Бълга́рия през ля́тото бе́ше съби́тието на годи́ната за ста́р и мла́д в на́шето семе́йство. Предчу́встваме, че за И́во и Я́на ориенти́р за дати́ранетo на вси́чки съби́тия ще ста́не и́дването на Е́мили и Ма́йк в Бълга́рия. Те́ ве́че по по́вод и без по́вод си спо́мнят за чуде́сните дни́, прека́рани зае́дно. Ако им спомена́т е́ди-коя́ си пе́сен, ка́зват, че са я чу́ли за пъ́рви пъ́т от Е́мили. Ако ги́ пи́тат дали́ са гле́дали е́ди-ко́й си фи́лм, ка́зват, че са го гле́дали с Ма́йк. Пи́там се за какво́ ли щя́ха да гово́рят с прия́телите си, ако Е́мили и Ма́йк не бя́ха дошли́ с ва́с та́я годи́на.

    Ни́е с Кали́на ми́слим, че ви́е видя́хте до́ста неща́ в Бълга́рия и сега́ ве́че зна́ете какво́ представля́ва на́шата страна́. Ако и́ма не́що, за кое́то да ни е мъ́чно, то́ е че така́ и не се́ нака́нихме да оти́дем зае́дно до Копри́вщица -- нали́ заради проли́вните дъждове́ отло́жиха фестива́ла с две́ се́дмици... Но Копри́вщица си́гурно ще́ше да е прекра́сна и в дъ́жд, и без фестива́л на бъ́лгарската наро́дна пе́сен. Поне́ за на́с е така́. Осве́н със свoя́ неподража́ем колори́т, тя́ ни привли́ча и с ро́лята, коя́то е изигра́ла в култу́рния живо́т на Бълга́рия. Копри́вщица, напри́мер, е ро́дното мя́сто на еди́н от най-оби́чаните бъ́лгарски пое́ти -- Ди́мчо Дебеля́нов. Не зна́м дали́ и́мето на то́зи пое́т ви говори́ не́що?

    Дру́гите голе́ми бъ́лгарски пое́ти осве́н сво́ите почита́тели и́мат и отрица́тели. Не́ в сми́съл, че им се отри́ча вели́чието, а защо́то за тя́х мо́же да се ка́же -- "то́й не е́ мо́ят ти́п, аз предпочи́там дру́ги пое́ти". А обича́ към Ди́мчо Дебеля́нов е всео́бща -- то́й е задължи́телната ю́ношеска бо́лест на мно́го бъ́лгарски поколе́ния. Дори́ в годи́ните на це́нностни размества́ния не́говият прести́ж оста́на неизме́нен.

    Като че ли предчу́вствайки ра́нната си смъ́рт по вре́ме на Пъ́рвата свето́вна война́ -- през 1916 г., кога́то е са́мо на 29 годи́ни, -- то́й така́ възпя́ва ро́дния си до́м:

Да се завърнеш в бащината къща,
когато вечерта смирено гасне
и тихи пазви тиха нощ разгръща
да приласкае скръбни и нещастни.
Кат бреме хвърлил черната умора,
що безутешни дни ти завещаха --
ти с плахи стъпки да събудиш в двора
пред гостенин очакван радост плаха.

Да те присрещне старата на прага
и сложил чело на безсилно рамо,
да чезнеш в нейната усмивка блага
и дълго да повтаряш: мамо, мамо...
Смирено влязъл в стаята позната,
последна твоя пристан и заслона,
да шъпнеш тихи думи в тишината,
впил морен поглед в старата икона:
аз дойдох да дочакам мирен заник,
че мойто слънце своя път измина...

О, скрити вопли на печален странник,
напразно спомнил майка и родина.

Стихотворението е написано още през 1912 г. Какво ли още би написал той, ако не беше загинал така делнично и нелепо в кървавата касапница на войната?

Едно от най-одухотворените, познато на всеки българин места в Копривщица е гробът на Дебелянов с известната на всички скулптура на Иван Лазаров -- майката, която безутешна чака сина си. А надписът гласи: "В кротък унес чака тя да дойде нейното дете".

Хем ни е мъчно, че не можахте тази година да видите Копривщица, хем се радваме, че ви остава нещо толкова хубаво за бъдещите посещения в България.

Защото вие ще дойдете пак, нали? Всички ние много ще се радваме да ви видим пак. Би било прекрасно да прекараме още едно лято заедно.

А засега пишете!
Сърдечни поздрави и целувки от четирима ни

Бойко

Двайсет и осми урок / Lesson 28

GLOSSARY

алпини́ст	mountaineer	какво́ представля́ва	what it is like
ба́щин	paternal, father's	кана́рче	canary
безси́лен	feeble, powerless	ка́пка	drop, spot
безуте́шен	inconsolable	карие́ра	career
бре́ме (*pl.* бремена́)	burden, load	каса́пница	butcher's; slaughter
		кате́ря се	climb, scramble up
веку́вам	live for ages	колори́т	color, picturesqueness
веку́вам та́м	live there forever	кря́сък (*pl.* кря́съци)	shout, yell
вели́чие	grandeur, greatness		
вися́	hang, hang about		
во́пъл	wail, lamentation	местопрестъпле́ние	scene of a crime
впи́вам / впи́я	sink, dig	ми́рен	peace (*adj.*), peaceable, gentle
впи́вам по́глед в	fix one's gaze on		
всео́бщ	universal, general	ми́рно	peacefully
възпя́вам / възпе́я	praise in song, glorify		
		нами́рам се в чу́до	be at one's wits' end
га́сна	die out, fade away	напра́зно	in vain
гле́зя	spoil, pamper	нара́мвам / нара́мя	shoulder
глу́пост	foolishness, nonsense		
го́стенин	guest (*archaic*)	неле́п	absurd, preposterous
го́стенка	guest (female)	неподража́ем	inimitable, unique
гостоприе́мство	hospitality	непока́нен	uninvited, unasked
		неща́стен	unhappy, ill-fated
да би́ ми́рно седя́ло не би́ чу́до видя́ло	that's what comes of asking for trouble	одухотворе́н	spiritual, exalted
деди́ (*pl. only*)	ancestors, forebears	о́питен	experienced, veteran
де́лничен	workaday, humdrum	опра́вям легло́	make a bed
допи́вам / допи́я	drink up, finish drinking	ориенти́р	landmark, reference point
доча́квам / доча́кам	wait for; live to see	отда́вам се / отда́м се (-даде́ш)	abandon oneself to
дъ́лго	[for] a long time		
		отрица́тел (ка)	detractor, denier
еди́н такъ́в	someone like	отри́чам / отрека́ (-че́ш)	deny, reject
завеща́вам / завеща́я	bequeath		
задължи́телен	compulsory	па́зва	bosom
за́ник	sunset, decline	па́зви	recesses
засло́н	shelter, refuge	патладжа́н	eggplant
		пи́пвам / пи́пна	touch; lay one's hands on
и през у́м не ми́ ми́на	I didn't dream of it	пи́пвам на местопрестъпле́нието	catch in the act
и́го	yoke; slavery		
изго́ра	sweetheart	пи́сък (*pl.* пи́съци)	shriek, squeal
изигра́вам / изигра́я	play, play out	пла́х	timid, shy, furtive
изни́квам / изни́кна	sprout; pop up	погъ́лщам / погъ́лна	swallow up, devour
ико́на	icon		
има́м-баялдъ́	spicy eggplant dish	по́ен, по́йна	song (*adj.*)

Двайсет и осми урок / Lesson 28

пойна птица	songbird	скулптура	sculpture
помирисвам / помириша (-еш)	smell, sniff	смирено	meekly, humbly
посещение	visit	споменавам / спомена	mention, refer to
почитател (ка)	admirer	странник	foreigner, wanderer
правя кариера	make it in the world	съпротивлявам се	resist, oppose, fight back
представлявам	represent, be		
предчувствувам (or предчувствам)	have a presentiment	термос	thermos bottle
престиж	prestige	ум, -ът (pl. умове)	mind
приласкавам / прилаская	befriend	унес	trance, reverie
		усмивка	smile
присрещам / присрещна	meet (poetic)		
		фльонга	bow, knot
пристан	wharf, moorage		
проливен	pouring	хор	choir, chorale
проливен дъжд	driving rain		
		целувка	kiss
разгръщам / разгърна	unfold, display	ценностен	pertaining to values
размествам / разместя	transpose, rearrange	ценностни размествания	changing values
разтварям / разтворя	open, open up wide	чезна	languish, pine
ранобуден	early riser		
родина	native land	шъпна (or шепна)	whisper
скръбен	sorrowful, mournful	юношески	adolescent

"Cyril and Methodius" high school, Koprivshtitsa

Двайсет и осми урок / Lesson 28

CULTURAL COMMENTARY

Geography: Vitosha

The final stop on the line of tram No. 5 in Sofia is called Knyazhevo (Княжево). It is here that many of the footpaths up Mount Vitosha begin. One of the two gondola lifts also leaves from here; the other leaves from Simeonovo (Симеоново). The chair lifts leave from Aleko (Алеко) and Dragalevtsi (Драгалевци). All of these localities, most of which were once separate villages, are now subsumed into the greater Sofia urban area.

Literature: Dimcho Debelyanov

A surprisingly large number of Bulgarians, when asked to name their favorite poet, will respond unhesitatingly with the name of Dimcho Debelyanov (Димчо Дебелянов, 1887-1916). Debelyanov, whose home town is Koprivshtitsa, completed only one volume of poems before his death, but practically all of these poems are now well known. Like many idealistic young men of his generation, Debelyanov insisted on going off to fight in the Balkan Wars, and then in World War I. Debelyanov was killed in northern Greece, and greatly mourned.

Many years passed, and much maneuvering was needed, before his remains could be brought home to Koprivshtitsa. He was interred in the town cemetery in 1934, and a fine scuplture by the well-known artist Ivan Lazarov (Иван Лазаров, 1884-1952) marks his grave. Both Lazarov and the writer Anna Kamenova (whose family was also from Koprivshtitsa) were instrumental in the success of the negotiations with Greece over Debelyanov's remains.

Grave marker of Dimcho Debelyanov, Koprivshtitsa (statue by Ivan Lazarov)

Двайсет и осми урок / Lesson 28

Guests

Bulgarians are proud of their hospitality and of their ability to entertain guests. Even the poorest family will do all it can to lay out a lavish spread of food and drink for the visitor.

Food and drink: foreign borrowings

Many typical Bulgarian dishes in fact originated elsewhere. The salad called "Russian" is a common dish: its primary ingredients are chopped cold ham, potatoes, peas and mayonnaise. "Imam bayildi" is a Turkish dish of stuffed eggplant, served at room temperature. The name means in Turkish "the imam fainted"; apparently the imam was so taken by the delicacy of the dish that when he saw it he collapsed with joy.

History: April uprising

The town of Koprivshtitsa is a favorite among Bulgarians not just because of its quaint picturesque beauty and clean mountain air, but also because of its historical importance. Although the great April uprising (априлското въстание) of 1876, which marked the beginning of Bulgaria's drive for freedom, took place in several different central Bulgarian towns, most Bulgarians connect this event primarily with Koprivshtitsa and Panagyurishte (Панагюрище). For some twenty days there was an independent republic in Koprivshtitsa; then the rising was crushed there and elsewhere with unspeakable cruelty. European indignation at the brutalities inflicted upon Bulgarians by the Ottomans at this time provided the impetus for the Russo-Turkish war of 1877-78, which finally led to Bulgarian independence.

Many famous Bulgarian revolutionary activists (most of whom were also writers) are from Koprivshtitsa, among them Lyuben Karavelov (Любен Каравелов, 1837-1879), Georgi Benkovski (Георги Бенковски, ca. 1841-1876), and Todor Kableshkov (Тодор Каблешков, 1853-1876). Their family homes have been made into museums; the Kableshkov museum displays the famous letter, signed in blood, which announced the start of the uprising.

The April uprising has been the subject of many stories and films. The most famous retelling is *Under the Yoke* (Под игото, 1894) by Ivan Vazov (Иван Вазов, 1850-1921).

Grave of Ivan Vazov, Sofia

LESSON 29

DIALOGUE

<u>Увлéкли са се в спóмени за добрóто стáро врéме</u>

// Нáшите екскурзиáнти са се изтéгнали на шáрена ся́нка на еднá вѝтошка поля́на. Веселѝн и Пéтър са се увлéкли в спóмени за добрóто стáро врéме. //

Петър: Ех, каквó не смé преживéли нѝе за тѝя пéт годѝни, когáто рабóтехме зáедно... Бя́хме като брáтя.

Веселин: Пóвече от брáтя. Дéн не é ѝмало да не сé срéщнем.

Петър: Тѝ на товá срéщи ли му вѝкаш. От сýтрин до вéчер бя́хме зáедно.

Веселин: Тáня, знáете ли, че вáшият мъ̀ж ми е спасѝл живóта? На нéго дължá възможносттá днéс да се рáдвам на вáшата компáния.

Таня: Пéтьо е тóлкова скрóмен. Нѝкога нѝщо не мѝ е споменáвал за товá.

Петър: Остави́, товá са стáри истóрии...

Веселин: Хѝч не разчѝтай на мълчáнието ми. Нéка женá ти знáе какъ̀в герóй ѝма до сéбе си.

Таня: Амá каквó е стáнало? Вѝе мнóго ме заинтригýвахте.

Веселин: Тъ̀й като чéсто пътýвахме до рáзни затъ̀нтени местá, къдéто пътѝщата са лóши и лéка колá не мóже да мѝне, в редáкцията ѝмаше двé джѝпки. Предполагáше се, че тря́бва да ги кáраме нé нѝе журналѝстите, а едѝн от шофьóрите към редáкцията. Не пóмня каквó бéше се слýчило тóчно в тóзи дéн, но шофьóр за нáс ня́маше. Пéтър токý-що бéше изкáрал шофьóрски кýрсове, а áз минáвах за óпитен шофьóр. От двé годѝни ѝмах кнѝжка, но налѝ ня́мах колá, слýчвало ми се бéше да кáрам за товá врéме сáмо на ня́колко пъ̀ти. А командирóвката ни бéше в Разлóжко. Зима, мнóго бъ̀рзо се мръ̀кна. Еднѝ завóи, не тѝ е рáбота. А пък и пътѝщата хлъ̀згави... И студéно... Джѝпката налѝ знáете каквó отоплéние ѝма -- нѝкакво. Ама áз не сé предáвам. Не взéма да си признáя: Пéшо, не съ̀м áз шофьóр за такѝва пътѝща, дáй да преношýваме в Разлóг, и ýтре е дéн, всé ще стѝгнем до сéлото. А наóколо жѝва душá ня́ма. И естéствено съм се блъ̀снал в едѝн стъ̀лб. Áз нѝщо не пóмня. Пéшо пóсле ми разкáзваше.

Петър: Ако знáете áз кáк се уплáших. На Вéско кръ̀в му течé от главáта. Вѝкам си: ще умрé. До нáй-блѝзкото сéло ѝма понé еднó двáйсет километра. Ни напрéд, ни назáд. Джѝпката обáче като че лѝ бéше оцеля́ла. И тогáва, мéчка стрáх, мéн не стрáх, решѝх да кáрам напрéд. Тря́бва да намéря бъ̀рзо лéкар за Вéско, налѝ такá. Кóлко чáса съм кáрал, да ме убѝеш, не мóга да си спóмня. Нáй-пóсле блéснаха светлинкѝ отпре́д. То всъ́щност не бе́ше къ́сно. Се́дем-о́сем часа́ вечерта́ да е било́. Разти́чаха се та́м хо́рата, наме́риха фе́лдшера, къде́ ще и́ма ле́кар в такова́ ма́лко селце́... Фе́лдшерът го прегле́да, превъ́рза го. Сърде́чен чове́к изле́зе, ця́ла но́щ стоя́ до Весели́н.

Весели́н: Ока́за се, че ра́ната е повъ́рхностна. И́маше опа́сност от сътресе́ние на мо́зъка, но ми се размина́. Докато́ съм би́л в безсъзна́ние, така́ стра́шно съм пъ́шкал, че деца́та на хо́рата, кои́то ни били́ приюти́ли, се разпла́кали и ма́йка им ни́как не мо́жела да ги утеши́.

Павли́на: Ня́мало е да се случи́ ни́що тако́ва, ако се бя́хте учи́ли като хо́рата да ка́рате кола́.

Весели́н: И да се у́чиш, и да не се́ у́чиш, все́ та́я. Ако ня́маш кола́, ня́маш и пра́ктика. Нау́ченото на шофьо́рския ку́рс бъ́рзо се забра́вя.

Де́йвид: У на́с в Аме́рика дне́с вси́чки хо́ра ка́рат кола́. Без кола́ не мо́же. А́з ве́че съм ми́нал с мо́ята де́сет хи́ляди ми́ли.

Джу́ли: По́-ра́но не все́ки чове́к е и́мал кола́. Шофьо́рска кни́жка получа́ваш на шестна́йсет годи́ни, но роди́телите че́сто не са́ разреша́вали на деца́та си да ка́рат, преди́ да завъ́ршат учи́лище. Поня́кога деца́та са си служи́ли с коли́те на роди́телите си, со́бствена кола́ са и́мали по́-ря́дко. Мо́ят баща́ е ку́пил пъ́рвата си кола́, кога́то е би́л два́десет и пе́т годи́шен. А на ме́не ма́ма и та́тко ми подари́ха кола́ за осемна́йсетия ми рожде́н де́н.

Весели́н: Каква́ ма́рка бе́ше кола́та?

Джу́ли: Тойо́та, те́ са по́-е́втини. Бя́ха я ку́пили на ста́ро.

Та́ня: Отка́кто го позна́вам, Пе́тьо е все́ зад корми́лото. Не се́ бя́х се́щала, че е и́мало вре́ме, кога́то не е́ мо́жел да ка́ра.

Петъ́р: Видя́ ли Ве́ско, какво́ напра́ви? На това́ му ка́зват мече́шка услу́га.

Весели́н: Защо́? Какво́ е ста́нало?

Петъ́р: Жена́ ми сега́, с тво́ята ле́ка ръка́, ще устано́ви, че и на слъ́нцето и́ма петна́.

Весели́н: Ти́ ли си слъ́нцето?

Петъ́р: А ко́й дру́г?

Весели́н: Та́ня, ако ме пока́ните да ви до́йда на го́сти, таки́ва исто́рии мо́га да ви разка́жа за благове́рния ви съпру́г.

Та́ня: Непреме́нно ще ви пока́ним.

Петъ́р: Зна́ех си а́з, че не би́ва да ви запозна́вам. Ведна́га се сдуши́хте за мо́я сме́тка...

Двайсет и девети урок / Lesson 29

GRAMMAR

29.1. Tense, mood, and aspect in Bulgarian: general review

Of the four moods of Bulgarian, two -- the conditional and the imperative -- are represented by a single paradigm each. The other two, the renarrated and the indicative, are represented by five and nine paradigms, respectively.

The nine tenses of the Bulgarian indicative specify the time of an action relative not only to the moment of speech, but usually to some other points on the time line as well. Eight of these nine tenses are paired such that one represents the projection of the other further into the past (along the vertical axis **A - B**). This pairing is repeated in the five paradigms of the reported mood: four of them represent an amalgam of each of these two pairs (along the horizonatal axis **X - Y**). The fifth corresponds to the aorist tense, which stands alone. Compare the chart from Lesson 25, repeated here:

		X INDICATIVE	Y RENARRATED
A.	present	чете́	четя́л
B.	imperfect	чете́ше	
A.	future	ще чете́	щя́л да чете́
B.	future in the past	ще́ше да чете́	
A.	future anterior	ще е че́л	щя́л да е че́л
B.	future anterior in the past	ще́ше да е че́л	
A.	past indefinite	че́л е	би́л че́л
B.	past anterior	бе́ше че́л	
*	aorist	че́те	че́л

There is thus almost a mirror-image relationship between tense (present vs. past / **A** vs. **B**) and mood (indicative vs. renarrated / **X** vs. **Y**). This final lesson considers the status of the third major verbal category, aspect, within this structure.

Verbal aspect is specified in nearly all verbs. It does not occur in all tenses with equal frequency, however. Rather, there is a correlation between the meaning of individual verbal tenses and the verbal aspect which is more likely to be used. The durative, habitual meaning inherent in the present and the imperfect, for instance, predisposes the choice of imperfect aspect. Perfective verbs are used in these tenses, but in much more limited and well-defined contexts than imperfective verbs. By contrast, the perfective aspect is the preferred choice in all the compound tenses, each of which tends by nature to focus more on the bounded nature of an action. Imperfective verbs do occur in these tenses, of course, but in more limited and specifically defined contexts.

The aorist alone stands outside this schema: there is nothing in its meaning which predisposes a marked choice of one aspect or the other. The aorist can therefore be called the purest of tenses, in that it refers to the fact of action alone. It is striking that the aorist is also the only tense which is not paired in terms of distancing, either along the temporal line (A - B) or the modal line (X - Y) in the above chart.

As all grammarians of Bulgarian are quick to point out, the dynamics of the Bulgarian verb are complex and multilayered. However, the system is even more elegant than current descriptions would indicate. This survey of Bulgarian grammar concludes by proposing a revised view of the interrelationships of tense, aspect and mood in Bulgarian.

29.2. Past narration and the renarrated mood

Forms of the renarrated mood are particularly frequent in the recounting of past events. Because the renarrated mood always includes an L-participle, it bears a certain formal similarity with one or more of the indicative compound tenses. This similarity is heightened in 1-2 person, where the copula (a form of **съм**) is always present. Only in the 3rd person forms of renarrated paradigms is this copula absent.

The 3rd person forms of the renarrated aorist and imperfect are the most striking, since each consists of an L-participle alone. These 3rd person forms are highly marked in narrative speech. Formally, they stand out as L-participles which are "bare" (lacking an auxiliary) and which carry the main verbal meaning of a sentence. Semantically they stand out because they specify one or more types of "distancing", the most common being the signal that it is someone else's words which are being transmitted.

There are significant descriptive problems connected with both of these forms. The relevant sections of this textbook have presented the basic facts about these two tenses and about their renarrated forms in accordance with what is stated in prescriptive Bulgarian grammars, omitting, as do most prescriptive grammars, any reference to these descriptive problems. This concluding lesson presents both a clear statement of these problems (normally mentioned only briefly, if at all, in the standard textbooks) -- and a solution.

Двайсет и девети урок / Lesson 29

The crux of the problem lies in the combination of two facts. The first is that 3rd person renarrated forms, by definition, occur *without* the auxiliary, and the second is that both aorist and imperfect renarrated forms actually occur frequently in the 3rd person *with* the auxiliary. That is, speakers are not supposed to use these forms. Nevertheless, it is quite clear that they do, and to such an extent that grammarians are forced to admit that they do. However, these same grammarians have not yet been able to account for this usage within the system of the Bulgarian verb as presently constituted.

To understand the nature of the problem, it is necessary to review these forms.

29.3. Renarrated forms of the aorist revisited

Given the importance of the aorist tense in the interlocking schema of tense, mood and aspect (as seen graphically in the chart presented above) it is surprising that the aorist renarrated forms are not more distinctly marked. If the aorist is as unique as this chart suggests, one would think that the grammatical system would allow speakers to identify aorist forms unambiguously whenever they choose the "distancing" option allowed by the renarrated mood. Instead, the aorist renarrated paradigm is almost exactly identical with the past indefinite indicative paradigm. Compare the following, repeated from Lesson 24, now with 3rd person highlighted:

	Aorist		*Past indefinite*
	indicative	**RENARRATED**	
1st singular	чётох	чёл съм	чёл съм
2nd singular	чёте	чёл си	чёл си
3rd singular	чёте	чёл	чёл е
1st plural	чётохме	чёли сме	чёли сме
2nd plural	чётохте	чёли сте	чёли сте
3rd plural	чётоха	чёли	чёли са

The forms are identical in 1st and 2nd persons, and are distinguished in the 3rd person solely by the presence or absence of the copula (singular: **е**; plural: **са**).

This situation is further complicated by the fact that Bulgarians often omit the copula in the past indefinite and add it in the renarrated. That is, speakers will use forms that look like the renarrated, such as **чёл**, in a context which clearly seems to lack the meaning of distancing. At the same time, they will use forms that look like the past indefinite, such as **чёл е**, in contexts that seem to be marked for distancing. Furthermore, speakers will on occasion shift back and forth between the two forms within a single narration. Here is an example of such a shift:

Двайсет и девети урок / Lesson 29

Óще преди мнóго годи́ни човéкът е и́скал да скъ́си растоя́нията, да намали́ врéмето за пъту́ване. Така́ се създа́ли превóзните срéдства. Отнача́ло тé били́ мнóго примити́вни, но в оснóвата на вси́чки оста́нало еднó от най-пъ́рвите откри́тия -- колелóто.	For many years, man has wished to bridge distances, and to shorten the time needed for travel. Thus were vehicles created. In the beginning they were very primitive, but at the basis of all of them lay one of the most basic discoveries, the wheel.

Although the passage begins with a verb in the past indefinite indicative (marked by the inclusion of the auxiliary), the main tense of narration in this passage, which is about events in the distant past, appears to be the renarrated aorist (marked by the exclusion of the auxiliary). How does one account for this? Either the writer of the text has shifted from one to the other for some unexplained reason, or the first verb is an example of an aorist renarrated with an optional addition of the copula.

Such shifts are in fact extremely common within individual texts. Grammarians have attempted to analyze these shifts and to systematize them, with varying degrees of success. Some of these shifts appear due to higher level discourse factors, connected with the overall structure of a narrative. Although a discussion of the discourse level of narrative is beyond the scope of this textbook, it is clear that the problem cannot be relegated completely to these higher levels of analysis. Simply stated, the aorist renarrated form frequently occurs with the 3rd person auxiliary added, which makes it indistinguishable from the 3rd person past indefinite indicative form. This is a basic conundrum which needs a solution at the level of grammar.

Although several explanations have been offered for this phenomenon, only two will be summarized here. That generally espoused by Bulgarian grammarians is that since the speakers "know" what they mean anyway, it is not really important whether the auxiliary is there or not in certain instances. The important thing is that it is there (or not) in the majority of instances as it ought to be. Thus, speakers have the option to add or omit the auxiliary as they wish without changing the underlying meaning. This point of view maintains the general theoretical distinction between renarrated and indicative within the system, but admits that in this one instance the formal distinction is not well observed.

A number of non-Bulgarian grammarians reject this account as unsatisfactory. If there is no consistent formal distinction, they say, then there can be no consistent distinction in meaning. According to the most well-known explanation offered by this group, the primary distinction within the past tense is between "confirmative" and "nonconfirmative". Two of the past tenses, aorist and imperfect, are marked as confirmative, in that they explicitly specify that the speaker has directly witnessed the action. The third, the past indefinite, lacks this specification. In its function as a very general past tense, it can signify a number of different ways that an action can be unconfirmed. One of these ways, in fact, is that an action was unwitnessed and is being reported from elsewhere. Others would cover inference, resultativity and the like. By grouping all these different meanings together as "lack of confirmativity", this explanation claims that the paradigms which are traditionally listed separately -- as aorist renarrated and past indefinite indicative -- are in fact one and the same. In so doing, this explanation accounts for the fact that the form чел е can be (and is on occasion) used with the meaning "renarrated".

Neither side has been convinced by the other's arguments. In brief, this is because the first makes a claim which is too weak (and is in fact no explanation at all), while the second makes a claim which although cogent is nevertheless too strong (since it threatens the existence of the entire system). A compromise solution will be proposed below. However, since the proposed solution concerns not just the aorist renarrated but rather the entire Bulgarian verbal system, it is necessary first to consider the other descriptive problem, that of the imperfect renarrated forms.

29.4. Renarrated forms of the imperfect revisited

In the 3rd person, both the aorist and the imperfect renarrated forms consist of a single L-participle. The L-participle used in the renarrated aorist occurs very frequently in Bulgarian, both as a past active participle used adjectivally and as a component part of four indicative tenses. The L-participle of the renarrated imperfect, however, is found only in renarrated forms (of the imperfect and present tenses). Here is the paradigm, repeated from Lesson 24:

	Present tense		*Imperfect tense*	
	indicative	**RENARRATED**	*indicative*	**RENARRATED**
1st singular	чета́	че́тял съм	четя́х	че́тял съм
2nd singular	че́теш	че́тял си	че́теше	че́тял си
3rd singular	че́те	че́тял	че́теше	че́тял
1st plural	чете́м	че́тели сме	четя́хме	че́тели сме
2nd plural	чете́те	че́тели сте	четя́хте	че́тели сте
3rd plural	чета́т	че́тели	четя́ха	че́тели

Historically, the imperfect L-participle **че́тял** appears to have been created for this purpose alone. Prescriptive grammars state that since this participle is formed from the *present* stem of the verb (**чете́-**), it cannot carry the meaning of a *past* participle. Therefore it must be something else. Indeed, this explanation continues, it *is* something else: it is the renarrated form and only that. According to prescriptive grammarians, whose job it is to instruct speakers of a language on correct usage, this participle cannot (and must not) occur with an auxiliary in the 3rd person.

As noted by descriptive grammarians, however, -- those who attempt to describe how educated people actually *do* write and speak -- forms such as **че́тял е** occur frequently. These grammarians call them the "inferential mood", claiming that their meaning is similar to that of the inferential past indefinite. They categorize them midway between the indicative imperfect (which signifies direct evidence) and the renarrated imperfect (which signifies transmission of another's words).

While this explanation is better than none, it fails to solve the problem in at least two ways. First, it does not succeed in integrating the so-called inferential into the verbal system of Bulgarian. The question of whether the form in question is a tense or a mood -- a very basic part of a grammatical description -- remains unclear. Furthermore, such a form cannot be considered a part of the language until it is included into prescriptive grammars and teaching grammars.

Second, the term "inferential" does not explain all the usages of this form. Compare the continuation of the passage quoted earlier, and note the usage of the imperfect L-participle движели се *with* the 3rd plural auxiliary. Its meaning, "used to be propelled", is clearly not renarrated, nor does it seem to specify that the writer has learned his information by inference. Rather, it conveys the generalized imperfective meaning of "durative, repeated action in the past".

Всички тези превозни средства служат за едно -- превозване на пътници и багажи, но се движат с помощта на различни горива и устройства. Например трамваят се движи с електричество, а леката кола -- с бензинов мотор; старите влакове са се движели с парна машина, а днес -- с дизелов мотор. Някои превозни средства вървят по релси, а други -- летят във въздуха или идват по вода.

All these vehicles serve the same purpose of transporting passengers and baggage, but they are propelled by different fuels and different mechanisms. For instance, a tram runs on electricity, and the passenger car with a gasoline engine. Old-fashioned trains used to be propelled by steam engines, but now with diesel engines. Some vehicles move along rails, and others fly through the air or travel on the water.

The imperfect L-participle, therefore, occurs often with the auxiliary. This usage is not accepted in the official grammars and textbooks of Bulgarian, nor is it yet fully understood by anyone. Descriptive Bulgarian grammarians have given it a name, but they have not yet successfully integrated it into their own view of the grammatical system. This is probably because at some level they share the opinion of the prescriptive grammarians, which is that the imperfect L-participle is still too strongly identified as the renarrated form to be called anything else.

Non-Bulgarian grammarians, for their part, have not proposed an explanation. For them, this second defect in the system seems sufficient proof that the entire system needs an overhaul. In any case, their primary attention is on the coalescence of aorist renarrated and past indefinite indicative, which in their view invalidates the existence of the renarrated mood as a separate category.

29.5. Towards a solution: transcending tense, aspect, and mood

Two verb forms need to be accounted for, therefore. One is composed of the imperfect L-participle plus the 3rd person auxiliary: **четя́л е, чете́ли са**. The other is identical to the 3rd person past indefinite (**чёл е, че́ли са**), but occurs in contexts where it is unclear whether the speaker's intended meaning is "past indefinite indicative" or "aorist renarrated".

It makes sense to view these not as isolated forms, but as part of an integrated paradigm. The obvious conjugations are as follows:

	(1)	(2)
1st singular	чёл съм	четя́л съм
2nd singular	чёл си	четя́л си
3rd singular	чёл е	четя́л е
1st plural	че́ли сме	чете́ли сме
2nd plural	че́ли сте	чете́ли сте
3rd plural	че́ли са	чете́ли са

Conjugation (1) is identical in form with the past indefinite. Conjugation (2) represents the imperfect inferential mood as defined by some grammarians. This second conjugation is not an accepted part of standard Bulgarian grammar. Those who do accept it as a functioning conjugation suggest that it is parallel to the past indefinite in form and in meaning (at least as far as the "inferential" meaning of the past indefinite). However, they still call it a mood rather than a tense. Yet the parallelism between the two is too striking to be ignored.

All the above difficulties can be transcended by allowing *both* sets of forms to stand outside the Bulgarian system of tense and mood as presently conceived. Their meaning is clear: they describe past action in the most generalized terms -- and nothing else. They are unspecified for either mood or tense. With respect to mood, their meaning covers the neutral zone between indicative and renarrated -- neither directly witnessed nor distanced. With respect to tense, this meaning also occupies the most neutral semantic space: it is marked neither for confirmative (as are the aorist and imperfect) nor for any of the meanings of the past indefinite (inference, relevance in the present, etc.).

The key to this interpretation is given by the aspectual marking of these conjugated forms. Both participles (both **чел** and **четял**) are formed from the imperfective verb **чета**. Logically, therefore, both conjugations ought to be assigned to the imperfective aspect. Yet the one clear distinction between conjugations (1) and (2) seems to be aspectual in nature: **четя́л е** signifies a generalized past action which is marked for durativeness or repetition, while **чёл е** carries no such specific marking. Examples demonstrating this usage will be given below.

This paired set of conjugations therefore, which we may call the "generalized past", stands outside and above all three of the parameters which structure the Bulgarian verbal system -- tense, mood *and* aspect. In terms of mood, it is neither indicative nor renarrated but something in between. In terms of tense, it means simply "past" in the most generalized sense, and does not participate in the complex set of semantic oppositions whereby the other past tenses are opposed to each other. Finally, in terms of aspect, it is formed only from simplex unpaired verbs, which by definition do not participate in the aspectual oppositions so pervasive throughout Bulgarian. At the same time these two conjugations are paired, and thus express a superordinate level of aspect. The participle formed from those tenses which most often express unbounded meaning, the present and the imperfect (**четял**), takes on the meaning of a durative or iterative (that is, unbounded) generalized past. The other participle (**чел**) takes on the remainder of the meanings by default.

29.6. Usage of the generalized past

When the generalized past takes the form of **чел съм**, it is identical to the past indefinite. Indeed, were it not for the distressing overlap between forms of the past indefinite indicative and those of the aorist renarrated, one would not need to propose any new name or description for the paradigm noted above simply as (1). Most descriptions of the past indefinite, in fact, emphasize its broad and general usage, which covers many different sub-meanings. Some grammarians even come close to saying that the distressing instances of overlap would seem better described as something in between the two. The generalized past is precisely this: a neutralization of the distinction between them *in certain contexts* which still allows each to retain its individual integrity within the system in all other contexts.

When the generalized past takes the form of **четял съм**, it follows the paradigm noted as (2) above, which has not yet received an unambiguously accepted place in the grammar of Bulgarian. Its usage is clear, however: it is the generalized past, in which the opposition between indicative and renarrated is neutralized in exactly the same way as in the forms of **чел съм** of paradigm (1). The only difference is that whereas **чел съм** (1) means "simple generalized past", **четял съм** (2) means "markedly durative or iterative generalized past". The meaning of **четял съм** is similar to the past indefinite in the most broad and general conception of that tense (and is notably *not* limited to the inferential sub-meaning of the past indefinite, as earlier grammarians have claimed). The fact that the two paradigms seem to complement each other according to the most basic conceptual frame of Bulgarian, that of an essentially aspectual distinction, allows the combined set to function as a basic neutral backdrop of past narration, against which the full complexity of the Bulgarian system of tense, mood and aspect can play itself out.

As an example, consider the following passage in which the primary narration is in the generalized past. The unpaired verbs **имам** and **служа** are in the generalized past (**имал е, имали са; служели са**); against this background the speaker slips into the historical present (**получаваш**) and the past indefinite (**разрешавали са**), both with derived imperfective verbs.

Двайсет и девети урок / Lesson 29

По́-ра́но не все́ки чове́к е и́мал кола́. Шофьо́рска кни́жка получа́ваш на шестна́йсет годи́ни, но роди́телите че́сто не са́ разреша́вали на деца́та си да ка́рат преди́ да завъ́ршат учи́лище. Поня́кога деца́та са си слу́жели с коли́те на роди́телите си, со́бствена кола́ са и́мали по́-ря́дко.	Earlier not everyone had his own car. You got your driver's license at 16, but parents often did not permit children to drive before they finished high school. Sometimes children used their parents' cars; more rarely they had their own.

Even within a very short narrative frame such as that below, a speaker can contrast the more specified tense forms of present (е) and past anterior (бях се сещала) with the generalized past (имало е, можел е):

Отка́кто го позна́вам, Пе́тьо е все́ зад корми́лото. Не́ се́ бях се́щала, че е и́мало вре́ме, кога́то не е́ мо́жел да ка́ра.	Ever since I've known him, Petyo has been behind the wheel. I tried to think, but couldn't, of a time when he wasn't able to drive.

Although the use of the generalized past is best seen in longer passages, two more examples can demonstrate both its broad meaning and the functioning within it of an aspectual-like complementarity. Forms below marked (1) denote general action in the past, and those marked (2) denote specifically durative action in the past.

(1)	Ти́я неща́ ни́кога не са́ му пра́вили впечатле́ние.	These things never made an impression on him.
(2)	Ти́я неща́ по́-ра́но ни́кога не са́ му пра́вели впечатле́ние.	These things never used to make an impression on him.
(1)	Не мо́жеш да ме изнена́даш с ни́що, пи́л съм вся́какви вина́.	You can't surprise me [with a new wine], I've drunk all sorts of wine.
(2)	А́з ця́л живо́т съм пи́ел на́й-изи́скани фре́нски вина́.	All my life I've drunk the finest French wines.

    The term "generalized past" is new, as is the concept of a verbal conjugation which stands outside the standard system of tense, mood and aspect. However, the forms themselves are regularly used by all Bulgarians. The goal of this final lesson has not been to introduce yet another paradigm into a system which already seems overloaded, but rather to describe more adequately the functioning of the overall system as an integrated whole. Indeed, it is the elegantly interwoven nature of the Bulgarian verbal system itself that has allowed the paradigms of the generalized past to crystallize as they have, and that has created the conceptual language by which they can be described.

Двайсет и девети урок / Lesson 29

EXERCISES

I. Rewrite in the past.

Ка́мен си игра́е с На́дка, са́мо кога́то прия́телите му ги ня́ма. И́наче те́ ще му се смея́т: такъ́в голя́м и серио́зен мъ́ж не би́ва да обръ́ща внима́ние на ма́лки деца́. А и На́дка ни́що не разби́ра от коли́. Не зна́е да́же какви́ гу́ми се купу́ват за фо́лксваген и какви́ за пежо́. Игра́е си са́мо с ку́кли. А Ка́мен о́ще па́зи коле́кцията си от коли́ и камио́ни. Ня́кои от не́говите прия́тели съ́що и́мат коле́кции и си разменя́т с не́го коли́. Най-це́нни са ме́рцедесите, но ме́рцедеси и́ма са́мо два́ -- еди́ният е на Пе́шо, а дру́гият -- на Я́вор.

II. Rewrite in the past.

Те́зи две́ съсе́дки мно́го се разби́рат. Те́ живе́ят от по́вече от три́йсет годи́ни в два́ съсе́дни апартаме́нта на о́смия ета́ж на еди́н софи́йски бло́к. Тя́хната дру́жба е надживя́ла вси́чки бу́ри и тру́сове. Те́ са по́вече от родни́ни. След като́ дъщери́те им завъ́ршат учи́лище, си́гурно ще оти́дат да рабо́тят на разли́чни места́, но засега́ са неразде́лни. Ма́йките им са ги ви́ждали ска́рани, но те́хните сръдни́ тра́ят де́н до пла́дне. По́сле или една́та ще позвъни́ на врата́та, или дру́гата. И до вечерта́ те́ ще са се сдобри́ли и ще са се́днали за́едно пред телеви́зора.

III. Rewrite as "potential", beginning the story with Ако бя́х дя́до Мра́з...

Най-голя́мата ми мечта́ е да се събу́дя една́ су́трин и да ви́дя, че е па́днал пъ́рвият сня́г. Тога́ва ще оти́да в киле́ра и ще изва́дя вси́чки писма́, кои́то ма́лките деца́ са ми напи́сали през годи́ната. Ще напра́вя спи́сък за Снежа́нка на кого́ какъ́в пода́рък да ку́пи. Мо́жех и са́м да оти́да на паза́р, но се боя́х, че продава́чите ще ме позна́ят с та́я бя́ла брада́ и че́рвените боту́ши. Дори́ и да им ка́жа, че не съ́м дя́до Мра́з, че и́мето ми по паспо́рт е Скре́жко, те́ ня́ма да ми повя́рват.

SAMPLE SENTENCES

1. Спо́мняш ли си, то́й да е но́сел със се́бе си голя́ма че́рна ча́нта?
2. Не зна́м, тя́ да е ка́звала такова́ не́що.
3. То́й зна́е и две́ и две́ста. Живя́л е и в коли́ба и в дворе́ц.

4. По това́ вре́ме те́ живе́ели мно́го скро́мно.
5. Ти́ си́гурно позна́ваш добре́ то́я кварта́л. А́з по́мня, че ня́кога си живя́л набли́зо.
6. Те́ живе́ли дъ́лго и щастли́во.

Двайсет и девети урок / Lesson 29

7. Докато са живéели тáм, са получáвали стипéндия.
8. Ако не бя́хте отстъ́пили редá си, досегá щя́хте да сте забрáвили, че сте чáкали на тáзи опáшка.

9. -- Ня́ма да мóжеш да си прóстиш, ако изпýснеш начáлото на фи́лма.
   -- Не сé притесня́вай. Ти́ не знáеш áз какви́ нещá съм си прощáвал.

10. Слъ́нцето ви́наги е свети́ло и ще продължáва да свети́.
11. Пó-рáно слъ́нцето е светéло пó-я́рко.

12. Не смé знáели, че тóй е сгóтвил вечéрята.
13. Не смé знáели, че досегá тóй е въ́ршел вси́чката домаки́нска рáбота.

14. Тóй разпрáвяше, че доскóро е пóмнел добрé рáзказите на дя́до си за войнáта.

15. Тóй бéше забрáвял и дрýг пъ́т кни́гите си в институ́та и затовá и сегá реши́, че тáм ги е остáвил.
16. Áз съм ши́л с такáва голя́ма иглá веднъ́ж като бя́х при бáба ми на сéло.

17. Бащá му бéше голя́м шивáч. Тóй е ши́ел дрéхите на вси́чки дáми от софи́йския хайлáйф преди́ войнáта.
18. Попáдал е и в пó-неприя́тни ситуáции, но не пóмни когá.

SENTENCES FOR TRANSLATION

1. A long time ago people lived in small villages like this one. Then they gradually moved to the cities. I can't imagine what made them do that. The cities aren't so bad, but all the storks stayed in the villages. They say storks are very wise.

2. If they had taught him to drive like a normal person, I wouldn't be so frightened by all the curves in the road. It's a shame Ivancho didn't come with us. We would have been able to count on his excellent driving.

3. In the good old days everyone always shared with his neighbor. Now each has to have his own.

4. While I was unconscious, they told all manner of stories about me. How terrible! If I weren't so afraid of mice, none of this would ever have happened!

5. It crossed my mind that he probably never lived in Sofia and that's why he is always getting lost. It really should have occurred to us to give him a map.

READING SELECTION

<u>Заха́ри Стоя́нов, "Хри́сто Бо́тев в се́ло Задуна́йка"</u>

Около кра́я на 1865 годи́на Бо́тев тря́бвало да се прости́ ве́че с Оде́са и с учени́ческите столо́ве. Изче́званeто му от Оде́са ста́нало съвсе́м незабеля́зано да́же и между друга́рите му бъ́лгарчета. Ни́кому не се́ оба́дил, не си́ взел да́же кни́гите, уче́бници и дру́ги.

-- Па ко́й ли се интересу́ваше от не́го по онова́ вре́ме? - гово́реше ни еди́н от не́говите оде́ски позна́йници. -- Ако го зна́ехме тога́ва, че той ще бъ́де Хри́сто Бо́тев, по́ет, революционе́р и войво́да, то да сме го но́сели в па́звата си.

Подир ме́сец-два́ чу́ли в Оде́са бли́зките му прия́тели, че то́й се настани́л учи́тел в едно́ бесара́бско бъ́лгарско се́ло, Задуна́йка. Тук бу́йната нату́ра въздъ́хнала от двего́дишния гра́дски живо́т, от те́жката учи́телска дисципли́на и от мора́ла на бъ́лгарското оде́ско настоя́телство. Най-напре́д то́й изяви́л жела́ние, да се преме́сти да живе́е в зда́нието на учи́лището. Това́ учи́лище било́ вън от се́лото, опустя́ло и развале́но, без прозо́рци и със счу́пени врати́. То́ било́ гнездо́ на кукумя́вки, на при́лепи и на дру́ги но́щни пти́ци, та и сред бя́л де́н хо́рата се боя́ли да го посетя́т. Съществу́вали о́ще и предразсъ́дъци, че това́ зда́ние не е́ чи́сто от зли́те ду́хове. Как да се случи пък, че та́м набли́зо и́мало ста́ри гро́бища, кои́то о́ще по́вече изла́гали това́ зда́ние на разли́чни преме́ждия; а кукумя́вките, ти́я гро́зни и подозри́телни гади́ни, о́ще по́вече гово́рели в по́лза на те́зи слу́хове.

Кога́то Бо́тев настоя́л, че е реше́н да си избе́ре за жи́лище учи́лището, то въпро́сът от уста́ на уста́ преми́нал на обсъ́ждане в ця́лото се́ло. Вси́чки ди́гали рамене́ и се чу́дели -- какъ́в чове́к е то́я учи́тел, ко́йто си е прежа́лил младини́те и оти́ва доброво́лно да ста́не же́ртва, защо́то ни́кой освен не́го не бил о́ще замръ́квал в учи́лището. Бо́тев, жа́ден за приключе́ние и за сюрпри́зи, оста́нал непрекло́нен. Пъ́рвата и вто́рата ве́чер се́лото било́ в безпоко́йство. Стоти́на кукумя́вки и то́лкова га́рги блоки́рали по въ́здуха зда́нието, ку́кали и гра́чили отча́яно през ця́лата но́щ.

А учи́телят споко́йно и дово́лно си отспи́вал под то́я див конце́рт, ко́йто напро́тив, му пра́вел о́ще и удово́лствие. Ако хвъркова́тите га́дове протести́рали, то това́ било́ по та́я еди́нствена причи́на, че то́й им наруши́л усаме́тното жи́лище със сво́ето прису́ствие. След та́я неустраши́мост Бо́тев от еди́н пъ́т придоби́л ня́какъв авторите́т в се́лото. Сва́тби, годе́жи, седе́нки, хора́, угоще́ния и дру́ги бъ́лгарски увеселе́ния не ста́вали без не́го. То́й пе́ел от вси́чки най-добре́, разка́звал боже́ствено подхо́дящи ра́зкази и при́казки, характеризи́рал позна́ти и изве́стни ли́чности с поети́ческа да́рба, коя́то била́ оценя́вана и от про́стите; игра́ел хоро́ и ска́чал най-мно́го; то́й кога́ пове́ждал хоро́то, то́ ста́вало най-жи́во и про́чее и про́чее. Бъ́лгарите в се́ло Задуна́йка, по насле́дство от ту́рците, на вся́ка сва́тба изва́ждали да се бо́рят пехлива́ни с га́йда и тъ́пани, на кои́то гле́дали с любопи́тство вси́чките от се́лото. И мо́жете ли да си предста́вите, че Бо́тев, пое́тът, основа́телят на една шко́ла, държа́л пъ́рво мя́сто между се́лските пехлива́ни? Като засви́рвали га́йдите, той по́чвал да трепе́ри, хвъ́рлял си дре́хите, събу́вал се бо́с, ма́зал се с ма́сло, плюща́л ръце́ и троши́л ко́кали на мегда́на! Где́ да се е подадя́л стро́гият му баща́ и ви́ди сво́ето че́до -- ко́лко то́ е отишло́ напре́д в нау́ката и възпита́нието! Ко́лкото за не́го сами́я, той би́л сто́ пъ́ти по́-дово́лен и по́-благода́рен на седе́нките, хора́та и пехлива́нския мегда́н, отко́лкото в оде́ската гимна́зия и в аристократи́ческите конце́рти.

Адаптирано от Захари Стоянов, <u>Христо Ботев, Опит за биография</u>.

Monument to the doctors who fell in the wars of liberation, Sofia

Двайсет и девети урок / Lesson 29

GLOSSARY

авторите́т	authority, prestige	дисципли́на	discipline
аристократи́чески	aristocratic	доброво́лно	voluntarily
		домаки́нски	household (adj.)
безпоко́йство	anxiety, unrest	домаки́нска ра́бота	housework
безсъзна́ние	unconsciousness	дължа́ (-и́ш)	owe
бензи́нов	gasoline (adj.)		
бесара́бски	Bessarabian	екскурзиа́нт	tourist, hiker
благове́рен	pious, faithful		
благове́рният съпру́г	[one's] lord and master	же́ртва	sacrifice, victim
блоки́рам	blockade	за/на мо́ята сме́тка	at my expense
блъ́скам се / блъ́сна се	hit, crash into	заво́й	turn, bend
бля́свам / бле́сна	flash, gleam	заинтригу́вам	intrigue, arouse curiosity
боже́ствен	divine, exquisite	замръ́квам / замръ́кна	be overtaken by night
боту́ш	high boot		
бу́ен	blazing, turbulent; unruly	засви́рвам / засви́ря	begin to play, strike up (instrument)
бу́ря	storm	зда́ние	building, edifice
		зли́ see зъл	
в безсъзна́ние съм	be unconscious	зна́я и две́ и две́ста	be adaptable
вди́гам рамене́	shrug [one's] shoulders	зъл	evil (adj.)
войво́да (or воево́да)	military leader	и про́чее и про́чее	etc., etc.
все́	surely	изи́скан	refined, distinguished
всъ́щност	actually, in fact	изла́гам на преме́ждия	expose to mishap/danger
въздъ́хвам / въздъ́хна	sigh		
възпита́ние	upbringing, education	изли́зам / изля́за	turn out
въ́рша (-иш)	do, commit	изте́глям се / изте́гля се	withdraw, retreat
гад	vermin	изявя́вам / изявя́	express, declare
гади́на	animal, brute		
га́рга	crow, rook	каква́ ма́рка е кола́та ти?	what make is your car?
где́ = де́, къде́			
гово́ря в по́лза на	argue in favor of	камио́н	truck
годе́ж	engagement, betrothal	киле́р	pantry, stockroom
годи́шен	[so many] years old; yearly	корми́ло	rudder; helm, wheel
гори́во	fuel	ку́кам	call (of a cuckoo-bird)
гоща́вам / гостя́	entertain, treat	кукумя́вка	screech owl
гра́ча (-иш)	croak, caw	курс	course, direction
гро́бища (pl.)	cemetery		
гу́ма	rubber; vehicle tire	любопи́тство	curiosity
да ме уби́еш	for the life of me	ма́рка	stamp; brand
двегоди́шен	two-year old (adj.)	ма́сло	butter; oil; grease
джип	jeep	ме́чешка услу́га	a doubtful service
див	wild	ме́чешки	bear's
ди́гам = вди́гам		ме́чка	bear
ди́зелов	diesel (adj.)		

Двайсет и девети урок / Lesson 29

мечка страх, мен не страх	here goes!	предавам се / предам се (-дадеш)	give up, surrender
миля	mile	предразсъдък	prejudice, bias
минавам за	pass for	прежалвам / прежаля	sacrifice, be reconciled to loss
младини	youth, tender years	премеждие	mishap, danger
морал	morals, ethics	преминавам / премина	pass, proceed
мотор	engine, motor	пренощувам	spend the night
мръква се / мръкне се (3d ps. only)	get dark	придобивам / придобия	acquire
мълчание	silence	прилеп	bat
		примитивен	primitive
на старо	secondhand	приютявам / приютя	shelter, give refuge to
най-напред	first of all	прости (хора)	common folk
напротив	on the contrary	протестирам	protest, remonstrate
нарушавам / наруша (-иш)	break, violate	прощавам се / простя се	bid farewell
настанявам се / настаня се	settle	пъшкам	groan, moan
настоятелство	board of trustees	разменям / разменя	exchange, trade
натура	nature	разстояние	distance, gap
незабелязан	unnoticed	разтичвам се / разтичам се	bestir; run about
непреклонен	inflexible, adamant		
неразделен	inseparable	рана	wound
неустрашимост	fearlessness	революционер (ка)	revolutionary
		релса	rail
одески	Odessa (adj.)	релси	track
опустял	deserted	решен	resolved, decided
основател (ка)	founder		
остави	never mind	с помощта на	by means of, thanks to
от/на един път	all at once	сдобрявам / сдобря	make peace, reconcile
отпред	in front	сдушавам се / сдуша се (-иш)	band together
отспивам си / отспя си	sleep well, catch up on sleep	седянка (pl. седенки)	village work party
отчаяно	desperately	скаран	on bad terms
оцелявам / оцелея	survive, be left standing	скъсявам / скъся	shorten, curtail
		служа си с	use
парна машина	steam engine	сметка	account; advantage
пехливан	wrestler	спасявам / спася	save, retrieve; rescue
пладне	noon	сред бял ден	in broad daylight
плющя	flap, lash	средство	means, medium
по наследство от	descended from	сръдня	quarrel, ill feelings
повърхностен	superficial	стипендия	scholarship, grant
подир	after	строг	strict, severe
подозрителен	suspicious	стълб	post, pole
поетически	poet's, poetic	сътресение	shaking, jolt
превозвам / превозя	transport	сътресение на мозъка	brain concussion
превозен	transport (adj.)	сюрприз	surprise
превозно средство	vehicle, conveyance		
превързвам / превържа (-еш)	tie up, bandage		

Двайсет и девети урок / Lesson 29

телеви́зор	television	фе́лдшер	paramedic
тра́я	last, endure	хайла́йф	uppercrust, beau monde
тра́я от де́н до пла́дне	be short-lived	характеризи́рам	characterize, describe
троша́ (-и́ш)	break, crush	хвъркова́т	flying, winged
тру́с	shock, tremor drum	це́нен	valuable
увеселе́ние	entertainment, merrymaking	че́до	child, offspring
увли́чам се / увлека́ се (-че́ш)	be absorbed	ша́рен	variegated, patterned; multi-colored
увли́чам се в спо́мени	get wrapped up in memories	ша́рена ся́нка	dappled shade
угоще́ние	feast	шива́ч (ка)	tailor; dressmaker
усамоте́н	secluded, isolated	шофьо́рски ку́рсове	driving school
устро́йство	structure, frame; system	я́рък	bright, vivid
утеша́вам / утеша́ (-и́ш)	comfort, console		
учени́чески	pupil's, student's		

CULTURAL COMMENTARY

Literature: Hristo Botev

The revolutionary and poet Hristo Botev (1848-1876) learned Russian early, and, like many young Bulgarian intellectuals at a time when Bulgaria was still part of the Ottoman Empire, went away to high school in Odessa. He was more interested in politics than in his studies, however, and after two years was dismissed. After a brief stint as a schoolteacher among Bulgarian émigrés in the Bessarabian village of Zadunajka (or Zadunaevka), he returned to Bulgaria to finish his schooling, and to work with his stern father, a schoolmaster. His devotion to revolutionary activities soon forced him to go abroad again, however, this time to Romania. There he worked actively for the Bulgarian cause, both in Brailia and Bucharest, as an organizer and spokesman. At the same time, he was actively involved in the arts, both literary (he completed numerous translations and began writing his own poetry) and dramatic (he was part of a theater troupe). He is best known today for his finely-crafted poems which express the fervor of the Bulgarian drive for independence. As the leader of a guerrilla band returning to Bulgaria to fight the Turkish oppressor in May, 1876, he died a hero's death quite similar to that described in his own poem "The Hayduk's Song" (Хайду́шка пе́сен).

Literature: Zahari Stoyanov

The writings of Zahari Stoyanov (1850-1889) provide some of the most invaluable insight into the history of Bulgaria's liberation in the 1870s. Not only was Stoyanov a keen observer and a prolific writer, but he was also sufficiently clever and wily to remain alive throughout the violent process of the liberation. He began publishing his memoirs in 1884, and lived long enough to write many volumes of memoirs. He is best known for his voluminous *Notes on the Bulgarian Uprising, Tales of Witnesses* (Запи́ски по бъ́лгарските въста́ния, разка́зи на очеви́дци), but as he was personally acquainted with most of the central figures of Bulgaria's liberation, his biographical sketches of these heroes are also of great interest. His "attempt" at a sketch of Botev's life (Христо́ Бо́тев, о́пит за биогра́фия) first appeared in Ruse in 1888.

Двайсет и девети урок / Lesson 29

Geography: Bessarabia

Bessarabia, now part of Moldova and the Ukraine, is located to the north of the province of Dobrudzha (which itself straddles Bulgaria and Romania). For many years, possession of the area was disputed between Ottoman Turkey, Russia, and Romania. The population is mixed, and includes a relatively large Bulgarian community who were settled there after the Russo-Turkish wars of 1792 and 1829.

Village life

Traditional Bulgarian village life was (and is) characterized by hard work, punctuated by festive celebrations whenever possible. Not only weddings but also engagements are celebrated with eating, music and dancing. The village work-party (**седянка**) was also an occasion for youth to meet, as it was one of the few times unmarried women and men could gather together. Singing, dancing and storytelling were an accompaniment to the work.

Wrestling as a sport is very popular in Bulgarian villages. The form of wrestling contests, where heavily greased fighters would encounter each other in the village square to the accompaniment of bagpipe and drum, is very similar to that in Turkish villages and is assumed to have been taken over from the Turkish model.

Traditional spinning and weaving

LESSON 30

DIALOGUE

<u>Ще се ви́дим ли догоди́на?</u>

// Ве́че е следо́бед. О́гънят, на ко́йто компа́нията е пе́кла ши́шчета, карто́фи и чу́шки, е уга́снал. Възрастните пи́ят ви́но, би́ра и разхлади́телни напи́тки -- ко́йто какво́то предпочи́та. Деца́та и ку́четата подска́чат след една́ то́пка нао́коло. //

Таня: Джу́ли, ви́е о́ще ко́лко ще оста́нете в Бълга́рия?

Джу́ли: Самоле́тът ни е на 31 а́вгуст. То́чно след де́сет де́на. Но то́й изли́та от Фра́нкфурт, така́ че ще тря́бва първо да сти́гнем до та́м.

Дейвид: Бълга́рия напу́скаме след една́ се́дмица.

Веселин: Защо́ не поо́стане́те по́вече?

Дейвид: На́шата вака́нция свъ́ршва. Запо́чва но́вата уче́бна годи́на. После́дната за на́с с Джу́ли.

Павлина: А какво́ сле́двате?

Джу́ли: Ни́е ве́че не сме́ студе́нти, ни́е сме аспира́нти.

Петър: Така́ ли? А на каква́ те́ма са дисерта́циите ви?

Дейвид: А́з съм археоло́г, а Джу́ли се занима́ва с наро́дна му́зика.

Веселин: Защо́ не ка́зваш, Джу́ли, че те интересу́ва бъ́лгарската наро́дна му́зика? А́з мо́жех таки́ва за́писи да ти презапи́ша от фо́нда на ра́диото. То́ о́ще не е́ къ́сно...

Джу́ли: Това́ е интере́сно. А́з впро́чем ве́че напра́вих мно́го ху́бави за́писи в ня́колко добруджа́нски села́. Мо́же би догоди́на...

Веселин: Зна́чи ви́е па́к ще до́йдете догоди́на?

Дейвид: Ху́баво би́ било́, но не се́ зна́е отсега́ дали́ ще е възмо́жно.

Павлина: Е́х, Весели́не, Весели́не. Светъ́т е то́лкова голя́м и е пъ́лен с наро́дна му́зика. Защо́ й тря́бва на Джу́ли вся́ко ля́то все́ на едно́ мя́сто да хо́ди?!

Димитър: Защо́ не? Къде́ ще наме́ри по́-ху́бава му́зика от на́шата?

Милена: Ела́ па́к, Джу́ли. Ела́те и двама́та с Де́йвид. Ще ни бъ́де дра́го да ви ви́дим дру́гото ля́то.

Веселин: Ня́ма са́мо му́зиката да гле́дате. И хо́рата са ва́жни...

Петър: Осо́бено ня́кои, нали́ така́, Ве́ско?

Веселин: Ха́йде сега́ и ти́. Вси́чки хо́ра са ва́жни...

Павлина: Ко́й зна́е, Джу́ли, ма́йка ти ка́к се е затъжи́ла за те́бе... И тво́ята ма́йка, Де́йвид. Ни́що о́ще не разби́рате ви́е, но като си роди́те сво́и деца́, ще разбере́те.

Дейвид: На́шите роди́тели са сви́кнали да ни ня́ма. А́з о́ще като завъ́рших гимна́зия, се изне́сох на кварти́ра. И дру́гите ми прия́тели живе́ят самостоя́телно.

Павлина: Не ми́ разпра́вяй ти на ме́не, че родителите ви били́ сви́кнали с ва́шето отсъ́ствие... Америка́нските ма́йки и те́ сърце́ но́сят. Ма́йки нали́ са... А́з зна́м какво́ е. Мо́ят си́н се е нака́нил да оти́де във Ва́рна да живе́е. Ва́рна ей я́ къде́ е, а на ме́н па́к ми е мъ́чно...

Милена: Ма́йко, ни́е ще пи́шем, ще се оба́ждаме.

Димитър: По два́ пъ́ти на де́н.

Павлина: Сме́й се ти́. Я се се́тиш еди́н пъ́т в се́дмицата да завърти́ш телефо́на, я не... В те́бе ми е наде́ждата, Миле́нче.

Веселин: А ти́, Джу́ли, по два́ пъ́ти на де́н ли ще ми пи́шеш, или веднъ́ж в се́дмицата?

Петър: А по́-наря́дко не мо́же ли, или дру́гите честоти́ се свъ́ршиха?

Дейвид: Ка́к така́ мо́же честоти́те да са се свъ́ршили?

Петър: Ами́ като в о́ня ви́ц. Дето ке́лнерът ка́зал на пия́ницата, който си би́л поръ́чал една́ ма́лка раки́я: "Ма́лките се свъ́ршиха, и́ма са́мо голе́ми". Нали́ разби́раш, домързя́ло го чове́ка през пе́т мину́ти да ти́ча да му но́си о́ще една́ раки́я...

Димитър: Накра́тко, да обобщя́ с две́ ду́ми ка́заното от преди́шните ора́тори: ако не се́ ви́дим, ще си пи́шем.

Павлина, Джули, и Веселин в един глас: Да́! Да́! Ще си пи́шем!

Трийсети урок / Lesson 30

POSTSCRIPT

30.1. Standard and literary languages: the Bulgarian literary standard

The preceding 29 lessons have presented the essentials of Bulgarian grammar. That which has been described is normally called the *contemporary Bulgarian literary language* (съвре́менен бъ́лгарски книжо́вен ези́к). This represents the form of the language which is described in language textbooks for foreigners, which is codified in dictionaries, which is taught in school, and which is used in the official media.

This version of a language is usually called a *standard language*. Leading cultural figures, such as linguists, language specialists, and politicians responsible for cultural affairs, agree on the specific form the accepted language should take, a process which involves making many decisions at many levels. For instance, at the level of orthography it must be decided what is the correct spelling for each word, and at the level of orthoepy it must be decided what is the correct pronunciation for every word (in the latter case, the most important information is the placement of the accent). Many of these decisions also involve the shape of the article, the shape of the vowel in instances of the я / е alternation, or the accent of the verb form.

Similar decisions must be made at the grammatical level, resolving such questions as: what is the correct form of the article for each noun? what is the correct imperfectivizing suffix for each derived imperfective? what is the correct plural form for certain masculine nouns? and the like. Finally and perhaps most crucially, decisions must be made at the level of usage and meaning. Because the system of tense, aspect and mood is so complex, the majority of these decisions concern the correct usage of the several tenses and moods. It is also necessary to define the precise meaning of individual words.

The completed set of decisions is codified and communicated to the public in lexical dictionaries, spelling and pronouncing dictionaries, and grammars. *Lexical dictionaries* are organized alphabetically, by word. Each entry is headed by what is called the *dictionary form* of a word (indefinite singular for nouns, masculine indefinite singular for adjectives, and first singular present for verbs). Simplex imperfectives are listed alone; derived imperfectives are usually listed followed by their perfective partner. If the formation of a word is irregular, sometimes the most basic irregularities are listed. Primarily, however, these dictionaries are intended to define the meanings and usage of words.

A spelling and *pronouncing dictionary* (правогово́рен ре́чник) is also organized alphabetically, by dictionary form. After the main entry are given all grammatical forms of a word, each with the correct accent. When variant forms are admitted in the standard, both are listed. The preferred pronunciation is also specified, such as those instances of stressed **-а** which must be pronounced as [-ъ].

Трийсети урок / Lesson 30

A *grammar* is intended to describe all levels of the language. Grammars traditionally begin with a description of the sounds, including accent. They then describe the formation of the several parts of speech (nouns, pronouns, adjectives, numbers, verbs, prepositions, adverbs, particles). Finally, they give as thorough a statement as possible of how and when these different forms (especially the verb tenses) should and should not be used.

The complex of descriptions given in grammars and dictionaries is generally referred to as *prescriptive grammar*: it prescribes how people should speak and write. Teachers, language learners, editors, publishers, journalists, and the like find it extremely useful to be able to refer to such rules.

Because language inevitably changes over time, these prescriptive rules are revised from time to time. The present set of decisions is essentially that formed during Bulgaria's socialist period (with some minor revisions). These decisions in turn rest upon those made by linguists and cultural leaders from the time of liberation (1878) throughout the first half of the present century. Prior to the middle of the 19th century, however, there was no one set written standard. It was part of the national revival movement to propose that educated Bulgarians write not in Greek (the language of Christian schools within Ottoman Bulgaria) nor in the church language (a very archaic form of written Bulgarian), but in the language that they actually spoke. There are several important names within the movement to create these language norms, the most significant of which is Naiden Gerov (Найден Геров, 1823-1900). Gerov compiled the first modern dictionary of Bulgarian and worked tirelessly for the cause of education and literacy.

Movements to create literary languages which would reflect the actual speech of the people (and not a written form reflecting a more elite cultural tradition, usually imposed from outside) were common in 19th century Europe. These movements usually were allied with political causes, either of unification (as in the case of Italy and Germany) or of liberation from foreign rule (as in the case of Serbia and Bulgaria). Defining the "language of the people", therefore, also meant defining the cultural vehicle of the new state. Thus, the various cultural leaders responsible for these decisions strove to find the particular form of that language which would represent what they took to be its purest incarnation, and would consequently best represent and transmit the indefinable "spirit of the people".

There were different ways to achieve this aim. Sometimes it was decided to elevate a single dialect to the level of literary standard. In these cases the chosen dialect was either the language of what had already become the cultural center of the new nation, or was the dialect of a particular town or area which everyone (or at least everyone in power) recognized as exemplifying the "best" speech. Other times, an amalgam language was created, in which the so-called "best elements" of several different local variants were chosen. The first choice has the advantage of naturalness, in that the entire system represents a real, internally consistent spoken language. Its disadvantage is that it is actually natural (for speaking and learning) only to those living in the region where it is spoken. The second choice has the

Трийсети урок / Lesson 30

advantage of breadth but the disadvantage of unnaturalness. Neither choice, of course, is perfect.

The codifiers of Bulgarian chose the second option. This means that there is no one single spoken Bulgarian dialect which corresponds completely to modern standard Bulgarian. What is now the standard language is rather an amalgam of various central and northeastern dialects. This is in fact a true representation of the cultural facts of the 19th century: there was no one single center of the national revival, but rather several centers spread throughout central and northeastern Bulgaria.

30.2. Variation within standard languages, and the concept of "norm"

Not everyone speaks as in a book. In principle, however, all educated speakers of Bulgarian try to speak as they were taught in school. The level they strive to reach is thought of as *normative*, or "the way one ought to speak". It is nevertheless the case that many educated speakers of Bulgarian do not follow all the rules exactly as laid out in this book. Furthermore, there is often more than one way to express a given idea or grammatical construction, and most Bulgarians would accept either way as correct.

Certain of these variant possibilities are codified into the literary standard. Pronouncing dictionaries, for instance, accept both **писах** and **писах** (and, of course, **писал** and **писал**); they also accept both **столове** and **столове**, and **зная** and **знам**. Most Bulgarians will use only one or the other of these, but some will vacillate between them in their speech.

Other variant forms are not accepted, even though they are very widespread in speech. One example of this is the masculine definite article. Prescriptive grammars require that the subject form of this article be spoken (and written) with a final -т, and that the object form of the article lack this final consonant (e.g. градът е голям, but живея в града). Very few Bulgarians observe this distinction regularly, however, and some do not observe it at all. It is much more common to hear speakers drop the -т in all forms; conversely, a smaller number of speakers use the -т in all forms.

Similarly, few speakers use what has been termed the correct alternant of -я-/-е- in all instances. Some use the -е- more often and others use the -я- more often. A higher frequency of -е- forms (e.g. **млеко**, **место**) is especially common in the capital city, Sofia. Residents of Sofia are also more likely to use 1st plural verb forms in -ме (such as **играеме**) and to use a hard consonant before the 1st singular and 3rd plural endings -я and -ят, pronouncing **благодаря** and **правят** as [благодаръ] and [правът].

Many of the above instances of so-called "incorrect" usage stem from the decisions made by the 19th-century codifiers of the language, who created a language that some modern linguists have called unnatural. These linguists claim that since there is no existing Bulgarian dialect which distinguishes subject and object forms of the masculine definite forms, it is therefore unnatural to have created such a distinction, and unrealistic to expect modern speakers to make it naturally. Nevertheless, since this distinction has become codified into the language, educated speakers are expected to make it, and indeed, most attempt to do so in formal situations. Similarly, the codified system of я / е alternations is to a certain extent unnatural, in that there is no one dialect in which all the relevant forms are spoken exactly as in the standard language. The variation with respect to this phenomenon is in fact very great throughout Bulgarian dialects.

In these and other instances, speakers attempt (to varying degrees) to use the language as they ought. Nevertheless, it is clear that the underlying, more natural version of the language continues to surface in informal speech situations. Certain of these more informal elements are becoming increasingly more common, and it is likely that at least some of them will find their way into the prescribed norm some day. The very concept of "norm", in fact, admits of a certain fluidity, of which most speakers are aware. Thus, while they attempt to speak with textbook correctness in more formal contexts, they are content to speak (and to hear) numerous different (and technically incorrect) forms of the language on other occasions.

A more subtle level of this question surfaces when one turns to the complex issue of the Bulgarian verbal system. Certain aspects of this problem have been mentioned in Lesson 29, namely the dispute between native and foreign linguists over the degree of autonomy of the renarrated mood within the Bulgarian verbal system. Although in the case of the renarrated mood, the linguistic facts are much more complex, the basic issue is the same. Namely, the norm as prescribed defines and describes only part of what people actually say. In the case of the article, accentuation, or the я / е alternation, the question is relatively straightforward: there are a number of variant forms possible, some of which are more acceptable than others. In the case of the verbal system, things are much more complicated, and there is considerable debate among linguists and grammarians about the issues involved.

The central part of the debate was presented in descriptive terms in Lesson 29, and a new solution was proposed. The advantages of this solution are that it seems to describe what people actually do say, and that the changes it proposes in the overall conception of Bulgarian grammar are relatively slight. Language norms are highly conservative, however, and most native linguists and language teachers are convinced that the language must be (and must remain) as they were taught it. The unspoken attitude is that if people do not speak that way, then they should be taught to do so. Linguists who attempt to describe what people actually do say, and to force the normative standard to reflect this, face a fair degree of resistance. When (and whether) the prescriptive grammars of Bulgarian will be altered to reflect more closely what people actually do say is unknown. The important point to note is that in the case of the verbal system, it is not a question of variant forms, some of which are more acceptable than others. It is rather a question of interpretation, and the names given to various grammatical forms which are used by everyone with more or less agreed-upon meaning.

30.3. Dialectology and linguistic geography: the study of rural dialects

Much of the Bulgarian population remains very attached to the countryside, and in quite specific terms: each has a tie to a particular locale in the countryside. Some are now city dwellers but retain an emotional connection to the natal village of their forefathers; some of these city dwellers actualize this connection by returning to the village on short occasions when possible. For others, the village is their primary or only residence. This has a strong effect on their speech. Despite the fact that most of them have been to school and have been instructed in the standard norms, they rarely speak this standard variant. Put differently, the norm towards which they strive is not that which is described above. Rather, it is the language of their ancestors, many of whom never went to school at all. These several different languages, each defined by the village in which it is spoken, are called *dialects*.

For non-linguists, the term "dialect" usually has negative connotations, and conjures up a picture of economic and social backwardness, or at the most positive a romantic landscape colored with quaint and archaic associations. Linguists, however, view the many different local dialects as objects of study just like any language. Each dialect, in fact, is actually a separate language, with its own internally consistent system. The relationships between the several dialects are studied from several different points of view. In geographical terms, linguists plot the degrees of sameness and difference between the different dialects (with respect to different criteria such as sounds, grammatical forms, and lexical meanings) on dialect maps. In typological terms, linguists study the different ways in which a particular linguistic element can be expressed. In historical terms, linguists use the different existing expressions both to reconstruct a common ancestor, and to describe the probable mechanisms of change that have led to the several different existing states.

There are several major groups of Bulgarian dialects. They are usually called by geographical names, such as the *Rhodope* dialects, the *northwestern* dialects, etc. Within each of these larger groups are numerous smaller sub-groupings. Each of these separate groups is defined not by location, but by the degree of differences between it and its neighbors. These differences are reckoned in terms of linguistic criteria. The choice of criteria is by now traditional; like much else that has to do with modern Bulgarian linguistics, it came gradually into being in the last years of the previous century and the first years of this one.

The primary differentiating criterion is defined by the **-я-/-e-** alternation, and is called the *jat' boundary* (я́това грани́ца). In older Slavic, there was a separate sound which was represented by the letter called *jat'* (ѣ). Presumably, it was pronounced something like the vowel sound in modern English "at". It is still pronounced this way in some Bulgarian dialects. In most other dialects, it is pronounced either as [e] or [a] or as a combination of the two (i.e. sometimes as [e]

Трийсети урок / Lesson 30

and sometimes as [a]). When it is pronounced as [a], the consonant preceding it is usually soft, and this vowel is therefore usually written -я-.

Other criteria have to do with the vowel which appears in the masculine definite article (which can be -о-, -а- or -ъ-), the sequence of -ръ-/-ър-, or the consonant which appears in the future particle (which can be -щ-, -ш-, -к'- or the like). Dialects are also differentiated by grammatical criteria. Some dialects have maintained more case forms in nouns and pronouns. Others have a different system of definite articles; for instance, Rhodope dialects have three different definite articles depending on whether the speaker perceives the noun in question to be close to him, far away from him, or neither of the above. Others have a different way of expressing the future tense. Finally, the range of dialectal words is rich. One could spend an entire lifetime studying the differences in Bulgarian dialects.

30.4. Dialectology and sociolinguistics: the study of urban dialects

Until recently, the concept of dialect referred almost exclusively to rural dialects in the sense defined above. In recent years, however, the term dialect has taken on a broader meaning, and has come to refer to any variant speech system which may be associated with a particular group. That is, it has been recognized at a more official level that inhabitants of a particular city may speak a variant of the language which is marked as belonging to that city, or to a particular social class within that city (or to a particular social class over a wider segment of the population). Such speech systems are called *urban dialects*, and the study of variant speech systems which can be associated with different social classes or groups is called *sociolinguistics*.

It is not yet clear how the relatively new field of sociolinguistics will develop in Bulgaria. Until quite recently, the only accepted way one could describe the speech of educated speakers was in terms of the prescriptive grammars and dictionaries. If variation was to be described, it was either done in cautionary terms or in technical terms. In the first case, speakers were told what they should avoid saying (the fact they needed to be told this, of course, was proof that they actually *did* say the word or phrase in question frequently). In the second case, linguists attempted to come up with better descriptions for usages that admittedly occurred, did not seem particularly wrong, but did not seem sufficiently well described in the received prescriptive system (the prime example is the tense/mood question described in Lesson 29).

Simply to admit that there is something called a jargon, however -- that there are ways to say things that are highly informal, and that are associated in everyone's mind with a particular city and social milieu -- is very innovative for Bulgarians. There has been a spate of publications in and about these socially defined styles of speech recently. Most have been centered on the capital city of Sofia, but there have also been descriptions of the jargon associated with other larger cities.

It is true that the speech associated with certain other socially-defined groups, such as members of certain trades, or of certain minority religions, had been described earlier. These were seen as special cases of regional dialects, however. Properly speaking, of course, they are also a part of sociolinguistics. Eventually one hopes that everyone will realize that language only exists in a social context, and that this context must always be taken into account in language description. At that point the concept sociolinguistics will become part of the accepted realm of linguistics. Because linguistics in Bulgaria has been defined in such narrow terms up till now, and because the ideology of the socialist government insisted upon a certain descriptive model of social relations, it has been necessary to expand the horizons in both directions by focusing special attention on "socio-" linguistics as a separate discipline.

30.5. The Bulgarian language: conclusion

This course concludes by returning to the words with which it began:

"Bulgarian is the language of the Republic of Bulgaria, and as such is spoken by approximately ten million people. In global terms, this is a fairly small number. In geographical terms as well, Bulgaria is a relatively small country. It is thus unavoidable that both Bulgarians and those who teach and study Bulgarian become accustomed to thinking of it as a small or lesser-known language, since much of the world refers to it as such.

It is clear to all who know it, however, that Bulgarian is an extremely fascinating and complex language, and that it carries in its expression a cultural heritage of long duration and great richness. Linguists have many different reasons to learn Bulgarian, for both its structure and its dialectal variation hold treasure stores of data yet to be mined and analyzed. Cultural historians also have many reasons to learn Bulgarian, for it covers a vast and important history.

Finally, the people of modern Bulgaria are perhaps the best reason to learn Bulgarian. Communication is the purpose of language, after all, and they are a people eminently worth speaking with."

May the student who has finished this course enjoy many profitable hours, days, and years communicating with Bulgarians and their history!

READING SELECTION

Стойко Стойков, "Българският книжовен език и българските диалекти"

През пъ́рвата половина на XIX в. българското занаятчи́йско произво́дство и българската търгови́я взе́мат национа́лни разме́ри. Така́ се създа́ва национа́лен паза́р, кой́то свъ́рзва българската наро́дност от вси́чки кра́ища на българската терито́рия в едно́ икономи́ческо ця́ло. У́споредно с това́ под влия́ние на ре́д конкре́тни истори́чески усло́вия се офо́рмя и българският национа́лен ези́к.

То́й се изгра́жда върху осно́вата на североизто́чните балка́нски го́вори, но то́й не е́ отде́лен североизто́чен диале́кт, напри́мер тъ́рновският, ка́кто непра́вилно се твърди́, или пъ́к га́бровският, изди́гнат до национа́лен ези́к. Терито́рията на центра́лния балка́нски го́вор, т.е. областта́ от две́те страни́ на Сре́дна Ста́ра планина́ и Сре́дна гора́, и́ма по това́ вре́ме ръково́дна ро́ля в икономи́ческия и културния живо́т и затова́ североизто́чните балка́нски го́вори ля́гат в осно́вата на българския национа́лен ези́к.

Значи́телно влия́ние оказва и съществу́ващата по́-ра́но пи́сменост на църковнославя́нски ези́к, кой́то на́шите пъ́рви книжо́вници смя́тат за ста́р и и́стински бъ́лгарски ези́к и кой́то се опи́тват да застъ́пват в една́ или дру́га сте́пен в книжо́вната си де́йност. През трийсе́тте и четиридесе́тте годи́ни на ми́налия ве́к у на́с се разга́рят оживе́ни спо́рове за хара́ктера на литерату́рния ни ези́к, кой́то завъ́ршват с пъ́лна побе́да на наро́дната разгово́рна ре́ч с не́йните на́й-характе́рни осо́бености в грамати́чния строе́ж: чле́нна фо́рма, ли́пса на паде́жи и пр. -- и ти́я осо́бености през петдесе́тте и шестдесе́тте годи́ни се възприе́мат като еди́нни но́рми на литерату́рния ези́к.

Ва́жна осо́беност на българския книжо́вен ези́к е, че то́й се офо́рмя гла́вно като ези́к пи́сан, т.е. в пи́смената си фо́рма, а не́ в говори́мата. До Освобожде́нието, а и дъ́лго след не́го са́мо пи́смената фо́рма на литерату́рния ези́к се възприе́ма като задължи́телна и стреме́жът е една́ково да се пи́ше. Едва́ по́-къ́сно се поста́вя въпро́сът за правого́вора. Затова́ пи́сането е ока́зало значи́телно влия́ние върху зву́ковото офо́рмяне на българския литерату́рен ези́к и във фонети́чно отноше́ние то́й значи́телно се отлича́ва от североизто́чните балка́нски го́вори.

Кога́то се гово́ри за българския национа́лен ези́к като за но́во явле́ние, офо́рмило се през пъ́рвата полови́на на ми́налия ве́к, и кога́то то́й се съпоста́вя с българските диале́кти, тря́бва да се и́мат пред ви́д ня́колко ва́жни положе́ния.

Българският национа́лен ези́к не е́ съвсе́м но́во явле́ние, но́в ези́к, а е са́мо по́-ви́сша фа́за в развоя́ на общонаро́дния български ези́к. То́й се отлича́ва от отде́лните български диале́кти, в това́ число́ и от централния балка́нски го́вор, на пъ́рво мя́сто по своя́ <u>речников съста́в</u>, след това́ и по своя́ <u>фонети́чен о́блик,</u> но е една́къв с тя́х по грамати́чен строе́ж и осно́вен речников фо́нд. Затова́ отноше́нието между литерату́рния ези́к и териториа́лните диале́кти не е́ отноше́ние между две́ ези́кови систе́ми, а

Трийсети урок / Lesson 30

отношéние на еднá пó-обрабóтена фóрма към еднá пó-необрабóтена. В истóрията на бъ́лгарския езѝк бъ́лгарският национáлен езѝк не é нóв, отдéлен перѝод, а заéдно с диалéктите влѝза в т.нар. новобъ́лгарски перѝод, който запóчва от XVI в. и който по отношéние на старобъ́лгарския езѝк ѝма дóста нóви специфѝчни осóбености в граматѝчния строéж, на пъ́рво мя́сто аналитѝчно изразя́ване на граматѝчните отношéния между именáта.

Рáзликите между отдéлните бъ́лгарски диалéкти съвсéм не сá такá значѝтелни, кáкто обикновéно се мѝсли и кáкто мóже да се заключѝ от ня́кои диалектолóжки проу́чвания. Фáктите я́сно покáзват, че териториáлните диалéкти на езѝка образу́ват здрáво едѝнство, офóрмена ця́лост, защóто ѝмат еднáкъв граматѝчен строéж, óбщ основéн рéчник и до голя́ма стéпен еднáкъв рéчников състáв, а се отличáват едѝн от дру́г сáмо по фонетѝчните си осóбености.

Изгрáждането на бъ́лгарския литерату́рен езѝк като срéдство за общу́ване на нáцията, като срéдство, на коéто се творѝ пó-висóка култу́ра, литерату́ра, нау́ка, е стáнало бáвно и постепéнно с усѝлията на редѝца поколéния, и то глáвно чрез обогатя́ване на рéчника. При изгрáждането лéксиката на бъ́лгарския национáлен езѝк се проявя́ва еднá интерéсна осóбеност. Пъ́рвите нáши просвéтни и книжóвни дейцѝ запóчват да гóнят системно ту́рските ду́ми и да ги замéстват с домáшни или чу́жди. Ѝзточник на мнóго такѝва заéмки стáва ру́скиятезѝк. Освéн товá от ру́ски езѝк тé заéмат и необходѝмите им нóви ду́ми за означáване на нóви поня́тия. Посрéдством ру́ски в бъ́лгарския езѝк навлѝза съ́що такá и пó-голя́мата чáст от междунарóдната еврoпéйска лéксика.

И тъ́й бъ́лгарският литерату́рен езѝк е реáлно езѝково явлéние, коéто образу́ва едѝнство, ця́лост с бъ́лгарските диалéкти. Бъ́лгарският литерату́рен езѝк и диалéктите представя́т двé странѝ на общонарóдния бъ́лгарски езѝк, двá етáпа в нéговия развóй. Тé си сътру́дничат, при коéто диалéктите постепéнно се сближáват и слѝват с едѝнния национáлен литерату́рен езѝк.

Адаптирано от Стойко Стойков, <u>Българска диалектология</u>, Трето издание.

Трийсети урок / Lesson 30

GLOSSARY

аналитичен	analytical (grammar: lacking cases)
в един глас	unanimously
в това число и	as well as
вземам национални размери	take on national proportions
влияние	influence
впрочем	incidentally; in fact
габровски	Gabrovo (adj.)
говорим	spoken
граматичен (and граматически)	grammatical
деец	worker, figure
диалектоложки	dialectological
добруджански	Dobrudzha (adj.)
домашен	domestic
едва по-късно	only later
един от друг	from one another
единство	unity, uniformity
еднакво	equally, alike
еднакъв	identical, the same
езиков	language (adj.), linguistic
етап	stage, degree
заемка	loanword
замествам / заместя	replace, substitute
занаятчийски	craft (adj.)
занаятчийско производство	craft industry
застъпвам / застъпя	step over; propound
затъжавам се / затъжа се (-иш)	begin to miss
значителен	considerable, significant
излитам / излетя	take off, fly away
изнасям се / изнеса се	move out
източник	source; origin
име (pl. имена)	noun
келнер	waiter
конкретен	concrete, specific
липса	lack, absence
литературен	literary
литературен език	standard language
навлизам / навляза	enter, penetrate
нарядко	seldom, at rare intervals
нация	nation
неправилно	incorrectly
норма	standard, norm
облик	aspect, shape
обобщавам / обобщя	generalize, draw a conclusion
обогатявам / обогатя	enrich
обогатявам речника [си]	enlarge [one's] vocabulary
обработвам / обработя	cultivate, finish
образувам	form, constitute
общонароден	nationwide, general
общуване	association, dealings
оживен	animated
оживен спор	lively debate
оказвам / окажа (-еш)	render, give
оказвам влияние	exert influence
оратор	speaker, speech-maker
освобождение	liberation
основен речников фонд	core vocabulary
особеност	peculiarity, feature
от двете страни	on both sides
отсега	from now on
оформен (and оформен)	formed
падеж	(grammatical) case
по-голямата част	most, the bulk
по отношение на	as regards
победа	victory
подскачам / подскоча (-иш)	jump, leap about
понятие	concept, notion
поостaвам / поостана	stay a little longer
посредством	by means of, through
поставям / поставя	put, produce
поставям въпрос	pose a question

Трийсети урок / Lesson 30

правоговор	orthoepy, correct pronunciation	средство за общуване	means of communication
презаписвам / презапиша (-еш)	make copies of recordings	съпоставям / съпоставя	juxtapose, compare
производство	production, manufacture	сътруднича (-иш)	collaborate, cooperate
просветен	educational	териториален	territorial
просветен деец	educationalist	т.нар. = така наречен(ият)	so-called
проучвам / проуча (-иш)	study, investigate		
		успоредно	simultaneously, in parallel
разгарям се / разгоря се	burn, run high	учебен	school (adj.)
разговорен	colloquial, conversational	учебна година	academic year
размер	size, scale	фаза	phase, stage
разхладителен	cooling, refreshing	факт (pl. факти)	fact
речник	lexicon	фонд	stock; fund
речников	lexical	фонетичен	phonetic
ръководен	leading, guiding		
		цяло	entity, whole
с две думи	in short	цялост	entirety, totality
сближавам се / сближа се (-иш)	draw closer		
североизточен	northeastern	честота	frequency
системно	systematically		
сливам / слея	fuse, combine	членна форма	definite article

Relaxing in a gazebo on Mount Vitosha, outside Sofia

CUMULATIVE GLOSSARY

INDEX

Homage to women practitioners of traditional textile arts, Ethnographic Museum, Nesebăr

CUMULATIVE GLOSSARY

Lessons 1-30

The following glossary contains all the Bulgarian words used in both volumes 1 and 2 of *Intensive Bulgarian.* Each entry is indexed to the lesson where the word or phrase first appeared. Idioms or other phrasal usage are fully cross-referenced; for instance, the phrase **имам нужда от** (need, have need of) is glossed under **имам, нужда,** and **от**.

All entries are accented. Accentual doublets are given where they are mentioned in all major dictionaries (such as **чело** or **чело**); other accentual variants are not noted. Accepted accentual variations in the aorist and L-participle of unprefixed verbs are not noted, either in glossaries or in textual usage. Stress shifts onto the masculine definite article are noted: **дим, -ът**.

Plural forms for nouns are given only when not predictable from grammar rules presented in the lessons. Thus, only plural forms in **-ове** where either ending syllable is stressed, plurals in **-и** of masculine monosyllables, feminine plural forms with shifted stress, or unpredictable neuter plural forms are specifically noted. Gender is noted only when not predictable: feminine nouns in a consonant other than in **-ост** are given with the article (**вечер, -та**) and neuter nouns ending in other than **-о** or **-е** are given with the gender specified: **меню** *(neuter)*.

Adjectives are given in the masculine singular indefinite form. The absence of a fleeting vowel is noted only when it is not predictable from rules presented in the lessons (thus **червен**, but **вълнен, -ена**). In the case of shifting vowels in the root (as in **верен, вярна** or **рядък, редки**), the non-masculine form is cross-referenced to the main entry.

Simplex imperfectives are given a single entry; all other verbs are given as aspect pairs with the imperfective listed first. All verbs are given in the standard 1st singular present form. The conjugation class of verbs whose stems end in **-ш, -ч,** or **-ж,** or which is not predictable from the citation form, is noted: **пиша (-еш), пуша (-иш), къпя (-еш)**.

English glosses are given as simply as possible; for a larger range of meanings, the full Bulgarian-English dictionary (the source taken as standard for this glossary listing) should be consulted. When the English noun and adjective forms are homonymous, the notation *adj.*, or an explanatory note such as (female) is added. Grammatical information such as *interrogative* or *relative conjunction* has been given in the relevant instances.

This glossary list consolidates and reproduces the separate glossary listings given at the end of each of the lessons in volume 1 (1-15) and volume 2 (16-30). The form is slightly different, in that idioms and phrases are listed here under each of their major components (as opposed to alphabetically according to the first element in the phrase, as in the lessons). A somewhat fuller listing is given herein: certain definitions are more detailed, and certain phrases are given here which were omitted from the lesson glossaries.

Българо-английски речник (урок 1-30)

а [1] and
абони́рам [11] subscribe
а́вгуст [5] August
австри́ец [23] Austrian (male)
австри́йка [23] Austrian (female)
автенти́чен [13] authentic
автобиогра́фия [17] autobiography, CV
автобу́с [2] bus
автогра́ф [13] autograph
автомоби́лен [17] automobile *(adj.)* ; автомоби́лна катастро́фа [17] auto accident
а́втор [23] author
авторите́т [29] authority, prestige
а́вторски [12] author's ; а́вторско пра́во [12] copyright
а́гне [21] lamb
а́гнешки [21] lamb *(adj.)*
адвока́т (ка) [2] lawyer
адре́с [9] address
аеро́бика [8] aerobics
а́з [1] I ; а́з се ка́звам my name is
а́збука [21] alphabet
акаде́мия [17] academy ; Бъ́лгарската акаде́мия на нау́ките [17] Bulgarian Academy of Sciences
ако́ [4] if ; ако́ оби́чате [4] if you please ; ако́ и да [22] even though
акордео́н [16] accordion
актьо́р [14] actor
акъ́л [16] mind, brain, sense
албу́м [9] album, picture-book
алкохо́л [2] alcohol
алкохо́лен [20] alcoholic
а́ло [12] hello (on the phone)
алпини́ст [28] mountaineer, mountain climber
ама́ [12] but
америка́нец [3] American (male)
американизи́рам [22] Americanize, become American
америка́нка [3] American (female)
америка́нски [8] American *(adj.)*
ами́ [7] but, well
аналити́чен [30] analytical (grammar: without case endings)
англи́йски [2] English (language)
англича́нин [3] Englishman
англича́нка [3] Englishwoman
анекдо́т [24] anecdote
антре́ [20] entryway
антрополо́г [26] anthropologist
апандиси́т [18] appendix, appendicitis
апара́т [5] [piece of] apparatus, equipment
апарату́ра [17] apparatus, equipment
апартаме́нт [8] apartment
апети́т [9] appetite
април́ [9] April

апропо́ [13] apropos, by the way
ара́бин [23] Arab (male)
ара́бка [23] Arab (female)
ара́бски [11] Arab *(adj.)*
аристокра́т [23] aristocrat, noble
аристократи́чески [29] aristocratic
аристокра́ция [23] aristocracy, nobility
арома́тен [10] aromatic
а́рмия [12] army
арха́ичен [23] ancient, archaic
археоло́г [3] archaeologist
археологи́чески [23] archaeological
архитекту́ра [7] architecture
асансьо́р [11] elevator
асма́ [16] trellis vine
аспира́нт (ка) [17] graduate student
аспиранту́ра [17] graduate studies
аспири́н [12] aspirin
асфа́лт [19] paving, asphalt
атмосфе́ра [3] atmosphere
аха́ [5] aha

ба́ба [8] grandmother
Ба́ба Ма́рта [11] Granny March (harbinger of spring)
бава́рец [22] Bavarian
ба́вен [3] slow
бага́ж [2] baggage, luggage
баджана́к [22] brother-in-law (wife's sister's husband)
байр [26] hill, mound
ба́й [1] uncle, old man *(term of address)*
балдъ́за [22] sister-in-law (wife's sister)
балка́нски [18] Balkan *(adj.)*
балко́н [13] balcony
БАН = Бъ́лгарска акаде́мия на нау́ките [17] Bulgarian Academy of Sciences
бана́тски [22] from the Banat
ба́ница [10] banitsa (baked pastry) ; ба́ница с късме́ти [10] banitsa filled with fortunes
ба́нка [22] bank
банке́р [23] banker, money-agent
банке́т [14] banquet
ба́нски [13] bathing; swimming suit ; по ба́нски [13] wearing swimsuits
ба́ня [3] bath, bathroom
баро́к [10] Baroque
баро́ков [9] baroque *(adj.)*
басе́йн [26] pool, reservoir
баща́ [8] father ; ти́ баща́, ти́ ма́йка [18] you're my only hope
ба́щин [28] paternal, father's
бе [6] *(vocative particle)* ; ка́к се ка́зваш, бе? [6] what's your name, fella?

Българо-английски речник (урок 1-30)

бебе [18] baby
беден [27] poor, meager
бедро [12] thigh
без [6] without ; пет без десет [6] ten to five (4:50)
без да [14] without *(relative conjunction)*
безделник [25] idler, indolent
бездна [18] abyss
безкраен [20] endless
безмесен [7] vegetarian (i.e. without meat)
безпартиен (-ийна) [17] [someone who is] not a party member
безплатен [22] free of charge, gratis
безпокойство [29] anxiety, unrest
безсилен [28] feeble, powerless
безсъзнание [29] unconsciousness ; в безсъзнание съм [29] be unconscious
безутешен [28] inconsolable
бележа (-иш) [7] mark
бележка [7] note; remark ; критични бележки [19] criticisms
бележник [7] notebook, notepad
бели *see* бял
белорусин [23] Belorussian (male)
белоруска [23] Belorussian (female)
бензинов [29] gasoline *(adj.)*
бера [12] pick, gather
бесарабски [29] Bessarabian
бетонен [27] concrete *(adj.)*
беше [6] was *(2sg., 3sg.)*
би [27] would *(2sg., 3sg.)*
библиотека [5] library
бивам [20] occur, be ; така не бива [20] that won't do/can't be ; не бива да пие [23] [one] mustn't drink [it]
бивш [17] ex, former
билет [11] ticket
билка [26] herb
биография [22] biography
биолог [19] biologist
биологичен [18] biological
бира [4] beer
бистря [20] clarify ; бистря политиката [20] discuss politics
бих [27] would *(1sg.)*
биха [27] would *(3pl.)*
бихме [27] would *(1pl.)*
бихте [27] would *(2pl.)*
бия [18] beat
благ [27] gentle, kindly
благоверен [29] pious, faithful ; благоверният съпруг [29] [one's] lord and master; [one's] old man
благодарен [17] grateful
благодарност [9] thanks, gratitude ; Ден на благодарността [9] Thanksgiving Day
благодаря [10] thank, pay gratitude ; благодаря [2] thank you
благоприятен [21] favorable, auspicious
благородство [18] nobility
благоухание [26] fragrance, aroma
блаженство [22] bliss, beatitude
блатенски [21] of the Blaten kingdom area
блед [11] pale
блестя [19] shine, sparkle
близнак [23] twin
близък [10] close ; близки са [10] they are very close friends
блок [8] apartment building
блокирам [29] blockade
блъскам се / блъсна се [29] hit, crash into
блясвам / блесна [29] flash, gleam
блясък [18] brilliant, sparkling
боаз [18] defile, gorge
боб [10] beans
бог [9] god, God ; слава Богу [9] thank God ; Боже [9] Oh God, Oh my God ; Бог да я прости [16] may she rest in peace
богат [7] rich
богатство [23] riches, wealth
богиня [23] goddess
богослужебен [21] liturgical
бодлив [26] prickly; barbed
бодрост [17] liveliness, cheer
бодър [13] lively, cheerful
Боже *see* бог
божествен [29] divine, exquisite
божество [23] divinity, deity
божи [27] God's, divine
бой [17] battle, beating
боклук [14] rubbish, garbage
боледувам [10] be ill ; боледувам от грип [23] have the flu
болен [2] sick, ill ; болен от грип [13] down with the flu ; болни [17] sick people, patients
болест [23] illness, ailment ; тежка болест [27] grave illness
боли *(3d person only)* [12] hurt ; боли ме главата [12] I have a headache ; болят ме очите [12] my eyes hurt
болка [12] pain
болница [6] hospital
бонбон [10] candy
боря се [26] fight, strive
бос [13] barefoot ; ходя бос [13] go barefoot
ботаника [26] botany
ботанически [13] botanical ; ботаническа градина [13] botanical garden
ботуш [29] high boot

Българо-английски речник (Урок 1-30)

боя́ [10] paint
боя́ се [8] fear ; не се́ бо́й [8] don't be afraid ; боя́ се от [24] be afraid of ; не бо́й се [26] don't be afraid
бояджи́я, -и́йка [10] house painter; paint or dye merchant
бояди́свам [10] paint, color; dye
бра́во [10] bravo
брада́ (*also* бради́чка) [12] chin
брада́ [12] beard; chin
брада́т [21] bearded
бра́два [25] axe
бра́к [10] marriage
бра́т (*plural* бра́тя) [8] brother
братовче́д (ка) [2] cousin
брашно́ [20] flour ; цареви́чно брашно́ [20] cornmeal
бреза́ [26] birch
бре́ме (*plural* бремена́) [28] burden, load
бри́дж [14] bridge (card game)
броя́ [3] count
бръ́мбар [26] bug, beetle ; ма́йски бръ́мбар [26] May-bug, chafer (*Melolontha melolontha*)
бря́г, брегъ́т (*plural* брегове́) [20] coast, bank ; на брега́ на море́то [23] on the seacoast
БСП (*pron.* бесепе́) [14] BSP (Bulgarian Socialist Party)
буди́лник [27] alarm clock
бу́дя [18] awaken, arouse
бу́ен, бу́йна [29] blazing, turbulent; unruly
бу́за [12] cheek
бу́ква [8] letter [of alphabet] ; чета́ до после́дната бу́ква [8] read every last word ; кири́лски бу́кви [18] Cyrillic [alphabet] letters
бу́квен [21] letter (*adj.*) ; бу́квени зна́ци [21] alphabet letters, characters
булева́рд [16] boulevard
бу́лка [10] bride
бу́рен [20] stormy, tempestuous
буркан [6] jar, can
бу́ря [29] storm
бу́т [25] leg, round; thigh
бу́там [6] push, shove
бути́лка [22] bottle
бу́чка [25] small lump
бъ́да [7] be
бъ́дещ [9] future (*adj.*) бъ́деще вре́ме [9] future tense ; бъ́деще предвари́телно (вре́ме) [22] past anterior (tense) ; бъ́деще в ми́налото (вре́ме) [22] future in the past (tense) ; бъ́деще предвари́телно в ми́налото [23] future anterior in the past (tense)
Бъ́дни ве́чер [10] Christmas Eve
бъднина́ [23] days to come ; бъднини́ [23] the future ; све́тли бъднини́ [23] a bright future
бъ́зе [19] danewort (*Sambucus ebulus*) ; пра́вя на бъ́зе и копри́ва [19] make mincemeat of
бъ́лгарин [3] Bulgarian (male)
бълг̀ари́ст (ка) [17] specialist in Bulgarian studies
бъ́лгарка [3] Bulgarian (female)
бъ́лгарски [1] Bulgarian; Bulgarian language
бъ́лгарче [13] young Bulgarian
бълха́ [25] flea
бъ́рз [6] [27] fast, quick; urgent ; ста́ва бъ́рзо [6] it's quick, it goes quickly ; на бъ́рза ръка́ [18] hastily ; бъ́рза по́мощ [18] first aid, ambulance
бъ́рзам [4] hurry, be in a hurry
бъ́рша (-еш) [13] wipe, rub
бъ́чва [18] barrel, cask
бюфе́т [22] sideboard, buffet, refreshment bar
бя́гам [24] run, run away; avoid; flee
бя́л, бе́ли [2] white ; бя́л дро́б [12] lung [*see also* дро́б] ; бя́л като платно́ [21] white as a sheet ; сред бя́л де́н [29] in broad daylight
бя́х [6] was (*1sg.*)
бя́ха [6] were (*3pl.*)
бя́хме [6] were (*1pl.*)
бя́хте [6] were (*2pl.*)

в [1] [6] in, into, on. at
в. = ве́к [20]
ваго́н [6] wagon, car
ва́дя [18] take out, get issued
ва́жен [8] important
ва́жност [17] importance
ва́за [17] vase
вака́нция [6] vacation
вали́ (*3d person only*) [12] rain, etc. (precipitation) ; вали́ (дъ́жд) [12] it's raining ; вали́ сня́г [12] it's snowing ; вали́ гра́д [12] it's hailing ; валя́т си́лни дъждове́ [12] it's raining heavily ; вали́ като из ведро́ [12] it's raining buckets
вампи́р [24] vampire
вампирджи́я [24] vampire fighter
вампиря́свам [24] turn into a vampire
вариа́нт [16] variant
варя́ [3] boil, cook
ва́с [10] you (*plural/polite; direct object pronoun*)

Българо-английски речник (урок 1-30)

варя́ [3] boil, cook
вас [10] you (plural/polite; object pronoun)
ваш [8] your, yours (plural/polite)
вглеждам се / вгледам се [26] stare, peer closely
вгра́ждам / вградя́ [26] build in, wall up; immure
вди́гам / вди́гна [6] raise, lift ; вди́гам шу́м [6] make noise ; вди́гам рамене́ [29] shrug shoulders
вди́швам / вди́шам [26] inhale
вдру́гиден [24] the day after tomorrow, the following day
вдълбоча́вам се / вдълбоча́ се (-и́ш) [27] be absorbed, be engrossed
вди́хвам / вди́хна [27] breathe in; inspire
вдя́сно [11] on the right
вегетериа́нец [3] vegetarian (male)
вегетериа́нка [3] vegetarian (female)
ведна́га [4] immediately, at once
веднъ́ж [7] once ; о́ще веднъ́ж [16] again, once more
ведро́ [12] bucket ; вали́ като из ведро́ [12] it's raining buckets
ве́жда [12] eyebrow ; гъ́сти ве́жди [27] bushy eyebrows
век, -ъ́т (plural векове́) [12] century ; XIX в. [20] the 19th century
веку́вам [28] live for ages ; веку́вам та́м [28] live there forever
вели́к [21] great
вели́кден [21] Easter
вели́чие [28] grandeur, greatness
велосипе́д [14] bicycle
вера́нда [23] veranda, porch
ве́рен, вя́рна [10] true, faithful
вя́рно е, че [10] it's true that ; изразя́вам се вя́рно [22] say [it] right
ве́рност [17] truthfulness, veracity
вероя́тен [17] probable
вероя́тно [17] probably
ве́сел [9] happy, gay, lively
ве́стник [6] newspaper
ветрове́ [7] see вя́тър
ве́че [3] already, by now ; сти́га ве́че [16] that's enough already! ; ве́че не се́ ви́жда [20] one can no longer see [it]
ве́чен [18] eternal
ве́чер, -та́ [9] evening ; до́бър ве́чер [9] good evening (fixed phrase) ; ве́чер, вечерта́ [9] in the evening ; та́зи ве́чер [9] this evening ; у́тре ве́чер [9] tomorrow evening
вече́рен [9] evening (adj.)
вече́ря [26] dinner, supper
вече́рям [9] eat dinner
взаимоде́йствие [20] interaction

взи́дан [18] "walled-in"
взи́мам (or взе́мам) / взе́ма [4] take; begin, take to ; вземи́ мо́ливите! [4] pick up the pencils! ; взе́мам си дови́ждане [13] make one's farewells ; взе́мам реше́ние [18] arrive at a decision ; ще ми взе́ме здра́вето [20] it'll be the death of me ; взе́мам ме́рки [20] take steps, take precautions ; взе́мам национа́лни разме́ри [30] take on national proportions
взи́рам се / взра́ се [25] peer
ви [5] you (plural/polite, direct object pronoun)
ви [7] (to) you (plural/polite, indirect object pronoun)
вид, -ъ́т [11] [12] aspect; view, appearance ; (не)свъ́ршен ви́д [12] (im)perfective aspect ; и́мам пред ви́д [19] bear in mind
видеока́мера [5] videocamera
ви́деокасета [12] video cassette
ви́е [1] you (plural/polite subject pronoun)
ви́ждам / ви́дя [3] [4] see ; ви́ж какво́ [12] look, well (topic focuser in conversation) ; де́то (or къде́то) ми очи́ ви́дят [25] wherever my feet lead me ; да би́ ми́рно седя́ло, не би́ чу́до видя́ло [28] that's what comes of asking for trouble
византи́йски [8] Byzantine
ви́кам [12] shout, yell ; ви́кам на во́ля [12] shout to one's heart's content
ви́квам / ви́кна [20] call to, yell at
ви́ла [10] pitchfork
ви́ла [23] villa
ви́лица [10] fork
ви́наги [4] always
ви́но [2] wine
виря́ [20] thrive, flourish
виртуо́з [17] virtuoso
виртуо́зен [18] masterly
висо́к [5] tall, high; elevated; loud
височина́ [20] height, elevation
ви́сш [16] high, supreme ; ви́сше образова́ние [16] higher education ; във ви́сша сте́пен [22] eminently, in the highest degree
вися́ [28] hang, dangle; hang about
ви́тошки [27] of or pertaining to Vitosha
витри́на [27] window [of a shop or public establishment]; showcase
виц [12] joke ; разпра́вям ви́ц [12] tell a joke
ви́я [20] curve, wind
вка́рвам / вка́рам [12] push in, drive in ; вка́рвам го́л [12] score [a goal]
включвам / включа (-иш) [14] include

Българо-английски речник (урок 1-30)

вкус, -ът [7] taste ; по вкуса на всеки човек [7] to everyone's taste
вкусен [6] tasty, delicious
вкъщи [6] home, at home
влага [18] dampness, moisture
владетел [20] [23] ruler, owner
владетелски [23] ruling, ruler's
владея [20] rule, control ; владея език [20] have command of a language
влак [2] train ; пътувам с влак [2] travel by train
власт [20] power, authority
влахо-молдавски [21] Wallacho-Moldavian
влечуго (*plural* влечуги) [26] reptile
вливам / влея [26] infuse, pour into
вливам се / влея се [26] flow into, empty into
влизам / вляза [4] enter, go in
влитам / влетя [26] dash, rush (в into)
влияние [30] influence ; оказвам влияние [30] exert influence
влияя [25] influence
влюбен [14] in love ; влюбени [16] lovers
вляво [11] on the left
вмъквам / вмъкна [21] insert
внасям / внеса [19] import, bring in
внимавам [6] pay attention ; внимавайте, бутате човека [6] careful, you're pushing someone
внимание [14] attention ; вниманието му се притъпи [14] his attention wandered ; обръщам внимание на [23] pay attention to
внимателен [14] attentive
внос [20] import
внук [10] grandson
внучка [10] granddaughter
вода [4] water
водя [8] lead, take
военен [19] military
воин [18] warrior
воистина [22] in truth (*archaic Slavonic*)
воистина воскресе [22] in truth Christ has risen (*ritual Easter formula*)
войвода (*or* воевода) [29] military leader, chieftain
война [7] war
войник [7] soldier ; служа войник [24] do military service
вол [24] ox
волен [18] free, independent
воля [12] will, desire ; викам на воля [12] shout to one's heart's content
вопъл [28] wail, lamentation
воскресе [22] arose (*3sg. aorist, archaic Slavonic*)
впечатление [22] impression ; с впечатление съм [22] be left with the impression
впивам / впия [28] sink, dig ; впивам поглед в [28] fix one's gaze on
впрочем [30] incidentally; in fact
врабче [22] sparrow
врат [12] back of the neck
врата [2] door
вратовръзка [13] necktie
вреден [20] harmful, injurious
вредя [20] harm ; вредя на здравето [20] be bad for one's health ; вредя на очите [20] be hard on one's eyes
време (*plural* времена) [2] [9] time; weather; season ; времето е топло [2] the weather is warm ; в последно време [6] recently ; по това време [7] at about that time ; годишните времена [9] seasons (of the year) ; доброто старо време [11] the good old days ; от време на време [14] from time to time ; време му е [16] it's time for him [to go/do it, etc.] ; по време на [25] during ; в наше време [26] nowadays ; времето не ми стига [26] I'm hard pressed for time ; открай време [27] from time immemorial
време [9] verbal tense ; сегашно време [9] present tense ; бъдеще време [9] future tense ; минало свършено време [12] aorist tense ; минало несвършено време [14] imperfect tense ; минало предварително време [19] past anterior tense
временен [23] temporary
временно [23] for the time being
връзка [13] tie, string, shoelace ; връзки [19] connections
връх, върхът (*plural* върхове) [11] summit; tip
връчвам / връча (-иш) [18] hand, deliver, present
връщам / върна [5] [20] return; turn away (*transitive*)
връщам се / върна се [11] return, go back
вря [9] boil (*intransitive*)
все [10] [29] always, constantly; surely ; все ме няма [10] I'm never there ; все още избирам [10] I'm still looking ; все едно и също [10] [it's] always the same thing ; все ми е едно [16] it doesn't make any difference ; все пак [18] nevertheless
всевъзможен [22] all sorts of, every possible

Българо-английски речник (урок 1-30)

всéки, всяка, всяко [6] every ; всéки момéнт [6] any minute ; на всяка ценá [12] at any price, at all costs, absolutely
всеóбщ [28] universal, general
всúчко [2] all, everything ; всúчко шéст [6] six in all ; всúчко хýбаво [2] all the best
вслýшвам се / вслýшам се [18] listen closely
всъщност [29] actually, in fact
всякакъв [17] all sorts of
втóри [8] second ; втóра мáйка [10] stepmother ; втóри бащá [10] stepfather
втóрник [9] Tuesday
вýйна [22] aunt (mother's brother's wife)
вýйчо (*plural* вýйчовци) [10] uncle (mother's brother)
вхóд [8] entrance
входящ [23] incoming ; входящ нóмер [23] "incoming number" on official correspondence
вчéра [9] yesterday ; вчéра следобéд [9] yesterday afternoon ; вчéра сутринтá [9] yesterday morning
вчéрашен [9] yesterday's
във = в [7]
въвéждам / въведá [20] bring in, introduce
въглища [27] coal
въдица [22] fish-hook; fishing rod
въжé [22] rope, line
въздéйствие [21] influence, impact
въздух [4] air ; на въздух [24] outdoors, in the open air
въздъхвам / въздъхна [29] sigh
възлáгам / възлóжа (-иш) [21] assign, delegate [a task]
възмóжен [23] possible
възмóжност [27] possibility, chance
възнúквам / възнúкна [21] arise, originate, come into being
възпалéние [23] inflammation
възпúтавам / възпúтам [20] bring up, educate
възпитáние [29] upbringing, education
възпрепятствувам (*or* възпрепятствам) [22] prevent, hinder
възприéмам / възприéма [18] perceive, apprehend
възпявам / възпéя [28] praise in song, glorify
възраст, -тá [27] age ; отúвам на [нéчия] възраст [27] be appropriate to [one's] age
възрастен [4] adult; elderly
възрастни [4] grownups

възстановявам / възстановя [23] restore, rebuild
възтóрг [10] delight, rapture ; предизвúквам възтóрг у [10] enrapture
възхищáвам / възхитя [17] enrapture, fill with admiration
възхищáвам се / възхитя се [22] admire, be enraptured by
вълк (*plural* вълци) [8] wolf
вълна [21] wool
вълнен, -ена [13] woolen
вълнýвам [17] excite, agitate, disturb
вълнýвам се [17] be agitated, excited ; не сé вълнýвай [17] take it easy
вълшéбник [11] magician, wizard
вън [11] out
външен [24] outside, outward, external
въобщé [11] in general; at all
въпрéки [19] despite ; въпрéки че [19] despite the fact that
въпрóс [11] question ; постáвям въпрóс [30] pose a question
вървя [3] walk, move, go ; вървя с [10] go well with ; вървя си [10] get going ; вървя под ръкá [14] walk arm in arm ; днéс нáма да ми вървú [14] today's not going to be my day
върлýвам [24] rage, run rampant
въртя [22] turn, spin ; въртя опáшка [22] wag tail
въртя се [14] turn around, rotate; move
върху [17] on, over ; градя върху оснóвата на [21] build on the foundations of
върша (-иш) [29] do, commit ; върша домакúнска рáбота [29] do housework
въстáние [20] uprising, rebellion
вътре [11] in, inside
вътрешен [18] internal
вяра [20] faith, belief
вярвам [7] believe
вярване (*plural* -ния) [24] belief
вярно [22] right, correctly
вятър (*plural* ветровé) [2] [7] wind ; úма сúлен вятър [2] there's a strong wind, it's very windy ; вятър рáбота [25] nonsense, baloney

г. = годúна [9]
г. = грáд [17]
гáбровски [30] Gabrovo (*adj.*)
гад [29] vermin
гадúна [29] animal, brute

Българо-английски речник (уроk 1-30)

газѝран [20] fizzy, carbonated
гàзя [26] wade, tread on ; гàзя калтà [26] flounder through the mud
г-жа = госпожà [21]
гàйда [16] bagpipe
гàма [18] scale, gamut
гàра [5] station
гàрга [29] crow, rook
гарнитỳра [4] garnish ; пържòла с гарнитỳра [4] steak with the trimmings
гàсна [28] die out, fade away
гàф [19] gaffe, blunder
гдè = дè, къдè [29]
ГДР (*pron.* гèдерè) [14] GDR (DDR, former East Germany)
гердàн [14] necklace, collar
гермàнец [23] German (male)
гермàнка [23] German (female)
гермàнски [14] German
герòй [23] hero; character (in a literary work)
ги [5] them *(direct object pronoun)*
гѝздав [27] pretty, comely
гимнàзия [3] academically oriented high school
гимнастѝк, -ѝчка [19] gymnast
главà [12] head ; двè децà на главàта [17] two kids to support ; трѝя му сòл на главàта [25] haul him over the coals
глàвен [9] main, chief ; глàвна рòля [27] the lead
глàвно [9] mainly
главобòлие [25] headache
глагòл [21] verb
глагòлен [21] verbal
глагòлица [21] Glagolitic [alphabet]
глàд [7] hunger
глàден [2] hungry ; на глàдно сърцè [22] on an empty stomach
глàс, -ът (*plural* гласовè) [12] voice ; на глàс [26] aloud ; в едѝн глàс [30] unanimously
гласỳвам [25] vote
глася̀ [24] state, indicate; intend, prepare
глèдам [4] [9] look at; look after ; глèдам на кàрти [18] read one's fortune
глèдна тòчка [22] point of view
глèзен [12] ankle
глèзя [28] spoil, pamper
глòба [17] fine, penalty
глобя̀вам / глобя̀ [19] fine, impose a penalty
глòждя [27] gnaw; rankle
глỳпав [20] stupid, foolish
глỳпост [28] foolishness, nonsense

глътвам / глътна [7] [take a] swallow
глътка [3] swallow, gulp
г-н = господѝн [19]
гнездò [13] nest
гнỳс ме е [12] feel nauseated
го [5] him, it *(direct object pronoun)*
гòвор [18] speech, dialect
говорѝм [30] spoken
говòря [3] speak, talk ; говòря в пòлза на [29] argue in favor of
годèж [29] engagement, betrothal
годенѝк [10] fiancé
годенѝца [10] fiancée
годѝна [3] year ; през 1975 г. [9] in 1975 ; мѝне не мѝне годѝна [19] every year or so ; днèс навършвам 20 годѝни [23] I'm 20 years old today ; учèбна годѝна [30] academic year
годѝшен [9] yearly, annual ; годѝшните временà [9] seasons [of the year] ; 25 годѝшен съм [29] be 25 years old
годѝшнина [10] anniversary
гòзба [5] dish
гòл [12] goal (in sports) ; вкàрвам гòл [12] score [a goal] ; изпỳскам гòл [12] miss [a goal]
гòл [17] naked
големинà [20] size, magnitude
голя̀м, голèми [2] large, big ; голèмите [4] big ones, adults ; голя̀мо движèние [12] lots of traffic ; до голя̀ма стèпен [17] to a great extent ; голя̀м лъжèц [25] consummate liar, swindler ; ѝмам голя̀м успèх [27] be wildly successful ; пò-голя̀мата чàст [30] most, the bulk
гòня [21] chase; persecute; seek after
горà [3] wood, forest
гòрд [17] proud
гордèя се [20] take pride in ; гордèя се с [20] be proud of
гòрдост [22] pride
гòре [11] up ; гòре-дòлу [11] more or less
гореизлòжен [17] aforementioned
гòрен [26] upper, higher, top
горèщ [11] hot
горещинà [20] heat
горѝво [29] fuel
горкѝят, горкàта [18] wretched one, poor thing
гòрко [17] woe (to someone)
гòрски [26] wood, forest *(adj.)*
гòрски [26] forest ranger
гòрък (*and* горчѝв) [17] bitter
горя̀ [11] burn
Гòспод [27] God, the Lord ; едѝн Гòспод знàе [27] God only knows

Българо-английски речник (урок 1-30)

господа́ [3] gentlemen ; да́ми и господа́ [3] ladies and gentlemen (*vocative*)
господа́р [20] master
господи́н [1] Sir, Mr.
госпожа́ (*plural* госпо́жи) [1] Ma'am, Mrs.
госпо́жица [1] Miss
гост (*plural* го́сти) [5] [8] guest ; и́двам на го́сти [5] come/go over to visit
го́стенин [28] guest (male)
го́стенка [28] guest (female)
гостоприе́мство [28] hospitality
госту́вам [25] stay with, visit ; то́й ми госту́ва [25] he's staying with me
готва́рски [7] cooking, culinary ; готва́рска кни́га [7] cookbook
го́твя [4] prepare, cook
го́твя се [9] prepare, get ready
гото́в [6] prepared, ready
гоща́вам / гостя́ [29] entertain, treat
гра́бвам / гра́бна [18] snatch up, carry off
град [12] hail
град, -ъ́т (*plural* градове́) [6] [7] town, city ; в г. Со́фия [17] in the city of Sofia ; затъ́нтено градче́ [25] godforsaken little town
гради́на [3] garden ; зоологи́ческа гради́на [19] zoo ; гра́дска гради́на [22] town garden
гради́нка [18] small garden
гра́дски [22] town, municipal; urban ; гра́дска гради́на [22] town garden
граждани́н [22] citizen
гра́жданка [23] citizen (female)
грамати́чен (and грамати́чески) [30] grammatical
грани́ца [24] border, boundary; limit
гранича́р [18] border guard
граф [26] count, earl
графи́чен [21] graphic
гра́ча (-иш) [29] croak, caw
гре́йвам / гре́йна [18] come out, start to shine (of sun)
грехо́вност [24] sinfulness, wickedness
греша́ (-и́ш) [7] sin, err
гре́шен [26] sinful; wrong
гре́шка [3] mistake
гре́я [9] warm, heat up; shine ; слъ́нцето гре́е [9] the sun is shining
гри́ва [26] mane
гри́жа се (-иш) [23] care ; гри́жа се (за) [23] look after/take care of
грип [13] influenza, flu ; бо́лен от грип [13] down with the flu
гроб [16] grave
гро́бища (*plural*) [29] cemetery
гробни́ца [23] tomb
гро́зде [9] grapes (*collective*)
гроздобе́р [24] grape-gathering, grape harvest
гро́здов [2] [made] of grapes
гро́зен [24] ugly, hideous
гръб, гърбъ́т (*plural* гърбове́) [12] back ; обръ́щам се с гръб [17] turn one's back
гръд, -та́ (*or* гърди́) [12] chest
грък, гъркъ́т (*plural* гъ́рци) [6] [23] Greek (male)
гръм, гърмъ́т (*plural* гръмове́ *or* гърмове́) [16] thunder(bolt)
гръмоте́вица [24] peal of thunder
гръ́мък [27] loud, high-sounding ; гръ́мка сла́ва [27] resounding fame
гръ́цки [20] Greek (*adj.*)
гря́х, грехъ́т (*plural* грехове́) [18] sin
гу́бя [14] lose
гу́ма [29] rubber; tire (for vehicle)
гу́ша [12] neck, throat
гу́щер [24] lizard
гъ́ба [4] mushroom ; омле́т с гъ́би [4] mushroom omelet
гъба́р [19] gatherer, grower or seller of mushrooms
гъдула́р [26] gudulka player
гъду́лка [16] gudulka (folk violin similar to rebec)
гъ́лтам [8] swallow ; гъ́лтам лека́рство [8] take medicine
гъ́мза [22] particular sort of dark red wine
гъ́рбом [26] with/on one's back
гърда́ [12] breast, bosom
гъркѝня [23] Greek (female)
гъ́рло [12] throat
гъ́рци *see* грък
гъст [27] thick, heavy ; гъ́сти ве́жди [27] bushy eyebrows
гюве́ч [20] earthenware pot; Balkan one-pot stew

да [5] (*subordinating/modal conjunction*) ; и́скам да до́йда [5] I want to come ; не мо́га да до́йда [5] I can't come ; ако и да [9] even though ; да сте жи́ви и здра́ви [11] here's to your life and health ; и то́й да до́йде [13] he should come too ; да вле́зе ли? [16] should he come in? ; да ме уби́еш [29] for the life of me
да [27] if ; да зна́ех [27] had I known
да́ [1] yes
да́вам / дам (даде́ш) [9] give; allow ; дай [4] give (*imperative*) ; да́вам под на́ем [12] rent out ; да́вам на

Българо-английски речник (урок 1-30)

заем [12] loan ; дадено явление [20] the given phenomenon ; давам душа за [27] be crazy about
давя [24] drown; suffocate
даже [11] even
дай *see* давам
дайчово хоро [16] Daicho's dance (name of a folkdance)
далече (and далеч) [4] far ; far away
далечина [26] distance
дали [11] whether, if *(relative/question particle)* ; дали има смисъл? [11] does it make any sense? ; не зная дали има смисъл [11] I don't know whether it makes any sense
дама [3] lady ; дами и господа [3] ladies and gentlemen *(vocative)*
данни [17] data
дано [10] let's wish, if only, I hope ; дано пристигне навреме [10] let's hope it gets there on time
дантела [16] lace
данък [17] tax
дар, -ът *(plural* дарове) [23] gift, donation; talent
дарба [27] gift, talent
датирам [23] date, go back to
датчанин [23] Dane (male)
датчанка [23] Dane (female)
два [6] two *(masculine)*
двайсет [6] twenty
двама [6] two *(masculine animate)*
дванайсет [6] twelve
две [2] [6] two *(feminine, neuter; in counting)* ; зная и две и двеста [29] adapt to circumstances ; с две думи [30] in short ; от двете страни [30] on both sides
двегодишен [29] two-year old *(adj.)* ; two-year long *(adj.)* ; biennial
двеста [9] two hundred ; зная и две и двеста [29] be adaptable
движа се (-иш) [14] move, go
движение [12] movement; traffic ; голямо движение [12] lots of traffic ; правила на пътното движение [12] traffic laws, rules of the road
двойка [10] [13] pair; "2" (failing mark in school)
двойкаджия, -ийка [10] high school dropout
двор [11] yard ; играя на двора [11] play in the yard
дворец [19] palace ; Народен дворец на културата [19] People's Palace of Culture
двуцветен [13] two-colored

де [10] *(intensifying particle)* ; вземете де! [10] so take [some] already!
дебел [22] thick, fat ; с дебели очи [22] shameless
дебют [23] debut, opening
девер [22] brother-in-law (husband's brother)
девет [6] nine
деветдесет [6] ninety
девети [8] ninth
деветнайсет [6] nineteen
деветстотин [9] nine hundred
деди *(pl. only)* [28] ancestors, forebears
деец [30] worker, figure ; просветен деец [30] educationalist
дежурен [10] on duty
дежурство [10] duty
дейност [21] activity
декан [18] dean
декември [9] December
декларация [23] declaration
декламирам [7] declaim, recite
делничен [28] workaday, humdrum
дело [20] deed, achievement; case
деля [20] divide, split up
демократически [14] democratic
демокрация [13] democracy
демонстрирам [23] demonstrate, display
ден -ят, *(plural* дни, 2 дена *or* деня) [4] [6] day ; рожден ден [5] birthday ; добър ден *(fixed accent)* ; [6] hello, good day ; днешен ден [9] this very day ; други ден [9] the day after tomorrow ; онзи ден [9] the day before yesterday ; през деня [9] in the daytime ; Ден на благодарността [9] Thanksgiving Day ; тези дни [22] one of these days ; трая от ден до пладне [29] be short-lived ; сред бял ден [29] in broad daylight
дера [12] skin, fleece, tear, scratch
десен, дясна [11] right (as opposed to left)
десерт [6] dessert
десет [6] ten
десетилетие [23] decade
десетина [23] ten or so; half a score
десетки [20] ten ; няколко десетки думи [20] a few score words
дете *(plural* деца) [1] [3] child ; от дете [12] since childhood
детински [13] childish ; детински работи [13] kid's stuff
детинство [22] childhood
дето [16] where[ever], who, for ; дето *(or* където) ми очи видят [25] wherever my feet lead me
джафкам / джафна [23] yap

Българо-английски речник (урок 1-30)

джами́я [24] mosque
джи́нси [13] jeans
джип [29] jeep
диале́кт [21] dialect
диалектоло́жки [30] dialectal, dialectological
див [29] wild
ди́гам = вди́гам [29]
ди́зелов [29] diesel *(adj.)*
дика́ня [18] threshing board
дикту́вам [14] dictate
дим, -ът [4] smoke
ди́плома [18] diploma
дире́ктен [8] direct
дире́ктор (ка) [13] director
дисерта́ция [17] dissertation
дисципли́на [29] discipline
длан [12] palm of the hand
длъ́жен [16] indebted, obliged
дне́вник [10] diary
днес [1] today
дне́шен [9] today's ; дне́шен ден [9] this very day
до [2] [5] [6] by, near, next to; [up] to; until ; то́ е до врата́та [2] it's by the door
доби́вам / доби́я [27] get, acquire
доби́тък [18] cattle, livestock
добре́ [2] well, fine; O.K. ; добре́ дошли́! [2] welcome! ; добре́ ли си сега́? [3] are you O.K. now? ; добре́ зава́рили [27] well-found *(answer to добре́ дошли́)*
доброво́лно [29] voluntarily
добродушен [22] good-natured, kind-hearted
добросъ́вестен [26] conscientious
добруджа́нски [30] Dobrudzha *(adj.)*
добъ́р [2] good ; до́бър ве́чер [9] good evening *(fixed phrase)* ; до́бър ден *(fixed accent)* [6] hello, good day ; добро́ у́тро [9] good morning ; добро́то ста́ро вре́ме [11] the good old days
дове́ждам / доведа́ [23] bring; bring about, lead to
дове́рие [26] confidence, trust ; отна́сям се с дове́рие към [26] put trust in, rely on
доверя́вам / доверя́ [17] entrust ; доверя́вам се на [17] confide in
дове́чера [9] this evening
дови́ждане [8] goodbye ; взе́мам си дови́ждане [13] make one's farewells
дово́лен [6] pleased, satisfied ; дово́лен до блаже́нство [22] blissfully content
довъ́ршвам / довъ́рша (-иш) [22] finish off, bring to a close
дога́рям / догоря́ [26] burn low, burn out
догоди́на [7] next year
дого́нвам / дого́ня [26] run after, overtake
доживя́вам / доживе́я [24] live to see
до́йда *see* дохо́ждам
дока́рвам / дока́рам [10] drive to, bring to
докато́ [9] while, until ; докато́ не [13] until
докла́д [12] report, [scholarly] paper ; изна́сям докла́д [19] read/deliver a paper ; плена́рен докла́д [19] keynote paper
доко́лкото [20] as far as
до́ктор [17] doctor
докуме́нт [17] document ; срок за пода́ване на докуме́нти [20] application deadline
докъ́м [21] until approximately
дола́вям / доловя́ [26] catch, detect, make out
до́лен [20] lower
доли́вам / доле́я [26] top up, pour in more
долина́ [20] valley
доли́там / долетя́ [13] come flying
до́лу [11] down ; го́ре-до́лу [11] more or less
дом, -ът *(plural* домове́*)* [7] home, house ; у до́ма [10] at home
домаки́н [23] householder, proprietor, manager, host
домаки́нски [29] household *(adj.)* ; върша́ домаки́нска ра́бота [29] do housework
домаки́ня [23] householder (female), proprietress, housewife, hostess
дома́т [6] tomato
дома́тен [20] tomato *(adj.)*
дома́шен [2] [7] [30] homemade; home *(adj.)*; domestic
дома́шно [8] homework
доми́там / домета́ [26] sweep up, finish sweeping
домързя́ва ме / домързи́ ме [18] *(3rd person only)* not feel like, be too lazy
дона́сям / донеса́ [7] bring
допи́вам / допи́я [28] drink up, finish drinking
допу́скам / допу́сна [27] allow, admit; suppose
допъ́лвам / допъ́лня [17] supplement, expand
допълне́ние [8] addition, supplement
допълни́телен [23] additional, supplementary
доразви́вам / доразви́я [21] develop fully, elaborate

Българо-английски речник (урок 1-30)

дори́ [8] even
досега́ [6] until now
доско́ро [23] until recently
досмеша́ва ме / досмеше́е ме *(3d person only)* [13] feel like laughing
досрамя́ва ме / досраме́е ме *(3d person only)* [13] feel ashamed
до́ста [22] fairly; a good deal
доста́тъчен [7] enough
дости́гам / дости́гна [18] reach, achieve
достиже́ние [21] achievement
досто́йнство [18] worth, dignity
досто́ен [25] worthy, well-deserved, just
досто́йно [25] with dignity, in a fitting manner
дотога́ва [22] until then, by that time ; дотога́ва, докато [22] until
дохо́ждам / до́йда [5] come, arrive
доча́квам / доча́кам [28] wait for; live to see
дочу́ване [12] goodbye (on the phone)
дошъ́л / дошла́ / дошли́ [11] come *(active participle)* ; добре́ дошъ́л [11] welcome *(to a male friend)* ; добре́ дошла́ [11] welcome *(to a female friend)* ; добре́ дошли́! [11] welcome *(to group or formal acquaintance)*
дра́г [2] [3] dear ; Дра́ги Бо́б, [2] Dear Bob, *(beginning of a letter)* ; дра́го ми е [21] I'm pleased
дра́зня [23] irritate
дре́вен [20] ancient
треси́рам [16] train, break in
дре́ха [10] article of clothing ; дре́хи [10] clothes
дро́б, -ъ́т *(plural* дро́бове *or* дробо́ве*)* [12] lung *(see also* бя́л дро́б*)* ; че́рен дро́б [12] liver
дро́бче [23] liver [food] ; пи́лешки дро́бчета [23] chicken livers
дру́г [2] [7] other, another; next ; на дру́гата спи́рка [7] at the next stop ; дру́ги де́н [9] the day after tomorrow ; дру́гата но́щ [9] tomorrow night ; дру́гия пъ́т [17] the next time (adverb of time) ; една́ до дру́га [23] next to each other ; еди́н от дру́г [30] from one another
дру́гаде [19] elsewhere ; ни́къде дру́гаде [19] nowhere else
друга́р (ка) [1] comrade
друга́рче [13] playfellow, playmate
дру́го [16] other, rest ; дру́гото ще е наре́д [16] the rest will be O.K.
другове́рец [24] person of another faith
дру́жба [20] friendship; society
дръ́нкам / дрънча́ (-и́ш) [27] rattle, clank
дръ́пвам / дръ́пна [22] pull, tug

дръ́пвам се / дръ́пна се [27] stand clear
ду́ма [7] word ; за какво́ ста́ва ду́ма? [11] what's the matter, what's it about? ; ста́ва ду́ма за [16] it's about ; с две́ ду́ми [30] in short
ду́пка [24] hole, gap
ду́х, -ъ́т *(plural* ду́хове *or* духове́*)* [18] spirit
ду́хам blow ; ду́ха [1] it's blowing, there is air coming
душа́ [27] soul, heart ; да́вам душа́ за [27] be crazy about
ду́ши [6] people *(counting form)* ; ко́лко ду́ши [6] how many people
дъ́жд, -ъ́т *(plural* дъждове́*)* [12] rain ; валя́т си́лни дъждове́ [12] it's raining heavily ; проли́вен дъ́жд [28] driving rain
дълбо́к [19] deep
дълбочина́ [20] depth
дъ́лг, -ъ́т [16] debt
дъ́лго [8] [28] [for] a long time
дължина́ [20] length
дължа́ (-и́ш) [29] owe
дъ́лъг [2] long
дъне́р [26] trunk, stump
дъ́но [26] bottom
дърве́н (-ена) [13] wooden
дърво́ *(plural* дърве́та*)* [7] tree
дърво́ *(plural* дърва́*)* [11] wood
държа́ (-и́ш) [11] hold, keep
държа́ се здра́во [21] hold tight, hold fast
държа́ва [20] state
държа́вен [20] state, public
дъ́х [8] breath, wind ; пое́мам [си] дъ́х [8] catch one's breath
дъщеря́ [10] daughter
дя́до *(plural* дя́довци*)* [8] [10] grandfather ; Дя́до Мра́з [10] Jack Frost ; Дя́до Ко́леда [10] Santa Claus
дя́сна *see* де́сен

е [1] is *(3d singular); see* съм
европе́ец [23] European (male)
европе́йка [23] European (female)
европе́йски [8] European
е́втин [9] cheap, inexpensive
егои́зъм [22] egotism
едва́ [19] with difficulty, hardly, just ; едва́ ли [19] hardly, not likely ; едва́ по́-къ́сно [30] not until later
е́ди [17] ; е́ди-ко́й си [17] so-and-so ; е́ди-ка́к си [17] such-and-such ; е́ди-какво́ си [17] in such-and-such a way ; е́ди-кога́ си [17] at such-and-

Българо-английски речник (урок 1-30)

such a time
един [2] [3] one, a *(masculine)* ; един и същ [10] the same, one and the same ; един Господ знае [27] God only knows ; един такъв [28] someone like, one such as ; от/на един път [29] all at once ; в един глас [30] unanimously ; един от друг [30] from one another
единайсет [6] eleven
единен [21] uniform, united
единствен, -ена [11] single, only
единство [30] unity, uniformity
една [3] one *(feminine)* ; в една стая с [10] in the same room as ; една до друга [23] next to each other
еднакво [30] equally, alike
еднакъв [30] identical, the same
едно [2] [3] one *(neuter; in counting)* ; все ми е едно [16] it doesn't make any difference
едновременен [11] simultaneous
едър [9] large, robust ; на едро [9] wholesale
езеро [3] lake, pond
език [3] language, tongue ; роден език [22] native language ; литературен език [30] standard language
езиков [30] language *(adj.)*, linguistic
ей! [1] hey, oh ; ей толкова [24] this much *(conversational device)* ; ей там [25] all the way over there
екземпляр [19] copy
екзотика [7] exotica, exoticism
екзотичен [5] exotic
екскурзиант [29] tourist, hiker
екскурзия [8] excursion
експедиция [17] expedition, field trip
ела [5] come *(imperative of* дойда*)* ела да ти полея [13] come let me pour water [over your hands]
елегантен [5] elegant
електрически [20] electrical
електричество [20] electricity
елемент [20] element
елен [8] deer, stag
елинистичен [23] Hellenic
елха [13] fir tree ; новогодишна елха [13] New Year's tree
емоционален [18] emotional
епиграфика [23] epigraphy
епизод [22] episode
епоха [23] epoch
ера [9] era ; преди н.е. [9] B.C. ; от н.е. [9] A.D.
ерген [11] bachelor
есен, -та [9] fall, autumn
естествен [18] natural

естествено [21] naturally, of course
естетически [23] aesthetic
етаж [8] floor (of a multi-story building)
етап [30] stage
етнически [20] ethnic
ето [2] here *(pointing)*
етърва [22] sister-in-law (husband's brother's wife)
ефектен [5] effective
ефенди [1] effendi, sir *(archaic term of address)*

жаден [2] thirsty
жал [19] pity, sorrow ; жал ми е [19] I'm sorry, it grieves me
жалко [11] too bad, pity
жега [27] sweltering heat
желание [14] wish, desire
желая [7] wish, desire
железен, желязна [22] iron, steel-like
желязо [27] iron, iron bar
жена [2] woman, wife
женен, -ена [10] married
женски [16] women's, female, feminine
женя [11] marry off
женя се [11] get married
жертва [29] sacrifice, victim
жив [11] live, living; lively ; жив да го оплачеш [11] it makes your heart bleed to see him ; да сте живи и здрави [11] here's to your life and health
живея [3] live
живот [9] life ; в живота [16] in the course of life, in daily life
животинче [13] little animal
животно [8] animal ; права на животните [12] animal rights
живущ [17] resident, residing
жилетка [12] waistcoat, cardigan sweater
жилище [27] lodging, residence ; самостоятелно жилище [27] separate quarters
жилищен [8] residential ; жилищен комплекс [8] housing development, block of apartments
житие [21] saint's life
ЖК = жилищен квартал [17] residential district
журналист (ка) [5] journalist
жълт [8] yellow

Българо-английски речник (урок 1-30)

за [1] [6] [10] [11] for, to; about; here's to ; за къде́ пъту́вате [1] where are you traveling to ; за съжале́ние [1] unfortunately ; за две́ се́дмици [6] for two weeks ; кажи́ ни за тя́х [10] tell us about them ; зна́я за не́го [10] I know about him ; за мно́го годи́ни [11] many happy returns ; за какво́ ста́ва ду́ма? [11] what's it about? ; за разнообра́зие [16] for a change ; за ра́злика от [16] as opposed to ; са́мо за ня́колко годи́ни [20] in the space of just a few years ; гласу́вам за́ [25] vote in favor of

за да [11] (purpose) ; за да не ста́ва тече́ние [11] so there won't be a draft

заба́вен [11] amusing

забеле́жка [19] note, observation

забеля́звам / забеле́жа (-иш) [5] notice, spot

забо́ждам / забода́ [13] stick, pin

заболя́ва (ме) / заболи́ (ме) (3d person only) [12] start to hurt

заболя́вам / заболе́я [12] get sick

заболя́вания [19] [cases of] illness ; онкологи́чни заболя́вания [19] [cases of] cancer

забра́вям / забра́вя [7] forget

забра́дка [16] scarf, head covering

забраня́вам / забраня́ [18] forbid

забръмча́вам, забръмча́ (-и́ш) [22] begin to buzz

завали́ва / завали́ (3d person only) [12] begin to precipitate

зава́рвам / зава́ря [27] find ; добре́ зава́рили [27] well-found (answer to добре́ дошли́)

заведе́ние [24] establishment, enterprise; public place

заве́ждам / заведа́ [10] take somewhere, lead

заверя́вам / заверя́ [17] notarize, endorse

заве́са [26] curtain

завеща́вам / завеща́я [28] bequeath

зави́вам / зави́я [6] turn, bend, wrap ; зави́вам зад ъ́гъла [26] turn the corner

зави́вка [25] blanket, wrap

зави́наги [16] forever

завися́ [14] depend ; зави́си от ва́с [14] it depends on you ; зави́си то́й какво́ ще ка́же [14] it depends what he will say ; зави́си от гле́дната то́чка [22] it depends on your point of view

завли́чам / завлека́ (-че́ш) [18] drag off, wash away

заво́д [23] factory, plant

заво́й [29] turn, bend

завръ́щам се / завъ́рна се [18] turn, return

завъ́рзвам / завъ́ржа (-еш) [13] tie ; завъ́рзвам връ́зките на обу́вки [13] tie [one's] shoelaces

завъртя́вам / завъртя́ [26] turn, spin

завъ́ршвам / завъ́рша (-иш) [17] finish, wind up

зага́дъчен [26] enigmatic, mysterious

заги́вам / заги́на [17] perish, die

загла́вие [13] title

загле́ждам / загле́дам [26] begin to look at; look steadily at ; загле́ждам се по [26] stare at

загря́вам / загре́я [19] heat up; catch on

загу́бвам / загу́бя [19] lose; waste

загу́бвам се / загу́бя се [19] get lost

зад [13] behind, beyond ; зад ъ́гъла [14] around the corner

зада́вам / зада́м (-даде́ш) [17] give, assign ; зада́вам въпро́с [17] ask a question

зада́вам се / зада́м се (-даде́ш) [25] appear, come into view

зада́ча [16] task, assignment

за́ден [14] back, rear (adj.)

за́дник [12] behind, rear end

заду́шен [4] stuffy

задължа́вам / задължа́ (-и́ш) [20] oblige, bind

задълже́ние [20] duty, obligation

задължи́телен [28] compulsory, obligatory

задъ́лго [23] for a long time

задъ́ржам / задържа́ (-и́ш) [21] keep, hold back

за́едно [5] together

за́ек [22] rabbit

зае́мам, зае́ма [12] take up, occupy

зае́мка [30] loanword

зае́т [7] busy, occupied

заинтересо́ван [23] concerned, partial ; заинтересо́вани лица́ [23] parties concerned

заинтригу́вам [29] intrigue, arouse curiosity

зака́рвам / зака́рам [23] take, drive over

зака́чвам / закача́ (-и́ш) [13] hang, suspend

зака́чвам се / закача́ се (-и́ш) [22] get caught on

закипя́вам / закипя́ [18] begin to boil; be in full swing

заклю́чвам / заклю́ча (-иш) [8] lock

закра́тко [11] for a short while

закри́вам / закри́я [23] hide, shelter; shut down

заку́свам / заку́ся [11] eat breakfast

заку́ска [10] [22] breakfast; snack, hors d'oeuvre

Българо-английски речник (урок 1-30)

закъснéние [14] delay; tardiness ; с мáлко закъснéние [14] a little late
закъснявам / закъснéя [7] be late
зáла [12] hall ; всé еднó си в зáлата [12] it's just like being in the concert hall
залáвям се / заловя́ се [22] catch hold of; set about
залúвам / залéя [23] overflow
залúвам се от смях [23] roar with laughter
залиня́вам / залинéя [26] languish, pine
зáлък [26] bite, mouthful; morsel
заля́зва / залéзе (3d person) [9] set (of the sun)
заменя́м / заменя́ [19] substitute, replace
замéствам / замéстя [30] replace, substitute
заминáвам / замúна [9] leave, depart
замúрам / замрá [23] die away, decline ; [23] живóтът в градá замря́ the town was dead
замúслен [27] thoughtful, preoccupied
замúсленост [27] pensiveness, reverie
замрáквам / замрáкна [29] be overtaken by night
занáсям / занесá [7] carry, take to
занаят [23] craft, trade; vocation
занаятчúйски [30] craft (adj.) ; занаятчúйско произвóдство [30] craft industry
зáник (poetic) [28] sunset, decline
занимáвам [11] interest, occupy
занимáвам се (с) [11] be occupied [with]
зáпад [16] west
зáпаден [21] western
зáпадноевропéйски [17] West European
запáлвам / запáля [16] light, turn on
зáпис [13] recording
запúсвам / запúша (-еш) [17] write down, record
зáписка [20] note, recording
запúтвам / запúтам [21] inquire [of]
заплáха [23] threat
заплáщам / заплатя́ [22] pay, pay up
заплúтам / заплетá [16] braid, intertwine
заплýвам [26] begin to swim
заповя́двам / заповя́дам [5] command, order ; заповя́дай [5] help yourself
запознáвам / запознáя [14] acquaint someone with
запознáвам се / запознáя се [10] meet, get acquainted
запóмням / запóмня [9] remember
запóчвам / запóчна [6] begin
заприлúчвам / заприлúчам [18] begin to resemble
запълвам / запълня [16] fill, fill up

запътвам се / запътя се [22] set out, be off
запъхтя́н [22] out of breath
запя́вам / запéя [22] begin to sing, break into song
зарáвям / заровя́ [23] bury
зарáдвам [19] please, delight
зарáдвам се [12] cheer up
зарáди [13] for the sake of, because of
зарáствам / зарáсна [27] heal, close up
заря́звам / зарéжа (-еш) [25] abandon, give up
засвидéтелствувам [20] testify, bear witness, certify
засвúрвам / засвúря [29] begin to play, strike up (instrument)
засегá [9] at present; for the time being
заслепя́вам / заслепя́ [19] blind, dazzle
заслóн [28] shelter, refuge
заслужáвам / заслýжа (-иш) [11] deserve, be worthy of
засмя́н [22] smiling ; засмя́н до ушú [22] grinning from ear to ear
заспúвам / заспя́ [14] fall asleep
застъпвам / застъпя [30] step over; represent, propound
затвáрям / затвóря [3] [4] close ; затвáрям вратáта под носá [на] [13] shut the door in [someone's] face
затвóр [24] prison; imprisonment
затвóрен, -ена [2] closed
затовá [5] therefore, thus
затрýпвам / затрýпам [11] cover up, bury under; pile up ; затрýпвам с въпрóси [11] burden with questions
затъжáвам се / затъжá се (-úш) [30] begin to miss
затънтен [25] obscure, desolate ; затънтено градчé [25] godforsaken little town
зáхар, -тá [12] sugar
захладня́вам / захладнéя [27] turn cool
захъ́рквам / захъ́ркам [25] start snoring
зашúвам / зашúя [19] sew up, sew in ; зашúвам кóпче [19] sew on a button
защúта [12] defense
защищáвам / защитя́ [17] defend
защó [3] why
защóто [3] because
заявя́вам / заявя́ [25] declare, announce; testify
звáние [25] rank, title
звездá [17] star
звук [20] sound
звýков [21] sound (adj.)
звучá (-úш) [12] sound, resound ; звучú добрé [12] that sounds good
звънéц [5] bell

Българо-английски речник (урок 1-30)

звъня́ [5] ring ; звъня́ по телефо́на [10] telephone
зда́ние [29] building, edifice
здра́в [2] healthy, lasting, strong ; здра́ви обу́вки [20] sturdy shoes
здра́ве [2] health ; поле́зно за здра́вето [8] good for you [for one's health] ; вредя́ на здра́вето [20] be bad for one's health ; ще ми взе́ме здра́вето [20] it'll be the death of me
здраве́й [6] hi
здра́во [21] well, soundly ; държа́ се здра́во [21] hold tight, hold fast
зе́ле [4] cabbage ; сала́та от зе́ле [4] cabbage salad
зеле́н [8] green
зелене́я [21] appear green
зеленчу́к [7] vegetable
земеде́лски [17] agricultural
земя́ [20] earth, land
зе́т, -ят (*plural* зе́тьове) [22] son-in-law; brother-in-law (sister's husband)
зи́ма [9] winter
зи́мен [11] winter *(adj.)* ; зи́мен куро́рт [11] ski resort
зимо́рничав [11] sensitive to the cold
зла́тен [9] golden
зла́то [24] gold
зле́ [13] bad, badly ; пък не́ка ми е зле́ [16] I should have it so bad
зли́ *see* зъл
зло́ [23] evil
злоче́ст [27] miserable, unfortunate
зна́к [9] sign ; бу́квени зна́ци [21] alphabet letters, characters ; пъ́тни зна́ци [26] road signs
зна́м [4] *see* зна́я
знамени́т [14] famous, renowned
знаха́р (ка) [26] folk healer
зна́ча (-иш) [17] mean ; зна́чи [1] that means, so, thus
значе́ние [9] meaning ; ня́ма значе́ние [9] it doesn't matter
значи́телен [30] considerable, significant
зна́я [3] know ; еди́н Го́спод зна́е [27] God only knows ; зна́я и две́ и две́ста [29] be adaptable
зо́на [23] zone, region
зоологи́чески [19] zoological ; зоологи́ческа гради́на [19] zoo
зооло́гия [26] zoology
зо́р [25] effort; need ; като́ ви́ди зо́р [25] when it gets hard
зре́ли *see* зря́л
зре́я [9] ripen
зрънце́ [16] grain, granule
зря́л (*plural* зре́ли) [23] ripe, mature
зъ́б, -ът (*plural* зъ́би) [6] [8] tooth
зъболе́кар [12] dentist
зъл [29] evil *(adj.)*
зъ́лва [22] sister-in-law (husband's sister)
зърно́ [16] grain, cereals

и [1] and, also ; и а́з [1] me too ; и то [11] at that ; ако́ и да [22] even though ; и про́чее и про́чее [29] etc., etc.
ѝ [7] (to) her *(indirect object pronoun)*
и ... и [8] both...and
игла́ [26] needle; thorn, quill
и́го [28] yoke; slavery
игра́ [14] play, game; playing
игра́чка [26] toy
игра́я [5] play ; игра́я на дво́ра [11] play in the yard
игра́я си [11] play around
и́да [5] come, go ; иди́ за хля́б [5] go get some bread
и́двам [5] come
идеа́лен [5] ideal
идеоло́гия [23] ideology
иде́я [5] idea ; хру́мна ми една́ иде́я [25] I just got an idea
идили́чен [3] idyllic
иди́лия [7] idyll
из [11] [22] around, throughout; out of ; пъту́ване из Бълга́рия [11] a trip throughout Bulgaria ; разхо́дка из града́ [11] city tour ; из къ́щи [11] around the house *(fixed phrase)* ; изхвъ́рквам из врата́та [22] fly out the door
избави́тел [23] savior, deliverer
изби́рам / избера́ [4] choose, select ; изби́рам но́мер [26] dial a telephone number
и́збор [7] selection, choice
избу́хвам / избу́хна [22] burst, explode ; избу́хна война́ [22] war broke out
избъ́рсвам / избъ́рша (-еш) [13] wipe, dry
избя́гвам / избя́гам [22] run away, get loose
избя́гвам / избя́гна [25] escape, avoid
изва́ждам / изва́дя [14] take/bring out, produce, extract
изведнъ́ж [5] suddenly
изве́ждам / изведа́ [9] take out, lead away ; изве́ждам ку́чето на разхо́дка [9] walk the dog
изве́стен [18] known, familiar; well-known
известя́вам / известя́ [20] notify, inform
изви́квам / изви́кам [13] cry, call out
извине́ние [13] excuse, pardon

Българо-английски речник (урок 1-30)

извиня́вам / извиня́ [5] pardon, excuse ; извине́те [2] excuse me
извъ́н [10] out of, outside
извънре́ден [20] extraordinary, special; additional
изга́рям / изгоря́ [14] get burned, burn up
изгле́ждам [4] look, appear, seem ; изгле́жда [6] it seems
изгле́ждам / изгле́дам [26] examine, scrutinize
изго́нвам / изго́ня [26] chase away; expel, kick out
изго́ра [28] sweetheart
изгра́ждам / изградя́ [21] build, construct
изгря́ва / изгре́е (3d person) [22] rise, come up (of the sun)
изгу́бвам / изгу́бя [16] lose
изда́вам / изда́м (-даде́ш) [19] give out, reveal; betray; publish
изда́ние [19] edition, publication ; отде́лно изда́ние [19] separate edition, book form
изда́тел [20] publisher
изда́телство [19] publishing house
изде́лие [23] article, product, handicraft
изди́гам / изди́гна [23] raise, build, put up
изди́гам се / изди́гна се [27] rise, advance ; изди́гам се над тя́х [27] tower over them
изди́швам / изди́шам [26] exhale
издока́рвам се / издока́рам се [14] dress up
издъ́ржам / издържа́ (-и́ш) [7] stand, endure
иззвъня́вам / иззвъня́ [14] ring (out)
изигра́вам / изигра́я [28] play, play out
изи́скан [29] refined, distinguished
изи́скване [19] requirement
изка́звам / изка́жа (-еш) [22] express; reveal
изка́рвам / изка́рам [17] take out, finish, spend
изкипя́вам / изкипя́ [14] boil over
изклю́чвам / изклю́ча (-иш) [23] exclude; turn off
и́зконен [20] ancient, original
изку́ствен [22] artificial, unnatural
изку́ство [23] art; skill
изкъ́пвам се / изкъ́пя се (-еш) [14] take a bath
изла́гам / изло́жа (-иш) [19] exhibit; set forth ; изла́гам на преме́ждия [29] expose to mishap/danger
и́злет [3] excursion
изли́вам / излея́ [26] pour out
изли́зам / изля́за [4] [29] leave, go; turn out
изли́там (or излетя́вам) / излетя́ [30] take off, fly away
изли́шен [20] superfluous; surplus
изло́жба [19] exhibition
излъ́гвам / излъ́жа (-еш) [19] lie, deceive
излъ́чвам / излъ́ча (-иш) [18] radiate, emanate
изма́мвам, изма́мя [24] deceive, swindle; betray
изма́мен [26] deceptive, misleading
изме́жду [21] among
изме́ствам / изме́стя [21] move away, displace
изми́вам / изми́я [13] wash up
измина́вам / измина́ [20] cover; elapse
изми́слям / изми́сля [12] think up, invent
изми́там / измета́ [16] sweep, sweep off
измо́крям / измо́кря [12] drench, soak ; измо́крям се до ко́сти [12] get soaked to the skin
измръ́звам / измръ́зна [22] freeze, die from cold
измъ́квам се / измъ́кна се [18] make off, slip away
измъ́чвам / измъ́ча (-иш) [24] torment
измъ́чвам се / измъ́ча се (-иш) [23] suffer, have a terrible time
изна́сям / изнеса́ [19] take out, export; make public ; изна́сям докла́д [19] read/deliver a paper
изна́сям се / изнеса́ се [30] move out
изнена́да [12] surprise ; по изнена́дите съм [14] I like surprises
изнена́двам / изнена́дам [24] surprise, take by surprise
изни́квам / изни́кна [28] sprout; pop up
изобразя́вам / изобразя́ [23] portray, depict
изо́бщо [8] in general, at all ; те́ изо́бщо не мо́гат да ча́кат [8] they can't wait at all
изоста́вам / изоста́на [25] lag behind, be slow ; часо́вникът ми изоста́ва с пе́т мину́ти [25] my watch is five minutes slow
изпи́вам / изпи́я [5] drink up
изпи́рам / изпера́ [12] do laundry
и́зпит [5] exam, test
изпи́твам / изпи́там [21] examine, test; experience
изпла́швам се / изпла́ша се (-иш) [25] get frightened, be afraid
изпли́там / изплета́ [12] knit, twist
изплъ́звам се / изплъ́зна се [14] slip out, slip through
изпо́д [25] from under
изпо́лзувам (also изпо́лзвам) [17] use, take advantage of

Българо-английски речник (Урок 1-30)

изпотя́вам се / изпотя́ се [27] sweat, perspire
изпочу́пвам / изпочу́пя [19] break [all up]
изпра́вен [17] erect ; изпра́вен пред [23] confronted with
изпра́вям / изпра́вя [17] set upright ; correct ; straighten
изпра́вям се / изпра́вя се [25] stand up, straighten up
изпра́звам / изпра́зня [22] empty, drain
изпра́щам / изпра́тя [8] send off, see off, accompany
изпраща́ч (ка) [19] sender, shipper; one who sees someone off
изпрева́рвам / изпрева́ря [24] outrun; anticipate, get ahead of
изпря́гам / изпря́гна [24] unharness
изпу́скам / изпу́сна [7] drop, let go; miss
изпъ́ждам / изпъ́дя [24] chase away
изпълни́м [19] feasible
изпълни́тел (ка) [16] performer; executor
изпълня́вам / изпъ́лня [21] carry out, fulfill
изпя́вам / изпе́я [11] sing [to the end]
израбо́твам / израбо́тя [23] produce, work out, form, make
и́зраз [18] expression
изразя́вам / изразя́ [18] express, manifest ; изразя́вам се вя́рно [22] say [it] right
изра́ствам / изра́сна (or израста́) [16] grow, shoot up
изска́чам / изско́ча (-иш) [25] jump out
изслу́швам / изслу́шам [16] listen to the end, hear out
изсти́вам / изсти́на [8] grow/become cold
изсъ́хвам / изсъ́хна [22] dry out, become dry
изте́глям се / изте́гля се (and отте́глям се / отте́гля се) [29] withdraw, retreat
изти́чвам / изти́чам [16] run [out, over, around]
и́зточен [20] eastern
и́зточник [30] source; origin
изтри́вам / изтри́я [20] erase, obliterate, rub [out]
изтръ́пвам / изтръ́пна [14] fall asleep (of a body part) ; изтръ́пвам от у́жас [14] freeze with terror ; изтръ́пвам от страх [24] get shudders down one's spine
изтъка́вам / изтъка́ (-че́ш) [16] weave to completion
изтъ́квам / изтъ́кна [23] emphasize
изуми́телен [13] amazing, astounding
изуча́вам / изу́ча (-иш) [2] [4] study, make a study of
изхвъ́рквам / изхвъ́ркна [22] fly out
изхвъ́рлям / изхвъ́рля [22] throw out, eject
и́зход [20] exit
изхо́ждам / изхо́дя [23] travel all over; originate, be based on ; изхо́дящ но́мер [23] "outgoing number" on official documents
изца́пвам / изца́пам [26] soil, stain
изча́квам / изча́кам [19] await, wait for
изче́звам / изче́зна [10] disappear
изчервя́вам се / изчервя́ се [24] blush, turn red
изче́рпвам / изче́рпя [18] exhaust, wear out
изчи́ствам / изчи́стя [14] clean up, clean out
изя́ва [18] manifestation
изявя́вам / изявя́ [29] express, declare
изяви́телен [24] declarative ; изяви́телно наклоне́ние [24] indicative mood
изя́ждам / изя́м (-я́деш) [9] eat up
изясня́вам / изясня́ [14] clear up ; след като неща́та се изясня́т [14] when things get clarified
ико́на [28] icon
иконогра́фия [23] iconography
иконо́мически [23] economic
иконо́мия [22] economy, saving
или ... или [8] either ... or
им [7] [to] them (indirect object pronoun)
и́ма [2] there is, there are ; какво́ и́ма в ча́нтата? [2] what is there in the bag? ; и́ма ма́лко вре́ме [2] there's not [very] much time ; и́ма о́ще мно́го ра́бота [2] there's still a lot of work [to do] ; и́ма си́лен вя́тър [2] it's very windy, there's a strong wind ; и́ма сми́съл [11] it makes sense
и́мам [2] [3] have ; и́мам ну́жда от [4] need, have need of ; и́мам пред вид [19] bear in mind ; и́мам голя́м успе́х [27] be very successful
има́м-баялдъ́ [28] spicy eggplant dish
и́ме (plural имена́) [6] [30] name; noun
име́ние [23] estate
и́менно [20] namely, exactly
импера́тор [18] emperor
ина́че (archaic ина́к) [27] otherwise
индивидуа́лен [18] individual, personal
инжене́р [14] engineer
институ́т [17] institution, institute
интере́с [7] interest ; проявя́вам интере́с към [8] take an interest in
интере́сен [2] interesting
интере́сно [1] interesting ; мно́го интере́сно [1] that's very interesting ;

Българо-английски речник (урок 1-30)

интере́сно, ти́ как си [3] I wonder how you are
интересу́вам [8] interest *(transitive)*
интересу́вам се от [11] be interested in
информа́ция [19] information; news item
ирла́ндец [23] Irishman
ирла́ндка [23] Irishwoman
и́скам [5] want, wish, intend
и́скра *(and* искра́*)* [27] spark
и́скрен [22] sincere, genuine
испа́нец [23] Spaniard
испа́нка [23] Spaniard (female), Spanish(woman)
и́стина [1] truth
и́стински [8] real, true
истори́чески [20] historical
исто́рия [7] history, story
италиа́нец [23] Italian (male)
италиа́нка [23] Italian (female)
италиа́нски [20] Italian *(adj.)*

к.м.н. = кандида́т на медици́нските нау́ки [17]
к.ф.н. = кандида́т на филологи́ческите нау́ки [17]
кабине́т [4] office [e.g. doctor's]
каби́нка [17] gondola (ski-lift)
кава́л [16] wooden flute
кавале́р [25] cavalier, knight; gentleman
кавга́ [10] quarrel, dispute
кавгаджи́я, -и́йка [10] quarrelsome person, brawler
каза́н [25] cauldron, vat
ка́звам / ка́жа (-еш) [1] [4] say
ка́звам се [1] my name is ; ка́зва се [1] his/her name is ; как се ка́звате? [1] what is your name?
кайма́ [6] ground meat
как [1] how ; как се ка́звате? [1] what is your name? ; как така́? [11] how is it that, how can that be? ; как не те́ е срам! [12] you should be ashamed!
какво́ [1] [4] what, what for ; какво́ е "тече́ние"? [1] what's a "тече́ние", what does "тече́ние" mean? ; какво́ е това́? [3] what's this? ; какво́ гле́даш то́лкова в..? [4] why are you so absorbed in..? ; какво́ рабо́тите? [5] what [kind of] work do you do? ; какво́ ще ка́жеш [7] what do you think ; какво́ ли не́ [12] whatever, whatnot
какво́то [12] whatever ; какво́то и да [17] no matter what
ка́кто [9] as ; ка́кто и да е [17] no matter how; never mind
ка́ктус [23] cactus
какъ́в [3] what kind of, what ; какъ́в е то́й? [3] what [work] does he do? ; каква́ ху́бава къ́ща! [3] what a nice house! ; какъ́в ли е то́й [5] what's he like, I wonder
какъ́вто [17] such [...as] ; какъ́вто и да е [17] whatever/however
кал, -та́ [19] mud ; га́зя калта́ [26] flounder through the mud
ка́лен [22] muddy
кале́н [25] hardened, seasoned
ка́лфа [27] journeyman
каля́вам / каля́ [25] temper, harden, toughen
кама́ра [25] heap, pile
камио́н [29] truck
ка́мък *(plural* ка́мъни*)* [21] stone
камъна́к [27] stones, stony ground
ка́на [23] pitcher, jug
кана́л [23] canal, drain
кана́рче [28] canary
кандида́т [17] candidate ; кандида́т на филологи́ческите нау́ки [17] Ph.D. degree equivalent ; кандида́т на медици́нските нау́ки [17] M.D. equivalent
канди́ло [26] icon-lamp; grave-lamp
кано́н [23] canon, rule
канцела́рия [16] office
ка́ня [10] invite
ка́ня се [11] plan, intend
ка́пвам / ка́пна [21] drop ; ка́пнал от умо́ра [21] exhausted
капиталовложе́ние [23] capital investment
капри́зен [13] capricious
ка́пя (-еш) [11] [23] drip, dribble; leak
ка́рам [6] drive, ride, push ; ка́рам кола́ [6] drive a car ; ка́рам го да я донесе́ [20] get him to bring it
ка́рам се [11] scold; quarrel
карие́ра [28] career ; пра́вя карие́ра [28] make it in the world
карикату́ра [19] cartoon, caricature
карнава́лен [12] carnival *(adj.)*
ка́рта [5] [23] card; map, chart ; гле́дам на ка́рти [18] read one's fortune
карти́на [27] picture
карти́нка [3] small picture ; като́ карти́нка [18] pretty as a picture
карти́чка [11] [22] postcard; business card, visiting card
карто́ф [17] potato
карто́фен, -ена [21] potato *(adj.)*
кару́ца [18] cart, carriage

Българо-английски речник (урок 1-30)

касáпница [28] butcher's; slaughter, carnage
касетофóн [5] cassette player; tape recorder
катастрóфа [17] accident, disaster ; автомобúлна катастрóфа [17] auto accident
катéдра [17] department, (academic) chair
кáтеричка [18] squirrel
катéря се [28] climb, scramble up
като [3] like, as; when ; áз прáвя като лéлята [3] I'm doing [just] like auntie ; като бях [6] when I was ; като мáлък [11] when he was little
като че ли [14] as if, apparently ; като че ли се смéеше [14] he appeared to be laughing
кафé [5] coffee, cup of coffee ; умúрам за еднó кафé [25] be dying for a cup of coffee
кафéен, -ейна [6] coffee (adj.)
кафéн, -ена [6] coffee (adj.) ; кафéна лъжúчка [6] coffee spoon
кафенé [25] cafe, coffeehouse
кафя́в [21] brown
кáца [24] cask, vat
качамáк [20] hominy, polenta
кáчвам / качá (-úш) [7] carry up, take up
кáчвам се / качá се (-úш) [7] ascend, get on
кашкавáл [4] kashkaval (yellow cheese) ; омлéт с кашкавáл [4] cheese omelet
квартáл [9] district, living area ; ЖК = жúлищен квартáл [17] residential district
квартúра [14] apartment, quarters
кг = килогрáм [23]
кебáп [13] grilled or stewed meat
кебáпче [6] kebab
кéлнер [30] waiter
килéр [29] pantry, stockroom
килúм [21] carpet, rug
килогрáм [6] kilogram
километър [24] kilometer
кúно [5] cinema, movies
киноактрúса [25] movie actress
кир [1] sir (archaic term of address)
кúра [1] ma'am (archaic term of address)
кирúлица [21] Cyrillic [alphabet]
кирúлски [18] Cyrillic (adj.) ; кирúлски бýкви [18] Cyrillic [alphabet] letters
кúсел [6] sour ; кúсело зéле [6] sauerkraut ; кúсело мля́ко [6] yogurt
китáец [23] Chinese (male)
китáйка [23] Chinese (female)
китáйски [21] Chinese

кúтка [12] wrist
кúхам (or кúхвам / кúхна) [14] sneeze
клас, -ът (plural класовé) [7] class, grade in school ; от класá [7] from the same (school) class
класá [16] social class ; от класá [16] "classy", high-grade
класúчески [3] classical ; класúческа литератýра [25] "the classics"
кла́тя [23] shake, roll
клéтка [24] cage
клéчка [26] stick
клиéнт [18] client, customer
клúмат [11] climate
клон [25] branch
клóнка [25] twig
клуб [18] club, clubhouse
клюн [13] beak
ключ [7] key
кнúга [2] book
кня́жество [21] kingdom
княз (plural князé) [8] prince
кнúжка [10] booklet; driver's license ; шофьóрска кнúжка [26] driver's license
книжóвен [21] literary, learned
книжóвник [21] man of letters
ковá [27] forge, hammer
ковáч [27] smith, blacksmith
когá [6] when (interrogative)
когáто [11] when (relative conjunction)
когó [8] whom (interrogative)
когóто [17] whom (relative conjunction)
кóжа [12] skin; hide, fur; leather
кóжен, -ена [21] leather
кожухáр (archaic кожухáрин) [22] furrier
кой, коя́, коé, кои [3] [5] who, which (interrogative) ; коé врéме стáна [16] [look] what time it's gotten to be
кóйто, коя́то, коéто, кóйто [17] who, which (relative conjunction) ; whoever, whichever ; кóйто и да [17] no matter who ; товá, коéто [17] what
кóкал [12] bone
кокéтка [19] flirt, coquette
кокóшка [11] hen, fowl ; кокóшка с кúсело зéле [11] chicken and sauerkraut casserole
колá [4] car, automobile ; кáрам колá [6] drive a car
колебáя се [17] hesitate, vacillate, fluctuate
колéга [10] colleague
Кóледа [10] Christmas
кóледен [10] Christmas (adj.)
колéжка [10] female colleague
колéкция [7] collection
колелó [14] wheel; bicycle

Българо-английски речник (урок 1-30)

колет [5] parcel, package
колиба [26] cabin, lodge; hut
количка [7] pushcart
колко [4] [6] how much, how many ; колко струва това? [4] how much does this cost? ; колко струва? [4] how much is it? ; колко души сме? [6] how many of us are there? ; на колко сте години? [6] how old are you? ; колко е часът? [6] what time is it? ; в колко часа? [6] when, at what time?
колкото [17] as much as
колония [20] colony
колорит [28] color, picturesqueness
коляно (plurals колена or колене) [12] knee
командировка [10] business trip
комбинат [17] works (factory)
комедия [11] comedy
комин [13] chimney
комитет [23] committee
компакт диск [12] compact disk
компания [27] company, crowd
комплекс [8] complex ; жилищен комплекс [8] block of apartments
композиция [23] composition, construction
компютър (plural компютри) [20] computer
комунистически [17] communist (adj.)
кон, -ят (plural коне) [8] horse
конгрес [19] congress
кондуктор (ка) [5] conductor
конкретен [30] concrete, specific
конкурс [17] competition
конник [23] horseman, rider
консервирам [6] preserve, can
консервиран [6] preserved, canned
консолидирам [20] consolidate
конституция [20] constitution
консумация [22] consumption, use
контролен [8] control (adj.) ; контролна работа [8] exam, quiz
контролно [8] exam, quiz
конференция [12] conference
концерт [19] concert
копач [19] digger; hoe
копая [10] dig
копие [13] copy ; пълно копие [14] exact replica
копие [26] spear, javelin
коприва [19] nettle ; правя на бъзе и коприва [19] make mincemeat of
коприна [21] silk
копринен, -ена [21] silken
копче [19] button, knob
копър [6] dill

кореец [23] Korean (male)
корейка [23] Korean (female)
корем [12] abdomen, belly
корен [26] root
коридор [2] corridor, passageway; entryway
корито [18] trough; bed (of a river)
кормило [29] rudder; helm, wheel
коса [12] hair
косвен [23] indirect
кост, -та [12] bone ; измокрям се до кости [12] get soaked to the skin
костенурка [9] turtle
костилка [18] pit, stone
костюм [14] suit ; ушивам си костюм [23] have a suit made; sew oneself a suit
косъм [26] hair, filament
котенце [18] kitten
котка [10] cat
кофа [14] pail, bucket ; кофа за боклук [14] garbage can
кошмар [6] nightmare
кошче [17] basket ; кошче за боклук [17] wastebasket
крава [21] cow
крави [21] cow (adj.)
краен, крайна [19] endmost, final, extreme ; краен срок [19] deadline ; за крайно удивление [22] to [their] utter amazement
край [7] edge, end ; работата край няма [25] [there's] no end of work
край (plural краища) [8] district
край [20] along, by
крак, -ът (plural крака) [8] leg ; на крак [12] hastily
крал, -ят (plural крале) [8] king
кран [23] faucet
красив [22] beautiful, handsome; noble
красота [18] beauty
краставица [6] cucumber
кратък [9] short
краче [26] tiny leg
крачка [26] step ; на две крачки [26] very close by
крив [3] crooked
криза [23] crisis
крило (plural крила or криле) [23] wing
критерий [23] criterion
критикувам [26] criticize; review
критичен [19] critical ; критични бележки [19] criticisms
крия [20] hide
кротувам [20] keep quiet
кротък [13] gentle
кръв, -та (plural кърви) [12] blood
кръг, -ът [10] circle ; тесен семеен кръг [10] immediate family

Българо-английски речник (урок 1-30)

кръ́гъл [10] round, circular ; кръ́гла годи́шнина [10] decade anniversary
кръжа́ (-и́ш) [23] circle, go around
кръст [21] cross; waist; small of back
кръстопъ́т, -ят [24] crossroads
кръстосло́вица [8] crossword puzzle ; реша́вам кръстосло́вица [8] do a crossword puzzle
кръ́чма [18] pub, tavern
кръща́вам / кръ́стя [25] christen, name
кря́сък (*plural* кря́съци) [28] shout, yell
куби́нски [8] Cuban
ку́кам [29] call (of a cuckoo-like bird)
ку́кла [13] doll, puppet
кукумя́вка [29] screech owl
култ [23] cult
култу́ра [9] culture
култу́рен [12] cultural ; култу́рна обще́ственост [20] cultural circles
кум, -ъ́т [14] godfather
кума́ [14] godmother
ку́па [17] bowl
купе́ [2] compartment ; купе́ № 7 [2] compartment No. 7 ; купе́то е тя́сно [2] the compartment is cramped
купу́вам / ку́пя [5] buy, purchase
куро́рт [11] resort ; зи́мен куро́рт [11] ski resort
курс [29] course, direction ; шофьо́рски ку́рсове [29] driving school
кусу́р [25] fault, flaw ; това́ ще ни е кусу́рът [25] that'll be the last straw
кути́я [10] box ; по́щенска кути́я [10] mailbox
ку́хня [5] [7] kitchen; cuisine
ку́фар [2] suitcase
ку́че [4] dog
ку́ченце [16] puppy
къде́ [1] [18] where (*interrogative*); far, infinitely ; къде́ ти [18] how could that be
къде́то [17] where (*relative conjunction*)
към [8] toward
къ́мпинг [25] camping site
къ́пя (-еш) [3] bathe
къ́рвав [24] bloody
къ́рпа [13] cloth, towel
къ́рша (-иш) [25] break; wring
къс [12] short
къ́сен [4] late
къ́сно [4] late ; едва́ по́-къ́сно [30] only later
късме́т [10] fortune, luck ; ба́ница с късме́ти [10] banitsa filled with fortunes
късметли́я [17] fortunate [person]
кът (*plural* къ́тища) [26] nook, recess
къ́ща [2] house
къ́щичка [7] little house
къщо́вница [18] sterling housewife
кьопоолу́ [18] eggplant caviar
кюфте́ [22] meatball

ла́вица [26] shelf, rack
ла́кът, ла́кътят (*plural* ла́кти) [8] elbow
лале́ [26] tulip
ла́мпа [18] lamp, light
ламя́ [25] dragon
лати́нски [21] Latin
ла́я [11] bark
лев [4] lev (Bulgarian currency) ; 120 ле́ва [4] 120 levs/leva
ле́ви [11] *see* лев
леге́нда [27] legend, myth
легло́ [4] bed ; опра́вям легло́ [28] make a bed
ле́гна *see* ля́гам
лед, -ъ́т (*plural* ледове́) [18] ice
ле́ден, -ена [8] ice (*adj.*), frozen
лежа́ (-и́ш) [4] lie, be lying ; лежа́ в бо́лница [16] be in hospital ; лежа́ в осно́вата на [21] underlie, be at the root of
лек [9] light, easy ; ле́ка нощ [9] good night
лек, -ъ́т (*plural* ле́кове *and* лекове́) [19] remedy, cure
ле́кар (ка) [1] doctor, physician
лека́рство [8] medicine ; гъ́лтам лека́рство [8] take medicine
лекови́т [26] curative, medicinal
ле́ксика [30] lexicon, vocabulary
леку́вам [27] cure, treat
ле́кция [6] lecture, class
ле́ля [3] aunt (father's sister) ; "auntie"
лен [21] linen, flax
ле́нен, -ена [21] linen (*adj.*), flaxen
ле́сен [6] easy
лесниче́й [26] forester
ле́тен, ля́тна [17] summer (*adj.*)
лету́вам [20] spend the summer
летя́ [26] fly, soar
лече́ние [19] treatment, cure
ле́шник [24] hazelnut
ле́я [27] pour
ли [1] [5] (*question particle*) ; от Ва́рна ли сте? [1] are you from Varna? ; какъ́в ли е то́зи чове́к [5] what is this person like, I wonder ; какво́ ли не́ [12] all sorts of [things] ; едва́ ли [19] hardly, not likely
ли́жа (-еш) [18] lick
ликьо́р [25] liqueur

Българо-английски речник (урок 1-30)

ли́ния [20] line, course ; ОФ-ли́ния [25] party line of the Fatherland Front coalition
ли́пса [30] lack, absence
ли́псвам / ли́псам [19] be missing, lack, be lacking in
лист [4] sheet of paper
лист (*plural* листа́) [6] leaf
листо́вка [26] news sheet, flyer
литерату́ра [17] literature ; класи́ческа литерату́ра [25] "the classics"
литерату́рен [30] literary ; литерату́рен ези́к [30] standard language
лифт [17] ski-lift
лице́ [12] [23] face; person ; заинтересо́вани лица́ [23] parties concerned
ли́чен [21] prominent; personal, particular
ли́чност [20] personality, character
лиша́вам / лиша́ (-и́ш) [23] deprive of, rob ; лиша́вам от насле́дство [23] disinherit
ловджи́йка [23] huntress
ло́вен [23] hunting *(adj.)*
ловя́ [9] catch ; ловя́ ри́ба [9] fish, catch fish
логи́чен [12] logical
ло́дка [22] boat, dinghy
лоза́ [6] vine
ло́зе (*plural* лозя́) [10] vineyard
ло́зов [6] grape, vine *(adj.)* ; ло́зови листа́ [6] grape leaves
локализи́рам [23] localize, locate
лош [3] bad
лук [6] onion
лу́ковица [26] bulb, tuber
луна́ [9] moon
лъ́жа (-еш) [18] tell a lie, deceive ; ако не ме́ лъ́же паметта́ [18] if memory serves me correctly
лъжа́ [25] lie, falsehood ; скроя́вам лъжа́ [25] concoct a lie
лъже́ц [25] liar ; голя́м лъже́ц [25] consummate liar, swindler
лъжи́ца [6] spoon, spoonful
лъжи́чка [6] teaspoon, teaspoonful
лъ́скав [10] shining, bright
лъ́скам / лъ́сна [17] polish, shine
лъ́хащ [18] smelling of, giving off
лъч, -ъ́т (*plural* лъчи́) [27] ray, glimmer
любя́ [13] love, be in love with
любе́зен [2] kind
люби́м [8] favorite
люби́тел [8] lover, fan
любопи́тство [29] curiosity
ляв (*plural* ле́ви) [11] left, Left
ля́гам / ле́гна [4] lie down, go to bed
ля́гам си / ле́гна си [8] go to bed
ля́то (*plural* лета́) [9] summer

ма́! [20] *(appellative particle addressed to a woman)* ; Ма́мо, ма́! [20] hey Mom!
магази́н [5] store
магаре́ [17] donkey
маги́я [24] magic, sorcery
ма́жа (-еш) [23] spread, smear
мазо́л [18] corn, callous, blister ; хва́щам мазо́ли [18] get blisters
май [9] May
май [12] it seems, in all probability ; май оста́ва да оти́дем та́м [12] I guess we have to go there
ма́йка [2] mother ; ти́ баща́, ти́ ма́йка [18] you're my only hope
майму́на [24] monkey, ape
ма́йски [26] May *(adj.)* ; ма́йски бръ́мбар [26] May-bug, chafer *(Melolontha melolontha)*
ма́йстор [18] master (worker), craftsman
мака́р [14] at least; although ; мака́р (и) да [17] although, even though
мака́р че [14] although, even though
македо́нец [20] Macedonian (male)
македо́нски [23] Macedonian *(adj.)*
мали́на [3] raspberry
ма́лко [1] [2] a little, [very] little ; той е ма́лко бо́лен [2] he's a bit under the weather
малоази́йски [23] Anatolian, of Asia Minor
малоле́тен [20] minor, underage
ма́лък [2] small ; ма́лко вре́ме [2] not much time ; ма́лките [4] small ones, children ; като́ ма́лък [11] when he was little ; от ма́лък [13] since he was little/a child ; с ма́лко закъсне́ние [14] a little late
ма́ма [2] Mom ; ма́мо [2] Mom *(when addressed)* ; а ни́е, ма́мо? [2] and what about us, Mom?
манасти́р [8] monastery
ма́нджа [18] dish, food
марато́нка [18] training shoe
ма́рка [29] stamp; brand ; каква́ ма́рка е кола́та ти? [29] what make is your car?
март [1] March
ма́ртеница [13] entwined red and white tassels worn as sign of spring
ма́ртеничка [13] small martenitsa
ма́са [7] table
ма́сичка [13] little table
масли́на [18] olive
ма́сло [29] butter; oil; grease

Българо-английски речник (Урок 1-30)

математик, -ичка [19] mathematician
материал [19] material
матура [8] matriculation (exam)
махам [14] wave ; махам с ръка [24] wave one's hand
махмурлия : махмурлия съм [24] have a hangover
мач [12] [sports] match
машина [17] machine, engine ; пишеща машина [26] typewriter ; парна машина [29] steam engine
мащеха [10] stepmother
ме [4] [5] me *(direct object pronoun)*
мегдан [18] [public] square
мед, -ът [24] honey
медицински [17] medical, health *(adj.)* ; медицинска сестра [17] nurse ; кандидат на медицинските науки [17] M.D. equivalent
между [12] between, among
международен [19] international
мек [15] soft, mild
мелнишки [27] Melnik *(adj.)*
мен [12] *(same as* мене*)* ; мечка страх, мен не страх [29] here goes!
мене [10] me *(direct object pronoun)*
меню *(neuter)* [4] menu
мери *see* мяра
мерки *see* мярка
месец [9] month
месо [6] meat
места *see* място
местен [20] local, native
местопрестъпление [28] scene of a crime ; пипвам (or хващам) на местопрестъплението [28] catch in the act
местя [20] move *(transitive)*
местя се [20] move, change residence
мета [19] sweep
металургичен [17] metallurgical
металургия [23] metallurgy
метач (ка) [19] sweeper; scavenger
метафизически [18] metaphysical
метла [26] broom
метод [19] method
метър [15] meter
механа [18] tavern
мече [11] bear cub
Мечо Пух [11] Winnie the Pooh
мечешки [29] bear's ; мечешка услуга [29] a doubtful service
мечка [29] bear ; мечка страх, мен не страх [29] here goes!
мечта [16] dream, fantasy
мечтая [25] dream, yearn
мешана салата [18] garden salad
ми [7] [to] me *(indirect object pronoun)*
мигвам / мигна [25] wink ; цяла нощ не мигвам [25] not sleep a wink [all night]
мигла [12] eyelash
мил [4] dear ; добре, мило [4] all right, darling
милея [13] hold dear, care for
милост [17] mercy, compassion
миля [29] mile
минавам / мина [5] pass ; мине не мине година [19] every year or so ; и през ум не ми мина [28] I didn't dream of it ; минавам за [29] pass for
минал [9] past ; миналата нощ [9] last night ; минало свършено време [12] aorist tense ; минало несвършено време [14] imperfect tense ; минало неопределено [16] past indefinite (tense) ; минало предварително [19] past anterior [tense] ; бъдеще в миналото [22] future in the past [tense] ; бъдеще предварително в миналото [23] future anterior in the past (tense)
министерство [14] ministry
министър [20] minister
минувач [26] passer-by
минута [6] minute
мир, -ът [25] peace
мирен [28] peace *(adj.)*, peaceable, gentle
мирно [28] peacefully ; да би мирно седяло не би чудо видяло [28] that's what comes of asking for trouble
миризма [11] smell, scent
мирише *(3d person only)* [17] smell of
мисля [5] think
мисъл, -та [26] thought, idea
митнически [23] customs *(adj.)*
митология [23] mythology
мишка [11] mouse
мия [8] wash
млад [7] young
младеж [17] youth, young man
младежки [17] youth *(adj.)*
младини [29] youth, tender years
младоженец [10] bridegroom, newlywed
младоженка [10] bride, newlywed
младост [17] youth
млекар [19] milkman
млечност [10] milkiness
млъквам / млъкна [22] fall silent, hush up
мляко *(plural* млека*)* [6] milk
мнение [20] opinion
много [1] [2] many; very; much ; много работа [2] a lot of work ; много интересно [1] very interesting

Българо-английски речник (Урок 1-30)

мнозинство́ [18] majority
мо́га (-жеш) [4] can, be able
моги́ла [18] hill, mound
могъ́щество [23] power, might
мо́да [21] fashion
мо́ден [13] fashionable ; мо́дно ревю́ [13] fashion show
модернизи́рам [25] modernize
мо́же [4] [11] possible, OK; it's possible ; би́ра мо́же [4] OK, I can [have a] beer
мо́же би [9] maybe
мо́зък (*plural* мо́зъци) [12] brain ; сътресе́ние на мо́зъка [29] [brain] concussion
мой [8] my, mine
молба́ [17] request ; пода́вам молба́ [19] submit a [formal] request
молда́вски [21] Moldavian
мо́лив [2] pencil
моли́тва [22] prayer
мо́ля [4] please ; мо́ля ви се, господи́не [4] please, sir ; мо́ля! [4] at your service
мо́ля [20] ask, beseech
моме́нт [5] [20] moment; point, feature ; в то́зи моме́нт [5] then, at that point in time ; в моме́нта [10] at the moment ; ва́жен моме́нт [20] an important point ; в после́дния моме́нт [22] at the last minute
моми́че [1] girl
момче́ [1] boy
мо́мък (*plural* момци́) [13] young man
моне́та [10] coin ; сека́ моне́ти [20] mint coins
мора́вски [8] Moravian
мора́л [29] morals, ethics
море́ [6] sea ; на море́то [6] at the seaside; at the Black Sea ; на море́ [20] at the seaside
море́на [25] moraine
мо́рков [4] carrot ; сала́та от мо́ркови [4] carrot salad
мо́рски [15] sea (*adj.*) ; мо́рското равни́ще [15] sea level
мост (*plural* мосто́ве) [6] bridge
мо́там се (*or* мотая́ се) [14] fool around
моти́в [17] motive, motif
мотиви́ровка [21] motivation
мото́р [29] engine, motor
мощ, -та́ [23] power, might; vigor
мра́вка [26] ant
мраз [10] frost, chill ; Дя́до Мра́з [10] Jack Frost
мръ́ква се / мръ́кне се (*3d person only*) [29] get dark
мръ́сен [9] dirty

му [7] [to] him, [to] it (*indirect object pronoun*)
му [18] (*conversational particle*) ; без да му ми́сля [18] without a second thought
музе́й [19] museum
му́зика [5] music
мусака́ [20] moussaka (Balkan dish)
му́скул [12] muscle
муста́ци (*plural*) [14] mustache
мъгла́ [22] mist, fog
мъдре́ц [27] wise man, sage
мъж, -ъ́т (*plural* мъже́) [8] man, husband
мъ́жки [8] male, masculine
мъ́ка [16] pain, suffering, difficulty
мълча́ (-и́ш) [10] be silent, fall silent
мълчали́в [22] silent, tacit
мълча́ние [29] silence
мързели́в [17] lazy
мързели́вец [25] lazybones, lazy person
мързи́ (*3d person only*) [17] be lazy ; мързи́ го [17] he's lazy
мъртве́ц [24] dead person, corpse
мъ́тен [18] muddy, dull
мъ́ча (-иш) [27] torment, bother
мъ́ча се (-иш) [26] suffer, agonize, have a hard time
мъ́чен [13] hard, difficult
мъ́чно [13] hard, with difficulty ; ста́на ми мъ́чно [13] I had a hard time
мъче́ние [18] torment, torture
мя́ра (*plural* ме́ри) [18] measure, fit
мя́рка (*plural* ме́рки) [20] measure; step ; взе́мам ме́рки [20] take steps, take precautions
мя́ркам се / мя́рна се [21] show, put in an appearance
мя́сто [2] place, seat ; мя́стото е свобо́дно [2] the seat is not taken ; стоя́ на мя́сто [17] stay in one place ; на мя́сто [20] on the spot

н.е. = но́вата е́ра [9]
на [1] [2] [3] [7] of; in, on, at; per; for (*indirect object*) ; ти́ си на № 2 [2] you've got No. 2 ; на село́ [3] in the village ; на бъ́лгарски [3] in Bulgarian ; на [...] годи́ни [6] [...] years old ; на ко́лко сте годи́ни? [6] how old are you? ; на едро́ [9] wholesale ; на телефо́на [12] speaking! [on the phone] ; по три пъ́ти на де́н [13] three times a day ; на бъ́рза ръка́ [18] hastily ; на гла́с [26] aloud ; на ста́ро [29] second-hand

Българо-английски речник (Урок 1-30)

на́ [18] here, there *(emphatic particle)* ; на́ ти пари́ [18] here's some money for you ; и на́! [18] and there you are!
наби́рам / набера́ [26] gather, compose ; наби́рам но́мер [26] dial a telephone number
наближа́вам / наближа́ (-и́ш) [17] approach, draw near
набли́зо [4] nearby
наблюда́вам [26] observe, examine
наве́ждам / наведа́ [19] bow, bend ; suggest
наве́ждам се / наведа́ се [19] bend down, lean over
навече́рие [10] the eve of; vigil
нави́вам / нави́я [17] wind up, roll up
на́вик [11] habit
навли́зам / навля́за [30] enter, penetrate
навре́д [24] everywhere
навре́ме [5] on time ; съвсе́м навре́ме [5] at exactly the right moment
нався́къде [19] everywhere, every nook and cranny
навъ́н [11] outside *(directional)*
навъ́ршвам / навъ́рша (-иш) [23] complete ; дне́с навъ́ршвам 20 годи́ни [23] I'm 20 years old today
навъ́тре [11] inside *(directional)*
навя́рно [14] probably
нагле́ждам / нагле́дам [26] inspect; look after
наго́ре [11] up *(directional)*
нагореща́вам / нагореща́ [27] heat, heat up
награ́да [13] reward, prize ; удостоя́вам с награ́да [20] confer a prize
награжда́вам / наградя́ [16] award [a prize]
над [15] above
надале́че (or надале́ч) [20] far
надби́гвам / надбя́гам [26] outdistance, outrun
надбя́гвам се / надбя́гам се [26] race, run in competition with
на́две-на́три [22] helter-skelter, in a disorganized manner
надве́сен [26] overhanging
надви́квам / надви́кам [20] outshout, outcry
надгро́бен [23] sepulchral, pertaining to grave or tomb
наде́жда [8] hope
наджи́вявам / наджи́вея [26] outlive, survive; outgrow
нади́гам се / нади́гна се [24] rise
надмина́вам / надмина́ [21] outdistance, surpass
надо́лу [11] down *(directional)*
на́дпис [14] inscription
надпи́свам / надпи́ша (-еш) [18] inscribe
надсви́рвам / надсви́ря [26] outplay, excel in playing
надсви́рвам се / надсви́ря се [26] compete in playing
надя́вам се [19] hope
надя́сно [11] to the right
на́ем [12] rent ; да́вам под на́ем [12] rent out
нае́сен [9] in the fall
наза́д [23] back, backwards ; обръ́щам се наза́д [23] turn back, look back
наза́ем [12] loan ; да́вам наза́ем [12] loan
наздра́ве [11] cheers, to your health! *(toast)*
назря́вам / назре́я [21] ripen, mature; come to a head
наи́вен [24] naive, guileless
наизу́ст [4] by heart, verbatim ; зна́м меню́то наизу́ст [4] I can recite the menu by heart
наи́стина [2] really, truly
най- [10] most... *(superlative degree particle)* ; най-по́сле [1] finally ; най-мно́го [10] the most ; най-разли́чни неща́ [10] all sorts of things ; най-накра́й [16] finally ; най-се́тне [19] finally ; най-напре́д [29] first of all
нака́нвам се / нака́ня се [22] get round to, find time to
нака́рвам / нака́рам [16] make [someone] do, induce
накла́ждам / наклада́ [22] make, light ; накла́ждам о́гън [22] light a fire
наклоне́ние [24] mood ; изяви́телно наклоне́ние [24] indicative mood ; повели́телно наклоне́ние [24] imperative mood ; усло́вно наклоне́ние [24] conditional mood ; преизка́зно наклоне́ние [24] renarrated mood
накра́я [17] finally
накра́тко [10] in short, in brief
накъде́ [11] to where
нала́гам / нало́жа (-иш) [18] put, impose, force
нала́гам се / нало́жа се (-иш) [18] impose, necessitate, get one's way ; нала́га се / нало́жи се *(3rd person only)* [18] be necessary
нали́ [3] *(added to form negative question)* ; нали́ ви́ждаш [3] don't you see ; нали́ зна́еш, че а́з съм... [3] you know, don't you, that I'm... ; голя́м е, нали́? [3] it's big, isn't it?

Българо-английски речник (урок 1-30)

наливам / налея [22] pour out, fill [a glass]
наливам се / налея се [24] drink heavily, booze
наляво [11] to the left
намалявам / намалея [21] decrease, dwindle
намалявам / намаля [21] decrease, reduce
наметна *see* намятам
наминавам / намина [18] drop in
намирам / намеря [5] find
намирам се / намеря се [17] be, be located ; намирам се в чудо [28] be at one's wits' end
намирисвам [16] smell [slightly] of
намислям / намисля [25] think of, set one's mind to
намръщен (-ена) [13] sullen, gloomy
намятам / наметна [27] throw on, throw over
нанизвам / нанижа (-еш) [14] string together
наоколо [9] around, round about
нападки [23] attacks, incrimination
напазарувам [27] do the shopping
напакостявам / напакостя [25] harm, injure
напевен [27] melodious, lilting
напервам се / наперя се [26] strut, become perky
напет [27] sprightly, handsome
напивам се / напия се [26] get drunk
написвам / напиша (-еш) [5] write, write down, finish writing
напитка [4] beverage, drink
наполовина [17] in half ; не и наполовина толкова тежка [17] not even half as heavy
напор [26] pressure
напоследък [8] lately
направо [18] directly, openly
направя [6] do, make ; направя място на този човек [6] make room for this man ; направя на прах [25] reduce to dust
напразно [28] in vain
напред [14] ahead, forwards
напредък [9] progress, gain
напрежение [14] pressure, tension
наприказвам се [22] talk one's fill, talk to one's heart's content
например [8] for example
напролет [9] in the spring
напротив [29] on the contrary
напускам / напусна [23] leave
напълно [20] completely
нарамвам / нарамя [28] shoulder
наред [7] [25] in order; in succession ; всичко е наред [7] everything's O.K. ; другото ще е наред [16] the rest will be O.K.
нареждам / наредя [6] set up, arrange
наричам / нарека (-чеш) [13] call, name
народ [7] people, folk
народен [5] national, folk ; народна носия [16] folk costume ; Народното събрание [18] Parliament ; Народен дворец на културата [19] People's Palace of Culture
народност [20] nationality
народностен [20] national, pertaining to nationality matters
нарочно [17] on purpose
нарушавам / наруша (-иш) [29] break, violate
нарядко [30] seldom, at rare intervals
нарязвам / нарежа (-еш) [18] cut into pieces
нас [8] [10] us *(object pronoun)*
насаждам / насадя [26] plant, set out
насам [24] this way, over here
насекомо (*plural* насекоми) [26] insect
насила [23] by force, under protest
насип [23] mound, embankment
насищам / насития [18] saturate
наскоро [17] recently
наслагам / насложа (-иш) [22] put out, lay ; наслагам всевъзможни закуски [22] serve all sorts of snacks
наследство [23] inheritance ; лишавам от наследство [23] disinherit ; по наследство от [29] descended from
наспивам се / наспя се [25] have enough sleep, sleep one's fill
настанявам се / настаня се [29] settle
настивам / настина [20] catch cold ; настинал съм [20] have a cold ; нещо съм настинал [20] have a bit of a cold
настигам / настигна [23] overtake, catch up with
настоявам / настоя [24] insist
настоятелство [29] board of trustees
настъпвам / настъпя [13] come, set in, occur; step on; advance
нататък [26] thither, further
нататъшен [23] far ; по-нататъшна съдба [23] subsequent fate
натоварвам / натоваря [17] burden, load down
натрупвам / натрупам [23] heap up, amass, hoard
натура [29] nature
натъжавам / натъжа (-иш) [19] sadden

Българо-английски речник (урок 1-30)

натъквам се / натъкна се (на) [23] come across, run into
наука [17] science; scholarship, learning ; кандидат на филологическите науки [17] Ph.D. degree equivalent ; кандидат на медицинските науки [17] M.D. equivalent
наумявам си / наумя си [17] take it into one's head
научавам / науча (-иш) [6] [9] learn; teach
научавам се / науча се (-иш) [14] learn to, learn about; get used to
научен [17] scientific ; старши научен сътрудник [17] senior research associate
нафталин [16] mothballs
нахален [25] insolent, impudent
находка [23] find
нахранвам / нахраня [11] feed
нахранвам се / нахраня се [22] eat one's fill
национален [18] national ; вземам национални размери [30] take on national proportions
нация [30] nation
нацъфтявам / нацъфтя [21] burst into bloom
начален [3] beginning, elementary ; начално образование [3] elementary education
начало [19] beginning
начертавам / начертая [21] draw, sketch, outline
начин [6] way, manner ; по този начин [6] in this way
наш [8] our, ours ; в наше време [26] nowadays
наяждам се / наям се (-ядеш) [9] eat one's fill, gorge on
НДК = Народен дворец на културата
не [1] not ; не те е срам [12] shame on you ; не бива да се пие [23] [one] musn't drink [it]
не́ [3] [5] no; *(contrastive negation)* ; не́ там [5] not there [but somewhere else]
небе́ (*poetic plural* небеса́) [17] sky
небце [12] palate (roof of mouth)
невероятен [26] improbable; inconceivable
невзрачен [26] unseemly, insignificant
неволно [27] involuntarily, instinctively
невяста (or невеста) [26] bride, wife
него [10] him *(object pronoun)*
негов [8] his
недей [16] don't...
неделен [18] Sunday *(adj.)*
неделя [6] Sunday
недоразумение [26] misunderstanding

недостигнат [18] unattained
неестествен [24] unnatural
незабелязан [29] unnoticed
неизменно [25] constantly, always
неин, нейна [8] her, hers
нека [16] let, let's
некропол [24] necropolis
нелеп [28] absurd, preposterous
немец [22] German (male)
неми *see* ням
неминат [18] "untrodden"
немкиня [22] German (female)
немногоброен [20] not numerous
немски [17] German
необходим [21] necessary
необходимост [20] necessity ; по необходимост [20] of necessity
неопределен [16] indefinite, unspecified ; минало неопределено (време) [16] past indefinite (tense)
неочакван [27] unexpected, sudden
неподозиран [27] unsuspected, unexpected
неподражаем [28] inimitable, unique
непознат [5] unknown
непоканен [28] uninvited, without being asked
непокорен [18] disobedient, rebellious
непостижен [18] unattainable
неправилно [30] incorrectly, mistakenly
непреклонен [29] inflexible, adamant
непрекъснат [17] continuous, unbroken
непрекъснато [17] constantly, always
непременен [13] indispensable, necessary
непременно [13] by all means
неприятен [23] unpleasant
неразделен [29] inseparable
нервен [17] nervous
несвършен [12] incomplete, imperfect ; несвършен вид [12] imperfective aspect ; минало несвършено време [14] imperfect tense
несигурност [23] insecurity, uncertainty
неспокоен [4] uneasy, restless
несравним [11] incomparable
нестинар [11] fire-dancer
нестинарство [11] fire-dancing, fire-walking
несъмнен [25] undoubted, undeniable
несъмнено [25] undeniably, without question
нетърпение [8] impatience ; чакам с нетърпение [8] await eagerly
неудобен [13] inconvenient, uncomfortable
неуморим [16] tireless
неустрашимост [29] fearlessness
нечетен [11] odd-numbered
нещастен [28] unhappy, ill-fated

Българо-английски речник (урок 1-30)

нещо [5] something ; нещо съм настинал [20] I have a bit of a cold
нея [10] her *(direct object pronoun)*
ни [5] us *(direct object pronoun)*
ни [7] [to] us *(indirect object pronoun)*
ни [8] not, neither
ни ... ни [8] neither...nor
нива [10] (corn)field
ниво [18] level
ние [1] we
нижа (-еш) [14] thread, string together
никак [8] not at all
никакъв [8] none, no kind of
никога [8] never
никого [8] no one *(object)*
никой [8] no one
никъде [8] nowhere ; никъде другаде [19] nowhere else
нисък [22] low, short, of short stature
нито [8] not, neither ; нито една дума [8] not a single word
нищо [8] nothing ; нищо, че няма [10] no matter that there isn't [any] ; няма нищо [17] no problem
но [2] but
нов [7] new ; Нова година [10] New Years
новина [5] [a piece of] news
новогодишен [11] New Year's *(adj.)* ; новогодишна честитка [11] New Year's greeting ; новогодишна елха [13] New Year's tree ; новогодишен празник [27] New Year's celebration
нога [12] leg *(dialectal, poetic)*
ноември [9] November
нож *(plural* ножове*)* [7] knife
ножче [13] [razor] blade
нокът, нокътят *(plural* нокти*)* [8] nail (on finger or toe)
номадски [20] nomadic
номер *(plural* номера*)* [2] [3] [8] number; size ; правя номера на [8] play dirty tricks on ; смален с два номера [20] shrunk two sizes ; изходящ / входящ номер [23] "outgoing/incoming number" on official documents
норвежец [23] Norwegian (male)
норвежка [23] Norwegian (female)
норма [30] standard, norm
нос, -ът *(plural* носове*)* [11] nose ; затварям вратата под носа [на] [13] shut the door in [someone's] face
носия [16] dress ; народна носия [16] folk costume
нося [3] carry; wear
нотариален [17] notarized

нощ, -та [9] night ; през нощта [9] at night ; тази нощ [9] tonight ; цяла нощ не мигвам [25] not sleep a wink [all night]
нощем [24] at night
нощен [9] night *(adj.)* ; нощно време [9] nighttime
нужда [2] need ; няма нужда [2] there's no need, it's not necessary ; имаме нужда от въздух [4] we need air ; имате нужда от преглед [4] you need to be examined
нужен [17] necessary ; нужно е (да) [17] it's necessary, you have to
нула [17] zero
някак [8] somehow
някакъв [8] some sort
някога [8] [26] sometime; at one time, formerly
някого [8] someone *(object)*
някой [8] someone
няколко [6] several
някъде [8] somewhere
ням *(plural* неми*)* [22] mute, silent, dumb
няма [2] there isn't/aren't any ; няма нужда [2] there's no need, it's not necessary ; няма място за паника [3] there's no need to worry ; няма значение [9] it doesn't matter ; няма нищо страшно [11] there's nothing to be afraid of ; няма нищо [17] no problem
няма да [7] won't *(negative future particle)* ; нямаше да [16] wasn't/weren't going to
нямам [2] [3] not have

о [26] against
обаждам се / обадя се [10] [12] call, get in touch; come to the phone ; обаждам се по телефона [11] call on the phone ; може ли да се обади [12] can s/he come to the phone
обаче [7] however
обвинение [24] accusation
обвинявам / обвиня [25] accuse, blame ; обвинявам в [25] accuse [someone] of
обед *(or* обяд*)* [8] lunch
обеден [9] lunch, noon *(adj.)* ; обедно време [9] lunch time
обединявам / обединя [20] unify
обект [18] object, project, site
обективен [18] objective
обесвам / обеся [24] hang (by the neck)
обещавам / обещая [10] promise

Българо-английски речник (урок 1-30)

обеща́ние [21] promise
обзаве́ждам / обзаведа́ [16] equip, furnish
обзаве́ждам се / обзаведа́ се [16] get settled in, get installed
обзо́р [20] survey
оби́да [14] insult ; пона́сям оби́да [14] bear/sustain an insult
оби́ждам / оби́дя [17] offend, insult
оби́ждам се / оби́дя се [17] take offense
обикнове́н [8] usual
обикнове́но [2] usually
оби́лен [23] abundant
оби́рам / обера́ [8] plunder, pick
о́бич, -та́ [22] love
обича́ен, -а́йна [14] customary
обича́й [13] custom, convention
оби́чам [2] [3] like, love
о́блак [18] cloud
о́бласт, -та́ [19] region, sphere, domain
облекло́ [27] clothing, apparel ; скро́мно облекло́ [27] simple clothes
облекча́вам / облекча́ (-и́ш) [17] lighten, facilitate
обле́чен, -ена [14] dressed
обли́звам / обли́жа (-еш) [18] lick
о́блик [30] aspect, shape
обли́чам / облека́ (-че́ш) [13] dress [someone]
обли́чам се / облека́ се (-че́ш) [13] put on, don ; обли́чам се спо́ртно [13] dress casually, wear casual clothing
обме́ням / обменя́ [22] exchange
обмя́на [19] exchange ; обмя́на на о́пит [19] pooling [of] experience
обобща́вам / обобщя́ [30] generalize, draw a conclusion
обогатя́вам / обогатя́ [30] enrich ; обогатя́вам ре́чника [си] [30] enlarge [one's] vocabulary
обрабо́твам / обрабо́тя [30] cultivate, finish, polish
о́браз [18] image, form ; све́тъл о́браз [18] a noble figure
образе́ц [23] model, pattern
образова́ние [3] education ; сре́дно образова́ние [16] secondary education ; ви́сше образова́ние [16] higher education
образу́вам [30] form, constitute
обра́тно [23] back, the other direction
о́бред [22] ritual, ceremony
обръ́щам / объ́рна [24] turn, turn over
обръ́щам се / объ́рна се [14] turn ; обръ́щам се с гръ́б [17] turn one's back ; обръ́щам се наза́д [23] turn back, look back ; обръ́щам внима́ние на [23] pay attention to

обслу́жвам / обслу́жа (-иш) [20] serve, cater for
обстано́вка [25] situation, context
обстоя́телство [19] circumstance
обсъ́ждам / обсъ́дя [23] discuss, debate, consider
обу́вам / обу́я [13] put someone's shoes, stockings, etc. on
обу́вам се / обу́я се [13] put on shoes, stockings, etc.
обу́вка [3] shoe ; здра́ви обу́вки [20] sturdy shoes
обу́ща [13] footwear
обуща́р [19] shoemaker
обши́рен [22] wide, extensive, spacious
о́бщ [7] general, common ; с о́бщи уси́лия [19] working all together
общество́ [12] [23] society; community
обще́ствен [23] social, public
обще́ственост [20] public ; култу́рна обще́ственост [20] cultural circles
общонаро́ден [30] nationwide, general
общу́ване [30] association, dealings ; сре́дство за общу́ване [30] means of communication
объ́рквам / объ́ркам [24] confuse, perplex, bewilder, frustrate
обя́ва [23] announcement, advertisement
обявя́вам / обявя́ [19] announce, proclaim
обя́д [9] (see also о́бед) lunch, noon ; след обя́д [9] afternoon, after lunch
обя́двам [17] have lunch
обясня́вам / обясня́ [17] explain
обясне́ние [24] explanation
ово́щен [25] fruit (adj.) ; ово́щна гради́на [25] fruit orchard
овца́ [19] sheep
овча́р (ка) [19] shepherd(ess)
о́вчи [21] sheep (adj.)
огладня́вам / огладне́я [4] get hungry
огледа́ло [11] mirror
о́глед [25] view, inspection ; с о́глед на [25] with an eye to
огле́ждам / огле́дам [14] survey, examine
огле́ждам се / огле́дам се [14] look at one's reflection
оглуша́вам / оглуше́я [21] go deaf
огни́ще [27] fireplace, hearth; center
огра́да [18] fence
огро́мен [18] huge, enormous
огря́вам / огре́я [19] illuminate, light up
о́гън (plural огньо́ве) [7] fire ; накла́ждам о́гън [22] light a fire
оде́ски [29] of or pertaining to Odessa
одея́ло [23] blanket
одобре́ние [23] approval
одухотворе́н [28] spiritual, exalted
оже́нвам / оже́ня [11] marry (transitive)

Българо-английски речник (Урок 1-30)

оже́нвам се / оже́ня се [11] get married
оживе́н [30] animated ; оживе́н спо́р [30] lively debate
означа́вам / означа́ (-и́ш) [21] mark; mean, signify
ока́звам / ока́жа (-еш) [30] render, give ; ока́звам влия́ние [30] exert influence
ока́звам се / ока́жа се (-еш) [22] turn out, prove to be
ока́чвам / окача́ (-и́ш) [24] hang, suspend
оки́чвам / оки́ча (-иш) [13] adorn, decorate
око́ (*plural* очи́) [12] eye ; ка́звам му в очи́те [20] tell him to his face ; вредя́ на очи́те [20] be hard on one's eyes ; с дебе́ли очи́ [22] shameless ; де́то (ог къде́то) ми очи́ ви́дят [25] wherever my feet lead me
око́лен [23] neighboring, adjacent, surrounding; roundabout
о́коло [21] around, in the vicinity of
оконча́телен [19] final, definitive
окостеня́вам / окостеня́ [24] take skeletal shape
окръ́жен [23] county, regional
окто́мври [6] October
окъ́пвам се / окъ́пя се (-еш) [14] bathe
олимпиа́да [20] Olympic games
о́лио [6] cooking oil
оме́квам / оме́кна [11] soften, grow milder
оми́там / омета́ [25] sweep clean; polish off
омле́т [4] omelet
омръ́звам / омръ́зна [12] tire, bore ; омръ́зна ми [12] I'm bored
омърлу́шен [20] down in the mouth, low-spirited
она́зи [8] that *(feminine)*
она́я [11] that (*variant of* она́зи)
оне́зи [8] those
о́нзи [8] that (*masculine*) ; о́нзи де́н [9] the day before yesterday
они́я [11] those (*variant of* оне́зи)
онкологи́чен [19] oncological, cancer-related ; онкологи́чни заболя́вания [19] [cases of] cancer
онколо́гия [19] oncology, cancerous diseases
онова́ [8] that *(neuter)*
ону́й [11] that (*variant of* онова́)
о́ня [11] that (*variant of* о́нзи)
опа́сен [4] dangerous
опа́сност [17] danger
опа́шка [11] tail; line, queue ; ча́кам на опа́шка [11] wait in/on line ; въртя́ опа́шка [22] wag tail
о́пера [12] opera

опера́ция [17] operation
операцио́нен [17] operating ; операцио́нна (за́ла) [17] operating room/theater
опери́рам [16] operate
опи́свам / опи́ша (-еш) [7] describe
о́пит [19] attempt, try; experience ; обмя́на на о́пит [19] pooling [of] experience
опи́твам / опи́там [16] try, taste
о́питен [28] experienced, veteran; experimental
опи́чам / опека́ (-че́ш) [22] roast, bake
опла́квам / опла́ча (-еш) [11] mourn, lament, weep ; жи́в да го опла́чеш [11] it makes your heart bleed to see him
опла́квам се / опла́ча се (-еш) [11] complain, grumble
опозна́вам / опозна́я [7] recognize, get to know
опо́мням се / опо́мня се [12] bring to [one's] senses ; опо́мни се! [12] snap out of it!
оправда́ние [25] justification
опра́вям / опра́вя [18] settle, put in order ; опра́вям легло́ [28] make a bed
опра́вям се / опра́вя се [27] work out, get better; find one's way, manage
определе́н [23] definite, precise
определя́м / определя́ [26] define, specify
оприлича́вам, оприлича́ (-и́ш) [27] liken, compare [to]
опростя́вам / опростя́ [21] simplify
опустя́л [29] deserted
ора́ [19] plough, till
ора́тор [30] speaker, speech-maker,
ора́ч [19] ploughman
организа́тор [19] organizer, sponsor
организи́рам [12] organize
оре́л (*plural* орли́) [20] eagle
о́рех [6] walnut
оригина́лен [17] original
ориенти́р [28] landmark, reference point
ориенти́рам [19] orient, put on the right track
ориенти́рам се [19] get one's bearings
ори́з [6] rice
о́рлов [20] eagle's
орнаме́нтика [23] ornamentation
о́с, -та́ [27] axis; axle
освежи́телен [18] refreshing
освободи́тел [16] liberator
освобожде́ние [30] liberation, emancipation
освен [4] except [for]; in addition to ; освен това́ [4] besides, in addition
освен че [17] not only

Българо-английски речник (урок 1-30)

осем [6] eight
осемдесет [6] eighty
осемнайсет [6] eighteen
осемнайсети [8] eighteenth
осемстотин [9]· eight hundred
оскъден [23] scarce, meager
осми [8] eighth
основа [21] base, grounding ; лежа в основата на [21] underlie, be at the root of ; градя върху основата на [21] build on the foundations of
основавам / основа [20] found, establish
основател (ка) [29] founder
основен [16] basic, fundamental ; основен речников фонд [30] basic word stock
особен [10] special, particular
особено [8] especially
особеност [30] peculiarity, feature
оспорвам / оспоря [19] contest, dispute
оставам / остана [3] [4] remain, stay ; остава още малко [3] there's still a little left ; остава да [16] it remains to
останал [9] remained, left, left-over
оставям / оставя [8] leave (transitive) ; остави [29] never mind, leave it be
остарявам / остарея [17] grow old
остров [26] island
осъществявам / осъществя [23] realize, fulfill, carry out
от [1] [4] [6] [8] from; of; since (time) ; than ; салата от зеле [4] cabbage salad ; имам нужда от [4] need, have need of ; от всички страни [6] from/on all sides ; от един час само [6] for only an hour ; от н.е. [9] A.D. ; от дете [12] since childhood ; от ваша страна [15] on your part ; от един път [29] all at once
отбивам се / отбия се [18] drop in
отблясък [27] reflection, gleam
отбор [12] team
отварям / отворя [2] [3] [4] open
отведнаж (or отведнъж) [27] suddenly, all at once
отвеждам / отведа [24] lead off, take away
отворен, -ена [2] open
отвратителен [27] disgusting, abominable
отвън [11] from outside
отвътре [9] from within
отглеждам / отгледам [20] grow, cultivate, breed, nourish
отговарям / отговоря [10] answer
отговор [7] answer
отговорност [17] responsibility
отгоре [11] from above
отдавам се / отдам се (-дадеш) [28] abandon oneself to
отдавна [6] long ago ; отдавна вече [6] for a long time now
отдалечен [26] remote, distant
отделен [3] separate ; отделно издание [19] separate edition, book form
отделно [2] separately, under separate cover
отделям / отделя [18] separate, detach
отдолу [11] from below
отдясно [11] from the right
отечествен [22] of one's native land; patriotic ; Отечествен Фронт [25] Fatherland Front
отечество [22] native land
отзад [3] in back, in the rear, behind
отивам / отида [5] [26] go; suit ; тази шапка много ти отива [26] that hat fits you well ; отивам на [нечия] възраст [27] be appropriate to [one's] age
отказвам / откажа (-еш) [13] cancel, renounce, refuse
отказвам се / откажа се (-еш) [21] give up, cancel
откакто [10] [ever] since
отключвам / отключа (-иш) [16] unlock
откога [16] since when (interrogative)
отколкото [10] than, in as much
открай [27] from the beginning ; открай време [27] from time immemorial
откривам / открия [20] uncover, reveal; open
откриване [19] opening [ceremony]
открито [13] openly, overboard, without hiding
откритие [18] discovery
откъде [1] whence, from where (interrogative) ; откъде да мина [17] which way to go ; откъде да знам? [18] how should I know?
откъдето [18] whence, from where (relative)
откъсвам / откъсна [22] tear, break off, uproot
отлагам / отложа (-иш) [27] put off, postpone
отлитам / отлетя [26] fly away ; птиците отлитат на юг [26] the birds migrate south
отличавам / отлича (-иш) [18] distinguish
отличие [17] distinction ; пълно отличие [17] high honors
отляво [11] from the left
отменям / отменя [22] abolish, cancel
отмерен [27] measured, deliberate

Българо-английски речник (урок 1-30)

отминавам / отмина [14] pass by, leave behind
отнасям / отнеса [20] take away
отнасям се / отнеса се [20] [26] apply to; treat ; същото се отнася до/за него [20] the same applies to him ; отнасям се с доверие към [26] put trust in, rely on
отначало [14] at the beginning
отнемам / отнема [17] take away, deprive
отново [2] again, once more
относно [19] concerning, with respect to
отношение [23] attitude, relationship; regard ; отрицателно отношение [23] disapproval ; по отношение на [30] as regards
отопление [11] heating
отпадъци [17] garbage, trash, waste
отпечатвам / отпечатам [19] print up
отплувам [26] set sail, embark
отпразнувам [20] celebrate
отпред [29] in front
отпуска [2] break, time off, vacation ; в отпуска [2] on a break, on vacation
отпътувам [7] set off for, depart
отражение [21] reflection; repercussion
отразявам / отразя [21] [22] reflect; refute
отраствам / отрасна [26] grow up
отрицател (ка) [28] detractor, denier
отрицателен [23] negative ; отрицателно отношение [23] disapproval
отричам / отрека (-чеш) [28] deny, reject
отровен [20] poisonous
отръки [18] ; иде ми отръки [18] I'm good at, handy at
отрязвам / отрежа (-еш) [18] cut off, cut out
отсега [30] from now on
отсичам / отсека (-чеш) [26] cut off; cut down ; отсичам глава [26] behead
отскачам / отскоча (-иш) [26] jump off, rebound
отскоро [11] [since] quite recently ; женени сме съвсем отскоро [11] we've just gotten married
отскубвам / отскубна [26] pluck out; wrest from
отспивам си / отспя си [29] sleep well, catch up on sleep
отсреща [18] across the way
отстранявам / отстраня [24] remove, eliminate
отстъпвам / отстъпя [8] step back, yield, give up
отсъствие [23] absence
отсядам / отседна [18] put up, stay at
оттам [3] from there
оттеглям се / оттегля се [22] withdraw, retire
оттогава [18] from that time
оттука, оттук [5] from here
отчайвам се / отчая се [26] get discouraged, despair
отчаяно [29] desperately
отървавам се / отърва се [23] get rid of, get off
ОФ-линия [25] party line of the Fatherland Front coalition
официален [21] official, formal
оформен (and оформен) [30] formed
оформям / оформя [21] shape, fashion ; draw up
охлюв [14] snail shell
оцелявам / оцелея [29] survive, be left standing
оценявам / оценя [20] value, estimate
оцет [20] vinegar
очаквам [7] await, expect
очаквам се [19] be liable to occur, be expected
очакване (plural -ния) [21] expectation
очаровам [17] charm, fascinate
очертание [21] outline, delineation
очи see око
очила (plural) [11] eyeglasses
още [2] still, yet ; още много [2] a lot more, still a lot ; още не говоря [3] I don't/can't speak yet ; тя още не чете [3] she doesn't [know how to] read yet ; още не [5] not yet ; още веднъж [16] again, once more ; още повече [19] all the more

па [22] and, but
паве [19] paving-stone, cobble
падам / падна [7] fall ; пада голям сняг [7] ; it's snowing heavily
падам се [17] fall to, go to ; какъв ти се пада той? [17] what [relation] is he to you?
падеж [30] (grammatical) case
пазар [16] market
пазаря [27] hire
пазач [24] guard, keeper
пазва [28] bosom ; пазви [28] recesses
пазя [8] guard, preserve
пак [9] again ; все пак [18] nevertheless
пакет [23] pack, package

Българо-английски речник (Урок 1-30)

па́кост [24] mischief, harm, damage ; пра́вя па́кост [24] make mischief, cause damage
па́костен [18] harmful, pernicious
пакостли́в [24] mischievous, naughty
пала́тка [25] tent
па́лец [12] thumb, big toe
палто́ [13] coat
па́мет, -та́ [18] memory ; ако не ме́ лъ́же паметта́ [18] if memory serves correctly
па́метник [17] monument; manuscript
паму́к [21] cotton
паму́чен [21] cotton (adj.)
па́ника [3] panic, worry ; ня́ма мя́сто за па́ника [3] there's no need to worry
панталон (or панталони) [14] pants
пантео́н [23] pantheon
папага́л [9] parrot
пара́ [11] coin
па́рен [11] steam (adj.) ; па́рно отопле́ние [11] central heating ; па́рна маши́на [29] steam engine
пари́ [11] money ; пе́т пари́ не да́вам [14] I don't give a damn
па́рк [16] park
па́ркинг [18] parking lot, carpark
па́ртия [14] party
парца́л [14] rag
парфе́ [26] parfait, ice-cream dish
парче́ [19] piece, portion
паса́ж [21] passage
паспо́рт [18] passport
па́ста [26] cake, pastry ; paste
патладжа́н [28] eggplant
патриа́рх [17] patriarch
па́уза [18] pause, break
па́фта [16] buckle
пацие́нт (ка) [4] [medical] patient
певе́ц [10] singer
певи́ца [23] female singer
пейза́ж [3] landscape, natural scene
пе́йка [3] bench
пека́ (-че́ш) [13] bake, roast
пека́ се (-че́ш) [13] warm oneself, sun ; пека́ се на слъ́нце [13] sunbathe
пенсионе́р (ка) [17] retired [person]
пера́ [12] wash ; пера́ на ръка́ [16] wash out by hand
пери́од [17] period (of time)
перо́ [22] feather
перо́н [7] (railway) platform
перси́йски [23] Persian
пе́сен, -та́ (plural пе́сни) [9] song
пе́т [6] five ; пе́т пари́ не да́вам [14] I don't give a damn
пета́ [12] heel
петвеко́вен [20] five centuries long (adj.)
петдесе́т [6] fifty
пете́л (plural петли́) [24] cock, rooster
пети́ма [6] five (masculine animate)
пе́ти [8] fifth
пети́ца [10] [25] "5" (next to top mark in school); № 5 tram or bus
петна́йсет [6] fifteen
петно́ [14] spot
пе́тстотин [9] five hundred
пе́тък [9] Friday
пехлива́н [29] wrestler
пехлива́нски [29] wrestler's
печа́лен [16] sad
печа́т [23] stamp, seal; printing press ; у́дрям печа́т на [23] put seal to
печеля [20] earn, gain
пе́чка [23] stove
пеша́ [9] on foot ; хо́дя пеша́ [9] go for a walk, walk (not ride)
пещера́ [26] cave, grotto
пе́я [11] sing
пиа́но [21] piano
пи́вница [22] pub, saloon
пи́ене [20] drinking ; не е́ за пи́ене [20] not fit to drink
пие́са [12] play (theater)
пи́йвам / пи́йна [18] have a drink, a shot
пи́ле [18] chick, chicken; sweetheart
пи́лешки [23] chicken (adj.) ; пи́лешки дро́бчета [23] chicken livers
пи́пам / пи́пна [9] touch, handle
пи́пвам / пи́пна [28] touch; lay one's hands on ; пи́пвам (or хва́щам) на местопрестъпле́нието [28] catch in the act
пипе́р [17] pepper (spice)
писа́тел (ка) [10] writer
писќюл [13] tassel, pendant
пи́смен [21] written; for writing
пи́сменост [20] writing, literacy
писмо́ [8] [21] letter; [system of] writing
пи́сък (plural пи́съци) [28] shriek, squeal
пи́там [4] ask
пи́там се [18] wonder
пи́тка [24] cake, flat loaf
пихти́я [24] jelly; pulp
пи́ца [21] pizza
пи́ша (-еш) [3] write
пи́шеща маши́на [26] typewriter
пи́я [3] drink
пия́ница [10] drunkard
плагиа́тство [25] plagiarism
пла́дне [29] noon ; тра́я от де́н до пла́дне [29] be short-lived
пла́ж [14] beach
пла́н [7] plan
планина́ [3] mountain ; на планина́ [20] in the mountains

Българо-английски речник (урок 1-30)

планински [16] mountain (adj.)
платно́ [16] cloth, fabric ; бял като платно́ [21] white as a sheet
плах [28] timid, shy, furtive
пла́ча (-еш) [16] weep, cry
пла́ша (-иш) [9] frighten
пла́ша се (-иш) [11] be frightened
пла́щам / платя́ [4] pay
пле́ме (*plural* племена́) [20] tribe, clan
пле́менник [10] nephew
пле́менница [10] niece
плена́рен [19] plenary ; плена́рен докла́д [19] keynote paper
пленя́вам / пленя́ [18] take captive, captivate
плета́ [18] knit, braid, plait
пле́щи [27] shoulders
пли́свам / пли́сна [21] pour; fling
пли́тък [23] shallow
плод (*plural* плодове́) [7] fruit
плодоро́ден [20] fertile
пло́ча [7] [13] tile, slab; phonograph record
пло́чка [3] tile
пло́чкаджия [18] tile-layer
площа́д [18] [city] square
плу́вам [9] swim
плуве́ц [23] swimmer
плувки́ня [23] female swimmer
плъ́нка [16] filling
плът, -та́ [24] flesh, body
плющя́ [29] flap, lash
по [3] [5] [7] each; along, down; according to, in the manner of; about ; ха́йде по една́ глъ́тка [3] let's each have a drink ; по коридо́ра [5] down the corridor ; преподава́тел по бъ́лгарски [5] teacher of Bulgarian ; по това́ вре́ме [7] at about that time ; по та́я рабо́та [18] on that score
по́- [8] [10] more... (*comparative degree particle*) ; по́-ху́бав [8] nicer, prettier ; по́-голя́м [10] older ; по́-ма́лък [10] younger ; по́-ра́но [14] before, earlier ; "used to..." ; по́-ми́налата годи́на [18] the year before last
побе́да [30] victory
победи́тел (ка) [19] victor, winner
побежда́вам / победя́ [19] conquer, defeat, win
побра́тим [25] blood brother
побъ́рзвам / побъ́рзам [7] hurry up
поведе́ние [18] behavior, conduct
пове́ждам / поведа́ [26] lead, conduct
повели́телен [24] authoritative ; повели́телно наклоне́ние [24] imperative mood
повели́телка [23] lady sovereign, queen
по́вече [7] more ; по́вечето [11] the majority ; о́ще по́вече [19] all the more
пови́квам / пови́кам [13] call, call out
повлия́вам / повлия́я [19] influence, affect
по́вод [13] occasion, cause ; по по́вод [13] regarding, in connection with
повта́рям / повторя́ [12] repeat
повторе́ние [12] repeat, replay
повъртя́вам се / повъртя́ се [25] rotate for a while; hang around for a while
повъ́рхностен [29] superficial
повя́рвам [8] believe, give credence to
по́глед [20] look, glance; view ; скри́вам се от по́гледа [20] drop out of sight; hide from view
погле́ждам / погле́дна [14] have a look, look at ; погледни́ [14] look! look over there!
поглъ́щам / поглъ́на [28] swallow up, devour
погово́рвам / поговоря́ [12] talk for a bit
погре́бвам / погреба́ [16] bury
погребе́ние [23] funeral, burial
погри́жвам се / погри́жа се (-иш) [11] take care of, look after
поглъ́на *see* поглъ́щам
под [3] under ; затва́рям врата́та под но́са [на] [13] shut the door in [someone's] face ; хва́щам под ръка́ [22] take [someone's] arm
под [4] floor
пода́вам / пода́м (-даде́ш) [11] hand, pass, reach ; пода́вам молба́ [19] submit a [formal] request ; срок за пода́ване на докуме́нти [20] application deadline ; пода́ваме си ръце́ [22] join hands
пода́рък [7] present, gift
подаря́вам / подаря́ [9] give [away], give a present
подви́вам / подвия́ [26] bend, tuck under ; не подви́вам крак [26] be constantly on the move
подго́нвам / подго́ня [26] chase, drive away
подго́твям / подго́твя [12] prepare, make ready
подгото́вка [5] preparation ; подгото́вката върви́ [5] the preparation's coming along
поде́м [23] upsurge, progress, revival
подир [29] after
по́диум [16] platform, dais
подкопа́вам / подкопа́я [26] undermine
подкре́па [21] support

Българо-английски речник (урок 1-30)

подлагам / подложа (-иш) [26] put under, subject to
подмамвам / подмамя [24] entice, lure
поднасям / поднеса [6] present, offer, serve
подобавам [17] befit ; както подобава [17] in a proper manner
подобен [8] similar ; нищо подобно [8] nothing of the sort
подобрявам / подобря [20] improve, ameliorate
подозирам / подозра [14] suspect, be suspicious
подозрителен [29] suspicious
подпалвам / подпаля [24] set fire to, ignite
подпирам / подпра [14] prop up, support ; подпирам си брадичката [14] [sit] with chin in hand
подпис [17] signature
подписвам / подпиша (-еш) [18] sign [one's name]
подписвам се / подпиша се (-еш) [17] affix one's signature
подпора [18] support, pillar
подправка [6] spice (cooking)
подреждам / подредя [23] arrange, put in order
подробен [13] detailed
подробно [13] in detail
подробност [17] detail ; пълни подробности [17] complete details
подсещам / подсетя [4] remind, call to mind ; това ме подсеща [4] that reminds me
подсказвам / подскажа (-еш) [13] hint, prompt
подскачам / подскоча (-иш) [30] jump, leap about
подслушвам / подслушам [24] eavesdrop, listen in on
подхлъзвам се / подхлъзна се [22] slip, trip
подходящ [17] suitable, appropriate
подчинявам / подчиня [23] subordinate, subject
подъл [26] base, vile
поезия [18] poetry
поемам / поема [8] take, take up ; поемам [си] дъх [8] catch one's breath ; поемам ръководството на съюза [24] take on union leadership
поен, пойна [28] song (adj.) ; пойна птица [28] songbird
поет [18] poet
поетеса [18] poetess
поетичен [18] poetic
поетически [29] poet's, poetic

пожелавам / пожелая [8] wish ; пожелавам от сърце [10] send heartfelt wishes
пожелание [23] wish ; сърдечни пожелания [23] best wishes
поза [18] posture, attitude
позволение [22] permission
позволявам / позволя [6] allow
позвънявам / позвъня [9] call
поздрав [2] greeting
поздравителен [23] congratulatory ; поздравителна телеграма [23] telegram of congratulations
поздравявам / поздравя [18] greet
позеленявам / позеленея [21] turn green
позлата [23] gilt, gold-leaf
познавам [3] know, be acquainted with
познавам / позная [1] [3] [7] know; guess ; познавам по очите [7] tell by [some]one's eyes ; познавам число [14] pick/guess a number
познайник [13] male acquaintance
познайница [13] female acquaintance
познат [8] acquaintance
позор [19] disgrace ; срам и позор! [19] for shame!
поигравам / поиграя [10] play for a while
поисквам / поискам [12] want, wish, ask for
показвам / покажа (-еш) [7] show
покана [19] invitation
поканвам / покана [10] invite
покоен, покойна [20] late, deceased
поколение [16] generation
покрай [10] [26] because of; alongside, past
покрив [3] roof
покривам / покрия [22] cover, overlay
покривка [22] cover (tablecloth, bedspread)
покровител (ка) [20] patron
покръствам / покръстя [20] convert to Christianity
покупка [23] purchase ; отивам на покупки [23] go shopping
пола [19] skirt
полагам / положа (-иш) [21] lay, put
поле [15] field, plain
полезен [8] useful ; полезно за здравето [8] good for you [for one's health] ; мога ли с нещо да бъда полезен? [13] can I help in some way?
полза [12] use, advantage ; каква е ползата [12] what's the use ; говоря в полза на [29] argue in favor of
поливам / полея [13] pour ; ела да ти полея [13] let me pour water (over

your hands) ; поли́вам цветя́та [13] water the flowers ; това́ тря́бва да се поле́е [22] this calls for a drink
поликли́ника [17] clinic, polyclinic
поли́там / политя́ [26] fly off, soar
политик [20] politician
поли́тика [20] politics ; би́стря поли́тиката [20] discuss politics
полити́чески [23] political
поли́ция [21] police
полови́н(а) [6] half
положе́ние [19] position
положи́телен [20] positive
полуно́щ [9] midnight
получа́вам / полу́ча (-иш) [8] receive, get
полюбопи́тствувам [22] inquire, show curiosity
поля́ [23] (*poetic plural of* поле́)
поля́к [23] Pole (male)
поляки́ня [23] Pole (female)
поля́на [16] meadow, clearing
пома́гам / помо́гна [7] help
помеще́ние [22] premises, room
помири́свам / помири́ша (-еш) [28] smell, sniff
поми́слям / поми́сля [12] think about
поми́слям си / поми́сля си [25] think it over, think twice
помо́лвам / помо́ля [13] beg, ask
по́мня [13] remember
по́мощ, -та́ [9] help ; бъ́рза по́мощ [18] first aid, ambulance ; с помощта́ на [29] by means of, thanks to
помръ́двам се / помръ́дна се [19] budge
понаболя́ва (*3d person*) [20] hurt a little; ache from time to time
понастоя́щем [17] at present
поня́сям / понеса́ [14] carry off; sustain, endure ; поня́сям оби́да [14] bear/ sustain an insult
поне́ [9] at least
понеде́лник [9] Monday
поня́кога [8] sometimes
поня́тие [30] concept, notion
пооста́вам / пооста́на [30] stay a little longer
поотде́лно [19] separately, individually
попа́дам / попа́дна [17] fall, land, happen on
попа́рвам / попа́ря [25] steam, scald
попи́твам / попи́там [14] ask, inquire
попи́твам се / попи́там се [13] ask oneself, wonder
попра́вка [16] correction, repair ; но́ся на попра́вка [16] take in for repairs
попра́вям / попра́вя [19] fix, correct, mend

попрекаля́вам / попрекаля́ [25] overdo, go a bit too far
поприка́звам [11] have a chat
популя́рен [12] popular
попъ́лвам / попъ́лня [23] replenish; fill in, complete
попя́вам / попе́я [11] sing a little
поради [20] because of
поразхо́ждам / поразхо́дя [11] take for a brief stroll
пора́ствам / пора́сна [14] grow up
поро́да [19] breed, race ; ра́сова поро́да [19] pedigreed
по́рта [18] gateway
портмоне́ [25] purse, change-purse
портока́л [10] orange
портока́лов [10] orange (*adj.*)
портре́т [17] portrait
по́рция [7] portion, serving
поръ́свам / поръ́ся [17] sprinkle
поръ́чвам / поръ́чам [4] order
поръ́чка [27] order, commission
поря́звам / поре́жа (-еш) [21] cut
поса́ждам / посадя́ [8] seat, plant
посве́твам / посве́тна (*or* посветя́) [18] shine for a while
поседя́вам / поседя́ [26] stay or sit for a while
посети́тел [22] visitor; patron, customer
посеща́вам / посетя́ [11] visit
посеще́ние [28] visit
по́сле [2] [6] later, afterwards; then
после́двам [18] follow
после́ден [6] last ; в после́дно вре́ме [6] lately ; чета́ до после́дната бу́ква [8] read every last word ; в после́дния моме́нт [22] at the last minute
после́дица [23] consequence
последова́телност [21] sequence, order; consistency
после́дствие [19] consequence
послу́швам / послу́шам [20] take advice, listen to, obey
посмя́вам / посме́я [16] dare
посо́ка [6] direction ; пи́там за посо́ката [6] ask directions
посоля́вам / посоля́ [9] salt
посо́чвам / посо́ча (-иш) [21] indicate, point out
посре́дством [30] by means of, through
посре́щам / посре́щна [5] meet, greet, entertain
пост [10] Lent; fast
поста́вям / поста́вя [30] put, produce ; поста́вям въпро́с [30] pose a question

постара́вам се / постара́я се [20] try, do one's best
по́стен [10] Lenten, pertaining to fasting
постепе́нен [21] gradual
постоя́вам / постоя́ [16] stay for a bit
постоя́нен [10] constant
постоя́нно [10] constantly
построя́вам / построя́ [16] construct, build
постъ́пвам / постъ́пя [17] proceed, act, enter ; постъ́пвам в университе́т [17] enter university
постя́гам / постегна [11] tighten, fasten; prepare, fix up
пота́ен, пота́йна [26] secret, mysterious
поте́глям / поте́гля [22] set out, set off
по́тен [19] sweaty, perspiring
поти́чам / потека́ (-че́ш) [12] start flowing
потъ́нал [27] sunk, absorbed
потърпя́вам / потърпя́ [27] have a little patience
потъ́рсвам / потъ́рся [7] look for, seek
поусми́хвам се / поусми́хна се [25] smile faintly, force a smile
похо́д [23] campaign, march
поча́квам / поча́кам [7] wait
по́чва [22] soil, ground
по́чвам / по́чна [10] begin, start, commence
почервеня́вам / почервене́я [21] turn red
поче́рпвам / поче́рпя [6] [23] treat someone to; draw from ; поче́рпвам вси́чки с по две́ [6] treat everyone to two each ; поче́рпен от архаи́чна тради́ция [23] drawn from ancient tradition
по́четен [19] honored; honorary
почи́вам / почи́на [3] [4] rest, go on holiday
почи́вам си / почи́на си [8] rest
почи́вен [8] rest (adjective) ; почи́вен де́н [8] day off, holiday
почи́вка [3] vacation trip, rest
почи́на [8] die
почи́ствам / почи́стя [22] clean, clean up
почи́там / почета́ [11] read for a bit
почита́тел (ка) [28] admirer
почти́ [8] almost
почти́телен [27] respectful, reverential
почу́вствувам (or почу́ствам) [14] have the feeling, realize, become aware
по́ща [3] mail, post office
пощаджи́я, -и́йка [10] letter carrier
по́щенски [10] postal ; по́щенска кути́я [10] mailbox
появя́вам се / появя́ се [14] appear
праба́ба [16] great-grandmother
пра́българи [20] proto-Bulgarians

пра́в [4] straight, upright ; стоя́ пра́в [4] stand, remain standing
правдоподо́бен [23] likely, probable
пра́вилен [19] right, straight, true
пра́вилно [19] correctly, rightly so
пра́вило [12] rule ; правила́ на пъ́тното движе́ние [12] traffic laws, rules of the road
пра́во [12] [legal] right ; и́мам пра́во [12] have the right ; а́вторско пра́во [12] copyright ; правата́ на живо́тните [12] animal rights
пра́во [17] straight, directly
правого́вор [30] orthoepy, correct pronunciation
правосла́вен [8] Orthodox [religion] (adj.)
правота́ [26] rightness, justice
пра́вя [3] do, make ; пра́вя и́злет [3] go on an excursion ; пра́вя номера́ на [8] play dirty tricks on ; пра́вя па́кости [24] make mischief, cause damage ; пра́вя карие́ра [28] make it in the world
пра́г [20] threshold
пра́зен [6] empty
пра́зник [10] [27] holiday; feast ; новогоди́шен пра́зник [27] New Year's celebration
празну́вам [10] celebrate
пра́ктика [21] practice
практи́чески [21] practical
пране́ [16] wash, laundry
прароди́на [20] first homeland; land of origin
прасе́ [18] pig
прасе́нце [18] piglet
пра́х, -ъ́т (plural прахове́) [25] dust ; напра́вя на пра́х [25] reduce to dust
пра́щам / пра́тя [2] [3] [4] send
пребива́вам [20] stay, sojourn
преброя́вам / преброя́ [6] count out
преве́ждам / преведа́ [18] translate
превиша́вам / превиша́ (-и́ш) [19] exceed, surpass
пре́вод [14] translation
преводач (ка) [21] translator
прево́звам / прево́зя [29] transport
прево́зен [29] transport (adj.) ; прево́зно сре́дство [29] vehicle, conveyance
превръ́щам / превъ́рна [18] transform
превъ́рзвам / превъ́ржа (-еш) [29] tie up, bandage
пре́глед [4] examination ; и́мате ну́жда от пре́глед [4] you need to be examined
прегле́ждам / прегле́дам [8] examine
преглъ́щам / преглъ́тна [25] swallow down, gulp

Българо-английски речник (Урок 1-30)

прегръщам / прегърна [16] embrace
прегърбвам се / прегърбя се [27] stoop
пред [19] in front of, before ; имам пред вид [19] bear in mind
предавам / предам (-дадеш) [27] deliver, transmit
предавам се / предам се (-дадеш) [29] give up, surrender
предан [22] devoted, faithful
предание [24] legend
предварителен [18] preliminary ; минало предварително време [19] past anterior tense ; бъдеще предварително [22] future anterior [tense] ; бъдеще предварително в миналото [23] future anterior in the past [tense]
предварително [18] in advance
предвиждам / предвидя [20] foresee; provide for
предводителство [20] leadership
преден [10] front, anterior
преди [6] ago ; преди 1 час [6] an hour ago
преди [6] [26] before; previously ; преди 1 ч. [6] before one o'clock ; преди н.е. [9] B.C. ; преди Р.Хр. [9] B.C.
преди да [14] before (relative conjunction)
предизвиквам / предизвикам [10] [25] provoke, defy; cause, evoke, induce
предимно [9] primarily
предимство [20] priority, advantage
предисторически [24] prehistoric
предишен [9] previous
предлагам / предложа (-иш) [8] proffer, propose
предложение [9] proposition, suggestion
предмет [23] object, article
предоставям / предостави [23] give, concede
предпазвам / предпазя [26] protect, safeguard
предписвам / предпиша (-еш) [18] prescribe
предполагам / предположа (-иш) [19] suppose, presume
предпочитам / предпочета [4] prefer
предразсъдък [29] prejudice, bias
предрешавам / предреша (-иш) [24] decide in advance, predetermine
представа [24] notion, concept
представителен [14] representative; personable, distinguished
представлявам [28] represent, be ; какво представлява [28] what it is like
представям / представя [13] present, offer
представям се / представя се [22] arise; introduce oneself, present oneself
представям си / представя си [13] imagine
предстоящ [9] forthcoming, impending
предупреждавам / предупредя [19] warn, caution; advise
предчувствувам [28] have a presentiment
прежалвам / прежаля [29] sacrifice, be reconciled to a loss
преживявам / преживея [19] experience, live through
преживяване [26] experience
през [4] [8] [9] during; through; at intervals ; гледам през прозореца [6] look out the window ; през седмица [8] every other week ; през деня [9] in the daytime ; през нощта [9] at night
презаписвам / презапиша (-еш) [30] make copies of recordings
презглава [25] headlong
президент [23] president
преизказвам (rare) [24] renarrate, retell
преизказно наклонение [24] renarrated mood
преки see пряк
прекален [13] too great, unconscionable ; прекалено голям [13] way too big
прекарвам / прекарам [7] spend
прекрасен [16] magnificent, splendid
прекратявам / прекратя [27] cease, suspend; break off
прелиствам / прелистя [23] turn the pages, leaf through
прелитам (or прелетявам) / прелетя [23] fly over
преждие [29] mishap, danger
премествам / преместя [17] move/put somewhere else
премествам се / преместя се [26] move, change residence
преминавам / премина [29] pass, proceed
премислям / премисля [23] think over, ponder
пренасям / пренеса [21] transfer, spread; transport
пренебрегвам / пренебрегна [23] neglect, ignore ; пренебрегвам съвет [23] disregard [someone's] advice
пренощувам [29] spend the night
преобладавам [23] predominate, prevail
препис [21] copy, transcript
преписвам / препиша (-еш) [13] rewrite, copy

Българо-английски речник (урок 1-30)

препита́ние [26] subsistence, livelihood ; тъ́рся препита́ние [26] try to make a living
преплитам / преплета́ [20] interweave
преплу́вам [26] swim/sail across
преподава́тел (ка) [1] teacher (university level)
преполовя́вам / преполовя́ [27] halve, be halfway through
препоръ́чвам / препоръ́чам [17] recommend
препрочи́там / препрочета́ [26] reread
препъ́вам се / препъ́на се [26] stumble, trip; falter
препъ́лнен [17] overfilled
преразгле́ждам / преразгле́дам [24] reconsider, re-examine
преря́звам / преря́жа (-еш) [21] cut through ; преря́зва ме [21] I feel a sharp pain
пре́сен, пря́сна [8] fresh
пресе́чка [11] intersection
преси́тен [22] satiated; fed up
преси́чам / пресека́ (-че́ш) [19] intercept, interrupt; cross [the street]
преска́чам / преско́ча (-иш) [23] jump over
преста́вам / преста́на [21] cease, stop
прести́ж [28] prestige
прести́лка [16] apron
преувелича́вам / преувелича́ (-и́ш) [27] exaggerate, overstate
преуморя́вам се / преуморя́ се [17] overwork, get overtired
префуча́вам / префуча́ (-и́ш) [18] rush past
прехвъ́рлям се / прехвъ́рля се [12] transfer; shift
пре́ходен [21] transitional
преценя́вам / преценя́ [18] estimate, assess
пре́ча (-иш) [8] bother
при [7] at, by
приба́вям / приба́вя [22] add, supplement
приби́рам / прибера́ [8] gather, collect
приби́рам се / прибера́ се [8] arrive home
приближа́вам / приближа́ (-и́ш) [14] approach
приблизи́телен [23] approximate
приблизи́телно [23] approximately, roughly
привли́чам / привлека́ (-че́ш) [9] attract, draw
привъ́рзан [11] tied, bound, attached
приго́твям / приго́твя [10] prepare, make ready

прида́вам / прида́м (-даде́ш) [26] add, lend; impart
придоби́вам / придоби́я [29] acquire
прие́мам / прие́ма [10] accept, adopt
прѝживе [16] during [one's] lifetime
призна́вам / призна́я [16] acknowledge, confess
призна́ние [21] acknowledgment, recognition
призна́телен [19] grateful
при́зрачен [26] ghostly, shadowy
прика́звам [9] talk, converse; say
при́казка [12] tale, story; chat, talking ; сла́дка при́казка [22] pleasant chat
приклю́чвам / приключа́ (-иш) [20] end, conclude
приключе́ние [14] adventure
прикля́квам / прикле́кна [25] squat
прикре́пвам / прикрепя́ [19] attach, join; support
прилиска́вам / прилиска́я [28] befriend
при́леп [29] bat
прили́чам [10] look like
прима́мвам / прима́мя [18] entice, allure
при́мер [18] example
примиря́вам / примиря́ [18] reconcile
примити́вен [29] primitive
принадлежа́ (-и́ш) [23] belong to, pertain to
принужда́вам / прину́дя [26] compel, coerce
приобща́вам / приобщя́ [21] incorporate
приобща́вам се / приобщя́ се [21] affiliate with ; приобща́вам се към [21] join
приро́да [7] nature
присви́вам / присви́я [23] bend ; присви́ва ме ко́рем [23] feel sharp pains in my abdomen
присре́щам / присре́щна [28] meet (poetic)
при́стан [28] wharf, moorage
присти́гам / присти́гна [6] arrive
присъединя́вам се / присъединя́ се [22] join, associate with
прису́ствие [20] presence
прису́ствувам (or прису́ствам) [16] be present, attend
притежа́тел (ка) [23] owner, possessor
притесня́вам / притесня́ [8] worry, cause concern to, embarrass
притесня́вам се / притесня́ се [7] worry ; не се́ притесня́вай [7] don't worry
притъпя́вам / притъпя́ [14] blunt, dull ; внима́нието му се притъпи́ [14] his attention wandered
приче́ска [12] haircut, hairstyle
причи́на [20] reason, cause

Българо-английски речник (урок 1-30)

приютя́вам / приютя́ [29] shelter, give refuge to
прия́тел (ка) [1] friend
прия́тен [9] pleasant ;
прия́тно [17] pleasant, pleasantly ; мно́го ни е прия́тно [17] we're very pleased
про́бвам [21] try
пробо́ждам / пробода́ [26] pierce, transfix ; пробо́ждам в сърце́то [26] stab in the heart
пробу́ждам се / пробу́дя се [22] awaken, be aroused
провѐждам се / проведа́ се [14] be conducted, be implemented
прове́рка [17] control, verification
проверя́вам / проверя́ [13] check, verify, test
прови́квам се / прови́кна се [25] exclaim, call out
прогимна́зия [16] junior high
прогно́за [19] prognosis ; прогно́за за вре́мето [19] weather forecast
програ́ма [8] program
продава́м / прода́м (-даде́ш) [6] sell
продава́ч (-ка) [7] salesperson
проду́кция [23] production, output
проду́мвам / проду́мам [22] utter, say a word
продължа́вам / продължа́ (-и́ш) [5] continue
продълже́ние [23] continuation, renewal; sequel ; в продълже́ние на [23] during, throughout
продължи́телност [26] duration ; продължи́телност на живо́та [26] life expectancy
прое́кт [23] project
прожекти́рам [20] show, project ; прожекти́рам филм [20] show a film
прозвуча́вам / прозвуча́ (-и́ш) [18] sound, ring out
прозо́рец (*plural* прозо́рци) [3] window
прозо́рче [13] small window
прозя́вам се / прозя́на се [25] yawn
произвѐждам / произведа́ [24] produce, make; cause
произво́дство [30] production, manufacture ; занаятчи́йско произво́дство [30] craft industry
произхо́д [20] origin, descent
произхо́ждам [23] come from; descend from
про́лет, -та́ [9] spring
про́летен [13] spring (*adj.*) ; про́летно равноде́нствие [13] vernal equinox
проли́вен [28] pouring ; проли́вен дъжд [28] driving rain

проло́жен [21] of or pertaining to a prologue
проме́ням / променя́ [11] change, alter
проме́ням се / променя́ се [11] change
промя́на (*plural* проме́ни) [13] change
прони́квам / прони́кна [20] penetrate, infiltrate
про́паст, -та́ [11] abyss, cavern
про́повед [21] sermon
про́пуск [19] clearance, pass; omission ; на про́пуска [19] at the clearance point
пропу́скам / пропу́сна [10] skip, let pass; miss
просве́тен [30] educational ; просве́тен де́ец [30] educationalist
прост [16] simple ; про́стите [29] common folk
про́сто [16] simply, just
прости́рам / простра́ [12] stretch out ; прости́рам дре́хи [12] hang clothes out to dry
просто́рен [18] spacious, roomy
простра́нен [21] spacious, extensive
просту́да [2] cold [illness]
простя́ *see* проща́вам
протести́рам [29] protest, remonstrate
про́тив [25] against ; про́тив съм [25] to be against [something]
проу́чвам / проу́ча (-иш) [30] study, investigate
професо́р [13] professor
прохла́ден [15] cool
проце́с [20] process
проце́сия [23] procession
про́чее [29] and so ; и про́чее и про́чее [29] etc., etc.
прочи́там / прочета́ [5] read (to completion)
прочу́т [27] famous, renowned
проща́вам / простя́ [16] forgive ; Бог да я прости́ [16] may she rest in peace ; проща́вай [17] excuse me
проща́вам се / простя́ се [29] bid farewell
проя́ва [21] manifestation, act
проявя́вам / проявя́ [8] appear, show ; проявя́вам интере́с към [8] take an interest in
пръв, пъ́рви [16] first
пръ́жки [20] cracklings, suet
пръст (*plural* пръ́сти) [12] finger, toe
пръст, -та́ [24] earth, soil
пръ́чка [20] stick, switch
пряк, пре́ки [17] direct
пря́сна *see* пре́сен
псевдони́м [18] pseudonym
психоло́г [26] psychologist

птица [7] bird ; пойна птица [28] songbird
публика [10] public
публикувам [19] publish
пуканка (*singular rare*) [9] popcorn
пуловер [12] sweater
пускам / пусна [10] let, allow; drop ; пускам писмо [10] mail a letter
пуст [10] empty; wretched, damned
пухкав [16] fluffy
пуша (-иш) [4] smoke
пушене [4] smoking
пушка [26] rifle, gun
пък [11] but, yet, and, while
пълен [5] [22] full; plump ; пълно копие [14] exact replica ; пълно отличие [17] high honors ; пълни подробности [17] complete details
пълноценен [18] complete, of full value
пълня [6] fill
пъпля (-еш) [26] creep, crawl
първенство [10] championship
първи [4] first
първоизточник [20] prime source, origin
първоначален [19] original, initial
първоучител [21] first teacher, founder of a doctrine
пържа (-иш) [6] fry
пържен, -ена [14] fried ; пържени филийки [14] French toast
пържола [4] chop, steak ; пържола с гарнитура [4] steak with the trimmings
пъстърва [9] trout
път (*plural* пъти) [4] [6] time (instance) ; за първи път съм тука [4] this is the first time I've been here ; другия път [17] the next time ; често пъти [27] time and again ; от (or на) един път [29] all at once
път, -ят (*plural* пътища) [6] [8] way, path, road ; дълъг път [6] a long way [to go] ; имам 6 часа път [6] have 6 hours to go ; по пътя [8] along the way
пътека [11] [foot]path
пътен [12] road (*adj.*), traveling ; правила на пътното движение [12] traffic laws, rules of the road ; пътни знаци [26] road signs
пътешествие [11] trip
пътник [7] traveler
пътувам [1] [3] travel
пътуване [7] travels, trip
пъшкам [29] groan, moan
пясък [20] sand

работа [2] [11] [17] work, job; matter; thing ; на работа съм [4] be at work ; ще свърши работа [11] it'll do the job ; имам си работа [14] have things to do ; не разбирам тези работи [17] I don't understand these things ; по тая работа [18] on that score ; работата край няма [25] [there's] no end of work ; вятър работа [25] nonsense, baloney ; върша домакинска работа [29] do housework
работен [6] work (*adj.*) ; работно време [6] office hours, hours of operation
работилница [23] workshop
работнически [24] worker's, workers' ; labor (*adj.*)
работлив [17] hard-working, industrious
работник [17] worker
работоспособен [9] efficient, productive
работя [4] [11] work, be in operation ; какво работите? [5] what [kind of] work do you do? ; не работи [11] it's out of order
равен [15] even, flat; equal
равнина [20] level plain
равнище [15] level, standard, plain ; морското равнище [15] sea level
равноденствие [13] equinox
радвам [17] make happy
радвам се [5] rejoice, be happy
радиация [25] radiation
радио [14] radio ; съобщавам по радиото [14] announce on the radio
радост [10] joy, pleasure
радостен [5] happy, joyful
раждам / родя [10] bear, give birth to, be fruitful
разбивам / разбия [17] break, beat
разбирам / разбера [1] [3] [4] understand
разбирам се / разбера се [12] come to an understanding, agree ; разбира се [3] of course
разбиране [12] understanding ; широко разбиране [12] liberal interpretation
разболявам се / разболея се [23] fall ill
развален [11] spoiled, rotten
развалям / разваля [17] [27] spoil, destroy; damage, break
развеждам / разведа [17] take about; divorce ; развеждам се с [17] get divorced from ; разведен [17] divorced
развивам, развия [21] develop, cultivate ; развива се лоза [21] the vine is putting out leaves
развитие [20] development, progress
развлечение [12] amusement

Българо-английски речник (урок 1-30)

развóй [18] development
разгáрям се / разгоря́ се [30] burn, run high
разглéждам / разглéдам [4] examine, study
разговáрям [10] converse
рáзговор [19] conversation
разговóрен [30] colloquial, conversational
разгрýщам / разгърна [28] unfold, display
раздáвам / раздáм (-дадéш) [8] give out, distribute
раздавáч (ка) [19] postman, letter-carrier
раздéлям / разделя́ [16] divide, split
рáзказ [14] story
разкáзвам / разкáжа (-еш) [8] relate, tell
разказвáч [24] narrator, storyteller
разкóпки [24] excavations
разкóш [23] luxury, splendor
разкупýвам / разкýпя [20] buy up
разлúвам / разлéя [17] spill, pour out
рáзлика [16] difference ; за рáзлика от [16] as opposed to
разлúствам се / разлúстя се [18] burst into leaf
разлúчен [10] different, various ; най-разлúчни нещá [10] all sorts of things
размáхвам / размáхам [17] swing, brandish ; размáхвам ръцé [17] wave one's hands about
размéням / разменя́ [29] exchange, trade
размéр [30] size, scale ; взéмам национáлни размéри [30] take on national proportions
размéствам / размéстя [28] transpose, rearrange
размéстване (*plural* -ния) shift ; цéнностни размéствания [28] changing values
разминáвам се / размúна се [15] pass each other, blow over
размúслям / размúсля [18] ponder; change one's mind
размишля́вам [18] speculate
рáзни [22] various, diverse ; рáзни хóра [22] all sorts of people
разновúдност [26] variety
разнообрáзен [16] varied
разнообрáзие [16] variety, diversity ; за разнообрáзие [16] for a change
разотúвам се / разотúда се [19] disperse, go different ways
разочарóвам [19] disappoint
разпáлвам се / разпáля се [27] flame up, become intense
разпéрвам / разпéря [26] spread, stretch out
разпúтвам / разпúтам [18] inquire, interrogate
разплáквам се / разплáча се (-еш) [14] burst into tears
разпознáвам / разпознáя [8] distinguish, discern
разполáгам се / располóжа се (-иш) [22] settle down
разположéние [22] situation, disposition ; на тя́хно разположéние съм [22] be at their disposal, be available to them
разпрáвям / разпрáвя [12] tell, relate ; разпрáвям виц [12] tell a joke
разпространя́вам / разпространя́ [19] distribute, disseminate
разпýждам / разпýдя [24] drive away, disperse
разпя́вам се / разпéя се [21] burst into song
разрешáвам / разрешá (-иш) [18] allow, permit
разрешéние [13] permission
разсáждам / разсадя́ [26] set out [seedlings]
разсмúвам се / разсмéя се [14] burst out laughing
разстоя́ние [29] distance, gap
разсъ́рдвам се / разсъ́рдя се [14] get angry
разтвáрям / разтвóря [28] open, open up wide
разтúчвам се / разтúчам се [29] bestir; run about
разтрошáвам / разтрошá (-иш) [18] break up, crumble
разýмен [13] sensible, rational
разýмно [25] judiciously, sensibly
разхвъ́рлям / разхвъ́рля [17] throw about, scatter
разхладúтелен [30] cooling, refreshing
разхóдка [9] walk, stroll ; извéждам кýчето на разхóдка [9] walk the dog ; разхóдка из градá [11] city tour
разхóждам / разхóдя [10] take for a walk
разхóждам се / разхóдя се [8] walk around, take a walk
разцвéт [23] bloom, flowering; zenith
разчúствам / разчúстя [25] tidy up, clear away
разчúтам [12] rely, count on ; мóжеш да разчúташ на мéне [12] you can count on me
разчúтам / разчетá [23] make out, decipher
разчýвам се / разчýя се [24] get out, get around

Българо-английски речник (урок 1-30)

разширявам / разширя [21] extend, broaden
район [16] district, region
рак [23] [25] crayfish, crab; cancer ; червен като рак [23] red as a lobster
ракия [2] rakia (strong brandy from fruits)
рамо (*plurals* рамена *or* рамене) [12] shoulder ; вдигам рамене [29] shrug shoulders
рана [29] wound
ранен [13] early
рано [9] early ; рано-рано [14] very early ; по-рано [14] before, earlier; "used to..."
раница [17] backpack, knapsack
ранобуден [28] early riser
расов [19] racial ; расова порода [19] pedigreed
растение [26] plant
реакция [19] reaction
реален [19] real, practicable
реваншрам се [5] make up, return a favor ; с нещо да се реваншрам [5] make [it] up with/by doing something
ревер [13] lapel
революционер (ка) [29] revolutionary
ревю (*neuter*) [13] revue, show ; модно ревю [13] fashion show
ред, -ът (*plural* редове) [17] row, range, line; series (of) ; идва ми редът [17] my turn is coming ; не е написал нито ред [21] he hasn't written a word
редактор (ка) [19] editor
редакция [19] editor's office
редица [21] row, series
редки *see* рядък
редовен [13] regular; in order
редовно [13] at regular intervals, regularly
редя [12] arrange, put in order ; редя се на опашка [12] get/wait in line
режа (-еш) [12] cut, slice
режисьор [12] director
резултат [18] result ; в резултат на [20] as a result of
резюме [19] summary, resumé
река (-чеш) [7] say, utter
река [9] river
ректорат [21] rector's office
релса [29] rail ; релси [29] track
ремонт [20] repairs
ремонтирам [2] redo, make repairs
репортаж [20] reporting, descriptive report
република [14] republic
ресторант [4] restaurant
рецепта [6] recipe
реч, -та [18] speech
речник [7] [30] dictionary; lexicon ; обогатявам речника [си] [30] enlarge [one's] vocabulary
речников [30] lexical ; основен речников фонд [30] basic word stock
реша (-еш) [13] comb
решавам, реша (-иш) [8] [11] solve; decide ; решавам кръстословица [8] do a crossword puzzle ; твърдо решавам [11] firmly resolve
решен [29] resolved, decided
решение [18] decision, solution ; вземам решение [18] arrive at a decision
решето [24] screen; colander
риба [9] fish ; ловя риба [9] fish, catch fish ; ходя за риба [9] go fishing
рибар [19] fisherman, fishmonger
рибен, -ена (*or* рибна) [21] fish *(adj.)*
риза [13] shirt, chemise
рилски [8] Rila *(adj.)*
рисувам [3] draw
рисунка [3] drawing
ритам [18] kick
ритвам / ритна [18] take a kick
ритъм [23] rhythm
роб [20] slave
робство [20] slavery, bondage ; турско робство [20] the Ottoman yoke
рогозенски [23] of or pertaining to Rogozen
род -ът (*plural* родове) [23] family, clan; genus, sort; gender
роден [11] one's own, native ; родно място [11] birthplace ; роден град [18] hometown ; родна сестра [18] birth sister (same parents) ; роден език [22] native language
роден [17] born ; роден(а) съм [17] I was born
родина [28] native land
родител [9] parent
роднина [10] relative
родов [23] family, lineal; generic
родя *see* раждам
рожден [5] birth *(adj.)* ; рожден ден [5] birthday
рождество [9] Christmas ; Рождество Христово [9] Christmas ; преди Р.Хр. [9] B.C. ; след Р.Хр. [9] A.D.
рой, роят (*plural* роеве) [22] swarm, host
рокля [12] dress
роля [20] role ; главна роля [27] the lead
роман [3] novel
романтичен [26] romantic
румънец [23] Romanian (male)
румънка [23] Romanian (female)

Българо-английски речник (урок 1-30)

рус [25] blond, fair
русин *(archaic)* [23] Russian (male)
руски [16] Russian *(adj.)*
рускиня [23] Russian (female)
руснак [23] Russian (male)
ръка (*plural* ръце) [12] hand, arm ; на ръка [16] by hand ; на бърза ръка [18] hastily ; хващам под ръка [22] take [someone's] arm
ръкавица [9] glove
ръководен [30] leading, guiding
ръководство [24] leadership ; поемам ръководството на съюза [24] take on union leadership
ръкопис [21] manuscript
ръкувам се [22] shake hands
ръченица [16] folk couple dance
рядкост [27] rarity
рядък, редки [10] rare
рядко [10] rarely

с [2] [9] with; by ; пътувам с влак [2] travel by train ; с всички сили [9] with all one's strength, full tilt ; с една дума [9] in a word ; с часове [9] for hours [on end] ; с малко закъснение [14] a little late
са [1] are *(3rd plural)* ; *see* съм
садя [26] plant
сако [13] jacket
саксонка [22] Saxon (female)
салам [11] sausage
салата [4] salad
сам, сама, само, сами [12] alone, [the] very, by oneself ; самият аз [12] I myself
само [1] only
само че [17] except *(conjunction)*
саможертва [17] self-sacrifice
самолет [11] airplane
самолетен [24] airplane *(adj.)*
самонадеян [25] self-reliant; self-confident, presumptuous
самообслужване [20] self-service
самостоятелен [27] independent, self-contained ; самостоятелно жилище [27] separate quarters
самосъзнание [18] self-awareness
самоутвърждаване [20] self-affirmation ; народностно самоутвърждаване [20] national self-determination
сандвич [9] sandwich
сандък [16] box, chest
сантименталност [22] sentimentality
сарми [6] stuffed cabbage or vine leaves
сатира [5] satire

САЩ = Съединените американски щати [1] USA (United States of America)
сближавам се / сближа се (-иш) [30] draw closer, become intimate
сбогувам се [18] say goodbye, take leave of
сборник [12] collection
сбърквам / сбъркам [20] err, get confused
Св. = Свети, Света
свако [22] uncle (aunt's husband)
свалям / сваля [18] remove, throw down
сварявам / сваря [5] cook, boil
сват (*or* сватя) [10] in-law
сватба [10] wedding
сватбен, -ена [11] wedding *(adj.)* ; сватбено пътешествие [11] honeymoon
сведение [23] a piece of information ; сведения [23] information, knowledge
свеж [26] fresh
свекър [10] father-in-law (to bride)
свекърва [9] mother-in-law (to bride)
свестен [17] decent
свети *see* свят
свети [21] saint ; Свети Константин [21] St. Constantine ; Св.Св. Кирил и Методий [20] Sts. Cyril and Methodius
светвам / светна [18] flash, go on (of a light)
светец [20] saint
светкавичен [20] like lightning
светкавично [20] with lightning speed
светлина [19] light ; слаба светлина [20] poor light
световен [10] world *(adj.)*
светост [18] sanctity
светоусещане [23] world outlook, conception of the world
светофар [19] traffic light
светъл [10] light *(adj.)* ; светъл образ [18] a noble figure ; светли бъднини [23] a bright future
светя [18] shine
свещ, -та [16] candle
свивам / свия [13] bend, fold, roll ; свивам гнездо [13] build a nest
свидетел [21] witness
свидетелство [21] certificate; evidence; proof
свиквам / свикна [15] get used to, grow accustomed to
свиря [16] play (musical instrument)
свирня [16] playing, tune
свобода [7] freedom
свободен [2] free ; мястото е свободно [2] the seat is not taken ; свободен съм сега [2] I'm free [not busy] now

Българо-английски речник (урок 1-30)

своеобра́зен [21] original; odd
свой [10] own *(adj.)*
свойство [26] characteristic, attribute
свъ́рзвам / свъ́ржа (-еш) [20] [21] tie, bind; connect; put someone in touch
свъ́ршвам / свъ́рша (-иш) [6] complete, finish ; ще свъ́рши ра́бота [11] it'll do the job
свъ́ршвам се / свъ́рша се (-иш) [22] end, run out, sell out
свъ́ршен, -ена [12] complete, perfect ; ми́нало свъ́ршено вре́ме [12] aorist tense ; свъ́ршен вид [12] perfective aspect
свят, све́ти [18] holy, sacred
свят, светъ́т *(plural* светове́) [18] world
сгот́вям / сгот́вя [5] cook, make
сгра́бчвам / сгра́бча (-иш) [25] clutch, grasp
сгра́да [19] building
сгу́швам се / сгу́ша се (-иш) [24] huddle together, nestle down
сдобря́вам / сдобря́ [29] make peace, reconcile
СДС *(pron.* седесе́) [14] SDS (UDF, Union of Democratic Forces)
сдуша́вам се / сдуша́ се (-и́ш) [29] band together
сдъ́ржаност [18] reserve, restraint
се [1] *(verbal particle)*
се [5] oneself *(direct object pronoun)*
се [7] oneself, themselves, itself, etc.
себе си [11] oneself *(reflexive object form)*
се́верен [20] northern
североизто́чен [30] northeastern
сега́ [1] now ; сега́ изли́зам [4] I'll go out right away
сега́шен [9] present-day, current ; сега́шно вре́ме [9] present tense
се́дем [2] seven
седемгоди́шен [26] seven-year old *(adj.)*
седемдесе́т [6] seventy
седемна́йсет [6] seventeen
се́демстотин [9] seven hundred
се́дми [8] seventh
се́дмица [6] week
седми́чно [20] weekly ; по два́ фи́лма се́дмично [20] two films a week
се́дна *see* ся́дам
седя́ [4] sit, be seated ; седя́ на тече́ние [4] sit in a drafty place ; да би́ ми́рно седя́ло, не би́ чу́до видя́ло [28] that's what comes of asking for trouble
седя́нка [29] village work party
сезо́н [20] season
сека́ (-че́ш) [9] cut ; сека́ моне́ти [20] mint coins
секрета́р (ка) [1] secretary

се́лище [23] settlement
село́ [2] village
селя́нин [16] villager, peasant
селя́нка [16] villager, peasant woman
семе́ен [10] family, domestic ; те́сен семе́ен кръг [10] immediate family
семе́йство [11] family
семина́р [17] seminar
се́мка [24] seed
септе́мври [5] September
серви́рам [4] serve, have available ; не зна́м какво́ серви́рат ту́ка [4] I don't know what they have here
сервитьо́р (ка) [4] waiter
серио́зен [21] serious
сестра́ [10] sister ; медици́нска сестра́ [17] nurse ; ро́дна сестра́ [18] birth sister (from the same parents)
се́тне [19] afterwards ; най-се́тне [19] finally
се́щам се / се́тя се [11] recall, come to mind, think of, remember
си [1] are *(2nd singular)* ; *see* съм
си [5] [7] to oneself *(indirect object pronoun)* ; ка́звам си [5] say to oneself
си́гурен [6] sure
си́гурно [9] surely, certainly
си́гурност [17] certainty, security
си́ла [7] strength, force
си́лен [2] strong ; и́ма си́лен вя́тър [2] it's very windy, there's a strong wind ; валя́т си́лни дъждове́ [12] it's raining heavily
симбио́за [20] symbiosis
символизи́рам [23] symbolize, stand for
симво́личен [23] symbolic
симпо́зиум [19] symposium
син (си́ня, си́ньо, си́ни) [8] blue
син, -ъ́т *(plural* синове́) [9] son
си́рене [7] white cheese
сири́ец [23] Syrian (male)
сири́йка [23] Syrian (female)
систе́ма [21] system
систе́мно [30] systematically, methodically
си́то [24] sieve
ситуа́ция [27] situation
сия́я [23] shine, be radiant
скала́ [14] rock, cliff
ска́ра [18] grill
ска́ран [29] on bad terms
скари́да [25] shrimp
ска́чам / ско́ча (-иш) [9] jump
ски́тане [22] wandering
ски́тница [18] wanderer
скок [25] jump, leap
ско́ро [1] soon
ско́рост [19] speed

Българо-английски речник (урок 1-30)

скоча *see* скачам
скривам / скрия [13] hide *(transitive)*
скривам се / скрия се [20] hide ; скривам се от погледа [20] drop out of sight ; hide from view
скромен [27] modest; humble ; скромно облекло [27] simple clothes
скроявам / скроя [25] cut out; fabricate ; скроявам лъжа [25] concoct a lie
скръб, -та [18] grief, sorrow
скръбен [28] sorrowful, mournful
скулптура [28] sculpture
скучая [22] be bored
скучен [13] boring
скъпоценен [23] precious
скъсан [14] torn
скъсвам / скъсам [19] tear, break; break off
скъсявам / скъся [29] shorten, curtail
скътвам / скътам [16] put by, store away
слаб [14] weak, thin ; слаба светлина [20] poor light
слава [9] [25] glory; reputation ; слава Богу [9] thank God ; гръмка слава [27] resounding fame
славист (ка) [17] specialist in Slavic studies
славянин [20] Slav (person)
славянски [17] Slavic
слагам / сложа (-иш) [4] put ; слагам да легне [5] put [someone] to bed
сладолед [6] ice cream
сладкарница [14] sweet shop
сладко [3] thick sweet preserves
сладък [3] sweet ; сладки [22] pastries, sweetmeats ; сладка приказка [22] pleasant chat
след [6] after ; след 15 минути [6] in 15 minutes ; след обяд [9] in the afternoon, after lunch ; след Р.Хр. [9] A.D.
след като [14] after *(relative conjunction)*
следа [18] trace, track
следвам [21] follow, pursue; study
следване [21] college studies
следващ [8] next, following
следобед [4] afternoon ; следобед съм на работа [4] I have to work this afternoon
следобеден [9] afternoon *(adj.)*
слива [20] plum
сливам / слея [30] fuse, combine
сливица [12] tonsil
слизам / сляза [7] get off, go down, descend
слисвам / слисам [20] amaze, astound
словак [23] Slovak (male)
словачка [23] Slovak (female)

слово [18] word, speech
сложен [5] difficult, complex
служа (-иш) [24] serve, work ; служа войник [24] do military service
служа си (-иш) ; служа си с [29] use, make use of
служба [14] service, position ; в службата [14] at work
служещ [17] [state] employee
слух, -ът *(plural* слухове) [17] hearing, ear; rumor ; има слухове [17] there's gossip
случаен, -айна [12] accidental, chance
случайно [12] by chance, accidentally
случай [12] instance; chance ; в такъв случай [12] in that case
случвам / случа (-иш) [20] run across, happen on
случвам се / случа се (-иш) [20] happen
слушалка [21] [telephone] receiver; headphone
слушам [4] listen, obey
слушател [17] listener ; слушатели [17] audience
слънце [9] sun ; слънцето грее [9] the sun is shining
слънчев [10] sunny
слънчоглед [24] sunflower
смачквам / смачкам [17] crush, crease
сме [1] are *(1st plural)* ; *see* съм
смалявам / смаля [20] diminish, reduce in size, shrink ; смален с два номера [20] shrunk two sizes
сменям / сменя [3] [4] change, replace
сметка [29] account; advantage ; за *(or* на) моята сметка at my expense
смешен [13] funny, humorous
смея се [13] laugh
смилам / смеля [17] grind, mill
смирено [28] meekly, humbly
смисъл [11] sense, meaning ; има смисъл [11] it makes sense
смущавам се / смутя се [13] get confused, be embarrassed
смърт, -та [16] death
смъртен [4] mortal
смятам / сметна [13] reckon, count ; смятам за [13] consider to be
смях, смехът *(plural* смехове) [11] laughter ; умирам от смях [11] burst one's sides/die laughing ; заливам се от смях [23] roar with laughter
снага [26] body, figure
снаха [22] daughter-in-law; sister-in-law (brother's wife)
снегове *see* сняг
снежен [11] snow *(adj.)* ; снежен човек [11] snowman

Българо-английски речник (урок 1-30)

снежи́нка [10] snowflake
сни́мка [6] photograph
сно́щен [9] last night's
сно́щи [9] yesterday evening, last night
сняг, снегъ́т (*plural* снегове́) [3] [7] snow ; бя́л като сня́г [3] white as snow
со́бствен, -ена [12] one's own ; ви́ждам със со́бствените си очи́ [12] see with one's own eyes
со́бственост [23] property
со́к [7] juice
со́л, -та́ [9] salt ; три́я му со́л на глава́та [25] haul him over the coals
соле́н [9] salted
соли́ден [21] solid, firm, substantial
солни́ца [9] salt shaker
со́лунски [20] from Solun (Greek Thessalonike)
солунча́нин [21] native of Solun (Greek Thessalonike)
софи́йски [8] of Sofia
софия́нец [14] Sofia resident
софия́нка [14] Sofia resident (female)
социалисти́чески [14] socialist
социоло́г [26] sociologist
спа́звам / спа́зя [19] observe, adhere to
спася́вам / спася́ [29] save, retrieve; rescue
спекта́къл [25] performance, show
специа́лен [9] special
специа́лно [16] especially ; специа́лно за целта́ [16] just for that reason
специали́ст (ка) [17] specialist
специа́лност [17] specialty; university major
специфи́чен [21] specific
спе́шност [23] urgency ; по спе́шност [23] as an emergency case
спече́лвам / спече́ля [14] win, gain, earn
спи́рам / спра́ [11] stop
спи́рка [7] bus or tram stop ; на дру́гата спи́рка [7] at the next stop
списа́ние [8] magazine, journal
спи́сък (*plural* спи́съци) [19] list, roll
споде́лям / споделя́ [20] share
споко́ен [21] calm, peaceful
споко́йствие [22] calm, quiet ; на споко́йствие [22] at leisure
сполу́чвам / сполу́ча (-иш) [17] succeed
спо́мен [18] memory, recollection ; увли́чам се в спо́мени [29] get wrapped up in memories
споменáвам / спомена́ [28] mention, refer to
спо́мням си / спо́мня си [8] recall
спо́р [18] argument ; спо́р ня́ма [18] that goes without saying ; оживе́н спо́р [30] lively debate
споре́д [20] according to
спо́рт [20] sport
спо́ртен [9] sports (*adj.*)
споря́ [13] dispute, contend ; не спори́ [13] don't argue
спра́вям се / спра́вя се [27] cope with, manage
сприятеля́вам се / сприятеля́ се [20] make friends
спу́скам / спу́сна [26] let down, drop
спъ́тник [19] fellow traveler
спъ́тничка [24] fellow traveler (female)
спя́ [4] sleep
сравне́ние [25] comparison ; в сравне́ние с [25] compared to
сраже́ние [26] battle
сра́м, -ъ́т (*plural* сра́мове *or* срамове́) [12] shame, modesty ; сра́м ме е [12] I'm ashamed, I'm too shy ; не те́ е сра́м [12] you should be ashamed ; ка́к не те е сра́м [12] shame on you ; сра́м и позо́р! [19] for shame!
сре́бърен [16] silver (*adj.*)
сред [19] among, amidst ; сред бя́л де́н [29] in broad daylight
среда́ [2] middle
сре́ден [3] middle (*adj.*) ; сре́дно образова́ние [16] secondary education
среди́ще [9] center
среднобъ́лгарски [17] medieval Bulgarian
средновеко́вен [9] medieval
средновеко́вие [8] Middle Ages
среднощ [24] midnight, middle of the night
сре́дство [29] means, medium ; прево́зно сре́дство [29] vehicle, conveyance ; сре́дство за общу́ване [30] means of communication
сре́свам / сре́ша (-еш) [19] comb
сре́ща [9] meeting, appointment
сре́щам / сре́щна [10] meet
срещу́ [12] against, opposite; across from
сро́к [19] term, time limit ; кра́ен сро́к [19] deadline ; сро́к за пода́ване на докуме́нти [20] application deadline
сро́чен [23] urgent, pressing
сръ́бвам / сръ́бна [22] take a nip, sip
сръбки́ня [23] Serb (female)
сръ́бски [22] Serbian
сръдня́ [29] quarrel, ill feelings
сря́да [9] Wednesday
ста́вам / ста́на [1] [4] [10] get up, stand up; become, happen; be ; ста́ва тече́ние [1] there's a draft ; ста́ваме мно́го [10] there gets to be a lot of us ; синъ́т им ста́на на че́тири [10] their son has turned four ; ще ти ста́не

Българо-английски речник (урок 1-30)

то́пло [11] you'll be/get [too] hot ; за какво́ ста́ва ду́ма? [11] what's it about? ; ста́на ме мъ́чно [13] I had a hard time ; кое́ вре́ме ста́на [16] [look] what time it's gotten to be ; за ни́що не ста́ва [18] isn't worth anything ; не ста́ва за я́дене [20] isn't for eating
стадио́н [12] stadium
станда́рт [17] standard
ста́р [7] old ; добро́то ста́ро вре́ме [11] the good old days ; на ста́ро [29] secondhand
стара́я се [19] try, take pains
старобъ́лгарски [17] Old Bulgarian, Old Church Slavic
ста́рост [17] old age
ста́рши [17] senior ; ста́рши нау́чен сътру́дник [17] senior research associate
ста́туя [21] statue
ста́я [9] room
сте [1] are *(2nd plural)* ; *see* съм
сте́ля се [26] drift, spread
стена́ [17] wall
сте́пен, -та́ [17] degree ; сте́пен к.ф.н. [17] Ph.D. equivalent ; до голя́ма сте́пен [17] to a great extent ; във ви́сша сте́пен [22] eminently, in the highest degree
сти́га [3] [16] enough, that's enough ; сти́га с то́зи прозо́рец [3] enough about that window ; сти́га то́лкова [10] that's enough ; сти́га си я гле́дал [16] stop looking at her ; сти́га ве́че [16] that's enough already ; сти́га да мо́га [17] to the extent that I can ; вре́мето не ми́ сти́га [26] I'm hard pressed for time
сти́гам / сти́гна [13] reach, arrive at
стипе́ндия [29] scholarship, grant
сти́скам / сти́сна [18] squeeze, press ; сти́скаме си ръце́те [18] shake hands ; сти́скам ръка́та [на ия́кого] [18] shake [someone's] hand
сти́х, -ъ́т [17] verse
стихотворе́ние [3] poem
сти́чам се / стека́ се (-че́ш) [20] flow down; flock together
сто́ [5] (a) hundred
сто́йност [21] value, worth
сто́ка [9] goods, commodity
стома́х [12] stomach
сто́л [4] chair
сто́п [10] stop-sign, hitchhiking
сто́паджия, -и́йка [10] hitchhiker
стопа́нин [22] owner, proprietor
сто́плям се / сто́пля се [17] get warm

стоти́на [24] a hundred or so
стоя́ [4] [11] stand, be standing; stay (in one place) ; стоя́ пра́в [4] stand, remain standing ; стоя́ на мя́сто [17] stay in one place
страда́м [23] suffer
страна́ [6] [7] [15] side; country; part ; от вси́чки страни́ [6] from /on all sides ; от ва́ша страна́ [15] on your part ; от дру́га страна́ [17] on the other hand ; от две́те страни́ [30] on both sides
стра́нен [18] strange, unusual
страни́ца [3] page
стра́нник [28] foreigner, wanderer
стра́ст, -та́ [27] passion
стра́х, -ъ́т *(plural* страхове́) [12] fear, dread ; стра́х ме е (от) [12] I'm afraid (of) ; изтръ́пвам от стра́х [24] get shudders down one's spine ; ме́чка стра́х, мен не стра́х [29] here goes!
страхли́в [24] cowardly, timid
страхо́тен [5] horrible, dreadful, terrifying ; страхо́тна иде́я [5] (a) terrific idea
страху́вам се [14] fear, be afraid of
стра́шен [9] terrible, fearful ; ня́ма ни́що стра́шно [11] there's nothing to be afraid of
стра́шно [16] awfully, terrifically
стре́лям [17] shoot
стреме́ж [23] striving, aspiration
стри́на *(or* стри́нка) [16] aunt (father's brother's wife)
стро́г [29] strict, severe
строе́ж [20] structure, construction
строи́телен [17] construction *(adj.)*
стро́й [26] system, order
строша́вам / строша́ (-и́ш) [25] break, smash
строя́ [18] build
стру́вам [4] cost ; това́ ко́лко стру́ва? [4] how much does this cost? ; ко́лко стру́ва? [4] how much is it?
стру́вам се [20] seem ; стру́ва ми се [20] it seems to me
стря́скам / стре́сна [11] startle, scare
стря́скам се / стре́сна се [11] be startled, take fright
стря́ха *(plural* стре́хи) [18] eaves
сту́д, -ъ́т *(plural* студове́) [7] cold, chill
студе́н [4] cold
студенина́ [22] cold, frigidity
студе́нт (ка) [1] university student
студе́нтски [17] student *(adj.)*
стъ́лб [29] post, pole
стъ́лба [11] step, ladder ; ка́чвам се по стъ́лбите [11] climb the stairs

373

Българо-английски речник (урок 1-30)

стълбище [17] staircase
стъпало [12] sole (of the foot)
стъпвам / стъпя [16] step, set foot
стъписвам се / стъписам се [26] be startled, be taken aback
стъпка [16] step
стърча (-иш) [22] stand out; hang about
сукман [16] (folk) tunic
сурвакар [10] survakar (New Year's wassailer)
суров [11] severe
сутрин, -та [9] morning ; сутрин, сутринта [9] in the morning ; утре сутринта [9] tomorrow morning
сух [16] dry ; на сухо [16] in/to a dry place
сушен [10] dried
схващам / схвана [20] grasp, comprehend
схващам се / схвана се [20] get stiff, cramped ; гърбът ми е схванат [20] my back is stiff
сцена [20] scene
счетоводител [17] bookkeeper, accountant
счува се / счуе се (3d person) [20] seem to hear ; счува ми се [20] I think I hear
счупен, -ена [11] broken
събирам / събера [3] [4] gather, collect
събирам се / събера се [19] congregate, gather together
събитие [20] event
събличам / съблека (-чеш) [13] undress [someone]
събличам се / съблека се (-чеш) [13] undress, get undressed
събор [20] fair; convention, council
събота [8] Saturday
събрание [18] meeting, gathering ; Народното събрание [18] Parliament
събувам / събуя [13] take [something] off [someone's] foot
събувам се / събуя се [13] take [something] off one's foot
събуждам / събудя [11] wake
събуждам се / събудя се [11] wake up, awaken
съвет [10] advice ; пренебрегвам съвет [23] disregard [someone's] advice
съветвам [5] advise
съвпадам / съвпадна [10] coincide, concur
съвременен [18] contemporary; modern
съвсем [5] completely ; съвсем навреме [5] at exactly the right moment ; женени сме съвсем отскоро [11] we've just gotten married
съвършен [21] perfect, consummate
съвършенство [18] perfection
съгласен [12] in agreement
съглеждам / съгледам [25] notice, catch sight of
съд [16] vessel, container ; съдове [16] dishes
съдба [23] fate, destiny
съдина [24] vessel, container; pan
съдържам [22] contain, hold
съдя [23] judge; put on trial
съжаление [1] pity ; за съжаление [1] unfortunately
съжалявам / съжаля [8] regret, be sorry
създавам / създам (-дадеш) [17] make, create, establish
създател (ка) [19] creator, founder
съзнание [18] consciousness, awareness
съкращавам / съкратя [17] curtail, reduce, lay off; shorten
съкровище [13] treasure
сълза (plural сълзи or сълзи) [12] tear (from the eye)
съм [1] am (1sg.); to be (citation form)
съмва се / съмне се (3d person only) [24] dawn, day breaks
сън (plural сънища) [8] dream
сън, -ят [8] sleep ; унасям се в сън [26] drift off to sleep
сънувам [6] dream ; сънувам кошмари [6] have nightmares
съобщавам / съобщя [5] announce, inform
съобщение [5] announcement ; съобщение за колет [5] postal notice (for a package)
съответен [19] corresponding; appropriate
съпоставка [17] comparison ; в съпоставка с [17] compared with
съпоставям / съпоставя [30] juxtapose, compare
съпротивлявам се (or съпротивявам се) [28] resist, oppose, fight back
съпруг, съпруга [3] [10] spouse
сърби (3d person only) [12] itch
сърбин [22] Serb
сърдечен [2] hearty ; сърдечни пожелания [23] best wishes
сърдя се [19] be/get angry
сърна [8] deer, doe
сърце [10] heart ; пожелавам от сърце [10] send heartfelt wishes ; на гладно сърце [22] on an empty stomach
със [7] = с with
съсед (ка) [5] neighbor
съседен [20] neighboring, adjacent
съседство [23] neighborhood, vicinity
състав [21] composition, structure
съставям / съставя [17] compose, make up

Българо-английски речник (урок 1-30)

състоя́ се [14] consist of; take place
състоя́ние [19] state, condition
сътресе́ние [29] shaking, jolt ; сътресе́ние на мо́зъка [29] brain concussion
сътру́дник [17] collaborator ; ста́рши нау́чен сътру́дник [17] senior research associate
сътру́днича (-иш) [30] collaborate, cooperate
съ́щ [3] same ; съ́щото [4] the same thing
существо́ [24] being, creature
существу́вам [24] exist
съ́що [1] also
съю́з [14] union
сюже́т [23] subject, subject-matter
сюрпри́з [29] surprise
ся́дам / се́дна [4] sit down, take a seat ; седне́те, господи́не! [4] have a seat, sir!
ся́каш [18] as if
ся́нка [23] shade, shadow ; ша́рена ся́нка [29] dappled shade

та [13] and; so that
тава́н [24] ceiling; attic
та́ен, та́йна [25] secret, covert
та́зи [3] this *(feminine)*
така́ [4] that way, like that ; ка́к така́? [11] how is it that; how can that be?
та́кса [23] charge, fee
такси́ *(neuter)* [14] taxi
та́кт [16] beat, rhythm
такъ́в (така́ва, такова, такива) [11] such ; такива неща́ [11] such things ; еди́н такъ́в [28] someone like, one such as
талантли́в [17] talented
та́м [4] there
тамбура́ [16] (folk) lute or mandolin
та́нц [16] dance
танцу́вам [23] dance
танцьо́р [16] dancer
тара́леж [9] hedgehog
тарато́р [6] yogurt and cucumber soup
та́тко *(plural* та́тковци) [10] Dad
та́ча (-иш) [13] respect
та́я [11] this *(variant of* та́зи)
тво́й [8] your, yours *(singular)*
творе́ц [18] creator; artist
тво́рчески [18] creative
тво́рчество [18] creation, creative work
творя́ [17] create
твъ́рд [11] firm, steadfast ; твъ́рдо реша́вам [11] firmly resolve

твъ́рде [24] rather, very
твъ́рдо [11] firmly, staunchly ; твъ́рдо реша́вам [11] firmly resolve
твърдя́ [17] assert, claim
те [5] you *(direct object pronoun)*
те́ [1] they
театра́лен [19] theater *(adj.)*
теа́тър *(plural* теа́три) [6] theater
те́бе [10] you *(object pronoun)*
тегло́ [23] weight
тежа́ (-и́ш) [17] weigh, be heavy
те́жко [17] difficult ; те́жко е [17] it's hard
те́жък [2] heavy; difficult, serious ; не вди́гам те́жко [17] not lift anything heavy ; те́жка бо́лест [27] grave illness
те́зи [3] these
тека́ (-че́ш) [9] flow
те́кст [19] text
те́ле [21] calf
телеви́зия [6] television
телеви́зор [29] television
телегра́ма [23] telegram ; поздрави́телна телегра́ма [23] telegram of congratulations
те́лешки [21] veal *(adj.)*
телефо́н [5] telephone ; на телефо́на съм [5] be (talking) on the phone
телефо́нен [13] telephone *(adj.)*
те́ма [17] subject, theme
те́нджера [6] (cooking) pot
те́нис [13] tennis
те́ниска [20] T-shirt
теорети́к, -и́чка [19] theoretician
териториа́лен [30] territorial
терито́рия [27] territory, area
терми́т [26] termite
те́рмос [28] thermos bottle
те́сен, тя́сна [2] tight, cramped, narrow ; те́сен семе́ен кръ́г [10] immediate family
тетра́дка [7] notebook
тефте́р [26] register, account book
тефте́рче [26] notebook
те́хен, тя́хна [8] their, theirs
те́хник [19] technician
те́хника [12] technology
те́хникум [3] technical high school
тече́ние [1] current, draft ; ста́ва тече́ние [1] there's a draft ; в тече́ние на два́ ме́сеца [19] within two months ; а́з съм в тече́ние на [22] I'm up on, I'm informed about
ти́ [1] you *(singular, familiar)*
ти [7] [to] you *(indirect object pronoun)*
ти́п [7] type
типи́чен [3] typical

Българо-английски речник (урок 1-30)

тих [18] quiet
тихо [18] quietly; quiet!
тичам [8] run
тичешком [26] at a run
тишина [26] silence, quiet
тия [11] these *(variant of* тези)
т.нар. = така наречен(ият) [30] so-called
то [11] then *(particle)* ; и то [11] at that
то́ [1] it *(rarely,* he *or* she)
това [2] [3] this *(neuter)* ; това не е ли шише? [2] isn't that a bottle? ; това е [13] that's that
тогава [4] then, in that case; at that point ; пий една бира тогава [4] have a beer, then
тогавашен [19] of that time
тоз = този
този [3] this *(masculine)*
той [1] he, it
току [19] just, suddenly; forever
току-що [14] just now
толкова *(or* толкоз) [4] [27] so much, so many, to such a degree
топвам / топна [25] immerse, dip
топка [8] ball
топъл [2] warm
торба [11] bag, sack
торта [18] cake
тоталитаризъм [20] totalitarian rule
тото [14] lottery, pool
точен [6] exact, precise
точно [6] [12] exactly; just
точка [22] point, dot ; гледна точка [22] point of view
тоя [11] this *(variant of* този)
традиция [20] tradition
трайност [26] stability, endurance
тракам [13] rattle
траки [20] Thracians
тракийски [23] Thracian *(adj.)*
тракторист [23] tractor driver
трамваен, -айна [7] tram *(adj.)*
трамвай [2] tram
трамплин [26] trampoline, springboard
трая [29] last, endure ; трая от ден до пладне [29] be short-lived
трева [16] grass
тревожа (-иш) [17] bother, worry
трепвам / трепна [21] wince, flinch
треперя [19] tremble ; треперя за него [26] be anxious about him
треса [12] shake ; тресе ме [12] I've got the shakes; I've got a fever
трети [8] third
третирам [8] treat
три [2] three

трибали [23] an ancient people living within Thrace, one of the Thracian tribes
трийсет *(or* тридесет) [6] thirty
трима [6] three *(masculine animate)*
тринайсет [6] thirteen
триста [9] three hundred
трия [25] rub ; трия му сол на главата [25] haul him over the coals
трогателен [26] touching, moving
трогвам / трогна [16] move, touch, affect
тромав [18] clumsy, ungainly
тропвам / тропна [17] rap, knock ; тропвам с крак [17] stamp one's foot
тротоар [14] sidewalk
троша (-иш) [29] break, crush
труд, -ът [25] labor, work
труден [5] difficult
трудност [17] difficulty ; големи трудности [17] big problems
трудолюбив [19] industrious, hardworking
трус [29] shock, tremor
тръгвам / тръгна [1] [4] set out, leave ; тръгвам на училище [5] start school
трябва *(3d person only)* [12] must, should ; той трябва да дойде [12] he needs to come
трябвам [12] be necessary to ; трябва му адвокат [12] he needs a lawyer
ту ... ту [17] now...now
туй [11] this *(variant of* това)
тук *(or* тука) [2] here *(location)*
тунел [17] tunnel
турист [8] tourist
туркиня [23] Turk (female)
турски [20] Turkish ; турско робство [20] the Ottoman yoke
турци [6] Turks *(see* турчин)
турчин *(plural* турци) [23] Turk
туршия [10] pickles; pickled vegetables
тутакси [22] immediately, right off
тъжен [21] sad
тъй [11] thus *(variant of* така)
тъй като [17] inasmuch as *(relative conjunction)*
тъка (-чеш) [16] weave
тъкмо [10] just, exactly; only ; тъкмо сега [10] just this minute
тъмен [17] dark
тъпан [16] drum
търговец [9] merchant
търговия [24] trade, commerce
тържествен [20] solemn, official, ceremonial
търновски [17] of or pertaining to Търново
търпелив [3] patient
търпение [16] patience ; нямам търпение [16] not be able to wait

Българо-английски речник (урок 1-30)

търпя́ [17] endure
тъ́рся [7] seek, look for ; тъ́рся препита́ние [26] try to make a living
тъст [10] father-in-law (to husband)
тъ́ща [10] mother-in-law (to husband)
тю́ркски [20] Turkic
тя [1] she, it
тя́ло (*plural* тела́) [18] body
тях [10] them (*object pronoun*)

у [10] at the home of ; у дома́ [10] at home, at one's house
убежда́вам / убедя́ [11] persuade ; убежда́вам [14] try to convince
убедя́ [14] succeed in convincing
уби́вам / уби́я [24] kill, murder ; да ме уби́еш [29] for the life of me
убо́ждам / убода́ [24] prick, stab
уважа́вам [20] respect, honor
уважа́ем [17] honored, esteemed
уваже́ние [27] respect, esteem
увелича́вам / увелича́ (-и́ш) [21] increase
увере́ние [17] assurance ; в увере́ние на вернотта́ на [17] in certification of
уверя́вам / уверя́ [22] assure
увеселе́ние [29] entertainment, merrymaking
увеща́ние [27] admonition; coaxing
уви́ [23] alas
увлече́ние [27] enthusiasm, animation
увли́чам се / увлека́ се (-че́ш) [29] be absorbed, be carried away ; увли́чам се в спо́мени [29] get wrapped up in memories
увя́хвам / увя́хна [22] wither, fade
уга́ждам / угодя́ [20] indulge, humor, please
уга́свам / уга́сна [18] go out
угово́рен [22] stipulated, agreed-upon
угоще́ние [29] feast
уда́вям / уда́вя [24] drown
удиви́телен [18] amazing
удивле́ние [22] amazement ; за кра́йно удивле́ние [22] to the utter amazement
удо́бен [11] convenient, comfortable ; не ми́ е удо́бно [17] I feel awkward
удо́бство [21] convenience
удово́лствие [18] pleasure
удостоя́вам / удостоя́ [20] honor, vouchsafe ; удостоя́вам с награ́да [20] confer a prize
у́дрям / уда́ря [18] hit, strike ; у́дрям печа́т на [23] put seal to
удължа́вам / удължа́ (-и́ш) [19] prolong, lengthen
уж [24] as if, ostensibly

у́жас [14] horror
ужа́сен [12] terrible
ужася́вам / ужася́ [18] horrify, appall
уи́ски [22] whiskey
украи́нец [23] Ukrainian (male)
украи́нка [23] Ukrainian (female)
украся́вам / украся́ [23] decorate, adorn, trim
ула́вям / уловя́ [22] catch, seize
улесня́вам / улесня́ [21] facilitate
у́лица [3] street
у́личка [18] small street
ум, -ъ́т (*plural* умове́) [28] mind ; и през ум не ми́ мина [28] I didn't dream of it
у́мен [10] smart
уме́ние [16] ability, skill
уми́рам / умра́ [11] die ; уми́рам от смя́х [11] die laughing, die from laughter
умо́ра [21] fatigue ; ка́пнал от умо́ра [21] exhausted
уморе́н [8] tired
уморя́вам се / уморя́ се [12] get tired, become exhausted
уна́сям / унеса́ [19] carry away, transport ; уна́сям се в съ́н [26] drift off to sleep
унга́рец [23] Hungarian (male)
унга́рка [23] Hungarian (female)
у́нес [28] trance, reverie
универса́лен [24] universal
университе́т [7] university
университе́тски [12] university (*adj.*)
уника́лен [18] unique
унищожа́вам / унищожа́ (-и́ш) [24] destroy, annihilate, wipe out
упла́швам / упла́ша (-иш) [19] frighten
упла́швам се / упла́ша се (-иш) [25] take fright, be scared
упори́т [26] tenacious, stubborn
упо́рство [19] tenacity
употребя́вам / употребя́ [21] use; use up
упражне́ние [17] exercise, drill
упъ́твам се / упъ́тя се [18] make one's way to
уре́ждам / уредя́ [9] arrange, settle
уро́к [5] lesson
усамоте́н [29] secluded, isolated
усе́щам / усе́тя [27] feel, notice
уси́лено [3] intensively
уси́лие [19] effort ; с о́бщи уси́лия [19] working all together
ускоря́вам / ускоря́ [20] hasten, accelerate
услажда́м се / усладя́ се [23] give pleasure ; това́ ми се усла́жда [23] I enjoy that

Българо-английски речник (урок 1-30)

усло́вен [24] provisional, conditional ; усло́вно наклоне́ние [24] conditional mood
усло́вие [21] condition
услу́га [17] favor ; ме́чешка услу́га [29] a doubtful service
услу́жвам / услу́жа (-иш) [26] do a service, oblige ; услу́жвам ви с не́го [26] lend it to you
усми́вка [28] smile
усми́хвам се / усми́хна се [26] smile ; усми́хнат [26] smiling
успе́х [5] success ; успе́х на и́зпита [5] good luck on the test ; и́мам голя́м успе́х [27] be wildly successful
успе́шно [17] successfully
успи́вам се / успя́ се [27] oversleep
успокоя́вам / успокоя́ [17] soothe
успокоя́вам се / успокоя́ се [17] calm down, soothe
успоре́дно [30] simultaneously, in parallel
успя́вам / успе́я [8] succeed, manage to
уста́ [12] mouth [22]
установя́вам / установя́ [20] determine, establish
у́стна [12] lip
усто́и (*plural only*) [26] buttress; mainstay ; усто́ите на обществото́ [26] the pillars of society
устро́йвам / устро́я [13] arrange, organize
устро́йство [29] structure, frame; system
утвържда́вам / утвърдя́ [20] confirm, endorse, approve
утеша́вам / утеша́ (-и́ш) [29] comfort, console
у́тре [4] tomorrow ; у́тре ве́чер [9] tomorrow evening ; у́тре сутринта́ [9] tomorrow morning
у́трешен [9] tomorrow's
у́тринен [9] morning (adj.)
у́тро [9] morning ; добро́ у́тро [9] good morning
уха́ние [26] scent, aroma
ухо́ (*plural* уши́) [12] ear ; засмя́н до уши́ [22] grinning from ear to ear
у́ча (-иш) [5] learn, teach
у́ча се (-иш) [17] study, learn
уча́ствувам (*and* уча́ствам) [17] participate
уча́стие [20] participation
уча́стник [19] participant
уче́бен [30] school (adj.) ; уче́бна годи́на [30] academic year
уче́бник [2] textbook, manual
учени́к [7] student, pupil
учени́чка [7] female student or pupil
учени́чески [29] pupil's, student's
учи́лище (*plural* учи́лища) [5] [6] school ; тръ́гвам на учи́лище [5] start school
учи́лищен [10] school (adj.) ; учи́лищен звъне́ц [10] school bell
учи́тел (ка) [1] teacher (up to 12th grade)
учи́телски [19] teacher's
учти́в [26] polite
учу́двам / учу́дя [19] surprise, astonish
уши́ *see* ухо́
уши́вам / уши́я [23] sew, tailor ; уши́вам си костю́м [23] have a suit made; sew oneself a suit

фа́за [30] phase, stage
факт (*plural* фа́кти) [30] fact
факулте́т [17] faculty, university division
фане́лка (*or* флане́лка) [14] sweatshirt, T-shirt
фантасти́чен [23] fantastic, fabulous
февруа́ри [9] February
фе́лдшер [29] paramedic; surgeon's assistant
фестива́л [5] festival
фиа́ла [23] broad flat bowl or saucer for drinking or pouring libation
фигу́ра [18] figure
фида́нка [26] sapling
физи́к, -и́чка [19] physicist
фили́йка [14] little slice ; пъ́ржени фили́йки [14] French toast
фили́я [14] slice
филм (*plural* фи́лми) [8] film, movie ; прожекти́рам филм [20] show a film
филоло́гия [17] philology
филологи́чески [17] philological ; кандида́т на филологи́ческите нау́ки [17] Ph.D. equivalent
филосо́ф [21] philosopher
финла́ндец [23] Finn (male)
финла́ндка [23] Finn (female)
флане́лка *see* фане́лка
фльо́нга [28] bow, knot
фоайе́ [19] foyer, lobby
фолкло́р [17] folklore
фолкло́рен [17] folklore (adj.)
фонд [30] stock; fund ; основе́н ре́чников фонд [30] core vocabulary
фонети́чен [30] phonetic
фо́рма [20] form ; чле́нна фо́рма [30] definite article
форми́рам [21] form, shape, set up
формули́рам [18] formulate, phrase
фотоапара́т [5] camera
фотогени́чен [23] photogenic
фра́за [22] phrase
францу́зин [23] Frenchman

Българо-английски речник (урок 1-30)

французо́йка [23] Frenchwoman
фре́нски [18] French
фро́нт [25] front; facade ; Оте́чествен Фро́нт [25] Fatherland Front
фуро́р [13] furor ; предизви́квам фуро́р [13] cause a ruckus
фу́ста [16] (folk) skirt
фу́тбол [10] soccer
фуча́ (-и́ш) [24] whiz; rage

ха́ [25] now, well; ha
хабилити́рам се [17] attain higher academic rank (past Ph.D.)
хаза́йка [15] landlady
ха́йде [3] come on, let's ; ха́йде по една́ глъ́тка [3] [come on,] let's each have a drink ; ха́йде да се чу́кнем [11] let's have a toast
хайла́йф [29] uppercrust, beau monde
халва́ [24] halva, sesame candy
ха́мстер [9] hamster
ха́н [20] khan
ха́пвам / ха́пна [15] eat, have a bite
ха́пя [18] bite
характе́рен [18] characteristic
характеризи́рам [29] characterize, describe
харе́свам / харе́сам [7] [12] like
хармони́чен [18] harmonious
хармо́ния [18] harmony
харти́я [8] paper
ха́рча (-иш) [17] spend
хва́ля [19] praise
хва́щам / хва́на [9] grasp, seize, catch ; хва́щам мазо́ли [18] get blisters ; хва́нати за ръка́ [20] hand in hand ; хва́щам под ръка́ [22] take [someone's] arm
хвъркова́т [29] flying, winged
хвъ́рлям / хвъ́рля [20] throw, toss
хе́м (хем ... хем) [12] and; both...and...; not only..., but...
хиля́да (plural хи́ляди) [9] thousand
хими́к, -и́чка [19] chemist
хиру́рг [17] surgeon
хи́тър [25] sly, clever
хич [18] nothing, not at all
хи́щник [26] predator; beast/bird of prey
хла́ден [22] cool; wintry
хлади́лник [7] refrigerator
хлапа́к [14] kid ; но се появи́ о́нзи хлапа́к [14] and then this kid appeared
хло́пам / хло́пна [27] knock, clatter
хлъ́згав [19] slippery
хляб [5] bread ; иди́ за хля́б! [5] go buy some bread!
хо́д [20] walk, gait

хо́дя [6] go ; хо́дя на ки́но [6] go to the movies ; хо́дя на учи́лище [6] go to school ; хо́дя за ри́ба [9] go fishing ; хо́дя пеша́ [9] go on foot, walk (and not ride) ; хо́дя бо́с [13] go barefoot
хор [28] choir, chorale
хо́ра [4] people ; като хо́рата [22] properly
хоризо́нт [20] horizon
хоро́ [16] folk line dance
хорово́дец [16] leader of line dances
хоте́л [9] hotel
хралу́па [18] cavity in a tree
хра́ня [8] feed, nourish
храст [20] bush, shrub
христия́нин [20] Christian
христия́нство [20] Christianity
Христо́в [9] Christ's ; Рождество́ Христо́во [9] Christmas ; преди́ Р.Хр. [9] B.C. ; след Р.Хр. [9] A.D.
Христо́с [22] Christ ; Христо́с воскре́се [22] Christ has risen
хру́мва / хру́мне (3rd person only) [25] occur ; хру́мна ми една́ иде́я [25] I just got an idea
ху́бав [2] fine, nice, beautiful, pretty ; вси́чко ху́баво [2] all the best
хубави́ца [5] beauty
хубостни́к [19] scamp, good-for-nothing
худо́жник [23] artist; painter
ху́квам / ху́кна [25] bolt, dart off
хулига́н [27] hoodlum, hooligan
ху́мор [5] humor
хърва́тин [23] Croat
хърва́тка [23] Croat (female)

цар, -ят (plural царе́) [8] tsar, emperor
царе́вичен [20] corn (adj.) ; царе́вично брашно́ [20] cornmeal
ца́рство [20] kingdom, realm
цве́те (plural цветя́) [6] flower ; цъ́фнали цветя́ [27] flowers in bloom
цве́тен [3] colored
цвят, цветъ́т (plural цветове́) [21] color
цел, -та́ [16] purpose ; специа́лно за целта́ [16] just for that reason
целу́вам / целу́на [5] kiss
целу́вка [28] kiss
цена́ [12] price ; на вся́ка цена́ [12] at any price, at all costs, absolutely
це́нен [29] valuable
це́нностен [28] pertaining to values ; це́нностни размества́ния [28] changing values

Българо-английски речник (урок 1-30)

централен [12] central
център (*plural* центрове) [7] center
ценя [17] esteem, value
цивилизация [21] civilization
цигара [4] cigarette
цигулар [17] violinist
цикъл [18] cycle, series
цирк [6] circus
ЦУМ = Централен универсален магазин [24] Central universal store (department store)
църква [3] church
цъфвам / цъфна [27] blossom, burst ; цъфнали цветя [27] flowers in bloom
цъфтя [9] bloom
цял, цели [7] whole, entire ; цяла нощ не мигвам [25] not have a wink of sleep [all night]
цяло [30] entity, whole
цялост [30] entirety, totality
цялостен [18] entire, total

ч. = часът, часа [9]
чадър (*plural* чадъри) [12] umbrella
чаен, чаена (*or* чайна) [7] tea *(adj.)*
чай (*plural* чаеве) [7] tea
чайник [7] teapot
чак [27] only; right; that much ; чак от Америка [27] all the way from America
чакалня [15] waiting room
чакам [3] await, wait, wait for
чанта [2] bag, briefcase
час, -ът, 2 часа (*plural* часове) [6] [7] [25] hour; class ; колко е часът? [6] what time is it? ; в колко часа? [6] at what time? ; в 1 ч. [6] at 1:00 ; с часове [24] for hours
часовник [7] watch, clock ; часовникът ми изостава с пет минути [25] my watch is five minutes slow
част, -та [16] part, portion ; по-голямата част [30] most, the bulk
чаша [3] [7] glass, cup
че [3] that *(subordinate conjunction)*
чедо [29] child, offspring
чезна [28] languish, pine
чейндж [10] currency exchange office
чейнчаджия, -ийка [10] unofficial money changer
чекрък [24] spinning wheel
чело (*or* чело) [12] forehead
червен [3] red ; червен като рак [23] red as a lobster
червенея [21] redden, grow red
черво [12] intestine
червя се [20] redden, blush; put on lipstick
черга [20] rug
чергило [18] awning
черен [11] black ; черен дроб [12] liver
череп [24] skull
череша [12] [25] cherry; cherry tree
черква [27] church *(archaic)*
черноризец [21] monk
черпя [4] treat ; утре черпя аз [4] it's my treat tomorrow
чест [3] frequent
чест, -та [18] honor
честен [12] honorable, honest ; честна дума [12] word of honor
честит [10] happy ; честито [11] congratulations! ; честита Нова Година [10] happy New Year ; честит празник [11] happy holiday ; честит рожден ден [11] happy birthday
честитка [10] greeting card
често [3] often ; често пъти [27] time and again
честота [30] frequency
чесън [6] garlic
чета [3] read
четвърт, -та [11] quarter
четвърти [8] fourth
четвъртък [9] Thursday
четен [11] even-numbered
четири [6] four
четиридесет *or* четирийсет [6] forty
четиринайсет [6] fourteen
четирима [6] four *(masculine animate)*
четиристотин [9] four hundred
чех [23] Czech (person)
чехкиня [23] Czech (female)
чешки [21] Czech *(adj.)*
чешма [23] fountain; tap
чий, чия, чие, чий [8] whose *(interrogative)*
чийто, чиято, чието, чийто [17] whose *(relative conjunction)*
чиния [19] plate, dish
чиновник [17] official, functionary
чирак [27] apprentice
число [14] number ; познавам число [14] pick/guess a number ; в това число и [30] as well as
чист [4] clean, pure
чисто [21] well, perfectly ; without an accent говоря чисто славянски [21] speak pure Slavic
чистач (ка) [19] cleaner, cleaning person
чистичък [22] neat
чистя [19] clean
читанка [26] school reader
читател (ка) [19] reader

Българо-английски речник (урок 1-30)

чифт [26] pair
чичеро́не [22] cicerone, guide
чи́чко [6] uncle (*diminutive*)
чи́чо (*plural* чи́човци) [10] uncle (father's brother)
член [17] member
чле́нен: чле́нна фо́рма [30] definite article
членѹ́вам [17] be a member
чове́к [4] man, person
човекоподо́бен [22] anthropoid
чове́че [13] dwarf
чове́шки [18] human; decent
чора́п [17] sock
чорба́ [20] soup
чува́л [24] sack
чу́вам / чу́я [10] hear, listen
чу́вство [26] feeling, emotion
чу́вствувам се (*or* чу́вствам се) [13] feel
чу́ден [18] wonderful; strange
чуде́сен [2] marvelous, wonderful
чу́до [27] miracle, wonder ; нами́рам се в чу́до [28] be at one's wits' end ; да би́ ми́рно седя́ло, не би́ чу́до видя́ло [28] that's what comes of asking for trouble
чу́дя се [5] wonder
чужби́на [12] abroad ; вси́чки са по чужби́на [12] they've all gone abroad
чужд [8] [26] foreign, alien; someone else's
чужде́нец [3] foreigner, stranger
чужденка́ [3] foreigner, stranger (female)
чуждестра́нен [17] from foreign countries
чук, -ът [27] hammer, mallet
чу́кам [18] knock
чу́квам / чу́кна [11] knock, clink (once) ; чу́кам на дърво́ [11] knock on wood
чу́кам се / чу́кна се [11] clink glasses, toast to ; ха́йде да се чу́кнем [11] let's have a toast
чу́пя [24] break
чу́шка [6] pepper (vegetable)

шампа́нско [11] champagne
шанс [17] chance
ша́пка [5] hat
ша́рен [29] variegated, patterned; multi-colored ; ша́рена ся́нка [29] dappled shade
шари́ло [27] painted decoration
швед [23] Swede (male)
шве́дка [23] Swede (female)
швейца́рец [23] Swiss (male)
швейца́рка [23] Swiss (female)
швепс [20] Schweppes, soft drink
шейсе́т (*or* шестдесе́т) [6] sixty

ше́па [21] hollow of hand; handful
шест [6] six
ше́ствие [12] procession, train
шестдесе́т *see* шейсе́т
ше́сти [8] sixth
шести́ма [6] six (*masculine animate*)
шести́ца [10] "6" (top mark in school)
шестна́йсет [6] sixteen
шестсто́тин [9] six hundred
ше́там [10] do housework; be active
шива́ч (ка) [29] tailor; dressmaker
ши́пка [24] briar, wild rose; rose hip
ши́пков [24] pertaining to wild rose; made of rose hips
широчина́ [20] width
широ́к [12] wide, broad ; широ́ко разби́ране [12] liberal interpretation
шише́ [2] bottle
ши́шче [25] skewer; grilled meat on a skewer
ши́я [12] neck
ши́я [19] sew
шкаф [6] cupboard
шко́ла [17] school ; Тъ́рновска шко́ла [17] Tărnovo school [of medieval literature]
шно́рхел [14] snorkel
шокола́д [5] chocolate
шо́пски [4] of the "Shope" area near Sofia ; шо́пска сала́та [4] "Shope salad"
шотла́ндец [23] Scotsman, Scot
шотла́ндка [23] Scotswoman, Scot
шофьо́р [19] driver
шофьо́рски [26] driver's ; шофьо́рска кни́жка [26] driver's license ; шофьо́рски ку́рсове [29] driving school
шпио́нин [27] spy
шум [6] noise ; вди́гам шум [6] make noise
шу́ма [25] foliage, leaves
шу́мен [10] noisy
шумоле́не [21] rustling
шумоля́ [26] rustle, murmur; ripple
шу́нка [4] ham ; омле́т с шу́нка [4] ham omelet
шуре́й [22] brother-in-law (wife's brother)
шурена́йка [22] sister-in-law (wife's brother's wife)
шъ́пна (*or* ше́пна) [28] whisper

ща [7] want ; ще не ще [7] whether one wants or not ; не ми́ се ще [20] I don't feel like
ща́стие [22] happiness, good fortune

Българо-английски речник (Урок 1-30)

щастли́в [12] happy
щат [1] state ; Ща́тите [1] the States
ще [7] will *(future particle)*
що́ [8] what
щом [11] as soon as, since, as, if, once
що́м като [17] as soon as, since *(relative conjunction)*
щъ́ркел [13] stork

ъ́глов [27] angular; corner *(adj.)*
ъ́гъл *(plural* ъ́гли*)* [14] corner ; зад ъ́гъла [14] around the corner ; зави́вам зад ъ́гъла [26] turn the corner

юг [13] south
ю́жен [20] southern
южнославя́нски [17] South Slavic
ю́ли [2] July
юмру́к [12] fist
юна́к [25] hero, brave fellow
ю́ни [9] June
ю́ношески [28] adolescent

я [5] her *(direct object pronoun)*
я́ [6] *(imperative particle)* ; я напра́ве́те мя́сто [6] come on, make space
я́бълка [6] apple
я́вен [11] open, obvious
я́вно [11] clearly
явле́ние [20] phenomenon ; да́дено явле́ние [20] the given phenomenon
явя́вам се / явя́ се [24] appear, show up
я́года [11] strawberry
яд [12] anger ; яд ме е на [12] I'm angry at
я́дене [9] food, meal; dish
я́здя [24] ride, straddle
яйце́ *(plural* яйца́*)* [11] egg
яка́ [22] collar
я́ке [13] jacket
ям (яде́ш) [9] eat
я́ма [23] pit
януа́ри [8] January
япо́нец [23] Japanese (male)
япо́нка [23] Japanese (female)
я́ростен [18] furious, fierce
я́сен [11] clear
я́сно [11] clearly, clear ; я́сно ми е [11] I get it, it's clear
я́сла [27] manger; crib
я́стие [18] dish

я́рък [29] bright, vivid
я́то [26] flock

INDEX

Note: alphabetic ordering in Cyrillic lists is as in Cyrillic.

Accent
- stress shifts
  - to theme vowel in certain L-participle forms: 6
  - in the past tense of идвам: 15

Adjectives
- participles functioning as adjectives: 168
- present active participle used adjectivally: 169-170
- contrast with verbal adverb: 171-172

Admirative, *see also* **Dubitative, Renarrated**
- definition: 213, 218
- place in scale of distancing: 220-221

Adverbs
- verbal adverb
  - formation: 171
  - usage: 171-172
  - contrast with present participle: 171-172

Agreement
- in the past indefinite: 6-7
- in relative clauses: 30

Aktionsarten, *see also* **Prefixation**
- defined: 232
- degrees of predictability: 240
- general system: 236-237
- usefulness of: 238

Aorist tense
- indicative vs. renarrated: 293
- renarrated mood of: 196-197
  - contrast with past indefinite: 295-297, 299-300

Aspect
- general review: 55
- and the generalized past: 299-300
- and imperatives: 9-10
- and motion verbs: 14
- and the past anterior: 84-85
- and subordinate clauses: 34-37
- contrast with tense and mood: 270, 293
- derived imperfectives
  - formation: 57-59, 64-65
  - meaning: 59-60, 65-66
- derived perfectives: 64-65
  - with instantaneous meaning: 64-65
  - with attentuated meaning: 64-65
- imperfect tense and perfective aspect: 36-37
- pairs
  - basic vs. derived: 55-59
  - formal relationships: 56-59

perfectives with conditional or habitual meaning: 134
prefixation: 57-59, 65
    and meaning shifts: 58, 60
primacy of in conditional constructions: 175
simplex imperfectives: 57, 300

Clitics, *see* **Word order rules**
past anterior auxiliary not a clitic: 85, 92

Complex sentences
and aspect differentiation: 34-37
and passive participles: 93
conditional constructions: 154, 173-174, 270-272
relative constructions: 29-30
technical terms defined: 173

Conditional, *see also* **Mood**
conditional constructions
    definition and general review: 154, 173-174, 270-272
    and aspect choice: 175
    concrete vs. theoretical: 276-277
    conditional mood in: 258-260
    hypothetical vs. factual: 273-275
    mood vs. tense: 258-259, 271-272, 278
    specific vs. broad: 277
    tense choice in: 154-155, 174-175, 271
    real and unreal conditions: 174-175, 271
    with да: 271-272, 279-280
conditional mood
    general review: 253
    describing hypothetical states: 254-255
    expressing attenuated commands or statements: 255-256
    formation: 253
    in conditional constructions: 258-260, 271-278
    in impersonal and modal constructions: 256-257
    word order: 253-254
conditional usage of ли: 134

Conjugation, *see also* **Verbs**; names of individual tenses
of aspect pairs related by prefixation: 57

Conjunctions, *see also* **Pronouns**, relative
compound: 34
relative: 29-33
без да: 279
да in place of че or как: 281
да не би да: 257, 279
дето: 41
докато: 35
защото: 33
как: 281
както: 33
какъвто, etc.: 32
като: 35-36, 41-42
като че ли: 42
когато: 33, 35
който, etc.: 29-31
колкото, etc.: 32-33, 279

където: 33
макар (и) да: 34
освен че: 34
преди да: 35, 279
само че: 34
след като: 35
това, което: 33
тъй като: 34
че: 281
чийто, etc.: 31-32
щом: 36
щом като: 34

Да-phrases
    as indirect commands: 10
    expressing degrees of hypotheticality: 279-281
    with който, etc.: 280-281
    with нека: 10
    with passive participles: 93

Definiteness
    definite article on nicknames: 71
    definite article with verbal nouns: 107
    indefinite relative pronouns ("whoever", etc.): 39-41

Derivation
    and ръ / ър alternation: 17
    multiple suffixes: 69
    of abstract nouns from adjectives: 43, 116
    of abstract nouns from nouns: 116
    of abstract nouns from verbs: 43
    of agentive nouns from nouns: 95, 116
    of agentive nouns from verbs: 94
    of animal-name adjectives from nouns: 138
    of borrowed agentive nouns: 95
    of causative verbs from adjectives: 136
    of diminutives: 69-71
        diminutives of personal names: 70-71
    of family-group possessives: 95
    of imperfective verbs by suffixation: 56, 58-59
    of imperfective verbs by consonant shift: 56, 58
    of imperfective verbs by root vowel shift: 57
    of imperfective verbs from nouns: 42
    of imperfective verbs from verbs: 42
    of nationality names: 179-180
    of nouns from nouns
    of perfective verbs by suffixation: 56
    of perfective verbs by prefixation: 56, 57-58, 65
    of stative verbs from adjectives: 136-137
    of substance adjectives from nouns: 137
    the "softening" suffix in adjectives: 138
    the suffixes -ава- or -ува- in verbs: 58
    the suffix -(а)к- in nationality names: 179-180
    the suffix -ар in nouns: 94-95
    the suffix -ач in nouns: 94
    the suffix -в- in verbs: 42, 56, 58, 64-65
    the suffix -ен- in adjectives: 137
    the suffix -енце in diminutives: 70-71

the suffix -ение in nouns: 43
the suffix -ец in nationality names: 179
the suffix -ец in nouns: 180
the suffix -ин- in nationality names: 179-180
the suffix -ин- in nouns: 180
the suffix -ин- in possessives: 95
the suffix -ина in nouns: 116
the suffixes -ич- + -к- in diminutives: 69-70
the suffix -к- in diminutives: 69-70
the suffix (-ка) in agentive nouns: 94-95
the suffix -ка in nationality names: 179
the suffix -киня in nationality names: 179
the suffix -на- in verbs: 56, 64-65
the suffix -ов- in possessives: 95
the suffix -ост in nouns: 43
the suffix -ство in nouns: 116
the suffix -тел in nouns: 94
verbs and nouns related by non-productive suffixes: 117

Diacritics, *see* **Spelling**

Dictionaries
    defined: 312
    lexical dictionaries: 312
    pronouncing dictionaries: 312-313

Distancing, *see also* **Mood; Renarrated, Point of View**
    general review: 221-222
    degrees of
        future anterior renarrated: 217
        gradation of dubitavity: 218
        full range from witnessed to strongest renarration: 220-221
    emotional aspects of: 213, 218-219
    expression of inference or assumption: 132
    in 1st and 2nd person renarrated: 213-214
    in the past indefinite: 129
    in the renarrated mood: 192, 197-201, 294
    "reality distancing": 253
    temporal distancing (tense) vs. "involvement distancing" (renarrated mood): 222, 293
    vs. vividness of direct verification: 129, 133

Dubitative, *see also* **Admirative, Distancing, Renarrated**
    defined: 218
    degrees of emotional distancing: 218-219, 220-221
    forms of "stronger renarration": 219-220

English, contrast with
    borrowed agentive suffixes: 95
    conditional constructions: 173-174, 259-260
    future in the past: 150
    "-ing" forms: 170-171
    passive constructions: 88
    past tense (simple past vs. present perfect): 8
    past tense (simple past, present perfect, pluperfect): 83
    point of view: 131
    relative constructions: 29-31
    relative conjunctions: 30-33
    scope of present vs. past: 86-88

sequence of tenses: 133
tense vs. aspect: 175
untranslatability of renarrated: 201
usage of diminutive constructions: 69
usage of "it": 62
usage of present active participle: 170
usage of passive participles: 86
usage of verbal nouns: 107

Fleeting vowels, *see* **Spelling**

Future tenses
    future tense
        indicative vs. renarrated: 293
        renarrated mood of: 195
    future anterior
        indicative vs. renarrated: 293
        general: 149
        formation: 149
        meaning: 149-150
        modal usage: 278-279
        renarrated mood of: 215-217
    future anterior in the past
        indicative vs. renarrated: 293
        formation: 172
        meaning: 172
        use in conditional constructions: 172
        renarrated mood of: 215-217
    future in the past
        indicative vs. renarrated: 293
        general: 150
        conditional usage
            general: 154-155
            tense vs. mood: 258-259, 271-272, 278
        form: 150-151
        meaning: 150-154
        renarrated mood of: 195
    "future-related" tenses: 176-177

Gender
    in kinship terminology: 157

Generalized past
    defined: 300
    place in schema of degrees of distancing: 220
    usage: 300-301

Glossary lists
    absence of diminutive formations in: 70

Imperative
    aspect in: 9-10
    and negation: 9, 241
    additional forms: 10

Imperfect tense
    and perfective aspect: 36-37, 134
    indicative vs. renarrated: 293

renarrated mood of: 194, 297-298

Impersonal (and related) constructions
"true" impersonals
general: 15
има: 15-16
може: 15-16
няма: 15-16
трябва: 15-16
impersonal verbs with without да: 15-16
impersonal constructions with се: 112-114
in conditional constructions: 256-257
"inclination" constructions (пие ми се): 113-114
indirect experiencer constructions (случва ми се): 114
past tense of impersonal verbs: 16

Indefinite article, *see* **Definiteness**

Indirect discourse, *see also* **Reported speech**
and usage of the past indefinite: 132-133

Infinitive
"truncated" infinitive: 14, 257

Kinship terms, *see also* **Names**
family-group possessive terms: 95, 103
overview and full list of kinship terms: 157

Mood, *see also* **Renarrated**
general review: 192
conditional mood
definition: 253
formation: 253
describing hypothetical states: 254-255, 259-260
use in attentuated commands and statements: 255-256
use in conditional constructions: 258-259
use in impersonal and modal constructions: 256-257
vs. tense: 270
word order: 253-254
indicative mood
definition: 192
summary: 176
vs. renarrated: 293
renarrated mood
definition: 192, 213
general principles of formation: 192-194
1st and 2nd persons: 213-214
review: 221-222
vs. indicative: 293

Names, *see also* **Kinship terms**
diminutives of personal names: 70-71
family-group possessive terms: 95, 103
in jokes: 229
nationality names: 179-180
patronymic: 229
place names: 209
to outwit Death: 210

surnames: 103, 229

Negation
    and the form of the future in the past: 151
    and relative constructions: 41
    and the past indefinite: 8-9, 130
    variation in word order of negative imperatives: 241

Nouns
    archaic case forms: 260
    plural
        of nationality names: 179-180
    verbal nouns
        formation: 106
        usage: 106-107
        definiteness in: 107

Participles
    general review: 170-171
    passive participles
        attributive usage: 86, 168
        formation: 27-28
        predicative usage: 28, 86-90, 168
        in passive constructions: 88-90, 110-111, 168
    past active (L-participle), aorist stem
        formation: 5-6, 193
        adjectival (attributive) use: 168
        predicative use: 168
        use as "form of stronger renarration": 219-220
        use with conditional mood: 253
        use within future anterior: 149, 169
        use within future anterior in the past: 169, 172
        use within past indefinite: 6-7, 169
        use within past anterior: 83, 169
        use within renarrated mood: 192-193, 294-296
        of съм: 6, 193
        of ща: 193
    past active (L-participle), imperfect stem
        formation: 193
        use within renarrated mood: 194, 294, 297-298
    present active participle
        formation: 169
        usage: 170

Past anterior tense
    formation: 83
    indicative vs. renarrated: 293
    renarrated mood of: 214-215
    usage: 83-85
    word order: 85, 92-93

Past indefinite tense
    general: 129
    and negation: 9
    expressing focus on present result: 129-130
    expressing inference or assumption: 132
    expressing point of view: 130-132
    in indirect discourse: 132-133

indicative vs. renarrated: 293
renarrated mood of: 214-215
usage: 7-9
vs. aorist/imperfect: 7-8, 133

Passive
agentive passive constructions: 89, 93
comparison of three passive constructions: 111-112
passive constructions, general: 88-89, 111
passive constructions with passive participles: 88-90, 110-112
passive constructions with ce: 109-112
3rd plural passives: 90, 111-112

Past tense
contrast between past indefinite and aorist: 8
contrast between past indefinite and aorist or imperfect: 7-8, 129-132
doubly marked past tense (past anterior): 83-84
generalized past: 299-301
joking about: 145
of impersonal verbs: 16
scope of past time vs. present: 87-88
shifting meanings of идвам in different past tenses: 14-15

Point of view, *see also* **Distancing**
determining choice of past indefinite vs. aorist or imperfect: 130-132
determining tense of passive constructions: 87-88
focus on present result: 129-130
projection of a future thought into the past: 151-153

Possessives
derived possessive nouns denoting family groups: 95
possessive constructions with indirect object: 61, 67-68
чийто, etc.: 31-32, 39

Prefixes
and aspect: 56-59

в-
   with spatial meaning ("into"): 232-234
   in *Aktionsart* chart: 237

до-
   expressing completion to an endpoint: 240-241
   in *Aktionsart* chart: 237

за-
   expressing the beginning of an action: 65
   in *Aktionsart* chart: 237

из-
   forming causatives: 136
   with spatial meaning ("out of"): 234-235
   with aspectual meaning ("thorough completion"): 235, 240-241
   in *Aktionsart* chart: 237

на-
   expressing general completion: 241
   expressing satiation: 241
   forming causatives: 136
   in *Aktionsart* chart: 237

над-
   expressing the idea "outdo": 240

Показалец / Index

о-
    in *Aktionsart* chart: 237

от-
    in *Aktionsart* chart: 237

по-
    expressing separation: 238-239
    expressing general boundedness: 239
    in *Aktionsart* chart: 237

    expressing limited duration: 65, 238
    expressing simple completion: 238, 241
    forming causatives: 136
    in *Aktionsart* chart: 237

пре-
    in *Aktionsart* chart: 237

при-
    forming causatives: 136
    in *Aktionsart* chart: 237

про-
    forming causatives: 136
    in *Aktionsart* chart: 237

раз-
    expressing dispersal: 238-239
    expressing general boundedness: 239
    forming causatives: 136
    in *Aktionsart* chart: 237

с-
    in *Aktionsart* chart: 237

у-
    forming causatives: 136
    in *Aktionsart* chart: 237

Prepositions
    and prefixes: 232, 234, 236-237, 240
    на + verbal noun: 107

Present tense
    "historical present" and verbal nouns: 107
    indicative vs. renarrated: 293
    renarrated mood of: 194, 297-298

Pronouns, *see also* **Adjectives**, possessive pronominal; **Conjunctions**
    personal
        indirect object
            general review: 61
            and word order: 66-68
            idiomatic, "non-personal" use: 69
            of "affect": 61-62, 67-68
            to express possession: 61, 67-68
            to express states: 61-62
    relative
        какъвто, etc.: 32
        когато: 33
        който, etc.: 29-31, 39-40
        колкото: 32-33
        където: 33
        на кого: 39
        чийто, etc.: 31-32, 39

and aspect differentiation: 35-37
    with да: 280-281
    with еди: 41
    with и да: 40
    with ли: 40
    with ли не: 41

Proverbs
    with който: 39-40
    archaic case forms in: 260

Questions
    attenuated form expressed with conditional: 255-256
    interrogatives and relatives: 31-33, 39, 41
    with да не би: 257
    word order: 7, 92

"Reflexive"
    general review: 108-109
    impersonal meaning: 112-114
    intransitive meaning: 108-109
    passive meaning: 109-112
    reciprocal meaning: 108
    reflexive meaning: 108
    verb-specific (idiomatic) meaning: 109

Relative constructions *see also* **Pronouns,** relative
    general: 29-31
    indefinite: 39-41
    relationship to present participles: 170

Renarrated
    formation
        general principles: 192-194
        aorist: 196
        future: 195
        future anterior: 215
        future anterior in the past: 216
        future in the past: 195
        imperfect: 194
        past anterior: 214
        past indefinite: 214
        present: 194
    optional usage of: 197
    overlap with indicative mood
        aorist renarrated vs. past indefinite indicative: 196-197, 295-297, 299-300
    and past tense narration: 294-295
    "stronger" renarration: 219-220
    usage
        future anterior and future anterior in the past: 216-217
        future and future in the past: 195
        past indefinite and past anterior: 215
        present and imperfect: 194
        in neutral narration: 197-201

Reported speech, *see also* **Renarrated**
    indirect discourse: 132-133

Показалец / Index

Russian, correspondences or contrast with
    agents in instrumental case: 93
    nouns in -ение: 43

Ce, *see* **"Reflexive"**

Spelling
    я / е alternation
        in the L-participle: 5-6
        in the passive participle: 28
        variation in: 313-314, 315-316
    ръ / ър alternation: 16-17
    additional vowels: 313
    commas: 30
    consonant shifts
        from т, д to nothing in L-participle: 5-6
        from д, т to жд, щ in aspect pairs: 56
        from к to ч in diminutives: 70
        from к, г to ч, ж before suffix -ина: 116
    fleeting vowels
        in the L-participle: 5-6
        in nationality names: 179
        NOT in the passive participle: 27-28
    hard/soft consonants: 314
    vowel alternations
        in root vowels of aspect pairs: 57

Standard language
    defined: 312
    codification thereof: 313-315
    variation within: 314-316

Subjectless sentences, *see also* **Impersonal constructions**
    active sentences without "actor": 112-113
    expressing inclination (пие ми се): 113-114
    third-person passives: 90, 111-112

Surprise, *see also* **Admirative**
    future in the past as expression of surprise or disappointment: 153-154
    1st and 2nd person renarrated: 214

"Third-person" verbs, *see* **Impersonal verbs** and related constructions

Usage of certain words, *see also* **Conjunctions**
    агнешко: 138
    би: 257
    бил: 219-221
    еди(-кой, etc.): 41
    горкият, etc.: 71
    идвам: 14-15
    има(ше): 15-16
    краве: 138
    може(ше): 15-16
    може би: 257
    му: 69
    недей: 10, 14
    нека: 10

Показалец / Index

нула: 51
няма(ше): 15-16
няма(ше) да: 16, 151
овче: 138
отишъл: 83
пиленце: 70
пиша and derivatives: 59
се: 108-114
стига: 10, 14
телешко: 138
трябва(ше): 15-16

Variation
    copula omission in past indefinite: 295-297, 299, 315
    copula presence in present/imperfect renarrated: 297-298, 299, 315
    in city speech: 317-318
    in dialects: 316-317
    in 1st plural present verbs: 314
    in hard and soft consonants: 314
    in я / е alternation: 314-315
    omission of -т in masculine definite: 314-315
    word order in past anterior: 85, 92
    word order in fixed phrases: 241
    in past active participle, imperfect stem: 193

Verbs (*see also* names of individual tenses)
    review of tense system: 176-177
    review of tense/mood system: 293-294
    compound vs. simple tenses: 83, 177
    future anterior: 149-150
    future anterior in the past: 172
    future in the past: 150-155
    future in the past vs. conditional mood: 258-259
    generalized past: 299-301
    of motion: 14-15
    past anterior tense: 83-85
    past indefinite tense: 5, 7-9, 129-133
    time axis
        relation of tenses: 83-85, 149, 150-152
        relation of verbal adverb and main verb: 171-172
    scope of past tense meaning: 7-9, 87-88
    съм
        L-participle: 6, 193
        conditional: 253
        truncated infinitive: 257

Word order
    in the conditional mood: 253-254
    in да-phrases: 93
    in questions: 7, 92
    in the past indefinite: 7, 12-13
    in the past anterior: 85
    variations in word order: 85, 241

Word order rules
    general review: 12
    definitions of notation
        general conventions: 12

Показалец / Index

COP (copula, съм): 12
DIR (direct object): 12
IND (indirect object): 12
INT (interrogative): 12
Neg. (negation): 12
part (the L-participle): 12
POS (possessive indirect object): 66
3ʳᵈ COP (3sg.auxiliary): 12
conditional mood: 253-254
"experiencer" constructions: 66
indirect object of "affect": 67-68
indirect object of verb: 66
past anterior tense: 92-93
past indefinite tense: 12-13
possessive constructions: 67-68
relational possessive constructions: 67

Sveta Nedelya Church and Square (formerly Lenin Square), Sofia

www.ingramcontent.com/pod-product-compliance
Lightning Source LLC
Chambersburg PA
CBHW081414230426
43668CB00016B/2236